ALL · IN · ONE

Network+®
Certification

EXAM GUIDE
THIRD EDITION

ALL·IN·ONE

Network+®
Certification

EXAM GUIDE
THIRD EDITION

Michael Meyers

McGraw-Hill/Osborne

New York • Chicago • San Francisco • Lisbon
London • Madrid • Mexico City • Milan • New Delhi
San Juan • Seoul • Singapore • Sydney • Toronto

The McGraw·Hill Companies

McGraw-Hill/Osborne
2100 Powell Street, 10th Floor
Emeryville, CA 94608
U.S.A.

To arrange bulk purchase discounts for sales promotions, premiums, or fund-raisers, please contact **McGraw-Hill**/Osborne at the above address. For information on translations or book distributors outside the U.S.A., please see the International Contact Information page immediately following the index of this book.

Network+® Certification All-in-One Exam Guide, Third Edition

1234567890 DOC DOC 01987654

Book p/n 0-07-225346-0 and CD p/n 0-07-225347-9
parts of
ISBN 0-07-225345-2

Publisher	**Copy Editor**
Brandon A. Nordin	Marcia Baker
Vice President & Associate Publisher	**Proofreaders**
Scott Rogers	Linda and Paul Medoff
Acquisitions Editors	**Indexer**
Tim Green, Nancy Maragioglio	Jack Lewis
Project Editor	**Composition**
Jenn Tust	Jean Butterfield, Peter F. Hancik
Acquisitions Coordinator	**Illustrators**
Jessica Wilson	Kathleen Edwards, Melinda Lytle
Technical Editor	**Series Designer**
Brian Schwarz	Peter F. Hancik

This book was composed with Corel VENTURA™ Publisher.

I dedicate this book to those who have the vision
and the guts to take chances in life.

ABOUT THE AUTHOR

Michael Meyers is the industry's leading authority on Network+ Certification. He is the president and founder of Total Seminars, LLC, a major provider of PC and Network repair seminars for thousands of organizations throughout the world, and a member of CompTIA.

Mike has written numerous popular textbooks, including the best-selling the *A+® Certification All-in-One Exam Guide* and *Introduction to PC Hardware and Troubleshooting*, part of the "Mike Meyers' Computer Skills" series.

CONTENTS AT A GLANCE

CONTENTS

ACKNOWLEDGMENTS

I'd like to acknowledge the many people who contributed their talents to make this book possible:

To Nancy Maragioglio and Tim Green, my sponsoring editors at McGraw-Hill: First billing goes to you, amigos! Thanks for the encouragement, cudgeling, and general derring-do that helped get this book off the ground.

To my in-house Editor-in-Chief, Scott Jernigan: Pamplona! Pamplona!

To Martin Acuña, wireless guru and Mr. MCSE: As always, your words and gentle (or not so gentle) suggestions made this a much better book. Thanks!

To Cindy Clayton, editor extraordinaire: You "needn't" worry about all those strange words!

To David Biggs, our marvelous in-house artist: Simply a bang-up job, Don Aeron!

To Brian Schwarz: First and ten, we did it again!

To Jenn Tust and Jessica Wilson: An outstanding job coordinating the production of this book. Simply a great joy to work with you!

To their crew at MHO on the Left Coast (Kathleen Edwards, Elizabeth Jang, Melinda Lytle, Kelly Stanton-Scott, John Patrus, Dick Schwartz, Marcia Baker, Susie Elkind, Paul Medoff, Linda Medoff, Jack Lewis, Mark Karmendy, Peter Hancik, Julie Smith, Jean Bodeaux): Thanks for the excellent work you did, copyediting, proofing, illustrating, indexing, typesetting…

CompTIA

The logo of the CompTIA Authorized Curriculum Program and the status of this or other training material as "Authorized" under the CompTIA Authorized Curriculum Program signifies that, in CompTIA's opinion, such training material covers the content of the CompTIA's related certification exam. CompTIA has not reviewed or approved the accuracy of the contents of this training material and specifically disclaims any warranties of merchantability or fitness for a particular purpose. CompTIA makes no guarantee concerning the success of persons using any such "Authorized" or other training material to prepare for any CompTIA certification exam.

The contents of this training material cover the new 2005 CompTIA Network+ exam objectives.

How to Become CompTIA Certified

This training material can help you prepare for and pass a related CompTIA certification exam or exams. To achieve CompTIA certification, you must register for and pass a CompTIA certification exam or exams.

To become CompTIA certified, you must do the following:

1. Select a certification exam provider. For more information, please visit www.comptia.org/certification/itprofessionals/get_certified.aspx.

2. Register for and schedule a time to take the CompTIA certification exam(s) at a convenient location.

3. Read and sign the Candidate Agreement, which will be presented at the time of the exam(s). The text of the Candidate Agreement can be found at www.comptia.org/certification/general_information/candidate_agreement.asp.

4. Take and pass the CompTIA certification exam(s).

For more information about CompTIA's certifications, such as their industry acceptance, benefits, or program news, please visit www.comptia.org/certification.

CompTIA is a nonprofit IT trade association. CompTIA's certifications are designed by subject matter experts from across the IT industry. Each CompTIA certification is vendor-neutral, covers multiple technologies, and requires demonstration of skills and knowledge widely sought after by the IT industry.

To contact CompTIA with any questions or comments:

Please call 1-630-678-8300
or e-mail questions@comptia.org

Introduction

The Network+ Certification exam expects you to know how to
- Understand the importance of Network+ certification
- Know the structure and contents of the Network+ certification exam
- Plan a strategy to prepare for the exam

CompTIA's Network+ exam has a unique position in the IT industry in that it is one of those certifications that act as a stepping-stone to so many other certifications. It does this by testing the core knowledge of how networks function without concentrating on any specific vendor. This non-vendor-specific attitude makes Network+ attractive to those who need to understand networking.

The networking side of our business clearly does not suffer from a lack of vendor-specific tests and certifications, and these certifications provide a great way to get (and keep) a job. The Microsoft Certified Professional (MCP), Microsoft Certified Systems Administrator (MCSA), Microsoft Certified Systems Engineer (MCSE), and Certified Novell Engineer (CNE), as well as a few niche players like the Cisco Certified Network Associate (CCNA) and Cisco Certified Internetwork Expert (CCIE), have opened doors for many who have decided to pursue those certifications. The vendor-specific certifications, however, fail to address one important group of people: those who have basic skills that apply to any type of network. These are the people who have taken the time to understand conceptually how computers and networks operate. These general practitioners form the cornerstone of the IT industry. They set up Windows systems to link into Windows, Novell, and Linux networks. They know how to set the TCP/IP information to access the Internet. They know a network cable from a telephone cable. The vendor-specific certifications fail to test these more generic skills comprehensively.

Further, attaining a vendor-specific certification can cost you a lot in terms of time and money. For many of these vendor-specific certifications, you must take a series of tests to get the full certifications. The tuition for courses or boot camps, or even the self-study programs, and the amount of work involved in getting those certifications, can be intimidating. By contrast, with the vendor-neutral Network+ Certification, you take only one test and get a lifelong certification that never needs updating.

Most techs get their Network+ Certification after becoming A+ certified. Network+ opens the way to several certification paths for those interested in continuing their certifications. Over the past several years, companies offering vendor-specific certifications have begun to respect the need for a Network+ Certification. In fact, many have adopted the Network+ certifications into their programs. If you pass CompTIA's A+ and Network+, you receive credit for one of the four exams needed to achieve your Microsoft Certified Systems Administrator (MCSA). Want another example? How about Novell certifications? After you become Network+ certified, Novell automatically notifies you that you have received credit for its Network Technologies test. Hence, if you decide to focus on Novell, you will already have one test under your belt!

Welcome to Network+ Certification!

Who Needs Net+?
I Just Want to Learn About Networks!

Whoa up there, amigo! Are you one of those folks who's either never heard of the Network+ exam or just doesn't have any real interest in certification? Is your goal only to get a solid handle on the idea of networking and get yourself a jumpstart on the basics? Are you looking for that "magic bullet" book that you can read from the beginning to the end, and then close the book and start installing and troubleshooting a network? Do you want to know what's involved with running network cabling in your walls or getting your new wireless network working? Are you tired of not knowing enough about what TCP/IP is and how it works? If these types of questions are running through your mind, then rest easy—you've got the right book. Like every book with the Mike Meyers name, you'll get solid concepts without pedantic details or broad, meaningless overviews. You'll look at real-world networking as performed by real techs. This is a book that understands your needs, well beyond the scope of a single certification.

If the Network+ exam isn't for you, you can skip the rest of this chapter, shift your brain into learn mode, and dive into Chapter 2. But then, if you're going to have the knowledge, why *not* get the certification?

What Is Network+ Certification?

Network+ Certification is an industry-wide, vendor-neutral certification program developed and sponsored by the Computing Technology Industry Association (CompTIA). The Network+ Certification shows that you have a basic competency in the physical support of networking systems and knowledge of the conceptual aspects of networking. The test covers the knowledge that a network technician with at least 9 months of networking experience should have. CompTIA recommends A+ knowledge or background, but does not require an A+ Certification to take the Network+ exam. You achieve a Network+ Certification by taking one computer-based, 72-question, multiple-choice examination. To date, nearly 140,000 technicians have become Network+ certified.

Network+ Certification enjoys wide recognition throughout the IT industry. At first, it rode in on the coat tails of the successful A+ Certification program, but it now stands on its own in the networking industry. Having a Network+ Certification notably improves your ability to get and keep a job. It also serves as a stepping stone to more networking certificate programs.

What Is CompTIA?

CompTIA is a nonprofit industry trade association based in Lombard, Illinois. More than 19,000 computer resellers, value-added resellers, distributors, manufacturers, and training companies from all over the world are members of CompTIA.

CompTIA was founded in 1982. The following year, CompTIA began offering the A+ Certification exam. A+ Certification is now widely recognized as a *de facto* requirement for entrance into the PC industry. Because the A+ exam covers networking only lightly, CompTIA decided to establish a vendor-neutral test covering basic networking skills. So, in April 1999, CompTIA unveiled the Network+ Certification exam.

CompTIA provides certifications for a variety of areas in the computer industry, offers opportunities for its members to interact, and represents its members' interests to government bodies. CompTIA certifications include A+, Network+, i-Net+, Security+, and Server+, to name a few. Check out the CompTIA web site at http://www.comptia.org for details on other certifications.

Virtually every company of consequence in the IT industry is a member of CompTIA. Here are a few of the biggies:

3COM	Fujitsu	Minolta	Rockwell
Adobe	Hayes	NEC	Toshiba
Apple	Hewlett-Packard	NETGEAR	Sun Microsystems
AST	IBM	Netscape	Symantec
AT&T	Intel	Novell	Total Seminars (LLC)(that's my company)
Canon	Iomega	Oracle	Xerox
Cisco	Lexmark	Panasonic	Plus more than 20,000 others!
Compaq	Lotus	Peachtree	
Epson	Microsoft	Ricoh	

The Current Network+ Certification Exam Release

CompTIA constantly works to provide tests that cover the latest technologies and, as part of that effort, they periodically update their test objectives, domains, and test questions. This book covers all you need to know to pass the newest version of the Network+ exam: the 2005 revision.

How Do I Become Network+ Certified?

To become Network+ certified, you simply pass one computer-based, multiple-choice exam. There are no prerequisites for taking the Network+ exam, and no networking ex perience is needed. You're not required to take a training course or buy any training materials. The only requirements are that you pay a testing fee to an authorized testing facility and then sit for the exam. Upon completion of the exam, you will immediately know whether you passed or failed. Once you've passed, you become Network+ certified. That's it—there are no annual dues and no continuing education requirements.

Now for the details:

CompTIA does recommend that you have at least nine months of experience and A+ knowledge, but this is not a requirement. Note the word "recommend." You may not need to have experience or A+ knowledge but, believe me, both of these help! The A+ exam has a strong degree of overlap with the Network+ and covers other issues, such as types of connectors. As for experience, keep in mind that Network+ is mostly a practical exam. Those who have been out there supporting real networks will find many of the questions reminiscent of the types of problems they have seen on *local area networks* (LANs). The bottom line is that you'll probably have a much easier time on the Network+ exam if you have some A+ experience under your belt.

What Are the Tests Like?

The Network+ test contains 72 questions, which you have 90 minutes to complete. To pass, you must score at least 646 on a scale of 100–900

This table lists the CompTIA Network+ domains and the percentage of the test that each represents.

Network+ Certification Exam Domain Areas	Percent of Examination
1.0 Media and Topologies	20 percent
2.0 Protocols and Standards	20 percent
3.0 Network Implementation	25 percent
4.0 Network Support	35 percent
Total	100 percent

The Network+ exam is extremely practical. Questions often present real-life scenarios and ask you to determine the best solution. Network+ loves troubleshooting. Let me repeat: many of the test objectives deal with direct, *real-world troubleshooting*. Be prepared to troubleshoot both hardware and software failures, and to answer both "What do you do next?" and "What is most likely the problem?" types of questions.

A qualified Network+ test candidate can install and configure a PC to connect to a network. This includes installing and testing a network card, configuring drivers, and loading all network software. The exam will test you on the different topologies, standards, and cabling.

Expect conceptual questions about the OSI seven-layer model. If you've never heard of the OSI seven-layer model, don't worry! This book will teach you all you need to know. While this model rarely comes into play during the daily grind of supporting a network, you need to know the functions and protocols for each layer to pass the Network+ exam. You can also expect questions on most of the protocol suites, with heavy emphasis on the TCP/IP suite.

 NOTE In the past, CompTIA has made changes to the content of the exams, as well as the score necessary to pass it! Count on that trend to continue. Do not assume they'll wait for a major revision! Always check the CompTIA web site before scheduling your exam. Be prepared!

How Do I Take the Tests?

To take the tests, you must go to an authorized testing center. You cannot take the test over the Internet. Prometric/Thomson and Pearson VUE administer the actual Network+ tests. You'll find thousands of Prometric and Pearson VUE testing centers scattered across the United States and Canada, as well as in over 75 other countries around the world. You may take the exam at any testing center. In the United States and Canada, call Prometric at 888-895-6116 or Pearson VUE at 877-551-7587 to locate the nearest testing center and schedule the exam. International customers should go to CompTIA's web site at www.comptia.org, navigate to the Network+ area of the site, and look under the General Information area for a heading called Exam Locations.

 NOTE While you can't take the exam over the Internet, both Prometric and Pearson VUE provide easy online registration. Go to www.prometric.com or www.vue.com to register online.

How Much Does the Test Cost?

CompTIA fixes the price, no matter what testing center you use. The cost of the exam depends on whether you work for a CompTIA member. At press time, the cost for non-CompTIA members is $207 (U.S.).

If your employer has a CompTIA membership, you can save money by obtaining an exam voucher. In fact, even if you don't work for a CompTIA member, you can purchase a voucher from member companies, and take advantage of significant member savings. You simply buy the voucher and then use the voucher to pay for the exam. Most vouchers are delivered to you on paper, but the most important element is the unique voucher number that you'll generally receive via e-mail from the company that sells you the voucher. That number is your exam payment, so protect it from prying eyes until you're ready to schedule your exam.

NOTE CompTIA requires any company that resells vouchers to bundle them with some other product or service. Because this requirement is somewhat vague, voucher resellers have been known to throw in some pretty lame stuff, just to meet the requirement and keep their overhead low. My company, Total Seminars, is an authorized CompTIA member and voucher reseller, and we bundle our Network+ vouchers with something you can actually use: our excellent test simulation software. It's just like the disc in the back of this book, but with hundreds more questions to help you prepare for the Network+ exam. If you're in the US or Canada, you can visit www.totalsem.com or call 800-446-6004 to purchase vouchers. As I always say, "You don't have to buy your voucher from us, but for goodness' sake, get one from *somebody!*" Why pay full price when you have a discount alternative?

You must pay for the exam when you schedule, either online or by phone. If you're scheduling by phone, be prepared to hold for a while. Have your Social Security number (or the international equivalent) and either a credit card or a voucher number ready when you call or begin the online scheduling process. If you require any special accommodations, both Prometric and VUE will be able to assist you, although your selection of testing locations may be a bit more limited.

International prices vary; see the CompTIA web site for international pricing. Of course, prices are subject to change without notice, so always check the CompTIA web site for current pricing!

How to Pass the Network+ Exam

The single most important thing to remember about the Network+ Certification is that CompTIA designed it to test the knowledge of a technician with as little as nine months of experience—so keep it simple! Think in terms of practical knowledge. Read the book, practice the questions at the end of each chapter, take the practice tests on the CD in the back of the book, review any topics you missed, and you'll pass with flying colors.

Is it safe to assume that it's probably been a while since you've taken an exam? Consequently, has it been a while since you've had to study for an exam? If you're nodding your head yes, you'll probably want to read the next sections. They lay out a proven strategy to help you study for the Network+ exam, and pass it. Try it. It works.

Obligate Yourself

The first step you should take is to schedule the exam. Ever heard the old adage that heat and pressure make diamonds? Well, if you don't give yourself a little "heat," you'll end up procrastinating and unnecessarily delay taking the exam. Even worse, you may end up not taking the exam at all. Do yourself a favor. Determine how much time you need to study (see the next section), then call Prometric or Pearson VUE and schedule the exam, giving yourself the time you need to study, adding a few extra days for safety. Afterward, sit back and let your anxieties wash over you. Suddenly, it will become a lot easier to turn off the television and crack open the book! Keep in mind that Prometric and Pearson VUE let you schedule an exam only a few weeks in advance, at most. If you schedule an exam and can't make it, you must reschedule at least a day in advance or lose your money.

Set Aside the Right Amount of Study Time

After helping thousands of techs get their Network+ Certification, we at Total Seminars have developed a pretty good feel for the amount of study time needed to pass the Network+ exam. Table 1-1 will help you plan how much study time you must devote to the Network+ exam. Keep in mind that these are averages. If you're not a great student or if you're a little on the nervous side, add another 10 percent. Equally, if you're the type who can learn an entire semester of geometry in one night, reduce the numbers by 10 percent. To use this table, just circle the values that are most accurate for you, and add them up to get the number of study hours.

A complete neophyte will need at least 120 hours of study time. An experienced network technician with A+ and MCSE or CNE will only need about 24 hours.

Keep in mind that these are estimates. Study habits also come into play here. A person with solid study habits (you know who you are) can reduce the number by 15 percent. People with poor study habits should increase that number by 20 percent.

The total hours of study you need is _____.

Type of Experience	Amount of Experience			
	None	Once or Twice	Every Now and Then	Quite a Bit
Installing a wireless (802.11) network	4	2	1	1
Installing network cards	8	7	2	1
Installing RAID devices	4	2	1	1
Building PCs from scratch	4	4	1	0
Installing NetWare using IP	8	8	6	1
Installing 2000/2003 server using IP	8	8	5	1
Configuring a DHCP server	1	1	0	0
Configuring a WINS server	1	1	0	0
Configuring Internet dial-ups	5	4	2	1
Supporting an NT/2000 Network	6	5	3	2
Supporting a NetWare network	6	5	3	1
Supporting a UNIX network	4	4	1	1
Supporting a Windows 9x/Me network	3	3	2	2
Supporting a Windows 2000/XP network	6	6	5	4
Installing/troubleshooting routers/firewalls	3	3	1	1
Installing/troubleshooting hubs/switches	2	2	1	1
Creating tape backups	1	1	0	0

Table 1-1   Study Hours Guide

Studying for the Test

Now that you have a feel for how long it's going to take, you need a strategy for studying. The following has proven to be an excellent game plan for cramming the knowledge from the study materials into your head.

This strategy has two alternate paths. The first path is designed for highly experienced technicians who have a strong knowledge of PCs and networking, and who want to concentrate on just what's on the exam. Let's call this group the Fast Track group. The second path, and the one I'd strongly recommend, is geared toward people like me: the ones who want to know why things work, those who want to wrap their arms completely around a concept, as opposed to regurgitating answers just to pass the Network+ exam. Let's call this group the Brainiacs.

To provide for both types of learners, I have broken down most of the chapters into two parts:

- **Historical/Conceptual**   It's not on the Network+ exam, but it's knowledge that will help you understand more clearly what is on the Network+ exam.

- **Test Specific**   Topics that clearly fit under the Network+ Certification domains.

The beginning of each of these areas is clearly marked with a large banner that looks like this:

Historical/Conceptual

If you consider yourself a Fast Tracker, skip everything but the Test Specific section in each chapter. After reading the Test Specific section, jump immediately to the End of Chapter questions, which concentrate on information in the Test Specific section. If you run into problems, review the Historical/Conceptual sections in that chapter. Be aware that you may need to skip back to previous chapters to get the Historical/Conceptual information you need for a later chapter.

After going through every chapter as described, do the free practice exams on the CD-ROM that accompanies the book. First, do them in practice mode, and then switch to final mode. Once you start hitting in the 80–85% range, go take the test!

Brainiacs should first read the book—the whole book. Read it as though you're reading a novel, starting on Page 1 and going all the way through. Don't skip around on the first read-through, even if you are a highly experienced tech. Because there are terms and concepts that build on each other, skipping around will make you confused, and you'll just end up closing the book and firing up your favorite PC game. Your goal on this first read is to understand concepts—to understand the whys, not just the hows.

It's helpful to have a network available while you're doing each read-through. This gives you a chance to see various concepts, hardware, and configuration screens in action when you read about them in the book. Nothing beats doing it yourself to reinforce a concept or piece of knowledge!

You will notice a lot of historical information—the Historical/Conceptual sections—that you may be tempted to skip. Don't! Understanding how some of the older stuff worked or how something works conceptually will help you appreciate the reason behind networking features and equipment, as well as how they function.

After you have completed the first read-through, cozy up for a second. This time, try to knock out one chapter at a sitting. Concentrate on the Test Specific sections. Get a highlighter and mark the phrases and sentences that bring out major points. Take a hard look at the pictures and tables, noting how they illustrate the concepts. Then, do the end of chapter questions. Repeat this process until you not only get all the questions right, but you also understand *why* they are correct!

Once you have read and studied the material in the book, check your knowledge with the practice exams included on the CD-ROM at the back of the book. The exams can be taken in practice mode or final mode. In practice mode, you are allowed to check references in the book (if you want) before you answer each question, and each question is graded immediately. In final mode, you must answer all the questions before you are given a test score. In each case, you can review a results summary that tells you which questions you missed, what the right answer is, and where to study further.

Use the results of the exams to see where you need to bone up, and then study some more and try them again. Continue retaking the exams and reviewing the topics you missed until you are consistently scoring in the 80–85% range. When you've reached that point, you are ready to pass the Network+ exam!

If you have any problems or questions, or if you just want to argue about something, feel free to send an e-mail to me at michaelm@totalsem.com.

For additional information about the Network+ exam, contact CompTIA directly at its web site: http://www.comptia.org.

Good Luck!

Mike Meyers

PART I

Everything You Ever Really Wanted to Know About Networking

Defining Networking

The Network+ Certification exam expects you to know how to

- Install, Configure, and Troubleshoot networks.
- Pass the Exam!

To achieve these goals, you must be able to

- Describe the birth of networking
- Explain the goal of networking
- Explain the difference between a server and a client system
- Define a network resource

If you ask the average person, "What's a network?" you'll usually get the same basic answer: "A *network* is a bunch of computers connected together so they can share information." This answer is absolutely correct—but how will it help you *fix* networks? Instead of concentrating on "What is a network?" a network tech might find thinking in terms of "What goal does a network achieve?" far more useful when installing, configuring, and repairing networks at any level.

If I'm doing any type of work, from frying an egg to building a 500-computer network from scratch, I find it helpful to remind myself of what I want as an end result. I need a goal. When I'm frying an egg, my goal isn't simply to get the egg cooked—that's just a step in my process. My goal is to make a *delicious* cooked egg. By concentrating on the goal instead of the process, I'm not limiting myself to just getting that egg cooked. I'm thinking about how I'd like to spice the egg, how to fry it, even the color of the plate I'll use to serve it. (I really do think this way—and I make great eggs!)

Goals don't just give you an overview of the end result; they also force you to think about the entire process of achieving that goal. Imagine you discover that your car makes a funny sound every time you hit the brakes, so you take it in to the garage for repair. The mechanic then says, "You need new brake pads" and immediately starts replacing them. Now, perhaps the brake pads *are* the cause of the noise problem, but the main goal of the brakes is to stop the car. If there's a problem with your brakes, wouldn't you prefer a mechanic who keeps that goal in mind, and makes sure to verify the entire braking system? Checking the entire process, as opposed to simply reacting to single problems, makes it more likely that the less obvious problems—which are just as likely to lead to disaster—will be caught and fixed.

I do the same thing when I'm working on a network. When someone pays me to install or fix a network, I'm not thinking about sharing information; I'm thinking how this network will serve the needs of the users. Do they want the network to share information? Sure, but that's not the network's goal. The goal might be for me to install a big laser printer and configure the network so that everyone can print. Perhaps a bunch of users suddenly can't get their e-mail, and they need me to get it going again. Maybe they need me to add a big computer that they use to save important files. Getting the users to access the printer so they can print, enabling them to send and receive e-mail messages, and saving files to a central computer are all goals.

Working on a network is a lot more complicated than frying an egg or fixing the brakes on a car. This complexity makes it too easy to concentrate on only one part of the process and forget other parts. By keeping a goal for your network job in mind, you'll remember all the steps you need to get every job done; you'll get your work done faster, and you'll do it with your users in mind.

After working on networks for more years than I care to admit, I've discovered that no matter what I'm doing on a network, the goal is always the same. Everything on a network involves getting some specific thing on another computer—a printer, some e-mail, a file—to work from the comfort of the computer where the user sits.

Having thought about this for so long, I've managed to refine the goal of networking into a single sentence. Are you ready? Here it is:

> *The goal of networking is to make a resource shared by a remote system function like a resource on a local system.*

Whoa! What is a resource? What is local? What is remote? The rest of this chapter has only one job: to clarify the goal of networking in such a way that you can use it in the Network+ exam—and more important, in the real networking world. Memorize this goal. No, you won't see a "What is the goal of networking?" question on the Network+ exam, but you'll see plenty of questions on the exam that will find you thinking about this goal to help you answer them correctly. And while this goal of networking won't exactly set the room on fire if you bring it up at a party, you'd do well to recite it to yourself every time you run into a networking problem—it works!

With that goal in mind, we have a big job ahead. To help you digest the goal of networking, I need to take you through some of the most fundamental aspects of how networks function. This means we'll begin with a bit of a history lesson. This is not because I'm a networking history fan—I am, by the way—but because, if you know the history, many aspects of what's happening on your current Windows machine will make a lot more sense.

Historical/Conceptual

The Birth of Networks

At the beginning of real computing, back in the late 1960s, the world used individual *mainframe* computers. Early mainframes were physically large (initially, the size of whole buildings!), expensive computers designed to handle massive number-crunching jobs and to support multiple users. Although the word "mainframe" in this context may sound impressive, the computers sitting in our offices and homes today have far more computing power than the archaic systems of that era. Nevertheless, those early mainframes were the cutting edge of technology at the time and capable enough to put men on the moon! This cutting-edge cachet, combined with the fact that mainframes always lived behind locked doors in faraway rooms tended by geeky people who didn't talk much, gave them an aura of exclusivity and mystery that still exists today.

One aspect of mainframes did make them special: there just weren't that many of them. So, how were the geeks of yesteryear able to share such a system, ensuring that as many people as possible could use it? The earliest answer was simple—they stood in line. Early mainframes didn't have a monitor and keyboard the way PCs do today. (If you're under 35, you probably think I'm making this up, but stay with me.) If a keyboard did exist, it was on a single, large typewriter-like console in the computer room, and the operators used it to give the system detailed operating commands, like telling it to look in a specific memory address for a piece of data or program code.

Most systems loaded programs using punch cards or magnetic tape. You, as the powerless user, stood in line with your tape or stack of cards and took a number. You submitted your "job" to a person behind a counter and came back an hour (or a day) later to receive a stack of readout paper, along with your cards or tape. If you were lucky, you got a meaningful and relevant result, and shouted "Eureka!" or some other dandy phrase, much to the annoyance of the other programmers. Just as often, however, you got a pile of gibberish or an error code, at which point you went back to the keypuncher and tried to figure out what you'd done wrong. In short, early mainframe computing wasn't pretty—but it beat the heck out of doing the calculations by hand!

Fairly quickly, mainframes began to use CRT terminals and keyboards. But let's get one thing straight: these were not networks in any way! The terminals were simply data entry devices, designed to enable you to compose your programs. (Forget about ready-to-go applications—if you wanted to run a computer program for some purpose, you usually had to write it first!) The terminals themselves had no CPUs or other computer chips; they were strictly *input/output (I/O) devices*—pieces of hardware through which data flows into or out of the computer, like the keyboard and monitor on a modern PC. That's why we use the term *dumb terminal* when referring to these ancient devices. (See Figure 2-1.)

Figure 2-1
Typical dumb
terminal from
the 1970s

In time, a single mainframe could support dozens of dumb terminals (Figure 2-2). From a distance this resembles networking, but in this case, looks deceive. You need more than one computer to make a network. Having multiple dumb terminals attached to a single mainframe computer is roughly analogous to having a single PC with multiple monitors and keyboards. Today's PCs aren't designed to do this, but the mainframes back then had the firepower and capability to separate each user's view of the system in such a way that it worked. You could add as many dumb terminals as you wanted, but all the work still took place back at the single mainframe computer.

NOTE PCs have replaced dumb terminals in today's mainframe environments. They use special terminal emulation software that looks and acts like a dumb terminal.

Mainframe computers grew more sophisticated during the late 1960s and 1970s, incorporating features such as mass storage (hard drives) and more sophisticated operating systems to enable multiple mainframe users, each sitting at his or her dumb terminal, to access common data on mass storage devices. Users enjoyed having the capability to access common data on one mainframe, but that still wasn't networking because the data was only on one computer. By the late 1960s, however, scientists and researchers saw the benefits of enabling users on one mainframe computer to share data with users on other mainframes.

Pre-Networking Issues

The great issue that motivated the development of networking was based on the academic world's desire to share information among scholars. As mainframes began to spread into almost every school of academic thought (okay, maybe not philosophy, but I promise you that philosophy profs liked to talk about computers, even though they

(Columbia University Academic Information Systems [1986], used by permission)

Figure 2-2   Multiple dumb terminals, from //www.columbia.edu/acis/history/

didn't use them much back in the mainframe days), the different universities wanted to enable other scholars at other locations to connect to their mainframes. Initially, the idea of networking simply didn't exist—the first idea was to come up with methods to provide dumb terminals wherever they were needed. This concept of "a terminal in every office" sounded great, but it presented two challenges that needed to be addressed before it could become a reality. First, how could they connect mainframes that were often hundreds, if not thousands, of miles apart? Second, by this time, many locations had acquired several mainframes, often from different manufacturers who used totally different operating systems, data formats, and interfaces. How could they get totally different machines—as depicted in Figure 2-3—to communicate? A lot of smart people had to work hard to come up with a way to hook computers together in this structure we eventually came to call a network.

The first great challenge was getting access to a computer physically far away from you. The answer came from an unlikely source: telephones. It took a little bit of magic,

Figure 2-3
What will it take
for us to be able
to talk?

 DEC

The world
before networks
was a lonely place...

 IBM

1. DEC is alone
in the world

2. IBM wants
someone
to talk to

but smart people developed special devices called *modems* that enabled users to connect a dumb terminal to a far-off computer via a regular phone line. These early modems couldn't send or receive quickly—at best only around 150 characters per second. Fortunately, dumb terminals only sent and received basic I/O data (such as what key was pressed on the keyboard, or what letters appeared on the screen), so these early modems did the job.

> **NOTE** Even though dumb terminals are virtually extinct, modems are still alive and well—in PCs!

Figure 2-4 gives you an idea of the typical computer interface on a dumb terminal. Note the lack of any graphics; the only items shown on the screen are characters—letters, numbers, and symbols. Many more years would pass before the graphical user interfaces like those in Windows were available to users!

The mainframe's primitive, character-based interface pales in comparison to a modern Windows PC's graphical desktop, but it worked well enough to get the type of work we needed done in a reasonable amount of time. While a remote terminal didn't provide networking, it did provide the idea that you could be far away from a computer and do work as though you were at a dumb terminal right next to the mainframe. This concept of long-distance connection would remain important in the minds of those who eventually began to create networks.

Remote terminals worked well for the times, but as more terminals began to appear in offices and computer rooms, another problem surfaced: different mainframe makers often required different terminals. In many situations, a school might require five or six different types of terminals just to connect to the mainframes of other schools. This be-

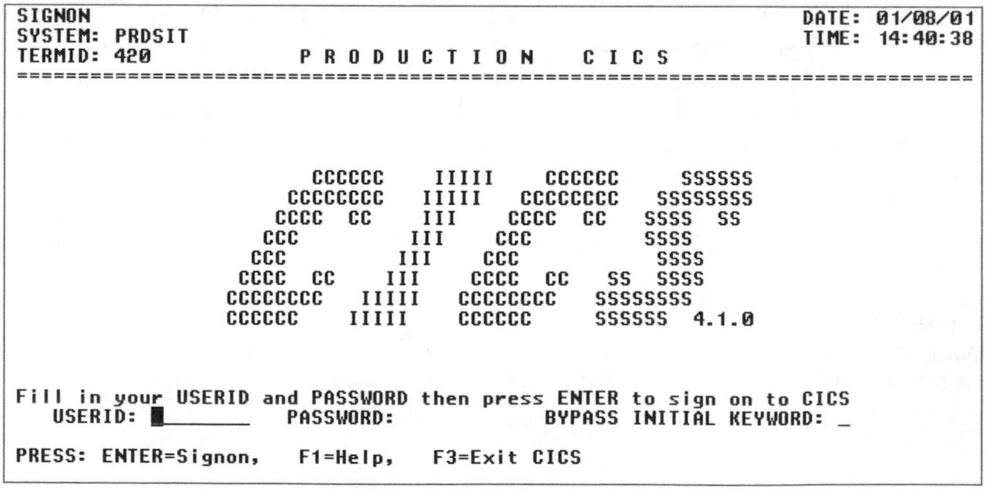

```
SIGNON                                                      DATE:  01/08/01
SYSTEM: PRDSIT                                              TIME:  14:40:38
TERMID: 420                P R O D U C T I O N    C I C S
============================================================================



                CCCCCC    IIIII    CCCCCC    SSSSSS
               CCCCCCCC   IIIII   CCCCCCCC   SSSSSSSS
              CCCC  CC     III    CCCC  CC   SSSS  SS
              CCC           III   CCC         SSSS
              CCC           III   CCC          SSSS
              CCCC  CC     III    CCCC  CC   SS  SSSS
              CCCCCCCC    IIIII   CCCCCCCC   SSSSSSSS
               CCCCCC     IIIII    CCCCCC    SSSSSS  4.1.0



Fill in your USERID and PASSWORD then press ENTER to sign on to CICS
    USERID: █_____    PASSWORD:           BYPASS INITIAL KEYWORD: _

PRESS: ENTER=Signon,   F1=Help,   F3=Exit CICS
```

Figure 2-4   Typical mainframe user interface

gan another important pre-networking step: *cross-platform support*. Terminal manufacturers began to develop standards that enabled different companies' terminals to interact with different mainframes. In this way, a professor or researcher at some remote location could use one terminal to connect to many different mainframes. This was an important idea that would later play a big part in the propagation of networks.

> **NOTE** Dumb terminals never reached the high level of integration we see in the PC world. Sometimes you had to buy the right dumb terminal for your type of mainframe.

The proliferation of dumb terminals enabled people to connect to individual mainframe computers, but after a while, some unknown person—no doubt sitting in front of his terminal—realized the inefficiency of having to access each mainframe as a separate entity. Instead of making users jump (via their terminals) from one system to the next, why not connect the mainframes in such a way that accessing the local mainframe would provide access to the others?

Just imagine the things those users could do with such an arrangement! A professor in Cambridge, Massachusetts, could send a message to another professor in San Jose, California, electronically instead of mailing a letter! It would be electronic mail! We could nickname it *e-mail*! A defense contractor could create a series of technical documents and then send them to a military procurement team, enabling the generals to make changes to the actual document without having to print the thing! By interconnecting the mainframes, no one would ever need more than one terminal! Heck, manufacturers had already started to think about cross-platform standards, so they were ready to work together to come up with a method to interconnect different mainframes. Throw in remote terminals, and you could sit in your house and do everything in your pajamas! A Brave New World! Paperless office! Information at your fingertips! Woo hoo!

There was only one little problem. No one had ever done this before. It landed on the plate of a United States government agency to create the first practical network, the now famous *ARPANET*.

ARPANET

Computer historians trace the beginnings of networking to a number of now-famous research papers that discussed the myriad issues involved in making a workable network. Long before any real network ever existed, researchers spent years theorizing about networking. Most people agree that the first practical network ever created was ARPANET. ARPANET was conceived by an organization called the Advanced Research Projects Agency (ARPA).

ARPA was created in 1958 by President Eisenhower, the same president who created another important network, the Interstate Highway System. ARPA is more commonly referred to as *DARPA* (Defense Advanced Research Projects Agency), and it still exists today (www.darpa.mil). Its name changed from ARPA to DARPA in 1972, back to ARPA in 1993, and back to DARPA again in 1996; so I'll refer to it as DARPA in this book. DARPA is a consortium of federal organizations and researchers who work on a number of highly technical projects for the U.S. government. DARPA was the organization that first funded a small project to pull together the existing mass of theoretical research and try to create a practical, working network.

 NOTE DARPA is still alive and well, developing advanced computer technologies for the U.S. government.

The earliest version of ARPANET successfully interconnected four mainframes in late 1969. Initially, ARPANET only provided two types of data transfer. First was the *File Transfer Protocol* (FTP). FTP, still popular today, enabled users to transfer files from one mainframe to another. The second was called *Telnet*. Telnet was a cool way to control another mainframe from the comfort of your own local mainframe session. You could log into your local mainframe, then Telnet into another mainframe and enter commands, just as if you were seated at a terminal connected directly to that mainframe. This was a tremendous advantage over the older idea of connecting to one mainframe, and then needing to connect to another mainframe over a separate line. One connection gave you access to all of the other computers. E-mail came soon after. Networking was born!

 NOTE From its early, four-computer start, ARPANET slowly evolved into what we now call the Internet. For a detailed history of the Internet, check out the excellent articles at the Smithsonian online, http://smithsonian.yahoo.com/ arpanet.html. Another good source is Michael Hauben's "History of ARPANET: Behind the Net—The untold history of the ARPANET" here: http://www.dei.isep.ipp.pt/docs/ arpa.html.

The idea of networking was old hat by the time PCs first appeared in the early 1980s. A level of expectation existed that PCs could network with other PCs, but unlike mainframes, the idea of having far-flung PCs interconnect to each other wasn't obvious when they first came out. Instead, early PC networks took on a far less ambitious niche. Groups of PCs, physically close to one another, were interconnected to form what we now call *local area networks (LANs)*. Yet, even though the first PC networks were humble compared to ARPANET, the legacy of ARPANET lives on in every PC network in existence. ARPANET defined almost the entire scope of networking concepts we use in today's networks. Concepts like "server" and "client" first came into existence with this now-ancient network. If you're unfamiliar with the terms "server" and "client" as they apply to networks, fear not—we cover them in the section "Servers and Clients."

NOTE Many people tend to separate LANs from the Internet. In the most basic sense, though, the major difference between the Internet and a LAN is nothing more than size!

Test Specific

The Goal of Networking

Folks often make two big mistakes when they initially attempt to understand networking. First, they fail to appreciate the phenomenal complexity of even the simplest networks. Second, they fail to understand the goal of networking. I'll deal with the complexity issue in a moment. Right now, let's think about the goal of networking. The magic word here is "sharing."

A single mainframe computer with a zillion terminals can't really share. Granted, all those terminals provide multiple access points to its data, but remember—all the data is on a single computer. For something to be a network, there must be more than one computer. This is a critical issue, and one that comes up even in today's post-mainframe world.

NOTE   A network must consist of more than one computer.

Let's get back to the concept of sharing. Assuming we have more than one system, what is there on the other system that we want to access? To put it another way, what do we want to share?

What to Share?

The designers of PC networks used ARPANET as a guide for how PC networks should work. By the mid-1980s, ARPANET had evolved into the Internet and there must have been a strong temptation to look to ARPANET for a model of what services to share in a PC network. But that's not what happened. The problem was this: ARPANET offered all sorts of services, such as FTP and Telnet, that went way beyond the conceivable scope of a little PC LAN. Why would you Telnet into a computer, for example, that was just around the corner in another office? It would make more sense to walk to the second machine, sit down, and start typing!

Rather than trying to re-create ARPANET on PC LANs, the companies that wrote the early versions of PC networking software—IBM, Microsoft, and Novell—concentrated on only two items to share: folders and printers, the two most obvious needs of a small LAN. It was not until the mid-1990s that we saw PC network makers develop the software to enable a PC to connect to the Internet. Even though early PC networks were separate from the Internet, Novell and Microsoft were smart enough to appreciate that they couldn't even begin to guess what else they might want to share in the far-off future. More than anything else, they wanted to create some type of standardized networking structure, hardware, and software that would enable a network to grow and adapt as new uses came to light. Almost no one could have imagined something as amazing as the World Wide Web way back then—but they still managed to create a networking methodology that enabled existing networks to integrate the technology of the World Wide Web easily when it later came along. So, even though PC networks are based in the idea of folder and printer sharing, they had the basic software underpinnings to enable a PC to access the Internet when consumers demanded that capability in the 1990s. Today, PCs share more than just folders and printers; they also share web pages, e-mail, FTP, and even each other's desktops.

How Do We Share?

Even though a PC network shares many types of data, all the sharing *processes* work basically the same way. Let's consider two seemingly different types of networking—surfing the World Wide Web and printing to a shared printer—and see how they share a number of important similarities. When you're checking the weather or a sports score on the Web, you are asking a computer at some other location to send data in the form of a web page to your computer. That web page may be just some text and graphics, or it might be something more complex like a sound file or a bit of java script that plays on your system. The important point is this: the information, be it a text file or a picture or something more complex, is not on your computer—it's far away on another computer, and you want it on your computer so you can experience it with your monitor and speakers. With that same thought in mind, consider the act of printing to a printer on the network. That printer might be across the room or across the country, but you want that printer to act as though it is connected to the back of your system.

What does that faraway (*remote*) web page have in common with that printer on the other side of the room? Well, they both have something that you want to access on your *local* computer; by local, I mean the computer you are physically using at this moment. Both the web page and the printer certainly require data transfers, but the data from a web page is completely different from the data you send to a printer. What we need is a better term than "data," one that's generic enough to cover anything we might want to send from one machine to another. This term must also stress the idea that another system has something we need to access and use on our system. The term I like to use for this is *resources*. Networks enable computers to share resources. A resource is anything that a particular device on a particular network wants to share with other systems on the same network. Typical resources include folders, web pages, and printers, but there are also other types of resources, ones that aren't nearly as simple to visualize. For example, e-mail is a resource for transferring messages: a system somewhere has your e-mail, and you need to go get that e-mail and bring it down to your machine to read it, send responses, and so on.

Here's an interesting little tidbit. Even though all operating systems provide ways for one system to access another system's folders, no OS lets you specify which individual files to share! All operating systems enable you to share folders, but not individual files. If you want to share a file, you must share the entire folder in which the file resides. Once a folder is shared, you can then make specific rules on how a file in that folder is shared. For example, you can set a file to be "read-only," so that no one may make changes to the file.

Servers and Clients

Okay, so a network centers around the concept of shared resources—so far, so good. Now we need to determine who shares and who simply accesses the shared resource. That's where the terms *server* and *client* come into play. A *server* is a system on a network that shares resources, while a *client* is a system that accesses a shared resource. To share a resource, you must have at least one serving computer and one client computer.

I can hear you right now: "But Mike, I thought a server was one of those big super PCs that hides in a closet!" Well, yes, we do call those servers, but that is a special use of the word. Any system that shares resources on a network will work best if it has extra power to handle all the incoming requests for its shared resources. In response to this need, the PC industry makes higher-powered systems specifically designed to meet the extra demands of serving up resources. These systems have powerful, redundant hard drives, incredibly fast network connections, and other super-powerful hardware that would be complete overkill on a regular PC. And everybody calls them . . . you guessed it: servers! (See Figure 2-5.)

The key addition you must make to create a network server is not special hardware, but rather software. Any system that wants to share its resources must run a serving program. By the same token, a client system must run a client program to access shared resources on a network. (See Figure 2-6.) Thus, even though servers tend to be the musclemen of the PC world, any system able to run a serving program can be a server. Each serving program is separate. If you want a system to share folders, it must have some type of folder-sharing software. If you want a system to share web pages, it must have some form of web page-sharing software. If you want a system to share a printer, it needs some type of printer-sharing software.

If any system running a server program is a server, then can there be more than one server on a network? For that matter, can one system run multiple serving programs?

Figure 2-5   Typical servers

Figure 2-6

Traditional roles of networked computers

Server   Client

Heck, yes! It's done all the time. In my office, for example, I have one computer that runs at least seven different serving programs, sharing everything from files to e-mail to a web site. Depending on the time of day, my office also contains roughly a dozen additional systems, each of which can serve up something.

Where do these sharing programs come from? Do you have to buy them? Well, many are built into the OS. Microsoft's many versions of Windows all have serving programs either built in or easily added from the installation CD. In other cases, you might have to buy serving programs separately. Microsoft has special server versions of Windows that include many serving programs not included in the more basic versions. These Windows server operating systems, such as Windows Server 2003, cost much more than the "regular" Windows we use on our personal systems.

The final thing to appreciate is that a system can be both a server and a client at the same time. With the exception of Novell NetWare, every OS that can do networking (Windows, UNIX/Linux, and Macintosh) enables systems to act as servers and as clients at the same time. (See Figure 2-7.)

Figure 2-7

Modern roles of networked PCs

A network of 6 servers/clients

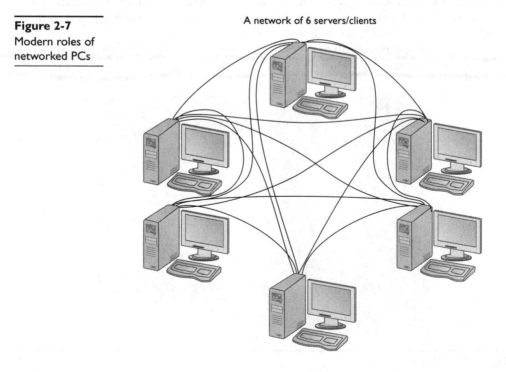

The PCs in my office are a combination of Windows 2000, Windows XP, and a few Linux computers. (I have some Windows 9*x* systems, but they're only used when people call and ask me questions about Windows 9*x*.) I have a few Microsoft Windows 2000 Server and Windows Server 2003 systems that I use to save important files. Each PC on the network, including these servers, can act as both a server and a client. This setup is common in office environments because it facilitates sharing both work files and common peripherals, like printers.

 EXAM TIP   The Network+ exam tests your understanding of clients and servers. Make sure you're comfortable with the fact that to share and access any type of resource, you need both a client and a server!

Making Shared Resources Usable

Okay, so servers share resources and clients access those shared resources. The last big conceptual question is this: how do we make sure that a client system—and the human using it—can use a shared resource? The better question would be this: how does a shared resource look and act as though it's local to the client system? The answer involves a two-part process. First we share the resource on the serving system, and then we access the shared resource on a client system.

Sharing a Resource

First, the serving system must ensure that its serving software is started. How this is done varies tremendously, but it must be done. In many cases, this is an automatic process. Figure 2-8, for example, shows the Services applet in a Windows 2000 Professional system. Note the highlighted Server service. This service, which starts automatically in all versions of Windows 2000, XP, and 2003, is the main service that must run to enable you to share folders and printers.

Once a serving program has started, you must then go through some process of defining what you want to share. In Windows, you alternate-click a folder and select the Sharing menu option. Every sharing program has this step, and one of the great challenges of a network support person is to determine how to start sharing a resource once the sharing software is turned on!

Part of sharing a resource is giving it some form of network name or address so that client systems can access the shared resource. These names manifest in many ways. A web site will need a name like www.slammo.net. A shared printer will need a name like LASER1 (see Figure 2-9). No matter what type of resource you share, at some point the shared resource must have a name.

The last part of sharing a resource is defining what those who access a resource may do with it. In most cases, this means creating account names and passwords with a defined set of what I generically call *permissions*. If I share a folder, I might define the permissions so that only a certain user account can change the files, while other accounts

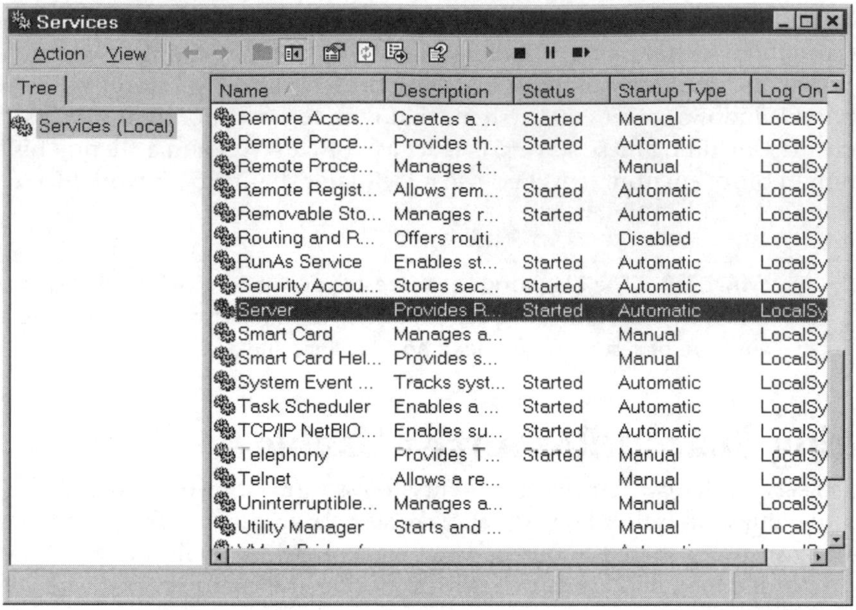

Figure 2-8   Windows Server Services

Figure 2-9

Giving a name to
a shared printer
in Windows

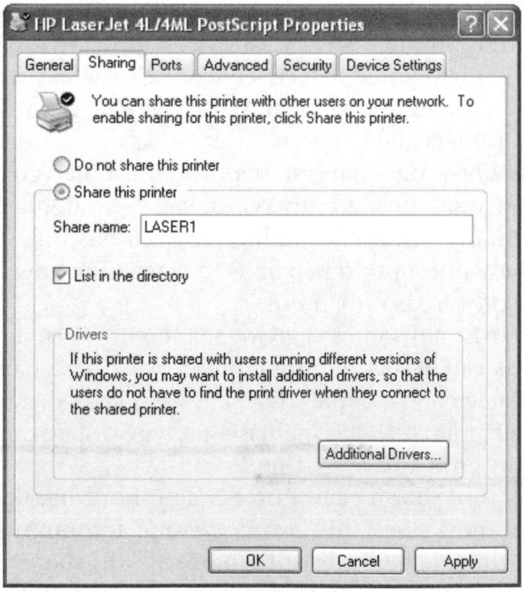

can only open and read them. If I have a web page, I might define that certain pages are only available to certain accounts. If I have an e-mail server, I might limit the amount or size of e-mails for certain accounts. Again, this permissions process varies tremendously based on the type of resource shared.

Accessing a Shared Resource

Once a serving system shares a resource, it's up to the client to go out and access that shared resource. As you might imagine, how this is done depends upon the shared resource. Remember the goal of networking: to make a shared resource look and act as though the resource were local to the client system. Let's use e-mail as an example. To access your e-mail, you need some form of e-mail client. I'll use the venerable Outlook Express as an example here. To get to your e-mail, you must know the name of the shared resource. For e-mail, this is usually a name like mail.slammo.net. In Figure 2-10, I've entered the name of the shared resource into the configuration panel. This enables me to access the shared resource.

After defining the name of the shared resource, you may have to set a username and password. Not all serving programs require this step, but more often than not, you will need to do this. Also, many serving programs use the Windows logon. It might seem you're not doing a logon, but Windows is doing it for you.

How do you know the name of the shared resource? Well, it depends on what's being shared. In a Windows network, you'll find shared printers and folders in your My Network Places—although you might have to dig a bit. You find the name of a web site by using a search engine—or simply by being told the name, reading it on a billboard, or seeing in on television. You can find out your e-mail server's name by asking the person

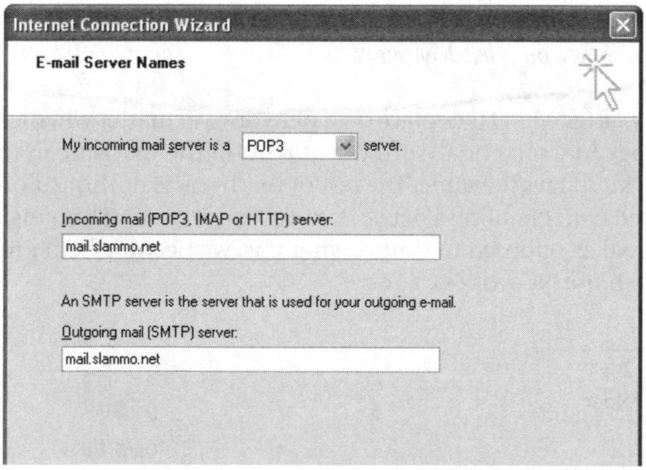

Figure 2-10

Setting the name of the e-mail server in Outlook Express

Internet Connection Wizard

E-mail Server Names

My incoming mail server is a [POP3 ▾] server.

Incoming mail (POP3, IMAP or HTTP) server:

mail.slammo.net

An SMTP server is the server that is used for your outgoing e-mail.

Outgoing mail (SMTP) server:

mail.slammo.net

who set up the server. Regardless of the specifics, the bottom line is that you must know the name to access the shared resource.

After you've accessed the resource, you're finally at a point to enjoy the fruits of your labor and begin using that resource as though it were local to your PC. In some cases, this is easy—you just type in the name of a web site and it appears or you click Send/Receive in your e-mail client and your e-mail just starts to show up.

In other cases—especially with shared folders and printers in Windows—a remote resource might not look precisely like a local resource, but it should *act* like a local resource when you access it. It may be okay and even useful, for example, if the icon of a shared folder looks slightly different on the screen—blue instead of yellow, say, or with an added symbol—but the shared folder should be similar enough to a local folder that you can tell it's a folder. Even though the shared folder may not look exactly like a local resource, it should interact with the client system's file manager or word processing software just as if it were local to that system. Figure 2-11 shows an example of how a shared folder appears in Windows 2000.

So, in some cases, the shared resource may not look exactly like a local resource—that's okay as long as that shared resource is comprehensible and usable to the local machine.

The Goal of Networking Redux

You are now armed with three critical pieces of information about what a network must do: it must have shared resources; there must always be a client and a server; and shared resources must look, or at least act, like local resources. With these three features in mind, let's once again see the goal of networking:

> *The goal of networking is to make a resource shared by a remote system act as a resource on a local system.*

No matter what takes place on a network, no matter whether you are trying to access a web page in China or a Word document on the machine in the next office, the goal of networking stays the same. The rest of this book is nothing more than learning processes involved with enabling a network to achieve its goal. Thinking about a network in terms of its goal as opposed to simply what it is, we become better network techs—and we do better on the Network+ exam!

Figure 2-11
Shared folder

Moe's files

Chapter Review

Questions

1. Which of the following statements are true of all servers? (Select two.)

   A. Servers access resources on client computers.

   B. Servers make resources available for client computers to access.

   C. Servers have special server hardware installed.

   D. Servers have special server software installed.

2. Which of the following is not a resource that can be shared by a server?

   A. Web page

   B. Printer

   C. Folder

   D. Individual files

3. Which of the following network operating systems cannot act as both a client and a server simultaneously?

   A. Windows 2000

   B. Linux

   C. Macintosh

   D. Novell NetWare

4. Which of the following is necessary to have a network?

   A. A modem

   B. At least one server and two clients

   C. More than one computer

   D. A remote terminal

5. The goal of networking is

   A. To enable remote systems to connect to each other efficiently and to access each other's files.

   B. To make a resource shared by a remote system function like a resource on a local system.

   C. To enable servers to access resources on one or more client systems in such a way that the shared resources are comprehensible to the accessing systems.

   D. To enable users on remote terminals to access mainframe systems as if they were directly connected to those systems.

Answers

1. **B, D.** Servers must have server software installed. This software is what enables them to serve up resources to client computers. Hardware upgrades can help a server handle its workload, but are not required.

2. **D.** Interestingly, no operating system shares individual files, so we share folders instead.

3. **D.** Novell NetWare cannot act as both a client and a server simultaneously. All of the other operating systems can.

4. **C.** To have a network, you must have more than one discrete system. A mainframe connected to dumb terminals, whether remote or local, is still just a single system.

5. **B.** The goal of networking is to make a resource shared by a remote system function like a resource on a local system.

Building a Network with OSI

The Network+ Certification exam expects you to know how to
- 2.1 Identify a MAC (Media Access Control) address and its parts
- 2.2 Identify the seven layers of the OSI (Open Systems Interconnect) model and their functions
- 2.3 Identify the OSI (Open Systems Interconnect) layers at which the following network components operate: Hubs, Routers, NICs (Network Interface Card)

To achieve these goals, you must be able to
- Explain the major functions of network hardware
- Describe the functions of network software
- Define each of these functions as part of the OSI seven-layer model

A functional PC network needs to do a number of jobs, using both hardware and software, to make a remote resource look like a local resource. Even though networking is fairly simple from a user's standpoint—most folks find getting a document to print to a networked printer trivially easy as long as everything is working properly—the design of this hardware and software to make them work together is a huge undertaking. You'll need to understand this huge undertaking if you're going to install, configure, or troubleshoot networks.

Before I begin any big job in my life, I find it beneficial to break that job down into discrete chunks or functions. Let's say I decide to move my family from Houston, Texas to Miami, Florida; this certainly counts as a big job in my book! I would start by breaking the moving job into discrete functions, such as choosing what to move, deciding how to go about packing, loading the van, choosing whether to move it myself or hire a driver, unloading the van, unpacking, and so forth—the usual tasks that anyone deals with when changing residences. Breaking a big job down into separate functions enables me both to grasp the overall task and to address each function separately.

Note that at this point, I'm not deciding any details within each function, such as how many boxes I need or what size moving van to use. Of course, these issues will eventually need addressing, but initially, I only want to understand and appreciate the scope of the necessary major functions to get my family moved! Each function may have many optional methods—all of them perfectly acceptable—but right now, the idea is to grasp the big picture of this big job and nothing else.

Anyone who has ever moved his or her residence could probably do a pretty good job of breaking the entire home-moving process into a few major chunks—experience is a wonderful teacher! Unfortunately, few of us ever consider the big job of moving data from one computer to another. Sure, we use networks every day—but the movement of a web page to your PC is akin to walking out of your old house and driving to your new one, only to find all your furniture already neatly arranged, dinner on the stove, and your favorite football game on the television!

This chapter breaks down networking into a series of discrete steps called the OSI seven-layer model. The *OSI seven-layer model* is a guideline for what it takes to make a network. Learning about OSI in networking is about the same as learning your multiplication tables in arithmetic: it's important, but its importance isn't obvious until after you learn it. To make OSI a bit more interesting, let's not even consider it at first. Instead, let's first concentrate on the steps required to make a network function—then we can talk about this OSI thing-a-ma-bob.

Just as the process of moving your home is best learned by going through a move, the best way to learn the steps of moving data in a network is to observe the move as it takes place in a real network. For this reason, I'll begin this chapter by introducing you to a small network that needs to get a file copied from one computer to another. Using this example, we will go through each of the steps needed to get that file moved, taking time to explain each step and why it is necessary. Finally, you'll see that these steps are defined under the important OSI seven-layer model.

Historical/Conceptual

Welcome to MHTechEd!

Mike's High-Tech Educational Supply Store and Post Office, or MHTechEd for short, has a small network of PCs running Windows XP—a situation typical of many small businesses today. Windows XP runs just fine on a PC unconnected to a network, but it also comes with all the network software it needs to connect to a network, making Windows XP a *network operating system (NOS)*, as well as just an operating system. All the computers in the MHTechEd network are connected by special network cabling.

I can see some questions forming from those of you with some networking experience: "Hey Mike, what's the difference between an operating system and a network operating system?" "What type of cabling is the network using?" Well, just hang on, buckaroo! The specific type of operating system and cabling used by our example network doesn't matter for the purposes of this chapter. We could use any operating system and any type of cabling for this chapter's goal of a conceptual overview. Trust me, by the time you close this book, you'll have all the details you can imagine—but for now, think "big picture." We have to start with something! So sit back, gather your wits about you, and join me as we take a look inside the visible network.

NOTE This section is a conceptual overview of the hardware and software functions of a network. Your network may have different hardware or software, but it will share the same functions!

Without further ado, let's head over to MHTechEd and start by taking a look at the overall network. As in most offices, virtually everyone has his or her own PC. Figure 3-1 shows two workers, Janelle and Dana, who handle all the administrative functions at MHTechEd. Because of the kinds of work they do, these two often need to exchange data between their two PCs. At the moment, Janelle has just completed a new employee handbook in Microsoft Word, and she wants Dana to check it for accuracy. Janelle could transfer a copy of the file to Dana's computer by the tried-and-true *Sneakernet* method, saving the file on a floppy disk and walking it over to her, but thanks to the wonders of computer networking, she doesn't even have to turn around in her chair. Let's watch in detail each piece of the process that gives Dana direct access to Janelle's computer, so she can copy the Word document from Janelle's system to her own.

Long before Janelle ever saved the Word document on her system—when the systems were first installed—someone who knew what they were doing set up and configured all the systems at MHTechEd to be part of a common network. All this setup activity resulted in multiple layers of hardware and software that can now work together behind the scenes to get that Word document from Janelle's system to Dana's. Let's examine the different pieces of the network, and then return to the process of Dana grabbing that Word document.

Figure 3-1
Janelle and Dana—happy workers!

Test Specific

Let's Get Physical

Clearly the network needs a physical channel through which it can move bits of data between systems. Most networks use a cable like the one shown in Figure 3-2. This cable, known in the networking industry as *unshielded twisted pair (UTP)*, contains either four or eight wires that transmit data. The MHTechEd network's UTP cable uses only four: two for sending data and two for receiving.

Another key piece of hardware the network uses is a special box-like device called a *hub* (Figure 3-3), often tucked away in a closet somewhere. Each system on the network has its own cable that runs to the hub. Think of the hub as being like one of those old-time telephone switchboards, where operators created connections between persons who called in wanting to reach other telephone users. A hub departs from the switchboard/operator analogy in one way: the hub doesn't connect the "caller" to one specific "callee." Instead, the hub passes along the data received from one system to *all* the other systems, leaving each system with the job of determining whether a piece of data is meant for it. Remember this fact, because it becomes an important concept later.

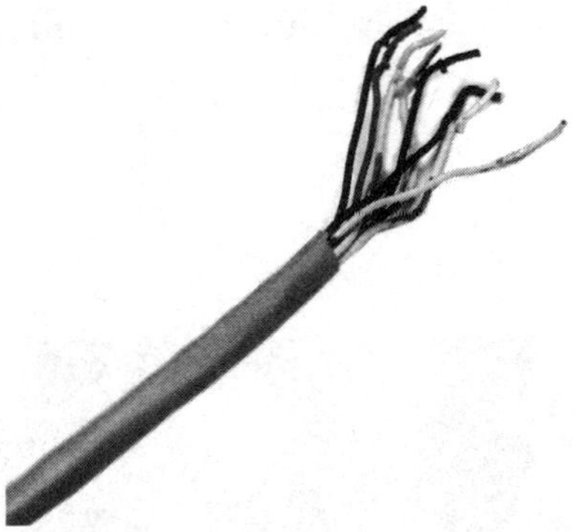

Figure 3-2
UTP network
cable showing
wires

Figure 3-3
Typical hub

Figure 3-4
Typical NIC

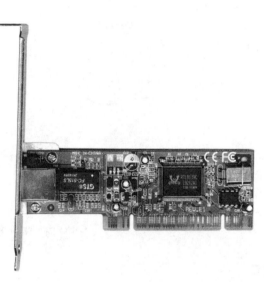

Let's get back to the hardware, because there's another key piece you will be hearing a lot about: the *network interface card*, or *NIC* (pronounced "nick"). The real magic of a network starts with the NIC, which serves as the interface between the PC and the network. While NICs come in a wide array of shapes and sizes, the ones at MHTechEd look like Figure 3-4.

When installed in a PC, the NIC looks like Figure 3-5. Note the cable running from the back of the NIC into the wall; inside that wall is another cable running all the way back to the hub.

Now that you have a picture of all the pieces, Figure 3-6 shows a diagram of the network cabling system. I'll build on this diagram as I delve deeper into the network process.

Figure 3-5
NIC installed
in a PC

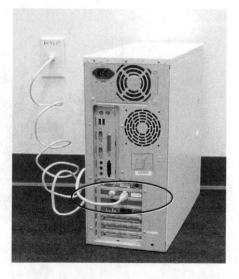

Figure 3-6
The MHTechEd
network

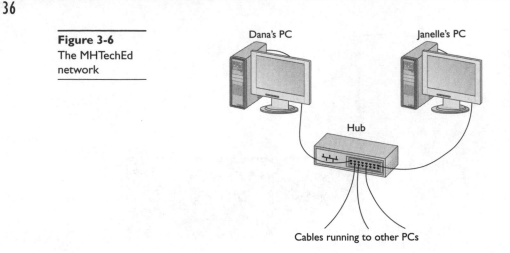

The NIC

To understand networks, you must understand what takes place inside a NIC. If you look at the previous diagram, you'll notice that all the networked systems connect to the same hub. The network must provide a mechanism that gives each system a unique identifier—like a telephone number—so that data is delivered to the right system. That's one of the most important jobs of a NIC. Inside every NIC, burned onto some type of ROM chip, is special firmware containing a unique identifier with a 48-bit value called the *media access control address*, or *MAC address*. No two NICs ever share the same MAC address—ever. Any company that makes NICs must contact the Institute of Electrical and Electronics Engineers (IEEE) and request a block of MAC addresses, which they then burn into the ROMs on their NICs. Many NIC makers also print the MAC address on the surface of each NIC, as shown in Figure 3-7. Note that the NIC shown here displays the

Figure 3-7
NIC with printed
MAC address

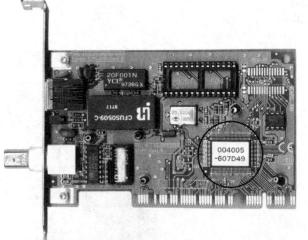

MAC address in hexadecimal notation. Count the number of hex characters—because each hex character represents four bits, it takes 12 hex characters to represent 48 bits.

The MAC address in Figure 3-7 is 004005-607D49, although in print, we represent the MAC as 00–40–05–60–7D–49. The first six digits, in this example 00–40–05, represent the number of the manufacturer of the NIC. Once the IEEE issues a manufacturer those six hex digits—often referred to as the *organizationally unique identifier*, or *OUI*—no other manufacturer may use them. The last six digits, in this example 60–7D–49, are the manufacturer's unique serial number for that NIC; this portion of the MAC is often referred to as the *device ID*.

Would you like to see the MAC address for your NIC? If your system uses Windows 9*x* or Me, run the **winipcfg** command from Start | Run to see the MAC address (Figure 3-8).

If you have a Windows NT/2000/XP system, run **ipconfig /all** from a command prompt to display the MAC address (Figure 3-9).

Okay, so every NIC in the world has a unique thingy called a MAC address, but how is it used? Ah, that's where the fun begins! Recall that computer data is binary, which means it's made up of streams of ones and zeroes. NICs send and receive this binary data as pulses of electricity, light, or radio waves. The NICs that use electricity to send and receive data are the most common, so let's consider that type of NIC. The exact process by which a NIC uses electricity to send and receive data is exceedingly complicated, but lucky for you, not necessary to understand. Instead, just think of a *charge* on the wire as a *one,* and *no charge* as a *zero.* A chunk of data moving in pulses across a wire might look something like Figure 3-10.

If you put an oscilloscope on the wire measuring voltage, you'd see something like Figure 3-11.

Now, remembering that the pulses represent binary data, visualize instead a string of ones and zeroes moving across the wire (Figure 3-12).

Once you understand how data moves along the wire, the next question becomes this: how does the network get the right data to the right system? All networks transmit data by breaking whatever is moving across the network (files, print jobs, web pages, and so forth) into discrete chunks called *frames.* A frame is basically a container for a chunk of data moving across a network. The NIC creates and sends, as well as receives and reads, these frames. I like to visualize an imaginary table inside every NIC that acts as a frame creation and reading station. I see frames as those pneumatic canisters you see

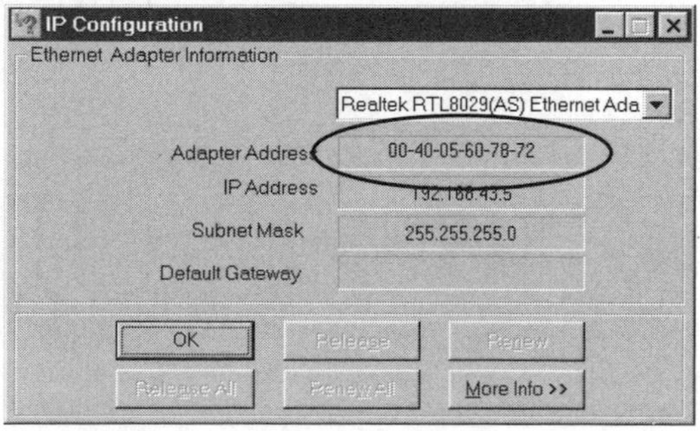

Figure 3-8
WINIPCFG
(showing MAC
address circled)

```
C:\WINDOWS\System32\cmd.exe

Microsoft Windows XP [Version 5.1.2600]
(C) Copyright 1985-2001 Microsoft Corp.

C:\>ipconfig /all

Windows IP Configuration

        Host Name . . . . . . . . . . . . : scott64
        Primary Dns Suffix  . . . . . . . : totalhome
        Node Type . . . . . . . . . . . . : Unknown
        IP Routing Enabled. . . . . . . . : No
        WINS Proxy Enabled. . . . . . . . : No
        DNS Suffix Search List. . . . . . : totalhome

Ethernet adapter Local Area Connection:

        Connection-specific DNS Suffix  . : totalhome
        Description . . . . . . . . . . . : 3Com Gigabit LOM (3C940)
        Physical Address. . . . . . . . . : 00-0C-6E-B3-3C-68
        Dhcp Enabled. . . . . . . . . . . : Yes
        Autoconfiguration Enabled . . . . : Yes
        IP Address. . . . . . . . . . . . : 192.168.4.5
        Subnet Mask . . . . . . . . . . . : 255.255.255.0
        Default Gateway . . . . . . . . . : 192.168.4.152
        DHCP Server . . . . . . . . . . . : 192.168.4.155
        DNS Servers . . . . . . . . . . . : 192.168.4.155
                                            192.168.4.156
                                            192.168.4.154
                                            192.168.4.157
        Lease Obtained. . . . . . . . . . : Wednesday, February 18, 2004 11:22:4
9 AM
        Lease Expires . . . . . . . . . . : Thursday, February 26, 2004 11:22:49
  AM

C:\>
```

Figure 3-9   IPCONFIG/ALL (MAC address is listed as Physical Address)

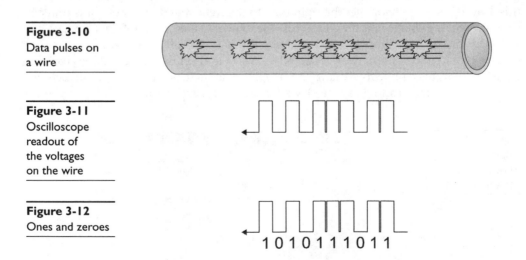

Figure 3-10
Data pulses on
a wire

Figure 3-11
Oscilloscope
readout of
the voltages
on the wire

Figure 3-12
Ones and zeroes

1 0 1 0 1 1 1 0 1 1

when you go to a drive-in teller at a bank. A little guy inside the network card—named Nick, naturally!—builds these pneumatic canisters (the frames) on the table, and then shoots them out on the wire to the hub (Figure 3-13).

> **NOTE** A number of different frame types are used in different networks. All NICs on the same network must use the same frame type or they will not be able to communicate with other NICs.

Here's where the MAC address becomes important. Figure 3-14 shows a representation of a generic frame. Even though a frame is a string of ones and zeroes, we often draw frames as a series of rectangles, each rectangle representing a part of the string of ones and zeroes. You will see this type of frame representation used quite often, so you should become comfortable with it (even though I still prefer to see frames as pneumatic canisters!). Note that the frame begins with the MAC address of the NIC to which the data is to be sent, followed by the MAC address of the sending NIC. Then comes the data, followed by a special bit of checking information called the *cyclic redundancy check (CRC)* that the receiving NIC uses to verify that the data arrived intact.

Most CRCs are only four bytes long, yet the average frame carries around 1,500 bytes of data. How can four bytes tell you if all 1,500 bytes in the data are correct? That's the

Figure 3-13
A frame-building table inside a NIC

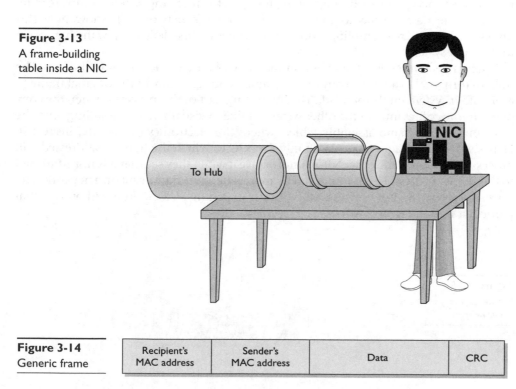

Figure 3-14
Generic frame

Recipient's MAC address	Sender's MAC address	Data	CRC

magic of CRCs. Without going into the grinding details, think of the CRC as just the remainder of a division problem. (Remember learning remainders from division back in elementary school?) The NIC sending the frame does a little math to make the CRC. Using binary arithmetic, it works a division problem on the data using a divisor called a *key*. This key is the same on all the NICs in your network—it's built in at the factory. The result of this division is the CRC. When the frame gets to the receiving NIC, it divides the data by the same key. If the receiving NIC's answer is the same as the CRC, it knows the data is good.

So, what's inside the data part of the frame? We neither know nor care. The data may be a part of a file, a piece of a print job, or part of a web page. NICs aren't concerned with content! The NIC simply takes whatever data is passed to it via its device driver and addresses it for the correct system. Special software will take care of *what* data gets sent and what happens to that data when it arrives. This is the beauty of imagining frames as little pneumatic canisters (Figure 3-15). A canister can carry anything from dirt to diamonds—the NIC doesn't care one bit (pardon the pun).

Like a canister, a frame can hold only a certain amount of data. Different networks use different sizes of frames, but generally, a single frame holds about 1,500 bytes of data. This raises a new question: what happens when the data to be sent is larger than the frame size? Well, the sending system's software must chop the data up into nice, frame-sized chunks, which are then handed to the NIC for sending. As the receiving system begins to accept the incoming frames, it's up to the receiving system's software to recombine the data chunks as they come in from the network. I'll show how this disassembling and reassembling is done in a moment—first, let's see how the frames get to the right system!

When a system sends a frame out on the network, the frame goes into the hub. The hub, in turn, makes an exact copy of that frame, sending a copy of the original frame to every other system on the network. The interesting part of this process is when the copy of the frame comes into all the other systems. I like to visualize a frame sliding onto the receiving NIC's "frame assembly table," where the electronics of the NIC inspect it. Here's where the magic takes place: only the NIC to which the frame is addressed will process that frame—the other NICs simply erase it when they see that it is not addressed to their MAC address. This is important to appreciate: *every* frame sent on a network is received by *every* NIC, but only the NIC with the matching MAC address will process that particular frame (Figure 3-16).

Figure 3-15
Frame as a
canister

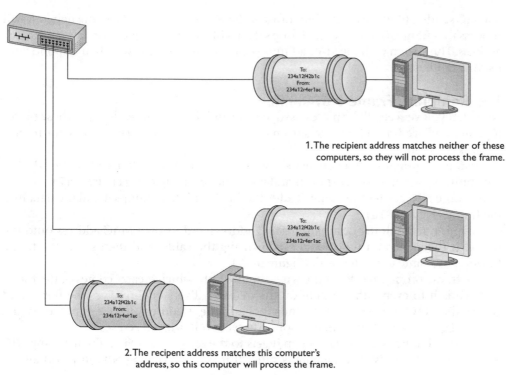

1. The recipient address matches neither of these computers, so they will not process the frame.

2. The recipient address matches this computer's address, so this computer will process the frame.

Figure 3-16   All NICs getting a frame, but only one processing it

Getting the Data on the Line

The process of getting data onto the wire, and then picking that data off the wire, is amazingly complicated. For instance, what happens to keep two NICs from speaking at the same time? Because all the data sent by one NIC is read by every other NIC on the network, only one system may speak at a time. Networks use frames to restrict the amount of data a NIC can send at once, giving all NICs a chance to send data over the network in a reasonable span of time. Dealing with this and many other issues requires sophisticated electronics, but lucky for us, the NICs handle these issues completely on their own without our help. So, thankfully, while the folks who design NICs worry about all these details, we don't have to!

Getting to Know You

Using the MAC address is a great way to move data around, but this process raises an important question. "How does a sending NIC know the MAC address of the NIC to which it's sending the data?" In most cases, the sending system already knows the destination MAC address, as the NICs had probably communicated earlier and each system stores that data. If it doesn't already know the MAC address, a NIC may send a *broadcast* onto the network to ask for it. The MAC address of FF-FF-FF-FF-FF-FF is the *broadcast address*—

if a NIC sends a frame using the broadcast address, every single NIC on the network will process that frame. That broadcast frame's data will contain a request for a system's MAC address. The system with the MAC address your system is seeking will then respond with its MAC address.

The Complete Frame Movement

Now that you've seen all the pieces used to send and receive frames, let's put these pieces together and see how a frame gets from one system to another. The basic send/receive process is as follows.

First, the sending system network software hands some data to its NIC. The NIC begins building a frame to transport that data to the receiving NIC (Figure 3-17).

After the NIC creates the frame, it adds the CRC, and then dumps it and the data into the frame (Figure 3-18).

Next, it puts both the destination MAC address and its own MAC address onto the frame. It then waits until no other NIC is using the cable, and then sends the frame through the cable to the network (Figure 3-19).

The frame propagates down the wire into the hub, which creates copies of the frame and sends it to every other system on the network. Every NIC receives the frame and checks the MAC address. If a NIC finds that a frame is addressed to it, it processes the frame (Figure 3-20); if the frame is not addressed to it, the NIC erases it.

So, what happens to the data when it gets to the *correct* NIC? First, the receiving NIC uses the CRC to verify that the data is valid. If it is, the receiving NIC strips off all the

Figure 3-17
Building the frame

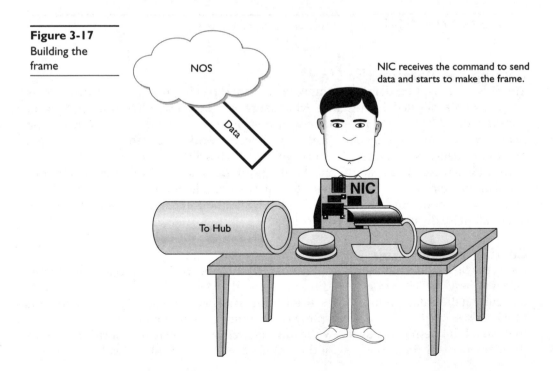

NIC receives the command to send data and starts to make the frame.

Figure 3-18
Adding the data
and the CRC to
the frame

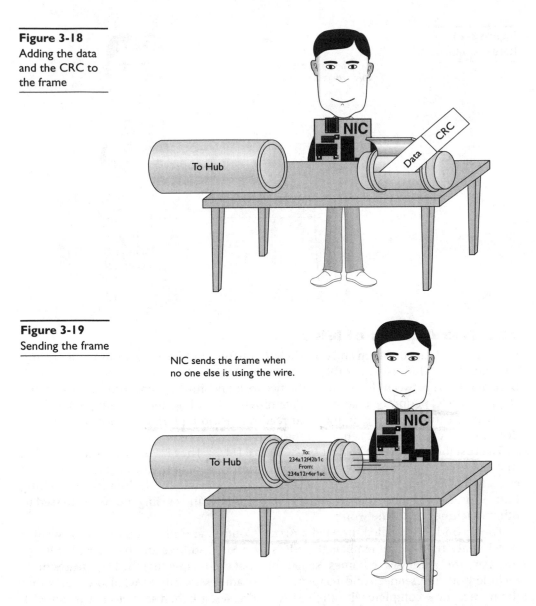

Figure 3-19
Sending the frame

NIC sends the frame when
no one else is using the wire.

framing information and sends the data to the software—the NOS—for processing. The receiving NIC doesn't care what the software does with the data; its job stops the moment it passes on the data to the NOS. *We*, however, are interested! For now, let's continue our conceptual overview—you'll learn what happens to that data when I talk about the NOS in more depth in Chapter 12, "Network Operating Systems."

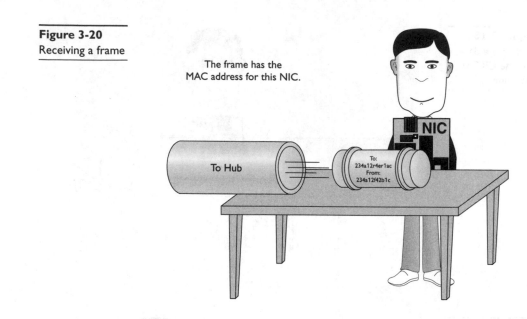

Figure 3-20
Receiving a frame

The frame has the
MAC address for this NIC.

To Hub

To:
234a12r4er1ac
From:
234a12f42b1c

NIC

The Two Aspects of NICs

Consider how data moves in and out of a NIC. On one end, we have frames moving into and out of the NIC's network cable connection. On the other end, we have data moving back and forth between the NIC and the network operating system software. The many steps your NIC performs to keep this data moving—sending and receiving frames over the wire, creating outgoing frames and reading incoming frames, attaching MAC addresses—are classically broken down into two distinct jobs.

The first job is called the Logical Link Control (LLC). The LLC is the aspect of the NIC that talks to the operating system, places data coming from the software into frames, and creates the CRC on each frame. The LLC is also responsible for dealing with incoming frames: processing those that are addressed to this NIC and erasing frames addressed to other machines on the network.

The second job is called the Media Access Control, and I bet you can guess what it does! That's right—it remembers the NIC's own MAC address and handles the attachment of MAC addresses to frames. Remember that each frame that the LLC creates must include both the sender's and recipient's MAC addresses. The MAC also ensures that the frames, now complete with their MAC addresses, are then sent along the network cabling.

Beyond the Single Wire—Network Software

Getting data from one system to another in a "simple" network (defined as one in which all the computers connect to one hub) takes relatively little effort on the part of the NICs. But what happens when you start to use the network for more complex functions? What if someone wants to use a modem to dial into Janelle's system? Modems connect to a network in a totally different way: they don't use MAC addresses and their frame types are completely different from the frames we use in networks. Or what if MHTechEd merges with a company that uses Macintosh computers and a different type of cabling? In these situations, you can't put these different systems on the same cable—the different frame types alone make them incompatible! (Figure 3-21.)

Figure 3-21
Computers using different frame types can't communicate on a network.

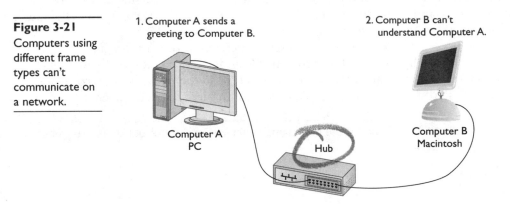

1. Computer A sends a greeting to Computer B.

2. Computer B can't understand Computer A.

Computer A
PC

Hub

Computer B
Macintosh

Even a network that uses the same frame and cabling runs into problems with MAC addresses. A single network, connecting to a single hub, cannot support more than a maximum of roughly 1,000 computers. As you add more computers to a single network, the amount of traffic becomes so great that you reach a point where the network runs unacceptably slow.

The answer to these problems comes in the form of magic little boxes called routers. *Routers* enable you to take one big network and chop it up into smaller networks. Routers also let you connect networks with different types of cabling or frames. Figure 3-22 shows a typical router. This router enables you to connect up to four computers to a cable network. Cable networks are popular for Internet connections. The connecter on the right side of the router is only for configuration.

The router in Figure 3-22 connects to a cable network and cable networks don't use MAC addresses—they have their own hardware-addressing scheme that is completely different from MAC addressing. So, when you start to connect multiple networks together with routers, each system on the network needs a more universal addressing method than MAC addresses. They need an addressing system to provide each system on the network with a unique identifier that works with any type of hardware.

Figure 3-22
Typical cable router

This other addressing scheme shows up as special software loaded onto every computer on the network. This special software—usually called a *network protocol*—exists in almost every network-capable operating system. A network protocol not only has to create unique identifiers for each system, it must also create a set of communication rules for issues like how to handle data chopped up into multiple packets, and how to deal with routers. Let's take a moment to learn a little bit about one famous network protocol—TCP/IP and its unique universal addressing system. Then we'll return to the router to see how this all works together.

To be accurate, TCP/IP is really two sets of network protocols designed to work together—that's why there's a slash between TCP and IP. TCP stands for *Transmission Control Protocol*, and IP stands for *Internet Protocol*. IP is the network protocol I need to discuss first; rest assured, however, I'll cover TCP in plenty of detail later!

NOTE   TCP/IP is the most famous network protocol, but there are plenty of others!

The IP protocol makes sure that a piece of data gets to where it needs to go on the network. It does this by giving each device on the network a unique numeric identifier. Every network protocol uses some type of naming convention, but no two protocols do it the same way. IP uses a rather unique *dotted-octet* numbering system based on four 8-bit numbers. Each 8-bit number ranges from 0 to 255, and the four numbers are separated by periods. (If you don't see how 8-bit numbers can range from 0 to 255, don't worry. By the end of this book, you'll understand these in more detail than you ever believed possible!) A typical IP address might look like this:

192.168.4.232

No two systems on the same network share the same IP address; if two machines accidentally receive the same address, a nasty error will occur. These IP addresses don't just magically appear—they must be configured. Sometimes, these numbers are typed into each system manually, but most IP networks take advantage of a groovy tool called Dynamic Host Configuration Protocol (DHCP) to configure these values automatically on each computer. We cover DHCP in Chapters 14 and 15.

What's important here is for you to appreciate that in a TCP/IP network, each system now has two unique identifiers: the MAC address and the IP address. The MAC address is literally burned into the chips on the NIC, while the IP address is simply stored in the software of the system. MAC addresses come with the NIC—we don't need to configure MAC addresses—while IP addresses must be configured through software. Here's the MHTechEd network diagram again, this time showing the IP and MAC addresses for each system (Figure 3-23).

This two-address system enables IP networks to do something really cool and powerful: using IP addresses, systems can send each other data without regard to the physical connection!

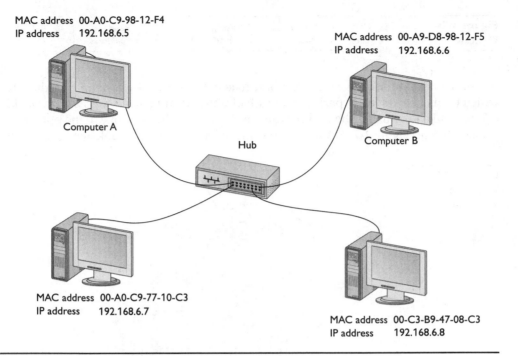

MAC address 00-A0-C9-98-12-F4
IP address 192.168.6.5

MAC address 00-A9-D8-98-12-F5
IP address 192.168.6.6

Computer A

Computer B

Hub

MAC address 00-A0-C9-77-10-C3
IP address 192.168.6.7

MAC address 00-C3-B9-47-08-C3
IP address 192.168.6.8

Figure 3-23 IP and MAC addresses for each system on the network

This capability requires more than the simple assignment of an IP address for each computer. The network protocol must also know where to send the frame, no matter what type of hardware the various computers are running. To do this, a network protocol also uses frames—actually, frames within frames!

There's Frames in Them Thar Frames!

Whoa! Frames within frames? What are you talking about, Mike? Never fear—I'll show you. Visualize the network protocol software as a layer between the system's software and the NIC. When the IP network protocol gets hold of data coming from your system's software, it places its own frame around that data. We call this inner frame an IP *packet*, so it won't be confused with the *frame* that the NIC will add later. Instead of adding MAC addresses to its packet, the network protocol adds sending and receiving IP addresses. Figure 3-24 shows a typical IP packet; notice the similarity to the frames you saw earlier.

NOTE This is a highly simplified IP packet—I am not including lots of little parts of the IP packet in this diagram because they are not important to what you need to understand right now—but don't worry, you'll see them later in the book!

Figure 3-24
IP packet

Data type	Packet count	Recipient's IP address	Sender's IP address	Data

But IP packets don't leave their PC home naked. Each IP packet is handed to the NIC, which then encloses the IP packet in a regular frame, creating, in essence, a *packet within a frame*. I like to visualize the packet as an envelope, with the envelope in the pneumatic canister frame (Figure 3-25). A more conventional drawing would look like Figure 3-26.

Figure 3-25
An IP packet
in a frame

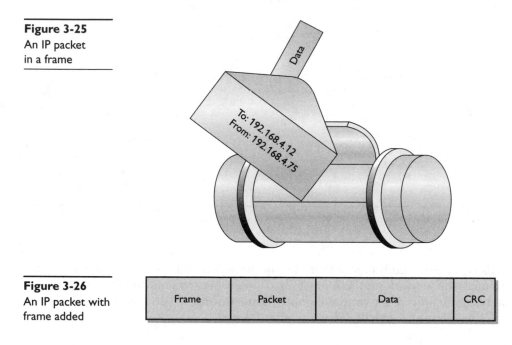

Figure 3-26
An IP packet with
frame added

Frame	Packet	Data	CRC

All very nice, you say, but why hassle with this *packet in a frame* business when you could just use MAC addresses? For that matter, why even bother with this IP thing in the first place? Good question! Let's get back to talking about routers!

Let's say that Janelle wants to access the Internet from her PC using her telephone line. We could just add a modem to her computer, but we'd rather create a way for everyone on the network to get on the Internet. To make this possible, we will connect the MHTechEd network to the Internet by adding a router (Figure 3-27).

The router that MHTechEd uses has two connections. One is just a built-in NIC that runs from the router to the hub. The other connection links the router to a telephone line. Therein lies our answer: telephone systems *don't* use MAC addresses. They use their own type of frame that has nothing to do with MAC addresses. If you tried to send a regular network frame on a phone line—well, I don't know exactly what would happen, but I assure you, it doesn't work! For this reason, when a router receives an IP packet inside a frame added by a NIC, it peels off that frame and replaces it with the type of frame the phone system needs (Figure 3-28).

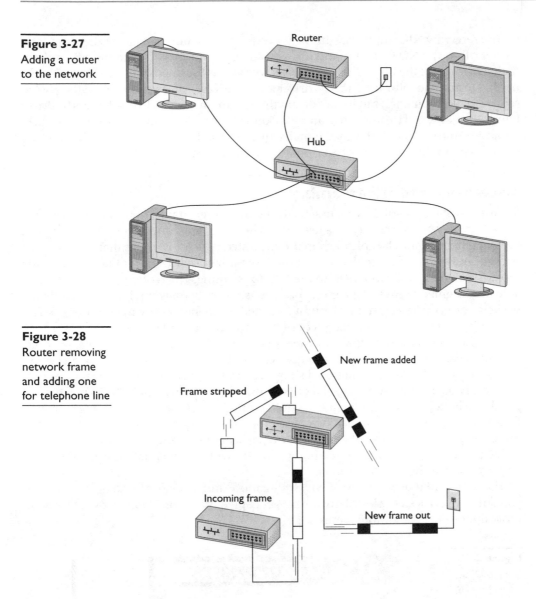

Figure 3-27
Adding a router
to the network

Router

Hub

Figure 3-28
Router removing
network frame
and adding one
for telephone line

New frame added

Frame stripped

Incoming frame

New frame out

Once the network frame is gone, so are the MAC addresses! Thus, you need some *other* naming system the router can use to get the data to the right computer—and that's why you use IP addresses on a network! After the router strips off the MAC addresses and puts on whatever type of addressing used by the telephone system, the frame flies through the telephone system, using the IP address to guide the frame to the router connected to the receiving system. At this point, the process reverses. The router rips off the telephone frame, adds the MAC address for the receiving system, and sends it on the network where the receiving system picks it up.

The receiving NIC strips away the MAC header information and passes the remaining packet off to the NOS. The networking software built into your operating system handles all the rest of the work. The NIC's driver software is the interconnection between the hardware and the software. The NIC driver knows how to communicate with the NIC to send and receive frames, but it can't do anything with the packet. Instead, the NIC driver hands the packet off to other programs that know how to deal with all the separate packets and turn them into web pages, e-mails, files, and so forth. Software handles the rest of the network function described from this point forward.

Assembly and Disassembly

Because most chunks of data are much larger than a single frame, they must be chopped up before they can be sent across a network. When a serving computer receives a request for some data, it must be able to chop the requested data into chunks that will fit into a packet (and eventually into the NIC's frame), organize the packets for the benefit of the receiving system, and hand them to the NIC for sending. The receiving system must be able to recognize a series of incoming packets as one data transmission, reassemble the packets correctly based on information included in the packets by the sending system, and verify all the packets for that piece of data arrived in good shape.

This part is relatively simple—the network protocol breaks up the data into packets and gives each packet some type of sequence number. I like to compare this process to the one that my favorite international shipping company uses. I receive boxes from UPS most every day; in fact, some days I receive many, many boxes from UPS! To make sure I get all the boxes for one shipment, UPS puts a numbering system, like the one shown in Figure 3-29, on the label of each box. A computer sending data on a network does the same thing. Embedded into the data of each packet is a sequencing number. By reading the sequencing numbers, the receiving system knows both the total number of packets and how to put them back together.

The MHTechEd network just keeps getting more and more complex, doesn't it? And you still haven't seen the Word document get copied, have you? Don't worry; you're almost there—just a few more pieces to go!

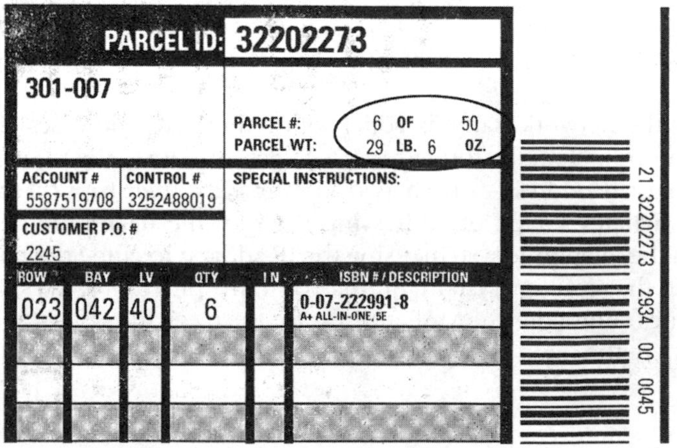

Figure 3-29
Sample UPS label showing sequencing number

Talking on a Network

Now that you understand that the system uses software to assemble and disassemble data packets, what's next? In a network, any one system may be talking to many other systems at any given moment. For example, Janelle's PC has a printer used by all the MHTechEd systems, so there's a better than average chance that as Dana tries to access the Word document, another system will be sending a print job to Janelle's PC (Figure 3-30). Janelle's system must know where to direct these incoming files, print jobs, web pages, and so on to the right programs (Figure 3-31). Additionally, the NOS must enable one system to make a connection to another system to verify that the other system can handle whatever operation the initiating system wants to perform. If Bill's system wants to send a print job to Janelle's printer, it first contacts Janelle's system to ensure that it is ready to handle the print job. We typically call the software that handles this part of networking the *session software*.

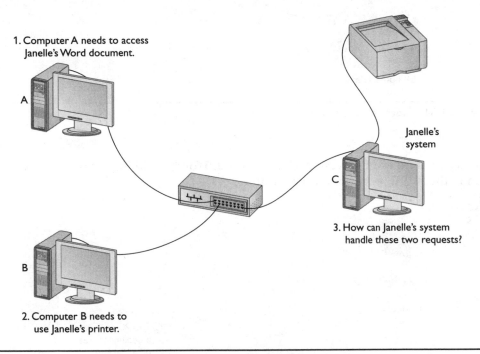

Figure 3-30   The system needs a way to handle multiple resource requests at the same time.

Standardized Formats

One of the most powerful aspects of a network lies in the fact that it works with (almost) any operating system. Today's networks easily connect, for example, a Macintosh system to a Windows 2000 PC, despite the fact that these different operating systems use different formats for many types of data. Different data formats used to drive us crazy back in

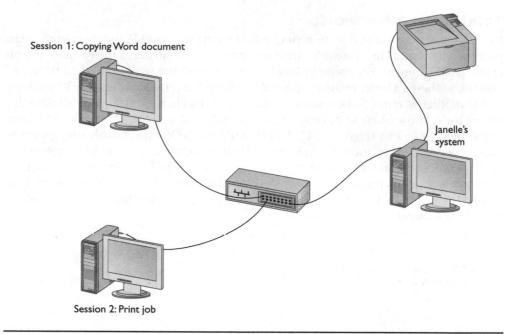

Figure 3-31 Each request becomes a session.

the days before word processors (like Microsoft Word) could import or export a thousand other word processor formats (Figure 3-32).

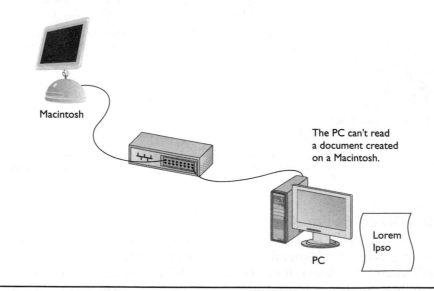

Figure 3-32 In the bad old days, differing formats could make file sharing difficult or impossible.

This created the motivation for standardized formats that anyone—at least with the right program—could read from any type of computer. Specialized file formats, such as Adobe's popular Portable Document Format (PDF) for documents and PostScript for printing, provide standard formats that any system, regardless of the operating system, can read, write, and edit (Figure 3-33).

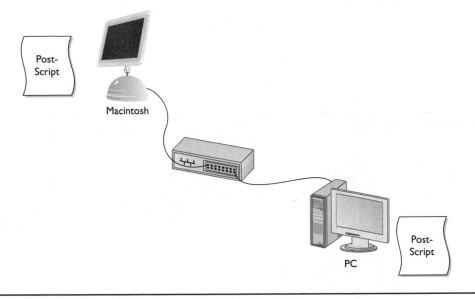

Figure 3-33   Macs and PCs both recognize Adobe PostScript.

Another function that comes into play at this point is encryption. Many networks encrypt data to prevent unauthorized access. One great example is a *Virtual Private Network (VPN)*. A VPN enables a system to access a private network via the Internet. Folks who live on the road love VPNs, because they eliminate the need to dial directly into the private network's server via a telephone line. Traveling employees can link securely into their company's private network using whatever Internet access is available to them locally. A common way VPNs manifest is through client software and server hardware (Figure 3-34).

The big problem with sending data over the Internet is security. Even a low-end hacker knows how to intercept data packets as they float by, and can look inside to see what those packets contain. Encryption stops these hackers cold—they may get the file, but they won't be able to read it if it is encrypted. For encryption to work, both the sending and the receiving system must know the encryption method, and they must be able to encrypt and decrypt on the fly (Figure 3-35).

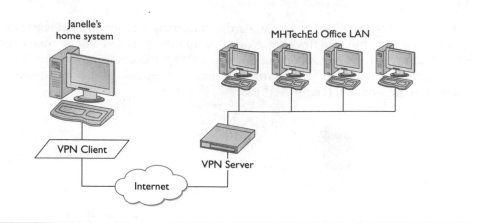

Figure 3-34   VPN diagram

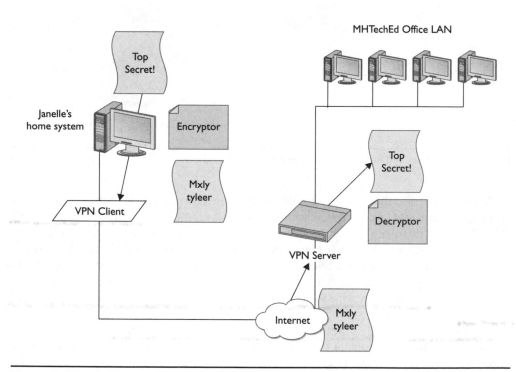

Figure 3-35   The same VPN diagram, showing encryption/decryption

Network Applications

The last, and most visible, part of any network is the software applications that use it. If you want to copy a file residing on another system in your network, you need an application like My Network Places in Windows that lets you access files on remote systems. If you want to view web pages, you need a web browser like Internet Explorer or Netscape Navigator. The people who use a network experience it through an application. A user who knows nothing about all the other parts of a network may still know how to open an e-mail application to retrieve mail (Figure 3-36).

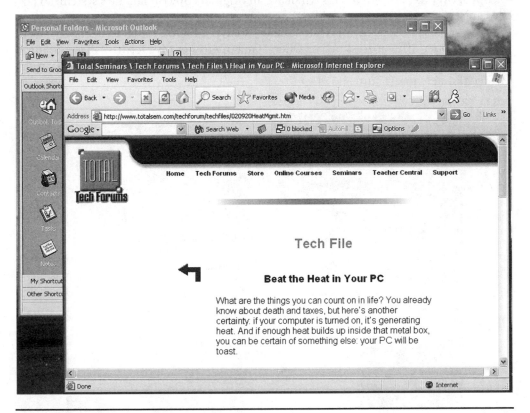

Figure 3-36 Network applications at work

Applications may include a number of additional functions, such as encryption, user authentication, and tools to control the look of the data. But these functions are specific to the given applications. In other words, if you want to put a password on your Word document, you must use the password functions of Word to do so.

How Dana Gets Her Document

Okay, you've now seen all the different parts of the network; keep in mind that not all networks contain all these pieces. Certain functions, such as encryption, may or may not be present, depending on the needs of the particular network. With that understanding, let's watch the network do its magic as Dana gets Janelle's Word document.

Dana has two choices for accessing Janelle's Word document. She can access the document by opening Word on her system, selecting File | Open and taking the file off Janelle's Desktop; or she can use My Network Places, My Computer, or Windows Explorer to copy the Word file from Janelle's Desktop to her computer, and then open her own copy of the file in Word. Dana wants to make changes to the document, so she chooses to copy it over to her system. This will leave an original copy on Janelle's system, so Janelle can still use it if she doesn't like Dana's changes.

Dana's goal is to copy the file from Janelle's shared Desktop folder to her system. Let's watch it happen. The process begins when Dana opens her My Network Places application. The My Network Places application shows her all the sharing computers on the MHTechEd network (Figure 3-37).

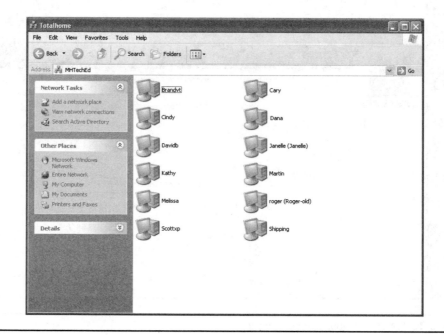

Figure 3-37   My Network Places in Windows XP

Both systems are PCs running Word, so Dana doesn't need to worry about incompatible data formats. This network does not use any encryption, but it does use authentication. As soon as Dana clicks the icon for Janelle's system in My Network Places, the two systems begin to communicate. Janelle's system checks a database of user names and privileges to see what Dana can and cannot do on Janelle's system. This checking process takes place a number of times during the process as Dana accesses various shared folders on Janelle's system. By this time, a session has been established between the two machines. Dana now opens the shared folder and locates the Word document. To copy the file, she drags and drops the Word document icon from her My Network Places onto her Desktop (Figure 3-38).

Figure 3-38 Copying the Word document

This simple act starts a series of actions. First, Janelle's system begins to chop the Word document into packets and assign each a sequence number, so that Dana's system will know how to reassemble them when they arrive on her system (Figure 3-39).

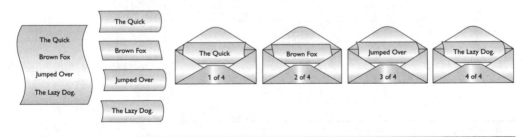

Figure 3-39 Janelle's system chopping packets

After Janelle's system chops the data into numbered packets, each packet gets the address of Dana's system, as well as Janelle's address (Figure 3-40).

The packets now get sent to the NIC for transfer. The NIC adds a frame around each packet that contains the MAC addresses for Dana's and Janelle's systems (Figure 3-41).

Figure 3-40   Adding packet headers

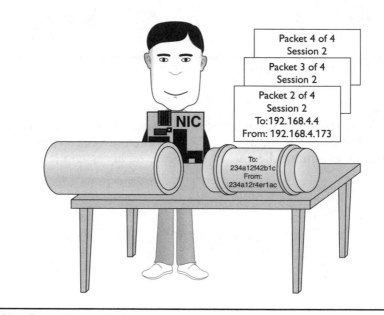

Figure 3-41   Frame being assembled

As the NIC assembles each frame, it checks the network cabling to see if the cable is busy. If not, it sends the frame down the wire. The frame goes through the hub and off to every other NIC in the network. Each NIC looks at the MAC address. All the other systems discard the frame, but Dana's system sees its MAC address and grabs it (Figure 3-42).

Figure 3-42
Dana's system
grabbing a frame

The frame has the correct
MAC address for the NIC.

NIC

To:
234a12r4er1ac
From:
234a12f42b1c

To Hub

As Dana's NIC begins to take in frames, it checks each one using the CRC to ensure
the validity of the data in the frame. After verifying the data, the NIC strips off both the
frame and the CRC and passes the packet up to the next layer (Figure 3-43).

Figure 3-43
Stripping off the
frame and CRC

The packet goes from
the NIC to the NOS.

NOS

NIC

To Hub

Packet 1 of 4
Session 2
To: 192.168.4.4
From: 192.168.4.173

Dana's system then begins to reassemble the individual packets back into the complete Word document. If Dana's system fails to receive one of the packets, it simply requests that Janelle's computer resend it (Figure 3-44).

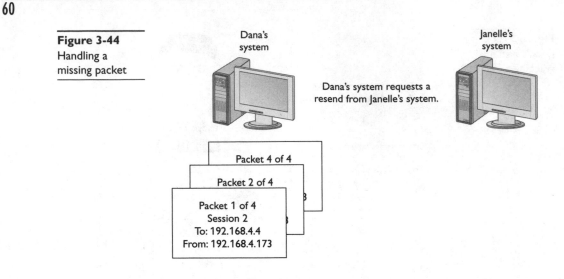

Figure 3-44
Handling a
missing packet

Dana's
system

Janelle's
system

Dana's system requests a
resend from Janelle's system.

Packet 4 of 4

Packet 2 of 4

Packet 1 of 4
Session 2
To: 192.168.4.4
From: 192.168.4.173

Once Dana's system reassembles the completed Word document, it sends the document to the proper application—in this case, Windows Explorer, better known as the Desktop. Once the system copies the file to the Desktop, the network applications erase the session connection information from each system and prepare for what Dana and Janelle may want to do next.

The most amazing part of this process is that the users see virtually none of it. Dana simply opened her My Network Places, located Janelle's system, located the shared folder containing the Word document, and then just dragged and dropped the Word document onto her Desktop. This is the beauty and mystery of networks. The complexities of the different parts of software and hardware working together aren't noticed by users—nor should they be!

The OSI Seven-Layer Model

As much as I'd love to take credit for defining these steps, I admit that I'm simply using a special concept called the *OSI seven-layer model*. Folks who want to understand networks—and who want to pass the Network+ exam—must memorize and understand this handy method for conceptualizing computer networks.

Biography of a Model

In the early days of networking, lots of different folks made their own unique types of networks. For the most part, they worked well, but because each was created separately, these different networks were incapable of working together. Each one had its own hardware, drivers, naming conventions, and many other unique features that created a lot of headaches and heartaches for anyone who had to try to get them to work together. Additionally, the proprietary nature of these early networks made it difficult for other companies to create hardware or software that worked with them. It was common for one company to supply cabling, NICs, hubs, and drivers, as well as the NOS for their brand of network, in one complete and expensive package! If the world of networking was going to grow, someone needed to create a guide, a model that described the functions of a network, so that people who made hardware and software could work together to make networks that worked together well.

The International Organization for Standardization, known as the ISO, proposed the *Open System Interconnection (OSI)* model. The OSI seven-layer model provides a precise terminology for discussing networks.

> **NOTE** ISO may look like a misspelled acronym, but it's actually a word, derived from the Greek word *isos*, which means equal.

The Seven Layers

Most network documentation uses the OSI seven-layer model to define more precisely the role played by each protocol. The OSI model also provides a common jargon that network techs can use to describe the function of any network protocol. The model breaks up the task of networking computers into seven distinct layers, each of which addresses an essential networking task. The seven layers are

- **Layer 7** Application
- **Layer 6** Presentation
- **Layer 5** Session
- **Layer 4** Transport
- **Layer 3** Network
- **Layer 2** Data Link
- **Layer 1** Physical

> **EXAM TIP** Be sure to memorize both the name and the number of each OSI layer. Network techs use terms such as "Layer 4" and "Transport layer" synonymously.

Each layer defines a challenge in computer networking, and the protocols that operate at that layer offer solutions to those challenges. The OSI model encourages modular design in networking, meaning that each protocol is designed to deal with a specific layer and to have as little to do with the operation of other layers as possible. Each protocol needs to understand the protocols handling the layers directly above and below it, but it can, and should, be oblivious to the protocols handling the other layers.

NOTE Keep in mind that these layers are not laws of physics—anybody who wants to design a network can do it any way they want. While many protocols fit neatly into one of the seven layers, others do not.

Layer 7: How Do Programmers Write Applications That Use the Network? The Application Layer

The *Application layer* in the OSI model defines a set of tools that programs can use to access the network. Application layer programs provide services to the programs that the users themselves see. Web browsing is a good example. Bob launches his web browser to access a web site. Web browsers use the HyperText Transfer Protocol (HTTP) to request data (usually HTML documents) from a web server. HTTP is not an executable program. It is a protocol, a set of rules that enables two other programs—the web browser and the web server—to communicate successfully with each other.

The APIs used by Microsoft networking also operate at the Application layer. An *API* is an Application Program Interface, a special set of commands that enables programmers to create applications (such as Microsoft Word) to request services from an operating system. When Microsoft Word displays My Network Places in a Save As dialog box, for example, it does not access the network directly. Instead, it uses the networking APIs. By providing a standard set of APIs that operate at the OSI's Application layer, Microsoft makes it easy for programmers writing applications like Microsoft Word to access the network without knowing any of the details of the network.

Layer 6: What Language Is This? The Presentation Layer

The job of the *Presentation layer* is to present data from the sending system in a form that the applications on the receiving system can understand. This enables different applications—Word and WordPerfect, for example—to communicate with each other, despite the fact that they use different methods to represent the same data.

Most computer systems store some form of text files for many different uses. A DOS or Windows 9x system usually stores text using a series of 8-bit codes known as ASCII (American Standard Code for Information Interchange), but a Windows NT, 2000, or XP system uses 16-bit Unicode to store text. A Windows 9x system stores the letter A as 01000001, while a Windows XP system stores the same letter A as 0000000001000001. The end users, of course, do not care about the difference between ASCII and Unicode—they just want to see the letter A. The Presentation layer smoothes over these differences.

The OSI model treats the Presentation layer as a distinct layer, but most real-world network operating systems fold its functions into programs that also handle either Application or Session layer functions. In fact, most network operating systems ignore the Presentation layer completely. Why? Because modern versions of Word and WordPerfect, to use my earlier example, now do this job for themselves!

NOTE Although not purely network protocols, Adobe Systems' PostScript printer language and Acrobat/PDF file format handle a typical Presentation layer problem: enabling users to view or print the same file, even if they use different operating systems or printers. *PostScript* is a device-independent printer language designed to ensure that any two PostScript-compatible printers will produce exactly the same output, regardless of the manufacturer. Adobe's PDF file format takes device independence a step further, enabling any system running an Acrobat viewer to view and print a PDF file precisely the way the author intended, regardless of what operating system or printer it uses. PostScript and Acrobat are both Presentation layer tools that hide the differences between systems.

Layer 5: How Do Machines Keep Track of Who They're Talking To? The Session Layer

The *Session layer* manages the connections between machines on the network. Suppose machine A receives one file from machine B, another from machine C, and sends a third file to machine D. Machine A needs some means to track its connections so that it sends the right response to the right computer. A computer managing connections is like a short-order cook keeping track of orders. Just as a cook must track which meals go with which ticket, a computer on a network must track which data should be sent out to which machine.

Layer 4: Breaking Data Up and Putting It Back Together: The Transport Layer

The *Transport layer* breaks up data it receives from the upper layers into smaller pieces—the packets—for transport. On the receiving side, the Transport layer reassembles packets from lower layers and hands the reassembled data to higher layers. The Transport layer also provides for error checking. ✔

The Transport layer is the pivotal layer that guarantees smooth communication between the lower layers (1 through 3) and the upper layers (5 through 7). The lower layers concern themselves with moving data from point A to point B on the network, without regard for the actual content of the data. The upper layers deal with specific types of requests involving that data. This separation allows applications using the network to remain blissfully unconcerned about the workings of the underlying hardware.

Layer 3: How Do Packets Get from A to B? The Network Layer

The *Network layer* adds unique identifiers (such as the IP address described earlier) to the packets. These unique identifiers enable special devices called routers to make sure the packets get to the correct system without worrying about the type of hardware used for transmission.

Layer 2: How Do Devices Use the Wire? The Data Link Layer

The *Data Link layer* defines the rules for accessing and using the Physical layer. The majority of the Data Link functions take place inside the NIC. The Data Link layer specifies the rules for identifying devices on the network, determining which machine should use the network at a given moment, and checking for errors in the data received from the Physical layer. Note that the functions performed at this layer affect only one sender and recipient. Data Link information does not persist beyond that single transaction, but is re-created each time the packet is transmitted to a new host.

The Data Link layer is divided into two sublayers, which you read about earlier in this chapter: Media Access Control (MAC) and Logical Link Control (LLC). The LLC sublayer is important enough to have its own IEEE standard, called 802.2. (You'll get to know the important IEEE 802.x series of networking standards in Chapter 4, "Hardware Concepts"; Chapter 5, "Ethernet Basics"; and beyond.) The LLC sublayer is conceptually *above* the MAC sublayer, that is, between it and the Network layer (OSI Layer 3). The MAC sublayer controls access to the Physical layer, or shared media. It encapsulates (creates the frames for) data sent from the system, adding source and destination MAC addresses, error-checking information, and decapsulates (removes the MAC addresses and CRC from) data received by the system. The LLC sublayer provides an interface with the Network layer protocols. It is responsible for the ordered delivery of frames, including retransmission of missing or corrupt packets, and for flow control (moderating data flow so one system doesn't overwhelm the other).

Layer 1: What Do These Electrical Signals Mean? The Physical Layer

Layer 1, the *Physical layer*, defines the physical form taken by data when it travels across a cable. While other layers deal with ones and zeroes, the physical layer defines the rules for turning those ones and zeroes into actual electrical signals traveling over a copper cable (or light passing through a fiber-optic cable, or radio waves generated by a wireless network, and so on). Figure 3-45 shows a sending NIC turning a string of ones and zeroes into an electrical signal, and a receiving NIC turning it back into the same string of ones and zeroes. Unless both ends of the transmission agree in advance on the physical layer rules, successful communication is not possible. The Physical layer adds no additional information to the data packet—it is concerned solely with transmitting the data provided by the layers above it.

Most networking materials that describe the OSI seven-layer model put NICs squarely into the Data Link layer of the model. It's at the MAC sublayer, after all, that data gets encapsulated into a frame, destination and source MAC addresses get added to that frame, and error checking occurs. What bothers most students with placing NICs solely in the Data Link layer is the obvious other duty of the NIC—putting the ones and zeroes on the network cable. How much more physical can you get?

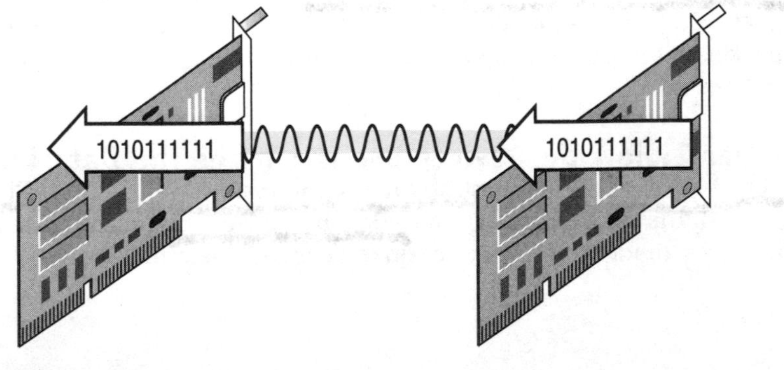

Figure 3-45

The Physical layer turns binary code into a physical signal and then back into ones and zeroes.

Many teachers will finesse this issue by defining the Physical layer in its logical sense—that it defines the rules for the ones and zeroes—and then ignore the fact that the data sent on the cable has to come from *something*. My question for a teacher who does this would be, "What component does the sending?" It's the NIC, of course, the only device capable of sending and receiving the physical signal.

Network cards, therefore, operate at both Layer 2 and Layer 1 of the OSI seven-layer model. If cornered to answer one or the other, however, go with the more common answer, Layer 2.

OSI Is the Key

The networking industry relies heavily on the OSI seven-layer model to describe the many functions that take place in a network. This chapter introduced these layers to you. Throughout the rest of the book, you'll find plenty of references to these layers as you examine every part of the network.

Chapter Review

Questions

1. Where does a hub send data?

   A. Only to the receiving system.

   B. Only to the sending system.

   C. To all the systems connected to the hub.

   D. Only to the server.

2. The unique identifier on a NIC is known as a(n)

   A. IP address

   B. Media access control address

   C. ISO number

   D. Packet ID number

3. What Windows 9x/Me utility do you use to find the MAC address for a system?

   A. WINIPCFG

   B. IFCONFIG

   C. PING

   D. MAC

4. On a Windows NT, 2000, or XP system, what utility do you use to find its MAC address? (Select the best answer.)

   A. WINIPCFG

   B. IPCONFIG

C. PING

D. MAC

5. A NIC sends data in discrete chunks called

A. Segments

B. Sections

C. Frames

D. Layers

6. A frame begins with the MAC address of the

A. Receiving system

B. Sending system

C. Network

D. Router

7. A frame ends with a special bit called the cyclic redundancy check (CRC). The CRC's job is

A. To cycle data across the network

B. To verify that the MAC addresses are correct

C. To verify that the data arrived correctly

D. To verify that the IP address is correct

8. Which of the following is an example of a MAC address?

A. 0—255

B. 00–50–56–A3–04–0C

C. SBY3M7

D. 192.168.4.13

9. Which layer of the OSI seven-layer model controls the assembly and disassembly of data?

A. Application layer

B. Presentation layer

C. Session layer

D. Transport layer

10. Which layer of the OSI seven-layer model keeps track of a system's connections to send the right response to the right computer?

A. Application layer

B. Presentation layer

C. Session layer

D. Transport layer

Answers

1. **C.** Data comes into a hub through one wire, and is then sent out through all the other wires. A hub sends data to all the systems connected to it.

2. **B.** The unique identifier on a network interface card is called the Media Access Control (MAC) address.

3. **A.** All versions of Windows 9x can use the WINIPCFG command to find the MAC address. The last 9x versions (SE and ME) could also use IPCONFIG from the command line.

4. **B.** You can use IPCONFIG/ALL from the command line to determine the MAC address of any system running Windows NT, Windows 2000, and Windows XP. You can also use WINIPCFG from the Start | Run field in Windows XP to see network settings.

5. **C.** Data is sent in discrete chunks called frames. Networks use frames to keep any one NIC from hogging the wire.

6. **A.** The frame begins with the MAC address of the receiving NIC, followed by the MAC address of the sending NIC, followed in turn by the data.

7. **C.** The data is followed by a special bit of checking information called the cyclic redundancy check, which the receiving NIC uses to verify that the data arrived correctly.

8. **B.** A MAC address is a 48-bit value, and no two NICs ever share the same MAC address—ever. 00–50–56–A3–04–0C is a MAC address. Answer D (192.168.4.13) is an IP address.

9. **D.** The Transport layer controls the assembly and disassembly of data.

10. **C.** The Session layer keeps track of a system's connections, to ensure that it sends the right response to the right computer.

PART II

The Basic LAN

## CHAPTER 4

Hardware Concepts

The Network+ Certification exam expects you to know how to

- Recognize the following logical or physical network topologies given a diagram, schematic, or description: star, bus, mesh, ring
- Recognize the following media types and describe their uses: Category 3, 5, 5e, and 6; UTP (Unshielded Twisted Pair); STP (Shielded Twisted Pair); coaxial cable; SMF (Single Mode Fiber) optic cable; MMF (Multimode Fiber) optic cable

To achieve these goals, you must be able to

- Explain the different types of network topology
- Describe the different types of network cabling
- Describe and distinguish among the 802.2, 802.3, and 802.5 IEEE networking standards

---

Every network must provide some method to get data from one system to another. In most cases, this method consists of some type of cabling (usually copper or fiber-optic) running between systems, although many networks skip wires and use wireless methods to move data. Stringing those cables brings up a number of critical issues you need to understand to work on a network. How do all these cables connect the computers together? Does every computer on the network run a cable to a central point? Does a single cable snake through the ceiling, with all the computers on the network connected to it? These questions need answering! Furthermore, we need some standards so that manufacturers can make networking equipment that works well together. While we're talking about standards, what about the cabling itself? What type of cable? What quality of copper? How thick should it be? Who will define standards for cables so that they'll all work in the network?

This chapter answers these questions in three parts. First, you will learn about the critical, magical concept called *network topology*—the way that cables and other pieces of hardware connect to one another. Second, you will tour the most common standardized cable types used in networking. Third, you will discover the all-important IEEE committees that combine these issues into solid standards.

Topology

If a bunch of computers connect together to make a network, there must be some logic or order to the way that they connect. Perhaps each computer connects to a single main line that snakes around the office. Each computer might have its own cable, with all the cables coming together to a central point. Or maybe all the cables from all the computers connect to a main loop that moves data along like a merry-go-round, picking up and dropping off data like a circular subway line.

A network's *topology* describes the way that computers connect to each other in that network. The most common network topologies are called *bus, ring, star,* and *mesh.* Figure 4-1 shows all four types: a *bus topology,* where all computers connect to the network via a main line called a bus cable; a *ring topology,* where all computers on the network attach to a central ring of cable; a *star topology,* where the computers on the network connect to a central wiring point (usually called a hub); and a *mesh topology,* where each computer has a dedicated line to every other computer. Make sure you know these four topologies!

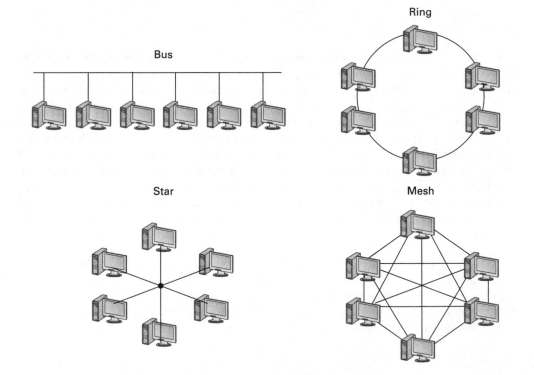

Figure 4-1   Clockwise from top left: bus, ring, mesh, and star topologies

If you're looking at the figure and thinking that a mesh topology looks amazingly re-silient and robust, it is—at least on paper. Because every computer physically connects to every other computer on the network, even if half the PCs crash, the network still functions as well as ever (for the survivors). In a practical sense, however, implementing a true mesh topology network would be an expensive mess. For example, even for a tiny network with only 10 PCs, you would need 45 separate and distinct pieces of cable to connect every PC to every other PC. What a mesh mess! Because of this, mesh topologies have never been practical in a cabled network.

But what if you didn't have to use physical wires to connect the PCs? You wouldn't have the expense of buying the wires, or the mess of having a zillion cables lying around. In fact, most *wireless* networks can use a mesh topology if configured to do so! You'll learn more about wireless networks in Chapter 9, "Wireless Networking."

While a topology describes the method by which systems in a network connect, the to-pology alone doesn't describe all of the features necessary to make a cabling system work. The term *bus topology*, for example, describes a network that consists of some number of machines connected to the network via the same piece of cable. Notice that this definition leaves a lot of questions unanswered. What is the cable made of? How long can it be? How do the machines decide which machine should send data at a specific moment? A net-work based on a bus topology can answer these questions in a number of different ways.

Most techs make a clear distinction between the *logical topology* of a network—how the network is laid out on paper, with nice straight lines and boxes—and the physical to-pology. The *physical topology* describes the typically messy computer network, with cables running diagonally through the ceiling space or snaking their way through walls. If someone describes the topology of a particular network, make sure you understand whether they're talking about the logical or physical topology.

Over the years, particular manufacturers and standards bodies created several specific network technologies based on different topologies. A *network technology* is a practical application of a topology and other critical technologies to provide a method to get data from one computer to another on a network. These network technologies have names like Ethernet, Token Ring, and FDDI. The next three chapters describe all these network technologies in great detail, but for now, concentrate on learning the different topologies.

TIP   Make sure you know your topologies: bus, ring, star, and mesh!

Test Specific

Hybrid Topologies

Of the four types of topologies just described, the bus topology was by far the most com-mercially successful. But bus topologies have a problem: the bus itself. *Ethernet*, the first network technology that used the bus topology, literally had a single cable—the bus—running around the networked area, usually up in the ceiling (see Figure 4-2). Each computer on the network connected to the bus.

Figure 4-2
Ethernet bus-topology network

If someone or something broke the bus cable (see Figure 4-3), the entire network would no longer function. The amount of network traffic would explode and packets would trample all over each other. (I'll explain why in detail in Chapter 5, "Ethernet Basics.") A true bus network has no *fault tolerance*, which means it cannot survive a problem on *any* node or cable.

Figure 4-3
A single break wreaking havoc on an Ethernet network

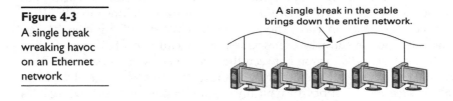

A single break in the cable brings down the entire network.

In the real world, bus breaks happened enough to motivate the Ethernet folks to develop an improved, fault-tolerant Ethernet network technology that shrunk the entire bus into a box called a *hub* (see Figure 4-4). Each computer connected to the hub with its own cable. If one of those cables broke, only the one computer connected to that hub was affected (see Figure 4-5); the rest of the network continued to run normally.

Figure 4-4
Improved Ethernet put the entire bus into the hub.

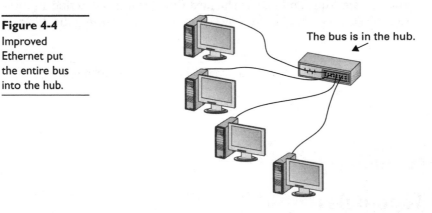

The bus is in the hub.

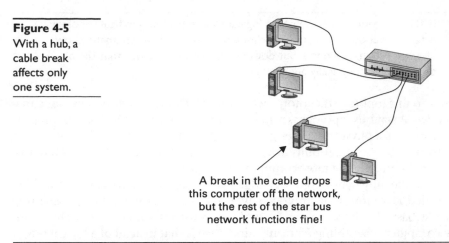

Figure 4-5
With a hub, a cable break affects only one system.

A break in the cable drops
this computer off the network,
but the rest of the star bus
network functions fine!

NOTE Fault tolerance refers to a system's capability to continue functioning even when some part of the system has failed. When bad things happen, a robust or fault-tolerant system continues to operate, at least to some degree.

This new type of Ethernet (see Figure 4-6) completely messed up the idea of topology. Physically, this new Ethernet had a central hub with wires coming out of it, so it looked like a star topology. But the hub was nothing more than a drastically shortened bus, so from an electronic (we like to use the term *logical*) standpoint, the network used a bus topology.

Figure 4-6
Star or bus?

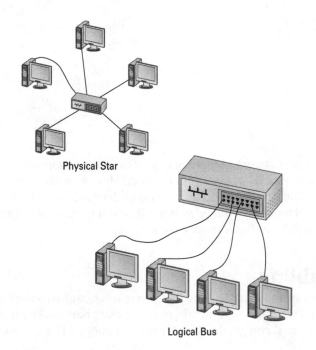

Physical Star

Logical Bus

NOTE A good way to separate logical topology from physical topology is to think about an electronic schematic diagram. The schematic shows how everything connects, but does not represent the way that the piece of electronics physically appears.

The answer to this topology dichotomy was simple—this type of topology was christened the *star bus*. A star bus topology is a *hybrid*, or blend, of the star and bus topologies. Star bus networks use a physical star design, which provides improved reliability, and a logical bus to maintain compatibility with existing bus-topology Ethernet standards. Star bus is overwhelmingly the most common topology used today.

Star bus is not the only hybrid topology. Many years ago, IBM invented a networking technology called *Token Ring* that employs a hybrid topology called *star ring*. A star ring topology works basically the same way as star bus. As with star bus, a central hub connects to the computers via cabling. The only difference is that instead of a logical bus, it uses a logical ring. Token Ring once held a large part of the installed base of networks, but this has slipped considerably over the years as many networks have switched to Ethernet. Token Ring still has a fairly large installed base, however, and the Network+ exam expects you to know its topology. Be warned: in many cases the Token Ring topology is simply referred to as a "star," even though in reality it is a star ring (see Figure 4-7)—be prepared to see it written either way!

Figure 4-7
Token Ring
topology is
a star ring.

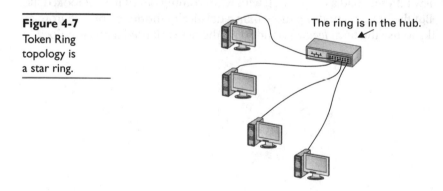

The ring is in the hub.

Every network uses some type of topology. A *topology* simply describes the method by which systems in a network connect. Make sure you know the four basic types of topology: star, ring, bus, and mesh. Also understand that many networks today use one of two hybrid types of topologies: star bus or star ring. Most networks use the star bus topology, but a substantial minority use star ring.

Cabling

The vast majority of networked systems are linked together using some type of cabling. Different types of networks over the years have used a number of different types of cables—and you get the job of learning about all these cables to pass the Network+ exam!

In this section, we'll explore both the cabling types used in older networks and those found in today's networks.

Some cabling types are used by a variety of networks, while other network types use their own unique cabling. Some of the cables I'll discuss have uses outside the networking industry; you'll probably recognize a number of them from their use in cable TV, recording equipment, and telephone systems. Don't assume that a particular cable type listed here is used only in networks!

All cables used in the networking industry separate into three distinct groups: coaxial (coax), twisted pair, and fiber-optic. Let's look at all three.

Coax

Coaxial cable contains a central conductor wire surrounded by an insulating material, which in turn is surrounded by a braided metal shield. The cable is referred to as coaxial (coax for short) because the center wire and the braided metal shield share a common axis or centerline (see Figure 4-8).

Figure 4-8
Cut-away view
of a coaxial cable

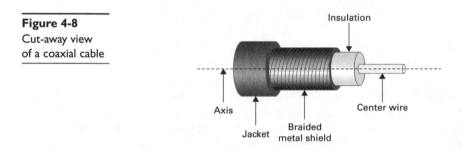

Coaxial cable is designed to shield data transmissions from *electro-magnetic interference (EMI)*. Many devices in the typical office environment generate magnetic fields, including lights, fans, copy machines, and refrigerators. When a metal wire encounters these magnetic fields, electrical current is generated along the wire. This extra current can shut down a network because it is easily misinterpreted as a signal by devices like NICs. To prevent EMI from affecting the network, the outer mesh layer of a coaxial cable shields the center wire (on which the data is transmitted) from interference (see Figure 4-9).

Figure 4-9
The braided
metal shield
prevents
interference
from reaching
the wire.

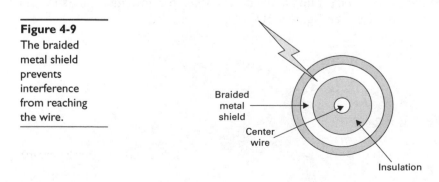

Only three types of coax cable have ever been used in networking: RG-8, RG-62, and RG-58. All coax cables have an *RG rating*; these ratings were developed by the military to provide a quick reference for the different types of coax. The only important measure of coax cabling is its *Ohm rating*, a relative measure of the resistance (or more precisely, characteristic impedance) on the cable. You may run across other coax cables, which may not have acceptable Ohm ratings although they look just like network-rated coax. Fortunately, most coax cable types display their Ohm ratings on the cables themselves (see Figure 4-10).

Figure 4-10
Ohm rating on
a coax cable

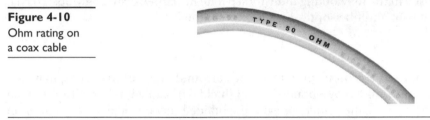

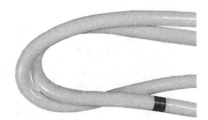 **TIP** Know the Ohm ratings for these cable types!

The Ohm rating of a particular piece of cable describes the impedance of that cable. *Impedance* describes a set of characteristics that define how much a cable resists the flow of electricity. This isn't simple resistance, though. Impedance also factors in things like how long it takes the wire to get a full charge—the wire's capacitance—and other things.

You'd think at first blush that the higher the Ohms rating, the worse the cable would be, but in practice, that's almost irrelevant. The most important aspect of Ohms ratings for network technicians is to use cables with the same rating within a network; otherwise, you'll run into data corruption and data loss. Because almost any kind of coax can use the same connector, take a moment to glance at the Ohms rating before plugging in that handy piece of cable you found lying around!

RG-8

RG-8, often referred to as *Thick Ethernet*, is the oldest coax cabling type still in use. It has the name Thick Ethernet because it is used exclusively with a network technology called—you guessed it—Thick Ethernet! You'll see more on Thick Ethernet (also called Thicknet) and how it uses RG-8 cabling in the next chapter; for now, just make sure you can recognize an RG-8 cable (see Figure 4-11).

Figure 4-11
Thick coaxial
cable (RG-8),
marked with a
black band every
2.5 meters

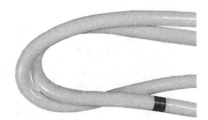

RG-8 is rated at 50 Ohms and has a distinct yellow or orange/brown color. The standardized color makes Thick Ethernet cabling unique, as almost all other types of cabling have no fixed color. Some cable types come in a veritable rainbow of colors!

RG-62

RG-62 cable, rated at 75 Ohms, is virtually never installed in networks these days, but you should know about it nonetheless (see Figure 4-12). If you think RG-62 resembles what your cable TV guy hitched up to your television, you aren't imagining things—cable TV uses the similar RG-6 coax. RG-62 cabling saw widespread use in a network technology called ArcNet, which is quite rare in today's networking world.

Figure 4-12
RG-62 coax cable

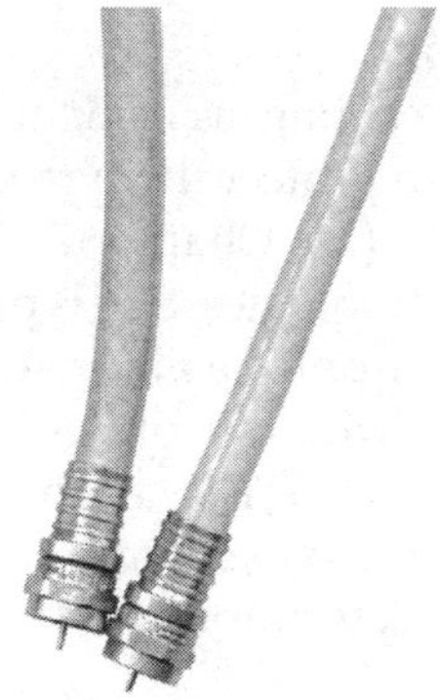

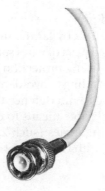

RG-58

Today, RG-58 stands alone as the only coax cable type still widely used in networks. It's often called *Thin Ethernet* or *Thinnet*, which is the name of the network technology that uses it. Thinnet technology is dated, but still used—in fact, I'll discuss it in detail in the next chapter—so you need to be able to recognize the cabling it uses. At first glance, RG-58 may look like RG-62 (see Figure 4-13), but its 50-Ohm rating makes it different on the inside.

Figure 4-13
RG-58 coax cable

Twisted Pair

The most overwhelmingly common type of cabling used in networks consists of twisted pairs of cables. Networks use two types of twisted-pair cabling: shielded twisted pair (STP) and unshielded twisted pair (UTP). Twisted-pair cabling for networks is composed of multiple pairs of wires, twisted around each other at specific intervals. The twists serve to reduce interference, called *crosstalk*: the more twists, the less crosstalk.

 NOTE Have you ever picked up a telephone and heard a distinct crackling noise? That's an example of crosstalk.

Shielded Twisted Pair

Shielded twisted pair (STP) cabling, as its name implies, consists of twisted pairs of wires surrounded by shielding to protect them from EMI. STP cabling is mostly confined to older Token Ring networks (see Chapter 7, "Non-Ethernet Networks") and a few rare high-speed networking technologies. STP is pretty rare, primarily because there's so little need for STP's shielding; it only really matters in locations with excessive electronic noise, such as a shop floor with lots of lights, electric motors, or other machinery that could cause problems for UTP. UTP is cheaper, and in most cases, does just as good a job as STP. Figure 4-14 shows the most common STP type: the venerable IBM Type 1 cable used in Token Ring network technology.

Figure 4-14
IBM Type 1
shielded
twisted-pair
cable

Unshielded Twisted Pair

Unshielded twisted pair (UTP) is by far the most common type of network cabling used today. UTP consists of twisted pairs of wires surrounded by a plastic jacket (see Figure 4-15). This jacket does not provide any protection from EMI, so some consideration must be used when installing UTP cabling to avoid interference from light, motors, and so forth.

Although more sensitive to interference than coaxial or STP cable, UTP cabling provides an inexpensive and flexible means to cable networks. UTP cable isn't exclusive to networks; many other technologies (such as telephone systems) employ the same cabling. This makes working with UTP a bit of a challenge. Imagine going up into a ceiling

Figure 4-15
UTP cabling

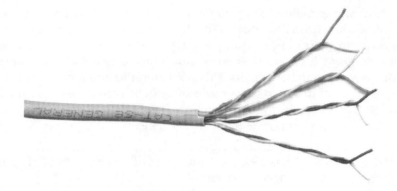

PART II

and seeing two sets of UTP cables: how would you determine which is for the telephones and which is for the network? Not to worry—a number of installation standards and tools exist to help those who work with UTP get the answer to these types of questions.

Not all UTP cables are the same! UTP cabling has a number of variations, such as the number of twists per foot, which determine how quickly data can propagate on the cable. To help network installers get the right cable for the right network technology, the cabling industry has developed a variety of grades called *categories* or *CAT ratings*. CAT ratings are officially rated in *megahertz (MHz)*, indicating the highest frequency bandwidth the cable can handle. Table 4-1 shows the most common categories.

UTP cables are rated to handle a certain bandwidth, such as 10 MHz or 100 MHz, which originally translated as the maximum throughput for a cable. On a one-for-one basis, for example, a 10 million cycle per second (10 MHz) cable could accommodate 10 million bits per second (10 Mbps)—1 bit per cycle. Through the use of *bandwidth-efficient encoding schemes*, such as MLT-3, manufacturers can squeeze more bits into the same signal, as long as the cable can handle it. Thus the CAT 5e cable can handle throughput of up to 1000 Mbps, even though it's rated to handle a bandwidth of only up to 100 MHz.

CAT Rating	Bandwidth	Typical Throughput in Networks
CAT 1	< 1 MHz	Analog phone lines—not for data communication
CAT 2	4 MHz	Supports speeds up to 4 Mbps
CAT 3	16 MHz	Supports speeds up to 16 Mbps[1]
CAT 4	20 MHz	Supports speeds up to 20 Mbps
CAT 5	100 MHz	Supports speeds up to 100 Mbps
CAT 5e (Improved CAT 5)	100 MHz	Supports speeds up to 1000 Mbps
CAT 6	200–250 MHz	Supports speeds up to 10,000 Mbps

[1] Note that the throughput for CAT 3 cable listed here applies only to network technologies that use two pairs of wires in the cable, not four pairs.

Table 4-1   UTP Categories

CAT ratings define the speed on a per-pair basis. CAT levels do not say how many pairs of wires are in the cable! UTP cable is made in many variations, with varying numbers of wire pairs. For example, you can purchase CAT 5 cable with two pairs, four pairs, or even more. It's impossible to say how much data a particular cable can carry unless you know the number of pairs. The speed examples listed here assume network technologies that use either two or four pairs of wires in a cable. As we go into different network technologies in later chapters, you'll see how the number of pairs becomes important. For now, simply appreciate that CAT ratings exist and that they have different speeds.

TIP Many people use the term *CAT level* instead of *CAT rating*. Be comfortable interchanging these terms!

As most networks are designed to run at speeds of up to 100 MHz, most new cabling installations use Category 5e (CAT 5e) cabling. CAT 5e cabling currently costs much less than CAT 6, although as CAT 6 gains in popularity, it will undoubtedly drop in price. Make sure you can look at UTP and know its CAT rating. There are two places to look. First, UTP is typically sold in boxed reels, and the manufacturer will clearly mark the CAT level on the box (see Figure 4-16). Second, look on the cable itself. The category level of a piece of cable is usually printed on the cable (see Figure 4-17).

Figure 4-16
Box of UTP showing CAT rating

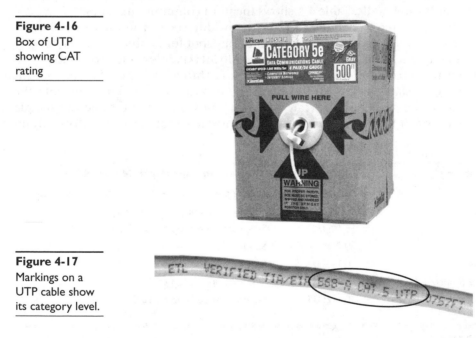

Figure 4-17
Markings on a UTP cable show its category level.

Fiber-Optic

Fiber-optic cabling transmits light rather than electricity, making it attractive for both high-EMI areas and long-distance transmissions. While most copper cables cannot carry data more than a few hundred meters at best, fiber-optic cabling will operate, depending on the implementation, for distances of up to 10 kilometers. A fiber-optic cable has three components: the fiber itself; the *cladding*, which is the part that makes the light reflect down the fiber; and the *insulating jacket*. Fiber-optic cabling is manufactured with many different diameters of fiber and cladding. In a convenient bit of standardization, cable manufacturers use a two-number designator to define fiber-optic cables according to their fiber and cladding measurements. The most common fiber-optic cable size is 62.5/125 µm. Almost all network technologies that use fiber-optic cable require pairs of fibers. In response to the demand for two-pair cabling, manufacturers often connect two fibers together like a lamp cord to create the popular duplex fiber-optic cabling (Figure 4-18).

Figure 4-18
Duplex fiber-optic cable

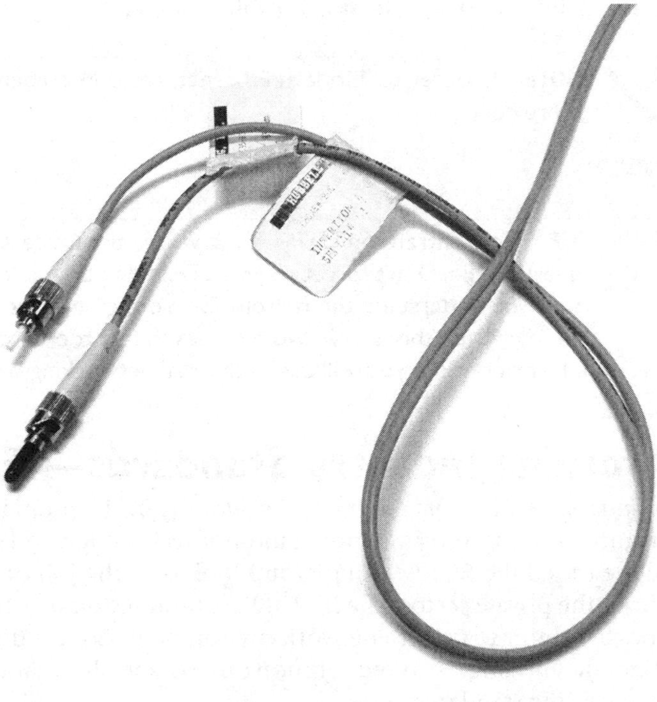

NOTE For those of you unfamiliar with it, the odd little u-shaped symbol describing fiber cable size (µ) stands for micro, or 1/1000th. Fiber cables are pretty tiny!

Light can be sent down a fiber-optic cable as regular light or as laser light. The two types of light require totally different fiber-optic cables. Most network technologies that use fiber optics use LEDs (light emitting diodes) to send light signals. Fiber-optic cables that use LEDs are known as *multimode*. Fiber-optic cables that use lasers are known as *single-mode*. Using laser light and single-mode fiber-optic cables enables a network to achieve phenomenally high transfer rates over incredibly long distances. It's difficult to differentiate between single-mode and multimode cable. Well, there's one easy way—single-mode cable is currently quite rare; if you see fiber-optic cabling, you can be relatively sure it's multimode.

Installing fiber-optic cabling is basically a love/hate arrangement. On the love side, fiber-optic cables don't carry electricity, so you can ignore the electrical interference issue. Also, fiber-optic cabling can reach up to 10,000 meters. This depends on the networking technology used, of course, and the most common network technology that uses fiber-optic cabling has a much lower limit of *only* 1000 meters! On the hate side of the fiber-optic equation is the chore of getting it into the walls. Fiber-optic cabling installations are tedious and difficult, although fiber-optic manufacturers continue to make new strides in easing the job. Fiber-optic cabling is fragile and will fail if it is bent much. My advice: leave this job to a professional cable installer.

NOTE Chapter 6, "Modern Ethernet," goes into fiber-optic technology in more detail.

TIP Concentrate on UTP—that's where the hardest Network+ questions lie. Don't forget to give STP and fiber a quick pass, and make sure you understand the reasons for picking one type of cabling over another. Even though Network+ doesn't test too hard on cabling, this is important information that you will use in the real networking world.

Networking Industry Standards—IEEE

The *Institute of Electrical and Electronics Engineers (IEEE)* defines industry-wide standards that promote the use and implementation of technology. In February of 1980, a new committee called the 802 working group took over the job of defining network standards from the private sector. The IEEE 802 committee defines frames, speed, distances, and types of cabling to use in a network environment. Concentrating on cables, the IEEE recognizes that no single cabling solution can work in all situations, and thus provides a variety of cabling standards.

IEEE committees define standards for a wide variety of electronics. The names of these committees are often used to refer to the standards they publish. The IEEE 1284 committee, for example, sets standards for parallel communication. Have you ever seen a printer cable marked "IEEE 1284-compliant," as in Figure 4-19? This means the manufacturer followed the rules set by the IEEE 1284 committee. Another committee you may have heard of is the IEEE 1394 committee, which controls the FireWire standard.

The IEEE 802 committee sets the standards for networking. Although the original plan was to define a single, universal standard for networking, it quickly became apparent that no single solution would work for all needs. The 802 committee was split into smaller subcommittees, with names such as IEEE 802.3 and IEEE 802.5. Table 4-2 shows the currently recognized IEEE 802 subcommittees and their areas of jurisdiction.

Figure 4-19
An IEEE 1284-
compliant printer
cable

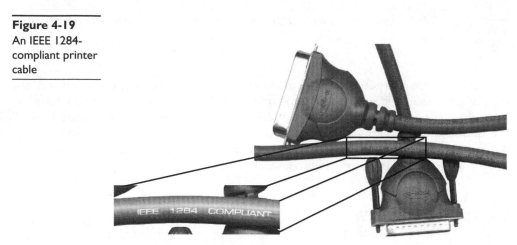

IEEE 802	LAN/MAN Overview & Architecture
IEEE 802.1	LAN/MAN Bridging and Management (Higher Layer LAN Protocols)
IEEE 802.1s	Multiple Spanning Tree
IEEE 802.1w	Rapid Reconfiguration of Spanning Tree
IEEE 802.1x	Port-based Network Access Control
IEEE 802.2	Logical Link Control (LLC)
IEEE 802.3	CSMA/CD access method (Ethernet)
IEEE 802.3ae	10 Gigabit Ethernet
IEEE 802.4	Token Passing Bus access method and Physical layer specifications
IEEE 802.5	Token Ring access method and Physical layer specifications
IEEE 802.6	Distributed Queue Dual Bus (DQDB) access method and Physical layer specifications (Metropolitan Area Networks)
IEEE 802.7	Broadband LAN
IEEE 802.8	Fiber Optic
IEEE 802.9	Isochronous LANs (standard withdrawn)
IEEE 802.10	Interoperable LAN/MAN Security
IEEE 802.11	Wireless LAN Medium Access Control (MAC) and Physical layer specifications
IEEE 802.12	Demand-priority access method, Physical layer, and repeater specifications
IEEE 802.13	Not used
IEEE 802.14	Cable modems (proposed standard withdrawn)
IEEE 802.15	Wireless Personal Area Network (WPAN)
IEEE 802.16	Wireless Metropolitan Area Network (Wireless MAN)
IEEE 802.17	Resilient Packet Ring (RPR) Access

Table 4-2   IEEE 802 subcommittees

TIP Memorize the 802.2, 802.3, 802.5, and 802.11 standards. Ignore the rest.

Some of these committees deal with technologies that didn't quite make it, and the committees associated with those standards, such as IEEE 802.4, Token Bus, have become dormant. When preparing for the Network+ exam—and more important, for real-life networking situations—concentrate on the IEEE 802.3, 802.5, and 802.11 standards. The others rarely impact the life of a network tech directly. You'll see each of the three main 802 standards in detail in later chapters.

Chapter Review

Questions

1. Which of the following standards defines Token Ring networks?

   A. IEEE 802.3

   B. IEEE 802.5

   C. EIA/TIA 568A

   D. IEEE 1284

2. Token Ring networks use a _____ physical topology and a _____ logical topology.

   A. Mesh, ring

   B. Ring, star

   C. Star, ring

   D. Ring, bus

3. Of the topologies listed, which one is the most fault-tolerant and has the most redundancy?

   A. Mesh

   B. Bus

   C. Star

   D. Ring

4. What term is used to describe the logical layout of network components?

   A. Segmentation

   B. Map

   C. Topology

   D. Protocol

5. Which of the following IEEE standards defines wireless networking?

   A. 802.8

   B. 802.9

   C. 802.10

   D. 802.11

6. Which IEEE standard defines the CSMA/CD access method?

   A. 802.2

   B. 802.3

   C. 802.4

   D. 802.5

7. Which of the following is *not* a type of coaxial cable?

   A. RJ-45

   B. RG-58

   C. RG-8

   D. RG-6

8. Which network topology connects nodes with a central ring of cable?

   A. Star

   B. Bus

   C. Ring

   D. Mesh

9. Which network topology uses a central hub?

   A. Star

   B. Bus

   C. Ring

   D. Mesh

10. Which of the following network topologies is the easiest to configure?

   A. Star

   B. Bus

   C. Ring

   D. Mesh

Answers

1. **B.** IEEE 802.5 defines Token Ring networks. EIA/TIA 568A is a cabling standard for UTP cabling that is used in both Token Ring and Ethernet networks.

2. **C.** Token Ring networks use a star physical topology and a ring logical topology.

3. **A.** Mesh topology is the most fault-tolerant and has the most redundancy because each computer has a dedicated connection to every other computer on the network.

4. **C.** *Topology* is the term used to describe the layout of a network: how computers connect to each other without regard to how they communicate.

5. **D.** The IEEE 802.11 standard defines wireless networking.

6. **B.** The IEEE 802.3 standard defines the CSMA/CD access method, part of the Ethernet standard.

7. **A.** RJ-45 is a type of connector used on unshielded twisted pair cables. All the others are types of coaxial cable.

8. **C.** The aptly named ring topology connects nodes with a central ring of cable.

9. **A.** A star topology uses a central hub.

10. **A.** A star topology is the easiest to configure.

Ethernet Basics

The Network+ Certification exam expects you to know how to
- 1.2   Specify the main features of 802.2 (Logical Link Control) [and] 802.3 (Ethernet) ... networking technologies, including speed, access method, topology, [and] media
- 1.5   Recognize the following media types and describe their uses: coaxial cable
- 1.6   Identify the purposes, features, and functions of bridges
- 2.3   Identify the OSI (Open Systems Interconnect) layers at which bridges operate

To achieve these goals, you must be able to
- Describe the concept of Ethernet
- Define Ethernet cabling systems
- Explain the function of repeaters and bridges

In the beginning, there were no networks. Computers were isolated, solitary islands of information in a teeming sea of proto-geeks. If you wanted to move a file from one machine to another—and proto-geeks were as much into that as modern geeks—you had to use Sneakernet, which meant you saved the file on a disk, laced up your tennis shoes, and hiked over to the other system. All that walking no doubt produced lots of health benefits, but frankly, proto-geeks weren't all that into health benefits—they were into speed, power, and technological coolness in general. (Sound familiar?) It's no wonder, then, that geeks everywhere agreed on the need to replace Sneakernet with a faster and more efficient method of sharing data. The method they came up with is the subject of this chapter.

Historical/Conceptual

In 1973, Xerox answered the challenge of moving data without sneakers by developing *Ethernet*, a networking technology standard based on a bus topology. The Ethernet standard, which predominates in today's networks, defines many issues involved in transferring data between computer systems. The original Ethernet used a single piece of coaxial cable to connect several computers, enabling them to transfer data at a rate of up to 3 Mbps. Although slow by today's standards, this early version of Ethernet was a huge improvement over Sneakernet methods, and served as the foundation for all later versions of Ethernet. It remained a largely in-house technology within Xerox until 1979, when Xerox decided to look for partners to help promote Ethernet as an industry standard. They worked with Digital Equipment Corporation (DEC) and Intel to publish what became known as the Digital-Intel-Xerox (DIX) standard. Running on coaxial cable, the DIX standard enabled multiple computers to communicate with each other at a screaming 10 Mbps. Although 10 Mbps represents the low end of standard network speeds today, at the time it was revolutionary. These companies then transferred control of the Ethernet standard to the IEEE, which in turn created the now famous *802.3 (Ethernet)* committee that continues to control the Ethernet standard to this day. The remainder of this book follows common parlance in using the terms Ethernet and IEEE 802.3 interchangeably.

TIP　The source for all things Ethernet is but a short click away on the Internet. Check out www.ieee802.org for starters.

Ethernet today is not a single network technology, but rather a standard for a family of network technologies that share the same basic bus topology, frame type, and network access method. Ethernet manufacturers have created a number of network technologies since Ethernet first came onto the scene more than 30 years ago. Different types of Ethernet use completely different cabling and NICs. This chapter shows you how Ethernet works, and then shows you the first generation of Ethernet technologies: Thick Ethernet (a.k.a. 10Base5) and Thin Ethernet (a.k.a. 10Base2). Both of these versions of Ethernet used a physical bus topology—a single cable that connected to all the computers on the network.

Providing a clear and concise definition of Ethernet has long been one of the major challenges in teaching networking. This difficulty stems from the fact that Ethernet has changed over the years to incorporate new and improved technology. Most folks won't even try to define Ethernet, but here's my best attempt at a current definition.

Ethernet is a standard for a family of network technologies that share the same basic bus topology, frame type, and network access method. Because the technologies share these essential components, you can communicate between them just fine. The implementation of the network might be different, but the frames remain the same.

How Ethernet Works

Ethernet's designers faced the same challenges as the designers of any network: how to send data across the wire, how to identify the sending and receiving computers, and how to determine which computer should use the shared cable at what time. The engineers resolved these issues by using data frames that contain MAC addresses to identify computers on the network, and by using a process called *CSMA/CD* to determine which machine should access the wire at any given time. You saw some of this in action in Chapter 3, "Building a Network with OSI," but now I need to introduce you to a bunch of new terms, so let's look at each of these solutions.

Physical Bus

The first generations of Ethernet used a physical and logical bus topology. A physical bus means a physical cable, and all early Ethernet networks were distinguished by a single coaxial cable snaking around the network, usually in the ceiling. Each computer on the network connected into the cable. This single cable had many interchangeable names, among them the *segment,* the *cable,* and the *bus.* Be comfortable using any of these terms to describe that single piece of cable that connects all the computers on an Ethernet network (Figure 5-1).

Organizing the Data: Ethernet Frames

All network technologies break data transmitted between computers into smaller pieces called *frames,* as you'll recall from Chapter 3. Using frames addresses two networking issues. First, it prevents any single machine from monopolizing the shared bus cable. Second, frames make the process of retransmitting lost data more efficient.

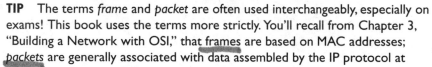 **TIP** The terms *frame* and *packet* are often used interchangeably, especially on exams! This book uses the terms more strictly. You'll recall from Chapter 3, "Building a Network with OSI," that frames are based on MAC addresses; packets are generally associated with data assembled by the IP protocol at Layer 3 of the OSI seven-layer model.

The process you saw in the previous chapter of transferring a word processing document between two computers illustrates these two issues. First, if the sending computer sends the document as a single huge frame, it will monopolize the cable and prevent other machines from using the cable until the entire file gets to the receiving system. Using relatively small frames enables computers to share the cable easily—each computer listens on the segment, sending a few frames of data whenever it detects that no other computer is transmitting. Second, in the real world, bad things can happen to good data. When errors occur during transmission, the sending system must retransmit the frames that failed to get to the receiving system in good shape. If a word processing

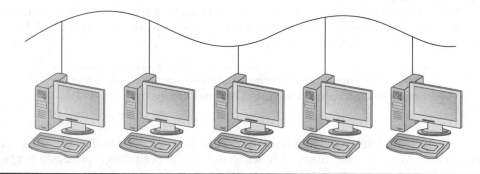

Figure 5-1   Ethernet segment

document were transmitted as a single massive frame, the sending system would have to retransmit the entire frame—in this case, the entire document. Breaking the file up into smaller frames enables the sending computer to retransmit only the damaged frames. Because of their benefits—shared access and reduced retransmission—all networking technologies use frames, and Ethernet is no exception to that rule.

In Chapter 3, you saw a generic frame. Let's take what you know of frames and expand on that knowledge by inspecting the details of an Ethernet frame. A basic Ethernet frame contains seven basic pieces of information: the preamble, the MAC address of the frame's recipient, the MAC address of the sending system, the length of the data, the data itself, a pad, and a frame check sequence. Figure 5-2 shows these components.

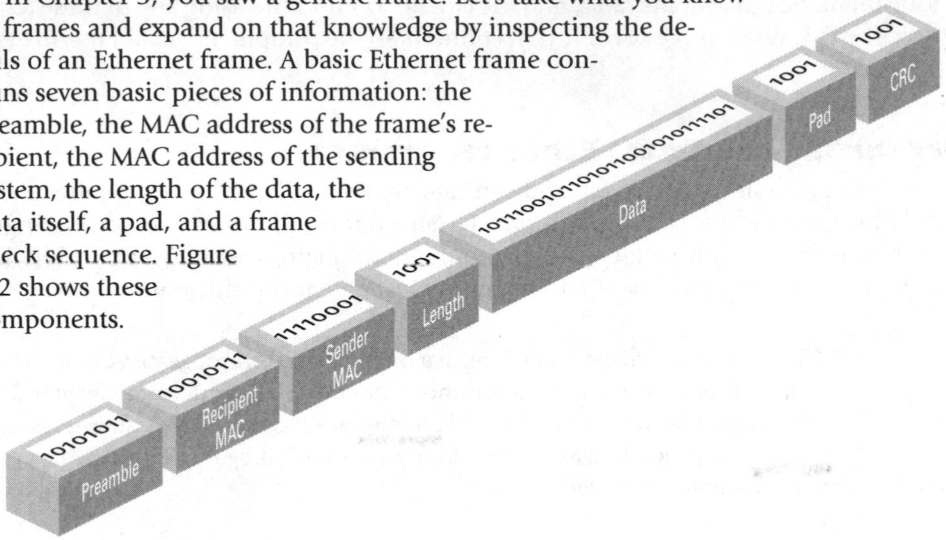

Figure 5-2   A simplified Ethernet data frame

Preamble
All Ethernet frames begin with a *preamble*, a 64-bit series of alternating ones and zeroes that ends with 11. The preamble gives a receiving NIC time to realize a frame is coming and to know exactly where the frame starts. The preamble is added by the sending NIC.

MAC Addresses
Each NIC, more commonly called a *node,* on an Ethernet network must have a unique identifying address. Ethernet identifies the NICs on a network using special 48-bit binary addresses known as *MAC addresses.*

TIP   There are many situations where one computer might have two or more NICs, so one system might represent more than one node!

MAC addresses give each NIC a unique address. When a computer sends out a data frame, it transmits it to every other node across the wire in both directions, as shown Figure 5-3. All the other computers on the network listen to the wire and examine the frame

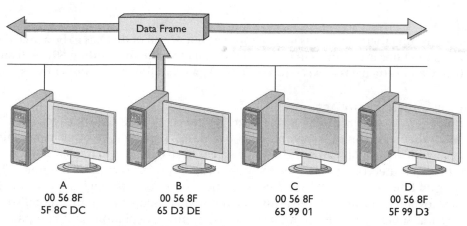

Figure 5-3 Sending out a frame

to see if it contains their MAC address. If not, they ignore the frame. If a machine sees a frame with its MAC address, it opens the frame and begins processing the data.

This system of allowing each machine to decide which frames it will process may be efficient, but because any device connected to the network cable can potentially capture any data frame transmitted across the wire, Ethernet networks carry a significant security vulnerability. Network diagnostic programs, commonly called *sniffers*, can order a NIC to run in *promiscuous mode*. When running in promiscuous mode, the NIC processes all the frames it sees on the cable, regardless of their MAC addresses. Sniffers are valuable troubleshooting tools in the right hands, but Ethernet provides no protections against their unscrupulous use.

NOTE You can find some software, such as AntiSniff, that can often detect when sniffers are in use on a network. None of the software hits close to 100 percent accuracy, but something is better than nothing. Good network administrators employ such countermeasures to stop malicious users from messing up the network.

Length

An Ethernet frame may carry up to 1500 bytes of data in a single frame, but this is only a maximum. Frames can definitely carry fewer bytes of data. The length field tells the receiving system how many bytes of data this frame is carrying.

Data

This part of the frame contains whatever data the frame carries. (If this is an IP network, it will include extra information, such as the IP addresses of both systems, sequencing numbers, and other information as well as data.)

Pad

The minimum Ethernet frame is 64 bytes in size, but not all of that has to be actual data. If an Ethernet frame has fewer than 64 bytes of data to haul, the sending NIC will automatically add extra data—a *pad*—to bring the data up to the minimum 64 bytes.

Frame Check Sequence

The *frame check sequence*—Ethernet's term for the cyclic redundancy check (CRC)—enables Ethernet nodes to recognize when bad things happen to good data. Machines on a network must be able to detect when data has been damaged in transit. To detect errors, the computers on an Ethernet network attach a special code to each frame. When creating an Ethernet frame, the sending machine runs the data through a special mathematical formula and attaches the result, the frame check sequence, to the frame. The receiving machine opens the frame, performs the same calculation, and compares its answer with the one included with the frame. If the answers do not match, the receiving machine will ask the sending machine to retransmit that frame.

At this point, those crafty network engineers have solved two of the problems facing them: they've created frames to organize the data to be sent, and put in place MAC addresses to identify machines on the network. But the challenge of determining which machine should send data at which time required another solution: CSMA/CD.

Test Specific

CSMA/CD

Ethernet networks use a system called *carrier sense, multiple access/collision detection (CSMA/CD)* to determine which computer should use a shared cable at a given moment. *Carrier sense* means that each node using the network examines the cable before sending a data frame (see Figure 5-4). If another machine is using the network, the node will detect traffic on the segment, wait a few milliseconds, and then recheck. If it detects no traffic—the more common term is to say the cable is "free"—the node will send out its frame.

Multiple access means that all machines have equal access to the wire. If the line is free, any Ethernet node may begin sending a frame. From the point of view of Ethernet, it doesn't matter what function the node is performing: it could be a desktop system running Windows XP, or a high-end file server running Windows 2003 Server or even Linux. As far as Ethernet is concerned, a node is a node is a node, and access to the cable is assigned strictly on a first-come, first-served basis.

So what happens if two machines, both listening to the cable, simultaneously decide that it is free and try to send a frame? When two computers try to use the cable simultaneously, a collision occurs, and both of the transmissions are lost (see Figure 5-5). A collision resembles the effect of two people talking at the same time: the listener hears a mixture of two voices, and can't understand either one.

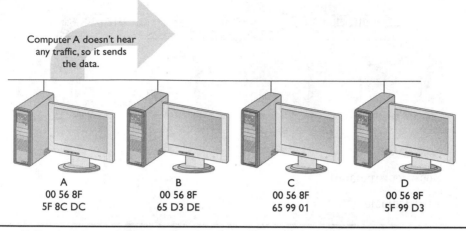

Computer A doesn't hear any traffic, so it sends the data.

A	B	C	D
00 56 8F	00 56 8F	00 56 8F	00 56 8F
5F 8C DC	65 D3 DE	65 99 01	5F 99 D3

Figure 5-4   A node on an Ethernet network listens for traffic before it sends out a data frame.

Both machines will detect the fact that a collision has occurred by listening to their own transmissions. People talking on the telephone use a similar technique to know whether they are the only ones speaking at a particular moment. By comparing the words they speak with the sounds they hear, they know whether other people are talking. If a person hears words he or she didn't say, he or she knows someone else is also talking.

Ethernet nodes do the same thing. They compare their own transmission with the transmission they are receiving over the cable, and use the result to determine whether another node has transmitted at the same time (Figure 5-6). If they detect a collision, both nodes immediately stop transmitting. They then each generate a random number to determine how long to wait before trying again. If you imagine that each machine rolls its magic electronic dice and waits for that number of seconds, you wouldn't be too far from the truth, except that the amount of time an Ethernet node waits to retransmit is much shorter than one second (see Figure 5-7). Whichever node generates the lowest random number begins its retransmission first, winning the competition to use the wire. The losing node then sees traffic on the wire, and waits for the wire to be free again before attempting to retransmit its data.

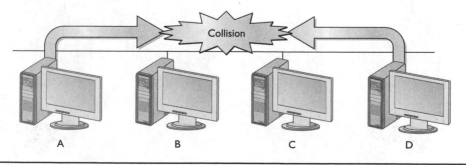

Collision

Figure 5-5   When two machines transmit simultaneously, their data frames collide.

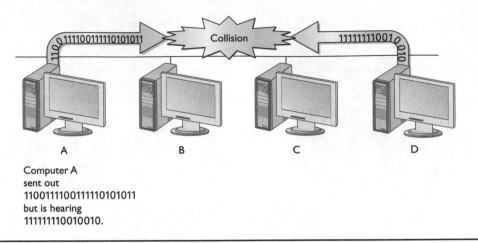

Computer A
sent out
110011110011110101011
but is hearing
111111110010010.

Figure 5-6   An Ethernet node detects a collision.

 NOTE   Because we're on the topic of collisions, a commonly used term in the Ethernet world is *collision domain*. A collision domain is a group of nodes that hear each other's traffic. A segment is certainly a collision domain, but there are ways to connect segments together to create larger collision domains. If the collision domain gets too large, you'll start running into traffic problems that manifest as general network sluggishness. That's one of the reasons to break up networks into smaller groupings. I'll discuss this in detail in Chapter 6, "Modern Ethernet."

CSMA/CD has the benefit of being simple to program into Ethernet devices, such as NIC cards. That simplicity comes at a price: an Ethernet node will waste some amount of its time dealing with collisions instead of sending data. To illustrate this waste, and the

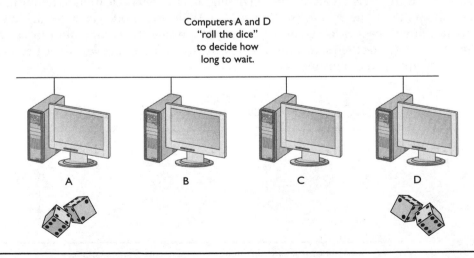

Figure 5-7   Following a collision, each node generates a random number and waits to try again.

chaos inherent to CSMA/CD, imagine a five-node network. Machines A and C both have outgoing data frames and begin the CSMA/CD process for sending traffic. They examine the cable and determine that no other node is currently sending out data (carrier sense). Because the cable is available, both A and C assume they are free to use it (multiple access). When they begin sending their respective data frames, they both detect that another station is also sending data (collision detection). Nodes A and C each generate a random number and begin counting down. Sticking with the dice analogy, assume node A rolls a 5 and node C rolls a 6. They begin counting down. 1, 2, 3, WAIT! Node E just started sending! Node E had no involvement in the original collision, and has no idea that nodes A and C are contending for the right to use the cable. All node E knows is that no device is using the cable at this moment. According to the CSMA/CD rules, E can begin sending. Nodes A and C have both lost out and now must wait again for the cable to be free.

The chaotic CSMA/CD method of determining access to the cable explains experiences common to users of Ethernet networks. At 9:00 on a Monday morning, 100 users sit down at approximately the same time, and type in their user names and passwords to log onto their Ethernet network. Virtually every station on the network contends for the use of the cable at the same time, causing massive collisions and attempted retransmissions. Only rarely will the end users receive any kind of error message caused by high levels of traffic. Instead, they will perceive that the network is running slowly. The Ethernet NICs will continue to retry transmission, and will eventually send the data frames successfully. Only if the collisions get so severe that a frame cannot be sent after 16 retries will the sending station give up, resulting in an error of some kind being reported to the user.

Collisions are a normal part of the operation of an Ethernet network. Every Ethernet network wastes some amount of its available bandwidth dealing with these collisions. A properly running average Ethernet network has a maximum of 10 percent collisions—for every ten frames sent, one will collide and require a resend. Collision rates greater than 10 percent often point to damaged NICs or out-of-control software.

Termination

The use of CSMA/CD in the real world has physical consequences for Ethernet networks. Most Ethernet networks use copper cabling to transmit their data frames as electrical signals. When an electrical signal travels down a copper wire, several things happen when the signal reaches the end of the wire. Some of the energy radiates out as radio waves, the cable functioning like the antennae on a radio transmitter. But some of the energy reflects off the end of the wire and travels back up the wire (see Figure 5-8).

Figure 5-8
When electricity hits the end of the wire, some of the electricity comes back up the wire as a reflection.

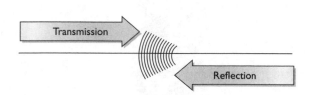

Figure 5-9
Reflections look like a busy signal to the computers attached to the network.

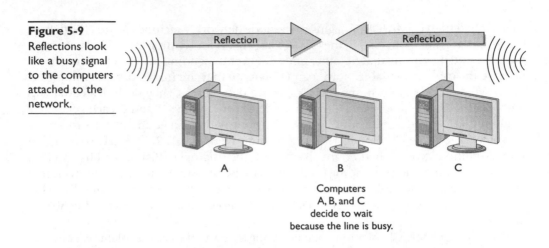

Computers
A, B, and C
decide to wait
because the line is busy.

This reflection might make a radio run well, but it spells disaster for an Ethernet network unless we do something about the reflection. Imagine this scenario: an Ethernet card sends out a frame, which propagates along the segment, reflecting off both ends of the segment. When the other Ethernet nodes on the network attempt to send, they check the cable and misinterpret that reflection as another node sending out data frames. They wait for the reflection to dissipate before sending. The reflections quickly build up to a point that the network looks permanently busy to all of the nodes attached to it (see Figure 5-9).

To prevent these reflections, all Ethernet segments require a *terminating resistor* connected at each end (see Figure 5-10). This resistor, usually just called a *terminator*, absorbs the reflections, thereby enabling the segment to function properly. A CSMA/CD network using copper cabling won't function properly unless both ends of the network bus cable are terminated with terminating resistors.

 NOTE Those of you who know something about networks might be wondering about star topologies and termination. I promise I'll cover all that in Chapter 6, "Modern Ethernet."

Figure 5-10
Two 50-Ohm terminating resistors of the type used with 10Base2 cable

Cable Breaks

The use of CSMA/CD in Ethernet networks causes some interesting behavior when the cable breaks. Figure 5-11 shows a five-node network connected to a single segment of cable. If the piece of cable between computer *A* and computer *B* breaks, computer *A* will not be able to communicate with the rest of the machines (see Figure 5-12). But that's not the end of the trouble, because a break anywhere in the bus cable causes a loss of termination in the cable. This results in reflections in both directions, prompting all the nodes on the network to go into perpetual waiting mode (see Figure 5-13), thereby shutting down the entire network.

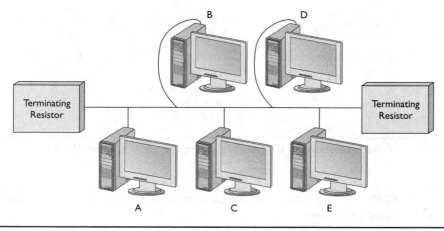

Figure 5-11   An Ethernet network with five computers

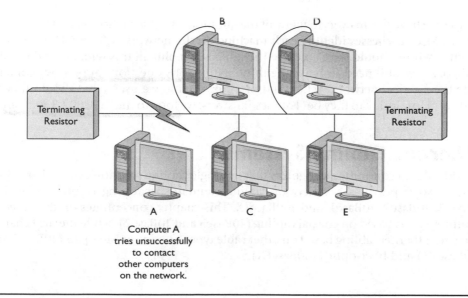

Figure 5-12   A cable break cuts computer A off from the rest of the network.

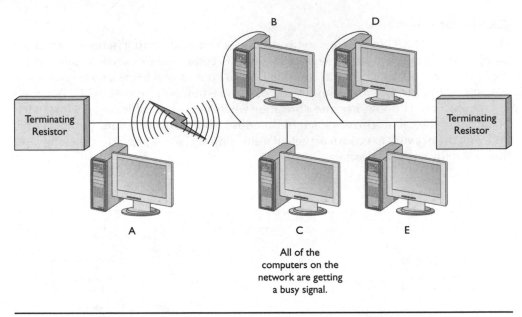

All of the
computers on the
network are getting
a busy signal.

Figure 5-13   Reflections caused by the cable break bring the whole network down.

NOTE   The bus cable to which computers on an Ethernet network connect is called a segment.

Now we have the answers to many of the questions that faced those early Ethernet designers. MAC addresses identify each machine on the network. CSMA/CD determines which machine should have access to the cable when. But all this remains in the realm of theory—we still need to build the thing! Numerous questions arise as we contemplate the physical network. What kind of cables should we use? What should they be made of? How long can they be? For these answers, we look to the IEEE 802.3 standard.

Ethernet Cabling Systems

The IEEE 802.3 committee recognizes that no single cabling solution can work in all situations, so it provides a variety of cabling standards, featuring cryptic names like 10Base5, 10Base2, 10BaseT, and 100BaseTX. This chapter concentrates on the Ethernet cabling systems based on coaxial cabling (10Base5 and 10Base2), while the next chapter discusses Ethernet cabling based on other cable types, such as twisted-pair (10BaseT and 100BaseTX) and fiber-optic (100BaseFX).

10Base5

In the beginning, the term "Ethernet" referred specifically to a CSMA/CD network running over a thick RG-8 coaxial cable, like the one shown in Figure 5-14. Although a specific color was not required by any standard, the cable was almost always yellow. Network techs refer to the original thick yellow cable used for Ethernet as Thick Ethernet, or Thicknet. Thicknet has the heaviest shielding of any cabling commonly used for 10-Mbps Ethernet, making it an excellent choice for high-interference environments. Because of its rigidity and typical color, the less formal among us occasionally refer to RG-8 cable as "yellow cable" or "frozen yellow garden hose."

Figure 5-14
Thick Ethernet cable (RG-8) is yellow, with a black band marking every 2.5 meters.

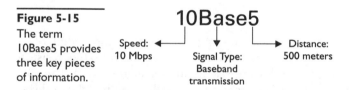

When the IEEE took charge of the Ethernet standard, it created a more structured way to refer to the various Ethernet cabling systems, and began referring to Thick Ethernet as 10Base5, a term that specifies the speed of the cabling system, its signaling type, and its distance limitations. 10Base5 breaks down as follows (see Figure 5-15):

Figure 5-15
The term 10Base5 provides three key pieces of information.

- **Speed** The *10* in 10Base5 signifies an Ethernet network that runs at 10 Mbps.

- **Signal type** The *Base* in 10Base5 signifies the use of baseband signaling, meaning a single signal is on the cable.

- **Distance** The *5* in 10Base5 indicates that cables may not be longer than 500 meters.

Baseband vs. Broadband

Data signals can be sent over a network cable in two ways: *broadband* and *baseband*. Cable television is an example of broadband transmission. The single piece of coaxial cable that comes into your home carries multiple signals, and a small box enables you to select specific channels. Broadband creates these separate channels through a process called *frequency division multiplexing*. Each channel is a different frequency of signal. Your television or cable box filters out all but the frequency you want to see. Baseband is a much simpler process: it sends a single signal over the cable (see Figure 5-16). Ethernet networks use baseband signaling that employs simple *transceivers* (the devices that transmit and receive signals on the cable) because they only need to distinguish among three states on the cable: one, zero, and idle. Broadband transceivers must be more complex because they have to be able to distinguish those three states on multiple channels within the same cable. Most computer networks use baseband signaling because of its relative simplicity.

Figure 5-16
Baseband signaling sends a single signal at any given instant, whereas broadband signaling sends multiple signals on separate frequencies.

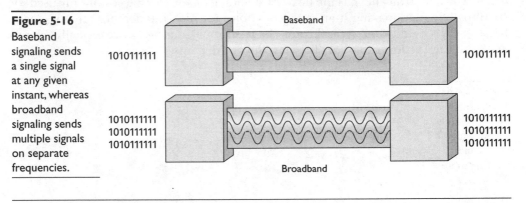

NOTE Cable modems are the only common networking devices that use broadband signaling.

Distance Limitations

10Base5 segments cannot be longer than 500 meters. A *segment* is the single length of cable to which the computers on an Ethernet network connect. The terminating resistors at each end of the segment define the ends of the segment (see Figure 5-17). The 500-meter segment limitation applies to the entire segment, not to the length of the cable between any two machines.

The distance limitations on Ethernet segments (of all sorts) provide a guideline, rather than a rigid rule for a properly functioning network. If you accidentally made a 10Base5 segment 501 meters long, the network would not suddenly cease to function or self-destruct! You would simply lower the possibility that data would get to the computers intact.

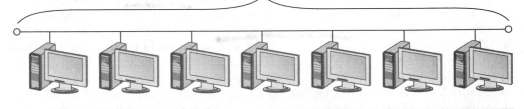

Figure 5-17 A 10Base5 Ethernet segment

The 10Base5 cabling standard strictly defines how nodes connect to the segment. Unlike nodes in many other cabling systems, 10Base5 nodes do not connect directly to the bus cable. Instead, 10Base5 NICs use a 15-pin female DB connector, called an *AUI connector*, to connect to an external transceiver (see Figure 5-18). This connector is physically identical to the MIDI and joystick connectors found on many sound cards. Confusing these connectors would not only drop the node off the network—it would also make your flight simulator game much more challenging!

Figure 5-18
An AUI
connector
(center) on a
10Base5 NIC

Remember that black band on the cable in Figure 5-14? Those black bands, spaced every 2.5 meters, were created to help technicians space the connections properly when installing a network. The cable between a NIC and a transceiver can be up to 50 meters long, but the external transceivers must be placed exactly at any one of those 2.5-meter intervals along the Ethernet cable (see Figure 5-19). Figure 5-20 shows the connection between a 10Base5 transceiver and a NIC. Because 10Base5 uses an extremely stiff cable, the cables were often run through the ceiling, with drop cables used to connect the cable to the individual NICs (see Figure 5-21). A maximum of 100 nodes can be attached to each 10Base5 segment.

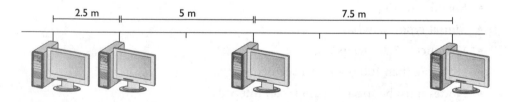

2.5 m   5 m   7.5 m

Figure 5-19   10Base5 requires that all nodes be attached at one of the 2.5-meter intervals.

Figure 5-20
A 10Base5
transceiver
connected to a
NIC drop cable

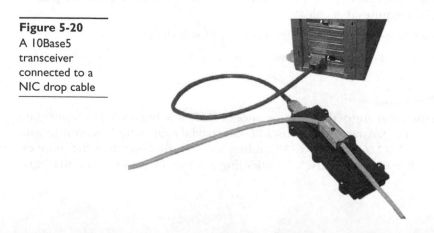

Figure 5-21
10Base5 uses drop cables to connect individual NICs to the segment, typically installed in the ceiling.

NOTE The fact that you must place every drop on one of the 2.5-meter intervals does *not* mean you must put a drop at every 2.5-meter interval. Don't get confused by this.

Goodbye 10Base5!

10Base5 is dead and gone. I'm sure that somewhere out there, there's still some 10Base5 working for a living, but with so many faster and cheaper options, 10Base5 has faded into the historical memory of the Ethernet world. After your Network+ exam, you have my permission to forget the following summary—but not until the end of the exam! Goodbye, good Thicknet. You served us well.

10Base5 Summary

- **Speed** 10 Mbps
- **Signal type** Baseband
- **Distance** 500 meters/segment
- No more than 100 nodes per segment
- Nodes must be spaced at 2.5 meter intervals
- Cables marked with a black band every 2.5 meters to ease installation
- Uses thick coaxial cable, which is almost always yellow (although nothing in the standard requires that color)
- Expensive cost per foot compared to other cabling systems
- Known as Thick Ethernet or Thicknet

10Base2

10Base2 can be used in many of the same instances as 10Base5, but it's much easier to install and much less expensive. 10Base2 uses RG-58 coaxial cable with BNC connectors, as shown in Figure 5-22. Although RG-58 cabling has less shielding than the more expensive RG-8 cabling used in 10Base5, its shielding is adequate for most installations.

Figure 5-22
A piece of RG-58
coaxial cabling
with BNC
connectors

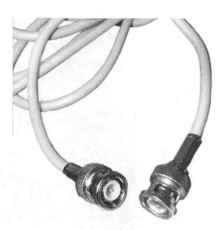

The IEEE 802.3 committee tried to stay consistent with its name-signal type-distance scheme for naming Ethernet. The term 10Base2 breaks down as follows:

- **Speed**   The *10* signifies an Ethernet network that runs at 10 Mbps.
- **Signal type**   *Base* signifies the use of baseband signaling, meaning a single signal is on the cable.
- **Distance**   The *2* indicates that cables may not be longer than 185 meters.

How does the 2 in 10Base2 translate into 185 meters? Don't ask—just live with it. Maybe at some point in the process, the distance limitation really was 200 meters and the IEEE later decided it had to be shortened. Maybe they thought 10Base1.85 looked funny and went for the closest round number. Who knows? Your job is to memorize the fact that the distance limitation for 10Base2 is 185 meters.

10Base2 has several advantages that make it the preferred choice for running Ethernet over coaxial cable. 10Base2 costs much less to install than 10Base5. RG-58 cabling costs significantly less per foot than 10Base5's RG-8 cabling. 10Base2's spacing requirements are also much less strict: computers must be spaced at least 0.5 meters apart, but they don't have to be spaced at specific intervals as required by 10Base5. RG-58's greater flexibility makes modifying and extending 10Base2 segments relatively painless. The only disadvantage is that 10Base2 allows only 30 computers per segment—far fewer than 10Base5.

Connectors

The connectors used with 10Base2 make it much easier to install and support than 10Base5. Unlike 10Base5's awkward requirement for external transceivers, 10Base2 NICs have a built-in transceiver and connect to the bus cable using a BNC connector (see Figure 5-23). The *BNC connector* provides an easy way to separate the center wire, which transmits data, from the outer shield, which protects the center wire from interference (see Figure 5-24).

Figure 5-23
Male and female
BNC connectors

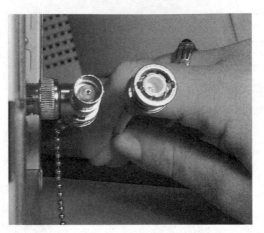

Figure 5-24
The BNC
connector keeps
the center wire
and the shield
from touching.

Traditional BNC connectors are crimped onto the wire using a crimping tool like the one shown in Figure 5-25. *Crimping* means bending the metal of the connector around the cable end to secure it to the cable. A properly crimped BNC connector keeps the center wire electrically insulated from the shield. An improperly crimped BNC connector allows the shield and the center wire to make electrical contact, creating a short in the cable (see Figure 5-26). A short, or *short circuit*, allows electricity to pass between the center wire and the shield. Because any current on the shield caused by interference will be conducted to the center strand, machines on the network will assume the network is busy and will not transmit data. The effect of a short circuit is the same as a break in the cable: the entire network goes down.

Figure 5-25
A typical crimping
tool used for
putting BNC
connectors on a
piece of RG-58
coaxial cable

Figure 5-26
A poorly crimped cable allows electricity to pass between the shield and the center wire, creating a short.

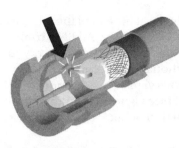

 NOTE The origins of the initials BNC have been lost. Some of the possible things it could stand for include Bayonet Nut Connector, Bayonet Navy Connector, British Naval Connector, Bayonet Neil Cofflin (purported inventor), and according to a long-time manufacturer of the devices, BNC stands for Bayonet Nut Coupling. My advice: If you can recognize a BNC connector, know what it's for, and know how to use one, then you don't need to worry about the initials!

If you find yourself in the (increasingly rare) position where you need a custom 10Base2 cable, but you have no crimping tool, all is not lost! For a quick connection on an RG-58 cable, you can dispense with the whole retro crimping scene and get a modern *twist-on* BNC connector. These convenient connectors install in seconds, and require no tools other than a pair of hands.

10Base2 requires the use of a T-connector (see Figure 5-27) when connecting devices to the cable. The stem of the *T-connector* plugs into the female connector on the Ethernet NIC, and the two pieces of coaxial cable are plugged into either end of the top bar (see Figure 5-28).

Figure 5-27
A T-connector

Figure 5-28
A T-connector with an RG-58 cable attached to either side

If an Ethernet node sits at the end of the cable, a terminating resistor takes the place of one of the cables (see Figure 5-29). All BNC connectors, including those on terminators and T-connectors, should be locked into place; you do this by turning their locking rings (see Figure 5-30). Although BNC connectors are basically easy to use, mistakes can happen. One frequent novice mistake is to connect a BNC connector directly to the female connection on a NIC (see Figure 5-31). While the connector locks in place just fine, the network will not function because there is no place to attach the terminating resistor.

Figure 5-29
A T-connector with a terminating resistor attached

Figure 5-30
The BNC connector on the right is locked into place; the one on the left is not.

Figure 5-31
BNC connectors should never be attached directly to the NIC.

10Base2 Summary

- **Speed**   10 Mbps
- **Signal type**   Baseband
- **Distance**   185 meters/segment
- No more than 30 nodes per segment
- Nodes must be spaced at least 0.5 meters apart
- RG-58 coaxial cable with BNC connectors connect to T-connectors on each node
- Nodes on the ends of the bus must have a terminator installed on one side of the T-connector
- Inexpensive cost per foot compared to 10Base5
- Known as Thin Ethernet, Thinnet, and sometimes Cheapernet

10Base2 offers a cheap and quick way to network a small number of computers using coaxial cable and Ethernet. Larger networks typically use twisted-pair wiring for Ethernet, but 10Base2 retains a strong installed base in smaller networks. 10Base2 retains the basic mechanisms of Ethernet: CSMA/CD, MAC addresses, and the Ethernet frame format. Rather than designing a new networking technology from scratch, 10Base2's designers built on proven, existing technology.

Although the network standards for Ethernet cabling lengths are commonly written in meters, I find that the distances make a lot more sense to most American students when they have the Standard English equivalents at hand. So here you go:

- 185 meters = approximately 607 feet
- 500 meters = approximately 1640 feet
- 1000 meters = approximately 6/10 of a mile

3.28 ft per Meter

Extending the Network: Repeaters and Bridges

Some networks function perfectly well within the limitations of 10Base2 and 10Base5. For some organizations, however, the limitations of these cabling systems are unacceptable. Organizations that need longer distance limits, more computers, more fault tolerance, or the capability to combine different cabling systems can add special devices called repeaters and bridges to their networks. Let's take a look at both of these devices to see how they work.

Repeaters

A *repeater* is a device that takes all data frames it receives from one Ethernet segment and retransmits them on another segment. (Talk about truth in advertising: repeaters *repeat*!) Figure 5-32 shows a typical Ethernet repeater. A repeater takes the incoming electrical signals, translates them into binary code, and then retransmits the electrical signals. A repeater does not function as an amplifier. *Amplifiers* boost signals, flaws and all, like a

Figure 5-32
A typical Ethernet repeater

copy machine duplicating a bad original. A repeater, in contrast, re-creates the signals from scratch. Repeaters address the need for greater distances, improved fault tolerance, and integration of different Ethernet cabling systems.

> **NOTE** Repeaters operate only at Layer 1 of the OSI model, the Physical layer (you *have* memorized these, right?).

Repeater Benefits

Repeaters have three key benefits. First, they extend the distance that a network can cover. Second, they provide a measure of fault tolerance, limiting the impact of cable breaks to the segment on which the break occurs. Third, they can link together segments using different types of Ethernet cabling.

A repeater increases the maximum possible distance between machines by linking together two segments. Each segment retains its own distance limitation. If a repeater connects two 10Base2 segments, for example, the maximum distance that can separate two machines

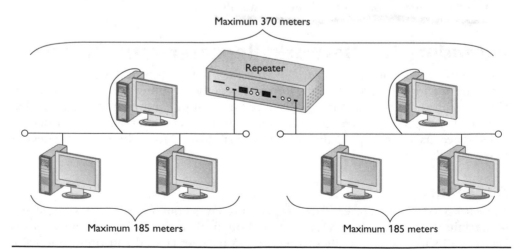

Figure 5-33   Two 10Base2 segments connected by a repeater can cover 370 meters.

on different segments is 2 × 185, or 370 meters (see Figure 5-33). Using this equation, two 10Base5 segments connected by a repeater can cover 1000 meters (2 × 500 meters).

Repeaters also add a degree of fault tolerance to a network. If one of the segments breaks, only that segment will fail. Computers on the adjacent segment will continue to function, unaffected when communicating within their own segment. The segment with the cable break fails because of reflections, but the segment on the far side of the repeater remains properly terminated and functions normally (see Figure 5-34).

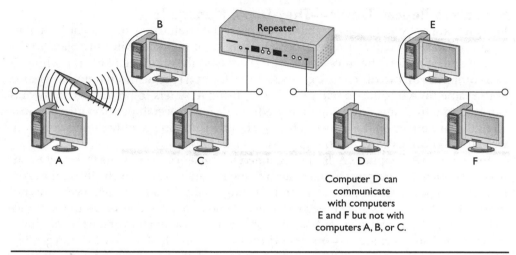

Computer D can
communicate
with computers
E and F but not with
computers A, B, or C.

Figure 5-34   Cable breaks affect only the segment on which the break occurs.

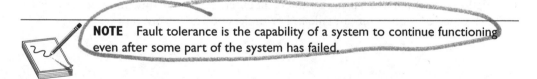

NOTE   Fault tolerance is the capability of a system to continue functioning even after some part of the system has failed.

As an added benefit, repeaters can give network designers the flexibility to combine different cabling types on the same network. Both 10Base5 and 10Base2 use exactly the

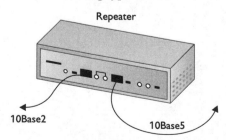

same frame structure (that is, the actual ones and zeroes used are identical). Thus a repeater can connect a 10Base5 segment and a 10Base2 segment without difficulty (see Figure 5-35). Many repeaters come with both AUI and BNC connectors for that purpose (see Figure 5-36).

Figure 5-35   A repeater can connect Ethernet segments that use different types of cabling.

Figure 5-36
A typical Ethernet
repeater with
both AUI
connectors for
10Base5 and
BNC connectors
for 10Base2

Repeaters Repeat Traffic—They Don't Manage It

Repeaters are not smart devices! They repeat every data frame they hear, regardless of its origin. Because the repeater repeats all frames that hit the wire, without regard to the source or destination, the rules of CSMA/CD apply to the entire network as a whole. If two computers on two different segments connected by a repeater both transmit a frame at the same time, a collision will result. Thus, using repeaters to build larger networks can lead to traffic jams, meaning more traffic and slower overall performance. Because all of the computers on this network hear each other and can possibly cause a collision, we call the entire network, both segments, a *single collision domain*.

In Figure 5-37, computers *A*, *B*, and *C* connect to segment 1; computers *D*, *E*, and *F* connect to segment 2. Computer *A* transmits a frame to computer *C*, which sits on the same side of the repeater. Computers *D*, *E*, and *F*, sitting on the far side of the repeater, do not need to hear the frames sent between computers *A* and *C*, but the repeater sends the frames to their network segment anyway. Machines on segment 1 cannot transmit while machines on segment 2 are using the network, and vice versa. Because all of the machines, regardless of the network segment to which they attach, can potentially have collisions with all of the other machines, segments 1 and 2 are both considered part of the same collision domain (see Figure 5-38). Even when using repeaters, an Ethernet network functions like a single CB radio channel: only one user can talk and be understood at any given time.

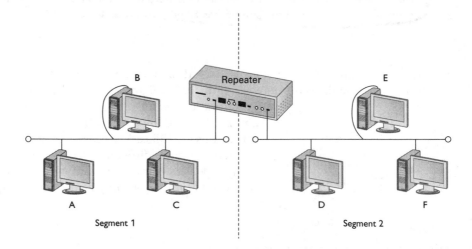

Figure 5-37   Two Ethernet segments connected by a repeater

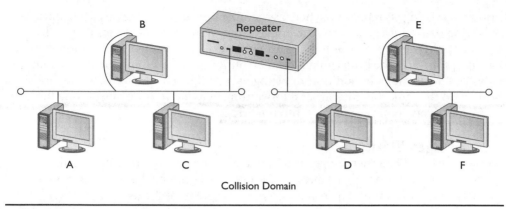

Collision Domain

Figure 5-38   A single collision domain

> **NOTE**   A set of Ethernet segments that receive all traffic generated by any node within those segments is a collision domain. Chapter 6, "Modern Ethernet," discusses devices that can break a network into multiple collision domains.

Repeater Summary

- Repeaters increase total network cable distance.

- Repeaters provide a measure of fault tolerance.

- Repeaters can provide interoperability between different Ethernet cabling systems.

- Repeaters operate only at the Physical layer (Layer 1) of the OSI model.

- Repeaters do not help reduce or manage network traffic, but their other attributes make them important tools for network technicians and architects.

Bridges

As the demands on network bandwidth grow, the number of machines that can peacefully coexist within an Ethernet collision domain shrinks. Fortunately, a special device called a *bridge* can link together Ethernet segments to form larger networks. At first you might say, "Isn't that what repeaters do?"—but bridges do not merely connect segments. They also filter traffic between the segments, preserving precious bandwidth. Let's look at bridges to see how they accomplish this amazing feat.

Bridges filter and forward traffic between two or more networks based on the MAC addresses contained in the data frames. To *filter traffic* means to stop it from crossing from one network to the next; to *forward traffic* means to pass traffic originating on one side of the bridge to the other. Figure 5-39 shows two Ethernet segments connected by a bridge. The bridge is represented here as a simple box, because the physical appearance of a bridge can vary a great deal. The bridge can be a stand-alone device that looks similar to an Ethernet repeater or hub, or it might be a PC with two NICs running special bridging software. The bridge might even be built into a multifunction device that provides other functions in addition to acting as a bridge. No matter how they look, all bridges do the same job: filtering and forwarding network traffic by inspecting the MAC address of every frame as it comes into the bridge.

How Bridges Work

A newly installed Ethernet bridge initially behaves exactly like a repeater, passing frames from one segment to another. Unlike a repeater, however, a bridge monitors and records the network traffic, eventually reaching a point where it can begin to filter and forward. This makes the bridge more "intelligent" than a repeater. The time for a new bridge to gather enough information to start filtering and forwarding is usually only a few seconds.

Let's watch a bridge in action. In the network shown in Figure 5-39, machine A sends a frame to machine D. When the frame destined for machine D hits the bridge, the bridge does not know the location of machine D, so it forwards the frame to segment 2. At this point, the bridge begins building a list of MAC addresses and the segment from which they came. As it forwards the packet to machine D, the bridge records that it received a frame from machine A's MAC address from segment 1. Now that the bridge knows the location of at least one machine, it can begin filtering. Eventually, each machine will have sent out at least some frames and the bridge will have a full list of each machine's MAC address and location. For the example used here, the table would look something like Table 5-1. (A real bridge's list would not have the machine letters—those are provided only for description.)

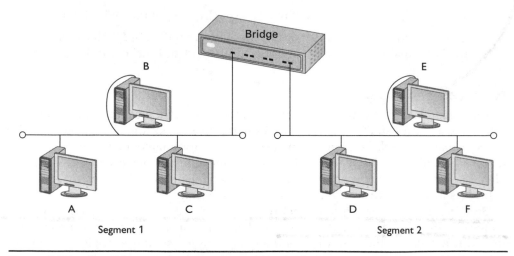

Figure 5-39   Two Ethernet segments connected by a bridge

	Segment 1	
Machine		**MAC address**
A		00 45 5D 32 5E 72
B		9F 16 C6 55 4D EE
C		9F 16 C6 99 DF F1
	Segment 2	
Machine		**MAC address**
D		9F 16 C6 85 E5 55
E		9F 16 C6 DD 41 11
F		00 45 5D 00 25 19

Table 5-1 Bridge's MAC Listing

Once the bridge has a complete table listing each machine's MAC address and the side of the bridge on which it sits, it looks at every incoming frame and decides whether or not to forward it to the other side. Let's see how a bridge uses this list. Let's say machine A decides to send another frame to machine D. When machine D responds to machine A, the bridge forwards the frame to segment 1 because it knows that machine A resides on segment 1 (Figure 5-40).

If machine C sends a frame to machine A, machine B will receive that frame as well because they all reside on the same segment. However, the bridge recognizes that no machine on segment 2 needs to see the frame being sent from machine C to machine A on segment 1. It filters this frame accordingly (Figure 5-41), so that the frame never makes it to segment 2.

Machines on either side of the bridge can remain blissfully unaware of the bridge's presence. When a bridge forwards a frame, it copies the frame exactly, even using the

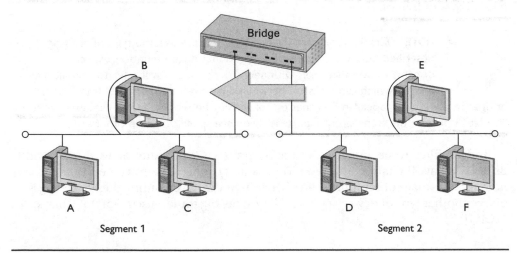

Figure 5-40   Bridge forwarding a frame

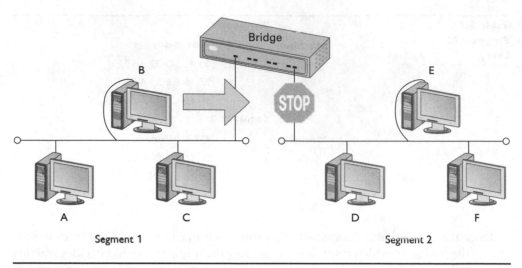

Figure 5-41   Bridge filtering a frame

originating machine's MAC address as the source MAC address in the new copy of the frame. Adding a bridge to a network does not require you to reconfigure any of the other nodes on the network. You simply rewire the cabling, and the bridge takes care of the rest.

Because bridges forward data frames without changing the frames themselves, the frame format used on each side of the bridge must be the same. The previous examples discuss bridges that connect two Ethernet networks. Bridges also exist for other technologies, such as Token Ring (see Chapter 7). Bridges cannot, however, connect an Ethernet network to a Token Ring network, because the two network technologies use totally different types of frames.

NOTE   Terminology alert! To be absolutely precise, the type of bridging described here is *transparent bridging.* Some documentation, especially documentation that deals with networking theory, will refer to *translational bridges,* which can translate between different frame formats. Translational bridges rarely, if ever, appear in Ethernet or Token Ring networks. You can assume the term "bridge" refers to the transparent type, unless you are specifically told otherwise.

Bridges filter some unnecessary traffic, preserving precious network bandwidth. Bridges do have limitations, however. They cannot connect dissimilar networks and cannot take advantage of multiple routes between nodes. Overcoming these challenges requires another type of device: a router. I'll save the big router discussion for Chapter 11, "TCP/IP."

Bridge Summary

- Bridges filter or forward traffic based on the MAC addresses contained in each data frame.
- Bridges operate at the Data Link layer of the OSI model.
- Bridges can connect two networks only if they use the same type of data frames (for example, Ethernet to Ethernet, or Token Ring to Token Ring).
- Bridges learn the MAC addresses of machines on each network by listening to the cable.
- Bridges cannot be used to provide multiple routes between machines.

Chapter Review

Questions

1. Which Ethernet cabling standard is limited to 10 megabits per second (Mbps) and can support cable segments up to a maximum distance of 185 meters?

    A. 10Base5

    B. 10Base2

    C. 10BaseT

    D. 10BaseF

2. Which Ethernet cabling standard is limited to 10 Mbps and can support cable segments up to a maximum distance of 500 meters?

    A. 10Base5

    B. 10Base2

    C. 10BaseT

    D. 10BaseF

3. At which layer of the OSI model do bridges operate?

    A. Physical

    B. Data Link

    C. Network

    D. Transport

4. Which of the following requires an external transceiver?

    A. 10Base5

    B. 10Base2

    C. 10BaseT

    D. 10BaseF

5. What kind of topology does 10Base2 use?

    A. Mesh

    B. Bus

    C. Star

    D. Ring

6. What kind of cable does 10Base2 use?

    A. RJ-45

    B. RJ-58

    C. RG-45

    D. RG-58

7. When a NIC is configured to accept all incoming packets, it is said to be running in _____:

    A. Master mode

    B. CSMA mode

    C. Promiscuous mode

    D. Multimode

8. An Ethernet segment is

    A. Any network connected by a bridge

    B. The same thing as an Ethernet network excluding any bridges

    C. The single length of cable that connects the computers on the network

    D. A grouping of network nodes running at a specific OSI layer

9. The type of connector used in 10Base2 is called a(n)

    A. AUI

    B. RJ-45

    C. BNC

    D. RG-8

10. The type of connector used in 10Base5 is called a(n)

    A. AUI

    B. RJ-45

    C. BNC

    D. RG-8

Answers

1. **B.** 10Base2 is the Ethernet cabling standard that is limited to 10 Mbps and can support cable segments up to a maximum distance of 185 meters.

2. **A.** 10Base5 is the Ethernet cabling standard that is limited to 10 Mbps and can support cable segments up to a maximum distance of 500 meters.

3. **B.** Bridges operate at the Data Link layer of the OSI model.

4. **A.** 10Base5 requires an external transceiver. 10Base2 transceivers are built into the NICs.

5. **B.** 10Base2 Ethernet uses a bus topology.

6. **D.** 10Base2 uses RG-58 coaxial cable. RJ-45 is a type of connector used with unshielded twisted-pair wiring. RJ-58 and RG-45 are not common network terms.

7. **C.** A NIC that is configured to accept all incoming packets is said to be running in promiscuous mode.

8. **C.** A segment is the single length of cable that connects the computers on the network.

9. **C.** 10Base2 networks use BNC connectors.

10. **A.** 10Base5 networks use AUI connectors.

Modern Ethernet

The Network+ Certification exam expects you to know how to

- 1.2   Specify the main features of 802.2 (Logical Link Control) [and] 802.3 (Ethernet): speed, access method, topology, media
- 1.3   Specify the characteristics (for example: speed, length, topology, and cable type) of the following cable standards: 10BaseT and 10BaseFL; 100BaseTX and 100BaseFX; 1000BaseTX, 1000BaseCX, 1000BaseSX, and 1000BaseLX; 10GBaseSR, 10GBaseLR, and 10GBaseER
- 1.4   Recognize the following media connectors and describe their uses: RJ-11, RJ-45, F-type, ST, SC, IEEE 1394, LC, MTRJ
- 1.6   Identify the purposes, features, and functions of the following network components: hubs, switches
- 2.3   Identify the OSI layers at which the following network components operate: hubs, switches

To achieve these goals, you must be able to

- Define the characteristics, cabling, and connectors used in 10BaseT and 10BaseFL
- Explain how to connect multiple Ethernet segments
- Define the characteristics, cabling, and connectors used with 100Base and Gigabit Ethernet

Historical/Conceptual

The first generation of Ethernet network technologies enjoyed substantial adoption in the networking world, but their bus topology continued to be their Achilles' heel—a single break anywhere on the bus completely shut down an entire network. In the mid-1980s, IBM unveiled a competing network technology called Token Ring. You'll get the complete discussion of Token Ring in the next chapter, but it's enough for now to say that Token Ring used a physical star topology. With a star topology, any single break in the network affected only the one system using that cable to connect to the network—he rest of the network continued to operate normally. As a result, Token Ring began to take substantial market share away from Ethernet through the second half of the 1980s.

In response to this threat, Ethernet manufacturers scrambled to make a new form of Ethernet that would have three major new features. First, this new Ethernet would use a physical star to match the robustness of Token Ring. Second, this new Ethernet would dump the use of more expensive coax and adopt inexpensive UTP cabling. Third, this new Ethernet would still use the same frame types and speeds of the older Ethernets, allowing for easy interconnections of this new Ethernet with older Ethernet networks. In 1990, working in close concert with the IEEE, the Ethernet manufacturers unveiled a new Ethernet standard: the now famous 10BaseT. From the moment of its introduction, 10BaseT's ease of installation, reliability, and low price reestablished Ethernet as the networking technology of choice, reducing Token Ring from market dominance to minor player today.

In the years since 1990, a series of faster Ethernet versions have come onto the networking scene, gradually pushing 10BaseT into the background. Even though its time in the spotlight has now passed, 10BaseT defined nearly every aspect of the Ethernet we use today, from cabling to topology. A solid understanding of 10BaseT is therefore an important part of your network tech foundation, as it will help you understand all the current Ethernet technologies. Let's take an in-depth look at 10BaseT, from its topology to its technology, and see why 10BaseT and the newer Ethernet technologies based on it now dominate the networking world.

Test Specific

10BaseT

The most important thing to remember about *10BaseT* is that it is still Ethernet. Except for the type of cabling and the topology, 10BaseT is identical to 10Base2 or 10Base5. 10BaseT uses the same frames as the earlier Ethernets. 10BaseT operates at the same speed of 10 Mbps. Machines still identify other machines by their MAC addresses and use CSMA/CD. The key difference between 10BaseT and its physical bus topology predecessors is the location of the Ethernet segment. Let's take a closer look at each of these issues.

10BaseT Topology

10Base2 and 10Base5 each use a physical bus topology. With a physical bus, you have a cable winding around the network and every computer connects to this single cable. Some might take exception to this—10Base5 may truly use a single cable, but isn't 10Base2 actually a number of cables connected together via the T-connectors at each PC? Yes, that's true—but in the case of 10Base2, all those cables connected together form a single bus. The existence of those T-connectors all along the 10Base2 bus doesn't detract from the fact that the bus carries the same signals in the same way as the truly single 10Base5 cable. As far as the network is concerned, both 10Base5 and 10Base2 use a single cable.

In the previous chapter, one of the words used to define that single cable was a "segment." Let's take the definition of a segment one step further. A *segment* is a single physical connection, terminated on both ends, to which computers may connect to form a network. In 10Base5 and 10Base2, the segment winds its way around the network, with terminators sitting at either end.

Figure 6-1
A 10BaseT
network with
each node
connected
to the hub

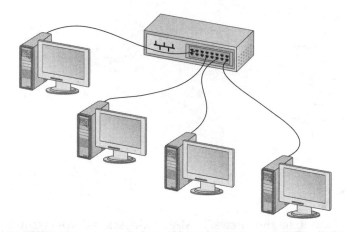

PART II

10BaseT also has a segment, but a 10BaseT segment doesn't wind all over the network. 10BaseT uses a physical star topology in which each node connects to a central hub (see Figure 6-1). The segment is still there—it's just shrunk into the hub (Figure 6-2).

  TIP Depending on who's talking, you may hear 10BaseT called a star topology, a bus topology, or a *star bus topology*. Which term a particular tech uses to describe 10BaseT's topology often depends on her job description. For someone whose primary job is installing cable, 10BaseT is a star. Similarly, a software engineer writing a device driver for an Ethernet NIC could not care less where the cables go; she thinks of 10BaseT as a bus. The right answer is star bus!

Why shrink the segment into the hub? By using this hybrid star bus topology, 10BaseT enjoys the key benefit of a star topology: fault tolerance. The hub is nothing more than a multiport *repeater*, in that it repeats the signal coming in from one port to all the other

Figure 6-2
A 10BaseT hub
contains the
segment.

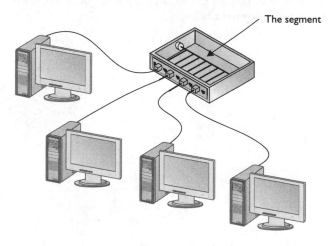

The segment

Figure 6-3
Because the Ethernet segment is protected inside the hub and remains unbroken, the break in the cable affects only one machine.

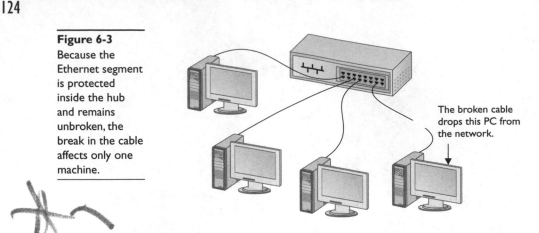

The broken cable drops this PC from the network.

ports. The hub has no interest in MAC addresses and works completely at the OSI Physical layer, just like 10Base2 or 10Base5 repeaters. If a cable running to a specific node breaks, the break affects only that computer because the Ethernet segment itself is unbroken (see Figure 6-3). If the segment itself breaks inside the hub, as shown in Figure 6-4, the entire network goes down.

10BaseT hubs come in a variety of shapes and sizes to support different sizes of networks. The biggest differentiator between hubs is the number of *ports*—connections—that a single hub provides. A small hub might have only four ports, while a hub for a large network might have 48 ports. As you might imagine, the more ports on a hub, the more expensive the hub. Figure 6-5 shows two hubs. On the top is a small, 8-port hub for small offices or the home. It rests on a 12-port rack-mount hub for larger networks.

NOTE Please don't crack open your Ethernet hubs looking for a piece of coaxial cable—it won't be there. The interior of an Ethernet hub contains a circuit board that serves the same function as the coaxial segments used in 10Base5 and 10Base2. When a hub fails, it's not because of a cable break; it's due to a failure in some part of the circuit board. The effect is the same, of course: if the hub fails, the entire segment fails.

Figure 6-4
If the segment inside the hub breaks, then the entire segment fails.

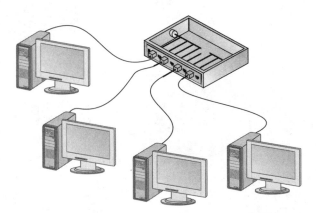

Figure 6-5
Two 10BaseT
hubs

Regardless of size, all 10BaseT hubs need electrical power. Larger hubs will take power directly from a power outlet, while smaller hubs often come with an AC adapter. In either case, if the hub loses power, the entire segment will stop working.

TIP   If you ever run into a situation on a 10BaseT or later network where none of the computers can get on the network, always first check the hub!

The name 10BaseT follows roughly the naming convention used for earlier Ethernet cabling systems. The number *10* refers to the speed: 10 Mbps. The word *Base* refers to the signaling type: baseband. The letter *T*, however, does not refer to a distance limitation like the *2* in 10Base2 or the *5* in 10Base5. Instead, it refers to the type of cable used: twisted-pair. 10BaseT uses unshielded twisted-pair (UTP) cabling.

UTP

Officially, 10BaseT requires the use of CAT 3 (or higher), two-pair, *unshielded twisted-pair (UTP)* cable. One pair of wires sends data to the hub while the other pair receives data from the hub. Although it is more sensitive to interference than coaxial cable, UTP cabling provides an inexpensive and flexible means to cable physical star networks. One minor difficulty with UTP stems from the fact that many other applications employ the same cabling. This can create some confusion when you're trying to determine if a piece of UTP in your ceiling is for your network or for your telephone system! Even though 10BaseT only requires two-pair cabling, for years, everyone has installed four-pair cabling to connect devices to the hub as insurance against the possible requirements of newer types of networking (see Figure 6-6). (Thank goodness they did! As you will see in the section "High-Speed Ethernet," newer forms of Ethernet need all four pairs.) Most UTP cables come with stranded Kevlar fibers to give the cable added strength, which in turn enables installers to pull on the cable without excessive risk of literally ripping it apart.

Figure 6-6
A typical
four-pair CAT
5e unshielded
twisted-pair cable

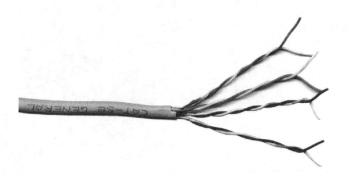

10BaseT also introduced the networking world to the *RJ-45 connector* (Figure 6-7). Each pin on the RJ-45 connects to a single wire inside the cable; this enables devices to put voltage on the individual wires within the cable. The pins on the RJ-45 are numbered from 1 to 8, as shown in Figure 6-8. The 10BaseT standard designates some of these numbered wires for specific purposes. As mentioned earlier, although the cable has four pairs, 10BaseT uses only two of the pairs. 10BaseT devices use pins 1 and 2 to send data, and pins 3 and 6 to receive data. Even though one pair of wires sends data and another receives data, a 10BaseT device cannot send and receive simultaneously. The rules of CSMA/CD still apply: only one device can use the segment contained in the hub without causing a collision. Later versions of Ethernet will change this rule.

An RJ-45 connector is usually called a *crimp*, and the act (some folks call it an art) of installing a crimp onto the end of a piece of UTP cable is called *crimping*. The tool we use to secure a crimp onto the end of a cable is a *crimper*. Each wire inside a UTP cable must connect exactly to the proper pin inside the crimp. Manufacturers color-code each wire

Figure 6-7
Two views of an
RJ-45 connector

Figure 6-8
The pins on an
RJ-45 connector
are numbered
1 through 8.

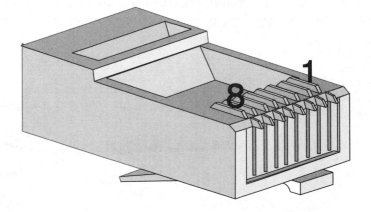

within a piece of four-pair UTP to assist in properly matching the ends. Each pair of wires consists of a solid-colored wire and a striped wire: blue/blue-white, orange/orange-white, brown/brown-white, and green/green-white.

The Telecommunications Industry Association/Electronics Industries Alliance (TIA/EIA) defines the industry standard for correct crimping of four-pair UTP for 10BaseT networks. Two standards currently exist: the TIA/EIA 568A and the TIA/EIA 568B. Figure 6-9 shows the TIA/EIA 568A color code standard, and Figure 6-10 shows TIA/EIA 568B. Note that the wire pairs used by 10BaseT (1 & 2; 3 & 6) come from the same color pairs (green/green-white and orange/orange-white). Following an established color-code scheme, such as TIA/EIA 568A, ensures that the wires match up correctly at each end of the cable.

The ability to make your own Ethernet cables is a real plus for a busy network tech. With a reel of CAT 5e, a bag of RJ-45 connectors, a moderate investment in a crimping tool, and a little practice, you can kiss those mass-produced cables goodbye! You can make cables to your own length specifications, replace broken RJ-45 connectors that would otherwise mean tossing an entire cable—and in the bargain, save your company or clients time and money. If you make cables with any regularity, you'll probably find yourself mentally reciting the order of wire colors in the standard that you use. For example, I use the 568A standard for cables in my company's network, so when I sit down to crimp a cable end, I'm thinking, "green-white, green; orange-white, blue; blue-white, orange; brown-white, brown." I've even been known to say this out loud as I separate out the wires and put them in the correct order—it may sound like I'm chanting some weird incantation, but I rarely have to recrimp a faulty cable end!

PART II

TIP An easy trick to remembering the difference between 568A and 568B is the word "GO." The green and orange pairs are swapped between 568A and 568B, whereas the blue and brown pairs stay in the same place!

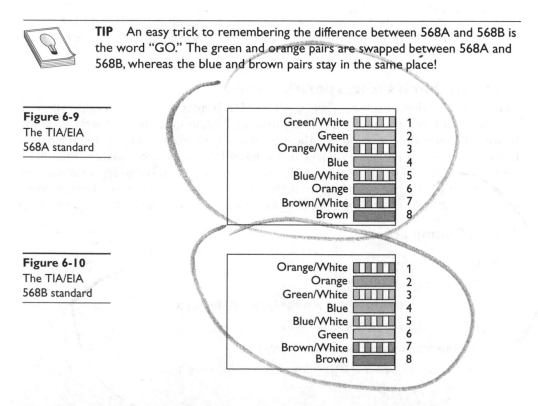

Figure 6-9
The TIA/EIA
568A standard

Green/White — 1
Green — 2
Orange/White — 3
Blue — 4
Blue/White — 5
Orange — 6
Brown/White — 7
Brown — 8

Figure 6-10
The TIA/EIA
568B standard

Orange/White — 1
Orange — 2
Green/White — 3
Blue — 4
Blue/White — 5
Green — 6
Brown/White — 7
Brown — 8

Why do the 568 standards say to split one of the pairs to the 3 & 6 position? Wouldn't it make more sense to wire them sequentially (1 & 2; 3 & 4; 5 & 6; 7 & 8)? The reason for this strange wiring scheme stems from the telephone world. A single telephone line uses two wires, and a typical RJ-11 connector has four connections. A single line is wired in the 2 & 3 positions; if the RJ-11 is designed to support a second phone line, the other pair is wired at 1 & 4. TIA/EIA kept the old telephone standard for backward compatibility. This standardization doesn't stop at the wiring scheme: you can plug an RJ-11 connector into an RJ-45 outlet.

Both the 568A and the 568B standards see a high quantity of use, but the 568A standard seems to be the most common in today's networks. Theoretically, as long as each end of each cable uses the same color code, many color codes could be used within the same building and everything would still work. 10BaseT devices do not care what color the wires are, they just need to have the pins on the RJ-45 connector match up at each end. Despite the fact that multiple color codes can work, the wise network tech will use a single color code throughout his or her entire organization. Consistency makes troubleshooting and repair easier by enabling network techs to assume the proper color code. If an end user trips over a cable and breaks the connector (of course, savvy network techs such as ourselves would never do such a thing), putting a new connector on the cable takes much less time if the tech knows with certainty which color code to use. If no standard color code exists, the poor network tech has to find the other end of the cable and figure out what color code was used on that particular cable. To save wear and tear on your techie tennis shoes, pick a standard color code and stick with it!

TIP   For the Network+ exam, you won't be tested on the TIA/EIA 568A or B color codes. Just know that they are industry standard color codes for UTP cabling.

10BaseT Limits and Specifications

Like any other Ethernet cabling system, 10BaseT has limitations, both on cable distance and on the number of computers. The key distance limitation for 10BaseT is the distance between the hub and the computer. The twisted-pair cable connecting a computer to the hub may not exceed 100 meters in length. A 10BaseT hub can connect no more than 1024 computers, although that limitation rarely comes into play. It makes no sense for vendors to build hubs that large—or more to the point, that *expensive*—because excessive collisions can easily bog down Ethernet performance with far fewer than 1024 computers.

10BaseT Summary

- **Speed**   10 Mbps
- **Signal type**   Baseband
- **Distance**   100 meters between the hub and the node
- No more than 1024 nodes per hub
- Star bus topology: physical star, logical bus
- Uses CAT 3 or better UTP cabling with RJ-45 connectors

10BaseFL

Just a few years after the introduction of 10BaseT, a fiber-optic version appeared, called *10BaseFL*. Fiber-optic cabling transmits data packets using pulses of light, rather than using electrical current. Using light instead of electricity addresses the three key weaknesses of copper cabling. First, optical signals can travel much farther. The maximum length for a 10BaseFL cable is up to two kilometers, depending how it is configured. Second, fiber-optic cable is immune to electrical interference, making it an ideal choice for high-interference environments. Third, the cable is much more difficult to tap into, making it a good choice for environments with security concerns. 10BaseFL uses a special type of fiber-optic cable called *multimode*, and employs one of two types of fiber-optic connectors: *SC connectors* or *ST connectors*. Figure 6-11 shows examples of these connector types.

The presence of two connector standards has led to a bit of confusion in 10BaseFL, as well as later versions of networking that use fiber-optic cabling. As a result, most manufacturers of fiber products are moving toward the SC connector over the ST connector, although both types are still in common use. Figure 6-12 shows a typical 10BaseFL card. Note that it uses two fiber connectors—one to send, and one to receive. While 10BaseFL enjoyed some popularity for a number of years, most networks today are using the same fiber-optic cabling to run far faster network technologies.

10BaseFL Summary

- **Speed**   10 Mbps
- **Signal type**   Baseband
- **Distance**   2000 meters between the hub and the node
- No more than 1024 nodes per hub
- Star bus topology: physical star, logical bus
- Uses multimode fiber-optic cabling with ST or SC connectors

Figure 6-11
ST (left) and
SC (right)
connectors for
fiber-optic cable

Figure 6-12
Typical 10BaseFL
card

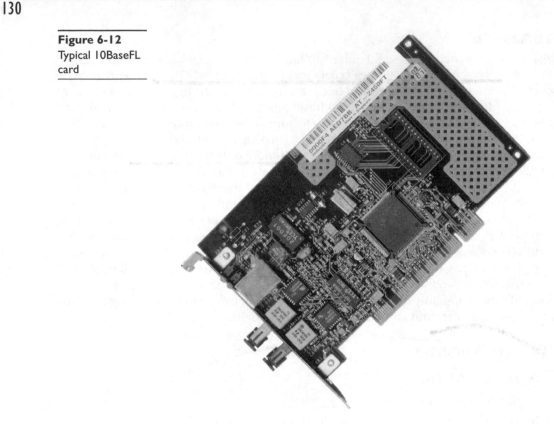

Connecting Ethernet Segments

Sometimes, one hub is just not enough. Once an organization uses every port on its existing hub, adding additional nodes requires additional hubs. Even fault tolerance can motivate an organization to add more hubs. If every node on the network connects to the same hub, that hub becomes a single point of failure—if it fails, everybody drops off the network. The 10BaseT standard provides two methods for connecting multiple hubs: coaxial cable and crossover cables.

Coaxial cabling, either 10Base2 or 10Base5, can link together multiple 10BaseT hubs. By definition, a 10BaseT hub is a repeater. It brings in signals from one port and repeats them on all other ports. Some 10BaseT hubs come with a BNC or AUI connector, as shown in Figure 6-13. With the addition of an AUI or BNC port, a hub can repeat packets onto a coaxial segment just as easily as it can repeat them on UTP cabling. The coaxial segment can be used to connect two 10BaseT hubs, or it can have nodes directly attached to it, as shown in Figure 6-14.

NOTE   A populated segment has one or more nodes directly attached to it.

Figure 6-13
10BaseT hub with
BNC connector

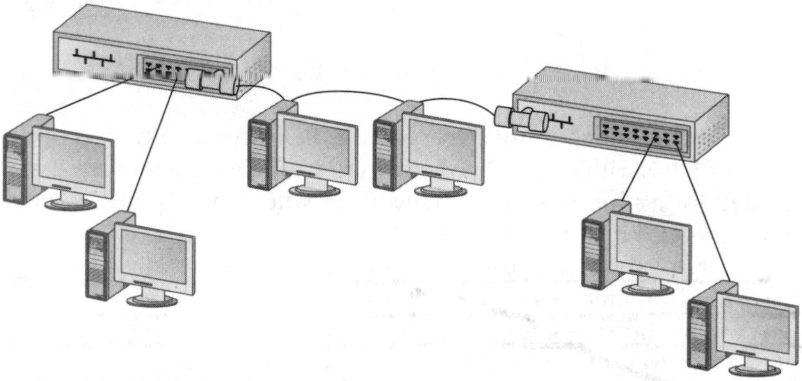

Figure 6-14
The segment
connecting two
hubs can be
populated with
machines.

Hubs can also connect to each other via special twisted-pair cables called crossover cables. A standard cable cannot be used to connect two hubs, because both hubs will attempt to send data on the second pair of wires (3 & 6) and will listen for data on the first pair (1 & 2). A *crossover cable* reverses the sending and receiving pairs on one end of the cable (see Figure 6-15). One end of the cable is wired according to the TIA/EIA 568A standard, while the other end is wired according to the TIA/EIA 568B standard. With the sending and receiving pairs reversed, the hubs can hear each other; hence the need for two standards for connecting RJ-45 jacks to UTP cables. To spare network techs the trouble of making special crossover cables, most older hubs have a special crossover port that crosses the wires inside the hub, as you can see in Figure 6-13, above. Unfortunately, when describing and labeling their crossover ports, hub manufacturers use a wide variety of terms, including crossover, uplink, in port, and out port. Most modern hubs have autosensing ports that turn themselves into crossover ports if necessary for communication (see Figure 6-16).

Figure 6-15
A crossover cable
reverses the
sending and
receiving pairs.

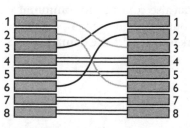

Figure 6-16
Hub with
autosensing
crossover ports

In a pinch, you can use a crossover cable to connect two computers together using 10BaseT NICs with no hub between them at all. This is handy for the quickie connection needed for a nice little home network or when you absolutely, positively must chase down a friend in a computer game!

Be careful about confusing crossover cables with crossover ports. First, never connect two hubs by their crossover ports. Take a regular cable; connect one end to the crossover port on one hub and the other end to any regular port on the other hub. Second, if you use a crossover cable, just plug each end into any handy regular port on each hub.

If you mess up your crossover connections, you won't cause any damage, but the connection will not work. Think about it. If you take a straight cable (that is, not a crossover cable) and try to connect two PCs directly, it won't work. Both PCs will try to use the same send wires and same receive wires. When you plug the two PCs into a hub, the hub electronically crosses the data wires, so one NIC sends and the other can receive. If you plug a second hub to the first hub using regular ports, you essentially cross the cross and create a straight connection again between the two PCs! That won't work. Luckily, nothing gets hurt (except your reputation if one of your colleagues notes your mistake!).

Multiple segments in a network provide greater fault tolerance than a single segment. Each segment functions or fails on its own. Figure 6-17 shows three segments: A, B, and C. Segments A and B are 10BaseT hubs; segment C is a 10Base2 segment. A failure of one segment does not cause other segments to fail. The failure affects only transmissions that rely on the failed segment. For example, if Cindy's pet rat Gidget escapes and chews through segment C, computers on segment A cannot communicate with computers on segment B, but computers on segment A can continue to communicate with each other, and computers on segment B can also continue to communicate with each other (see Figure 6-18). Of course, the poor computers on segment C must sit idle and twiddle their thumbs until some kind network tech repairs the damage wrought by the evil Gidget.

Figure 6-17
Two hubs
connected by a
10Base2 segment

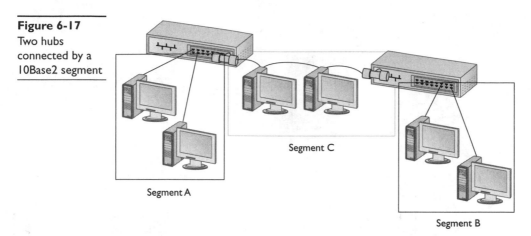

How Big Can an Ethernet Network Be? The 5-4-3 Rule

When multiple Ethernet segments connect to each other with hubs and repeaters, they remain part of the same collision domain (see Figure 6-19). As discussed in Chapter 5, "Ethernet Basics," a collision domain is a set of Ethernet segments that receive all traffic generated by any node within those segments. A set of restrictions known as the *5-4-3 rule* limits the size of an Ethernet collision domain.

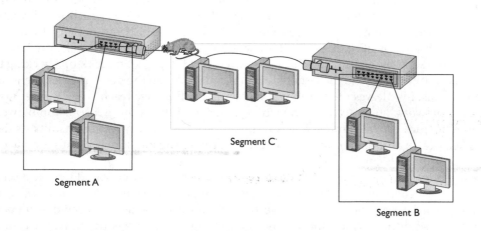

Figure 6-18   Segment C's failure prevents communication between segments A and B, but does not affect communication within segments A and B.

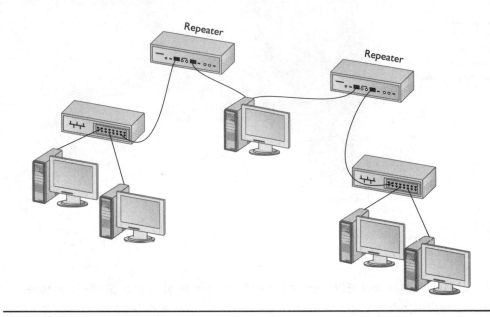

Figure 6-19   An Ethernet collision domain

A Useful Approximation

For Ethernet networks to function properly, each node must detect when its own transmissions collide with those of another node. When a node detects a collision, it waits a random period of time and then re-sends the packet. (Refer back to Chapter 5 for a more detailed discussion of CSMA/CD.) If the sending node fails to detect a collision, it won't know to resend the packet, and the packet will be lost. Ethernet nodes stop checking for collisions once they send the last byte of each data packet. If the network is large enough that the last byte leaves the sending node before the first byte reaches every other node on the network, an undetected collision can occur. In the event of a collision between two machines on the extreme edges of the network, neither node retransmits its data packet, causing the data packets to be lost. Clearly, a collision domain that's too big can be a serious problem!

The question, then, is: "How big is too big?" A precise answer would require a series of arcane calculations that determine variables with thrilling names like *round-trip signal propagation delay* and *interpacket gap*. Fortunately, the average network tech doesn't need to do these difficult calculations. The networking industry has developed a general rule—the so-called 5-4-3 rule—that enables technicians to build networks within safe size limits without needing to earn advanced math degrees.

The 5-4-3 rule is pretty easy to remember: it states that in a collision domain, no two nodes may be separated by more than 5 segments, 4 repeaters, and 3 populated segments.

To calculate a network's compliance with the 5-4-3 rule, trace the worst-case path between two machines—in other words, the path between two machines that will yield the highest number of segments, repeaters, and populated segments. We consider a segment populated if any systems are connected to that segment. This might then beg the question: "Why would anyone want to have a segment that isn't populated? That's easy—sometimes we use a separate segment as a way to connect other segments.

Figure 6-20 shows a network with 5 segments, 4 repeaters, and 3 populated segments. The path between machines *A* and *C* represents the worst-case path because the packets must pass through all of the segments and repeaters on the network. The paths between *A* and *B*, or *B* and *C*, are irrelevant for calculating compliance with the 5-4-3 rule because a longer path exists between two other machines. The path between machine *A* and machine *C* uses all five segments, all four repeaters, and all three populated segments.

> **NOTE** When calculating the 5-4-3 rule, a hub counts as both a repeater and a segment.

The 5-4-3 rule's limitations apply not to the entire network, but rather to the paths within the network. Figure 6-21 shows a network that complies with the 5-4-3 rule, but has 6 segments, 6 repeaters, and 5 populated segments within the entire network. Hub 1 counts as both a segment and a repeater, but not as a populated segment because no computers attach directly to it. Segments that link other segments together, but have no computers directly attached to them, are called *link segments*. This network follows the 5-4-3 rule because no path between two machines ever traverses more than 5 segments,

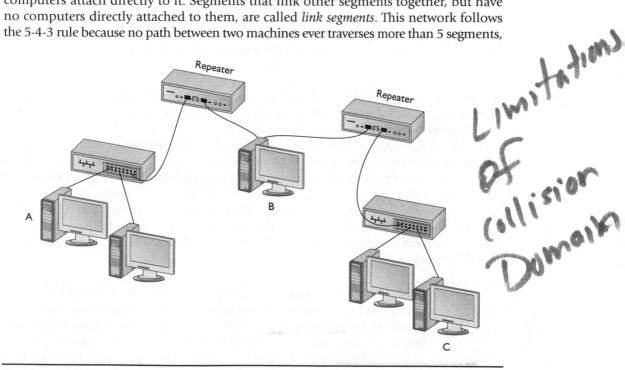

Figure 6-20 A network with 5 segments, 4 repeaters, and 3 populated segments

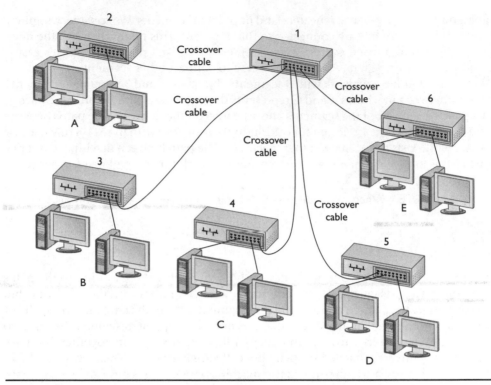

Figure 6-21   A network with 6 segments that complies with the 5-4-3 rule

4 repeaters, or 3 populated segments. For example, the path between computers *A* and *C* runs through 3 segments (hubs 2, 1, and 4), 3 repeaters (hubs 2, 1, and 4), and 2 populated segments (hubs 2 and 4).

The 5-4-3 rule imposes limits on the size of an individual Ethernet collision domain, but the limits are generous. The network shown in Figure 6-21 can contain thousands of individual machines. Remember that each hub can support up to 1024 PCs; because of the demands of modern operating systems and applications, however, 10-Mbps Ethernet networks with far fewer than 1024 machines can become too busy and congested to function well. Manufacturers have overcome congestion and size limitations using a number of fascinating improvements to the original 10BaseT standard that I'll call high-speed Ethernet.

NOTE   Rather than make 1024-port hubs that would have a limited market and be expensive to replace in the event of failure, manufacturers make stackable hubs. Stackable hubs are hubs with a special proprietary connection that enables them to function in groups, called *stacks*, as a single device. For the purposes of the 5-4-3 rule, all the hubs in a stack are considered a single segment, repeater, and populated segment.

High-Speed Ethernet

As any fighter pilot will tell you, sometimes you just feel the need—the need for speed. While plain-vanilla Ethernet performs well enough for basic file and print sharing, today's more demanding network applications, such as Lotus Notes, SAP, and Microsoft Exchange, as well as other vital office applications like Half-Life and Unreal Tournament, can quickly saturate a network running at 10 Mbps. Fortunately, those crazy kids over at the IEEE keep expanding the standard, providing the network tech in the trenches with new tools that provide additional bandwidth. These cool new tools include Fast Ethernet, full-duplex Ethernet, Gigabit Ethernet, and switched Ethernet.

100Base Ethernet

Fast Ethernet is not a single technology. The term *Fast Ethernet* refers to any of several Ethernet flavors that operate at 100 Mbps. Rather than limiting Ethernet to a single high-speed solution, the IEEE endorsed multiple standards for Fast Ethernet and allowed the marketplace to choose from among them. The major variations include 100BaseT and 100BaseFX.

100BaseT

The IEEE supports two variations of *100BaseT*: 100BaseTX and 100BaseT4. Both flavors physically resemble 10BaseT, using a star bus topology and connecting to hubs with UTP cabling. The 100 in their names reflects the fact that the cable connecting a device to a hub can send data at speeds up to 100 Mbps. The difference between 100BaseTX and 100BaseT4 lies in the quality of the cable required. 100BaseTX requires CAT 5 or better cabling to achieve a speed of 100 Mbps using only two pairs of wires. Like 10BaseT, 100BaseTX ignores the remaining two pairs. 100BaseT4 uses all four pairs to achieve 100 Mbps performance using lower quality CAT 3 or better cabling. Think of the cable as a highway: 100BaseTX increases capacity by raising the speed limit, while 100BaseT4 increases capacity by adding additional lanes.

NOTE 100BaseVG, also known as 100BaseVGAnyLAN, is not a flavor of Ethernet. Designed to run over Category 3 (voice grade) cabling, it does not use CSMA/CD to determine access to the cable. The IEEE 802.12 committee controls the standards for 100BaseVG. As the popularity of 100BaseTX has grown, the importance of competitors like 100BaseVG has diminished dramatically.

Both 100BaseTX and 100BaseT4 allow organizations to take advantage of their existing UTP cabling. If the existing UTP wiring was properly installed, you can upgrade a network from 10BaseT simply by replacing hubs and network cards, with no recabling required.

100BaseTX and 100BaseT4 are not interchangeable. If you have 100BaseTX hubs, then you must also have 100BaseTX NICs. Equally, if your hub is 100BaseT4, then you must have 100BaseT4 NICs. Over the past few years, 100BaseTX has pushed 100BaseT4 out of the market so completely that devices labeled as 100BaseTX are now practically impossible to find. When you purchase 100BaseTX equipment now, it usually just says 100BaseT.

UTP cabling cannot meet the needs of every organization, however, for three key reasons. First, the 100-meter distance limitation of UTP-based networks is inadequate for networks covering large buildings or campuses. Second, UTP's lack of electrical shielding makes it a poor choice for networks functioning in locations with high levels of electrical interference. Finally, the Maxwell Smarts and James Bonds of the world find UTP cabling (and copper cabling in general) easy to tap, making it an inappropriate choice for high-security environments. To address these issues, the IEEE 802.3 standard provides for a flavor of 100-megabit Ethernet using fiber-optic cable, called 100BaseFX.

NOTE Even though shielded twisted-pair cabling is available, its use is rare. Most installations will use fiber-optic cable in situations where UTP is not adequate.

100BaseFX

The *100BaseFX* standard saw quite a bit of interest for years, as it combined the high speed of 100Base Ethernet with the reliability of fiber optics. Outwardly, 100BaseFX looks exactly like 10BaseFL: both use the same multimode fiber-optic cabling, and both use SC or ST connectors. 100BaseFX is an improvement over 10BaseFL, however, supporting a maximum cable length of 400 meters.

Migrating to Fast Ethernet

Upgrading an entire network to 100BaseTX can be a daunting task. 100BaseTX requires new hubs, new NICs, and often upgrades to the existing cabling. For organizations with more than a few machines, upgrading every node can take months or even years. Fortunately, the conversion can be done slowly. In fact, organizations that want to do so can purchase 10/100BaseT devices. A 10/100BaseT device automatically functions as a 100BaseT device when plugged into another 10/100BaseT or 100BaseT device, but functions as a 10BaseT device when plugged into another 10BaseT device. The existence of these hybrid devices enables organizations to roll out 100BaseT in batches, providing high-speed access to the machines that need it.

Gigabit Ethernet

For the true speed junkie, an even more powerful version of Ethernet exists: *Gigabit Ethernet*. The IEEE has approved two different versions of Gigabit Ethernet. The first version, published under the 802.3z standard and known as 1000BaseX, is divided into a series of standards, with names such as 1000BaseCX, 1000BaseSX, and 1000BaseLX. The 802.3ab standard defines a single UTP solution called 1000BaseT. Of all these Gigabit standards, 1000BaseT has come out as the dominant Gigabit Ethernet standard.

1000BaseT uses four-pair UTP cabling to achieve gigabit performance. Like 10BaseT and 100BaseT, 1000BaseT has a maximum cable length of 100 meters. 1000BaseT connections and ports look exactly like the ones on a 10BaseT or 100BaseT network.

NOTE The term *Gigabit Ethernet* is more commonly used than *1000BaseT*.

The 802.3z standards require a bit more discussion. Let's look at each of these solutions in detail to see how they work.

1000BaseCX   1000BaseCX uses a unique shielded cable known as twinaxial cable (Figure 6-22). Twinaxial cables are special shielded 150-Ohm cables with a length limit of only 25 meters. 1000BaseCX has made little progress in the Gigabit Ethernet market. 1000BaseCX falls under the IEEE 802.3z standard.

1000BaseSX   Many networks upgrading to Gigabit Ethernet use the 1000BaseSX standard. 1000BaseSX uses multimode fiber optic cabling to connect systems, with a generous maximum cable length of over 500 meters; the exact length is left up to the various manufacturers. 1000BaseSX uses an 850-nm (nanometer) wavelength LED to transmit light on the fiber optic cable. Like 1000BaseCX, 1000BaseSX comes under the 802.3z standard. 1000BaseSX devices look exactly like the 100BaseFX products you read about earlier in this chapter, but they rely exclusively on the SC type of connector.

1000BaseLX   1000BaseLX is the long-distance carrier for Gigabit Ethernet. 1000BaseLX uses single-mode (laser) cables to shoot data at distances up to five kilometers—and some manufacturers use special repeaters to increase that to distances as great as 70 kilometers! The Ethernet folks are trying to position this as the Ethernet backbone of the future, and already some large carriers are beginning to adopt 1000BaseLX. You may live your whole life and never see a 1000BaseLX device, but odds are good that you will encounter connections that use such devices in the near future. 1000BaseLX looks like 1000BaseSX, and is also part of the 802.3z standard.

New Fiber Connectors

Around the time that Gigabit Ethernet first stated to appear, two problems began to surface with ST and SC connectors. First, ST connectors are relatively large, twist-on connectors, requiring the installer to twist the cable when inserting or removing a cable. Twisting is not a popular action with fiber-optic cables, as the delicate fibers may fracture. Also, big-fingered techs have a problem with ST connectors if the connectors are

Figure 6-22
Twinaxial cable

too closely packed: they can't get their fingers around them. SC connectors snap in and out, making them much more popular than STs. However, SC connectors are also large, and the folks who make fiber networking equipment wanted to pack more connectors onto their boxes. This brought about two new types of fiber connectors, known generically as SFF (Small Form Factor) connectors. The first SFF connector—the MTRJ, or Mechanically Transferable Registered Jack, shown in Figure 6-23—gained popularity with important companies like Cisco and is still quite common.

The second type of popular SFF connector is the LC, or Local Connecter, shown in Figure 6-24. LC-type connectors are very popular, particularly in the United States, and many fiber experts consider the LC connector to be the predominant fiber connector.

LC and MTRJ are the most popular types of SFF fiber connections, but many others exist. The fiber industry has no standard beyond ST and SC connectors, which means that different makers of fiber equipment may have different connections.

10-Gigabit Ethernet

The ongoing demand for bandwidth on the Internet means that the networking industry is continually reaching for faster LAN speeds. Not only must speeds increase, but they must increase while keeping strong backward compatibility—or no one will buy the technology! The progression of Ethernet from 10 Mbps up to 1 Gbps is a testament to that attitude. The other factor that comes into the minds of network hardware manufacturers is the degree of speed increase. Let's look at the different speeds of Ethernet over the years: 10 Mbps, 100 Mbps, and 1 Gbps. Note that every jump is a factor of ten—but why is that? There's no law of physics that says each generation must be ten times faster than the last. The amount of speed increase in each generation is the result of marketing, plain and simple. Most manufacturers of Ethernet hardware feel that customers aren't motivated to buy into any new Ethernet generation with less than a tenfold speed increase, and perhaps they're right—but it makes for increasingly tough increases in speed.

Figure 6-23
MTRJ connector

Figure 6-24
LC connector

This leads me to the newest and fastest Ethernet to date: 10 Gbps. Initially standard-ized in 2002 under the IEEE 802.3ae committee, 10-Gigabit Ethernet—commonly ab-breviated as 10GbE—is only now showing up in very high-level LANs and WANs. Did I say *WANs*? Yes, I did; one of the goals of the 10GbE standard was that it would work as both an Ethernet LAN and WAN solution. Certain versions of the 802.3ae standard pro-vide for segment lengths of up to 40 kilometers, so it's clear that the 802.3ae folks have taken a long-distance view for 10GbE.

10GbE is true Ethernet, although it is exclusively full-duplex and must run on fiber. There are 802 groups working to create 10GbE solutions that run on twinaxial and even UTP, but it will probably be quite some time before those technologies appear on store shelves. In order to wrap your mind around 10GbE, you need to remember that it was designed from the ground up as a fiber solution. When you use fiber, you're using light, not electricity, to send signals down the line. Light, unlike electricity, has multiple wave-lengths. Different wavelengths of light exhibit different qualities. Longer wavelength light tends to travel longer distances, but usually requires more complex circuitry or more power. Lower-bandwidth fiber optics tend to use LEDs as their light sources, as LEDs are inexpensive and easy to use. Higher-bandwidth fiber optics usually use lasers as their light source. Laser light travels much farther than regular light, but the hardware that produces it is considerably more difficult to manufacture.

The creators of 10GbE recognized the many different types of fiber optics in use, and wanted 10GbE to work on as many different types as possible. They achieved this goal by defining seven different media types to work with different types of fiber.

 NOTE Before reading about these different media types, be sure you understand that these are Physical layer issues. Each of these types transmits exactly the same type of Ethernet frames!

The 10GBaseSR and 10GBaseSW media types are designed for use over short wave-length (850 nm) multimode fiber. The maximum fiber length is 300 meters, although this will vary depending on the type of multimode fiber used. The 10GBaseSR media type is designed for typical Ethernet LAN connections. The 10GBaseSW media type is de-signed to connect to SONET equipment. 10GBaseSR has seen usage in co-location facili-ties to interconnect large networks that traditionally relied on ATM-type connections.

The 10GBaseLR and 10GBaseLW media types are designed for use over long wavelength (1310 nm) single-mode fiber. The maximum fiber length is 10 kilometers, although this will vary depending on the type of single-mode fiber used. The 10GBaseLR media type is designed for typical Ethernet LAN connections. The 10GBaseLW media type is designed to connect to SONET equipment. 10GBaseLR is the most popular 10GbE media type.

The 10GBaseER and 10GBaseEW media types are designed for use over extra long wavelength (1550 nm) single-mode fiber. The maximum fiber length is 40 kilometers, although this will vary depending on the type of single-mode fiber used. The 10GBaseER media type is designed for typical Ethernet LAN connections, while the 10GBaseEW media type is designed to connect to SONET equipment. 10GBaseER is expensive and has only seen substantial use in long-distance interconnects to replace a leased line.

10GBaseLX4 is the odd duck. The previous six media types all use a single wavelength of light, sending a serial signal. This media type uses wave division multiplexing technology, using four or more wavelengths of light over a single pair of either single-mode or multimode fiber-optic cable. 10GBaseLX4 has had little industry support.

10GBaseSW, 10GBaseLW, and 10GBaseEW only exist to allow 10GbE connections over existing SONET lines; see Chapter 16, "Remote Connectivity," for details on SONET. Many network experts see these 10GbE-over-SONET solutions as little more than short-term solutions until 10GbE lines replace the SONET lines. Replacing SONET lines with 10GbE provides two benefits: first, you no longer need equipment on each end to convert Ethernet to SONET and back again. Second, because SONET is no longer needed, anyone willing to make a large enough up-front investment can own their own native Ethernet fiber cables, in WAN and MAN situations where typically they would be at the mercy of the local SONET carriers' lease rates.

This hodgepodge of 10GbE Ethernet types might have been the ultimate disaster for hardware manufacturers. All types of 10GbE send and receive the exact same signal; only the physical medium is different. Imagine a single router that had to come out in seven different versions to match all these types! Instead, the 10GbE industry devised a very clever, very simple concept called *multisource agreements,* or *MSAs.* An MSA is a modular transceiver that you plug into your 10GbE equipment, enabling you to convert from one media type to another by inserting the right transceiver. Unfortunately, there have been as many as four different MSA types competing in the last few years. Figure 6-25 shows a typical MSA called XENPAK.

Figure 6-25
XENPAK MSA

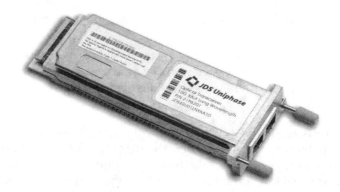

NOTE Not all 10GbE manufacturers use MSAs in their equipment.

For now, 10GbE equipment is the exclusive domain of extremely high-bandwidth LANs and WANs, including parts of the "big pipe" Internet connections.

Switched Ethernet

Don't feel like upgrading all your NICs and hubs to get more speed? How would you like to dramatically improve performance just by replacing your hub? *Switched Ethernet* may be the solution for you! An *Ethernet switch* is a special hub that can place some devices into their own collision domains. In essence, an Ethernet switch is a hub with a bridge built in. *Switches,* like bridges, work at the OSI Data Link layer, or Layer 2—in fact, they're often referred to as Layer 2 switches. Physically, an Ethernet switch looks much like any other Ethernet hub, except for the addition of one or more switched ports (see Figure 6-26). Logically, an Ethernet switch puts each device plugged into one of its switched ports into its own collision domain. As one system begins to send data to another system, a switch looks at the incoming MAC addresses and creates a single collision domain (see Figure 6-27).

Using an Ethernet switch provides two benefits. First, if both the sender and the receiver are on their own switched ports, the full bandwidth of that connection (10, 100, or 1000 megabits) is available to them—no other machine can cause a collision. Second, the switch can act as a buffer, enabling devices running at different speeds to communicate. Without this buffering capability, a Gigabit Ethernet card would overload a slow NIC.

Ethernet switches can also connect segments to a backbone. A *backbone* is a segment that connects other segments. Most backbones are lightly populated or unpopulated. In most cases, a backbone runs at a higher speed than the segments it connects. Figure 6-28 shows a network that supplies 10BaseT to networked desktops, and connects the hubs to a 100BaseT backbone segment. In some cases, heavily accessed machines, such as file servers, plug directly into the backbone, as shown in Figure 6-29.

Figure 6-26

An eight-port switch with two switched ports

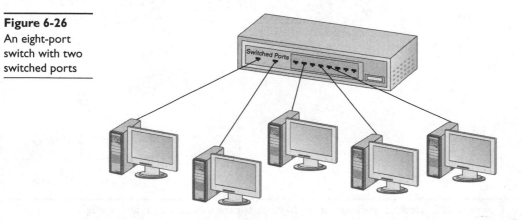

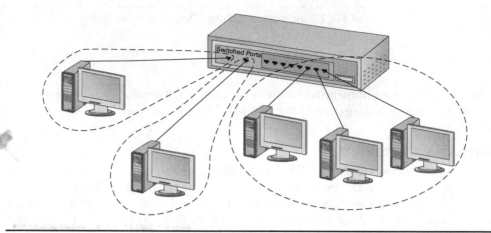

Figure 6-27   Devices plugged into switched ports are isolated on their own collision domains.

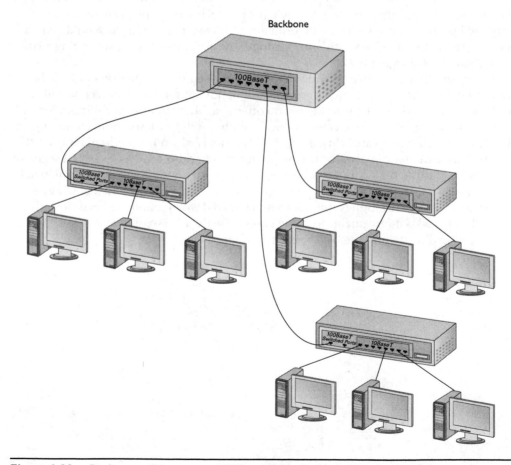

Figure 6-28   Desktop machines run at 10 Mbps, but the backbone runs at 100 Mbps.

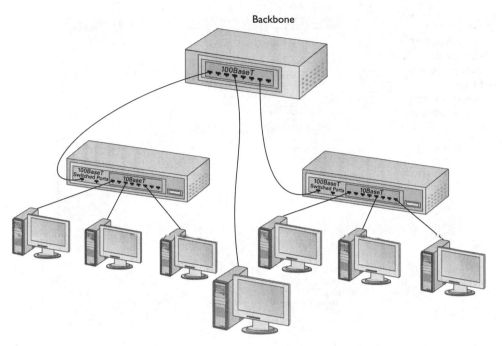

Figure 6-29   Heavily accessed machines can be plugged directly into the backbone.

Full-Duplex Ethernet

Ethernet switching opens up another avenue for improving the performance of the network: full-duplex Ethernet. *Full-duplex* means that a device can send and receive data simultaneously. Normally, Ethernet transmissions are *half-duplex*—in other words, at any given moment, a machine can either send or receive data, but not both. If a machine sends and receives simultaneously in half-duplex mode, a collision occurs. In the event of a collision, the CSMA/CD rules kick in, causing the machine to stop sending and wait a random period of time before trying again. CSMA/CD allows many machines to share the same segment, but requires all communication to be half-duplex.

A switched Ethernet connection running over UTP, however, not only creates a two-machine-only segment, it also uses separate pairs of wires for sending and receiving. Each pair of wires acts as a separate channel, enabling the devices at each end to communicate with one another in full-duplex mode. If the Ethernet NICs on each end of a switched connection support full-duplex mode, turn it on and enjoy the benefits! Note that not all Ethernet NICs support full-duplex operation; however, those that do will have a full-duplex option that you can turn on using their setup programs (see Figure 6-30).

Full-duplex Ethernet offers impressive performance gains. A 10BaseT full-duplex connection has a theoretical bandwidth of 20 Mbps (2 × 10 Mbps), while a 100BaseT full-duplex connection has a theoretical bandwidth of 200 Mbps (2 × 100 Mbps). Because there should never be collisions on a full-duplex connection, the real-world speeds of

Figure 6-30
If a card supports full-duplex mode, its setup program will have an option to switch between half- and full-duplex.

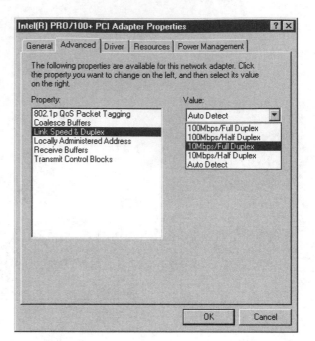

full-duplex Ethernet approach these theoretical maximums. Unfortunately, many older 10BaseT devices do not support full-duplex operation; however, most 100Base and 1000Base Ethernet standards require full-duplex operation, making it an assumed function on those devices.

 TIP For the exam, know that in half-duplex communication, a device cannot send when it is receiving and vice versa. In full-duplex communication, however, a device can send and receive at the same time.

 Here's a thought: if a switched network creates separate collision domains for all the nodes, does the 5-4-3 rule still apply? Good question! If you answered "No," that's even better! Once you start using switches, the entire concept of 5-4-3 goes out the window; there are no limitations due to collisions, except within individual collision domains.

The wonderful benefits of switches make them extremely common today. By replacing a hub with a switch, your network can take advantage of collision-free, full-duplex communication to achieve much higher speeds.

Conclusion

While 10Base2 and 10Base5 soldier on in some networks, the use of the star bus hybrid topology for UTP- and fiber-optic-based Ethernet networks enables techs to build more robust and flexible networks. The capability to use high-speed segments, full-duplex operation, bridging, routing, and switching gives the network architect a full toolkit with which to build fast, stable networks. For all these reasons, UTP and fiber dominate the networking industry today, leaving coaxial to dwindle away.

Chapter Review

Questions

1. Star bus networks use a _____ star and a _____ bus.

   A. Physical, logical

   B. Logical, physical

   C. Hub, Ethernet

   D. Ethernet, hub

2. The *T* in 10BaseT refers to

   A. Topology

   B. Ten-Mbps speed

   C. Twisted-pair cable

   D. Transport technology

3. Fault tolerance is the key advantage of what topology?

   A. Bus

   B. Ring

   C. Star bus

   D. Bus ring

4. The maximum distance that can separate a 10BaseT node from its hub is

   A. 50 meters

   B. 100 meters

   C. 185 meters

   D. 200 meters

5. When used for Ethernet, unshielded twisted pair uses what type of connector?

   A. RG-58

   B. RJ-45

   C. RJ-11

   D. RS-232

6. What is the maximum number of nodes that can be connected to a 10BaseT hub?

   A. 1024

   B. 500

   C. 100

   D. 185

7. Which of the following is not true of crossover cables?

    A. They are a type of twisted-pair cabling.

    B. They reverse the sending and receiving wire pairs.

    C. They are used to connect hubs.

    D. The ends of a crossover cable are wired according to the TIA/EIA 568B standard.

8. Which of the following connectors are used by 10BaseFL cable? (Select two.)

    A. SC

    B. RJ-45

    C. RJ-11

    D. ST

9. Which of the following cable types does not use CAT 3 cabling?

    A. 100BaseTX

    B. 10BaseT

    C. 100BaseT4

    D. 100BaseVG

10. Within an Ethernet collision domain, the 5-4-3 rule limits 10-megabit Ethernet networks to _____ between any two machines.

    A. 5 populated segments, 4 repeaters, and 3 hubs

    B. 5 segments, 4 repeaters, and 3 populated segments

    C. 5 tokens, 4 packets, and 3 broadcasts

    D. 5 segments, 4 repeaters, and 3 hubs

Answers

1. **A.** Star bus networks use a physical star, which provides improved stability, and a logical bus that maintains compatibility with existing Ethernet standards.

2. **C.** The *T* in 10BaseT refers to its use of twisted-pair cabling. This differs from 10Base2 and 10Base5, where the 2 and 5 refer to the maximum segment lengths. The *10* in 10BaseT refers to its 10-Mbps speed.

3. **C.** Fault tolerance is the key advantage of the star bus topology. Fault tolerance refers to a system's capability to continue operating when part of it is not working. In this case, a break in a network cable affects only the machine connected to that cable; the others can continue to communicate.

4. **B.** The maximum distance between a 10BaseT node and its hub is 100 meters.

5. **B.** UTP cable uses an RJ-45 connector when used for Ethernet. RG-58 is the type of coaxial cable used with 10Base2. RJ-11 is the standard four-wire connector used for regular phone lines. RS-232 is a standard for serial connectors.

6. **A.** A 10BaseT hub can connect no more than 1024 nodes (computers).

7. **D.** One end of a crossover cable is wired according to the TIA/EIA 568B standard; the other is wired according to the TIA/EIA 586A standard. This is what crosses the wire pairs and enables two hubs to communicate without colliding.

8. **A, D.** 10BaseFL uses two types of fiber-optic connectors called SC and ST connectors.

9. **A.** 100BaseTX requires CAT 5 or better cabling. 10BaseT, 100BaseT4, and 100BaseVG can all use CAT 3 cabling.

10. **B.** Within a collision domain, the 5-4-3 rule limits 10-megabit Ethernet networks to 5 segments, 4 repeaters, and 3 populated segments between any two machines.

Non-Ethernet Networks

The Network+ Certification exam expects you to know how to

- • 1.2   Specify the main features of 802.5 (Token Ring) and FDDI (Fiber Distributed Data Interface), including speed, access method, topology, and media
- • 1.4   Recognize the following media connectors and describe their uses: RJ-45, ST, SC

To achieve these goals, you must be able to

- • Define the characteristics, cabling, and connectors used in Token Ring
- • Describe the characteristics, cabling, and connectors used in ARCnet and LocalTalk
- • Explain the characteristics, cabling, and connectors used in FDDI and ATM

No one denies Ethernet's virtual monopoly as the network technology of choice in today's world. Depending on your choice of source, something like 80 to 90 percent of all network cables in the world run some derivation of Ethernet. Still, in the immortal words of Master Yoda in *The Empire Strikes Back*, "There is another." More precisely, "There are many others," and Network+ expects you to know them as well as you know Ethernet. Some of these network technologies, in particular IBM's famous Token Ring, still enjoy strong followings, especially in organizations that have invested heavily in installing these technologies. Despite their substantial installed bases, though, the chances of you seeing any of these technologies during the course of your networking career are pretty slim. So, look at this chapter as fulfilling two goals: introducing you to the final days of rapidly fading technologies, and getting you past the Network+ questions that address them. Read this chapter carefully—after the test, you may never hear of these technologies again!

Historical/Conceptual

Token Ring

Token Ring, also known as *IEEE 802.5*, competed directly—and in the long run, unsuccessfully—with Ethernet as an option for connecting desktop computers to a LAN. Although Token Ring possesses a much smaller share of the market than Ethernet, Token Ring's installed base has remained extremely loyal. The most common Token Ring networks offer greater speed (16 Mbps) and efficiency than 10BaseT Ethernet, and the Token Ring folks have even established 100- and 1000-Mbps Token Ring standards.

EXAM TIP   Expect questions on the Network+ exam about 16-Mbps Token Ring, but not about the 100-Mbps or 1000-Mbps versions.

Token Ring networks may look much like 10BaseT Ethernet networks, even using identical UTP cabling in some cases. Although these network types share the same physical star topology, Token Ring uses a logical ring topology, rather than a logical bus topology.

NOTE   Although Token Ring began as a proprietary IBM technology, today the IEEE 802.5 committee defines the standards for this technology. Just as there are minor differences between the original Xerox Ethernet standard and IEEE 802.3, the original IBM standard for Token Ring and the IEEE 802.5 standard also differ slightly from one another. These differences have little impact on the average network tech, so for all intents and purposes, Token Ring and IEEE 802.5 should be considered synonyms.

Test Specific

Logical Ring Topology

Token Ring networks use a logical ring topology (see Figure 7-1). Unlike an Ethernet node, which broadcasts its frames across a shared cable to every other computer on the segment, a Token Ring node communicates directly with only two other machines: its *upstream and downstream neighbors* (see Figure 7-2). To control access to the ring, Token Ring employs a system of *token passing*.

Figure 7-1
Token Ring networks use a logical ring topology.

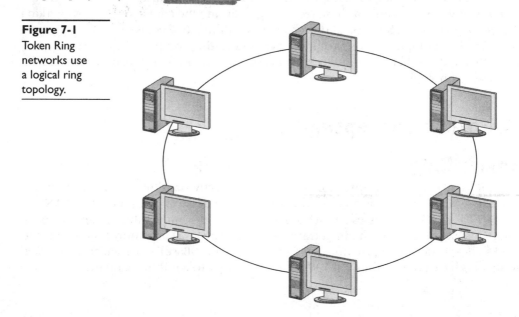

Figure 7-2
Node A's
downstream
neighbor is
node B and
its upstream
neighbor is
node F.

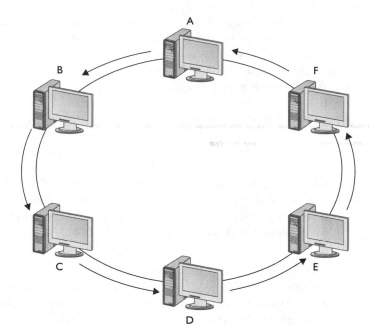

Token Passing

The cornerstone of token passing is a special frame called the *token*. This frame enables the systems on a Token Ring network to effectively "take turns" sending data. The rule is that no device can transmit data unless it's currently holding the token. Because collisions simply cannot occur under this system, Token Ring nodes can make full use of the network's bandwidth, and thus operate more efficiently than Ethernet networks using CSMA/CD.

A Token Ring frame begins with the token itself, but otherwise contains much the same information as an Ethernet frame: the source MAC address, the destination MAC address, the data to be transmitted, and a *frame check sequence (FCS)* used to check the data for errors (see Figure 7-3). When receiving a frame, a Token Ring node checks the destination MAC address to determine whether to process the data it contains or send the frame to its downstream neighbor. When the intended recipient processes the data, it creates a new frame that includes a special code indicating that the frame was received in good order. The receiving node then sends this frame around to the sending node. When the sending node gets the frame with the "received in good order" code, it removes the frame from the wire and sends out a new free token—that is, a new frame consisting of only a token.

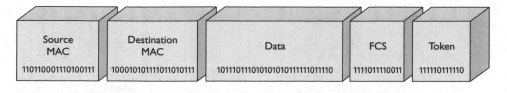

Figure 7-3   A Token Ring frame

The free token tells any node that receives it that the ring is available. A node with data to send must wait until it receives a free token; it then creates a data frame, which includes a token, and sends the new frame on to its downstream neighbor (see Figure 7-4). Again, when the sending node receives confirmation that the intended recipient received the frame, it generates a new free token, giving the next machine inline access to the ring.

A token-passing network sends data frames more efficiently than one using CSMA/CD because no collisions occur. A station may have to wait for a free token before it can send, but if it has the token, it knows no other station will try to send at the same time. In contrast, a CSMA/CD-based network, such as Ethernet, can waste significant bandwidth resolving collisions. Token passing is a deterministic method to resolve which machine should have access to the wire at a given moment. *Deterministic* means that access to the wire is granted in a predictable way, rather than through a random process like CSMA/CD. No virtual dice rolling here!

Token Ring Speed

Token Ring networks can run at either 4 or 16 Mbps, speeds that sound slow compared to the 10- and 100-Mbps Ethernet standards (again, newer versions of Token Ring improve on these speeds, but the Network+ exam has little interest, so for the moment at least, neither do we). The raw numbers, however, do not tell the full story. Token Ring networks use every bit of their bandwidth to send data. Ethernet networks, in contrast, waste significant amounts of bandwidth resolving collisions. Because of the wasted bandwidth inherent in Ethernet networks, many well-informed techs argue that a 4-Mbps Token Ring's performance is almost as fast as 10-Mbps Ethernet, and that a 16-Mbps Token Ring's performance is significantly faster. The speed at which the ring operates, however, depends on the slowest device on the ring. A Token Ring network consisting of five 4/16-Mbps Token Ring nodes and one 4-Mbps Token Ring node will run at 4 Mbps (see Figure 7-5).

Token Ring networks can be configured to give some systems higher-priority access to the token. Conceivably, a network architect could set a high priority for a particular PC, ensuring that it would get access to the token more often than other nodes on the network. Real-life Token Ring networks rarely take advantage of the capability to prioritize traffic, making the feature less useful than it might seem.

Figure 7-4

After receiving a free token, node A can send new data to its downstream neighbor.

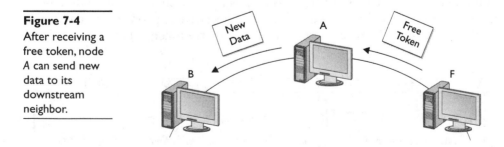

Figure 7-5

 The slowest device on the ring determines the speed of the ring.

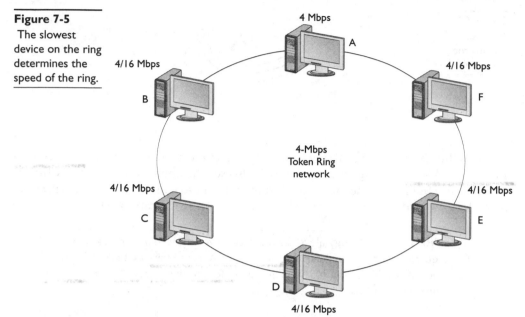

Physical Star

Physical ring topology shares the same vulnerability to cable breaks as physical bus topology. When the cable used by a physical bus topology such as 10Base2 breaks, the entire network shuts down due to electrical reflections. A physical ring topology would also fail completely from a cable break, but for a different reason. In a ring topology, all traffic travels in one direction. If the ring breaks, traffic can never complete the round trip around the network, so no node will generate a free token (see Figure 7-6). To avoid the problems inherent in a physical ring topology, Token Ring uses a physical star topology.

Figure 7-6

A physical ring topology cannot function if the ring breaks.

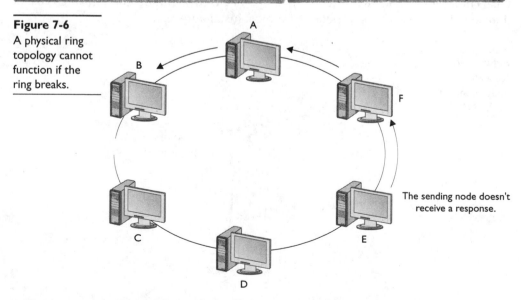

Figure 7-7
The MAU
contains the
logical ring.

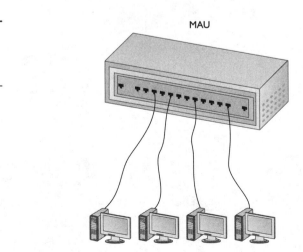

Token Ring hides the logical ring inside a hub, technically referred to as a *Multistation Access Unit (MAU)* (see Figure 7-7). You will also see the abbreviation *MSAU*, which is less common but means the same thing. Individual nodes connect to the hub via either unshielded twisted-pair (UTP) or shielded twisted-pair (STP) cabling (Figure 7-8).

NOTE   Terminology alert! To make our lives more difficult, Token Ring documentation can refer to Multistation Access Units by two different acronyms: MAU and MSAU. The terms Token Ring hub, MAU, and MSAU are synonymous.

Token Ring over STP

Originally, Token Ring networks used a heavily shielded version of twisted-pair cabling referred to as *shielded twisted pair (STP)*. STP consists of two pairs of copper wires surrounded by a metal shield (refer to Chapter 4, Figure 4-14). STP's metal shield serves the same function as the shield used in coaxial cables: preventing electrical interference from affecting the wires used to send signals. When using STP, a single Token Ring MAU can support up to 260 computers. The STP cable connecting a computer to the hub may not be longer than 100 meters. While the heavy shielding of STP cabling makes it an ideal choice for environments with high levels of electrical interference, the high cost of that shielding makes it too expensive for most installations.

Figure 7-8
Token Ring
nodes connect
to the MAU.

MAU

NOTE In one of the few variances between IBM Token Ring and the IEEE 802.5 standard, the latter states that a Token Ring network can support only up to 250 nodes per segment. The IEEE 802.5 standard does not, however, distinguish between STP and UTP. In real-world applications, the 260-node limit found in implementations of IBM Token Ring networks over STP has proven accurate. (The Network+ exam reflects the real world too!)

Token Ring uses a special *Type 1 connector* for STP (see Figure 7-9). Type 1 Token Ring connectors are not RJ-45. Instead, IBM designed a unique *hermaphroditic* connector called either an *IBM-type Data Connector (IDC)* or a *Universal Data Connector (UDC)*. These connectors are neither male nor female; they are designed to plug into each other. Token Ring network cards use a nine-pin female connector, and a standard Token Ring cable has a hermaphroditic connector on one end and a nine-pin connector on the other.

TIP Token Ring STP connectors are referred to as *Type 1* or *IDC/UDC*. Be prepared to use either term on the Network+ exam, although you'll most likely see them called Type 1.

Token Ring over UTP

UTP cabling offers a cost-effective alternative to STP for normal business environments. Because it lacks the heavy shielding of STP and is manufactured for use in a variety of applications, UTP cabling is relatively inexpensive.

Token Ring can run over UTP using the same cable and RJ-45 connectors as Ethernet. Like 10BaseT, Token Ring uses only two of the four wire pairs in the typical UTP cable: the 3/6 pair and the 4/5 pair, as shown in Figure 7-10. Provided the cable installer uses a proper wiring color code (such as the EIA/TIA 568A standard discussed in Chapter 6), the UTP cable and connectors used for Token Ring are identical to those used for Ethernet. Token Ring MAUs using UTP can support up to 72 nodes, each of which must be within 45 meters of the MAU. UTP is so common for Token Ring that you can purchase special media converters to connect UTP to MSAUs using the older style Type 1 connectors (see Figure 7-11).

Figure 7-9
An IBM Type 1 connector

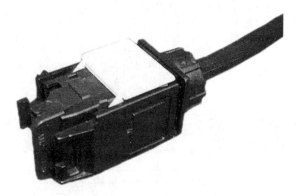

Figure 7-10
Token Ring uses two of the four pairs of available wires.

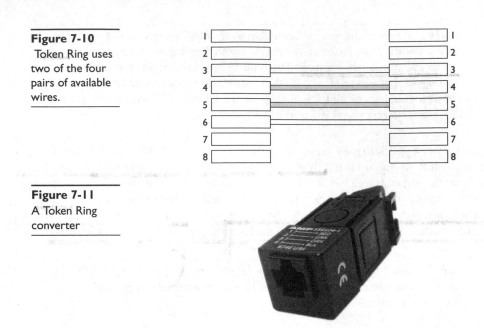

Figure 7-11
A Token Ring converter

Connecting MAUs

To connect multiple Token Ring hubs to form a larger network requires the extension of the ring. Token Ring MAUs, whether using UTP or STP, have two special ports, labeled *Ring In* and *Ring Out*. These special connections can link multiple MAUs together to form a single ring. The Ring In port on the first MAU must connect to the Ring Out port on the second MAU, and vice versa, to form a single logical ring. Figure 7-12 shows two

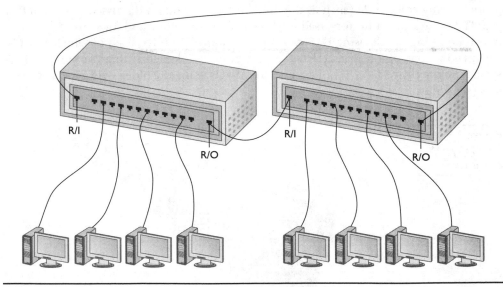

Figure 7-12 Two MAUs connected via Ring In and Ring Out ports

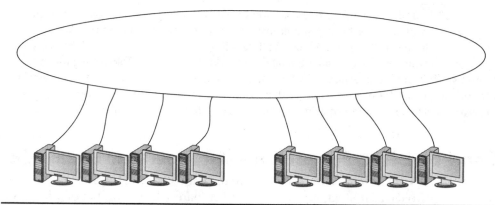

Figure 7-13 When linked together properly, the two MAUs form a single logical ring.

MAUs connected using the Ring In and Ring Out ports. Logically, the two MAUs look like a single ring to the devices attached to them (see Figure 7-13). Up to 33 MAUs can combine to form a single logical ring. Building a network with more than 33 MAUs requires the use of bridges or routers. Routers can also connect Token Ring LANs to other types of LANs, such as Ethernet.

Token Ring vs. Ethernet

The Token Ring vs. Ethernet debate was a fixture in computer networking journals for many years. Token Ring advocates argued that Token Ring's token-passing system used available bandwidth more efficiently than Ethernet's random CSMA/CD process. In addition, the token-passing system guaranteed that every node got some amount of bandwidth.

Ethernet advocates argued that even if Token Ring had technical advantages, it was too expensive to implement. Ethernet technology has always been cheaper than Token Ring for two reasons. First, Ethernet devices are simpler than Token Ring devices. CSMA/CD is a simple algorithm to program into a device, whereas Token Ring devices must deal with more complex issues, such as differing priority levels among the nodes on the ring. Second, economies of scale make Ethernet even less expensive. Because the market for Ethernet devices dwarfs the market for Token Ring devices, Ethernet manufacturers can make a smaller profit on each piece sold and still make money.

In addition, Ethernet overcomes the efficiency advantages of Token Ring by throwing bandwidth at the problem. While 16-Mbps Token Ring may be faster than 10BaseT, it runs significantly more slowly than 100BaseT. Plus, although high-speed Token Ring standards exist, Fast Ethernet and Gigabit Ethernet have achieved a far greater penetration of the market. Most industry pundits agree that Token Ring is a dying technology. While it will continue to exist in niche markets and in organizations with a large installed base of Token Ring equipment, Ethernet will retain and expand its dominance in the marketplace for the foreseeable future.

NOTE Token Ring manufacturers have not rolled over and given in to the pressure of Ethernet standards; instead, they have continued to adapt and innovate. Modern IEEE 802.5t Token Ring networks run at 100 Mbps or faster, which is certainly a respectable speed. In fact, because Token Ring technology doesn't suffer from the overhead of CSMA/CD, High-Speed Token Ring (HSTR) networks offer phenomenally faster performance than comparably speedy Ethernet. You can check out www.madge.com for information on these speedy Token Ring solutions.

Gone But Not Forgotten—ARCnet and LocalTalk

Oh, the 1980s were an interesting time to be in the networking business. Not only were Ethernet and Token Ring slugging it out for market share, a large number of other competitors were also on the market. Two in particular—ARCnet and LocalTalk—deserve mention for two reasons. While ARCnet has disappeared from the PC networking world, it is popular in a number of niche markets, such as robotics and industrial controls. LocalTalk is definitely gone, but its relation to AppleTalk, a popular piece of networking software found on every Apple brand computer, motivates us to mention it. The terms LocalTalk and AppleTalk are often confused, so it's important to get them straight in your mind.

ARCnet

During the late '70s and early '80s, a company called Datapoint Corporation invented a networking technology called *Attached Resource Computer Network (ARCnet)*. For many years, ARCnet enjoyed some degree of popularity in smaller networks, and it still has enough of an installed base to make it interesting for the Network+ exam.

The original ARCnet standard defines a true star topology—both the physical and logical topologies work as stars. ARCnet uses token passing to get frames from one system to another. Originally, ARCnet used a type of coaxial cable called *RG-62*; later versions, however, used good old two-pair UTP cable. ARCnet runs at a whopping 2.5 Mbps—acceptable in the early 1980s, but far too slow to be of any interest for a modern network application. Faster ARCnet standards, called ARCnet Plus, ran at speeds up to 20 Mbps, but were not successful in making ARCnet a serious competitor to either Ethernet or Token Ring in mainstream networking.

ARCnet uses hubs to propagate data between nodes (see Figure 7-14). These hubs provide either 8 or 16 ports, and like 10BaseT hubs, they can be *daisy-chained*—strung together—to handle more nodes. ARCnet networks can use more basic hubs, called passive hubs. These do not repeat the signal like regular (active) hubs; they just pass the signal along without re-creating the data. Because of this, passive hubs are much less common. Using RG-62 and regular hubs, ARCnet supports segment lengths up to 600 meters. Many folks found this substantial segment distance highly attractive; in fact, the majority of ARCnet implementations still in place today involve networking scenarios that needed to span longer distances.

Figure 7-14
An ARCnet hub

Like most other network technologies, ARCnet now supports UTP and fiber-optic cabling, and has increased its speed and maximum cable length dramatically. Like Token Ring, ARCnet has bowed to Ethernet's dominance in the PC networking industry, but lives on, hidden away in a myriad of other industries that enjoy its cheap price and simple function.

LocalTalk

When the folks at Apple decided to add networking to their computers, they created a unique networking technology called *LocalTalk* (see Figure 7-15). LocalTalk used a bus topology with each device daisy-chained to the next device on the segment, and proprietary cabling with small round DIN-style connectors. (*DIN connectors* look like modern keyboard connectors.) A later version called *PhoneTalk*, produced by a company called Farallon, used regular telephone cable and RJ-11 connectors and saw widespread popularity. The rise of Ethernet, along with LocalTalk's slow speed, led to the demise of LocalTalk.

Figure 7-15
LocalTalk
connectors

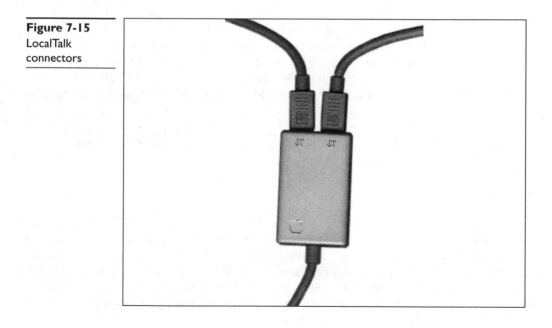

NOTE Many people confuse the terms AppleTalk and LocalTalk. *LocalTalk* is a networking technology, whereas *AppleTalk* is a network protocol. The networking technology defines the physical issues: what kind of cabling to use, the characteristics of the data frame, the signaling methods for sending frames through the cable, and so forth. A network protocol works at higher layers of the OSI seven-layer model, enabling the operating system to communicate effectively with the NIC, for example. You'll see a lot more on network protocols in Chapter 10, "Protocols."

LAN to WAN—FDDI and ATM

The increase in demand for bandwidth in the '80s motivated the creation of more powerful network technologies. Two different types of technologies, called FDDI and ATM, appeared in the early '90s. These were the *de facto* high-speed networking standards—at least for a few years, until the emergence of high-speed Ethernet. Like so many other network technologies, FDDI and ATM continue to lose market share to Ethernet, but both have found new life with the telephony and cable industries as methods for transferring data across long distances between networks, creating wide-area networks (WANs).

FDDI

Fiber Distributed Data Interface (FDDI) stands as one of the few network technologies that did not spring directly from private industry (although private industry had a lot of impact on its development). Instead, FDDI came directly from the American National Standards Institute (ANSI) as a high-speed, highly redundant technology, specifically designed to work as a high-speed backbone to support larger networks.

The best single word to describe FDDI is "unique." FDDI uses a unique dual token-passing ring topology. Each ring runs at 100 Mbps, making an aggregate speed of 200 Mbps. If one ring breaks, the other ring continues to operate. FDDI runs on either a true physical ring or a physical star topology. Figure 7-16 shows a typical FDDI installation. Note that the server is on the FDDI ring, while other machines connect to the ring via FDDI to Ethernet hubs.

 NOTE FDDI does not have to run dual rings. Single-ring FDDI is also commonly used.

FDDI connectors are also unique. Figure 7-17 shows a classic FDDI connector. To support two rings, every classic FDDI device needed two connectors, as shown in Figure 7-18. Using fiber-optic cabling, FDDI segments could reach up to two kilometers between systems, with a maximum ring size of 100 kilometers. A later version of FDDI moved to—you guessed it—CAT 5 UTP. Called Copper Distributed Data Interface or *CDDI*, this version uses the same frame types as FDDI, but it runs over copper cabling instead of fiber.

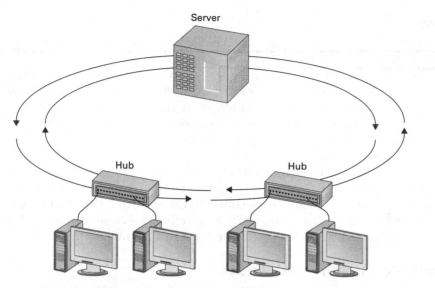

Figure 7-16   FDDI topology: two rings are better than one!

Figure 7-17
FDDI connector

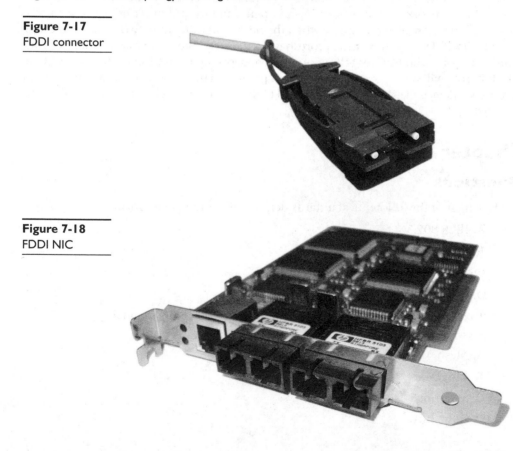

Figure 7-18
FDDI NIC

ATM

Asynchronous Transfer Mode (ATM) came into development at roughly the same time as FDDI. ATM runs at 155 Mbps using fiber-optic cabling or CAT 5 UTP.

While FDDI may be unique, ATM—at least from a topology and physical connection standpoint—is rather boring. ATM typically uses a physical star, just as 10/100/1000BaseT does. ATM supports a number of physical connection types. The most common ATM looks like any other fiber cabling system, using two fiber connectors per node. ATM can also run over CAT 5 or better cabling with RJ-45 connectors, making an ATM NIC look identical to any Ethernet NIC.

ATM didn't make a large mark in the high-speed networking world, but ATM's signaling method, which uses fixed-length frames on a point-to-point connection, became popular as a method for WAN connections. In Chapter 15, "TCP/IP and the Internet," you'll see ATM again. Even though ATM lost in the LAN connectivity wars to Gigabit Ethernet, its frames have found new life in the world of WANs.

Don't Be an Ethernet Snob!

For all Ethernet's popularity, failing to recognize that other network technologies exist can turn you into an Ethernet snob. Although Ethernet definitely rules the vast majority of installed networks today, by keeping an open mind toward other network technologies, you'll be more likely to notice when the next great thing in networking technology presents itself. Don't follow the unfortunate path worn bare by so many other network administrators, who blindly follow only the networking technologies they know. One day, Ethernet will no longer enjoy its current predominance, and when that happens, an alert network tech like you will be prepared to use the technology that best suits you and your network.

Chapter Review

Questions

1. Which of the following standards defines Token Ring networks?

   A. IEEE 802.3

   B. IEEE 802.5

   C. EIA/TIA 568A

   D. IEEE 1284

2. Token Ring networks use a _____ physical topology and a _____ logical topology.

   A. Mesh, ring

   B. Ring, star

   C. Star, ring

   D. Ring, bus

3. Which of the following are true about Token Ring networks? (Select all that apply.)

   A. Collisions occur as a normal part of their operation.

   B. Only a machine with a free token can transmit a new data frame.

   C. In the event of a break in the cable connecting a machine to the MAU, the entire network shuts down.

   D. Token Ring can use either UTP or STP cabling.

4. Token Ring nodes transmit data only when they receive a special frame called a free _____.

   A. Ring

   B. Frame

   C. MAU

   D. Token

5. Philip calls Bob, a tech support technician, for help with a networking problem. Bob asks Philip to tell him what kind of network he uses. Philip responds that he uses UTP. This tells Bob that Philip:

   A. Uses a Token Ring network.

   B. Uses a 10BaseT network.

   C. Uses a 10Base5 network.

   D. Has not provided enough information for Bob to know what kind of network Philip uses.

6. Token Ring MAUs using STP can support up to _____ nodes.

   A. 1024

   B. 260

   C. 100

   D. 72

7. Token Ring MAUs using UTP can support up to _____ nodes.

   A. 1024

   B. 260

   C. 100

   D. 72

8. Token Ring MAUs use special ports called _____ to connect to other MAUs.

   A. Crossovers

   B. Uplinks

   C. Ring In and Ring Out

   D. Repeaters

9. A node connected to its MAU using UTP can be _____ from the MAU.

   A. 100 meters

   B. 100 feet

   C. 45 meters

   D. 45 feet

10. Which of these technologies can run on a dual-ring topology?

   A. ARCnet

   B. ATM

   C. FDDI

   D. Token Ring

Answers

1. **B.** IEEE 802.5 is the IEEE standard for Token Ring. IEEE 802.3 is the standard for Ethernet. EIA/TIA 568A is a cabling standard for UTP cabling. IEEE 1284 is the IEEE standard for parallel communication.

2. **C.** Token Ring networks use a star physical topology and a ring logical topology.

3. **B and D.** Token Ring nodes transmit new data frames only if they have a free token. Token Ring can use either UTP or STP cabling. Although collisions are a normal part of the operation of an Ethernet network, Token Ring's token passing system prevents collisions from occurring. Because Token Ring uses a physical star topology, a break in the cable between the MAU and a device affects only that device, not the rest of the network.

4. **D.** Token ring nodes transmit data only when they receive a special frame called a free token.

5. **D.** Both Token Ring and Ethernet networks can use unshielded twisted-pair cabling.

6. **B.** Token Ring MAUs using STP can support up to 260 nodes.

7. **D.** Token Ring MAUs using UTP can support up to 72 nodes.

8. **C.** Token Ring MAUs use special ports called Ring In and Ring Out to connect to other MAUs.

9. **C.** A Token Ring node using UTP can be up to 45 meters from the MAU.

10. **C.** An FDDI network can run on a dual-ring topology as either a true physical ring or a physical star.

Installing a Physical Network

The Network+ Certification exam expects you to know how to

- 3.3 Identify the appropriate tool for a given wiring task (for example: wire crimper, media tester/certifier, punchdown tool, or tone generator)
- 4.3 Given a network scenario, interpret visual indicators (for example: link LEDs and collision LEDs) to determine the nature of a stated problem
- 4.7 Given a troubleshooting scenario involving a network with a particular physical topology (for example: bus, star, mesh, or ring) and including a network diagram, identify the network area affected and the cause of the stated failure

To achieve these goals, you must be able to

- Recognize and describe the functions of basic components in a structured cabling system
- Explain the process of installing structured cable
- Install a network interface card
- Perform basic troubleshooting on a structured cable network

In previous chapters, you toured the most common network technologies used in today's (and yesterday's) networks. At this point, you should be able to visualize a basic network setup. For bus topologies like 10Base2, visualize a cable running in a ceiling or along the floor with each PC connected somewhere along the bus. For star bus or star ring topologies like 10BaseT or Token Ring, visualize some type of box (hub, MSAU, or switch—whatever you like) with a number of cables snaking out to all of the PCs on the network (see Figure 8-1).

On the surface, such a network setup is absolutely correct, but if you tried to run a network using only a hub and cables running to each system, you'd have some serious practical issues. In the real world, you need to deal with physical obstacles like walls and ceilings. You also need to deal with those annoying things called *people*. People are incredibly adept at destroying physical networks! They can unplug hubs, trip over cables, and rip connectors out of NICs with incredible skill unless you protect the network from their destructive ways. Although the simplified hub-and-a-bunch-of-cables type of network we currently know would work in the real world, this simple network

Figure 8-1
What an orderly
looking network!

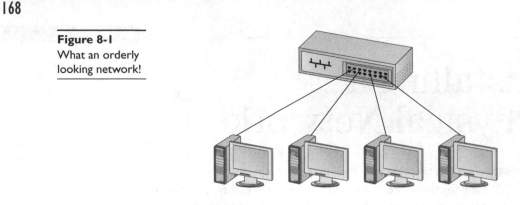

clearly has some problems that need addressing before it can work safely and efficiently (see Figure 8-2).

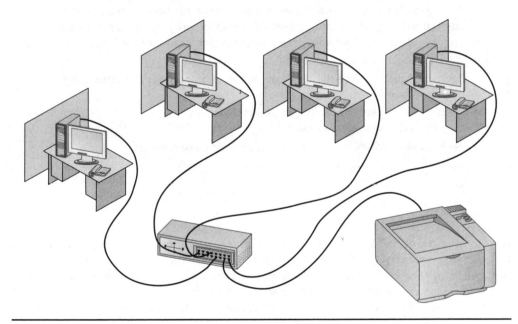

Figure 8-2   A real-world network

This chapter will take the abstract discussion of network technologies from previous chapters into the concrete reality of real networks. To achieve this goal, we'll be marching through the process of installing an entire network system from the beginning. To start, I'll introduce you to the magical world of *structured cabling*: the critical set of standards used all over the world to install physical cabling in a safe and orderly fashion. We'll then delve into the world of larger networks—those with more than a single hub—and see some typical methods used to organize them for peak efficiency and reliability.

Next, we'll take a quick tour of the most common NICs used in PCs, and see what it takes to install them. Finally, we'll look at how to troubleshoot cabling and other network devices—including an introduction to some fun diagnostic tools!

Historical/Conceptual

Structured Cabling

If you want a functioning, dependable, real-world network, you need a solid understanding of a set of standards, collectively called *structured cabling*. These standards, defined by the EIA/TIA (yup, the same folks who tell you how to crimp an RJ-45 onto the end of a UTP cable) give professional cable installers detailed standards on every aspect of a cabled network, from the type of cabling to use to the position of wall outlets. The Network+ exam requires you to understand the basic concepts involved in designing a network and installing network cabling, and to recognize the components used in a real network. Network+ does not, however, expect you to be as knowledgeable as a professional network designer or cable installer. Your goal is to understand enough about real-world cabling systems to support basic troubleshooting. Granted, by the end of this chapter, you'll have enough of an understanding to try running your own cable (I certainly run my own cable!), but consider that knowledge a handy bit of extra credit!

Cable Basics—A Star Is Born

With that goal in mind, let's explore the world of connectivity hardware, starting with the most basic of all networks: a hub, some UTP cable, and a few PCs—in other words, a typical physical star network (see Figure 8-3).

Okay, pop quiz! Is the network in Figure 8-3 a star bus or a star ring? Is it Token Ring, 100BaseT, or Gigabit Ethernet? Gotcha! It's a trick question—you can't tell from this picture. In fact, it could be any of these network technologies. If you have a 10BaseT network using CAT 5e cabling and you want to turn it into a Token Ring network, you simply replace the 10BaseT NICs in the PCs with RJ-45-equipped Token Ring NICs, and

Figure 8-3
A hub connected by UTP cable to two PCs

the 10BaseT hub with a Token Ring MSAU. The cable would stay the same, because as far as the cabling is concerned, there is no difference between these topologies. The physical star does not need to change; only the logical portion—bus or ring—needs to change.

Does this ability to switch network technologies completely, yet keep the same cabling, surprise you? Many people find the idea of totally different network technologies like 10BaseT and Token Ring using the same cables somehow just not right. They think that because the network technology is different, the cabling should also be different. To those people I say, "Open your mind to the idea of cabling options!" If you went back in time 15 years, you'd find that pretty much every networking technology had its own type of cabling. Ethernet used RG-8 or RG-58, and Token Ring used Type 1 STP. Today, that is no longer the case. Over the years, UTP has edged out other cabling options to become the leading type of cabling used today. If an organization already has UTP cabling installed, they're not going to be interested in deploying a network technology that doesn't use UTP. If a network technology wants to thrive today, it must work with UTP. All new network technologies employ UTP, even the new Gigabit Ethernet standards!

NOTE The one exception to the use of UTP is fiber. It's not that much of an exception—almost all fiber network technologies from 10BaseFL to fiber-based Gigabit Ethernet use a star topology and the same type of fiber cable: 62.5/125 multimode.

Not only does UTP reign supreme, but all of today's network technologies run UTP in a physical star. This means that in today's networking world, you're almost always going to run into the same cabling situation: UTP in a physical star topology. Let's discuss the ramifications of the standard networking cabling scenario—the basic star—and see how the network technology industry evolved a bunch of cables running from the hub/switch to each computer into something more realistic.

NOTE Anyone who makes a trip to a local computer store sees plenty of devices that adhere to the 802.11 (wireless networking) standard. There's little doubt about the popularity of wireless. This popularity, however, is giving too many people the impression that 802.11 is pushing wired networks into oblivion. While this may take place one day in the future, wireless networks' unreliability and relatively slow speed (as compared to 100BaseT and Gigabit Ethernet) make it challenging to use in a network that requires high reliability and speed. Wireless makes great sense in homes, your local coffeehouse, and offices that don't need high speed or reliability, but any network that can't afford downtime or slow speeds still uses wires!

The Basic Star

No law of physics prevents you from installing a hub in the middle of your office and running cables on the floor to all the computers in your network. This setup will work, but it falls apart spectacularly when applied to the real-world environment. Three problems present themselves to the real-world network tech. First, the exposed cables running along the floor are just waiting for someone to trip over them, causing damage to the network and giving that person a wonderful lawsuit opportunity. Possible accidents aside, simply moving and stepping on the cabling will, over time, cause a cable to fail due to wires breaking or RJ-45 connectors ripping off cable ends. Second, the presence of other electrical devices close to the cable can create interference that confuses the signals going through the wire. Third, this type of setup limits your ability to make any changes to the network. Before you can change anything, you have to figure out which cables in the huge rat's nest of cables connected to the hub go to which machines. Imagine *that* troubleshooting nightmare!

"Gosh," you're thinking (okay, I'm thinking it, but you should be), "there must be a better way to install a physical network." A better installation would provide safety, protecting the star from vacuum cleaners, clumsy co-workers, and electrical interference. It would have extra hardware to organize and protect the cabling. Finally, the new and improved star network installation would feature a cabling standard with the flexibility to enable the network to grow according to its needs, and then to upgrade when the next great network technology comes along.

As you have no doubt guessed, I'm not just theorizing here. In the real world, the people who most wanted improved installation standards were the ones who installed cable for a living. In response to this demand for standards, the EIA/TIA developed standards for cable installation. The EIA/TIA 568 standards you saw in earlier chapters are only part of a larger set of EIA/TIA standards, all lumped together under the umbrella of structured cabling.

NOTE Installing structured cabling properly takes a startlingly high degree of skill. Thousands of pitfalls await inexperienced network people who think they can install their own network cabling. Pulling cable requires expensive equipment, a lot of hands, and the ability to react to problems quickly. Network techs can lose millions of dollars—not to mention their good jobs—by imagining they can do it themselves without the proper knowledge. If you are interested in learning more details about structured cabling, an organization called BICSI (www.bicsi.org) provides a series of widely recognized certifications for the cabling industry.

Structured Cable Network Components

Successful implementation of a basic structured cabling network requires three essential ingredients: an equipment room, horizontal cabling, and a work area. All the cabling runs from individual PCs to a central location, the *equipment room* (see Figure 8-4). What equipment goes in there—a hub, MSAU, or even a telephone system—is not the important thing. What matters is that all the cables concentrate in this one area.

All cables run horizontally (for the most part) from the equipment room to the PCs. This cabling is called, appropriately, *horizontal cabling* (see Figure 8-5). A single piece of installed horizontal cabling is called a *run*. At the opposite end of the horizontal cabling from the equipment room is the work area. The *work area* is often simply an office or cubicle that potentially contains a PC you want on the network (see Figure 8-6).

Figure 8-4
An equipment
room

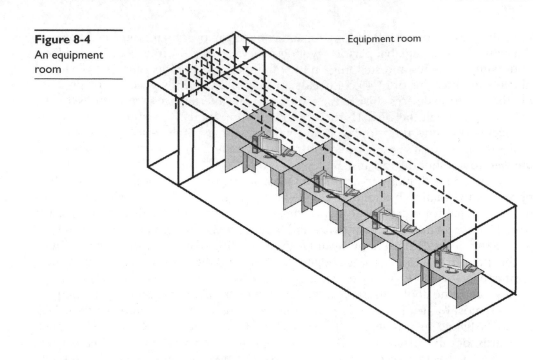

Equipment room

Each of the three parts of a basic star network—the horizontal cabling, the equipment room, and the work area(s)—must follow a series of strict standards designed to

Figure 8-5
Horizontal
cabling

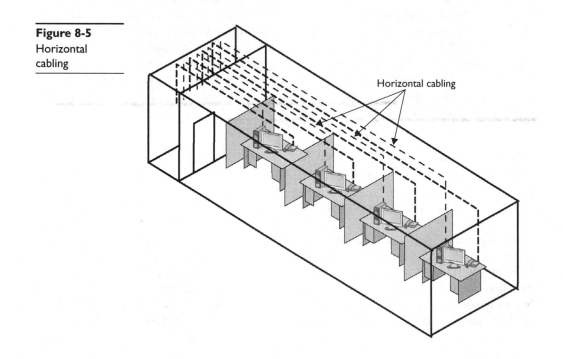

Horizontal cabling

Figure 8-6
The work area

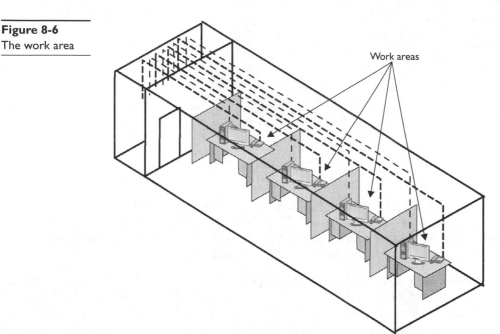

Work areas

ensure that the cabling system is reliable and easy to manage. Let's look at each of the parts individually, starting with the horizontal cabling.

Horizontal Cabling

A horizontal cabling run is the cabling that goes more or less horizontally from a work area to the equipment room. In most networks, this is a CAT 5e or better UTP cable, but when we move into the world of structured cabling, the EIA/TIA standards require a number of other aspects to the cable, such as the type of wires, number of pairs of wires, and fire ratings.

TIP A single piece of cable that runs from a work area to an equipment room is called a run.

Solid Core vs. Stranded Core   All UTP cable comes in one of two types: stranded core or solid core. Each wire in *solid core* UTP uses a single solid wire. With *stranded core*, each wire is a bundle of tiny wire strands. Each of these cable types has its benefits and downsides. Solid core is a better conductor, but it is stiff and will break if handled too often or too roughly. Stranded core is not quite as good a conductor, but it will stand up to substantial handling without breaking. Figure 8-7 shows a close-up of stranded and solid core UTP.

EIA/TIA specifies that horizontal cabling should always be solid core. Remember, this cabling is going into your walls and ceilings, safe from the harmful effects of shoes and

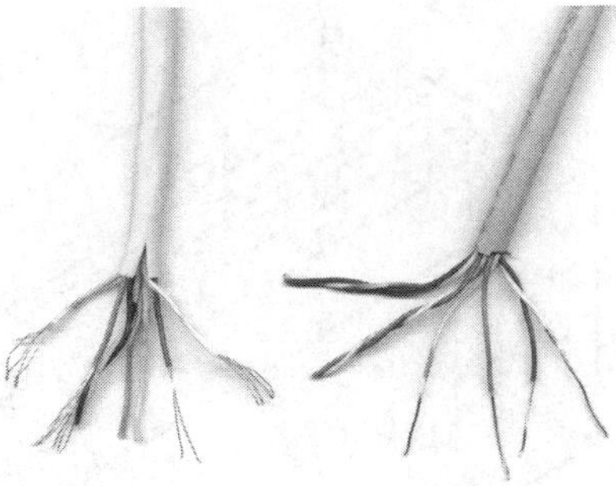

Figure 8-7
Stranded and
solid core UTP

vacuum cleaners. The ceilings and walls enable us to take advantage of the better conductivity of solid core without risk of cable damage. Stranded cable also has an important function in a structured cabling network, but we need to discuss a few more parts of the network before we see where to use stranded UTP cable.

Number of Pairs   Pulling horizontal cables into your walls and ceilings is a time-consuming and messy business, and not a process you want to repeat, if at all possible. For this reason, most cable installers recommend using the highest CAT rating you can afford. A few years ago, we would also mention that you should use four-pair UTP, but today, four-pair is assumed. Four-pair UTP is so common that it's difficult, if not impossible, to find two-pair UTP.

> **NOTE**   Unlike previous CAT standards, EIA/TIA defines CAT 5e and CAT 6 as four-pair-only cables.

Fire Ratings   Did you ever see the movie *The Towering Inferno*? Don't worry if you missed it—*The Towering Inferno* was one of the better infamous disaster movies of the 1970s, but it was no *Airplane!* Anyway, Steve McQueen stars as the fireman who saves the day when a skyscraper goes up in flames because of poor-quality electrical cabling. The burning insulation on the wires ultimately spreads the fire to every part of the building. Although no cables made today contain truly flammable insulation, the insulation is made from plastic, and if you get any plastic hot enough, it will create smoke and noxious fumes. The risk of burning insulation isn't fire—it's smoke and fumes.

To reduce the risk of your network cables burning and creating noxious fumes and smoke, Underwriters Laboratories and the National Electrical Code (NEC) joined forces to develop cabling *fire ratings*. The two most common fire ratings are PVC and plenum. Cable with a *PVC (polyvinyl chloride)* rating has no significant fire protection. If you burn a PVC cable, it creates lots of smoke and noxious fumes. Burning *plenum*-rated cable creates much less smoke and fumes, but plenum-rated cable—often referred to simply as "plenum"—costs about three to five times as much as PVC-rated cable. Most city ordinances require the use of plenum cable for network installations. Bottom line? Get plenum!

The space between the acoustical tile ceiling in an office building and the actual concrete ceiling above is called the plenum—hence the name for the proper fire rating of cabling to use in that space. A third type of fire rating, known as *riser*, designates the proper cabling to use for vertical runs between floors of a building. Riser-rated cable provides less protection than plenum cable, though, so most installations today use plenum for runs between floors.

Choosing Your Horizontal Cabling   In the real world, network people only install CAT 5e or CAT 6 UTP, even if they can get away with a lower CAT level. Installing rated cabling is done primarily as a hedge against new network technologies that may require a more advanced cable. Networking *caveat emptor* warning: many network installers take advantage of the fact that a lower CAT level will work on most networks, and bid a network installation using the lowest grade cable possible, so be sure to specify CAT 5e or even CAT 6 when soliciting bids for cable installation!

The Equipment Room

The equipment room is the heart of the basic star. This is where all the horizontal runs from all the work areas come together. The concentration of all this gear in one place makes the equipment room potentially one of the messiest parts of the basic star. Even if you do a nice, neat job of organizing the cables when they are first installed, networks change over time. People move computers, new work areas are added, network topologies are added or improved, and so on. Unless you impose some type of organization, this conglomeration of equipment and cables is bound to decay into a nightmarish mess.

Fortunately, the EIA/TIA's structured cabling standards define the use of specialized components in the equipment room that make organizing a snap. In fact, it might be fair to say that there are too many options! To keep it simple, we're going to stay with the most common equipment room setup, and then take a short peek at some other fairly common options.

Equipment Racks   The central component of every equipment room is one or more equipment racks. *Equipment racks* provide a safe, stable platform for all the different hardware components. All equipment racks are 19 inches wide, but they vary in height. You'll see two- to three-foot-high models that bolt onto a wall, as well as to the more popular floor-to-ceiling models (see Figure 8-8).

You can mount almost any network hardware component into a rack. All manufacturers make rack-mounted hubs and switches that mount into a rack with a few screws. These hubs and switches are available with a wide assortment of ports and capabilities. There are even rack-mounted servers, complete with slide-out keyboards, and rack-mounted uninterruptible power supplies (UPSs) to power the equipment (see Figure 8-9).

Patch Panels and Cables   Ideally, once you install horizontal cabling, it should never be moved. As you know, UTP horizontal cabling has a solid core, making it pretty stiff. Solid core cables can handle some rearranging, but if you insert a wad of solid core cables directly into your hubs, every time you move a cable to a different port on the hub, or move the hub itself, you will jostle the cable. You don't have to move a solid core

Figure 8-8
A bare
equipment rack

Figure 8-9
A rack-mounted
UPS

cable many times before one of the solid copper wires breaks, and there goes your network! Luckily for you, you can easily avoid this problem by using a patch panel. A *patch panel* is simply a box with a row of female connectors (ports) in the front and permanent connections in the back, to which you connect the horizontal cables (see Figure 8-10).

Not only do patch panels prevent the horizontal cabling from being moved, they are also your first line of defense in organizing the cables. All patch panels have space in the front for labels, and these labels are the network tech's best friend! Simply place a tiny label on the patch panel identifying each cable, and you will never have to experience that sinking feeling of standing in the equipment room of your nonfunctioning network, wondering which cable is which. If you want to be a purist, there is an official, and

Figure 8-10
Sample patch
panels

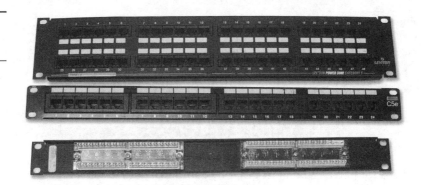

rather confusing, EIA/TIA labeling methodology you can use; but most real-world network techs simply use their own internal codes (see Figure 8-11).

Figure 8-11
A labeled
patch panel

NOTE The EIA/TIA 606 standard covers proper labeling and documentation of cabling, patch panels, and wall outlets. If you want to know how the pros label and document a structured cabling system, check out the EIA/TIA 606 standard.

Patch panels are available in a wide variety of configurations that include different types of ports and numbers of ports. You can get UTP, STP, or fiber ports, and some manufacturers combine several different types on the same patch panel. Panels are available with 8, 12, 24, 48, or even more ports. UTP patch panels, like UTP cables, come with CAT ratings, which you should be sure to check. Don't blow a good CAT 6 cable installation by buying a cheap patch panel—get a CAT 6 patch panel! Most manufacturers proudly display the CAT level right on the patch panel (see Figure 8-12).

Once you have installed the patch panel, you need to connect the ports to the hub through *patch cables*. Patch cables are short (two- to five-foot) UTP cables, similar to horizontal cabling (see Figure 8-13). Unlike horizontal cabling, patch cables use stranded rather than solid cable, so they can tolerate much more handling. Patch cables also differ from horizontal cables in their wiring scheme. EIA/TIA defines a straight-through

Figure 8-12
CAT level on
patch panel

wiring for patch cables: Pin 1 on one connector goes to Pin 1 on the other; Pin 2 to Pin 2, and so on. Even though you can make your own patch cables, most people buy pre-made ones. Buying patch cables enables you to use different-colored cables to facilitate organization (yellow for accounting, blue for sales, or whatever scheme works for you). Most prefabricated patch cables also come with reinforced RJ-45 connectors specially designed to handle multiple insertions and removals.

Figure 8-13
Typical patch
cables

An equipment room doesn't have to be a special room dedicated to computer equipment. You can use specially made cabinets with their own little built-in equipment racks that sit on the floor or attach to a wall, or use a storage room, as long as the equipment can be protected from the other items stored there. Fortunately, the demand for equipment rooms has been around for so long that most large office spaces come equipped with them.

At this point, our basic star installation is taking shape (Figure 8-14). We've installed the EIA/TIA horizontal cabling and configured the equipment room. Now it's time to address the last part of the structured cabling system: the work area.

The Work Area

What is a work area? From a cabling standpoint, a work area is nothing more than a wall outlet that serves as the termination point for horizontal network cables: a convenient insertion point for a PC. A wall outlet itself consists of a female jack to accept the cable, a mounting bracket, and a faceplate. You connect the PC to the wall outlet with a patch cable (Figure 8-15).

Figure 8-14
Complete
medium-sized
equipment room

Figure 8-15
A patch cable
connecting a
PC to an outlet

The female RJ-45 jacks in these wall outlets also have CAT ratings. You must buy CAT-rated jacks for wall outlets to go along with the CAT rating of the cabling in your network. In fact, many network connector manufacturers use the same connectors in the wall outlets that they use on the patch panels. These modular outlets significantly increase ease of installation. Make sure you label the outlet to show the job of each connector (see Figure 8-16). A good outlet will also have some form of label that identifies its position on the patch panel. Proper documentation of your outlets will save you an incredible amount of work later.

Figure 8-16
A typical
wall outlet

The last step is connecting the PC to the wall outlet. Here again, most folks use a patch cable. Its stranded cabling stands up to the abuse caused by moving PCs, not to mention the occasional kick.

Now, my young apprentice, let us return to the question of why the EIA/TIA 568 specification only allows UTP cable lengths of 90 meters, even though most UTP networking technologies allow cables to be 100 meters long. Have you figured it out? Hint: the answer lies in the discussion we've just been having. Ding! Time's up! The answer is…the patch cables! Patch cables add extra distance between the hub and the PC, so EIA/TIA compensates by reducing the horizontal cabling length.

TIP Watch out for the word *drop*, as it has more than one meaning. A single run of cable from the equipment room to a wall outlet is often referred to as a drop. The word *drop* is also used to define a new run coming through a wall outlet that does not yet have a jack installed.

The work area may be the simplest part of the structured cabling system, but it is also the source of most network failures. When a user can't access the network and you suspect a broken cable, the first place to look is the work area!

Structured Cabling—Use It!

As you can see, EIA/TIA structured cabling methods transform the basic star from the cabling nightmare shown at the beginning of this discussion into an orderly and robust network. Sure, you don't have to do any of this to make a network function; you only have to do it if you want the network to run reliably and change easily with the demands of your organization. The extra cost and effort of installing a properly structured cabling system pays huge dividends: you can avoid the nightmare scenario of having to find one bad cable in a haystack of unlabeled CAT 5, and you can protect the network from clumsy and/or clueless users.

Planning the Installation

A professional installer will begin a structured cabling installation by assessing your site and planning the installation in detail before a single piece of cable is pulled. As the customer, your job is to work closely with the installer. That means putting on old clothes and crawling along with the installer as he or she combs through your ceilings, walls, and closets. Even though you're not the actual installer, you must understand the installation process, so you can help the installer make the right decisions for your network.

Structured cabling requires a lot of planning. You need to know if the cables from the work areas can reach the equipment room—is the distance less than the 90-meter limit dictated by the EIA/TIA standard? How will you route the cable? What path should each run take to get to the wall outlets? Don't forget that just because a cable looks like it will reach, there's no guarantee that it will! Ceilings and walls often include nasty hidden surprises like firewalls—big, thick, concrete walls designed into buildings that require a masonry drill or a jackhammer to punch through. Let's look at the steps that go into proper planning.

Get a Floor Plan

First, you need a blueprint of the area. If you ever contract an installer and they don't start by asking for a floor plan, fire them immediately and get one who does! The floor plan is the key to proper planning; a good floor plan shows you the location of closets that could serve as equipment rooms, alerts you to any firewalls in your way, and gives you a good overall feel for the scope of the job ahead.

If you don't have a floor plan—and this is often the case with homes or older buildings—you'll need to create your own. Go get a ladder and a flashlight—you'll need them to poke around in ceilings, closets, and crawl spaces as you map out the location of rooms, walls, and anything else of interest to the installation. Figure 8-17 shows a typical do-it-yourself floor plan, drawn out by hand.

Map the Runs

Now that you have your floor plan, it's time to map the cable runs. Here's where you run around the work areas, noting the locations of existing or planned systems to determine where to place each cable drop. *A cable drop* is the location where the cable comes out of the wall. You should also talk to users, management, and other interested parties to try and understand their plans for the future. It's much easier to install a few extra drops now than to do it a year from now when those two unused offices suddenly find themselves with users who immediately need networked computers!

This is also the point where the nasty word "cost" first raises its ugly head. Face it: cables, drops, and the people who install them cost money! The typical price for a network

Figure 8-17
Hand-drawn
network
floor plan

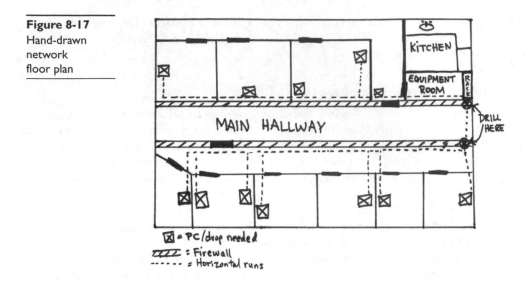

installation is around US $150 per drop. Find out how much you want to spend and make some calls. Most network installers price their network jobs by quoting a "per drop" cost.

Inside or Outside the Walls?

While you're mapping your runs, you have to make another big decision: Do you want to run the cables in the walls or outside them? Many companies sell wonderful external raceway products that adhere to your walls, making for a much simpler, though less neat, installation than running cables in the walls (see Figure 8-18). Raceways make good sense in older buildings, or when you don't have the guts or the rights to go into the walls.

Figure 8-18
A typical raceway

Even though I said you can run cables through a raceway, let's face it: most of us prefer the nice little outlets with the wires running in the walls. Once we finish mapping the runs, we'll see just what that takes.

The Equipment Room While mapping the runs, you should decide on the location of your equipment room. When deciding on this location, keep five issues in mind: distance, power, dryness, coolness, and access.

PART II

- **Distance**   The equipment room must be located in a spot that won't require cable runs longer than 90 meters. In most locations, keeping runs under 90 meters requires little effort, as long as the equipment room is placed in a central location.

- **Power**   Many of the components in your equipment room need power. Make sure you provide enough! If possible, put the equipment room on its own dedicated circuit; that way, when someone blows a circuit in the kitchen, it doesn't take out the entire network.

- **Dryness**   I imagine this one is obvious. Electrical components and water don't mix well. (Remind me to tell you about the time I installed a rack in an abandoned bathroom, and the toilet that later exploded.) Remember that dryness also means low humidity. Avoid areas with the potential for high humidity, such as a closet near a pool or the room where the cleaning people leave mop buckets full of water. Of course, any well air-conditioned room should be fine—which leads to the next big issue....

- **Coolness**   Equipment rooms tend to get warm, especially if you add a couple of server systems and a UPS. Make sure your equipment room has an air-conditioning outlet or some other method of keeping the room cool. Figure 8-19 shows how I installed an air-conditioning duct in my small equipment closet. Of course, I did this only after I discovered that the server was repeatedly rebooting due to overheating!

Figure 8-19
An A/C
duct cooling an
equipment closet

- **Access**   Access involves two different issues. First, it means preventing unauthorized access. Think about the people you do and don't want messing around with your network, and act accordingly. In my small office, the equipment closet literally sits eight feet from me, so I don't concern myself too much with unauthorized access. You, on the other hand, may want to consider placing a lock on the door of your equipment room if you're concerned that unscrupulous or unqualified people might try to access it. Figure 8-20 shows what happened to my equipment room when I allowed access to it!

Figure 8-20
Equipment room taken over by mops, brooms, and trash

The second access consideration is making sure the people who need to get at your equipment to maintain and troubleshoot it can do so. Take a look at my equipment room in Figure 8-21. Here's a classic case of not providing good access. Note how difficult it would be for me to get to the back of the server—I would literally need to pull the server out to check cables and NICs!

Figure 8-21
A server wedged into a closet

One other issue to keep in mind when choosing your equipment room is expandability. Will this equipment room be able to grow with your network? Is it close enough to be able to service any additional office space your company may acquire nearby? If your company decides to take over the floor above you, can you easily access another equipment room on that floor from this room? While the specific issues will be unique to each installation, keep thinking "expansion" as you design—your network will grow, whether or not you think so now!

Most equipment rooms require a floor-mounted equipment rack, but you do have other options. One option is a shorter rack, like the wall-mounted one shown in Figure 8-22.

Figure 8-22
A wall-mounted
short rack

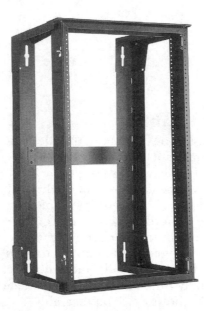

Serious equipment racks such as these must be mounted to the floor or the wall, usually with big concrete fasteners or other heavy-duty hardware. Installing a rack properly is a big job, and one I never do myself. A small network can dispense with a rack altogether and use a simple wall-mounted patch panel like the one shown in Figure 8-23.

 NOTE All racks use a unique height measurement called units, or U. One U equals 1.75 inches. When you purchase a rack, its height will be listed in terms of U, for example 44U. All rack-mounted equipment uses the U measurement; it's common to see rack-mounted servers, hubs, and patch panels with U dimensions, such as 2U (3.5 inches) or 4U (7 inches).

So, you've mapped your cable runs and established your equipment room—now you're ready to start pulling cable!

Figure 8-23
A wall-mounted
patch panel

Installing the Cable

Pulling cable is easily one of the most thankless and unpleasant jobs in the entire net-working world. It may not look that hard from a distance, but the devil is in the details. First of all, pulling cable requires two people if you want to get the job done quickly; three people are even better. Most pullers like to start from the equipment room and pull toward the drops. The pullers draw cable from a reel—many using a handy reel spindle to help the reel turn easily. In an office area with a drop ceiling, pullers will often feed the cabling along the run by opening ceiling tiles and stringing the cable along the top of the ceiling. Professional cable pullers have an arsenal of interesting tools to help them move the cable horizontally, including telescoping poles, special nylon pull ropes, and even nifty little crossbows and pistols that can fire a pull rope long distances! Figure 8-24 shows a tech pulling cable.

Figure 8-24
A tech pulling
cable

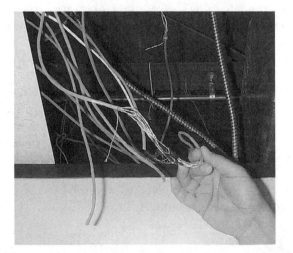

Professional installers no longer simply dump cabling onto the top of a drop ceiling. A previous lack of codes or standards for handling cables led to a nightmare of disorganized cables in drop ceilings all over the world. Any cable puller will tell you that the hardest part of installing cables is the need to work around all the old cable installations in the ceiling! (See Figure 8-25.)

Figure 8-25
My buddy Roger Conrad working in a messy ceiling

Local codes, the EIA/TIA, and the NEC all have strict rules about how you pull cable in a ceiling. A good installer will use either hooks or trays, which provide better cable management, safety, and protection from electrical interference (see Figure 8-26). The faster the network, the more critical good cable management becomes. You probably won't have a problem laying UTP directly on top of a drop ceiling if you just want a 10BaseT network, and you might even get away with this for 100BaseT—but forget about doing this with Gigabit. Cable installation companies are making a mint from all the CAT 5 and earlier network cabling installations that need to be redone to support Gigabit Ethernet.

Figure 8-26
Cable trays above a drop ceiling

PART II

Running cable horizontally requires relatively little effort, compared to running the cable down from the ceiling to a pretty faceplate at the work area, which often takes a lot of skill. In a typical office area with sheetrock walls, the installer first decides on the position for the outlet, usually using a stud finder to avoid cutting on top of a stud. Once the worker cuts the hole (see Figure 8-27), most installers drop a line to the hole using a weight tied to the end of a nylon pull rope (see Figure 8-28). They can then attach the network cable to the pull rope and pull it down to the hole. Once the cable is pulled through the new hole, the installer puts in an outlet box or a low-voltage *mounting bracket* (see Figure 8-29). This bracket acts as a holder for the faceplate.

Figure 8-27
Cutting a hole

Figure 8-28
Dropping
a weight

Figure 8-29
Installing a low-voltage mounting bracket

Back in the equipment room, the many cables leading to each work area are consolidated and organized in preparation for the next stage: making connections. A truly professional installer takes great care in organizing the equipment closet. Figure 8-30 shows a typical installation using special cable guides to bring the cables down to the equipment rack.

Figure 8-30
Cable guides
help organize the
equipment closet.

Making Connections

As the name implies, making connections consists of connecting both ends of each cable to the proper jacks. This step also includes the most important step in the entire process: testing each cable run to ensure that every connection meets the requirements of the network that will use it. Installers also use this step to document and label each cable run—a critical step too often forgotten by inexperienced installers, and one you need to verify takes place!

Connecting the Work Areas

Let's begin by watching an installer connect a cable run. In the work area, that means the cable installer will now crimp a jack onto the end of the wire and mount the faceplate to complete the installation (see Figures 8-31 and 8-32).

Figure 8-31
Attaching a jack
to the wire

Figure 8-32
Fitting the jack
into a faceplate

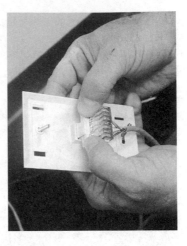

Note the back of the jack shown in Figure 8-31. This jack uses the popular *110-punchdown* connection. Other jack makers may use different types, but the 110 is the most common. Most 110 connections have a color code that tells you which wire to punch into which connection on the back of the jack. We use a special 110-punchdown tool to make these connections (see Figure 8-33).

Figure 8-33
The 110-
punchdown tool

Connecting the Patch Panels

Connecting the cables to patch panels requires you to deal with two issues. The first is patch cable management. Figure 8-34 shows the front of a small network's equipment rack—note the complete lack of cable management! This one is so messy, I challenge you to find the patch panels and the hubs. (Hint: The hubs are in the center of the picture.) Managing patch cables means using the proper cable management hardware. Plastic D-rings guide the patch cables neatly along the sides and front of the patch panel. Finger boxes are rectangular cylinders with slots in the front; the patch cables run into the open ends of the box, and individual cables are threaded through the fingers on their way to the patch panel, keeping them neatly organized. Creativity and variety abound in the world of cable-management hardware—there are as many different solutions to cable management as there are ways to screw up organizing them. Figure 8-35 shows a rack using good cable management—these patch cables are well secured using cable-management hardware, making them much less susceptible to damage from mishandling. Plus, it looks much nicer!

Figure 8-34
Bad cable
management

Figure 8-35
Good cable
management

The second issue to consider when connecting cables is the overall organization of the patch panel as it relates to the organization of your network. Organize your patch panel so that it mirrors the layout of your network. You can organize according to the physical layout, so the different parts of the patch panel correspond to different parts of your office space—for example, the north and south sides of the hallway. Another popular way to organize patch panels is to make sure they match the logical layout of the network, so the different user groups or company organizations have their own sections of the patch panel.

Labeling the Cable

Even if your installer doesn't use an official EIA/TIA 606 labeling scheme, you still must label your runs. Design a labeling scheme that matches your network's organization—for example, you could have all the connections on the north side of the building start with the letter *N* followed by a three-digit number starting with 001. After you have a labeling scheme—this part is critical!—you must *use it*. When you make a network connection, label the outlet at the work area and the jack on the patch panel with the same number. Figure 8-36 shows a typical equipment rack with a number of patch panels—a common setup for a small network. In this case, both the color of the patch cables and their placement on the panels tell you where they belong in the network.

Figure 8-36
Well-organized
patch panels

You must label, but you don't have to organize to this degree. In fact, many network installers choose not to, because they feel it wastes ports on the patch panel. What happens if one side of the network grows beyond the number of assigned ports, while the other side gets smaller? My answer: Get another patch panel. Other techs prefer to fill up the existing patch panels, even if it muddies their organizational scheme. This is a matter of personal choice, of course. Whatever the labeling scheme, only one thing matters. The most important part of labeling is that both ends of a given cable say the same thing. Figure 8-37 shows some labels on a typical patch panel.

Figure 8-37

Labels on a
patch panel

Take a look at the wall outlet in Figure 8-38. Note that the label on the outlet corresponds to the label on the patch panel in Figure 8-37. Failure to include this one simple step creates more problems than you can imagine. Good network installers always label the runs in this manner, not to mention a lot of other labeling that users do not see, such as labeling on the cable inside the wall. Proper labeling can save you from many potential disasters. Here's a classic example: John wants to install a second networked system in the unused office next door. He sees that the unused office has a network outlet, but he wants to make sure the wall outlet connects to the network hub. His problem: he can't determine which port on the patch panel he needs to use. Sure, he could guess, or use a special tool called a toner (we'll get to that later), but think how much faster it would be if all he had to do was read the label on the outlet and find the corresponding label on the patch panel! Make your life simpler than John's—label your patch panels and outlets.

Figure 8-38

Label on
an outlet

Test Specific

Testing the Cable Runs

Well, in theory, your cabling system is now installed and ready for a hub and some systems. Before you do this, though, you must test each cable run. Someone new to testing cable might think that all you need to do is verify that each jack has been properly connected. While this is an important and necessary step, the interesting problem comes after that: verifying that your cable run can handle the speed of your network.

Before we go further, let me be clear: a typical network admin/tech cannot properly test a new cable run. The EIA/TIA provides a series of incredibly complex and important standards for testing cable. Unless you want to get into a 75-page discussion of things like near-end crosstalk and the attenuation-to-crosstalk ratio, this is an area where employing a professional cable installer makes sense. The testing equipment alone totally surpasses the cost of most smaller network installations! Advanced network testing tools easily cost over $5000, and some are well over $10,000! Never fear, though—a number of lower-end tools work just fine for basic network testing. Let's look at some of them.

NOTE These tools are also used to diagnose network problems.

The best tool to start with is the cable tester. *Cable testers* perform a wide variety of functions, and can diagnose all manner of problems with the cabling. Most network admin types staring at a potentially bad cable want to know the following:

- How long is this cable?
- Are any of the wires broken?
- If there is a break, where is it?
- Are any of the wires shorted together?
- Are any of the wires not in proper order (in other words, are there split or crossed pairs)?
- Is there electrical or radio interference?

Various models of cable testers are designed to answer some or all of these questions, depending on the amount of money you are willing to pay. At the low end of the cable tester market are devices that only test for broken wires. A wire that can conduct electricity is said to have *continuity*; thus, a broken wire lacks continuity. These cheap (under $100) testers are often called continuity testers (see Figure 8-39). Some cheaper cable testers will also test for split or crossed pairs and for shorts. These cheap testers usually require you to insert both ends of the cable into the tester. Of course, this can be a bit of a problem if the cable is already installed in the wall!

Medium price testers (≈ $400) have the additional capability to determine the length of a cable, and can even tell you where a break is located. This type of cable tester (see Figure 8-40) is generically called a *Time Domain Reflectometer (TDR)*. A medium-priced tester will have a small loopback device that gets inserted into the far end of the cable, enabling the tester to work with installed cables. This is the type of tester you want to have around!

If you want a device that can test the electrical characteristics of a cable, the price shoots up fast. These professional devices test critical EIA/TIA electrical characteristics, and are used by professional installers to verify installations. These are generally known

Figure 8-39
A simple
cable tester

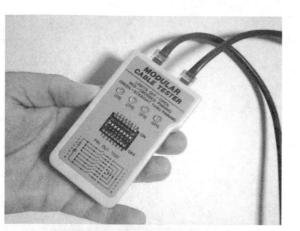

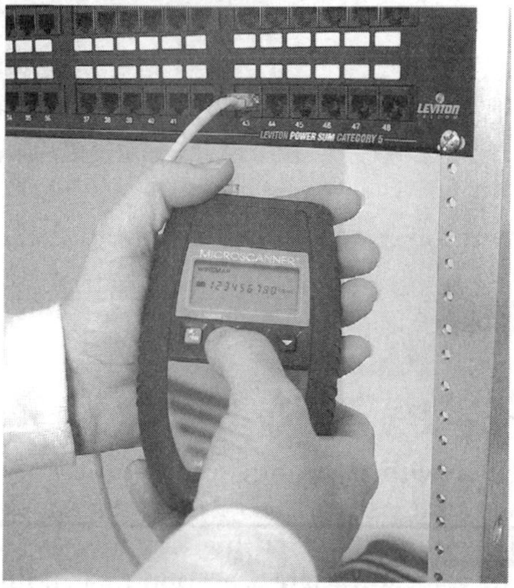

Figure 8-40
A typical
medium-priced
TDR—a
Microtest
Microscanner

as *media certifier tools*, as they generate a report that the installer can then print and hand to you as certification to prove that your cable runs pass EIA/TIA standards. Some of these high-end devices have powerful added features, such as the capability to plug into a network and literally draw a schematic of the entire network for you, including neat information like the MAC addresses of the systems, IP or IPX addresses, and even the operating system for each computer. Figure 8-41 shows an example of this type of scanner made by Microtest (www.microtest.com). These advanced testers are more than most network techs need, so unless you have some deep pockets or find yourself doing serious cable testing, stick to the medium-priced testers.

Getting Physical

The process of installing a structured cabling system is rather involved, requires a great degree of skill, and should be left to professionals. However, by understanding the

Figure 8-41
A typical media
certifier—
a Microtest
OMNIScanner

process, you'll find you're able to tackle most of the problems that come up in an installed structured cabling system. Make sure you're comfortable with the components of structured cabling!

Beyond the Basic Star

The basic single hub with star configuration only works acceptably in the simplest networks. In the real world, networks tend to have many hubs, and often span floors, buildings, states, and even countries. Starting with the basic star, and using structured cabling where applicable, you can progress beyond that rudimentary configuration using certain equipment and strategies designed for larger, more advanced, and more efficient networks.

To see the many ways we can progress beyond the basic star, let's look at an example. The Bayland Widget Corporation's network has three 10BaseT hubs. Each hub serves a different department: hub *A* is for accounting, hub *B* is for sales, and hub *C* is for manufacturing. Bayland's clever network tech has connected the three hubs, enabling any system on any of the three hubs to communicate with any other system on any of the three hubs (see Figure 8-42).

Switched Networks

As you add PCs to a 10BaseT network, your network traffic will increase. As network traffic increases, your users will begin to experience a perceptible slowdown in network

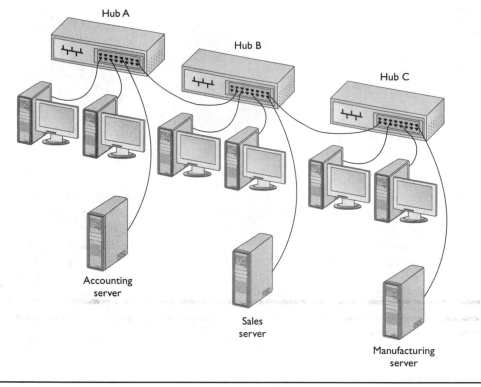

Figure 8-42   Bayland Widget Corporation's three cascaded 10BaseT hubs

performance. One of the fastest and cheapest hardware solutions for too much traffic on any star-bus Ethernet network is the addition of a switch. To switch (sorry, the pun was just hanging there!) to a switched 10BaseT network, simply remove a hub and replace it with a switch. You don't have to do anything to the cards or the cabling.

Like hubs, switches come in a dizzying variety of shapes and sizes. As you might have guessed, companies that make hubs tend to make switches, too, most of which use the same casing for equivalent hubs and switches. In fact, from 20 feet away, an equivalent hub and switch look identical. Figure 8-43 shows an Intel small office hub next to a small office switch; note that they are virtually identical.

In the past, switches were tremendously more expensive than hubs, but in the last few years, the price of switches has dropped immensely—from thousands of dollars to mere hundreds. Small eight-node switches are available at your local computer store for under $100. With the dramatic price drop, the switch has moved from a luxury technology to a standard part of all networks.

So, now you can buy a switch without selling your house to pay for it, but what do you do with it once you have it? You have many possibilities, depending on the type of network you have, but odds are you'll want to choose between two common implementation

Figure 8-43
Switches and hubs look the same.

strategies. The first option is to switch everything—forget about plain hubs and connect everything to a switch. The second option is to use the switch as a bridge between hubs. Let's look at both of these options, using Bayland Widget as the example.

Bayland's network has three hubs, each of which you can replace with a switch. This eliminates the collision domain problem: with three cascaded hubs, the packets sent from any PC go to all the other PCs on all three hubs, raising the likelihood of collisions. Because switches direct each packet only to the specified recipient PC, no collisions occur (after the switch determines the MAC addresses and creates a direct connection between the two computers). This is wonderful because it means that every connection runs at the full potential speed of the network—in this case, the full 10 Mbps of a 10BaseT network. Remember, the moment you start using switches, you can throw the 5-4-3 rule out the window!

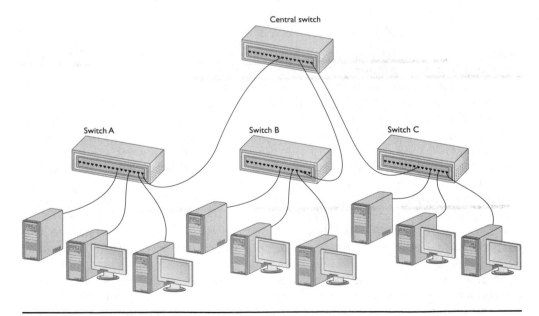

Figure 8-44   Bayland's network with three switches installed

Multispeed Networks

In the networking world, the fastest technology isn't always the best. My office uses a 100BaseT network. Even though Gigabit Ethernet is available with relatively inexpensive switches and NICs, the CAT 5 cable in our network simply was installed too poorly to handle it. The RJ-45 jacks were poorly crimped at the wall outlets and the horizontal cabling was laid too close to my fluorescent lights, so I'd need to replace all my structured cabling. The work we do is such that the vast majority of the users on the network wouldn't even notice the extra speed of Gigabit Ethernet. Computers that cruise the Web, pull down e-mail, and transfer an occasional Word document barely make use of 100-megabit connections, let alone gigabit! On the other hand, my hard-working servers handle almost 50 times as much traffic as my workstations, so they would benefit dramatically from a speed increase. How can I make my servers run at Gigabit Ethernet speeds, while my regular PCs run on 100BaseT?

The secret lies in a class of switches called *multispeed* switches. Multispeed switches come in two types. One type is a switch with some number of—for example—100BaseT ports. To the side of those ports lie one or two Gigabit ports. I can snap Gigabit Ethernet cards into my servers, and then plug those servers directly into the Gigabit ports (Figure 8-45).

Figure 8-45
High-speed ports on a multispeed switch

With the second type of multispeed switch, every port is capable of running at more than one speed. Figure 8-46 shows the link lights for the primary switch in my office. Every port on the switch can run at either 10 or 100 Mbps. These ports are *autosensing;* this means that when you connect a cable into any port, the port will detect the speed of the NIC on the other end of the cable and run at that speed. An autosensing port that runs at either 10 or 100 Mbps is referred to as a 10/100 port. A port that runs at 10, 100, or Gigabit is often referred to as a 10/100/1000 port.

Figure 8-46
Multispeed port lights on a multispeed switch

You'll also find switches that combine both of the types just described. For example, I have a switch with 24 multispeed 10/100 ports and two Gigabit ports.

NOTE Is there such a thing as a multispeed hub? Sure, there have been multispeed hubs, but today they're so rare that we consider them obsolete.

Multispeed networks are incredibly common, as they provide an easy way to support a few systems that need a high-speed connection, while also supporting lower-speed systems. Another big benefit to multispeed networks is that you can use the high-speed ports on one switch to interconnect other high-speed ports on other multispeed switches. This creates a special, separate, high-speed segment called a *backbone* that acts as the primary interconnection for the entire network. Backbones are popular in larger networks where systems are separated by floors and buildings. Let's talk about larger networks and see how backbones fit into this picture.

Multiple Floors, Multiple Buildings

Once you begin to expand a network beyond the basic star configuration by adding more hubs and switches, new demands arise. These can be summarized in a single statement: as networks grow, they take up more space! Adding significantly more PCs to a network usually implies adding more offices, cubicles, and other work areas. Adding work areas means adding more switches and hubs in more equipment rooms.

As a general rule, networks use one equipment room per floor. If the room is centrally located in the building, cabling within the 90-meter limit will completely cover the floor space in most buildings. If your office has work areas on more than one floor, you essentially now have multiple networks on multiple floors. This is a classic example of the need for a backbone network. Backbones tie all the floors together with a robust, high-speed network fast enough to support the demands of combined networks.

Enlarging a network usually also means adding more servers to handle the increased demand. As more servers are added to the network, the administrators who tend to them will find it more efficient to group mission-critical servers together in a single computer room. A computer room not only provides enhanced safety and security for expensive hardware, it also enables administrators to handle daily support chores like backups more efficiently. Bottom line: the larger the network, the larger the space needed to support it, and the more complex your network infrastructure will be.

The concept of structured cabling extends beyond the basic star. EIA/TIA provides a number of standards, centered on EIA/TIA 568 and another important EIA/TIA standard, EIA/TIA 569. These standards address cabling configuration and performance specifications (568), and cable pathways and installation areas (569) involving multiple equipment rooms, floors, and buildings. Slightly simplified, EIA/TIA's view of structured cabling in larger networks breaks down into six main components: the equipment room, the horizontal cabling, the work areas, the backbone, the building entrance, and the telecommunication closets. The first three were discussed earlier and perform the same roles in a more complex network as in a basic star, so I'll concentrate on the last three.

NOTE Don't bother memorizing these terms. Network+ is not going to quiz you on naming the six components of structured cabling. Do make it a point to understand the equipment required for each of these components, and how the different parts interrelate.

Backbones and Building Entrances

When you split a network into multiple floors or buildings, a common practice is to interconnect those floors or buildings with a single high-speed segment—a classic example of a backbone. EIA/TIA specifies using UTP or fiber-optic cable for backbones. While any cable that meets the criteria for a backbone can certainly serve as a backbone cable, EIA/TIA conceives of backbones more as cables that vertically connect equipment rooms (often called risers) or horizontally connect buildings (interbuilding cables).

EIA/TIA provides some guidelines for backbone cable distances, but the ultimate criterion for determining cable length is the networking technology used. Most riser backbones use either copper or fiber-optic cables. Because of its imperviousness to electrical interference, fiber-optic is the only cabling you should use for interbuilding connections (see Figure 8-47).

Figure 8-47
Fiber-optic backbone cables connecting into hubs

The *building entrance* is where all the cables from the outside world (telephone lines, cables from other buildings, and so on) come into a building (see Figure 8-48). EIA/TIA specifies exactly how the building entrance should be configured, but we're not interested in the building entrance beyond knowing that fiber-optic cable should be used between buildings.

Complexity Is Cool!

As networks grow beyond the basic star, they will also grow in complexity. A large network that is switched, multispeed, and multifloored requires a substantial time investment for proper management and support. Those who take the time to understand their large networks find a beauty—or as Bill Gates would say, an *elegance*—that stems from a well-running large network. Complexity is definitely cool!

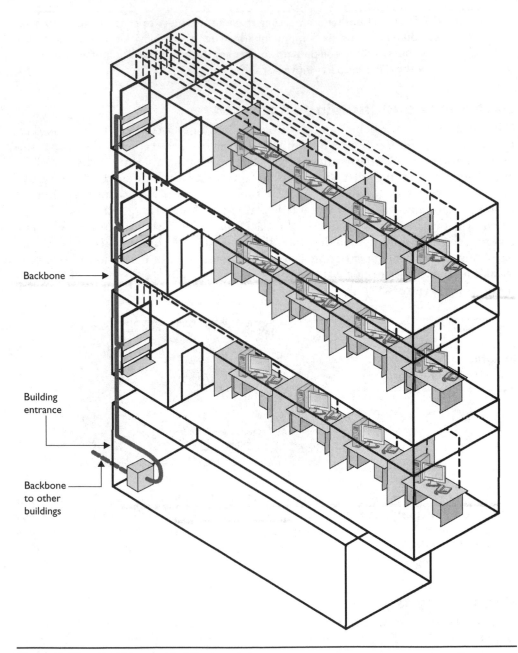

Figure 8-48 Backbone and building entrance

NICs

Now that the network's completely in place, it's time to turn to the final part of any physical network: the NICs. NICs are nearly as common as mice on today's PCs! A good network tech must recognize different types of NICs by sight and know how to install and troubleshoot them. Let's begin by reviewing the most common NICs.

Ethernet NICs

Ethernet NICs are by far the most common type of NIC used today. It's tough to get an absolutely dependable statistic, but it's probably safe to say that most of all new installations use Ethernet in one way or another. Ethernet installations are also the most complicated, because of the vast variety of cable types and speeds.

10Base5 (Thicknet)

As you've seen, 10Base5 (Thicknet) NICs use a female, 15-pin DB DIX connector, as shown in Figure 8-49. The Ethernet drop cable runs from the DIX connector on the NIC to the AUI, which also happens to have a DIX connector. Many techs erroneously refer to the DIX connector as the AUI, as in, "Hey, plug in that AUI before the coffee gets cold!"

Figure 8-49
A DIX connector

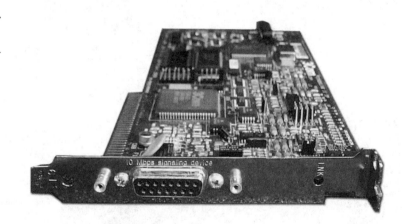

10Base2

10Base2 (Thinnet) NICs have a BNC connector (as shown in Figure 8-50) that attaches to the network cable via a T-connector.

10BaseT

10BaseT, 100BaseT, and Gigabit Ethernet NICs all use the RJ-45 connector. The cable runs from the NIC to a hub or a switch (see Figure 8-51). It is impossible to tell one from the other simply by looking at the connection.

Figure 8-50
A combo
Ethernet card
with BNC (left)
and RJ-45 (right)
connectors

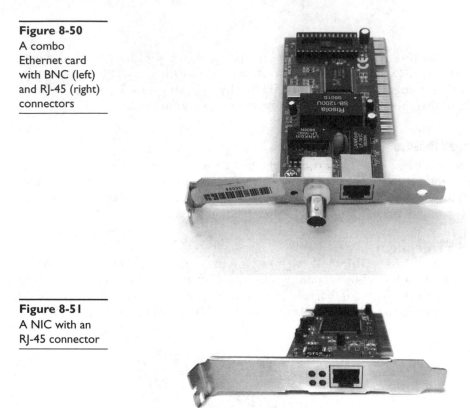

Figure 8-51
A NIC with an
RJ-45 connector

Fiber-optic

Fiber-optic NICs are the most challenging. Most fiber networking standards allow cards to use either SC or ST connections on these NICs, so be alert to variations, even among cards from the same manufacturer (see Figure 8-52).

Figure 8-52
Combination
ST fiber and
RJ-45 NIC

Token Ring NICs

In this Ethernet-centric world, many network folks tend to look at IBM's Token Ring as yesterday's news. This is a mistake. Granted, finding a *new* Token Ring installation is about as easy as getting 50-yard-line seats at the Super Bowl, but Token Ring continues to enjoy a huge installed base. If you need proof that Token Ring is alive and well, simply browse any of the leading NIC manufacturers' web sites. Notice that they all continue to sell Token Ring cards, because the demand still exists, suggesting that Token Ring is doing just fine.

Token Ring NIC connectors come in only two types. The older and much more rare connector is a female DB-9. The newer, and far more common, connector is an RJ-45. (See Figure 8-53.)

Figure 8-53
A combo Token Ring NIC with RJ-45 and DB-9 connectors

Gee, this Token Ring card suddenly looks a lot like a 10BaseT card, doesn't it? The problem of figuring out what type of connector goes with what NIC is complicated by the fact that lots of networking technologies use the same connector—in particular the RJ-45. How can you tell whether the NIC in your hand with an RJ-45 connection is for 10BaseT, 100BaseTX, or Token Ring? The bad news is that you can't always tell; the good news is that there are some clues. If you see an RJ-45/BNC combo card, for example, you can be pretty sure that the RJ-45 is for 10BaseT. In addition, most cards will have some information printed on them that can provide clues. Everybody who makes Token Ring cards gives them a Token Ring-sounding name. So, if you see a word like TokenLink printed on a card, you should at least start with the theory that it's a Token Ring card. Finally, there's the small factoid that the NICs you're examining are probably part of a Token Ring or an Ethernet network—a big clue indeed, wouldn't you say?

Distinguishing between Token Ring and Ethernet is usually fairly easy. But supposing you know you have an Ethernet RJ-45 NIC, how do you know if it is 10BaseT, 100BaseT, or something else altogether? This is tougher. First of all, know your network and the cards you buy. Second, know your model numbers. Every NIC has a manufacturer's model number you can use to determine its exact capabilities. The model number is nearly always printed on the card. Finally, pray that the NIC is Plug and Play (PnP) and stick it in a Windows 98/Me or Windows 2000/XP system. If you're lucky, the PnP application will recognize the card and give you some text clue as to what type of card it is (see Figure 8-54).

Figure 8-54
Windows 98
Plug and Play

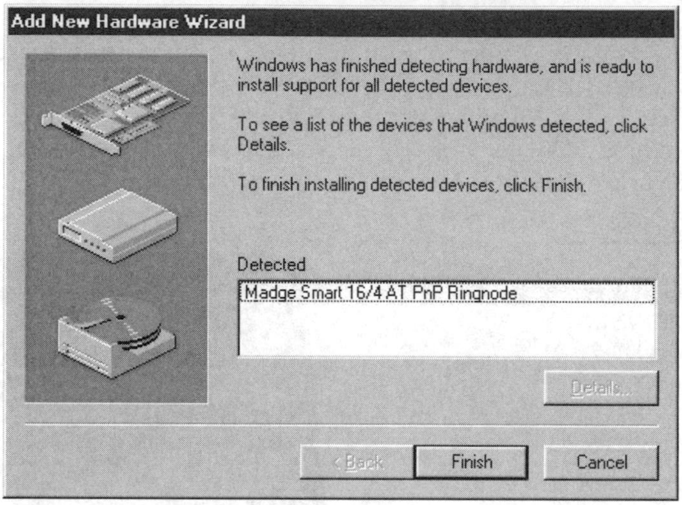

The model number is the real key to knowing your NICs. As you will soon see, if you have the model number of a NIC, you also know the right driver for that NIC. You need to deal with this issue before you drop the NIC into a system, though, because once the NIC is installed in a PC, it's difficult to determine the model number from a Windows screen. Many network techs use one of two methods for remembering the types of cards used in their systems. The best way is simply to ensure that the model number of the NIC is printed on the card. If the manufacturer chose not to put the model number on the NIC, a good network admin takes the time to attach the model number or some other number physically to the NIC, as shown in Figure 8-55.

Granted, some folks will complain, "What good is having the model number on the card once you close the PC?" Well, in the real world, NICs tend not to stay in PCs, and you will be glad you put the model number on the NIC when you have to swap it out later and no longer have any clue what it is. Sometimes PnP doesn't work, and the model number will tell you which driver you need—so slap that number on a label and save yourself some hassle later! The other method—one used for many years, but increasingly difficult to do—is to buy only certain models of NICs. Buying only one model of NIC makes knowing what you have trivially easy. For years, the predominance of 10BaseT gave certain models of NICs a multi-year lifespan, which made it easy for NIC purchasers to pursue this method; it also generally made dealing with NICs much easier. The recent influx of new technologies such as 100BaseT and even Gigabit, however, has caused most purchasers to move into newer models, especially 10/100 Ethernet cards—making this strategy less convenient.

Figure 8-55
A NIC with model number label added to outside

Installing NICs

Now that you have a basic understanding of the different types of NICs, let's march through the process of installing a NIC in a PC. Installing a NIC involves three distinct steps. First, you must physically install the NIC. Second, the NIC must be assigned unused system resources—either by PnP or manually. Third, you (or PnP) must install the proper drivers for the card.

NOTE Remember that manufacturers update their drivers often. Even if Windows loads a driver for you, get the latest from the manufacturer's web site or use the Windows Update tool.

Buying NICs

Some folks may disagree with this, but I always purchase name-brand NICs. For NICs, stick with big names, such as 3COM or Intel. The NICs are better made, have extra features, and are easy to return if they turn out to be defective. Plus, it's easy to replace a missing driver on a name-brand NIC, and to be sure that the drivers work well. The type of NIC you purchase depends on your network. Try to think about the future and go for multispeed cards if your wallet can handle the extra cost. Also, where possible, try to stick with the same model of NIC. Every different model you buy means another set of driver disks you need to haul around in your tech bag. Using the same model of NIC makes driver updates easier, too.

Many desktop systems and almost all laptops come with built-in Ethernet NICs with RJ-45 ports. Nothing is wrong with built-in NICs, as long as you know they will work with your network. Virtually all built-in NICs are autosensing and multispeed, so this is almost never an issue anymore—unless your network is all fiber-optic, or you're still running Token Ring!

NOTE Many people order desktop PCs with NICs simply because they don't take the time to ask if the system has a built-in NIC. Take a moment and ask about this!

Physical Connections

I'll state the obvious here: If you don't plug the NIC into the computer, it just isn't going to work! Many users happily assume some sort of quantum magic when it comes to computer communications, but as a tech, you know better. Fortunately, physically inserting the NIC into the PC is the easiest part of the job. Most PCs today have two types of expansion slots. The most common expansion slot is the Peripheral Component Interconnect (PCI) type (see Figure 8-56). PCI slots are fast, 32-bit, self-configuring expansion slots; virtually all new NICs sold today are of the PCI type, and with good reason: PCI's speed enables the system to take full advantage of the NIC.

Figure 8-56
PCI slots

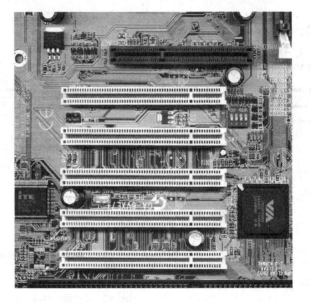

Another type of slot used for NICs is PCI-X. PCI-X is simply a faster PCI with a slightly longer (and brightly colored) slot. PCI-X is popular with Gigabit Ethernet due to its high speed, but it requires a motherboard with a PCI-X slot. Many higher-end motherboards now come with at least one PCI-X slot.

If you're not willing to open a PC case, you can get NICs with USB or PC Card connections. USB is convenient, but slow, and PC Card is only a laptop solution (see Figure 8-57). USB NICs are handy to keep in your toolkit. If you walk up to a machine that might have a bad NIC, test your suspicions by inserting a USB NIC and moving the network cable from the potentially bad NIC to the USB one. (Don't forget to bring your driver disc along!)

Figure 8-57
USB NIC

Drivers

Installing a NIC's driver into a Windows system is easy: just insert the driver CD when prompted by the system. The only problem is that this process is sometimes *too* automated! Windows will probably already have the driver if you use a more common model of NIC, but there are benefits to using the driver on the manufacturer's CD. The CDs that come with many NICs, especially the brand-name ones, include extra goodies such as enhanced drivers and handy utilities, but you'll only be able to access them if you install the driver that comes with the NIC!

Windows 2000 and XP give you the ability to show the status of the network connections in the taskbar. By default, only disconnected networks show up, but it's handy to have Windows always show the connection. To change this, go into Network Connections (in Windows 2000, it's called Network And Dial-Up Connections) in the Control Panel. Select the Properties for the network connection and check the "Show icon in notification area when connected" check box; note that this box is called "Show icon in taskbar when connected" in Windows 2000.

Lights

Most NICs made today have some type of lights, which are actually light-emitting diodes (LEDs—see Figure 8-58). Now that you know they are LEDs, call them "lights," just like all the other network techs. NICs with lights are mostly those for Ethernet network technologies that use RJ-45 (10BaseT, 100BaseT, and so on), and Token Ring cards. Don't be surprised if an old 10Base2 card has no lights. There is no guarantee that a NIC will have lights. In most cases, NICs with lights will have two of them. Sometimes there's only one, and they can be any color. More advanced cards might have four lights. These lights give you clues about what's happening, making troubleshooting a NIC much easier.

A *link light* tells you that the NIC is connected to a hub or switch. Hubs and switches also have link lights, enabling you to check the connectivity at both ends of the cable. If a PC can't access a network, look in the back to be sure the cleaning person didn't accidentally unplug the cable while vacuuming around the PC. Multispeed switches will also usually have an LED that tells you the speed of the connection (see Figure 8-59).

Figure 8-58

Typical lights on a 10BaseT NIC

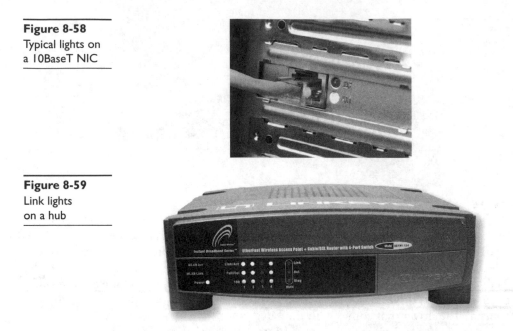

Figure 8-59

Link lights on a hub

The second light is the *activity light*. This little guy will flicker when the card detects network traffic. The activity light is a lifesaver for detecting problems, because in the real world, the connection light will sometimes lie to you. If the connection light says the connection is good, the next step is to try to copy a file or do something else to create network traffic. If the activity light does not flicker, there's a problem.

Another LED you will often find on multispeed NICs tells you the speed of the connection. This "speed" LED works in different ways depending on the NIC. On my 10/100 NICs, a single light is on when they run at 100 Mbps and off when they run at 10 Mbps. Some Gigabit Ethernet NICs have a single LED that glows in different colors, depending on the speed.

You might run into a fourth light on some much older NICs, called a collision light. As you might suspect from the name, the *collision light* flickers when it detects collisions on the network. Modern NICs don't have these, but you might run into the phrase on some test.

No standard governs how NIC manufacturers use their lights. When you encounter a NIC with a number of LEDs, take a moment and try to figure out what each one means. Although different NICs have different ways of arranging and using their LEDs, the functions are always the same.

Fiber-optic NICs rarely have lights, making diagnosis of problems a bit more challenging. Nevertheless, most physical connection issues for fiber can be traced to the ST or SC connection on the NIC itself. Fiber-optic cabling is incredibly delicate; the connectors that go into NICs are among the few places that anyone can touch fiber optics, so the connectors are the first thing to check when problems arise. Those who work with fiber always keep around a handy optical tester to enable them to inspect the quality of the connections. Only a trained eye can use such a device to judge a good fiber connection from a bad one—but once you learn how to do it, this kind of tester is extremely handy (Figure 8-60).

Figure 8-60
Optical tester

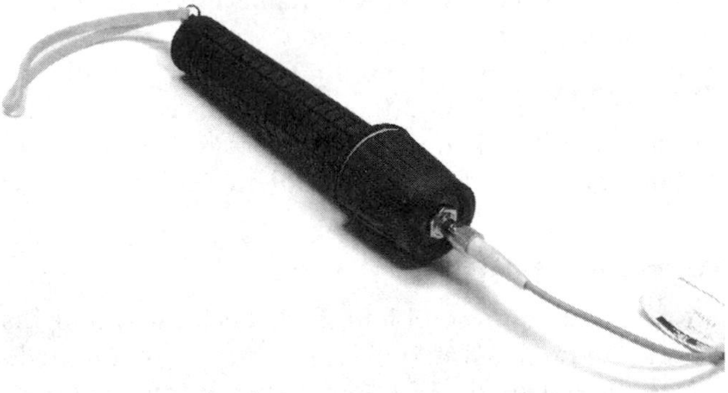

Direct Cable Connections

Without doubt, NICs and modems are overwhelmingly the most common method of connecting PCs. But there is one other method—called *direct cable connection*—that should be addressed for completeness. All recent versions of Windows come with software to enable direct serial-to-serial, parallel-to-parallel, or infrared-to-infrared port connections between two PCs. Parallel connections require a special IEEE 1284-rated bidirectional parallel cable.

To connect two PCs using their serial ports, you need to string a special cable called a *null modem cable* between the two PCs. They can then share hard drives, but nothing else. Serial direct cable connections are slow—a maximum of 115,600 bps—but they are a cheap and dirty network option when you don't have a pair of NICs handy.

Diagnostics and Repair of Physical Cabling

"The network's down!" is easily the most terrifying phrase a network tech will ever hear. Networks fail for many reasons, and the first thing to know is that good quality, professionally installed cabling rarely goes bad. Chapter 20, "Zen and the Art of Network Support," covers principles of network diagnostics and support that apply to all networking situations, but let's take a moment now to discuss what to do when you think you've got a problem with your physical network. The first question to ask yourself is, "Do I have a physical problem?"

Diagnosing Physical Problems

Look for errors that point to physical disconnection. A key clue that you may have a physical problem is that a user gets a "No server is found" error, or goes into My Network

Places and doesn't see any systems besides his own. In general, look for errors implying that some network device is not there. If one particular application fails, try another. If the user can't browse the Internet, but can get his e-mail, odds are good that the problem is with software, not hardware—unless someone unplugged the e-mail server! If possible, try the problem user's logon name and password on another system, to make sure that account can access the shared resource.

Multiple system failures often point to hardware problems. This is where knowledge of your network cabling helps. If all the systems connected to one switch can suddenly no longer see the network, but all the other systems in your network still function, you not only have a probable hardware problem, you also have a suspect—the switch.

Check Your Lights

If you suspect a hardware problem, first check the link lights on the NIC and hub or switch. If they're not lit, you know the cable isn't connected somewhere. If you're not physically at the system, the Windows network connection icon on your System Tray is helpful. A user who's unfamiliar with link lights (or who may not want to crawl under her desk in a skirt) will have no problem telling you if the "Network cable unplugged" error shows up (Figure 8-61).

Figure 8-61
Disconnected
cable

If your problem system is clearly not connecting, eliminate the possibility of a failed switch or other larger problem by checking to make sure other people can access the network, and that other systems can access the shared resource (server) that the problem system can't see. Make a quick visual inspection of the cable running from the back of the PC to the outlet. Finally, if you can, plug the system into a known good outlet and see if it works. A good network tech always keeps a long patch cable for just this reason! If you get connectivity with the second outlet, you should begin to suspect the structured cable running from the first outlet to the hub or switch. Assuming the cable was installed properly and had been working correctly before this event, a simple continuity test will confirm your suspicion in most cases.

Check the NIC

Be warned that a bad NIC can also generate this "can't see the network" problem. Go into Device Manager and verify that the NIC is working. If you've got a NIC with diagnostic software, run it—this software will check the NIC's circuitry. The NIC's female connector is a common failure point, so NICs that do come with diagnostic software often include a special test called a *loopback test*. A loopback test sends data out of the NIC and checks to see if it comes back. Some NICs perform only an internal loopback, which tests the circuitry that sends and receives, but not the actual connecting pins. A true external loopback requires a loopback plug inserted into the NIC's port. If a NIC is bad, replace it—preferably with an identical NIC so you don't have to reinstall drivers!

Despite many claims by many software makers, there is no such thing as a single utility program that will test any NIC. The programs that make these claims try to communicate with the NIC via the NIC's drivers to send packets. If the NIC is physically bad or if the driver isn't working, you get a failure. You don't need a special program to do this for you—not when you can come to the same conclusion just by trying to access a web page using your browser! If you want to test your NIC, you'll need a diagnostic program that was designed for that NIC; if you don't have the CD-ROM that came with the hardware, check the manufacturer's web site for a program that you can download.

Cable Testing

With the right equipment, diagnosing a bad horizontal cabling run is easy. Anyone with a network should own a midrange tester with TDR like the Microtest Microscanner. With a little practice, you can easily determine not only whether a cable is disconnected, but also where the disconnection takes place. Sometimes patience is required, especially if you've failed to label your cable runs, but you will find the problem.

In general, a broken cable must be replaced. A bad patch cable is easy, but what happens if the horizontal cable is to blame? In these cases, I get on the phone and call my local installer—if a cable's bad in one spot, the risk of it being bad in another is simply too great to try anything other than total replacement.

Ah, if only broken cables were the network tech's worst problem! The rarity of this situation, combined with the relative ease of cable diagnostics, makes the problem of bad cables both uncommon and easily fixed. Far more problematic than broken cables is an issue that comes up in every network installation: tracking cable. When you're faced with an "I don't know where this cable goes" problem, you need a special tool called a toner.

Toners

It would be nice to say that all cable installations are perfect, and that over the years, they won't grow into horrific piles of spaghetti-like, unlabeled cables. In the real world, though, you will eventually find yourself having to locate ("trace" is the term installers use) cables. Even in the best-planned networks, labels fall off ports and outlets, mystery cables appear behind walls, new cable runs are added, and mistakes are made counting rows and columns on patch panels. Sooner or later, most network techs will have to be able to pick out one particular cable or port from a stack.

When the time comes to trace cables, network techs turn to a device called a toner for help. *Toner* is the generic term for two separate devices that are used together: a tone generator and a tone probe. The *tone generator* connects to the cable using alligator clips, tiny hooks, or a network jack, and it sends an electrical signal along the wire at a certain frequency. The *tone probe* emits a sound when it is placed near a cable connected to the tone generator (see Figure 8-62). These two devices are often referred to by the brand name Fox and Hound, a popular model of toner made by the Triplett Corporation.

Figure 8-62
A tone probe
at work

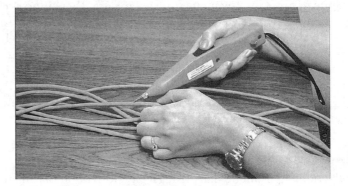

To trace a cable, connect the tone generator to the known end of the cable in question, and then position the tone probe next to the other end of each of the cables that might be the right one. The tone probe will make a sound when it's placed next to the right cable. More advanced toners include phone jacks, enabling the person manipulating the tone generator to communicate with the person manipulating the tone probe: "Jim, move the tone generator to the next port!" Some toners have one tone probe that works with multiple tone generators. Each generator emits a separate frequency, and the probe sounds a different tone for each one. Even good toners are relatively inexpensive ($\approx$ \$75); although cheapo toners can cost less than \$25, they don't tend to work well, so it's worth spending a little more. Just keep in mind that if you have to support a network, you'd do best to own a decent toner.

A good, medium-priced cable tester and a good toner are the most important tools used by folks who must support, but not install, networks. A final tip: be sure to bring along a few extra batteries—there's nothing worse than sitting on the top of a ladder holding a cable tester or toner that has just run out of juice!

Chapter Review

Questions

1. Which of the following cables should never be used in a structured cabling installation?

   A. UTP

   B. STP

   C. Fiber-optic

   D. Coax

2. Which type of fire rating should horizontal cabling have?

   A. Mil Spec

   B. Plenum

   C. PVC

   D. UTP

3. The CAT 5e rating defines how many pairs of wires in the cable?

   A. 2

   B. 4

   C. 8

   D. It doesn't specify.

4. The best type of cabling to use for interbuilding connections is

   A. UTP

   B. Coax

   C. Fiber-optic

   D. STP

5. A _____ organizes and protects the horizontal cabling in the equipment room.

   A. Rack

   B. Patch panel

   C. Outlet

   D. 110 jack

6. Which of the following would never be seen in an equipment rack?

   A. Patch panel

   B. UPS or SPS

    C. PC

    D. All of the above can be seen in an equipment rack.

7. What are patch cables used for? (Select all that apply.)

    A. To connect different equipment rooms.

    B. To connect the patch panel to the hub.

    C. They are used as crossover cables.

    D. To connect PCs to outlet boxes.

8. Which of the following network technologies use UTP cabling in a star topology? (Select all that apply.)

    A. 10Base2

    B. Fiber optics

    C. 10BaseT

    D. 100BaseT

9. Jane needs to increase network throughput on a 10BaseT network that consists of 1 hub and 30 users. Which of the following hardware solutions would achieve this most inexpensively?

    A. Add a fiber backbone.

    B. Upgrade the network to 100BaseT.

    C. Replace the hub with a switch.

    D. Add a router.

10. Which standard addresses cable pathways and installation areas involving multiple rooms, floors, and buildings?

    A. EIA/TIA 586

    B. EIA/TIA 587

    C. EIA/TIA 568

    D. EIA/TIA 569

Answers

1. **D.** Coax cable should not be used in structured cabling networks.

2. **B.** Plenum cabling should be used in horizontal cabling.

3. **B.** The CAT 5e rating requires four pairs of wires.

4. **C.** EIA/TIA specifies fiber-optic cabling as the preferred interbuilding cabling.

5. **B.** The patch panel organizes and protects the horizontal cabling in the equipment room.

6. **D.** All these devices can be found in equipment racks.

7. **B, D.** Patch cables are used to connect the hub to the patch panel and the PCs to the outlet boxes.

8. **C, D.** 10BaseT and 100BaseT use UTP cabling in a star topology. 10Base2 is an older, dying technology that doesn't use UTP in a star. Fiber-optic networking uses a star topology, but the name is a dead giveaway that it doesn't use UTP!

9. **C.** Upgrading to 100BaseT will work, but replacing the hub with a switch is much cheaper.

10. **D.** EIA/TIA 569 addresses cable pathways and installation areas involving multiple rooms, floors, and buildings. The EIA/TIA 568 standard defines acceptable cable types, the organization of the cabling system, guidelines for installation of the cable, and proper testing methods. The other two choices were made up to confuse you!

Wireless Networking

The Network+ Certification exam expects you to know how to

- 1.6 Identify the purposes, features, and functions of wireless access points
- 1.7 Specify the general characteristics (for example: carrier speed, frequency, transmission type, and topology) of the following wireless technologies: 802.11 (frequency-hopping spread spectrum), 802.11x (direct-sequence spread spectrum), infrared, Bluetooth
- 1.8 Identify factors that affect the range and speed of wireless service (for example: interference, antenna type, and environmental factors).
- 2.17 Identify the following security protocols and describe their purpose and function: WEP (Wired Equivalent Privacy), WPA (Wi-Fi Protected Access), 802.1x

To achieve these goals, you must be able to

- Explain wireless networking hardware and software requirements, and configure wireless networking hardware
- Define wireless networking IEEE standards and FCC operation frequencies
- Define wireless network operation modes, limits, and methods
- Configure wireless networking security
- Describe troubleshooting techniques for wireless networks

Historical/Conceptual

In the last couple of chapters, we've had detailed discussions of the most common network implementations on the market. Even though Ethernet, Token Ring, ARCnet, LocalTalk, FDDI, and ATM networks all use wildly different hardware and protocols, one thing ties all these technologies together—the wires! Every type of network we've talked about thus far assumes that your PCs are tethered to your network with some kind of physical cabling. Now it's time to cut the cord and look at one of the most exciting developments in network technology: wireless networking.

Instead of a physical set of wires running among networked PCs, servers, printers, or what-have-you, a *wireless network* uses radio waves to enable these devices to communicate with each other. This offers great promise to those of us who've spent time "pulling cable" up through ceiling spaces and down behind walls, and therefore know how time-consuming that job can be.

But wireless networking is more than just convenient—sometimes it's the only networking solution that works. For example, I have a client whose offices are housed in a building designated as a historic landmark. Guess what? You can't go punching holes in historic landmarks to make room for network cable runs. Wireless networking is the solution.

> **NOTE** Because the networking signal is freed from wires, you'll sometimes hear the term "unbounded media" to describe wireless networking.

Wireless networks operate at the same OSI layers and use the same protocols as wired networks. The difference lies in the type of media—radio waves instead of cables—and the methods for accessing the media. Different wireless networking solutions have come and gone in the past, but the wireless networking market these days is dominated by two technologies: those based on the most common implementation of the IEEE 802.11 wireless Ethernet standard—namely *Wireless Fidelity (Wi-Fi)* and *Home Radio Frequency (HomeRF)*—and those based on *Bluetooth*, a newer wireless technology that enables PCs to communicate wirelessly with each other, as well as with a wide variety of peripheral gadgets and consumer electronics.

> **TIP** The CompTIA Network+ exam focuses on Wi-Fi wireless networking, but I'm including HomeRF and Bluetooth because you're likely to see these wireless networking technologies in the field.

I'll start off the chapter with some wireless networking basics, and then discuss the accepted wireless networking standards. I'll also talk about how to configure wireless networking, and finish with a discussion of troubleshooting wireless networks. Let's get started!

Test Specific

Wireless Networking Basics

In this section, I'll talk about the basic things you need to know to get off the ground with wireless networking. I'll start with the hardware and software you need, and then talk about modes of wireless network operation, wireless security technologies, and wireless specifications, such as speed, range, and broadcast frequencies. Last, I'll discuss wireless network media access—that is, how wireless devices avoid stepping on each other's data packets.

Wireless Networking Hardware

Wireless networking hardware serves the same function as hardware used on wired PCs. Wireless Ethernet NICs and Bluetooth adapters take data passed down from the upper OSI layers, encapsulate it into data packets, send the packets out on the network media in strings of ones and zeroes, and receive data packets sent from other PCs. The only difference is that instead of charging up a network cable with electrical current or firing off pulses of light, these devices are transmitting and receiving radio waves.

Wireless networking capabilities of one form or another are built into many modern computing devices. Wireless Ethernet and Bluetooth capabilities are increasingly popular as integrated components, or can easily be added using PCI or PC Card add-on cards. In fact, many wireless PCI NICs are simply wireless PC Card NICs that have been permanently housed in a PCI component card. Figure 9-1 shows a wireless PCI Ethernet card.

You can also add wireless network capabilities using external USB wireless network adapters, as shown in Figure 9-2. The USB NICs have the added benefit of being *placeable*—that is, you can move them around to catch the wireless signal as strongly as possible, akin to moving the rabbit ears on old pre-cable television sets.

Wireless network adapters aren't limited to PCs. Many networked printers use wireless NICs or Bluetooth adapters. Most handheld computers and *Personal Digital Assistants (PDAs)* also have wireless capabilities built in or available as add-on options. Figure 9-3 shows an older Handspring PDA accessing the Internet through a wireless network adapter card.

Is the wireless network adapter all the hardware you need to connect wirelessly? Well, if your needs are simple—for example, if you're connecting a small group of computers into a decentralized workgroup—then the answer is yes. However, if you need to extend the capabilities of a wireless Ethernet network—say, connecting a wireless network segment to a wired network, or connecting multiple wireless network segments together—you need additional equipment. This typically means wireless access points and wireless bridges.

A *wireless access point* connects wireless network nodes to wireless or wired networks. A basic WAP operates like a hub and works at OSI Layer 1. However, many wireless access

Figure 9-1
Wireless PCI NIC

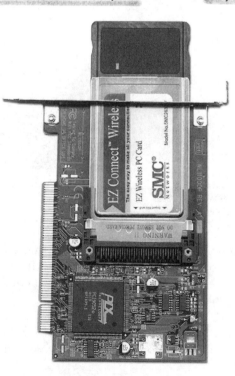

Figure 9-2   External USB wireless NIC

Figure 9-3   PDA with wireless capability

points are combination devices that act as high-speed hubs, switches, bridges, and routers, all rolled into one and working at many different OSI layers. The Linksys device shown in Figure 9-4 is an example of this type of combo device.

NOTE   Some manufacturers drop the word "wireless" from wireless access points and simply call them access points. Further, many sources abbreviate both forms, so you'll see the former written as WAP and the latter as AP.

Figure 9-4

Linksys device that acts as wireless access point, switch, and DSL router

Dedicated *wireless bridges* are used to connect two wireless network segments together, or to join wireless and wired networks together in the same way that wired bridge devices do. You can also use wireless bridges to join wireless networks with other networked devices, such as printers.

Wireless bridges come in two different flavors: point-to-point and point-to-multipoint. *Point-to-point* bridges can only communicate with a single other bridge, and are used to connect two wireless network segments. *Point-to-multipoint* bridges can talk to more than one other bridge at a time, and are used to connect multiple network segments. Some vendors also offer repeating bridges, and bridges with access point and router functions. Figure 9-5 shows a wireless bridge.

Wireless Bluetooth hardware is included as built-in equipment in many newer PCs, laptops, PDAs, and cell phones. When installed on a PC, Bluetooth add-on components almost always use the USB expansion bus, instead of an internally installed PCI card. Some devices use the PC Card bus, or even a Compact Flash socket. Bluetooth access points, hubs, and bridges are slowly making their way to the PC market, but haven't caught on as quickly as wireless Ethernet devices. Figure 9-6 shows a Bluetooth adapter plugged into a laptop USB port.

Figure 9-5

Linksys wireless bridge device

Figure 9-6
External USB
Bluetooth
adapter

Wireless Networking Software

Every wireless network adapter needs two pieces of software to function with an operating system: a driver and a configuration utility. Installing drivers for wireless networking devices is usually no more difficult than for any other hardware device, but you should always consult your vendor's instructions before popping that card into a slot. Most of the time, you simply have to let Plug and Play (PnP) work its magic and put in the driver disc when prompted, but some devices (particularly USB devices) require that you install the drivers beforehand. Windows XP Professional comes well equipped for wireless networking and has built-in drivers for many popular wireless NICs. Even so, it's always a better idea to use the drivers and configuration utilities that the vendor has supplied with your wireless adapter.

In addition to the driver, you also need a utility for configuring how the wireless hardware connects to other wireless devices. Windows XP has built-in tools for configuring these settings, but for previous versions of Windows, you need to rely on wireless client configuration tools provided by the wireless network adapter vendor. Figure 9-7 shows a typical wireless network adapter's client configuration utility. Using this utility, you can determine important things like your *link state* (whether your wireless device is connected) and your *signal strength* (a measurement of how well your wireless device is connecting to other devices); you can also configure items such as your wireless networking *mode*, security encryption, power-saving options, and so on. I'll cover each of these topics in detail later in this chapter.

Wireless access points and routers are configured through browser-based setup utilities. Wireless bridges usually need a vendor-supplied configuration utility to get them to talk to your wireless network initially, and then are set up using the browser-based tool. I'll talk about configuring adapters and access points in the section called "SSID." Now let's look at the different modes wireless networks use.

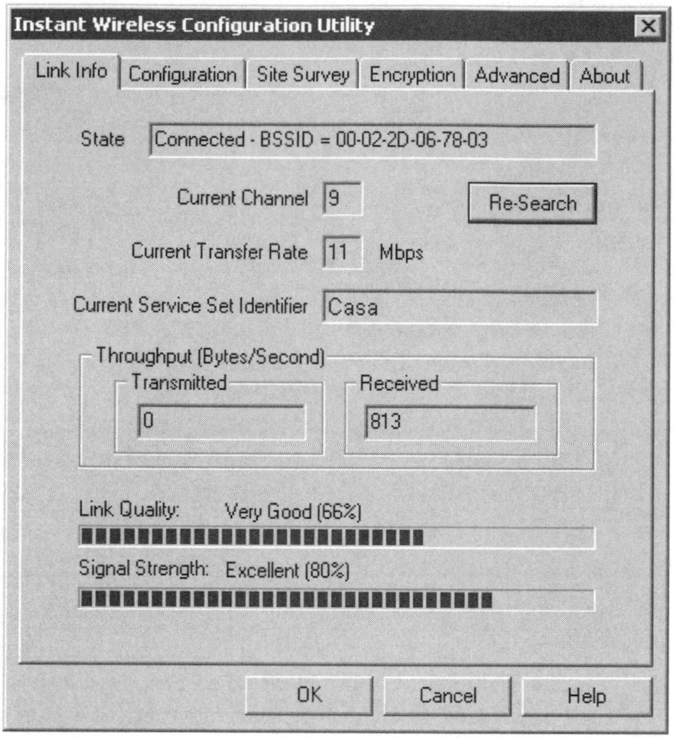

Figure 9-7
Wireless client
configuration
utility

Wireless Network Modes

The simplest wireless network consists of two or more PCs communicating directly with each other without cabling or any other intermediary hardware. More complicated wireless networks use an access point to centralize wireless communication, and to bridge wireless network segments to wired network segments. These two different methods, or *modes*, are called *ad-hoc* mode and *infrastructure* mode.

Ad-hoc Mode

Ad-hoc mode is sometimes called peer-to-peer mode, with each wireless node in direct contact with each other node in a decentralized free-for-all, as shown in Figure 9-8. Ad-hoc mode is similar to the *mesh* topology discussed in Chapter 4, "Hardware Concepts."

Two or more wireless nodes communicating in ad-hoc mode form what's called an *Independent Basic Service Set (IBSS)*. This is a basic unit of organization in wireless networks. Think of an IBSS as a wireless workgroup, and you're not far off the mark.

Ad-hoc mode networks are suited for small groups of computers (fewer than a dozen or so) that need to transfer files or share printers. Ad-hoc mode networks are also good for temporary networks, such as study groups or business meetings.

Hardly anyone uses ad-hoc networks for day-to-day work, simply because you can't use an ad-hoc network to connect to other networks unless one of the machines is running Internet Connection Sharing (ICS) or some equivalent. More commonly, you'll find wireless networks configured in infrastructure mode.

Figure 9-8
Wireless ad-hoc
mode network

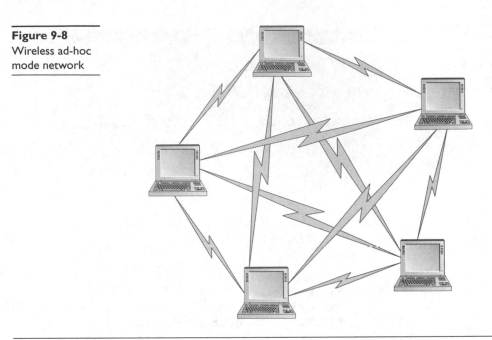

 NOTE Infrastructure mode is so much more commonly used than ad-hoc
mode that most wireless NICs come preconfigured to run on an
infrastructure mode network. Getting them to run in ad-hoc mode usually
requires reconfiguration.

Infrastructure Mode

Wireless networks running in *infrastructure mode* use one or more wireless access points
to connect the wireless network nodes centrally, as shown in Figure 9-9. This configuration is similar to the *star* topology of a wired network. You also use infrastructure mode
to connect wireless network segments to wired segments. If you plan on setting up a
wireless network for a large number of PCs, or you need to have centralized control over
the wireless network, infrastructure mode is what you need.

A single wireless access point servicing a given area is called a *Basic Service Set (BSS)*.
This service area can be extended by adding more access points. This is called, appropriately, an *Extended Basic Service Set (EBSS)*.

A lot of techs have begun dropping the word "basic" from the Extended Basic Service
Set. Accordingly, you'll see the initials for the Extended Service Set as ESS. Similarly to
the Token Ring issue of MAUs and MSAUs, either EBSS or ESS is correct.

Wireless networks running in infrastructure mode require a little more planning—
such as where you place the wireless access points to provide adequate coverage—than
ad-hoc mode networks, and they provide a stable environment for permanent wireless
network installations. Infrastructure mode is better suited to business networks or networks that need to share dedicated resources like Internet connections and centralized
databases.

Figure 9-9
Wireless
infrastructure
mode network

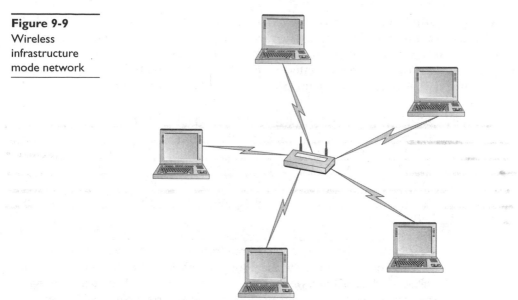

Wireless Networking Security

One of the biggest problems with wireless networking devices is that right out of the box, they provide *no* security. Vendors go out of their way to make it easy to set up their devices, so usually the only thing that you have to do to join a wireless network is turn your wireless devices on and let them find each other. Sure, from a configuration point of view, this is great—but from a security point of view, it's a disaster!

Further, you have to consider that your network's data packets are floating through the air instead of safely wrapped up inside network cabling. What's to stop an unscrupulous network tech with the right equipment from grabbing those packets out of the air and reading that data?

To address these issues, wireless networks use four methods: Service Set Identification (SSID), MAC address filtering, port-based access control, and data encryption. The first three methods secure access to the network itself, and the fourth secures the data that's moving around the network. All of these methods require you to configure the wireless networking device. Let's take a look.

SSID

The *Service Set Identification (SSID)*, sometimes called a *network name*, is a 32-bit identification string that's inserted into the header of each data packet processed by a wireless access point. When properly configured, only wireless clients whose SSID matches that of the wireless access point are able to gain access to the wireless network. Data packets that lack the correct SSID in the header are rejected. The SSID, therefore, provides the most basic unit of wireless security.

Unfortunately, this isn't the way wireless access points come out of the box. By default, they're given a generic SSID that's widely publicized in the vendor's literature and online. For example, the default SSID for Linksys wireless access points is "linksys,"

3COM uses "101," and Netgear uses "wireless" (although they're migrating to "netgear"). Just in case you think I only know this because I have some sort of secret industry insider information, keep in mind that I found these SSID names with a two-minute search on Google. It's that easy! To make matters worse, right out of the box, all wireless access points are configured to broadcast this SSID to make it easier for clients to join in on the wireless fun!

Generally speaking, if you want a secure network, you don't go around yelling the network name to everyone within earshot, so configuring a unique SSID name should be one of the first things you do to secure a wireless network. You should also change the default login names and passwords, and possibly turn off the name-broadcast option. Finally, make sure that you configure all of your clients with the new unique SSID name. I'll walk through the steps for doing this in the "Configuring Wireless Networking" section of this chapter.

 TIP Most wireless access points broadcast their SSIDs by default, creating a security hole that Andre the Giant (may he rest in peace) could walk through. Detecting the SSID of a wireless network is the hacker's first step for using the network without permission. Closing that security hole should be *your* first step to making your wireless network secure.

MAC Address Filtering

Most wireless access points support *MAC address filtering*, a method that enables you to limit access to your wireless network based on the physical, hard-wired addresses of the wireless network adapters you support. MAC address filtering is a handy way of creating a type of "accepted users" list to limit access to your wireless network. A table stored in the wireless access point lists the MAC addresses that are permitted to participate in the wireless network. Any data packets that don't contain the MAC address of a node listed in the table are rejected.

Many wireless access points also enable you to deny specific MAC addresses from logging onto the network. This works great in close quarters, such as apartments or office buildings, where your wireless network signal goes beyond your perimeter. You can check the wireless access point and see the MAC addresses of every node that connects to your network. Check that list against the list of your computers, and you can readily spot any unwanted interloper. Putting an offending MAC address in the "deny" column effectively blocks that system from piggybacking onto your wireless connection.

While both methods work well, a seriously determined hacker can "spoof" a MAC address and access the network. Then again, if you have data so important that someone would go to this extreme, you should seriously consider using a wired network, or separating the sensitive data from your wireless network in some fashion! MAC address filtering is also a bit of a maintenance nightmare, as every time you replace a NIC, you have to reconfigure your wireless access point with the new NIC's MAC address.

Encryption

The next step in securing a wireless network is encrypting the data packets that are floating around. With *encryption*, data packets are electronically scrambled and "locked" with a private encryption "key" before being transmitted onto the wireless network. The receiving network device has to possess the encryption key to unscramble the packet and process the data. Thus, any data packets surreptitiously grabbed out of the air are useless to the grabber unless they've got the encryption key. Enabling wireless encryption through either Wireless Equivalency Privacy (WEP) or Wi-Fi Protected Access (WPA) provides a good level of security to data packets in transit.

Data Encryption Using WEP Standard *Wireless Equivalency Privacy (WEP)* encryption uses a 64-bit encryption algorithm to scramble data packets, but most vendors now enable stronger 128-bit algorithms. If you have this option and are in a high-risk situation, you should always use the strongest encryption available for your wireless network devices.

Even with the strongest encryption enabled, WEP isn't considered to be a particularly robust security solution. Consider, for instance, that WEP doesn't provide complete encryption for data packets. That is, WEP works only on the two lowest OSI network layers: the Data Link and Physical layers. Encryption is stripped from the data packet before it travels up through the subsequent network layers to the application. Another problem with WEP is that the encryption key is both static (never changes from session to session) and shared (the same key is used by all network nodes). There is also no mechanism for performing user authentication. That is, network nodes that use WEP encryption are identified by their MAC address, and no other credentials are offered or required. With the right equipment, MAC addresses are fairly easy to "sniff" out and duplicate, thus opening up a possible "spoofing" attack. If you want true, end-to-end data encryption with authentication, you need to use WPA.

Data Encryption Using WPA *Wi-Fi Protected Access (WPA)* addresses the weaknesses of WEP, and acts as a sort of security protocol upgrade to WEP-enabled devices. WPA offers security enhancements such as dynamic encryption key generation (keys are issued on a per-user and per-session basis), an encryption key integrity-checking feature, user authentication through the industry-standard *Extensible Authentication Protocol (EAP)*, and other advanced features that WEP lacks.

The downside is that WPA isn't available on all wireless networking devices. Even on those that do include it (or for which it's available as an upgrade option), WPA can be difficult to configure, requiring firmware updates for all access points, network adapters, and client software. Keep in mind also that WPA is intended only as a temporary security solution until the new IEEE 802.11i security standard is ratified.

> **NOTE** WPA addresses the known weaknesses in the WEP encryption protocol, but it is not widely implemented.

Port Based Access Control: 802.1*x*

One other wireless security tool worth mentioning here is *802.1x*. This security measure (which is all about authentication, rather than encryption) is meant to control access to a wireless LAN. The 802.1*x* authentication standard uses various flavors of EAP, the same authentication protocol that WPA uses; these include EAP over LAN (EAPOL), Protected EAP (PEAP), and EAP-Transport Level Security (EAP-TLS).

Process

Basically, 802.1*x* uses the wireless access point as a kind of gatekeeper, keeping users out of the LAN until they have the approval of the network's 802.1*x authentication server,* typically a RADIUS server. When an 802.1*x*-enabled system tries to access the network, the client software (referred to in 802.1*x*-speak as the *supplicant* sends an EAP packet to the access point (called the *authenticator*), which immediately shuts down the port the supplicant is using to all traffic except EAP packets. The access point passes authentication messages back and forth as needed between the supplicant and the authenticating server. When the server is satisfied of the supplicant's identity, it instructs the access point to open the supplicant's port to other kinds of traffic, as predetermined by the network administrator.

To use 802.1*x*, all the hardware involved—supplicant, authenticator, and authenticating server—must be 802.1*x*-enabled. On the PC end, a Windows XP machine should have the native capability to use 802.1*x*; older Windows operating systems can have the Microsoft 802.1*x* Authentication Client software added. Be sure to configure your wireless NIC to use 802.1*x* as well. If the server that will be authenticating users is running Windows 2003 Server, you should be good to go; although, an older Windows server OS will need an upgrade. Finally, your wireless access points must be configured to use 802.1*x*; if you have doubts about the capability of an access point to use 802.1*x*, you can poke around all of the setup screens, or contact the manufacturer.

Wireless Networking Speed

Wireless networking data throughput speeds depend on a few factors. Foremost is the standard that the wireless devices use. Depending on the standard used, wireless throughput speeds range from a measly 2 Mbps to a respectable 54 Mbps.

One of the other factors affecting speed is the distance between wireless nodes (or between wireless nodes and centralized access points). Wireless devices dynamically negotiate the top speed at which they can communicate without dropping too many data packets. Speed decreases as distance increases, so the maximum throughput speed is only achieved at extremely close range (less than 25 feet or so). At the outer reaches of a device's effective range, speed may decrease to around 1 Mbps before it drops out altogether.

Finally, speed is affected by interference from other wireless devices operating in the same frequency range—such as cordless phones or baby monitors—and by solid objects. So-called *dead spots* occur when something capable of blocking the radio signal comes between the wireless network nodes. Large electrical appliances, such as refrigerators, are *very* effective at blocking a wireless network signal! Other culprits include electrical fuse boxes, metal plumbing, air conditioning units, and so on.

Exact wireless data transfer speeds are listed in the next section, where I describe the specific wireless networking standards.

Wireless Networking Range

Wireless networking range is hard to define, and you'll see most descriptions listed with qualifiers such as "*around* 150 feet" and "*about* 300 feet." This is simply because, like throughput speed, wireless range is greatly affected by environmental factors. Interference from other wireless devices affects range, as does interference from solid objects. The maximum ranges listed in the next section are those presented by wireless manufacturers as the *theoretical* maximum ranges. In the real world, you'll see these ranges only under the most ideal circumstances. True effective range is probably about half of what you see listed.

You have a couple of ways to increase wireless network range. First, you can install multiple wireless access points or bridges to permit "roaming" between one access point's coverage area and another—an EBSS, as described earlier in this chapter. Second, you can install a signal booster that increases a single wireless access point's signal strength, thus increasing its range.

Like wireless networking speeds, I'll discuss the ranges of each type of wireless standard in the section called "Wireless Networking Standards."

Wireless Network Broadcasting Frequencies

One of the biggest issues with wireless communication is the potential for interference from other wireless devices. To solve this, different wireless devices must operate in specific broadcasting frequencies. Knowing these wireless frequency ranges will assist you in troubleshooting interference issues from other devices operating in the same wireless band.

Wireless networks in the U.S. use a range of airwave bandwidth set aside by the *Federal Communications Commission (FCC)* in 1989 called the *Industrial, Scientific, and Medical,* or *ISM,* frequencies. FCC regulations allocate 83.5 MHz of bandwidth in the 2.4-GHz frequency band and 125 MHz of bandwidth in the 5.8-GHz band for usage by ISM equipment. In 1997, the FCC released an additional 300 MHz of bandwidth called the *Unlicensed National Information Infrastructure,* or *U-NII,* split into three 100-MHz frequency bands. The first band is in the frequency range of 5.15 to 5.25 GHz; the second is in the range of 5.25 to 5.35 GHz; and the third is in the range of 5.725 to 5.825 GHz.

Wireless Networking Media Access Methods

Because only a single device can use any network at a time, network nodes must have a way to access the network media without stepping on each other's data packets. Let's review the differences between the two most popular media access methods, *carrier sense media access/collision detection (CSMA/CD)* and *carrier sense media access/collision avoidance (CSMA/CA).*

How do multiple devices share the network media, such as a cable? This is fairly simple: each device listens in on the network media by measuring the level of voltage currently on the wire. If the level is below the threshold, the device knows that it's clear to send data. If the voltage level rises above a preset threshold, the device knows that the line is busy and it must wait before sending data. Typically, the waiting period is the length of the current frame plus a short, predefined silence period called an *interframe space (IFS).* So far, so good—but what happens when two devices both detect that the wire is free and try to send data simultaneously? As you probably guessed, packets transmitted on the network from two different devices at the same time will corrupt each other, thereby canceling each other out. This is called a *collision.*

Unless you're using Token Ring, collisions are a fact of networking life. So, how do network nodes deal with collisions? They either react to collisions after they happen or take steps to avoid collisions in the first place.

CSMA/CD is the reactive method. With CSMA/CD, each sending node detects the collision and responds by generating a random timeout period for itself, during which it doesn't try to send any more data on the network—this is called a *backoff*. Once the backoff period expires (remember that we're only talking about milliseconds here), the node goes through the whole process again. This approach may not be very elegant, but it gets the job done.

The problem with using CSMA/CD for wireless networking is that wireless devices simply can't detect collisions; therefore, wireless networks need another way of dealing with them. The CSMA/CA access method, as the name implies, proactively takes steps to avoid collisions. The 802.11 standard defines two methods of collision avoidance: *Distributed Coordination Function (DCF)* and *Point Coordination Function (PCF)*. Currently, only DCF is implemented.

> **TIP** Current CSMA/CA devices use the Distributed Coordination Function (DCF) method for collision avoidance.

DCF specifies much stricter rules for sending data onto the network media. For instance, if a wireless network node detects that the network is busy, DCF defines a backoff period on top of the normal IFS wait period before a node can try to access the network again. DCF also requires that receiving nodes send an *acknowledgement (ACK)* for every packet that they process. The ACK also includes a value that tells other wireless nodes to wait a certain duration before trying to access the network media. This period is calculated to be the time that the data packet takes to reach its destination based on the packet's length and data rate. If the sending node doesn't receive an ACK, it retransmits the same data packet until it gets a confirmation that the packet reached its destination.

Optionally, the 802.11 standard defines the rules for using the *Request to Send/Clear to Send (RTS/CTS)* protocol. When RTS/CTS is enabled, transmitting nodes send an RTS frame to the receiving node before sending any data, just to make certain that the coast is clear. The receiving node responds with a CTS frame, telling the sending node that it's okay to transmit. This process is decidedly more elegant, but using RTS/CTS introduces significant overhead to the process and can impede performance. Most network techs enable this option only on heavily populated wireless network segments where the collision rate is high.

Wireless Networking Standards

Like any other networking technology, wireless technology must conform to strict industry standards defined by the IEEE organization. This section describes the different 802.11 standards and the Bluetooth wireless standard.

IEEE 802.11-Based Wireless Networking

The IEEE *802.11* wireless Ethernet standard defines methods by which devices may communicate using *spread-spectrum* radio waves. Spread-spectrum broadcasts data in small, discrete chunks over the different frequencies available within a certain frequency range. All the 802.11-based wireless technologies broadcast and receive in the 2.4-GHz frequency, with the exception of 802.11a, which uses the 5-GHz band.

802.11 defines two different spread-spectrum broadcasting methods: *direct-sequence spread spectrum (DSSS)* and *frequency-hopping spread spectrum (FHSS)*. DSSS sends data out on different frequencies at the same time, while FHSS sends data on one frequency at a time, constantly shifting (or *hopping*) frequencies. DSSS uses considerably more bandwidth than FHSS—around 22 MHz as opposed to 1 MHz. DSSS is capable of greater data throughput, but it's also more prone to interference than FHSS. HomeRF wireless networks are the only type that use FHSS; all the other 802.11-based wireless networking standards use DSSS.

The original 802.11 standard has been extended to 802.11a, 802.11b, and 802.11g variations used in Wi-Fi wireless networks, and also *hybridized* (combined with another wireless communication technology) to form the *Shared Wireless Access Protocol (SWAP)* used in HomeRF networks.

Wi-Fi Wireless Networking Standards

Wireless Fidelity, or *Wi-Fi*, is by far the most widely adopted wireless networking type today. Not only do thousands of private businesses and homes have wireless networks, but many public places, such as coffee shops and libraries, also offer Internet access through wireless networks.

Technically, only wireless devices that conform to the extended versions of the 802.11 standard—802.11a, 802.11b, and 802.11g—are Wi-Fi certified. Wi-Fi certification comes from the Wi-Fi Alliance (formerly the Wireless Ethernet Compatibility Alliance, or WECA), a nonprofit industry group made up of over 175 member companies that design and manufacture wireless networking products. Wi-Fi certification ensures compatibility between wireless networking devices made by different vendors. First-generation devices that use the older 802.11 standard are not Wi-Fi certified, so they may or may not work well with devices made by different vendors.

Wireless devices can communicate only with other wireless devices that use the same standard. The exception to this is 802.11g, which is backward-compatible with 802.11b devices (although at the lower speed of 802.11b). The following paragraphs describe the important specifications of each of the popular 802.11-based wireless networking standards.

802.11 Devices that use the original 802.11 standard are a rarity these days. You're most likely to find them in service on some brave early adopter's network. 802.11 was hampered by both slow speeds (2 Mbps maximum) and limited range (about 150 feet tops), but 802.11 employed some of the same features that are in use in the current wireless standards. 802.11 uses the 2.4-GHz broadcast range, and security is provided by the use of industry-standard WEP and WPA encryption.

802.11a Despite the *a* designation for this extension to the 802.11 standard, *802.11a* was developed *after* 802.11b. 802.11a differs from the other 802.11-based standards in significant ways. Foremost is that it operates in a different frequency range, 5 GHz. The 5-GHz range is much less "crowded" than the 2.4-GHz range, reducing the chance of interference from devices such as telephones and microwave ovens. 802.11a also offers considerably greater throughput than 802.11 and 802.11b, at speeds up to 54 Mbps! Range, however, suffers somewhat, and tops out at about 150 feet. Despite the superior speed of 802.11a, it isn't widely adopted in the PC world.

802.11b The currently reigning king in wireless networking, *802.11b* is practically ubiquitous. The 802.11b standard supports data throughput of up to 11 Mbps—on par with

Standard	802.11	802.11a	802.11b	802.11g
Max. throughput	2 Mbps	54 Mbps	11 Mbps	54 Mbps
Max. range	150 feet	150 feet	300 feet	300 feet
Frequency	2.4 GHz	5 GHz	2.4 GHz	2.4 GHz
Security	SSID, MAC address filtering, industry-standard WEP, WPA	SSID, MAC address filtering, industry-standard WEP, WPA	SSID, MAC address filtering, industry-standard WEP, WPA	SSID, MAC address filtering, industry-standard WEP, WPA
Compatibility	802.11	802.11a	802.11b	802.11b, 802.11g
Spread-spectrum method	DSSS	DSSS	DSSS	DSSS
Communication mode	Ad-hoc or infrastructure	Ad-hoc or infrastructure	Ad-hoc or infrastructure	Ad-hoc or infrastructure
Description	The original 802.11 wireless standard. Only seen on first-generation wireless networking devices.	Products that adhere to this standard are considered "Wi-Fi Certified." Eight available channels. Less prone to interference than 802.11b and 802.11g.	Products that adhere to this standard are considered "Wi-Fi Certified." Fourteen channels available in the 2.4-GHz band (only 11 of which can be used in the U.S. due to FCC regulations). Three non-overlapping channels.	Products that adhere to this standard are considered "Wi-Fi Certified." Improved security enhancements. Fourteen channels available in the 2.4-GHz band (only 11 of which can be used in the U.S. due to FCC regulations). Three non-overlapping channels.

Table 9-1   802.11

older wired 10BaseT networks—and range of up to 300 feet under ideal conditions. 802.11b networks can be secured through the use of WEP and WPA encryption. The main downside to using 802.11b is, in fact, that it's so popular. The 2.4-GHz frequency is already a crowded place, so you're more likely to run into interference from other wireless devices.

802.11g   The latest-and-greatest version of 802.11, called *802.11g*, offers data transfer speeds equivalent to 802.11a—up to 54 Mbps—and the wider 300-foot range of 802.11b. More important, 802.11g is backward-compatible with 802.11b, so the same 802.11g wireless access point can service both 802.11b and 802.11g wireless nodes. Table 9-1 compares the main characteristics of the different versions of 802.11.

NOTE   Products that use the 802.16 wireless standard—often called *WiMax*—are expected on the market any time now. Although speed for 802.16-compliant devices is about the same as 802.11b, manufacturers claim a range of up to 30 miles! This kind of range would be perfect for so-called metropolitan area networks (MANs). Before you get too excited, though, keep in mind that the speed of the network will almost certainly decrease the farther away from the base station (the wireless access point) the nodes are. Effective range could be as little as three miles, but that still beats 300 feet in my book!

HomeRF
Home Radio Frequency or *HomeRF*, as the name implies, is intended for home use, not for use in large business network environments. It is easy to set up and maintain, but it does not offer much in the way of range, topping out at about 150 feet. Speed on early HomeRF devices was also nothing to write home about, clocking in at a maximum of 2 Mbps. The

Table 9-2	Standard	HomeRF
HomeRF	Max. throughput	2 Mbps, or 10 Mbps in version 2.0
	Max. range	150 feet
	Frequency	2.4 GHz
	Security	NWID, Proprietary 56-bit encryption algorithm (128-bit in version 2.0)
	Compatibility	HomeRF 2.0 is compatible with the earlier version of HomeRF.
	Spread-spectrum method	FHSS
	Communication mode	Ad-hoc or infrastructure
	Description	HomeRF is less prone to interference, and you can set up multiple HomeRF networks in the same area.

later version 2.0 of the HomeRF standard, however, bumps the speed up to a respectable 10 Mbps, and provides full backward compatibility with the earlier HomeRF technology. Also, because HomeRF devices use the FHSS spread-spectrum broadcasting method, they are less prone to interference and somewhat more secure than Wi-Fi devices.

HomeRF wireless networks use the *SWAP* protocol, a hybrid of the *Digital Enhanced Cordless Telecommunications (DECT)* standard for voice communication and the 802.11 wireless Ethernet standard for data. HomeRF uses seven channels in the 2.4-GHz range, six of which are dedicated to voice communication, with the remaining one used for data.

Security-wise, HomeRF uses a proprietary 56-bit encryption algorithm (128-bit in version 2.0) instead of the industry-standard WEP and WPA that 802.11 uses. Also, instead of an SSID name, HomeRF uses what's called a *Network ID (NWID)*. It serves the same purpose as an SSID, but is somewhat more secure. Table 9-2 lists HomeRF's important specifications.

Infrared Wireless Networking

Wireless networking using infrared technology is largely overlooked these days, due to the explosion of interest in the newer and faster wireless standards. Still, infrared technology is built into lots of existing devices, and it provides an easy and reasonably fast way to transfer data, often without the need to purchase or install any additional hardware or software on your PCs.

The Infrared Data Association Standard

Communication through infrared devices is enabled via the *Infrared Data Association*, or *IrDA, protocol*. The IrDA protocol stack is a widely supported industry standard, and has been included in all versions of Windows since Windows 95. Apple computers also support IrDA, as do Linux PCs.

In terms of speed and range, infrared isn't very impressive. Infrared devices are capable of transferring data at up to 4 Mbps—not too shabby, but hardly stellar. The maximum distance between infrared devices is 1 meter, and connections must be in direct line-of-sight, making them susceptible to interference. An infrared link can be disrupted

Table 9-3	Standard	Infrared (IrDA)
Infrared	Max. Throughput	Up to 4 Mbps
	Max. Range	1 meter (39 inches)
	Security	None
	Compatibility	IrDA
	Communication mode	Point-to-point ad-hoc
	Description	Infrared is best suited for quick, small transfers, such as zapping business card information from one PDA to another or sending print jobs to an infrared-capable printer.

by anything that breaks the beam of light; a soda can, a co-worker passing between desks, or even bright sunlight hitting the infrared transceiver can cause interference.

Infrared is only designed to make a point-to-point connection between two devices in ad-hoc mode—no infrastructure mode is available. You can, however, use an infrared access point device to enable Ethernet network communication using IrDA. Also, Infrared devices operate at half-duplex, so they can't talk and listen at the same time. IrDA has a mode that emulates full-duplex communication, but it's really half-duplex.

In terms of security, the IrDA protocol offers exactly nothing in the way of encryption or authentication. Infrared's main security feature is the fact that you have to be literally within arms' reach to establish a link. Clearly, infrared is not the best solution for a dedicated network connection, but for a quick file transfer or print job, it'll do in a pinch. Table 9-3 lists infrared's important specifications.

Bluetooth

Upon its introduction, there was some confusion among PC techs about what Bluetooth technology actually *does*. Much of the confusion has since been cleared up. *Bluetooth* creates small wireless networks, called *personal area networks (PANs)*, connecting PCs with peripheral devices such as PDAs and printers, input devices like keyboards and mice, and consumer electronics like cell phones, home stereos, televisions, home security systems, and so on. Interestingly, Bluetooth was *not* originally designed to be a full-function networking solution, although many vendors have adopted it for this purpose.

Bluetooth is the basis for the IEEE organization's forthcoming 802.15 standard for wireless PANs. Bluetooth uses the FHSS spread-spectrum broadcasting method, switching among any of the 79 frequencies available in the 2.45-GHz range. Bluetooth hops frequencies some 1600 times per second, making it highly resistant to interference. Bluetooth transfers data at rates from 723 Kbps to 1, count 'em, *1 Mbps*, with a maximum range of 10 meters (about 33 feet). At least, those are the specs according to the Bluetooth standard. Some high-powered Bluetooth devices have throughput speed and range on par with 802.11b, but these are still somewhat uncommon, so I'll concentrate on the published Bluetooth specifications.

Bluetooth Operation Modes

Bluetooth's operation mode is neither truly ad-hoc nor infrastructure. Bluetooth devices interoperate in a *master/slave* scheme, in which one master device controls up to seven active slave devices. Don't worry about having to designate these roles—Bluetooth handles that automatically.

A Bluetooth PAN is called a *piconet*—"pico" literally translating into "one trillionth," and loosely translating into "very small." Note that more than seven Bluetooth slave devices (up to 255) can participate in a piconet, but only seven of those devices can be active at one time. Inactive slave devices are referred to as *parked* devices.

Bluetooth Communication

Bluetooth devices go through four stages to find each other and start talking: device discovery, name discovery, association, and service discovery.

During *device discovery*, the Bluetooth device broadcasts its MAC address, as well as a code identifying what type of device it is (PDA, printer, and so on). Note that you have the option of setting your Bluetooth device to *non-discovery* mode, thus skipping this stage. During the *name discovery* stage, the device identifies itself by a "friendly" name, such as *iPAQ Pocket PC*. Next comes the *association* stage, also called *bonding, pairing, or joining*, depending on your device's vendor. This is the stage where the device officially joins your Bluetooth network. Some devices require that you input a PIN code, providing a level of security. Finally, during *service discovery*, the Bluetooth device tells what kind(s) of service (profiles) it provides.

From your PC's perspective, Bluetooth devices manifest as a separate network accessible through Windows Explorer, as shown in Figure 9-10.

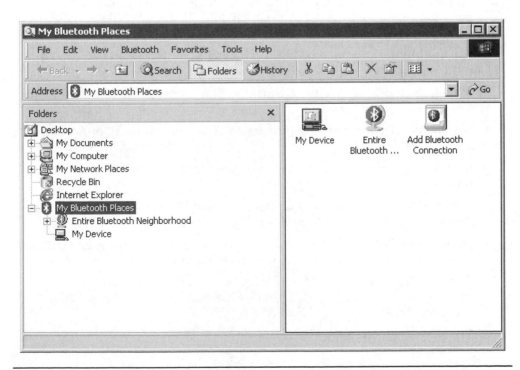

Figure 9-10   Windows Explorer showing My Bluetooth Places

Bluetooth uses two types of data transfer between master and slave nodes: *synchronous connection-oriented (SCO)* and *asynchronous connectionless (ACL)*. SCO connections guarantee that all data transmitted is received, and are better suited to things like file transfers during PDA-to-PC synchronization. ACL connections don't guarantee that all data is transferred successfully, but they're somewhat faster than SCO connections. ACL connections are suited to data transfers such as streaming media. Master nodes can support up to three SCO connections at a time with up to three slave units. ACL links are either *point-to-point* (master node to a single slave), or *broadcast* (master node to all slaves).

Bluetooth Services

The various services that are supported by Bluetooth, called *profiles,* are defined by Bluetooth specification 1.1. The 13 common Bluetooth profiles are as follows:

- **Generic Access Profile**   Defines how Bluetooth units discover and establish a connection with each other.

- **Service Discovery Profile**   Enables the Bluetooth device's Service Discovery User Application to query other Bluetooth devices to determine what services they provide. This profile is dependent on the Generic Access Profile.

- **Cordless Telephony Profile**   Defines the Bluetooth wireless phone functionality.

- **Intercom Profile**   Defines the Bluetooth wireless intercom functionality.

- **Serial Port Profile**   Enables Bluetooth devices to emulate serial port communication using RS232 control signaling, the standard used on ordinary PC serial ports. This profile is dependent on the Generic Access Profile.

- **Headset Profile**   Defines the Bluetooth wireless telephone and PC headset functionality.

- **Dial-up Networking Profile**   Defines the Bluetooth device's capability to act as, or interact with, a modem.

- **Fax Profile**   Defines the Bluetooth device's capability to act as, or interact with, a fax device.

- **LAN Access Profile**   Defines how the Bluetooth device accesses a LAN and the Internet.

- **Generic Object Exchange Profile**   Defines how Bluetooth devices exchange data with other devices. This profile is dependent on the Serial Port Profile.

- **Object Push Profile**   Bluetooth devices use this profile to exchange small data objects, such as a PDA's Vcard, with other Bluetooth devices.

- **File Transfer Profile**   Used to exchange large data objects, such as files, between Bluetooth devices. This profile is dependent on the Generic Object Exchange Profile.

- **Synchronization Profile** Used to synchronize data between Bluetooth PDAs and PCs.

Bluetooth devices have to support identical profiles to communicate; for example, your PDA and PC both have to support the Bluetooth Synchronization profile if you want them to synch up.

To use a particular Bluetooth service (profile), simply locate its icon in My Bluetooth Places and double-click it, as shown in Figure 9-11.

Bluetooth Security

Security-wise, Bluetooth offers proprietary 128-bit encryption and the capability to set per-user passwords to guard against unauthorized access to the Bluetooth network. Bluetooth also supports industry-standard *Point-to-Point Tunneling Protocol (PPTP)* and *Secure Sockets Layer (SSL)* security through browser-based remote access. Access to Bluetooth networks can be controlled through MAC address filtering, and Bluetooth devices can be set to non-discovery mode to effectively hide them from other Bluetooth devices. Table 9-4 lists Bluetooth's important specifications.

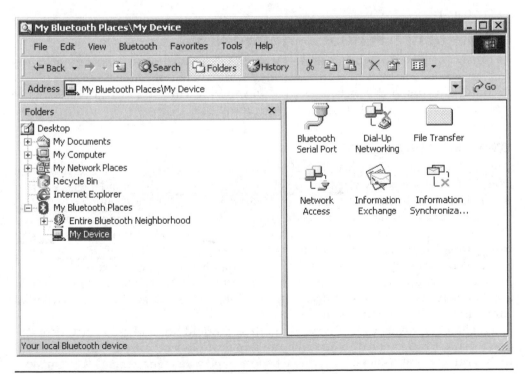

Figure 9-11 Bluetooth services listed in My Bluetooth Places

Standard	Bluetooth
Max. throughput	1 Mbps (some devices boast 2 Mbps)
Max. range	Typically 30 feet, but some high-powered Bluetooth devices have a maximum range of 300 feet
Frequency	2.45 GHz
Security	Proprietary 128-bit encryption, password-protected access, PPTP, SSL (through browser-based remote access client)
Compatibility	Bluetooth
Spread-spectrum method	FHSS
Communication mode	Master/slave: a single master device with to up to seven active slave devices. Connection links are either SCO (synchronous connection-oriented) or ACL (asynchronous connectionless).
Description	Bluetooth is designed to enable wireless communication between PCs and peripheral components, as well as consumer electronics. Bluetooth is not a full-fledged networking solution, and it is not intended to compete with or replace 802.11-based wireless networking technologies.

Table 9-4   Bluetooth

Configuring Wireless Networking

As I mentioned earlier, wireless devices want to talk to each other, so communicating with an available wireless network is usually a fairly straightforward process. The trick is in configuring the wireless network so that only specific wireless nodes are able to use it, and in securing the data that's sent through the air.

Wi-Fi and HomeRF

The mechanics of setting up a PC with a wireless network adapter aren't very different from installing a wired NIC. All modern Wi-Fi or HomeRF wireless adapters, whether they're internally installed PCI devices, PC Card devices, or USB, are completely PnP, so you won't have to spend your time setting jumpers and manually configuring resources. The key is to follow the manufacturer's instructions. Some makers insist that you install the device drivers and configuration utility software before you plug in the device. Failing to follow the vendor's instructions will almost certainly lead to problems later.

Once you've got the gadget plugged in, open Windows Device Manager and check to see if any errors or conflicts are listed. If everything's in the clear, then you're ready to configure the adapter to use your network.

Wi-Fi and HomeRF wireless networks both support ad-hoc and infrastructure operation modes. Which mode you choose depends on the number of wireless nodes you need to support, the type of data sharing they'll perform, and your management requirements.

Configuring a Network Adapter for Ad-hoc Mode

Configuring NICs for ad-hoc mode networking requires you to address four things: SSID, IP addresses, channel, and sharing. (Plus, of course, you have to set the NICs to

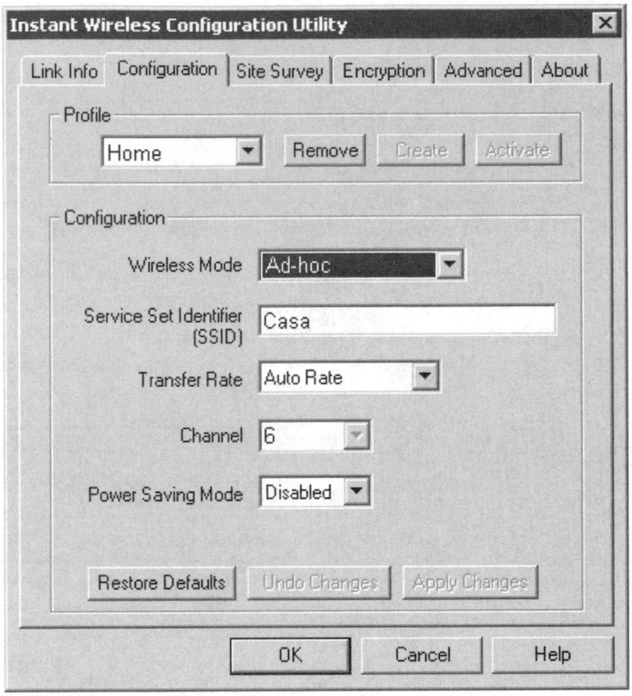

Figure 9-12

Selecting ad-hoc
mode in wireless
configuration
utility

PART II

Figure 9-12

Selecting ad-hoc
mode in wireless
configuration
utility

function in ad-hoc mode!) Each wireless node must use the same network name (SSID). Also, no two nodes can use the same IP address—although this is unlikely with modern versions of Windows and the Automatic Private IP Addressing (APIPA) feature that automatically selects a Class B IP address for any node not connected to a DHCP server or hard-coded to an IP address. Finally, ensure that the File and Printer Sharing service is running on all nodes. Figure 9-12 shows a wireless network configuration utility with ad-hoc mode selected.

Configuring a Network Adapter for Infrastructure Mode

As with ad-hoc mode wireless networks, infrastructure mode networks require that the same SSID be configured on all nodes and access points. Figure 9-13 shows a wireless network access point configuration utility set to Infrastructure mode.

Depending on the capabilities of your access point, you can also configure DHCP options, filtering, client channels, and so on.

Access Point Configuration

Wireless access points have a browser-based setup utility. Typically, you fire up your web browser on one of your network client workstations and enter the access point's default IP address, such as 192.168.1.1, to bring up the configuration page. You will need to supply an administrative password, included with your access point's documentation, to log in (see Figure 9-14).

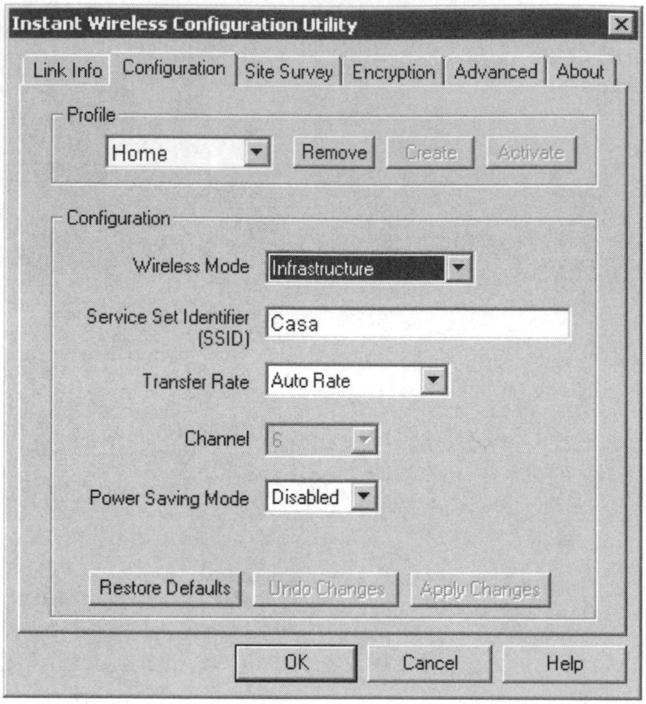

Figure 9-13

Selecting infrastructure mode in wireless configuration utility

Once you've logged in, you'll have configuration screens for changing your basic setup (with SSID and so on), access point password, security, and other options. Different access points offer different configuration options. Figure 9-15 shows the initial setup screen for a popular Linksys wireless access point/router.

Configuring Access Point SSID   The SSID option is usually located somewhere obvious on the configuration utility. On the Linksys model shown in Figure 9-15, it's on

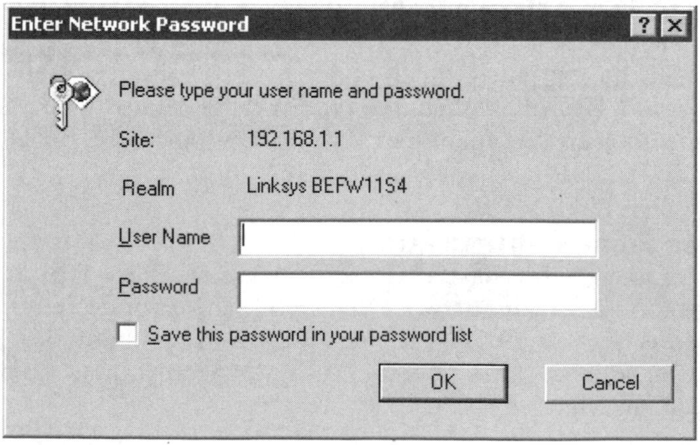

Figure 9-14

Security login for Linksys wireless access point

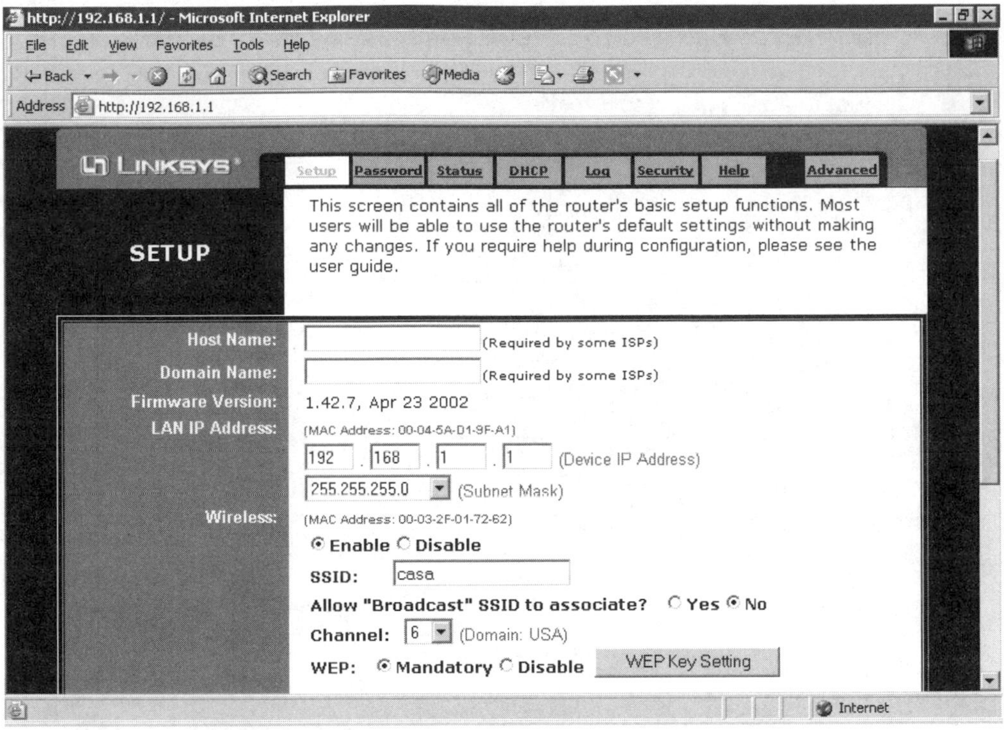

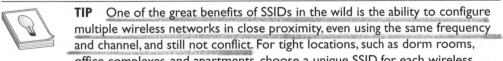

Figure 9-15   Linksys wireless access point setup screen

the Setup screen. Set your SSID to something unique, but not obvious. In other words, don't use "home" for your home network, or "office" for your work network, or anything else that's easy to guess. Why make a hacker's job easier?

In most circumstances, you should disable broadcasting of the SSID. This ensures that only wireless nodes specifically configured with the correct SSID can join the wireless network.

> **TIP**   One of the great benefits of SSIDs in the wild is the ability to configure multiple wireless networks in close proximity, even using the same frequency and channel, and still not conflict. For tight locations, such as dorm rooms, office complexes, and apartments, choose a unique SSID for each wireless network to avoid the potential for overlap problems.

Configuring MAC Address Filtering   Increase security even further by using MAC address filtering. This builds a list of wireless network clients that are permitted or denied access to your wireless network based on their unique MAC addresses.

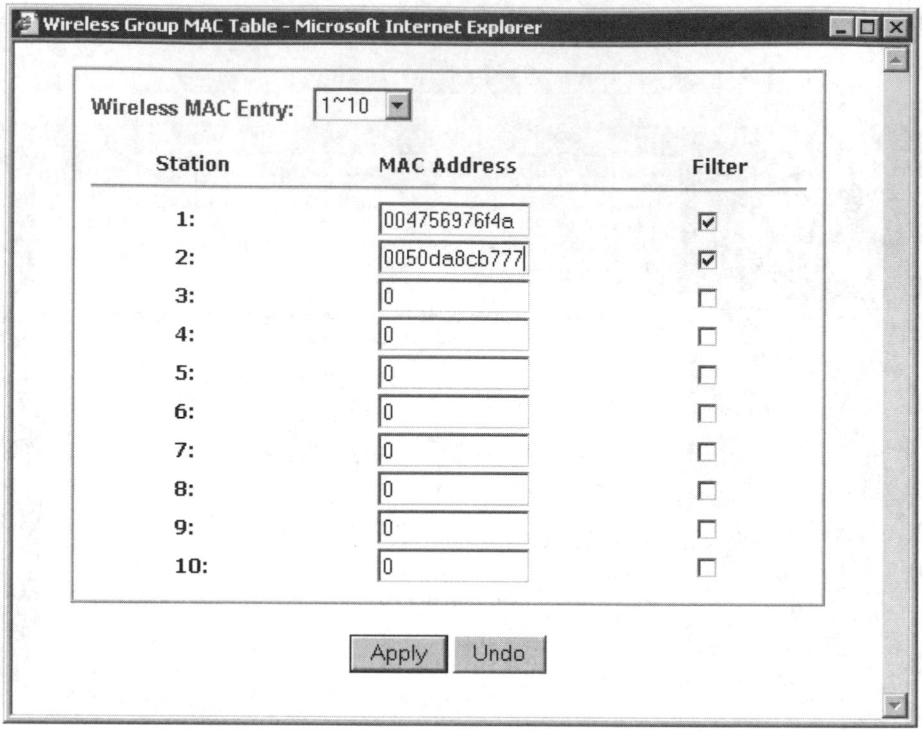

Figure 9-16   MAC address filtering configuration screen for a Linksys wireless access point

Figure 9-16 shows the MAC address filtering configuration screen on a Linksys wireless access point. Simply enter the MAC address of a wireless node that you want to allow (or deny) access to your wireless network.

Configuring Encryption   Enabling encryption ensures that data packets are secured against unauthorized access. To set up encryption, you turn on encryption at the wireless access point and generate a unique security key. Then you configure all connected wireless nodes on the network with the same key information. Figure 9-17 shows the WEP key configuration dialog for a Linksys access point.

You have the option of automatically generating a set of encryption keys or doing it manually. You can save yourself a certain amount of effort by using the automatic method. Select an encryption level—the usual choices are either 64-bit or 128-bit—and then enter a unique *passphrase* and click the Generate button (or whatever the equivalent button is called in your access point's software). Then select a default key and save the settings.

The encryption level, key, and passphrase must match on the wireless client node, or communication will fail. Many access points have the capability to export the encryption key data onto a floppy diskette for easy importing onto a client workstation, or you

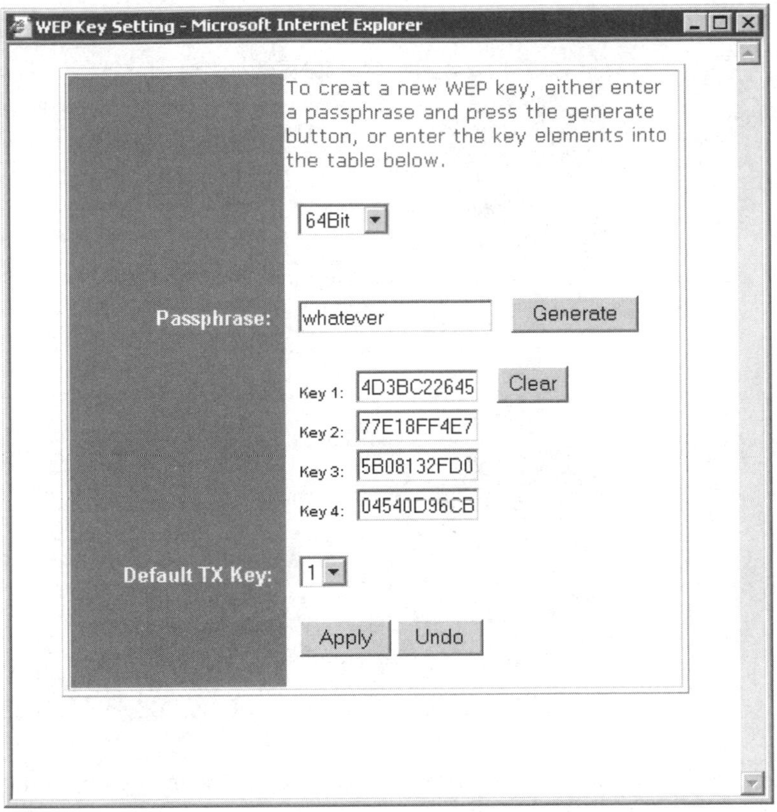

Figure 9-17   Encryption key configuration screen on Linksys wireless access point

can configure encryption manually using the vendor-supplied configuration utility, as shown in Figure 9-18.

WPA encryption, if supported by your wireless equipment, is configured in much the same way. You may be required to input a valid user name and password to configure encryption using WPA.

Configuring Infrared

IrDA device support is very solid in the latest versions of Windows, so there's not much for us techs to configure. IrDA links are made between devices dynamically, without user interaction. Typically, there's nothing to configure on an infrared-equipped PC, although in some cases you may need to enable your infrared port by assigning it to a COM port in the CMOS setup program. If an infrared port is already enabled on your

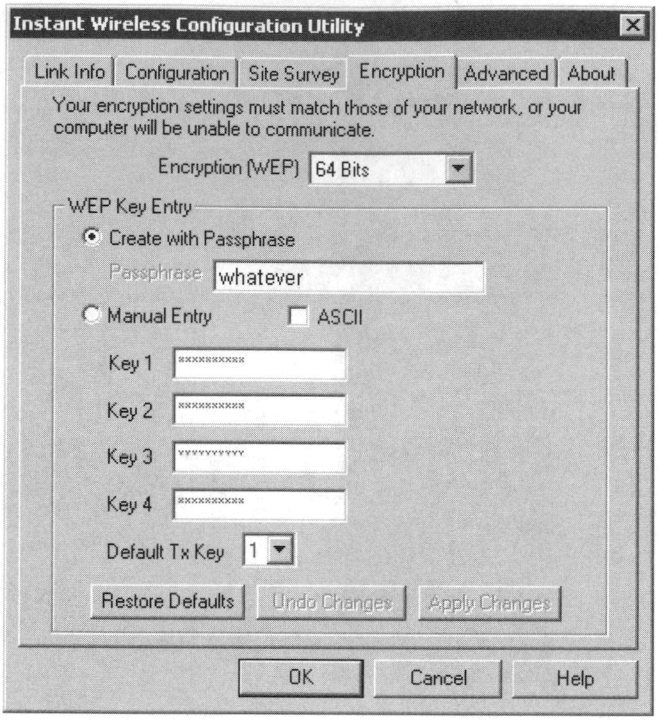

Figure 9-18
Encryption screen on client wireless network adapter configuration utility

system, you can find it under *Infrared devices* in Device Manager, and check its properties to see if it's working properly (see Figure 9-19).

As far as networking goes with infrared, your choices are somewhat limited. Infrared is designed to connect only two systems together in ad-hoc mode. This can be done simply to transfer files, or with a bit more configuration, you can configure the two PCs to use IrDA in *direct-connection* mode. You can also use a special infrared access point to enable Ethernet LAN access via IrDA.

Transferring Files via Infrared

File transfers via IrDA are as simple as can be. When two IrDA-enabled devices "see" each other, the sending (primary) device negotiates a connection to the receiving (secondary) device, and voilà. It's just "point and shoot"!

Figure 9-20 shows Windows XP's *Wireless Link* applet. Use this to configure file transfer options and the default location for received files.

You can send a file over the infrared connection in one of several ways:

- Specify a location and one or more files using the Wireless Link dialog box.
- Drag and drop files onto the Wireless Link icon.
- Using Windows Explorer, or My Computer, alternate-click a file or a selection of files, and then select Send To Infrared Recipient.
- Print to a printer configured to use an infrared port.

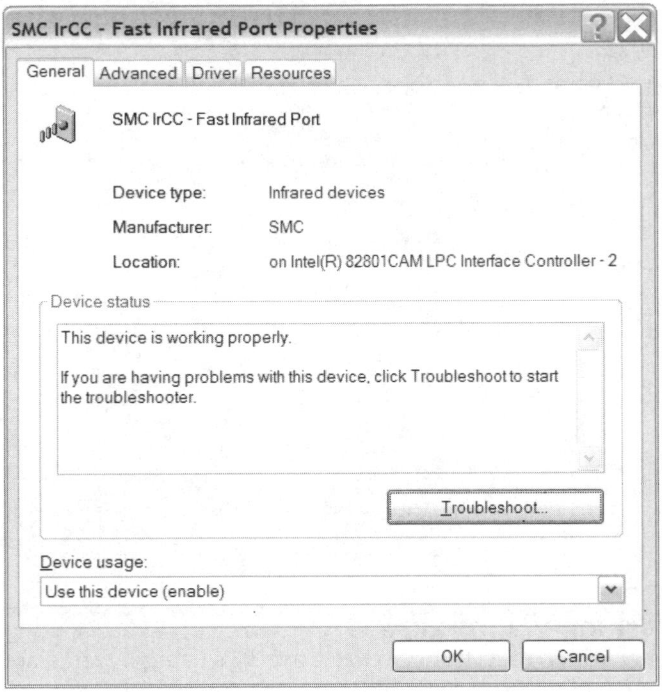

Figure 9-19
Properties for a
properly installed
infrared port

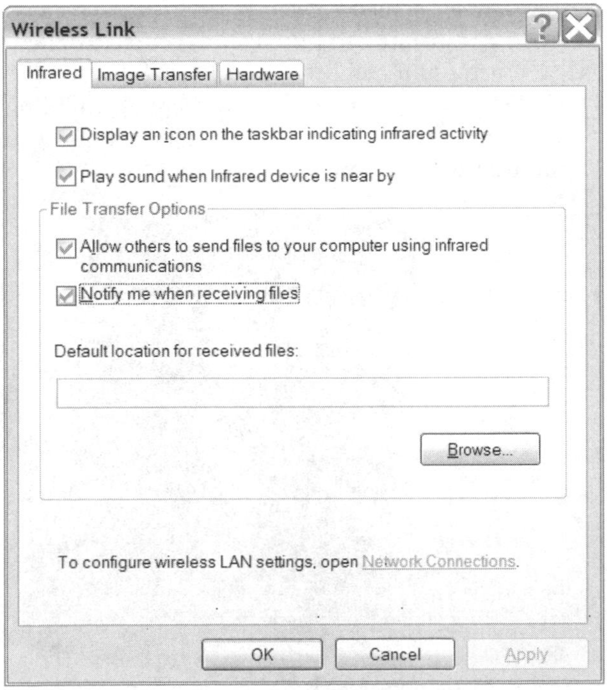

SMC IrCC - Fast Infrared Port Properties

General | Advanced | Driver | Resources

SMC IrCC - Fast Infrared Port

Device type: Infrared devices
Manufacturer: SMC
Location: on Intel(R) 82801CAM LPC Interface Controller - 2

Device status
This device is working properly.

If you are having problems with this device, click Troubleshoot to start
the troubleshooter.

Troubleshoot...

Device usage:
Use this device (enable)

OK   Cancel

PART II

Figure 9-20
Windows XP's
Wireless Link
applet

Wireless Link

Infrared | Image Transfer | Hardware

☑ Display an icon on the taskbar indicating infrared activity

☑ Play sound when Infrared device is near by

File Transfer Options
☑ Allow others to send files to your computer using infrared
   communications
☑ Notify me when receiving files

Default location for received files:

Browse...

To configure wireless LAN settings, open Network Connections.

OK   Cancel   Apply

Figure 9-21

The Connection
Device screen
of the New
Connection
Wizard

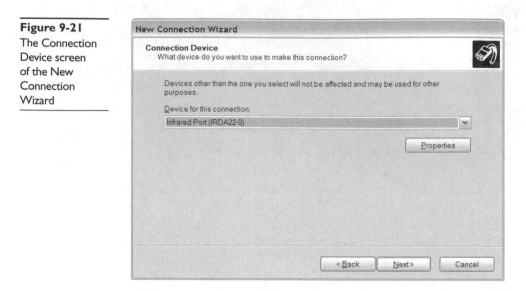

Networking via Infrared

Direct network connections between two PCs using infrared are similar to using a null-modem cable to connect two PCs together via a serial port. Modern versions of Windows make this type of connection extremely easy via wizard-driven dialogs. Using the Windows XP New Connection Wizard, first select *Set up an advanced connection*, then select *Connect directly to another computer* on the next screen. Continue to follow the prompts, choosing your infrared port as the connection device (see Figure 9-21).

An infrared access point combines an infrared transceiver with an Ethernet NIC and translates the IrDA protocol into an Ethernet signal, enabling you to log on to your network and access resources. Figure 9-22 shows a laptop accessing an Ethernet LAN through an infrared access point.

Figure 9-22

Laptop using
infrared access
point

Bluetooth

Before I jump into Bluetooth configuration, I want to give you a word of warning. Although by this point, Bluetooth is a well-established standard with wide vendor support, setting up Bluetooth devices can still be a hit-or-miss affair. Many Bluetooth vendors tweak their products up so much that the devices have trouble talking to products from other vendors. If you want to save yourself a headache, be sure to read all the documentation that comes with your Bluetooth gadget, check the vendor's web site for any updated info or drivers, and allow yourself plenty of time for troubleshooting.

Installing Bluetooth Wireless Networking Hardware

Bluetooth hardware comes integrated into many newer portable electronic gadgets, like PDAs and cell phones. To add Bluetooth capabilities to a laptop or desktop PC, you often need an adapter of some sort. USB and PC Card adapters are the most common type, but you'll also see Compact Flash and PCI add-on peripheral cards, and even specialized Bluetooth adapters that plug into legacy serial and parallel ports.

Bluetooth networking is enabled through ad-hoc styled PC-to-PC (or PDA, handheld computer, or cell phone-to-PC) connections, or in an infrastructure-like mode through Bluetooth access points. Bluetooth access points are similar to 802.11-based access points, bridging wireless Bluetooth PAN segments to wired LAN segments.

Bluetooth Configuration

Follow your manufacturer's instructions to install your Bluetooth adapter. You'll probably have to install your driver and configuration utility beforehand, particularly if your Bluetooth adapter attaches via USB. Once the adapter is installed, your work is basically done. Bluetooth devices seek each other out and establish the master/slave relationship without any intervention on your part.

Connecting to a Bluetooth PAN is handled by specialized utility software provided by your portable device or Bluetooth device vendor. Figure 9-23 shows a Compaq iPAQ

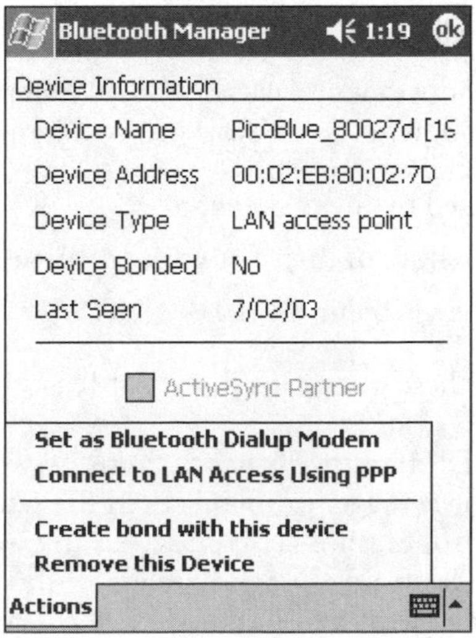

Figure 9-23
iPAQ Bluetooth Manager software connected to Bluetooth access point

Figure 9-24
Belkin Bluetooth
access point
setup screen

handheld computer running the Bluetooth Manager software to connect to a Bluetooth access point.

Like their Wi-Fi counterparts, Bluetooth access points use a browser-based configuration utility. Figure 9-24 shows the main setup screen for a Belkin Bluetooth access point.

Use this setup screen to check on the status of connected Bluetooth devices; configure encryption, MAC address filtering, and other security settings; and access other utilities provided by the access point's vendor.

Troubleshooting Wireless Networks

Wireless networks are a real boon when they work right, but they can also be one of the most vexing things to troubleshoot when they don't. Before I close out this chapter, I want to give you some practical advice on how to detect and correct wireless hardware, software, and configuration problems.

As with any troubleshooting scenario, your first step in troubleshooting a wireless network is to break down your tasks into logical steps. Your first step should be to figure out the scope of your wireless networking problem. Ask yourself *who, what,* and *when*:

- Who is affected by the problem?
- What is the nature of their network problem?
- When did the problem start?

The answers to these questions dictate at least the initial direction of your troubleshooting.

So, who's affected? If all machines on your network—wired and wireless—have lost connectivity, you have bigger problems than the wireless machines being unable to access the network. Troubleshoot this situation the way you'd troubleshoot any network failure. Once you determine which wireless nodes are affected, it's easier to pinpoint whether the problem lies in one or more wireless clients or in one or more access points.

After you narrow down the number of affected machines, your next task is to figure out specifically what type of error the users are experiencing. If they can access some, but not all, network services, then it's unlikely that the problem is limited to their wireless equipment. For example, if they can browse the Internet, but can't access any shared resources on a server, then they're probably experiencing a permissions-related issue, rather than a wireless one.

Finally, determine when the problem started. What has changed that might explain your loss of connectivity? Did you or somebody else change the wireless network configuration? For example, if the network worked fine two minutes ago, and then you changed the WEP key on the access point, and now nobody can see the network, you have your solution—or at least your culprit! Did your office experience a power outage, power sag, or power surge? Any of these might cause a wireless access point to fail.

Once you figure out the who, what, and when, you can start troubleshooting in earnest. Typically, your problem is going to center on your hardware, software, connectivity, or configuration. Let's look at troubleshooting steps for Wi-Fi and HomeRF wireless networks first, and then tackle Bluetooth wireless networking.

Troubleshooting Wi-Fi and HomeRF Wireless Networks

Wi-Fi and HomeRF take different approaches to their implementation, but troubleshooting procedures are practically identical for both technologies.

Hardware Troubleshooting

Wireless networking hardware components are subject to the same kind of abuse and faulty installation as any other hardware component. Troubleshooting a suspected hardware problem should bring out the A+ Certified technician in you.

Open Windows Device Manager and check to see if there's an error or conflict with the wireless adapter. If you see a big yellow exclamation point or a red X next to the device, you've got either a driver error or a resource conflict. Reinstall the device driver or manually reset the IRQ resources as needed.

If you don't see the device listed at all, it's possible that the device is not seated properly in its PCI slot, or not plugged all the way into its PC Card or USB slot. These problems are easy to fix. One thing to consider if you're using an older laptop and PC Card combination is that the wireless adapter may be a CardBus type of PC Card device. CardBus cards will not snap into a non-CardBus slot, even though both new and old cards are the same size. If your laptop is older than about five years, it may not support CardBus, meaning you need to get a different PC Card device. Or, if you've been looking for a reason to get a new laptop, now you have one!

NOTE As with all things computing, don't forget to do the standard PC troubleshooting thing and reboot the computer before you do any configuration or hardware changes!

Software Troubleshooting

Because you've already checked to confirm that your hardware is using the correct drivers, what kind of software-related problems are left to check? Two things come immediately to mind: the wireless adapter configuration utility and the wireless access point's firmware version.

As I mentioned earlier, some wireless devices won't work correctly unless you install the vendor-provided drivers and configuration utility before plugging in the device. This is particularly true of wireless USB devices. If you didn't do this, go into Device Manager and uninstall the device, then start again from scratch.

Some wireless access point manufacturers (I won't name names here, but they're popular) are notorious for shipping devices without the latest firmware installed. This problem often manifests as a device that enables clients to connect, but only at such slow speeds that the devices experience frequent timeout errors. The fix for this is to update the access point's firmware. Go to the manufacturer's web site and follow the support links until you find the latest version. You'll need your device's exact model and serial number—this is important, because installing the wrong firmware version on your device is a guaranteed way of rendering it unusable!

Again, follow the manufacturer's instructions for updating the firmware to the letter. Typically, you need to download a small executable updating program along with a data file containing the firmware software. The process takes only minutes, and you'll be amazed at the results.

Connectivity Troubleshooting

Confirm wireless connectivity using the same methods you use for a wired network. First, check the wireless NIC's link light to see whether it's passing data packets to and from the network. Second, check the wireless NIC's configuration utility. Typically, the utility has an icon in your System Tray that shows the strength of your wireless signal. Figure 9-25 shows Windows XP Professional's built-in wireless configuration utility displaying the link state and *signal strength*.

 NOTE If you're lucky enough to have a laptop with an internally installed NIC (instead of a PC Card), your device may not have a link light.

If your *link state* indicates that you're currently disconnected, you may have a problem with your wireless access point. If your signal is too weak to receive a signal, you may be

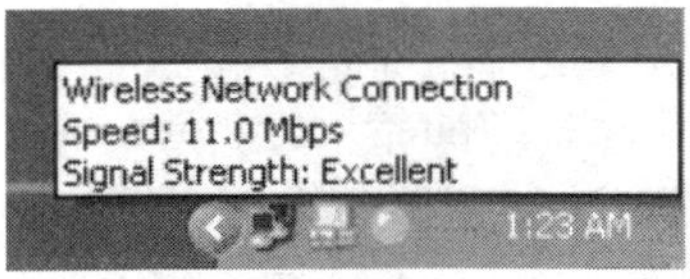

Figure 9-25
Windows XP's
wireless
configuration utility

Wireless Network Connection
Speed: 11.0 Mbps
Signal Strength: Excellent

1:23 AM

out of range of your access point, or there may be a device causing interference. Relocate the PC or access point, or locate and move the device causing interference.

Remember, other wireless devices that operate in the same frequency range as your wireless nodes can cause interference as well. Look for wireless telephones, intercoms, and so on as possible culprits. One fix for interference caused by other wireless devices is to change the channel your network uses. Another is to change the channel the offending device uses, if possible. If you can't change channels, try moving the interfering device to another area or replacing it with a different device.

Configuration Troubleshooting

With all due respect to the fine network techs in the field, the most common type of wireless networking problem is misconfigured hardware or software. That's right—the dreaded *user error*! Given the complexities of wireless networking, this isn't so surprising. All it takes is one slip of the typing finger to throw off your configuration completely. The things that you're most likely to get wrong are the SSID and WEP configuration.

Verify SSID configuration on your access point first, and then check on the affected wireless nodes. Most wireless devices allow you to use any characters in the SSID, including blank spaces. Be careful not to add blank characters where they don't belong, such as trailing blank spaces behind any other characters typed into the name field.

If you're using MAC address filtering, make sure the MAC address of the client that's attempting to access the wireless network is on the list of accepted users. This is particularly important if you swap out NICs on a PC, or if you introduce a new PC to your wireless network.

Check WEP configuration to make sure that all wireless nodes and access points match. Mistyping a WEP key prevents the affected node from talking to the wireless network, even if your signal strength is 100 percent! Remember that many access points have the capability of exporting WEP keys onto a floppy disk or other removable media. It's then a simple matter to import the WEP key onto the PC using the wireless NIC's configuration utility. Remember that the encryption level must match on access points and wireless nodes. If your wireless access point is configured for 128-bit encryption, all nodes must also use 128-bit encryption. Although it's not as secure, lowering the encryption level might solve an encryption-related connectivity issue.

Troubleshooting Bluetooth

Bluetooth technology might have outgrown its infancy, but it's still something of a toddler when it comes to industry-wide standard implementation. Like any toddler, Bluetooth falls down a lot. This section can help you get your Bluetooth wireless network back on its feet.

Hardware Troubleshooting

Check your Bluetooth hardware to make sure the device is detected and there are no driver or resource conflicts. Make sure the device is properly seated. Because practically all Bluetooth networking devices attach to the PC via USB, this should be a no-brainer, but check it anyway. Make sure the device is compatible with your USB version. Some newer Bluetooth devices only work with USB 2.0.

Typically, a Bluetooth device comes with its own configuration utility that enables you to confirm and change system resource usage. You can also look in Device Manager to see quickly if the device driver is incorrectly installed or missing, and if any resource conflicts need to be resolved.

Software Troubleshooting

More than most networking technologies, Bluetooth suffers from "proprietary-itis." Hence, you may find that one manufacturer's instructions for setting up a Bluetooth device differ completely from the setup instructions for another manufacturer's device. That's why it's particularly important for you to remember to RTFM—*Read The Furnished Manual*—when it comes to setting up software on Bluetooth networking devices. Check your documentation and make sure there are no special steps that you may have skipped or performed out of order.

An important consideration is whether your OS supports Bluetooth. Currently, the only desktop operating systems that offer native Bluetooth support are Windows XP (with Service Pack 1) and Apple OSX (with the Bluetooth software update installed). Support for Windows 9*x*/Me or 2000 is spotty and completely dependent on third-party drivers and utilities.

Connectivity Troubleshooting

Check connectivity on your Bluetooth device the same way you do with Wi-Fi and HomeRF devices. Chances are your Bluetooth device lacks a link light, so you'll have to trust the vendor-supplied configuration utility to tell you whether you're connected. Remember, Bluetooth range is only about 30 feet, so it's quite easy to lose connectivity by wandering too far away from your access point or other networked Bluetooth device.

Bluetooth tends to be more resistant to interference than other wireless solutions, but don't rule it out entirely. If you have other Bluetooth devices operating in the same area, shut them down one by one until you confirm that they aren't causing you to lose connectivity.

Configuration Troubleshooting

Once you confirm that your Bluetooth hardware is in good working order with the correct drivers installed and within range of your other networked devices, it's time to check your configuration.

Troubleshoot Profiles   I mentioned earlier that Bluetooth devices have to support the same services, or profiles, to communicate. The LAN Access profile is the most common networking profile for Bluetooth devices, though your device may use a different name for the same profile. Make sure all devices are configured to use the same networking profile.

Troubleshoot Bluetooth Association   Bluetooth devices are typically set to discover and associate with any other Bluetooth devices in range. As a security measure, you can set your Bluetooth device to *non-discovery mode* to keep it from automatically announcing its presence to other Bluetooth devices. If you're having trouble connecting to it from another device, confirm that your device isn't set to hide itself from the network.

If you receive a message telling you the discovery and association process has failed—typically something like "pairing unsuccessful"—you need to check your password or PIN.

Troubleshoot Bluetooth Power Options   Although Bluetooth devices consume very little power to begin with, some devices are configured by default to cut power usage even further by dropping into a sleep mode from time to time. If your device goes to sleep, you may have to wake it up manually by using the configuration utility to switch it back on. While you're there, you may want to disable the power-saving option.

Chapter Review

Questions

1. Which wireless networking technology uses the 5-GHz frequency range?

    A. 802.11

    B. 802.11a

    C. 802.11b

    D. 802.11g

2. The original 802.11 wireless specification enables a maximum throughput speed of _____.

    A. 2 Mbps

    B. 11 Mbps

    C. 54 Mbps

    D. 4 Mbps

3. Which of the following use DSSS broadcasting? (Select all that apply.)

    A. HomeRF

    B. 802.11a

    C. 802.11g

    D. 802.11b

4. What is the maximum range of current Bluetooth devices?

    A. 1 meter

    B. 3 feet

    C. 10 meters

    D. 300 feet

5. What function does CSMA/CA provide that CSMA/CD does not?

   A. Data packet collision detection

   B. End-to-end data packet encryption

   C. Data packet collision avoidance

   D. Data packet error checking

6. Why should you configure a unique SSID for your wireless network?

   A. A unique SSID enables backward compatibility between 802.11g and 802.11b.

   B. A unique SSID boosts wireless network range.

   C. A unique SSID boosts wireless network data throughput.

   D. A unique SSID prevents access by any network device that does not have the same SSID configured.

7. Which of these consumer electronics may cause interference with 802.11b wireless networks? (Select all that apply.)

   A. Wireless telephones

   B. Wireless baby monitors

   C. Bluetooth-enabled cellular telephones

   D. Television remote controls

8. Which of the following advantages does WPA have over WEP? (Select all that apply.)

   A. End-to-end data packet encryption

   B. EAP user authentication

   C. Encryption key integrity checking

   D. 128-bit data encryption

9. What hardware enables wireless PCs to connect to resources on a wired network segment in infrastructure mode? (Select all that apply.)

   A. An access point

   B. A router

   C. A hub

   D. A bridge

10. What do you call a wireless Ethernet network in infrastructure mode with more than one access point?

   A. BSS

   B. EBSS

   C. PAN

   D. Piconet

Answers

   1. **B.** 802.11a operates in the 5-GHz frequency range.

   2. **A.** Early 802.11 wireless networks ran at a maximum of 2 Mbps.

   3. **B, C, D.** HomeRF uses FHSS. 802.11a, b, and g all use DSSS.

   4. **C.** Current Bluetooth devices have a maximum range of 10 meters, or about 30 feet.

   5. **C.** CSMA/CA uses the RTS/CTS protocol to provide data packet collision avoidance.

   6. **D.** A unique SSID prevents wireless devices that do not have the same SSID from accessing the network.

   7. **A, B.** Many wireless telephones and baby monitors operate in the same 2.4-GHz frequency range as 802.11b wireless networking equipment and may cause interference. Bluetooth devices operate in the same frequency, but are unlikely to cause interference because they use FHSS instead of DSSS. Television remote controls use infrared signals.

   8. **A, B, C.** WPA upgrades WEP to provide end-to-end data packet encryption, user authentication via EAP, and encryption key integrity checking.

   9. **A, D.** A wireless access point or bridge enables you to connect wireless PCs to a wired network segment.

   10. **B.** A wireless network with more than one access point is called EBSS, or Extended Basic Service Set.

PART II

Protocols

The Network+ Certification exam expects you to know how to

- 2.4   Differentiate between the following network protocols in terms of routing, addressing schemes, interoperability, and naming conventions: TCP/IP, IPX/SPX, NetBEUI, AppleTalk
- 2.13   Identify the purpose of network services and protocols, such as SMB (Server Message Block)

To achieve these goals, you must be able to

- Understand the concept of protocols
- Learn about the NetBEUI protocol suite
- Learn about the IPX/SPX protocol suite
- Learn about the TCP/IP protocol suite

Everything you've learned up to now points to a single goal—getting the right packets to the right system. We've concentrated on hardware in the form of cabling, hubs, switches, and NICs that handle the majority of this job. Now it's time to move away from hardware and start looking at the software built into your operating system that handles the primary networking duties: the network protocols.

Using the OSI seven-layer model as a guide, this chapter defines network protocols and details exactly what network protocols do to make the network work on your system. Once you understand exactly what network protocols do, we'll take a deeper look at a number of different network protocols from both the past and today to see how they work and how to install them.

Historical/Conceptual

Network Protocols

The term *network protocol* describes all the software on a PC that enables your applications to share or access resources. Your first reaction might be "Cool! Where is this software?" Don't bother trying to look under My Computer to try to find these programs. Of course, they do exist, but every operating system stores them in different ways. These programs might be executable files or they might be support files, such as Windows Dynamic Link Libraries (DLLs). Some operating systems build these programs into the core of the operating system itself. Even though it's difficult to show the exact programs that do this work, you can understand what they do and see what you can do to make them work.

Only a handful of network protocols exist. Currently, the famous TCP/IP network protocol is by far the most commonly used in networks. Other network protocols, such as Novell's IPX/SPX and Microsoft's NetBIOS/NetBEUI, are also popular and well supported, although both of these have lost ground to TCP/IP. There's a simple reason for this: the biggest network in the world, the Internet, runs on TCP/IP.

 NOTE I'd like to apologize on behalf of the entire networking industry for its horrific use of the term "protocol." You know from the OSI seven-layer model that a network uses many different protocols and procedures to get data from one system to another in the proper format. The networking industry's flexible use of the term can cause a great deal of confusion. When a network tech, book, or FAQ uses the word "protocol," take the time to be sure you understand what type of protocol is involved.

Protocol Stacks

Notice that the network protocols I just named all have a slash in their names. Those slashes are there for a reason. Network protocols are groups of protocols designed to work together, but at different levels of the OSI seven-layer model. The TCP/IP label, for example, stands for the Transmission Control Protocol (TCP) and the Internet Protocol (IP). The TCP part of TCP/IP defines a set of protocols that run at the Session and Transport layers. The IP of TCP/IP defines the protocols that run at the Network layer. We use the terms *protocol stacks*—or less commonly, *protocol suites*—to describe these groups of network protocols.

 TIP A protocol stack is a group of protocols that work together from Layers 3 through 7 of the OSI seven-layer model to enable your applications to use the network.

In fact, the details get even a bit more complex. When you say TCP, you'd think that was a single protocol, but it's a number of protocols operating at the same OSI layers with names like TCP, UDP, and ICMP. So, even though a single network protocol might only have two names separated by a slash, that doesn't mean there are only two! Fear not! This chapter breaks these protocols down to show you their different functions. For now, get the idea into your head that a network protocol isn't a single protocol. A network protocol is many protocols, working together at the Application, Presentation, Network, Transport, and Session layers of the OSI.

Protocols by Layer

All network protocols perform basically the same functions at the Session, Transport, and (on some protocols) Network layers of the OSI seven-layer model. Network protocols also function at the Presentation layer and Application layer, although how they work at these layers differs tremendously, depending on the protocol.

Each of the major protocol suites provides a different mix of efficiency, flexibility, and scalability (*scalability* means the capability to support network growth). NetBIOS/ NetBEUI works best for small networks without routers; IPX/SPX provides support for integrating with Novell NetWare; and TCP/IP provides a complex, robust, open solution for larger networks. The rest of this chapter inspects these and a few other network protocols to help you understand which one to use, how to install them in Windows client PCs, how to configure them, and how to deal with network protocol suites when they fail. This is a big job, which we will break down by protocol. First, we need to cover a few critical points about network protocol suites in general. Let's do this by clarifying exactly what a network protocol does at the Session, Transport, and Network layers. We'll cover the Application and Presentation layers function in the section called "IPX/SPX," when we discuss individual network protocols.

A Network Protocol's Session-Layer Functions

From a conceptual standpoint, a network protocol's Session-layer functions are far more complex than the Transport and Network functions combined. Let's conquer the Session functions first—Transport and Network will be much shorter!

A system's *Session-layer software* has many jobs. It must create a connection—a session— between two systems. Second, it must determine the type of data being moved in that session and confirm the other system supports that particular type of data. Third, the Session software monitors the session as data moves from one system to another. Fourth, the Session software must have a method of handling multiple sessions at a single time. Last, the Session software must recognize when the data transfer completes, and then shut off that session. (See Figure 10-1.)

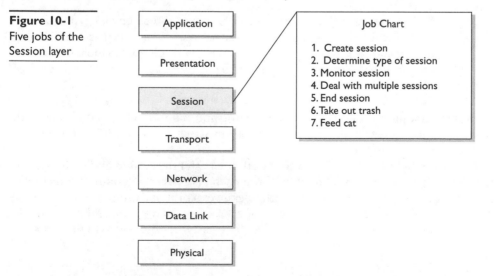

Figure 10-1
Five jobs of the
Session layer

Application

Presentation

Session

Transport

Network

Data Link

Physical

Job Chart

1. Create session
2. Determine type of session
3. Monitor session
4. Deal with multiple sessions
5. End session
6. Take out trash
7. Feed cat

Interestingly, an almost perfect analogy to the Session-layer functions is a family reunion. Don't laugh, this works! Imagine you're entering a pub, crowded full of family members you haven't seen in years, as well as their sundry significant others. To make this analogy work best, assume everyone is wearing those "Hi! My Name is ____" name tags. (It's been a few years or decades, after all, since you've been together!)

You enter the pub and begin to scan the room. Initially, your goal is to purchase a beverage. To secure a beverage, you need to create a conversation, a "session," with the bartender. You locate the bartender (she's wearing a name tag that says "bartender"). She's busy with another customer, so you wait, occasionally doing something (raising your hand or yelling "bartender!") to let her know you want to create a session. Eventually, the bartender finishes with a customer and notices you. She asks you what you need. You tell the bartender to pour a pint of Guinness for you. She says "Okay." Congratulations! You now have established a session!

Network session protocols work nearly the same way. Every network protocol uses some form of addressing function (the name tag) that goes beyond MAC addresses. This might be a number or it might be a word—but all network protocols will provide some form of addressing convention above and beyond MAC addresses.

What if you couldn't locate a bartender? In that case, perhaps you might yell out, "Where do I get a drink?" Assuming you didn't offend anyone, the bartender would yell back, "Right here! I'm the bartender!"

All network protocols realize that not every other computer will know the name of every other computer on the network. The network protocol must provide some method—we like to use the term *name resolution*—to enable one computer on the network to locate another to establish a session. All network protocols perform name resolution in one of two ways: *broadcasting*—the equivalent of yelling to the whole network, or by providing some form of *name server*—a computer whose job is to know the name of every other computer on the network. A name server would be analogous to an information booth in the corner of the pub. You could ask a person manning the booth to locate any other person in the room and he could point her out for you.

 NOTE Even though the Session-layer software of the network protocol needs the name of the other computer to create a session, that doesn't mean the Session-layer software performs the name resolution! In most network protocols, name resolution is handled by software at higher or lower levels of the OSI seven-layer model.

Most network protocols combine broadcasting and name serving in one way or another. The bottom line is that network protocols must give you a way to get the name of any other computer on the network.

Let's head back to the pub, shall we? In both the bartender's mind and yours, each of you realizes that a session is taking place. You each also assume certain actions to perform based on the type of session. The bartender gives a pint of Guinness to you. You ask the cost. The bartender tells you. You give money. You get change. You and the bartender know what to do for this type of session. If you had asked for directions to the restroom, you would still have a session, but both you and the bartender would assume a totally different set of actions.

All network protocols must not only establish a session, they must identify to the other system the type of session they want to initiate. All network protocols use some type of function-numbering system that identifies the type of session you want to perform. These numbers are embedded into the packet along with the name of the computer with which you want to create a session. Network protocols initiate a session by stating the name of the remote system, the name of the system making the request, and the function desired. It's as though you said to the bartender, "Hi, bartender, my name is Mike. Would you pour me a Guinness?"

It's important to appreciate that not all systems on a network perform every possible function. Imagine walking up to a huge, burly man sitting at a booth and saying, "Hello, Uncle Bruno. Could I have a Guinness?" In the human world (assuming he is the pleasant sort), he might say, "I'm sorry, I'm not a bartender." In the computer world, if you send a packet with a function number built into the packet for a type of data transfer the other computer doesn't know how to respond to, you usually just get silence (there are exceptions to this). A successful session requires both the name of the other computer and a function number that the other computer knows how to handle.

The bartender is capable of serving you a pint of Guinness. She looks at you and says, "Hi, Mike. I'll get you a Guinness!" and the session begins. In the networking world, the responding system must give you some form of function number in return. This function number may be the same in some network protocols, while in others, it may be a totally different number. Either way works perfectly well, as long as each system keeps track of the corresponding function numbers.

While waiting for your pint, you scan the room, only to discover a lady is looking right at you with a friendly smile on her face. A new session is taking place! You see her nametag says "Laura." Laura is initiating a session! You look back at her, smile, and casually stroll over for a chat. Seems that Laura is your long-lost cousin and you begin to converse. You two humans certainly don't need a function number here, but a network protocol would, of course. The session is successfully established—you and cousin Laura begin to catch up on family stories.

The interesting part (from a network protocol standpoint) is that you now have two sessions running—a session with cousin Laura and a session with the bartender (remember, you still haven't gotten your Guinness). In your mind, you must keep track of both sessions at the same time. This is also true of network protocols: the session software must keep track of multiple "open" sessions. Not only do you need to remember the session with the bartender, you must remember the current status of the active session—keeping up conversation with cousin Laura. At this point, you are simply waiting for your beer—there's nothing you need to do except listen for the bartender to tell you your beer is ready. The same is true in a network. Not all sessions need to be constantly active, just constantly monitored.

While speaking to Laura, you notice another person you want to speak to. Even though Laura and you are conversing, you turn to the other person and start to talk. In the human world, this would irritate cousin Laura no end (and probably result in a rather abrupt end to your session!), but in the networking world, there's no problem carrying on the same type of session with multiple computers at the same time. A good example is if you had two web browsers open at the same time, each going to a different web site (Figure 10-2). Even though the function numbers are the same for both sessions, the network session software lists them with different computer names and keeps each session separate from the other. So you can initiate a session with another person without fear of cousin Laura just walking away.

While speaking to this other person, you discover that he is poor cousin Martin and he starts asking for a loan. Given your "never loan money to family" policy, you politely break off the conversation with cousin Martin, each of you saying a pleasant goodbye. In the networking world, session software must recognize a session has ended and close that session. Sessions don't always end that cleanly, though, and so session software must also recognize when sessions end abruptly. Imagine if cousin Martin, miffed as you began to say you would not loan him money, simply walked away. You might stand there for a moment, perhaps call out to him, but eventually you would realize that the conversation was over and return to talking with cousin Laura. This is also true in the networking world. The session software waits for response, calls out to the other system to confirm the session has died—"Hey, wait!"—and then closes the session and removes it from memory.

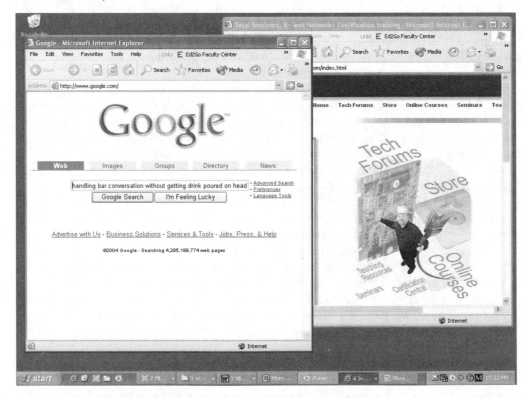

Figure 10-2 Two identical session types open

Returning your attention to cousin Laura, you notice her drink is almost empty. Without ending the current topic of conversation (Can you believe what happened to Uncle Bruno?), you ask her if you might buy her a drink. You now have two separate conversations running: one about Uncle Bruno and one about a drink. This is also a critical aspect of session software. The session software must enable two computers to run two totally separate sessions. In the networking world, this takes place constantly—for example, you might access two different shared folders on a single system. The session software tracks each session separately using the function numbers, even though the computer names are the same.

All the sessions discussed so far are *connection-oriented*: this means that both computers had to recognize by name and accept the function of the other computer before data could transfer. But now imagine that there's a pay telephone in the pub, and it rings. Niece Susan, quietly reading a book next to the telephone, picks up. It's that no-good Uncle Bruno's boss on the line. She tells poor Susan that Bruno had better get to the office quickly! Susan hangs up, and then yells to Bruno—without bothering to see if Bruno is listening, "Uncle Bruno, you better get to work! Your boss is angry!" Susan then returns to her book. Network protocols occasionally do the same thing. They send packets out without first creating a connection-oriented session. We call these *connectionless* sessions. Network protocols use connectionless sessions only for data that won't cause problems if it doesn't make it to the intended recipient; a great example of a connectionless session is the popular PING command. Like Susan in our example, who doesn't care much for Bruno and therefore doesn't care whether or not he hears her, a connectionless session might or might not get its point across.

TIP Make sure you understand the difference between connection-oriented and connectionless sessions.

Let's review the functions of the Session-layer software of every network protocol—I'll leave the end of the analogy to your imagination (have fun at the reunion!). The session software of a network protocol:

- Establishes sessions with another system
- Needs a name or number other than the MAC address to identify a destination system
- Needs a function number to determine what type of data transfer should take place
- Can support multiple sessions, both with multiple machines and multiple sessions on a single machine
- Must monitor open sessions and close completed sessions

The Session layer is easily the most complex, most visible part of the network protocol stack. Given this complexity, almost all operating systems give you tools to inspect sessions in one way or another. Even though Session-layer tools exist, most of these tools only enable you to inspect, not to make changes to your sessions. So where can you tweak the Session layer functions? Don't bother looking for a "Session Layer Configuration" program on your computer— no such program is on any operating system. Instead, think about what a session needs: a computer name (or number) and a function number—and those you can adjust! Every operating system has ways for you to name or number your computer and ways to define what functions your computer can ask for or accept. Where and how these settings take place, though, varies wildly by operating system and by the types of resources you want to share or access.

A Network Protocol's Transport-Layer Functions

Once the Session layer has done its magic and made the right kind of connection with a destination machine, the Transport-layer software steps in to handle the data. In Chapter 3, "Building a Network with OSI," you learned that the main job of the *Transport layer* is to chop up data into packet-sized chunks and add a sequence number before passing the packet down to the Network layer for further processing. On the receiving side, the Transport layer reassembles the packet passed up from the Network layer, inspecting the sequence numbers to verify proper data reassembly. See Figure 10-3.

Unlike the Session layer, no operating system has a way to open a hatch to show you the Transport layer at work. There is no utility program to run to show the assembly or disassembly of data into packets or packets into data. Perhaps this is a good thing: at least one part of every protocol stack works automatically without the need for us to make adjustment or changes.

Windows systems' Transport layer software, by default, will make packets using Ethernet's maximum frame data limitation of 1,500 bytes. This is called the Maximum Transmission Unit (MTU) and the value is stored in the Windows' Registry. Many systems, especially systems using ADSL or cable modems for Internet access, (See Chapter 16, "Remote Connectivity," for details on ADSL and cable modems) enjoy improved perfor-

Figure 10-3
The Transport layer at work

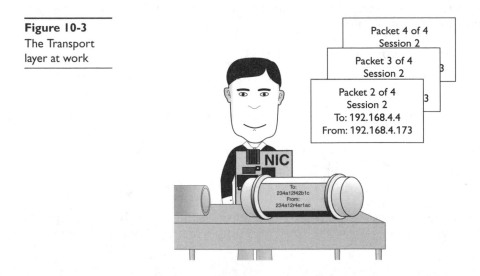

mance by adjusting the MTU size to a lower value. Check out the FAQ section of the wonderful web site—www.dslreports.com—to see if adjusting your MTU makes sense for your system. Included with this book's CD is a handy program called Dr. TCP that adjusts your MTU settings without forcing you to dig through your Registry. Try it!

A Network Protocol's Network-Layer Functions

Once the Transport layer has neatly divided and numbered the data into packets, the Network-layer software does its job. In Chapter 3, you saw how the *Network layer* of the OSI seven-layer model deals with the network protocol's capability to provide some form of universal addressing system enabling computers to communicate on any type of hardware technology. Actually, the network layer does more than just enable a system to communicate across platforms. By creating a universal numbering system, large networks can be broken down into smaller subnetworks (the hip term is *subnets*).

As networks get larger and larger, the simple number of machines trying to communicate on the same wire can create both performance problems for the network and difficulties for administration. The first resource for revving up a bogged-down network, as you'll recall from Chapter 4, is to replace the hubs with switches, but even that won't help enough if the network growth spirals out of control. By breaking a single big network into two or more *subnets*—groups of computers that are a subset of a larger network, defined most often numerically—administrators can reduce the overhead for all the machines. Thus, subnets provide a huge benefit for large networks, even large networks that share the same type of network technology.

Subnets are conceptually fairly easy to understand, although in real-world application, things get rather tricky. The secret lies in the universal numbing system. To break a network into subnets (through the process, conveniently called *subnetting*), the numbering system must work in such a way that specific groups of computers can be separated from the rest of the computers on the network. In the TCP/IP world, subnets of computers are identified by the part of their IP addresses that match each other. For example, a single subnet might be all the computers that share the first three octets of 192.168.4. So, computers 192.168.4.3 and 192.168.4.34 are on the same subnet. A computer with the IP address of 192.168.22.3 would not be part of the same subnet. See Figure 10-4.

You know from Chapter 3 that routers read incoming packets to determine which machine on the local network should receive the packet. Routers use the packet information to decide which port to route the packet. Chapter 3 used a single router connected to a cable modem, and then the Internet that enabled multiple PCs on the MHTechEd LAN to connect (remember Dana and Janelle?). A single router might have many connections. In fact, some routers have so many ports on them, they physically look like a switch. This makes for an interesting analogy. Switches decide where frames go based on their MAC addresses. Routers decide where frames go based on their subnet number. See Figure 10-5. This analogy is so strong that it's common to hear a router referred to as a *Layer 3 switch*.

The important point from the concept of a network protocol is to use routers, a network protocol must provide its own universal number convention. Not all network protocols do this! Only two protocols, IPX/SPX and TCP/IP, provide some form of universal

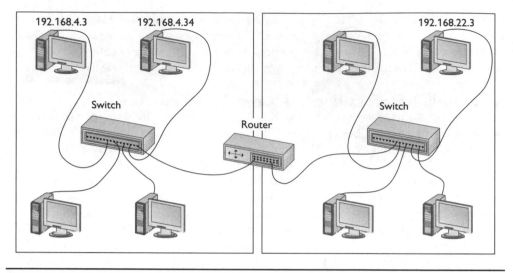

Figure 10-4   Two subnets

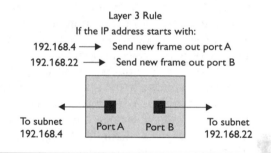

Figure 10-5   Layer 3 switch at work

numbering system. Some protocols, the most famous being NetBIOS/NetBEUI, have no universal numbering convention, making them unusable in networks that use routers.

Test Specific

Implementing Protocols

Now that you have a more detailed idea of what network protocols do for our networks, let's investigate some common issues shared by all network protocols. First, many networks use more than one protocol. Second, this creates a need to determine which protocols go with which NIC, a process called *binding*. Finally, you need to do the actual installation of network protocols.

Multiple Protocols

Most of the time, every system on the network will use the same protocol, but situations do exist where some systems are set up on purpose to run a different protocol from others. Figure 10-6 shows four networked systems. Systems *A* and *B* use the TCP/IP network protocol, while systems *C* and *D* use IPX/SPX. For any two systems to communicate on a network, they must use the same network protocol. Systems *A* and *B* can see each other, but not systems *C* and *D*; systems *C* and *D* can see each other, but not systems *A* and *B*. Why would anyone break their network like this on purpose? Well, they probably wouldn't—but it's important to understand that no computer can see another computer on the network unless they use the same protocols.

You may have more than one network protocol on the same system. Let's add another system, System *E*, to the previous diagram. System *E* has both the IPX/SPX and the TCP/IP network protocols installed. As a result, System *E* can see every system on the network! (See Figure 10-7.)

Hey! If System *E* sees both networks, can we fix System *E* so it acts as a kind of translator between the two sets of systems? Well, yes, you can—but hold onto that concept for just a moment as we discuss one more important concept: binding.

Binding

If a single system can have multiple NICs and multiple protocols, there needs to be a way to decide which NICs use which protocols for which transactions. The solution to this challenge is called *binding*. Every protocol installed on a system must be bound to one or more NICs, and every NIC must be bound to one or more specific protocols.

Figure 10-6

Systems *A* and *B* use TCP/IP, while systems *C* and *D* use IPX/SPX.

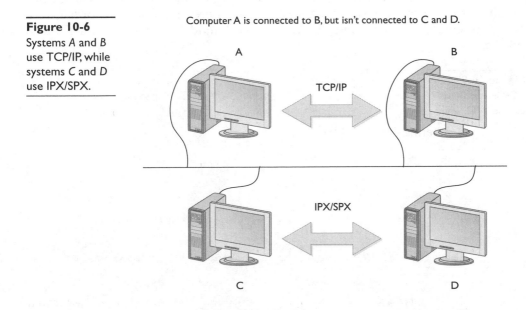

Computer A is connected to B, but isn't connected to C and D.

A   B

TCP/IP

IPX/SPX

C   D

Computer D is connected to C, but isn't connected to A and B.

PART II

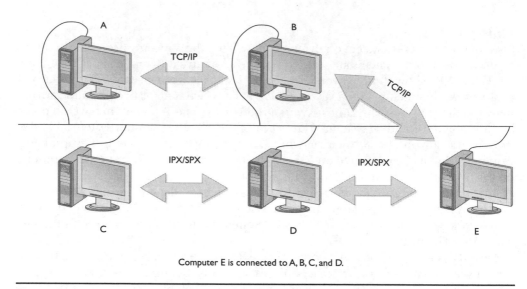

Computer E is connected to A, B, C, and D.

Figure 10-7 System *E* has both protocols installed and can thus see them all!

Look at Figure 10-7 and think about System *E* for a moment. You can correctly assume that both the IPX/SPX and TCP/IP protocols were bound to System *E*'s NIC. Now look at the situation shown in Figure 10-8. In this case, System *E* has two NICs —one connected to systems *A* and *B*, and the other connected to systems *C* and *D*. This situation calls for binding IPX/SPX to one NIC, and TCP/IP to the other. Fortunately, Windows makes this binding process extremely easy. We'll save the actual process of binding for later. For now, just remember, at least one protocol must be bound to each NIC in a networked system.

Figure 10-8
TCP/IP is bound
to one NIC, while
IPX/SPX is bound
to the other.

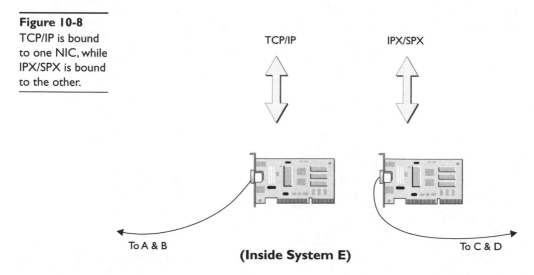

TIP At least one network protocol must be bound to each NIC in a networked system.

Before adding a new system to a network, you should check one of the existing systems to determine which network protocol the network uses. Almost all modern networks use TCP/IP, but older network operating systems tend to use other protocols. Older versions of Novell NetWare, for example, may use IPX/SPX, while a network containing only Windows 9*x* systems may use the NetBIOS/NetBEUI protocol.

Installation

Every computer on your network requires a network protocol and every network protocol needs installation. Despite the impression given to us by many operating systems, not every part of every network protocol's software is built into the operating system. Right now, TCP/IP is so predominant that every operating system preinstalls TCP/IP (assuming the operating system detects a NIC!), giving the impression that TCP/IP is somehow one and the same as the operating system. Preinstalling TCP/IP into your system is a pleasant convenience, but if you want to use another network protocol, you're probably going to have to do some installing and some configuring. Most versions of Microsoft Windows support all the common network protocols; depending on the version of Windows you use, you may or may not need to install a protocol. Regardless of the protocol you want to install, it's important to know where to go to do this on your Windows computers. In all Windows 9*x* systems, alternate-click (right-click) Network Neighborhood and select Properties to open the Network Properties dialog box. You may also click the Network Control Panel applet to get to this dialog box (Figure 10-9).

Look closely at Figure 10-9 and the line that starts with TCP/IP. Do you see the small arrow that points to the name of the NIC (AMD PCNET Family...)? That arrow shows TCP/IP is bound to that NIC.

NOTE Windows Me works the same way as Windows 9*x*, but Microsoft changed the name of Network Neighborhood to My Network Places.

Windows 2000, Server 2003, and XP have a different way to get to your protocols. Instead of a list showing all your networked devices and all your protocols, 2000 and XP separate each network connection into its own configuration dialog box. Alternate-click My Network Places and select Properties to open the Network Connections window (Figure 10-10). This window shows all the network devices on a system. Many computers have multiple network devices. Figure 10-11 shows a laptop system with lots of network connections!

To get to the protocols, alternate-click the connection you want to change and select Properties to get to that connection's Properties dialog box (Figure 10-12).

Figure 10-9
Windows 98
Network
Properties

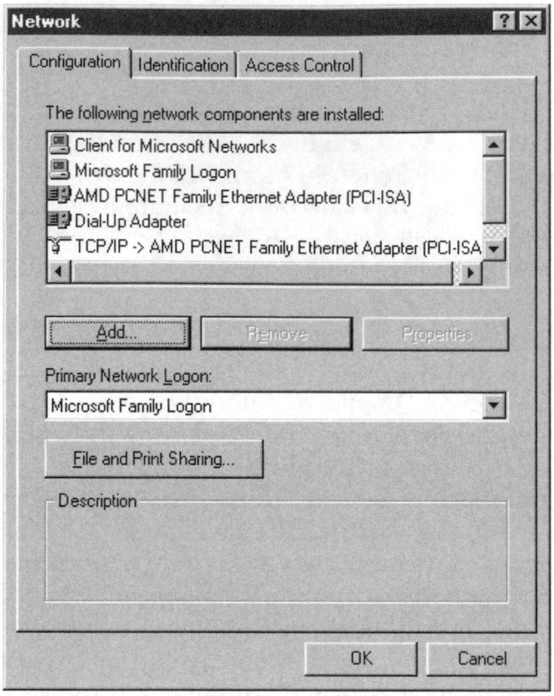

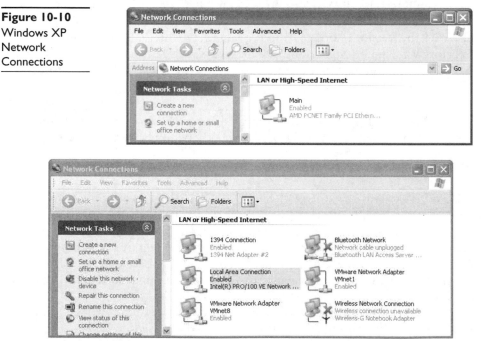

Figure 10-10
Windows XP
Network
Connections

Figure 10-11   Lots of network connections!

Along with installation comes configuration. As we dive into the different network protocols, you'll soon discover that with the exception of TCP/IP, network protocols re-

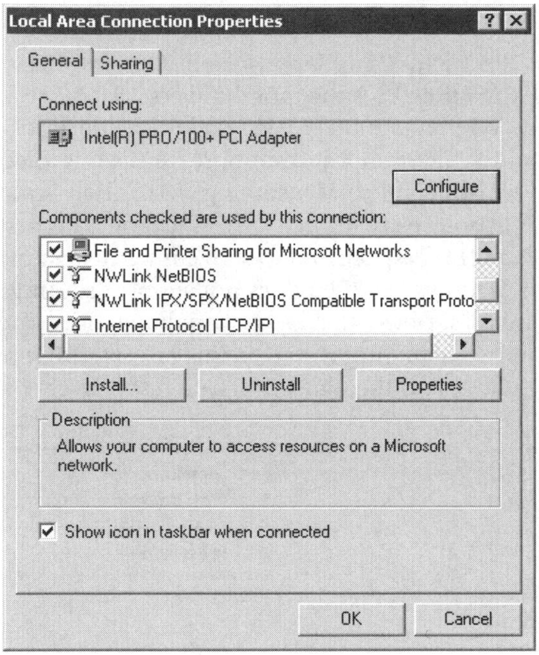

Figure 10-12
NIC Properties
box in Windows
2000

quire surprisingly little configuration. Almost anything you want to do to a network protocol in terms of configuration takes place under the Network Properties.

Protocol Concepts

In this section, you've learned about a number of important protocols concepts. Using the OSI seven-layer networking model as your guide, you now have a pretty strong understanding of exactly what the network protocol software's doing on your systems. Now it's time to stop talking concept and dive into the three most common protocol suites: NetBIOS/NetBEUI, IPX/SPX, and TCP/IP.

NetBIOS/NetBEUI

NetBIOS/NetBEUI provides a fast, simple set of network protocols appropriate for use in smaller LANs. NetBIOS/NetBEUI was the primary network protocol stack used in Windows 9x and NT systems. Today, NetBIOS/NetBEUI primarily exists to support Microsoft networking using Windows NT or Windows 9x systems.

NOTE NetBIOS stands for Network Basic Input/Output System; NetBEUI is short for NetBIOS Extended User Interface.

Windows 2000 and XP still support NetBIOS/NetBEUI, but Microsoft is moving away from NetBIOS/NetBEUI for the more universal TCP/IP. This moving away is best illustrated by how Windows 2000 and Windows XP support NetBIOS/NetBEUI. Both Windows 2000 and Windows XP still support NetBIOS. However, Windows 2000 does not install NetBEUI by default, and installing NetBEUI in Windows XP requires locating the NetBEUI protocol software from a special location on the XP installation CD.

NetBIOS/NetBEUI's speed and ease of configuration make it a good choice for small networks, but because NetBEUI does not support routing, it is totally unacceptable for any but the smallest (fewer than 30 systems) networks. The NetBIOS/NetBEUI protocol stack contains two main protocols—in this case, NetBIOS and NetBEUI—which operate at the Session layer and the transport layer, respectively (see Figure 10-13).

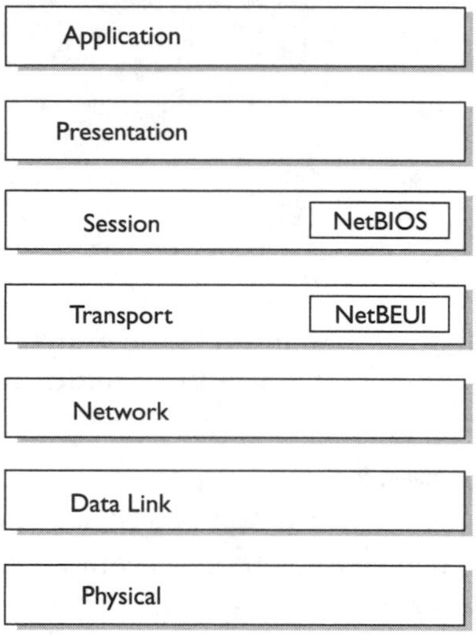

Figure 10-13
NetBIOS operates at the Session layer, while NetBEUI operates at the Transport layer.

Application

Presentation

Session	NetBIOS

Transport	NetBEUI

Network

Data Link

Physical

One big benefit of NetBEUI, and a reason this protocol remains popular, is this: for simple networks, NetBIOS/NetBEUI requires no configuration—it just works. You'll appreciate this more when you see how much configuration TCP/IP takes! Let's start with a little history, and then look at the two parts of NetBIOS/NetBEUI—first NetBIOS, and then NetBEUI—to see how it all works

In the Early Days

Starting with DOS and continuing to the latest Windows operating systems, Microsoft has enjoyed tremendous success in the PC world. One of the many reasons for

Microsoft's success stems from its concentration on the customer's needs. Microsoft has always tried hard to make computing as easy for the user as possible. This attitude certainly came into play as Microsoft was choosing how to make network protocols for PC networks. By the mid-1980s, TCP/IP was well established as a network protocol for the Internet, but back then, the Internet wasn't anything like it is today. Microsoft—like everyone other than the geekiest of geeks—saw no reason to use the free, but complex and difficult to configure, TCP/IP. Instead, they chose to design a much simpler protocol: NetBIOS/NetBEUI. The simplicity of NetBIOS/NetBEUI comes, in part, because it's designed to share only folders and printers—why would anyone want to share anything else?

When Windows rolled around, Microsoft made a corporate decision that still haunts us today. Microsoft decided to build NetBIOS into the core of the Windows operating system. When you installed Windows, you were prompted to give the computer a name. That name was the NetBIOS name. The problem was that no one (again, except for the geekiest of geeks) appreciated that this was taking place. Finding the word NetBIOS anywhere on the computer was hard, and as a result, people never tied in the fact that the name of the computer was the NetBIOS name—it was just the "name of the computer." While this tight integration made life easy for those who used the first generations of Windows networks, it put Microsoft in a bad place. By tying NetBIOS into the operating system so tightly, it made things challenging years later when people wanted to use other network protocols—like TCP/IP or IPX/SPX that used completely separate and incompatible naming conventions—on their Windows computers. While we'll delve into this naming fiasco in detail in the next two chapters, keep in mind that on the first generations of Windows: NT, 95, 98, and Me, you had no way to turn on or turn off NetBIOS—it was just there!

TIP   Over the years, separating NetBIOS from NetBEUI has become popular. This is because of a number of factors. First, Microsoft has always hidden NetBIOS from users. Second, Microsoft shows NetBEUI as a separate installable protocol. Third, NetBIOS most commonly now runs with TCP/IP. Despite the march of time, the fact remains that NetBIOS and NetBEUI were originally designed to work together as NetBIOS/NetBEUI.

NetBIOS at Session

Microsoft's NetBIOS handles the Session-layer functions for NetBIOS/NetBEUI networks. NetBIOS manages sessions based on the names of the computers involved. A NetBIOS name is based on a system's network name, which you can designate using the Network applet in the Control Panel. Figure 10-14 shows an example of the network name of a Windows 98 system, displayed by the Network applet.

NetBIOS names are made up of a system's network name, as specified in the Network applet, followed by a function-specific suffix. The system's network name can contain up to 15 characters. Each character is represented by a single 8-bit (one byte) ASCII code. For example, the 8-bit ASCII code 01100101 (65h in hexadecimal format), represents the capital letter A. NetBIOS limits the network name to 15 bytes, or characters, because it

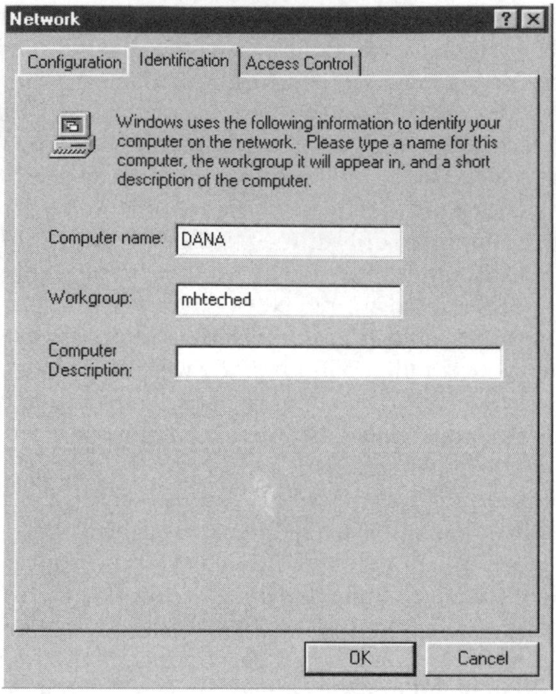

Figure 10-14
The Windows 98 Network Control Panel applet displays the computer's name.

Network	? X

Configuration | Identification | Access Control

Windows uses the following information to identify your computer on the network. Please type a name for this computer, the workgroup it will appear in, and a short description of the computer.

Computer name: DANA

Workgroup: mhteched

Computer Description:

OK | Cancel

reserves the 16th byte for the special number function code that defines the role the machine will play on the network in that particular session. A NetBIOS machine can take on several roles, depending on the needs of the session.

TIP Windows 2000 and XP use TCP/IP's *Domain Name Service (DNS)* to give individual computers more descriptive names than just an IP address. DNS names are much less restrictive than NetBIOS names, and this can cause some confusion with Windows. When you install a Windows XP system and give the new computer a name longer than 15 bytes or one that uses special characters, you'll get a warning screen that tells you the name is invalid or has been shortened. That's because NetBIOS systems cannot see any system that uses a name that does not fit into the NetBIOS naming convention.

Table 10-1 lists the common 16th byte codes used by NetBIOS to define the server and client functions of a machine.

Don't worry about memorizing all the functions and 16th byte codes listed in the table. Instead, let's look at an example using the three most commonly used extensions to understand how NetBIOS manages a session.

Hannah, a friendly neighborhood network tech, installs three Windows systems—named MHTECHED, JANELLE, and DANA—on her network. Hannah does not need to specify these NetBIOS names. NetBIOS, operating in the background, determines the

Table 10-1	16th byte	Function
NetBIOS Names and Functions	<00>	Workstation Service Name. The name registered by clients on the network.
	<03>	Messenger Service Name. Used by applications such as WINPOPUP and NET SEND to deliver messages.
	<1B>	Domain Master Browser
	<06>	RAS Server
	<1F>	NetDDE Service
	<20>	File and Printer Server
	<21>	RAS Client
	<BE>	Network Monitor Agent
	<BF>	Network Monitor Utility

NetBIOS names automatically based on the computer names (MHTECHED, JANELLE, and DANA) that Hannah selected for these systems. Even though these names are determined at installation, you can easily change them. In Windows 98, get to the Network Properties applet and click the Identification tab (refer to Figure 10-14).

You can also specify the *workgroup* name here. NetBIOS contains the capability to group computers together into workgroups. Workgroups are nothing more than a convenient way to organize computers under Network Neighborhood/My Network Places (Figure 10-15). They do not provide any form of security. More advanced versions of Windows provide a much more powerful grouping called a domain—we'll save the details of Windows workgroups and domains for the next chapter.

NetBIOS also supports an optional descriptive computer name. These descriptive names do as they are named, providing a handy method to describe the machine in more detail than the NetBIOS name provides.

By default, all Windows computers act as clients. Any Windows computer can also act as a server, but must first be configured. Hannah configures the MHTECHED and JANELLE systems to act as servers, leaving the DANA system as only a client. According to what you've just learned, MHTECHED now has at least two names: MHTECHED<00>,

Figure 10-15
Typical
Workgroups

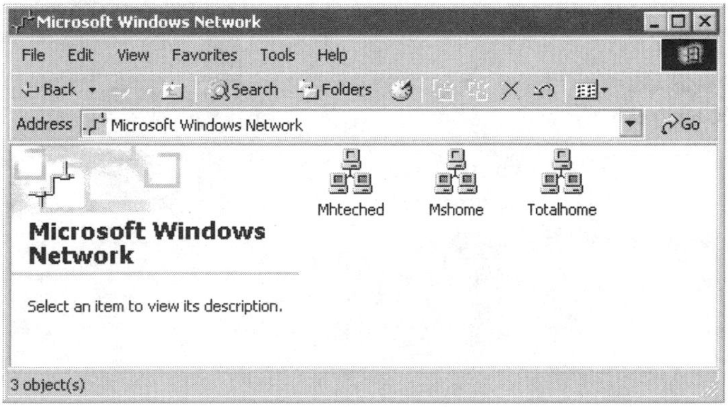

identifying MHTECHED as a client, and MHTECHED<20>, identifying MHTECHED as a file and print server. JANELLE also has two names: JANELLE<00>, identifying JANELLE as a client, and JANELLE <20>, identifying JANELLE as a file and print server. DANA, by contrast, registers only one name, as a client: DANA<00>.

> **NOTE** Any real machine using NetBIOS on a Microsoft Network will register several more names, to support other, less obvious functions. Those additional names have been left out of this discussion for the sake of simplicity.

When Hannah sits at JANELLE and accesses a file on MHTECHED, both JANELLE and MHTECHED must manage that connection. To open the connection, JANELLE the client, aka JANELLE<00>, opens a connection with MHTECHED the server, aka MHTECHED<20> (see Figure 10-16). As MHTECHED begins to send the requested file to JANELLE, another user, Barbara, sits down at DANA and opens another file on MHTECHED (see Figure 10-17). Each of the computers keeps track of these simultaneous conversations using their NetBIOS names (see Figure 10-18).

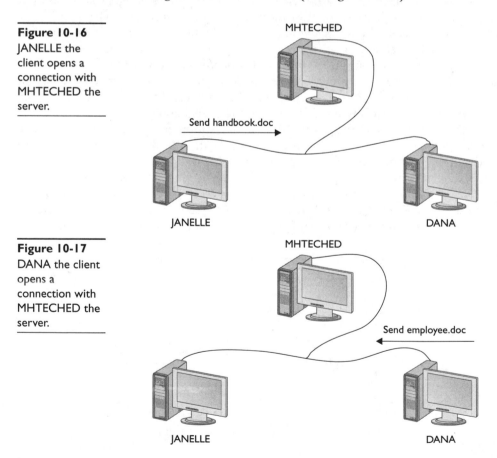

Figure 10-16
JANELLE the client opens a connection with MHTECHED the server.

Figure 10-17
DANA the client opens a connection with MHTECHED the server.

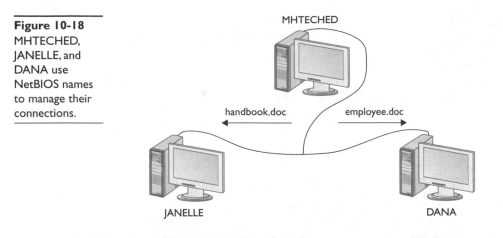

Figure 10-18
MHTECHED,
JANELLE, and
DANA use
NetBIOS names
to manage their
connections.

MHTECHED

handbook.doc

employee.doc

JANELLE

DANA

By using a different NetBIOS name for each function, networked systems can keep track of multiple connections among them simultaneously. For example, let's say Barbara sits at MHTECHED and opens a file on JANELLE, causing MHTECHED<00> to establish a connection with JANELLE<20>. At the same time, Hannah can sit at JANELLE and open a file on MHTECHED, causing JANELLE<00> to establish a connection with MHTECHED<20>. The capability to use unique NetBIOS names for each server (<20> suffix) and client (<00> suffix) function enables MHTECHED and JANELLE to hold two (or more) simultaneous conversations (see Figure 10-19).

Without a NetBIOS name for a particular function, a system cannot perform that function when requested by another node on the network. For example, if Hannah sits at JANELLE and attempts to open a file on DANA, JANELLE will be unable to establish the connection. Why? Because DANA is not configured to function as a server. The request from JANELLE for a connection to DANA is addressed to DANA<20>. But the NetBIOS name DANA<20> does not exist; DANA can respond only to the client NetBIOS name DANA<00> (see Figure 10-20). When it sees the message for DANA<20>, DANA just assumes it's for some other system and ignores it; DANA doesn't even send a refusal message back to JANELLE.

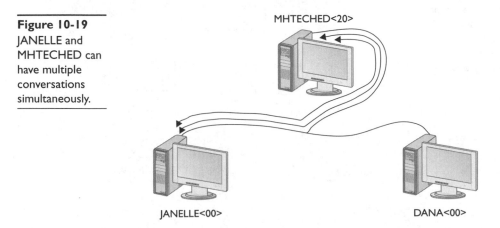

Figure 10-19
JANELLE and
MHTECHED can
have multiple
conversations
simultaneously.

MHTECHED<20>

JANELLE<00>

DANA<00>

Figure 10-20
DANA ignores
JANELLE because
DANA<20> is
not one of its
NetBIOS names.

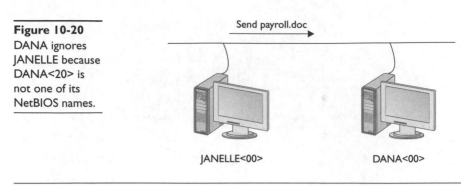

Send payroll.doc

JANELLE<00>   DANA<00>

NOTE Even though Windows 2000 and XP no longer use the NetBIOS
naming convention, all of the NetBIOS processes you've just learned—known
as Server Message Blocks (SMBs)—are still very much a part of these newer
operating systems. The way computers are named have changed, but
everything else still works the same!

NetBEUI at Transport

NetBEUI functions at the Transport layer within the NetBEUI protocol suite, breaking
larger chunks of data into smaller pieces on the sending machine, and reassembling
them on the receiving end (see Figure 10-21). The NetBEUI protocol requires no setup
beyond installation by the network tech. While its operational simplicity makes NetBEUI
attractive for smaller networks, it deprives NetBEUI of a capability vital to larger networks: routing.

The NetBEUI protocol skips the Network layer and communicates directly with the
data-link layer. When a router receives a NetBEUI packet, it doesn't find the routing information it needs, so it simply discards the packet (Figure 10-22).

Figure 10-21
NetBEUI breaks
the file into
smaller pieces for
transmission and
reassembles the
pieces on the
receiving end.

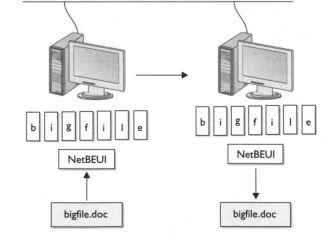

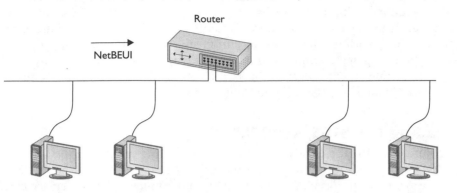

The Router discards the packet when there is no Network layer information in it.

Router

NetBEUI

Figure 10-22   Routers discard NetBEUI packets.

NOTE   The NetBEUI protocol suite's lack of any Network layer protocol illustrates the key weakness of the OSI model: not every network protocol follows the OSI completely.

NetBIOS/NetBEUI Naming Weaknesses

While NetBIOS provides an adequate means for managing connections on a small network, it does not scale well for larger networks. NetBIOS uses what is called a *flat name space*, meaning that the names for every machine in a network are drawn from one pool. Thus, the base NetBIOS name for each computer must be unique. Imagine a world where people only had first names. To prevent confusing any two people, no two people could have the name Mike, or Bob, or Johnny. Instead, people would have to come up with unique names like Johnny5, Fonzie, and Bluto. Finding unique names for a dozen people presents no problem. Placing a few thousand people in the same flat name space creates a big problem. In real life, most people have at least two, and sometimes as many as four or more names, and even then we often need other information, like addresses and identifying numbers, to tell people apart.

Network administrators working in a first-name-only NetBIOS world are often driven to give their systems bizarre, nondescriptive names, creating many administrative headaches. NetBIOS names are so restricted, it's hard to be usefully descriptive. On a network with only one server, simply calling that machine SERVER works fine. But let's take a more realistic example. Simon's network has 20 servers: ten accounting servers, five web servers, four file servers, and an e-mail server. Simon usually refers to one of his servers as "'Accounting Server 7"' in conversation, but he can't use that as the NetBIOS name for the machine. Remember, NetBIOS names must contain 15 or fewer characters (not counting the special 16th character that designates the machine's function). Instead of Accounting Server 7, Simon must name the server ACCOUNTSERV7. Not bad, but not optimal, and Simon's network is a relatively modest one by commercial standards.

The problem of ensuring name uniqueness is much more extreme in large WAN environments run by multiple administrators. In a large WAN run by 40 different administrators, guaranteeing that no two administrators ever assign the same name to any two of their 5000+ machines becomes an administrative nightmare, requiring extensive planning and ongoing communication. This is why network architects prefer a more scaleable naming scheme, such as the TCP/IP protocol suite's Domain Name Service (DNS—see Chapter 11, "TCP/IP"), for larger networks.

Installing NetBIOS/NetBEUI

The nature of NetBIOS's close connection in a Windows system compels us to install NetBIOS separately from NetBEUI. If you're using Windows NT or 9x, NetBIOS is automatically, permanently installed. Windows 2000 and Windows XP have replaced NetBIOS with TCP/IP's DNS (see Chapter 11). However, they respect the fact that you may want to connect to older computers that use NetBIOS and also install NetBIOS, but enable you to turn it off if you want to do so. Installing NetBIOS on a Windows computer is moot—you get NetBIOS. There is a way to remove NetBIOS, but it will also remove networking from your Windows machine!

NetBEUI is another issue entirely. Realizing long ago that NetBIOS might not run with NetBEUI, Microsoft treats NetBEUI as a standalone network protocol that must be installed via the Network Control Panel applet described earlier. Let's go through two installations of NetBEUI, once with Windows 98 and again with Windows 2000.

Windows 9x

To add the NetBEUI protocol to a Windows 9x system, click Add on the Configuration tab of the Network applet (see Figure 10-23). A Select Network Component Type screen appears. Select Protocol and click Add (see Figure 10-24). A Select Network Protocol screen appears. Select Microsoft as the Manufacturer and NetBEUI as the Network Protocol (see Figure 10-25).

NOTE The tradition in the industry of referring to entire protocol suites by the name of one or two of their constituent protocols has caused unnecessary confusion, pain, suffering, and gnashing of teeth. Read carefully whenever you see the word *protocol*—sometimes a writer means a specific protocol, but sometimes he or she means a protocol suite.

While you're still in the Network applet, head back to the Configuration tab and see if you can locate the Client for Microsoft Networks, and File and Print Sharing for Microsoft Networks (see Figure 10-26). Client for Microsoft Networks is NetBIOS, plus a few extra tools to make Windows networking function. Windows 98 calls its server component File and Printer Sharing for Microsoft Networks. To configure DANA as a client only, Hannah installs NetBIOS and the Client for Microsoft Networks. Hannah has created a three-node network, and she and her coworkers can sit down to do some serious gaming, errr . . . oops! I mean *work*.

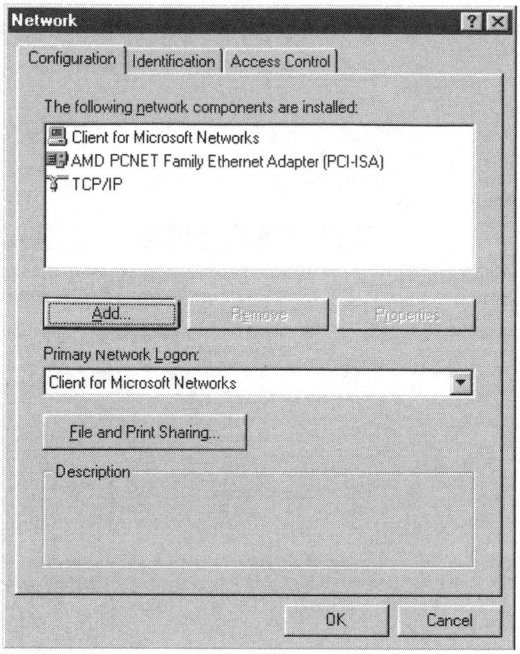

Figure 10-23

The Configuration tab of Windows 98's Network applet

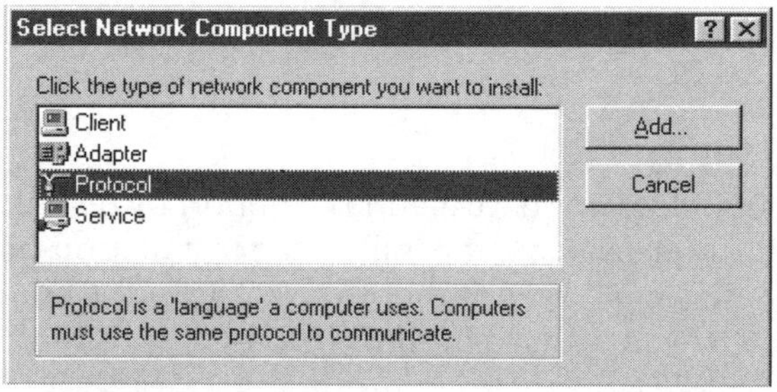

Figure 10-24

Selecting Protocol

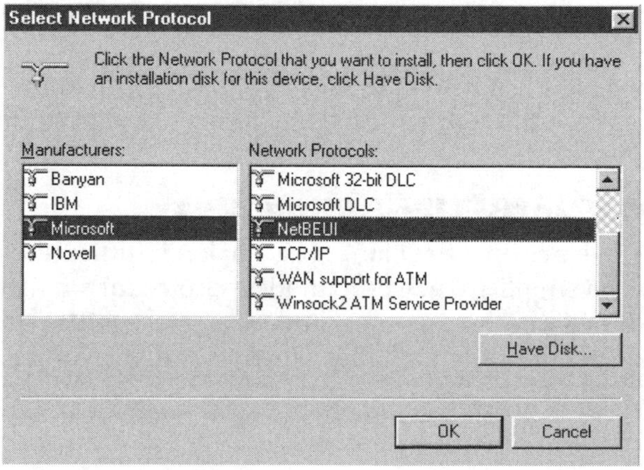

Figure 10-25

Selecting Microsoft, NetBEUI

PART II

Figure 10-26
Installing File and
Printer Sharing
for Microsoft
Networks

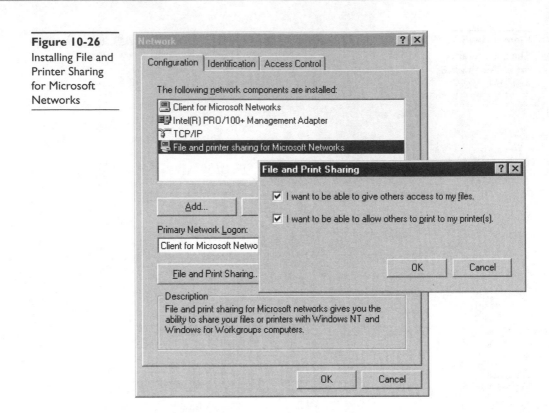

Windows 2000

Windows 2000 does not have NetBEUI support by default. Fortunately, installation is not difficult; in many ways, it parallels the installation process done in Windows 98. The big difference between Windows 2000 (and XP) and Windows 98 is you must choose the NIC you want to bind the protocol to, and then select properties for that NIC (Figure 10-27).

From this point, the process is pretty much identical to Windows 98. Click the Install button, select Protocol, and then select NetBEUI. You'll then see the NetBEUI protocol installed (Figure 10-28).

Installing NetBEUI in Windows is easy to do if you know where to go. In fact, this is the process to go through to install any protocol on a Windows system.

NetBIOS/NetBEUI—Fading Away

NetBIOS's reliance on a flat name space makes it difficult to use in large WAN environments, but its simplicity makes it an ideal choice for smaller LANs. As long as the network tech assigns every computer a unique name, NetBIOS does a fine job. Even though NetBIOS does a fine job on smaller networks and Microsoft has done some bits of magic

Figure 10-27
Selecting a NIC's
properties

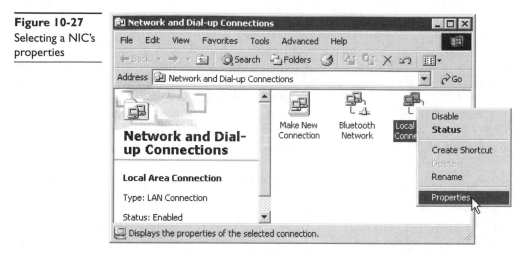

to make NetBIOS work on larger networks, NetBIOS is fading away, replaced by the more universal DNS. Equally, NetBEUI does a fine job at the Transport layer, but its lack of any Network layer functions make it unsuitable for larger networks.

Figure 10-28
NetBEUI installed
on Windows
2000

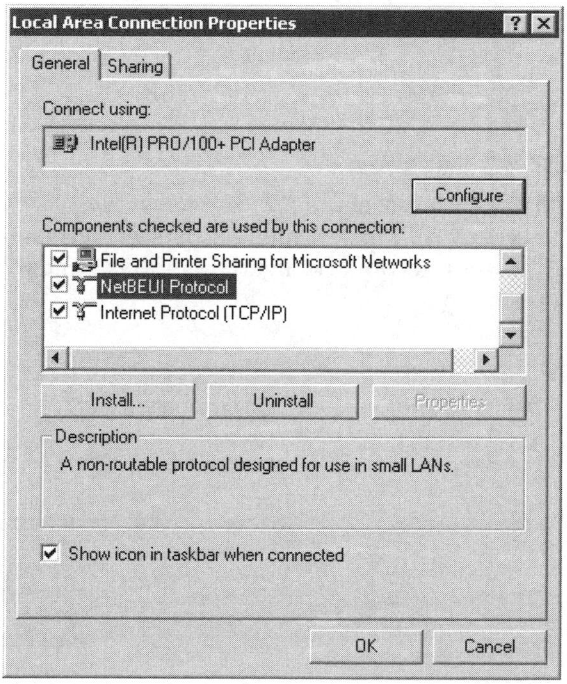

IPX/SPX

Novell's *IPX/SPX* protocol suite, used primarily by Novell NetWare-based networks, provides a more scaleable solution for networks compared to NetBIOS/NetBEUI. While the NetBIOS/NetBEUI protocol suite provides services at the Transport and Session layers, IPX/SPX includes a wide variety of protocols operating at OSI layers three through seven (the Network layer through the Application layer). Although more scaleable than NetBEUI, IPX/SPX bogs down in large networks due to excessive traffic. The latest versions of Novell NetWare still support IPX/SPX, but they default to TCP/IP.

 TIP Make sure you know that IPX/SPX is mainly for Novell NetWare!

In a Novell NetWare network, IPX/SPX operates at layers 3 through 7 of the OSI model. Figure 10-29 shows how various IPX/SPX protocols relate to the OSI layers. The *NetWare Core Protocol (NCP)* handles a variety of Presentation and Application layer issues, the *Server Advertising Protocol (SAP)* handles the Session layer. SPX works at the Transport layer and IPX handles all the network functions.

 NOTE The Network+ exam does not require knowledge of the individual protocols that make up the IPX/SPX suite.

NCP/SAP at Session

The most important aspect about IPX/SPX is that Novell invented this protocol to work in a client/server environment. Remember, Novell NetWare is not a client operating system, so most of your network configuration job is done to your NetWare servers. After

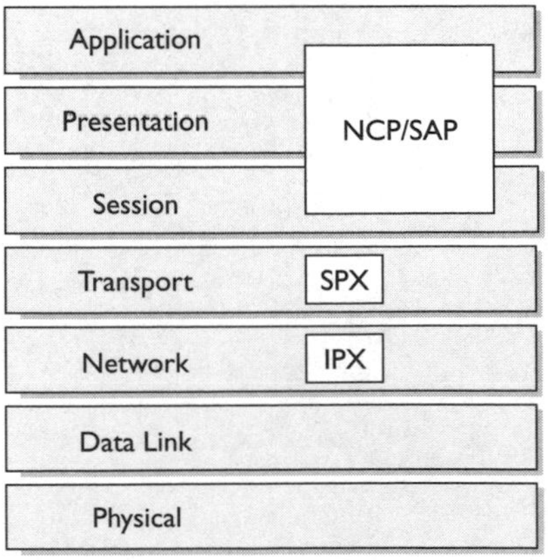

Figure 10-29
IPX/SPX includes protocols operating at OSI layers 3 through 7.

Application	
Presentation	NCP/SAP
Session	
Transport	SPX
Network	IPX
Data Link	
Physical	

you set up your servers, you then configure your clients to whatever settings you made. This is interesting because it makes networking a bit simpler as, like NetBIOS/NetBEUI, you have a limited number of functions to configure, and those functions are all centered on file and print sharing.

NetWare servers have NetBIOS-like names but that is only for ease of use. In reality, all NetWare servers have a unique, eight hexadecimal character, *internal network number* that identifies that one server. A server's internal network number, for example, might be 87654321. In a typical NetWare network, servers advertise their presence to all clients (and to other servers) by broadcasting their internal network numbers every 60 seconds. Clients keep a list of the known servers and use this information to contact the servers as needed.

NCP supports all the applications used in a NetWare IPX/SPX network. When a client makes a request to a service, the server's NCP functions handle the session, presentation, and application functions on its side to enable a data transfer.

IPX/SPX at Transport and Network

If you check the official NetWare documentation, you'll see that SPX works at the Transport layers, while IPX works at the network layer. However, these two protocols are closely intertwined and are best discussed together. NetWare running IPX/SPX creates subnets by adding a special *external network number* (often referred to as "network number" causing confusion with the earlier mentioned internal network number, or as "segment address") to the MAC address of every computer on the network. Internal network addresses define servers, while external network numbers define every computer on the network—a subtle, but important, difference (see Figure 10-30).

Figure 10-30
IPX/SPX naming
conventions

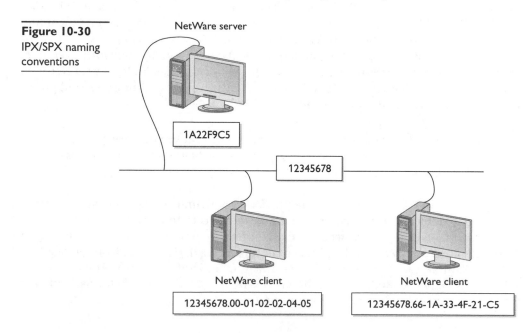

When you install NetWare client software on your Windows computer, you must enter the name of a preferred server. Each client's preferred NetWare server assigns this network number to the client computers. IPX/SPX network numbers are eight hexadecimal digits. So, a single subnet would be the entire set of computers that share the network number of 12345678. Computer 12345678.00-01-02-02-04-05 and Computer 12345678.66-1A-33-4F-21-C5 are on the same subnet.

IPX/SPX, although routable, does not scale well for large WANs. Novell designed IPX/SPX to support its NetWare operating system, which treats NetWare servers as the ultimate focus of the network. In a NetWare environment, servers are servers and clients are clients, and never the twain shall meet. Unlike NetBEUI, which assumes that a machine can function as both a client and a server, IPX/SPX assumes that a proper network consists of a few servers and a large number of clients. While this configuration works well on small- and medium-sized networks, when a network grows to include hundreds of servers and thousands of clients, the increase in SAP traffic will take down the network. Until relatively recently, the danger of excessive SAP broadcasts did not impact the typical network tech, because most networks simply did not have enough servers for SAP broadcasts to cause congestion. But, as large networks become more common, IPX/SPX's reliance on SAP broadcasts becomes more of a problem. This has led most WAN designers to adopt a more scaleable alternative: TCP/IP.

Installing IPX/SPX

Installing IPX/SPX usually means installing either the Microsoft or the Novell clients for NetWare. Microsoft takes advantage of the widespread industry support of IPX/SPX with its own version of the protocol suite, referred to as either IPX/SPX-compatible Protocol (Windows 9*x*) or NWLink IPX/SPX/NetBIOS Compatible Transport Protocol (Windows 2000/XP/2003) (see Figure 10-31). Microsoft network operating systems, including Windows 9*x*, Windows 2000, and Windows NT, use IPX/SPX for two purposes: to connect to NetWare servers (usually), and to provide the transport and network layer functionality for Microsoft Networking (rarely). In the latter case, Windows uses NetBIOS over IPX/SPX. Windows 2000/XP/2003 manifest this clearly by adding a second protocol called *NWLink* NetBIOS when you install IPX/SPX.

 TIP Rarely do techs manually install IPX/SPX in Windows systems. In most cases, they install either the Microsoft or the NetWare client and these clients, in turn, install IPX/SPX.

Unlike NetBIOS/NetBEUI, which requires no configuration beyond assigning each computer a name, IPX/SPX requires that a network tech potentially make configurations. The first area that may need configuration is the frame type. IPX packets vary in their format according to the data-link layer protocol used. IPX running on top of Ethernet, for example, can use one of four data structures, called frame types: Ethernet 802.3, Ethernet II, Ethernet 802.2, and Ethernet SNAP. If two network nodes use different frame types, they will be unable to communicate.

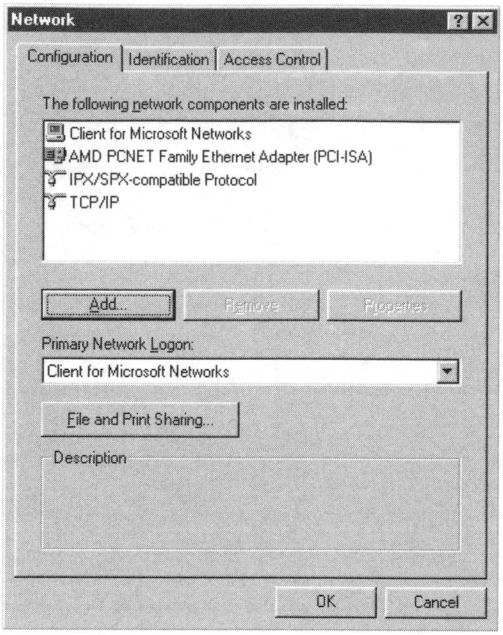

Figure 10-31

Microsoft calls its version of the IPX/SPX protocol suite either IPX/ SPX-compatible Protocol or NWLink IPX/ SPX/NetBIOS Compatible Transport Protocol.

[Network dialog box]

Network [? X]

Configuration | Identification | Access Control |

The following network components are installed:

- Client for Microsoft Networks
- AMD PCNET Family Ethernet Adapter (PCI-ISA)
- IPX/SPX-compatible Protocol
- TCP/IP

[Add...] [Remove] [Properties]

Primary Network Logon:

| Client for Microsoft Networks | ▼ |

[File and Print Sharing...]

Description

[OK] [Cancel]

NOTE Determining Ethernet frame types is not unique to IPX/SPX. All protocols need to identify the type of Ethernet frame used on the network. It's just that NetBIOS/NetBEUI and TCP/IP protocols determine the frame type automatically, while IPX/SPX traditionally does not.

In the days of DOS-based network clients, network techs set the frame type manually for each system on the network. All versions of Windows simplify the process by automatically detecting Ethernet traffic on the network and configuring themselves to use the first frame type they detect (see Figure 10-32). Because modern Windows systems automatically use whatever frame type they detect first, however, systems on networks using multiple types can end up trying to communicate using mismatched frame types. This is a rare situation, but one that is most probable to manifest itself in NetWare networks.

To ensure that every system on a network uses the same frame type, a system admin can set each system's frame type manually using the Network (Connections) applet (see Figure 10-33). The structural details of the different frame types do not affect the network tech—simply configure all systems to use the same frame type.

On some NetWare networks, you may need to enter the internal and external network numbers. This is usually done in the same dialog box as the frame type. Figure 10-34 shows the NWLink Windows XP dialog box setting the network numbers.

Splitting Protocols I: NetBIOS over IPX/SPX

Network protocol stacks aren't designed to work with anything but their own family of protocols. When Novell made IPX/SPX, for example, the company wasn't interested in it

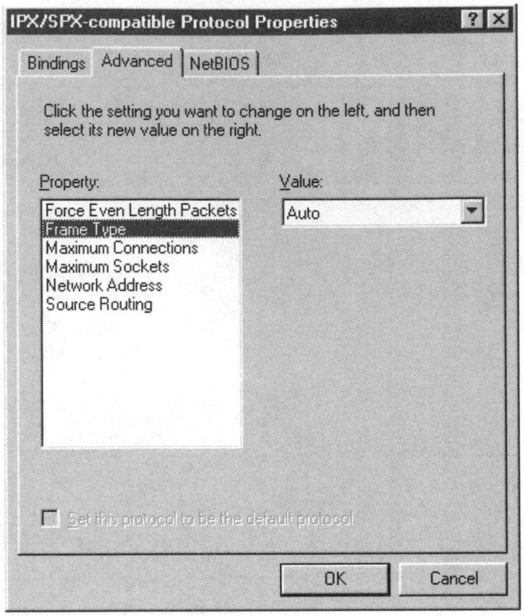

Figure 10-32
Modern
Windows
systems can
autodetect
the frame type
being used.

working with other network protocols. The folks who made TCP/IP assumed that you
would never use anything but TCP/IP, and Microsoft thought the same thing when they
adopted and developed NetBIOS/NetBEUI. But, over the years, situations developed to
change this attitude.

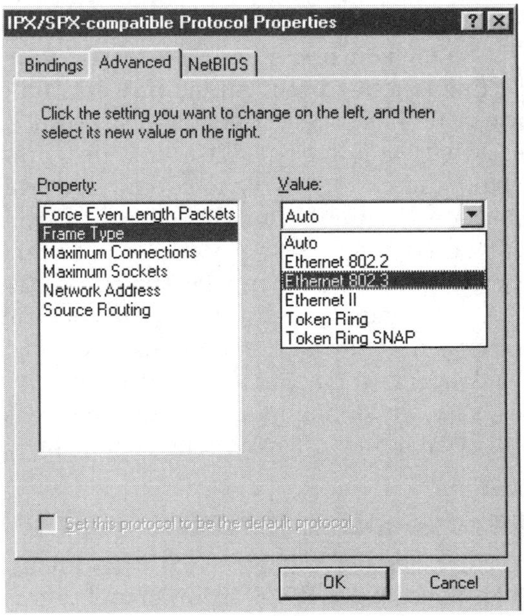

Figure 10-33
Setting the frame
type manually

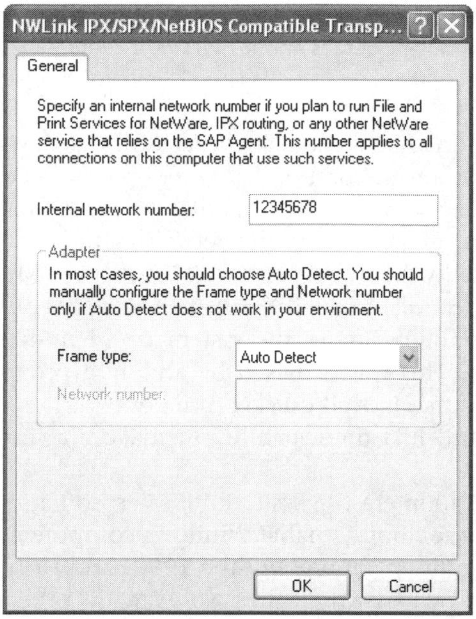

Figure 10-34
Setting NetWare
network numbers

NWLink IPX/SPX/NetBIOS Compatible Transp... [?] [X]

General

Specify an internal network number if you plan to run File and
Print Services for NetWare, IPX routing, or any other NetWare
service that relies on the SAP Agent. This number applies to all
connections on this computer that use such services.

Internal network number: `12345678`

Adapter
In most cases, you should choose Auto Detect. You should
manually configure the Frame type and Network number
only if Auto Detect does not work in your enviroment.

Frame type: `Auto Detect` ▼

Network number: `                    `

[OK] [Cancel]

PART II

NOTE Technically, Microsoft didn't invent NetBIOS. IBM was the originator
of NetBIOS, but Microsoft added much more functionality to NetBIOS, and
adopted it for DOS and Windows PCs.

Microsoft's idea to incorporate NetBIOS closely into the operating system created a
number of serious cross-platform issues. NetBIOS was designed to run with NetBEUI,
but other systems, running other protocols, forced Microsoft to realize that the NetBEUI
protocol was separating Windows computers from foreign systems running protocols
such as IPX/SPX and TCP/IP. Additionally, NetBEUI was incapable of routing, making it
useless in anything but small networks. Microsoft's solution was to dump NetBEUI, but
to keep NetBIOS. This resulted in split protocols where Windows would still run
NetBIOS, but instead of using NetBEUI, it would use the lower protocols the entire network used.

The first issue came about back in the days when Novell NetWare was the network operating system of choice. How do you make a bunch of Microsoft client computers running NetBIOS able to see the Novell NetWare servers running IPX/SPX?

When NetWare first became popular back in the 1980s, Microsoft simply ignored the
networking issue. Novell supplied special (and free) client software that you installed on
every system you wanted to see the Novell servers. When the first versions of Windows
came out, Novell was right there with graphical networking-client tools. These client
programs didn't use NetBIOS—they used the NetWare naming conventions.

TIP Chapter 18, "Interconnecting Network Operating Systems," discusses important details about NetWare clients.

Microsoft didn't like this one bit. Microsoft was developing the idea of the Windows Desktop and an integral part of that Desktop was Network Neighborhood, later called My Network Places. Microsoft didn't like the idea of Novell's client making its users go to a different program to access the network—Microsoft wanted everything in Network Neighborhood. By the time Windows 95 came out, Microsoft tried to beat NetWare to the punch by creating its own IPX/SPX software that could translate the NetWare Server's names into NetBIOS names the system could understand and place into Network Neighborhood. This was achieved by adding a program called Microsoft Client for NetWare. Of course, Novell quickly came out with its own client software that ran on Windows 9*x* and had the capability to make NetWare servers show up in Network Neighborhood.

This created an interesting issue. Both Microsoft and Novell now had client software that did the same thing—enable Windows computers to access NetWare servers. This created a competition throughout the 1990s and early 2000s, between Microsoft and Novell to get users to use their client software over the other. Fortunately, this competition recently came to a conclusion. Novell no longer uses IPX/SPX and has joined the TCP/IP bandwagon, making any special client software unnecessary.

TCP/IP

As usual, with greater functionality comes greater complexity. The *TCP/IP* protocol suite offers a more scaleable solution for the largest networks, but it requires significantly more configurations on the part of the network tech. TCP/IP began as a UNIX networking protocol suite, but its status as the Internet's *de facto* protocol suite has prompted both Microsoft and Novell to embrace it. Helping this along is the convenient fact that unlike NetBEUI and IPX/SPX, TCP/IP is an open standard, not controlled by any one company.

TCP/IP now stands as the network protocol of choice in the vast majority of today's networks, and certainly on any system that wants to connect to the Internet. This popularity, combined with the fairly high degree of complexity involved in making TCP/IP work properly and the fact that the Network+ exam really wants you to know TCP/IP in minute detail, requires several chapters just on the TCP/IP network protocol.

TCP/IP defines a large number of protocols that work from layers three through seven of the OSI seven layer model (Figure 10-35). In this section, we concentrate on conceptually how the TCP/IP works at multiple OSI layers and save the details for later chapters.

Applications

It's hard to talk about TCP/IP without taking time to talk about the Application layer. Unlike the proprietary protocols IPX/SPX and NetBIOS/NetBEUI, the designers of

Figure 10-35
TCP/IP protocols

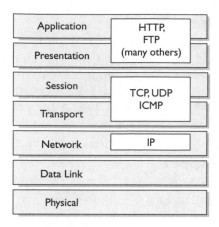

TCP/IP worked hard to make a protocol stack that worked well for any applications, not just file and print sharing. As a result, TCP/IP relies heavily on Application layer protocols for many critical network functions.

A great example is this DNS thing I keep referring to. DNS (as you'll see in great detail in the next two chapters) is what TCP/IP networks use to resolve a computer name like www.totalsem.com into the machine's actual IP address. This critical process runs at the Application layer.

All TCP/IP applications have their own distinct *port* number. DNS, for example, has port 53. Other famous Application layer functions have different port numbers. Your web browser uses port 80. E-mail uses ports 25 (outgoing) and 110 (incoming). TCP allows port numbers from 0 to 65,535. Port numbers from 0 to 1204 are called *well-known ports* and are used primarily by client applications to talk to server applications. No other application should use these ports. Some of the ports after 1204 are for less-known applications (and can be used by other applications), but most are for servers to use as an identifier to talk back to clients. The following line of text is cut from the NETSTAT -n command running on a Windows XP system. This shows a session running between my computer and the popular Google.com search engine on my web browser.

```
TCP    192.168.4.27:2357    216.239.41.104:80    ESTABLISHED
```

Ignore the words "TCP" and "ESTABLISHED" and concentrate on the IP addresses and ports. On the left is the IP address and port number used by the Google.com web server to talk to my system. On the right is the IP and port number my system uses to talk to the Google.com web server. Note that my system sends out on port 80, the well-known port used to talk to web servers. Note also that the web server uses the arbitrarily chosen port number 2357 to talk back to my system.

Earlier, we mentioned that TCP isn't one protocol, it's a family of protocols with names like TCP, UDP, or ICMP. The type of protocol is determined by the application.

TCP at Session

When you start an application on a TCP/IP computer, the application alerts the Session layer software to begin a session with a remote computer. Your system will send out a packet with the remote system's IP address and the port number of the service you are requesting. When that packet gets to the remote system, it will respond by assigning a port number for the session running from the serving system back to your system. This number is arbitrarily assigned from the pool of port numbers between 1024 and 49151.

TCP at Transport

TCP at the transport level is invisible. This layer, as already described, chops away at the outgoing data, breaking each piece into frames and adding sequence numbers. On the receiving side, the incoming packets are reassembled, checked, and then moved up to the next layer.

IP at Network

The cornerstone of TCP/IP's popularity is the robust and scalable IP addressing scheme. The IP addressing scheme, famous with its four dotted-decimal notation, has one quality unmatched in any other protocol—you can take a network, subnet it, subnet the subnets, and keep subnetting until you run out of numbers and TCP/IP can handle it! This, of course, assumes you know how to configure a complex TCP/IP network properly!

Take, for example, a block of IP addresses ranging from 10.0.0.0 up to 10.255.255.255. TCP/IP networks reserve the numbers 255 and 0 on the end of the IP address for special uses so you have all the IP addresses from 10.0.0.1 to 10.255.255.254. This would give you one network with ($256 \times 256 \times 254 =$) 16,646,144 different computers or *hosts*, as we would say in the TCP/IP vernacular. All the computers share the same first number: 10. We call that part of the IP address the network ID. The part that changes for every system is called the *host ID*. Let's pick one computer on our network: 10.168.43.7. Its network ID is 10.0.0.0 (we put zeroes on the end of network IDs) and the host ID is 168.43.7.

Here's where the power of IP shines. If we wanted to, we could take some of those IP addresses in the 10.0.0.0 network; let's pick all the addresses with the 10.14.0.0 network ID and make this a subnet of the bigger network. We could take the 10.14.0.0 network and subnet that into even smaller networks. Notice that each subnet has fewer host IDs than the larger network, so you eventually run out of numbers, but you get the idea. You'll see in Chapter 12, "Network Operating Systems," that you can subnet even more than what's shown here.

Installing TCP/IP

The first item to put into your head is that every modern OS installs TCP/IP by default, so it's rare for you to need to install TCP/IP. If, by some chance, you find yourself needing to install the TCP/IP protocol into Windows, just follow the installation examples shown in the earlier network protocols in this chapter.

The "joy" of TCP/IP comes from the configuration. TCP/IP, in its most basic form, takes a substantial amount of configuration. Fortunately, TCP/IP has evolved dramatically over the years to the point where most client systems need little or no configuration to work correctly.

Splitting Protocols II: NetBIOS over TCP/IP

It's been said that Bill Gates once called the Internet a passing fad. While I've never found a reliable reference for this quote, it is correct to say that Windows was the last major operating system to adopt TCP/IP. There was a good reason for this late entry—Windows had NetBIOS tightly embedded and NetBIOS just wasn't designed to work with TCP/IP.

The world continued to move toward TCP/IP and Microsoft, finally realizing the need for TCP/IP with Windows, responded to this issue in a series of steps. By the early 1990s, Microsoft provided a TCP/IP protocol—but you could not run a Microsoft network with the TCP/IP software provided from Microsoft. Back then, you added both the NetBEUI and the TCP/IP protocols to your Windows computers. NetBEUI handled your internal network and TCP/IP enabled you to run web browsers and such. It was inelegant, but it worked!

The next step was to take the flexibility of TCP/IP and add NetBIOS support. This was actually fairly simple, as long as you kept your networks small. Microsoft grabbed some unused port numbers and transformed NetBIOS into an Application-layer function on a TCP/IP network, using a process called *NetBIOS over TCP/IP (NetBT)*. It even invented a naming system called *Windows Internet Naming Service (WINS)* that enabled NetBIOS over TCP/IP to work over large networks. (See Chapter 11, "TCP/IP," for a discussion on WINS.) The vast majority of computers run TCP/IP and the vast majority of Windows computers run NetBIOS over TCP/IP.

The last step is still taking place: Microsoft is dropping support for NetBIOS. Networks composed exclusively of Windows 2000 and XP systems can turn off NetBIOS and still function as a network.

Also-Ran Protocols

Odds are good that you could spend your entire networking life and never see any protocols other than NetBIOS/NetBEUI, IPX/SPX, and TCP/IP. In fact, odds are good that you could go the rest of your life and only see TCP/IP! However, you need to know about a few other "also-ran" network protocols that are historically important and still supported by most operating systems.

AppleTalk

Just as IPX/SPX was invented in-house by Novell for its NetWare NOS, Apple invented the *AppleTalk* network protocol suite to run on Apple computers. AppleTalk was originally designed to run on top of the old LocalTalk networking technology. Roughly speaking, AppleTalk does for Macs what NetBIOS does for PCs. When two Macintosh computers communicate using AppleTalk, their conversation looks quite a bit like a NetBIOS session, in that each name has an associated number function assigned to it. I won't go through this in detail, but you should know that AppleTalk uses a special function called Name Binding Protocol (NBP). NBP binds each system's name to its AppleTalk address, so that other systems on the network can see it. Modern Macintosh systems still rely on AppleTalk. All but the earliest versions of Windows come with the capability to install the AppleTalk protocol, so they can talk to Macintosh systems that still use AppleTalk. For the Network+ exam, at least know that if you want to talk to a Macintosh computer, you'll want to install the AppleTalk protocol on your Windows system.

 TIP To communicate with an older Macintosh on a Windows-centric network, install the AppleTalk protocol on your Windows PCs.

DLC

The *Data Link Control (DLC)* network protocol was used for many years to link PCs to mainframe computers. Because Hewlett-Packard adopted the DLC protocol for use by network printers, DLC enjoyed a much longer life than it probably should have, given the existence of so many alternatives. All versions of Windows, including Windows XP, still support DLC, but unless you're installing an older network printer that only uses DLC, odds are good you'll never see it. Just know that DLC is a network protocol and you can install it if needed.

Chapter Review

Questions

1. What is the maximum length of a NetBIOS network name?

   A. 8 characters

   B. 23 characters

   C. 15 characters

   D. 256 characters

2. NWLink is Microsoft's version of which protocol suite?

   A. NetBEUI

   B. NetBIOS

   C. IPX/SPX

   D. TCP/IP

3. An IPX/SPX external network number is also known as

   A. The subnet mask

   B. An external node

   C. A segment address

   D. A default address

4. The NetBIOS protocol operates at which OSI layer?

   A. Data Link

   B. Network

   C. Transport

   D. Session

5. What part of the NetBEUI protocol suite operates at the Transport layer?

   A. IPX

   B. NetBIOS

   C. NetBEUI

   D. SPX

6. Travis, using a Windows 95 computer named TRACK3, complains that he cannot connect with another Windows 95 computer named SALES3. Jim, the friendly neighborhood network technician, determines that TRACK3 can connect successfully with other machines that reside on the same side of the router, but not with any machines on the far side of the router. Which of the following is the most likely cause of Travis's problem?

   A. TRACK3 is connected to the network with a bad cable.

   B. TRACK3's network card has failed and needs to be replaced.

   C. TRACK3 is running NetBEUI.

   D. TRACK3 is running NetBIOS.

7. Which of the following protocols are routable? (Select all that apply.)

   A. NetBEUI

   B. IPX/SPX

   C. TCP/IP

   D. NetBIOS

8. What do routers do with NetBEUI packets?

   A. Send the packets out over the Internet.

   B. Send the packets back to the sending machines.

    C. Hold the packets until they receive a resend request.

    D. Discard the packets.

9. The IPX/SPX protocol was originally designed for use with which network operating system?

    A. Novell NetWare

    B. Windows 3.1

    C. UNIX

    D. Linux

10. What are Ethernet 802.3, Ethernet II, Ethernet 802.2, and Ethernet SNAP?

    A. Types of NIC cards

    B. IPX/SPX data structures

    C. TCP/IP protocols

    D. OSI model layers

Answers

1. **C.** The maximum length of a NetBIOS network name is 15 characters. NetBIOS reserves the 16th byte for a special code that defines the function of the machine on the network.

2. **C.** NWLink is Microsoft's version of the IPX/SPX protocol. NetBIOS is part of the NetBEUI protocol.

3. **C.** An IPX/SPX external network address is also known as simply the network number or the segment address.

4. **D.** The NetBIOS protocol operates at the Session layer.

5. **C.** The NetBEUI protocol operates at the Transport layer. IPX and SPX are parts of a different protocol.

6. **C.** TRACK3 is running NetBEUI. NetBEUI is a nonroutable protocol. Because TRACK3 can communicate with some other machines on the network, a bad cable or NIC is unlikely to be the cause of the symptoms described.

7. **B, C.** IPX/SPX and TCP/IP are both routable protocols. NetBEUI is not a routable protocol, and NetBIOS is part of the NetBEUI protocol suite.

8. **D.** Routers discard NetBEUI packets because the packets lack the OSI Network layer routing information that routers use to do their job.

9. **A.** IPX/SPX was originally designed for use with Novell NetWare.

10. **B.** IPX running on top of Ethernet can use one of four data structures, called frame types: Ethernet 802.3, Ethernet II, Ethernet 802.2, or Ethernet SNAP.

TCP/IP

The Network+ Certification exam expects you to know how to

- 2.5 Identify the components and structure of IP (Internet Protocol) addresses (IPv4, IPv6) and the required setting for connections across the Internet
- 2.6 Identify classful IP ranges and their subnet masks (for example: Class A, B, and C)
- 2.7 Identify the purpose of subnetting
- 2.8 Identify the differences between private and public network addressing schemes
- 2.10 Define the purpose, function, and use of the following protocols used in the TCP/IP suite: TCP, UDP, FTP, TFTP, SMTP, HTTP, POP3/IMAP4, Telnet, ICMP, ARP/RARP, NTP, NNTP, LDAP, IGMP
- 2.11 Define the function of TCP/UDP (Transmission Control Protocol/User Datagram Protocol) ports

To achieve these goals, you must be able to

- Recognize properly formatted IP addresses
- Describe the function of subnet mask and default gateway
- Define and calculate classful and classless subnets
- Describe the functions of DNS, DHCP, and WINS
- Recognize the port numbers and the functions of popular TCP, UDP, and ICMP applications
- Describe the need for IPv6 and recognize properly formatted IPv6 addresses.

TCP/IP has the unique distinction of being the only popular network protocol designed from the ground up by the government of the United States. Like many government endeavors, TCP/IP is big, messy, ponderous, hard to configure (relative to other protocols, at least), and tries to be all things to all users. Compared to IPX/SPX or NetBIOS/NetBEUI, TCP/IP is a pain in the posterior at best. So why does every computer on the Internet use TCP/IP? Why do networks not even connected to the Internet almost exclusively use TCP/IP? Why is TCP/IP overwhelmingly the most popular network protocol on the face of the Earth? The answer is *flexibility*. TCP/IP works well for both small and large networks in a way that no other network protocol matches, and this chapter's job is to show you that flexibility.

In this chapter, you'll learn the components and configurations of TCP/IP. We'll go over IP addresses in detail. Next, we'll follow with a discussion of how a single TCP/IP network can divide itself into multiple subnetworks. Then we'll take a look at some other parts of the TCP/IP suite, including the all-important TCP and UDP protocols, to see what role they play in setting up systems to run in TCP/IP networks. Finally, we'll review the functions of various key ports, and take a quick look at the upcoming IPv6 protocol.

Historical/Conceptual

IP Address Basics

The greatest danger facing those learning about IP addressing stems from the fact that so much of TCP/IP has reached the common vernacular. The average user has heard words like "IP address" and "default gateway" and might already have an idea about what they mean and why TCP/IP networks use them. Odds are also good that many of you have an idea as to what an IP address looks like. In most cases, knowledge is a good thing, but in this case, we need to get on the same mental playing field. The best way to get there is to inspect the format of a typical IP address.

Test Specific

IP Address Format

Every system in an IP network (in TCP/IP parlance, every *host*) must have a unique IP address. IP addresses look complex, but are quite simple once you know how they work.

To see a typical IP address, go to a system that connects to the Internet (so you know it uses TCP/IP) and run *WINIPCFG* (Windows 9*x*/Me/XP) or *IPCONFIG* (Windows NT/98 SE/Me/2000/XP/2003) from the Start | Run menu. Both tools enable you to view network settings at a glance, making them invaluable as first-line troubleshooting tools. Figure 11-1 shows the IP address for a Windows 98 system.

Figure 11-1
WINIPCFG
showing a
system's IP
address

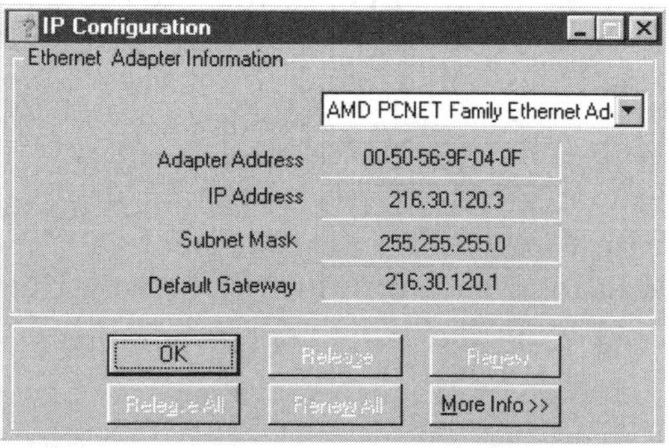

An IP address consists of four numbers, each number being a value between 0 and 255. We use a period to separate the numbers. No IP address may be all 0s or all 255s (I'll explain this in a moment). Here are a few valid IP addresses:

216.30.120.3

224.33.1.66

123.123.123.123

and here are a few invalid IP addresses:

216.30.120   (Must have four numbers)

255.255.255.255   (Can't be all 255s)

6.43.256.67   (Every number must be between 0 and 255)

32-1-66-54   (Must use periods between numbers)

These numbers are entered into every system on the IP network. Figure 11-2 shows where to enter these values in a Windows system: the Internet Protocol (TCP/IP) Properties dialog box.

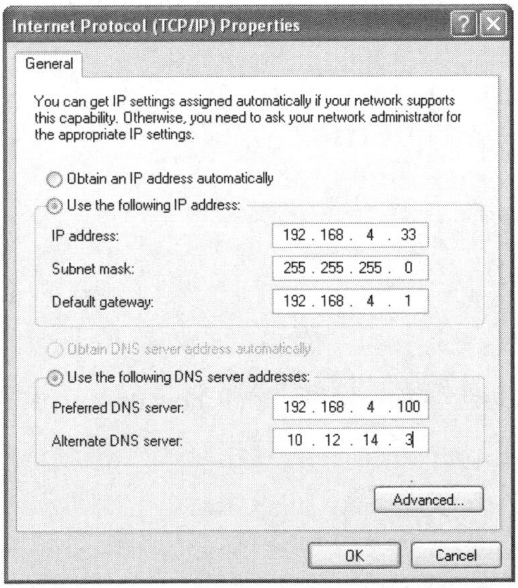

Figure 11-2

Internet Protocol (TCP/IP) Properties dialog box showing IP addresses

Note in Figure 11-2 the value labeled Subnet mask, as well as options that say Default gateway, Preferred DNS server, and Alternate DNS server. Then there's the Advanced button that leads to even more options. What are these all about? Hey, I told you IP is by far the messiest of all protocols to configure! That's what this chapter is all about: understanding these IP entries. But to understand how to configure these settings, you must understand what an IP address is. So, let's grab an arbitrary IP address and start tearing it up into its real components: binary numbers.

Converting IP Addresses

While we commonly write IP addresses as four groups of digits separated by periods, this is just convenient shorthand for a 32-bit binary address. Here's a typical IP address in its primeval binary form:

11000101101010010101111001010010

While computers have no difficulty handling long strings of ones and zeroes, most humans can't handle speaking in these terms. Instead, techs use a special shorthand for IP addresses called dotted decimal notation. Dotted decimal notation works as follows. First, divide the IP address into four pieces of eight bits:

11000101 10101001 01011110 01010010

A group of eight bits has a limited number of permutations of ones and zeroes, ranging from all zeroes (00000000) to all ones (11111111), with a lot of different combinations of ones and zeroes in between. The exact number of permutations is 2^8 or 256 different patterns of ones and zeroes. Each group of eight ones and zeroes corresponds to a number between 0 and 255. If you write down all of the possible permutations for eight bits, the list starts like this:

00000000 = 0

00000001 = 1

00000010 = 2

00000011 = 3

00000100 = 4

I'll skip about 246 entries here and show the end of the list:

11111011 = 251

11111100 = 252

11111101 = 253

11111110 = 254

11111111 = 255

Each value of 0 to 255 to represent eight bits is called an *octet*. Wait a minute! Isn't eight binary characters a byte? Then why not call them bytes? Well, they most certainly could be bytes, but the difference here is the numbering system. Normally when we discuss binary values, we use hexadecimal, but the TCP/IP folks wanted something easier than hexadecimal, so they instead use this 0-to-255 numbering system called octets. Any binary octet can be represented by the values 0 to 255. Let's take a look at the first example I just gave you:

11000101 10101001 01011110 01010010

We represent this number in dotted decimal notation as 197.169.94.82. While you may have some idea how I did this, let's take a moment to work through how to convert a true binary IP address into dotted decimal, and back again into binary. The trick is to convert the individual octets, one at a time.

The problem with using decimal notation to display an octet is that most folks find it difficult to convert between binary to decimal notation, at least without a calculator handy. The secret to success is to appreciate that each position in the binary value corresponds to a decimal value. Look at this list:

00000001 = 1

00000010 = 2

00000100 = 4

00001000 = 8

00010000 = 16

00100000 = 32

01000000 = 64

10000000 = 128

If you can memorize these eight binary/decimal equivalents, you can convert any binary octet into its decimal equivalent—not only useful in your networking duties, but an excellent trick you can use to amaze your friends at parties! To make conversion easier, every good IP network person memorizes the form in Figure 11-3.

Figure 11-3

Form to help with binary/decimal conversion

Position	8th	7th	6th	5th	4th	3rd	2nd	1st
Value	128	64	32	16	8	4	2	1

PART II

To convert an octet from binary to decimal, enter the binary number into the empty spaces at the bottom of the form, copy the decimal values of the columns where there are ones in the binary number, and add those decimal values together to get a final answer. Let's convert the binary value 10010011 to a decimal number (see Figure 11-4). In the 8th position enter a 1, and write down 128, which is the decimal value in that column. 128 is the first number in your decimal addition problem. In the 7th and 6th positions enter 0's, and for completeness, write down zeroes. Your decimal addition problem now reads 128 + 0 + 0. Enter a 1 in the 5th position, and write down 16, the decimal value of that column. In the 4th and 3rd positions, enter two more 0's, and write those down. In the 2nd position enter a 1, and add its value, 2, to your equation that follows. Finally, place a 1 in the 1st position, which we know equals 1. Add a 1 to the end of your addition problem, and then do the math! The decimal equivalent of 10010011 is 147. Converting binary numbers to decimal is easy with this handy form!

Figure 11-4

Converting the binary value of 10010011 into a decimal value

Position	8th	7th	6th	5th	4th	3rd	2nd	1st
Value	128	64	32	16	8	4	2	1
	1	0	0	1	0	0	1	1

128 + 0 + 0 + 16 + 0 + 0 + 2 + 1 = 147

Now let's return to our binary IP address example, and convert each binary octet to decimal:

11000101=197 10101001=169 01011110=94 01010010=82

Then separate the values with dots, like this:

197.169.94.82

You've now translated an IP address from binary to the more familiar dotted-decimal IP address format! Go drink the beverage of your choice in celebration—but only one, because you'll need your wits about you for the next step: converting a decimal value into binary!

You can use the same form to convert numbers from dotted decimal to binary. Let's use a sample decimal value of 49. Whip out a nice blank form and write the number 49 at the top. Start on the far left-hand side of the form and ask yourself, "How many 128s are there in 49?" You should answer yourself, "None, because 128 is larger than 49!" Because zero 128s fit into 49, place a zero in the 128 spot. Repeat this exercise with the next value, 64. Each time you hit a value that produces an answer of one, place a one in the corresponding position. Subtract that value from the decimal value and continue the procedure with the remainder.

Here's how it works with the 49 example:

• How many 128s in 49? None—so put a zero in the 128s place.

- How many 64s in 49? None—so put a zero in the 64s place.

- How many 32s in 49? One—put a one in the 32s place and subtract 32 from 49, leaving 17.

- How many 16s in 17? One—put a one in the 16s place and subtract 16 from 17, leaving 1.

- How many 8s in 1? None—so put a zero.

- How many 4s in 1? None—so put a zero.

- How many 2s in 1? None—so put a zero.

- How many 1s in 1? One—put a one in the 1s place and subtract 1 from 1, leaving zero.

This does—and because you've reached the end of the procedure, it most definitely should—leave you with zero (Figure 11-5). If you don't get zero at this point, you made a mistake. No big deal—it can take some practice to get the hang of it. Try it again!

Figure 11-5
Did yours come
out to zero?

Position	8th	7th	6th	5th	4th	3rd	2nd	1st
Value	128	64	32	16	8	4	2	1
	0	0	1	1	0	0	0	1

```
How many    128s  in  49?   0
How many     64s  in  49?   0
How many     32s  in  49?   1     49 - 32 =17
How many     16s  in  17?   1     17 - 16 =1
How many      8s  in   1?   0
How many      4s  in   1?   0
How many      2s  in   1?   0
How many      1s  in   1?   1     1 - 1 =0
```

Using this handy form, we've deduced that the decimal value 49 is 00110001 in binary. Because every IP address has four values, you must go through this process three more times to convert a typical IP address. You'll find that, with practice, this becomes a fast process. Stop here; make up some IP addresses, and practice converting back and forth with values you create until you're comfortable.

Now that you've toiled to learn conversion by hand, I have a confession to make: you can use the Calculator applet that comes with every version of Windows (Start | Run, type **calc**, and press ENTER). The Scientific mode of the calculator has a nice series of radio buttons on the top left. Make sure that the Decimal radio button is checked, type in the octet's decimal value, and then click the Binary radio button. Voilà! Instant conversion!

NOTE The Network+ exam does not expect you to know how to convert dotted-decimal IP addresses into binary and back, although any network tech worth his salt can do this in his sleep. Also, it's a skill you need to understand a number of other aspects of TCP/IP that you are about to learn.

I always laugh when I think about the first time I tried converting IP addresses from decimal to binary and back. When I first had to learn all this, it took me three solid days to get the whole thing straight in my head, while my friend Taylor had it nailed in about five minutes. Even though a calculator will do the conversions for you, don't give up too quickly on doing it yourself—you'll find that being able to do this manually brings some big benefits out in the real world!

Local vs. Remote

Back in the early 1970s, the world was waking up to the possibility of taking computing beyond individual systems. People began realizing the dream of a vast network of systems across the United States and, eventually, the world—what we now call the Internet. The U.S. Defense Advanced Research Projects Agency (DARPA) was tasked to create a series of protocols to support this massive network. This network needed a protocol, so DARPA had to get to work designing one—but not just any network protocol! The *D* in DARPA stood for "Defense." DARPA needed a protocol that could handle a crisis—in particular, the loss of one or more network interconnections from an atomic bomb hit (remember, this was during the Cold War). DARPA wanted a large network designed such that, in the event one piece suddenly went down, the remaining parts of the network would realize the break and automatically reroute network traffic to avoid the downed areas.

Thus came the birth of TCP/IP. TCP/IP was designed from the ground up to support groups of separate, interconnected networks. Each of the individual networks connected to one or more individual networks via special computers called routers. Routers direct network traffic by reading the IP addresses in each incoming packet, and then use that information to send the packet out on its way toward the intended recipient. (The creators of the TCP/IP protocol suite literally invented the concept of routers.)

In general, a single TCP/IP network consists of some number of computers connected together into a single collision domain. If this TCP/IP network wants to interconnect to other TCP/IP networks, it also needs a router connected to the same network, as shown in Figure 11-6.

If you're like most people, you look at Figure 11-6 and say, "What's with that cloud? Is that the Internet?" Let's get some misconceptions out of the way right now. The terms "Internet" and "TCP/IP" are so closely interwoven that most folks assume that all TCP/IP networks are part of the Internet. Not true! First, a TCP/IP network doesn't have to connect to any other TCP/IP network. Nothing prevents you from taking a few Windows computers, installing TCP/IP on them, and connecting them to a single switch. This little TCP/IP network will run perfectly and it's done all the time. Second, you can connect two or more TCP/IP networks together and not be on the Internet. For example, you can take two TCP/IP networks in the same room and connect them together with a router. These two interconnected networks use TCP/IP and a router, but they're not part of the Internet. The cloud is a representation of "the rest of the TCP/IP network." The cloud might represent one other network, a number of other networks, or even the Internet—it makes no difference.

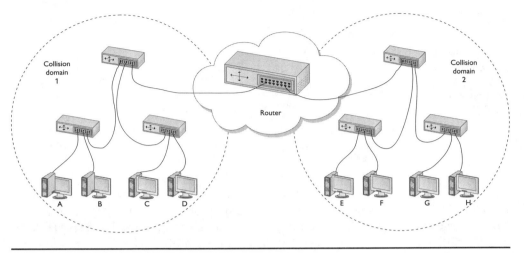

Figure 11-6   Typical TCP/IP network

TIP   Just because a computer runs TCP/IP, don't assume it's connected to the Internet!

If a single TCP/IP network connects to a group of interconnected networks, would it be safe to assume that some of the traffic going in and out of any one computer stays *local*—within its own network? Equally, won't all of the traffic destined for *remote* computers (outside the local network) need to go out through the router? This local vs. remote issue is the cornerstone of TCP/IP configuration: there must be a method to enable a system to know when it needs to send data to its local network and when it needs to send data to the router.

TCP/IP most certainly does have a method—an elegant one! To learn this method, let's begin by looking at a simple TCP/IP network, a network not connected to any other network, and see how TCP/IP works to send data from one system to another.

ARP

With all this talk about IP addresses, it's easy to forget that in a simple (no routers) TCP/IP network, all of the systems share the same network technology. In this case, the computers must put their packets inside of frames to move data from one system to another, and frames use MAC addresses—not IP addresses—to do that job.. So how does the sending system know the MAC address of the receiving system? The TCP/IP protocol suite has a neat little function called *address resolution protocol (ARP)* that performs this task.

To see how ARP works, let's add TCP/IP to Hannah's MHTechEd network you saw in the previous chapter. In this case, she configured DANA to use the IP address 216.30.120.2 and JANELLE gets the IP address 216.30.120.3. You also know that each system has a MAC address—let's give each system a MAC address, as shown in Figure 11-7.

Figure 11-7
MHTechEd network showing IP and MAC addresses for each system

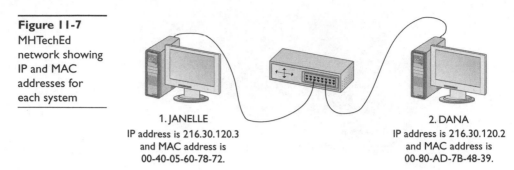

1. JANELLE
IP address is 216.30.120.3
and MAC address is
00-40-05-60-78-72.

2. DANA
IP address is 216.30.120.2
and MAC address is
00-80-AD-7B-48-39.

Let's say DANA wants to send data to JANELLE. It knows the IP address (216.30.120.3) but does not know the MAC address, and without the MAC address, it cannot make a frame. So, DANA sends out a special frame, addressed to a special MAC address called the broadcast address. This MAC address is all 1s (FFFFFFFFFFFF in hexadecimal). It's special because all systems on the network receive and process frames sent to the broadcast address. This frame asks every system on the local network: "What is the MAC address for IP address 216.30.120.3?" We call this frame an *ARP request*. The system with that IP address replies to DANA with an ARP reply (see Figure 11-8).

Figure 11-8
DANA sending an ARP request and getting an ARP reply

JANELLE   DANA

1. DANA asks all systems for the MAC
address for IP 192.168.4.3.

JANELLE   DANA

2. JANELLE replies with the MAC
address 00-40-05-60-78-72.

Once DANA gets the MAC information for JANELLE, it stores this in a cache. You can see the ARP cache in your system by typing the command **ARP -a** (note: the -a is case-sensitive) from a command prompt in any version of Windows. Figure 11-9 shows the **ARP** command in action!

In some situations, a computer knows another computer's MAC address, but needs an IP address—the exact opposite of an ARP. To get a MAC address, the system broad-

Figure 11-9
The ARP
command
in action

```
C:\WINNT\System32\cmd.exe

C:\>arp -a

Interface: 192.168.4.15 on Interface 0x1000003
  Internet Address      Physical Address     Type
  192.168.4.17          00-20-18-8b-54-80    dynamic
  192.168.4.18          00-40-95-00-2e-1c    dynamic
  192.168.4.21          00-c0-f0-2c-f7-0c    dynamic
  192.168.4.28          00-a0-c9-98-97-9e    dynamic
  192.168.4.150         00-01-02-c8-95-41    dynamic
  192.168.4.152         00-04-5a-d0-ca-6b    dynamic
  192.168.4.155         00-40-05-60-73-a6    dynamic

C:\>_
```

casts a RARP (Reverse ARP) command. While ARP is very common, RARP is rare in LAN environments as only a few applications need RARP.

ARP works perfectly well for a simple TCP/IP network, but what if you want to send data from a computer to another computer on a network connected to your network with a router? Routers cannot forward ARP requests because ARP requests are broadcasts. ARP alone fails the moment you want to send data outside your local network. This is where a special setting called a gateway comes into play.

Gateways

ARP works great when one IP system needs to know the MAC address of another IP system in the same local network, but remember that one of the cornerstones of IP is its assumption that your local network will be connected to a larger network. TCP/IP assumes—and this is important—that a system knows, or at least can find out on the fly (see the DNS discussion that follows), the IP address of any system on the Internet. It is not possible, however, for one system to know the MAC addresses of all the millions of other systems on the Internet. If a system wants to send data to another system on another network, a local network must connect to a larger network via a router. The router connecting a local network must know how to address packets for other systems that are not part of its local network—we call this router the *default gateway*, *gateway router*, or sometimes just *gateway*.

 NOTE The term "gateway" is used in a number of different, often unrelated ways in the networking world. In this case, I refer to a router that connects a local network to a larger network.

A gateway might be a router or it might be a PC that runs routing software. Most versions of Windows, as well as other operating systems like Linux, also have the capability to make a regular PC function perfectly well as a router. Whether your router is a special box or a PC, the gateway must have at least two network connections—one connecting to the local network and a second connecting to another network. Figure 11-10 shows

Figure 11-10
The Totalsem
gateway

the gateway system in my office. This little box connects to (a) my network and (b) the DSL line to the Internet. Note the two thicker network cables—one runs to the switch for my network and the other runs to my DSL line. (The third, thinner cable is the power cable. The other two projections are antennae for its wireless capabilities.)

When setting up a local network, you must enter the IP address of the gateway in the TCP/IP Properties dialog box of every system. The IP address of the gateway is called, somewhat confusingly, the default gateway. Figure 11-11 shows my TCP/IP Properties dialog box with the default gateway setting added.

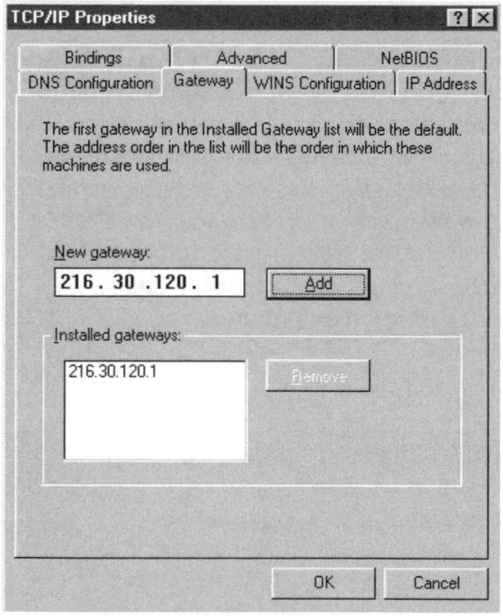

Figure 11-11
The TCP/IP
Properties dialog
box showing
the default
gateway setting

Continuing with our MHTechEd network, if DANA wants to talk to another system that is not part of the local network, it cannot ARP that far away system, because the Internet does not allow any form of broadcast frames. My gosh, imagine if it did! That would mean DANA would have to ARP every other computer on the Internet! Now imagine every system on the Internet doing this—there'd be no bandwidth left for data! Don't worry about this happening; every router on the Internet is designed to block ARP requests. Instead, the DANA system sends its data to the local network's default gateway, which will work with all of the other routers on the Internet to get the packet to the proper location.

NOTE Be careful at this point! You might think that remote data heading out of the local network doesn't need ARP. It does—but only to get data to the default gateway.

Okay, let's review. Any system that wants to send a data packet over a network must be able to tell whether the recipient system is local or remote, because it handles locally and remotely bound IP packets in two completely different ways. If the address is local, the sending system can use ARP. If the address is on a remote network, it creates packets with the remote system's IP address and runs an ARP to determine the MAC address of the default gateway. Armed with the default gateway's MAC address, the sending system tells its NIC to make frames with the gateway's MAC address and sends frames to the default gateway. As each frame comes into the default gateway, it strips off the frame, leaving the IP packets (which still have the IP address of the remote system as its destination). The default gateway then inspects the IP packets, wraps them up in whatever type of frame the outgoing connection needs, and sends them toward the intended system.

Well, the local vs. remote question is half-answered. You now know what your system will do if it determines a packet is local or remote, but now it's time for the other half of the big question: How does it know if the packet is local or remote?

Subnet Masks and Subnetting

Every system on a TCP/IP network needs a special binary value called a *subnet mask* to enable them to distinguish between local and remote IP addresses. But before we can dive into subnet masks, you need to understand how TCP/IP can organize networks into distinct chunks. Think about it, we've got all these IP addresses, from 0.0.0.0 all the way up to 255.255.255.255. That's over 4 billion IP addresses! Clearly it's not optimal to treat them all as one big network—you couldn't even daisy-chain enough switches together to do it! We need an organizational scheme to divvy up this huge pool of IP addresses into groups of IP addresses that make sense and that we can use. And lucky us, this has been done! The official term for these groups of addresses is *network IDs*.

Network IDs

In the earlier discussion, Hannah configured DANA to use the IP address 216.30.120.2 and JANELLE to use the IP address 216.30.120.3. Notice anything about these two IP addresses? Look carefully. They are almost identical—only the final octet is different, and that is not a coincidence! It has to do with the organization of networks. Consider postal addresses for a moment. Why is your address 305 Main Street, and your next-door neighbor's 306 (or 307, depending on how your street is numbered) Main Street? How about if we make your address 1313 Mulberry Lane, and your neighbor's address 451 Bradbury Avenue? Imagine the horror on the face of your mail carrier! For the same reason we group street addresses using street names and sets of consecutive numbers, we divide network addresses into two parts: one part designating a group of computers, and one part designating individual computers. Let's watch this happen. Here's an IP address in binary form: 11010101101010010101111001010010.

Which part is which? Ha! Not easy, is it? It's easier than it looks. (The answer to this lies in the *subnet mask*, but you need a bit more background for this to make sense.)

Look at the DANA and JANELLE IP addresses again. The first part, 216.30.120, is the same for each system. In fact, it's the same for every machine in the MHTechEd network! This part of the address, the part that's the same for all the MHTechEd systems, is called the *network ID*. It's the number by which the rest of the Internet knows the MHTechEd network. The last part of the IP address, the part that is—and must be—different for each host system on the MHTechEd network, is called—catch this originality—the *host ID*. So how many hosts can the MHTechEd network support, given that each one must have a unique IP address? Remember the binary conversion stuff we just did (I hope)? Each binary octet translates into a decimal number between 0 and 255, for a total of 256 possible IP addresses using MHTechEd's network ID, starting with 216.30.120.0 and running through 216.30.120.255.

Great. Only there's a small complication, courtesy of those quirky folks who designed the Internet: no host ID can be either all zeroes or all ones. So 216.30.120.0 and 216.30.120.255 are invalid IP addresses. The rest of them are okay, however, so the range of IP addresses available to the MHTechEd network starts at 216.30.120.1 and runs to 216.30.120.254, for a whopping total of 254 unique IP addresses.

If some other network admin asks the MHTechEd network admin for his network ID, the answer will be 216.30.120.0. This is just a convention among network folks—any time you see an IP address with a final octet of zero, you are looking at a network ID, not the address of any individual system.

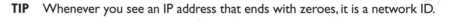

TIP Whenever you see an IP address that ends with zeroes, it is a network ID.

Okay, you're thinking, so the first three octets are the network ID, and the last one is the host ID, right? In MHTechEd's case that's true, but that's not always the case! Here are two more IP addresses, for two systems that share the same network ID: 202.43.169.55 and 202.43.67.123. Uh oh, this time only the first two octets are the same! Care to guess what the network ID is for this network? It's the first two octets: 202.43. Why would one network have a three-octet network ID, and the other only two? Because the one with the two-octet network ID has many more computers on its local network and needs a lot more IP addresses for its host systems. The two-octet network's IP addresses range from

202.43.0.1 to 202.43.255.254. Now, look carefully—what part of 202.43.0.1 is the host ID? The 1? Nope, it's the final two octets: 0.1!

Oh no, that host ID has a zero! A host ID can't have all zeroes or all ones, right? Granted, the first octet is 00000000 (all zeroes), but the second octet is 00000001 (not all zeroes). The IP address 202.43.0.0 won't fly, but 202.43.0.1 works just fine. By the same token, we can't use 202.43.255.255, because the final two octets would be 11111111 and 11111111 (all ones), but we can use 202.43.255.254, because its final two octets are 11111111 and 11111110 (not all ones). I never said that an octet in an IP address can't be all zeroes or all ones; what I said was that a host ID can't be all zeroes or all ones. Big difference!

We've established that MHTechEd has a network ID of 216.30.120.0. Where did it come from, and why is it a different size from the other one we just looked at? Because no two systems anywhere in the world on the Internet can have the same IP address, we need a single body to dispense IP addresses. The *Internet Assigned Numbers Authority (IANA)* is the ultimate source of all network IDs. You can't just call them up and ask for one, however; only the big boys play in that arena. Most small networks get their network ID assignments from their Internet service provider (ISP); the ISPs and some large end users can go directly to one of the IANA-authorized Regional Internet Registries that collectively provide IP registration services to all regions around the globe. Okay, so MHTechEd probably got its network ID from its ISP, but who decided what size it would be? MHTechEd's network admin did, by deciding how many individual IP addresses MHTechEd needed. MHTechEd is a small company, so it only asked its ISP for 254 IP addresses, and the ISP gave MHTechEd a three-octet network ID.

Subnet Mask

Now that you know where network IDs come from, let's return to the second part of the big question: how does a host system tell whether an IP address is local or remote? It compares the IP address to its own IP address to see if they have the same network ID. All machines with the same network ID are, by definition, on the same network, so if the IDs match, it knows the other system is local, not remote. Every TCP/IP computer uses the *subnet mask* to compare network IDs.

Subnet masks are always some number of ones, followed by enough zeroes to make a total of 32 bits. This is—not coincidentally—the same length as an IP address. Every network has a subnet mask, determined by the length of its network ID. Your system uses the subnet mask like a filter. Everywhere there is a 1 in the subnet mask, you are looking at part of the network ID (see Figure 11-12). Everywhere there is a zero, you are looking at part of the host ID. By placing a subnet mask on top of an IP address, a computer can tell which part of the IP address is the network ID and which part is the host ID. A sending system holds up its local network's subnet mask to both its own and the recipient's IP addresses, to see whether the part of the address under the 1's (the network ID) is the same for both systems. If the other system shares the sending system's network ID, it's local; if it does not, it's remote (see Figure 11-13). This process is technically called *ANDing*.

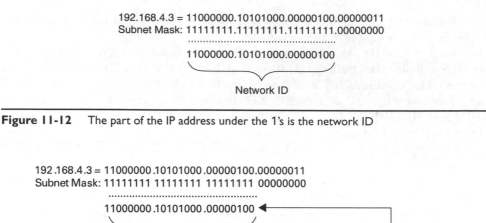

Figure 11-12   The part of the IP address under the 1's is the network ID

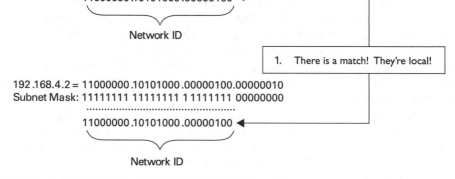

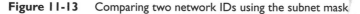

Figure 11-13   Comparing two network IDs using the subnet mask

Subnet masks are represented in dotted decimal just like IP addresses—just remember that both are really 32-bit binary numbers. All of the following (shown in both binary and dotted decimal formats) can be subnet masks:

11111111111111111111111100000000 = 255.255.255.0

11111111111111110000000000000000 = 255.255.0.0

11111111000000000000000000000000 = 255.0.0.0

Most network folks represent subnet masks using special shorthand: a / character followed by a number equal to the number of ones in the subnet mask. Here are a few examples:

11111111111111111111111100000000 = /24 (24 ones)

11111111111111110000000000000000 = /16 (16 ones)

11111111000000000000000000000000 = /8 (8 ones)

An IP address followed by the / and number is telling you the IP address and the subnet mask in one statement. For example, 201.23.45.123/24 is an IP address of 201.23.45.123, with a subnet mask of 255.255.255.0. Similarly, 184.222.4.36/16 is an IP address of 184.222.4.36, with a subnet mask of 255.255.0.0.

Fortunately, computers do all of this subnet filtering automatically. Network administrators need only to enter the correct IP address and subnet mask when they first set up their systems, and the rest happens without any human intervention.

 TIP   By definition, all computers on the same Network will have the same subnet mask and network ID.

Let's take another peek at the TCP/IP Properties dialog box on my system to see the subnet mask (see Figure 11-14). Are you getting the impression that this dialog box is an important place for configuring your IP settings? You bet it is!

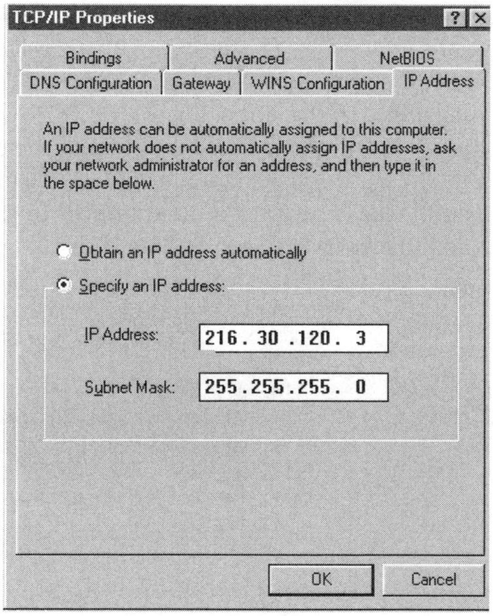

Figure 11-14
The TCP/IP Properties dialog box showing the subnet mask

> **TCP/IP Properties**
>
> | Bindings | Advanced | NetBIOS |
> | DNS Configuration | Gateway | WINS Configuration | IP Address |
>
> An IP address can be automatically assigned to this computer. If your network does not automatically assign IP addresses, ask your network administrator for an address, and then type it in the space below.
>
> ○ Obtain an IP address automatically
>
> ● Specify an IP address:
>
> IP Address: 216 . 30 .120 . 3
>
> Subnet Mask: 255 .255 .255 . 0
>
> OK   Cancel

Class Licenses

Until fairly recently, if you wanted to put some computers on the Internet, you (or your ISP) asked for a block of unused IP addresses from the IANA. The IANA passes out IP addresses in contiguous chunks called *class licenses* (see Figure 11-15). Classes *D* and *E* addresses were not distributed (only Classes *A, B,* and *C* were).

	First Decimal Value	Addresses	Hosts per Network
Class A	1–126	1.0.0.0–126.0.0.0	16.7 Million
Class B	128–191	128.0.0.0–191.255.0.0	65534
Class C	192–223	192.0.0.0–223.255.255.0	254
Class D	224–239	224.0.0.0–239.255.255.255	Multicast addresses
Class E	240–255	240.0.0.0–255.255.255.254	Experimental addresses

Figure 11-15   IP classes

 TIP   Make sure you memorize the Class A, B, and C IP class licenses! You should be able to look at any IP address and tell its class license. A trick to help: The first binary octet of a Class A address always begins with a 0 (0*xxxxxxx*); for Class B, it's 10 (10*xxxxxx*), and for Class C, 110 (110*xxxxx*).

In most cases, you get an address class that you need to subnet, which means the subnet always hits at one of the dots (/8, /16, or /24). Using this, you can make a chart showing the number of subnets created by moving the subnet mask from zero to eight places (see Figure 11-16). It makes subnetting a lot faster! Note that there are only certain numbers of subnets. If you need 22 subnets, for example, you need to move the subnet mask over 5 places to get 30. You then only use 22 of the 30 subnets.

Figure 11-16
Subnet possibilities

$.00000000 =$ 0 Subnets $2^8 - 2 = 254$ Hosts
$.10000000 = .128 = 2^1 - 2 = $ 0 Subnets $2^7 - 2 = 126$ Hosts
$.11000000 = .192 = 2^2 - 2 = $ 2 Subnets $2^6 - 2 = 62$ Hosts
$.11100000 = .224 = 2^3 - 2 = $ 6 Subnets $2^5 - 2 = 30$ Hosts
$.11110000 = .240 = 2^4 - 2 = $ 14 Subnets $2^4 - 2 = 14$ Hosts
$.11111000 = .248 = 2^5 - 2 = $ 30 Subnets $2^3 - 2 = 6$ Hosts
$.11111100 = .252 = 2^6 - 2 = $ 62 Subnets $2^2 - 2 = 2$ Hosts
$.11111110 = .254 = 2^7 - 2 = $ 126 Subnets $2^1 - 2 = 0$ Hosts
$.11111111 =$ 0 Subnets

The previous example used a Class C license, but subnetting works the same for Class A and Class B licenses, just with a larger number of hosts and subnets. Let's say you get a network ID of 129.30.0.0 and need to create 12 subnets. All IP addresses starting with 128.0.xxx.xxx up to 191.255.xxx.xxx are by definition Class B, so we can represent our network as 129.30.0.0/16. Just as you did before, first write out the starting subnet mask and start moving it to the right until you have enough subnets. If you move it over three places, you get $2^3 = 8 - 2$ (the two you can't use) = 6 subnets. Not enough. If you move the subnet mask four places, you get $2^4 = 16 - 2$ (again, minus the two you can't use) = 14 subnets (see Figure 11-17).

Figure 11-17
Moving the
subnet mask
four places

10000001.00011110·00000000.00000000
11111111.11111111·00000000.00000000

10000001.00011110|0000|0000.00000000 = 129.30.0.0 —Can't Use
10000001.00011110|0001|0000.00000000 = 129.30.16.0
10000001.00011110|0010|0000.00000000 = 129.30.32.0
10000001.00011110|0011|0000.00000000 = 129.30.48.0
10000001.00011110|0100|0000.00000000 = 129.30.64.0
10000001.00011110|0101|0000.00000000 = 129.30.80.0
10000001.00011110|0110|0000.00000000 = 129.30.96.0
10000001.00011110|0111|0000.00000000 = 129.30.112.0   Wow!
10000001.00011110|1000|0000.00000000 = 129.30.128.0   14 Subnets!
10000001.00011110|1001|0000.00000000 = 129.30.144.0
10000001.00011110|1010|0000.00000000 = 129.30.160.0
10000001.00011110|1011|0000.00000000 = 129.30.176.0
10000001.00011110|1100|0000.00000000 = 129.30.192.0
10000001.00011110|1101|0000.00000000 = 129.30.208.0
10000001.00011110|1110|0000.00000000 = 129.30.224.0
10000001.00011110|1111|0000.00000000 = 129.30.240.0   Can't Use

Just out of curiosity, can you figure out how many host numbers you get for each new network ID? As you can see from the previous figure, the host ID has a total of 12 places. For each network ID, you get $2^{12} - 2$ or 4094 hosts. Figure 11-18 lists some of the IP addresses for one of the new network IDs.

Figure 11-18
Some of the IP
addresses for
network ID
129.30.0.0/16

10000001.00011110.10010000.00000001 = 129.30.144.1
10000001.00011110.10010000.00000010 = 129.30.144.2
10000001.00011110.10010000.00000011 = 129.30.144.3
10000001.00011110.10010000.00000100 = 129.30.144.4
10000001.00011110.10010000.00000101 = 129.30.144.5

....
10000001.00011110.10010000.00011110 = 129.30.144.30
10000001.00011110.10010000.00011111 = 129.30.144.31
10000001.00011110.10010000.00100000 = 129.30.144.32
10000001.00011110.10010000.00100001 = 129.30.144.33
10000001.00011110.10010000.00100010 = 129.30.144.34

....
10000001.00011110.10010000.11111010 = 129.30.144.250
10000001.00011110.10010000.11111011 = 129.30.144.251
10000001.00011110.10010000.11111100 = 129.30.144.252
10000001.00011110.10010000.11111101 = 129.30.144.253
10000001.00011110.10010000.11111110 = 129.30.144.254

Subnetting has three secrets. First, remember to start with the given subnet mask and move it to the right until you have the number of subnets you need. Second, forget the dots. Never try to subnet without first converting to binary. Too many techs are locked into what I call Class-C-itis. They are so used to working only with Class C licenses that they forget there's more to subnetting than just the last octet. Third, practice subnetting. Use the questions at the end of this lesson as a guide. You should be able to create your own scenarios for subnetting. Stick to these three secrets and you'll soon find subnetting a breeze to do.

Now that you understand subnets, let's take a moment to understand why you can't use all zeroes or all ones in an IP address. First of all, you can use zeroes and ones—just not all zeroes and ones for the host ID. Let's look at a network of 201.44.13/24. The IP address of 201.44.13.0 is the network ID and is used by systems to determine how to ship a packet, so we can't use it. 201.44.13.255 is the IP broadcast address. This address is used by many different TCP/IP applications to broadcast packets to every other computer on the local network. This IP broadcast is similar to the ARP broadcast you saw at the beginning of this chapter. In an ARP broadcast, however, the destination IP address is the IP address of the computer the ARP is trying to locate. In an IP broadcast, in contrast, the destination IP address is the IP broadcast address itself.

[Mike switches to Evil Overlord mode] Cackle! Muhawhawhaw! Now that I've had some fun torturing your pathetic little minds with subnets, I'm going to let you in on a little secret. Few network administrators deal with subnetting anymore, because most systems nowadays don't need their own unique IP addresses. Instead, they use special IP addresses that are invisible outside of their local network, thanks to the machinations of special systems called NATs (I cover NATs in Chapter 15, "TCP/IP and the Internet"). Is that whimpering I hear? How satisfying! All that pain for nothing! Well, the folks who administer any network with routers, including the thousands of techs who work at every ISP, do this stuff every day. So, learn subnetting—and come visit me in my underground volcano complex when you've figured it out! Muhawhawhaw!!!

Classless Subnetting

At first glance, you may discount the network ID as relatively unimportant; most of us have never had to enter a network ID into anything. We enter the IP address, the gateway, and the subnet mask on each PC, but there's no place to type in the network ID. Nevertheless, the network ID is critical to making an IP network function. Individual systems don't use network IDs, but routers need them badly! Why do the routers need network IDs? Because routers use router tables, and router tables use network IDs. Let me explain. Figure 11-19 shows a typical router setup at a small office. I even added the IP addresses for each NIC in the router. (Each NIC in a router, by the way, is commonly referred to as an *interface*.) Below the diagram is the router table for that router. The router uses this table to determine the interface (the far-right column) through which it should route packets, based on the network ID of the recipient (the left-most column). As you can see, it needs the network ID of the receiving system to know how to route the packet. What if a packet's network ID doesn't match any of the routes in the table? Ah, those clever network designers are way ahead of you! If a router doesn't know what to do with a packet, it sends it along to its own default gateway, which will then distribute it to other routers, one of which will eventually know exactly where it should be routed. Very clever, and quite efficient, if you think about it for a minute!

This data in the router table doesn't just appear magically in the router. Someone needs to enter this information into the router when the router is first installed. But once this data is entered, the router will get the packets to the network.

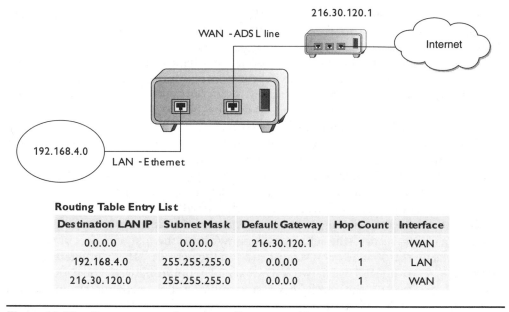

Routing Table Entry List

Destination LAN IP	Subnet Mask	Default Gateway	Hop Count	Interface
0.0.0.0	0.0.0.0	216.30.120.1	1	WAN
192.168.4.0	255.255.255.0	0.0.0.0	1	LAN
216.30.120.0	255.255.255.0	0.0.0.0	1	WAN

Figure 11-19   Router setup and corresponding router table

Now that you appreciate the importance of network IDs, let's complicate the networking situation. Let's use a more advanced router with three NICs to create two separate networks (see Figure 11-20). This type of setup is commonly used to reduce network traffic or increase security. We need to make all of this work!

Let's also assume for a moment that you are in charge of setting up this network. You have been given a total of 256 IP addresses: 216.30.120.0/24. This means you are in control of all the IP addresses from 216.30.120.0 to 216.30.120.255. If this were only one network, you wouldn't have any problems. You could simply set up each system with a unique IP address between 216.30.120.1 and 216.30.120.254.

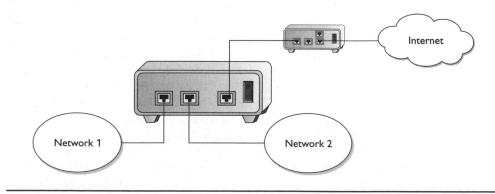

Figure 11-20   Adding another router to make separate networks—how does this work?

In this case, however, you can't do that. This router has two NICs—if each host system is randomly assigned an IP address from the total, how does the router decide which NIC to route packets through to be sure they get to the correct system? No, you can't just route everything through both NICs! The solution: divide those 256 IP addresses into two distinct groups in such a way that your router person can configure the router table to ensure that packets get to the right system. Just as we divide our neighborhoods into streets, we need to take this one Network ID with its Class C license and turn it into two distinct subnetwork IDs. Friend, you need to do classless subnetting!

Classless subnetting means to make subnets that aren't Class *A*, *B*, or *C* by defining the subnet mask at some point other than /8, /16, or /24. Classless subnetting is simple in concept, but complex in practice, largely because it requires us to break away from dividing our network IDs "at the periods." What does "at the periods" mean? I'm referring to the periods in a dotted decimal IP address, which you will recall are nothing more than a handy method for representing a set of binary values. So far, every network ID you've seen uses a *classful subnet*—the subnet mask always stops the first one, two, or three octets. There is no reason network IDs must end "on the periods." The computers, at least, think it's perfectly fine to have network IDs that end at points between the periods, such as /26, /27, or even /22. The trick here is to stop thinking about network IDs, and subnet masks just in their dotted decimal format, and instead go back to thinking of them as binary octets. Remember the binary/decimal conversion form? If I were you, I'd put this book on a photocopier right now and make yourself a bunch of copies of that form—you will need them!

We need to divide the Class C 216.30.120.0/24 network ID into two classless subnets. Note that the default subnet mask—the mask given to us by whoever gave use these IP addresses—is /24. We always start the classless subnetting process by writing out the default subnet mask in binary. The Class C subnet mask, equal to /24, is

11111111111111111111111100000000

To make classless subnets, we must extend the original subnet mask to the right, thereby turning our one network ID into multiple network IDs. The only downside is that we will have fewer host numbers in each of our new subnets. That's the cornerstone of understanding classless subnetting: you take the network ID you get from your ISP, and then chop it up into multiple, smaller network IDs, each of which supports fewer host numbers. The final step in this process is changing the IP addresses and subnet masks on all your systems, and entering the two (in this case) new network IDs into your gateway system. The hard part is knowing what to enter into the systems and routers.

If you order real, unique, ready-for-the-Internet IP addresses from your local ISP, you'll invariably get a classless set of IP addresses. More importantly, when you order them for clients, you need to be able to explain why their subnet mask is 255.255.255.192, when all the books they read tell them it should be 255.255.255.0!

Okay, let's stop and work from what you know. You know you need two subnets, right? So let's extend the subnet mask one place to the right (see Figure 11-21). This creates a three-section IP address: (1) the original network ID; (2) the now one-digit smaller host ID; and (3) nestled in between, what I call the subnet ID.

PART II

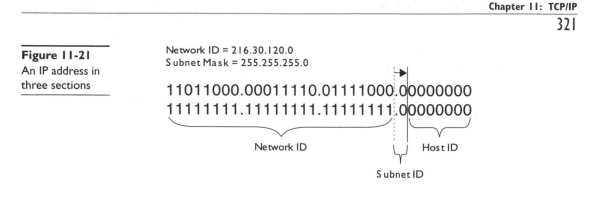

Figure 11-21
An IP address in
three sections

Network ID = 216.30.120.0
Subnet Mask = 255.255.255.0

11011000.00011110.01111000.00000000
11111111.11111111.11111111.00000000

Network ID   Host ID

Subnet ID

Uh oh. Sorry, you can't do that—by rule of the Internet powers that be, you're not allowed to have a subnet ID that is all ones, or all zeroes either! We get around this by moving the subnet mask two places, as shown in Figure 11-22. How many new network IDs does that create? That would be 2^2, which is four, did I hear you say? Careful— remember the "all ones or zeroes" prohibition! Two of the subnets (00 and 11) are useless according to the rules of subnetting, so we only get two new network IDs.

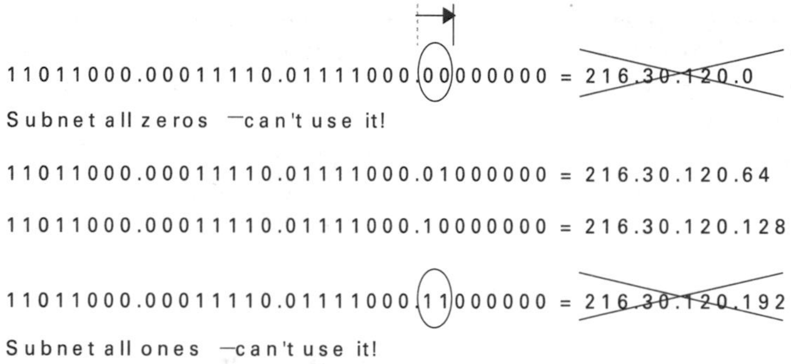

Figure 11-22
Extending the
subnet mask
two places

11011000.00011110.01111000.00000000 = 216.30.120.0
Subnet all zeros ⌐can't use it!

11011000.00011110.01111000.01000000 = 216.30.120.64

11011000.00011110.01111000.10000000 = 216.30.120.128

11011000.00011110.01111000.11000000 = 216.30.120.192
Subnet all ones ⌐can't use it!

NOTE Even though the official rules do not allow subnets with all zeroes or all ones, most networking systems—certainly all versions of Windows—run just fine if you use them. But for the test, stick to the rules!

Take a good look at the two new dotted decimal network IDs. Do you see how they no longer end in a zero? Earlier I said you could tell a dotted decimal network ID because it ends in a zero, but these do not! True enough, but convert those network IDs to binary form. They still end in zeroes, but not at the periods. Only the last *six* digits of the IP address, which in this example are the host ID, are zeroes.

Now think about the subnet masks for each of the new subnets—how would you write a subnet mask of /26? That would be 255.255.255.192! Hey, these new subnet masks don't end in a zero either, or do they? Yes indeedy, they do, too! Remember that we count zeroes in the binary version of the address. The last six values in the fourth binary octet are zeroes. 11000000 equals 192 (128 + 64) in decimal, so we represent that subnet mask in dotted decimal as 255.255.255.192.

This "dotted decimal ID must end in a zero" issue drives a lot of folks crazy when they're first learning this stuff—they just can't "get past the periods," as I like to put it. It takes effort to stop thinking in terms of classful network IDs and subnets masks and instead think in a classless way. With some effort you will be able to appreciate that whether or not the subnet masks and network ID end in a zero when you write them as dotted decimal, everything still works the same way. It's useful to memorize the fact that any time you see a dotted decimal network ID ending in 128, 192, 224, or 240, you are looking at a classless network ID which, in its binary format, ends in zero.

> **NOTE** I confess that this drove me crazy when I first learned subnetting years ago. Roll with it and you, too, can spend the rest of your life huddled next to a computer at odd hours writing books.

So, we now have two subnets: 216.30.120.64/26 and 216.30.120.128/26. If that isn't clear, stop reading now and go back to the previous text and graphics until it is clear. How do you use these two subnets in our example network? Well, the new subnet mask for every system is /26, so, first, we need to update the subnet mask settings in all our systems. We also know that our resident router geek must update the router to reflect the two new network IDs. The only question left is this: which IP addresses go to each subnet? Well, every IP address must include the network ID, leaving only six places for unique host numbers. In network ID 216.30.120.64/26, that gives us 64 different unique IP addresses. Just as no subnet may contain all zeroes or all ones, no host ID may be all zeroes and all ones, leaving a total of 62 usable IP addresses: 216.30.120.65 to 216.30.120.126 (see Figure 11-23). Contrast those with the IP addresses for the 216.30.120.128/26 network ID (see Figure 11-24).

Figure 11-23 Showing the IP addresses for 216.30.120.64	**Network ID: 216.30.120.64 =** 11011000.00011110.01111000.01000000 11011000.00011110.01111000.01000001 = 216.30.120.65 11011000.00011110.01111000.01000010 = 216.30.120.66 11011000.00011110.01111000.01000011 = 216.30.120.67 11011000.00011110.01111000.01000100 = 216.30.120.68 .... 11011000.00011110.01111000.01111011 = 216.30.120.123 11011000.00011110.01111000.01111100 = 216.30.120.124 11011000.00011110.01111000.01111101 = 216.30.120.125 11011000.00011110.01111000.01111110 = 216.30.120.126

Clearly, there is a relationship between the number of network IDs you create and the number of unique IP addresses available for each subnet. This is the tradeoff of subnetting: the more subnets, the fewer available host numbers per subnet. Also notice

Figure 11-24
Showing the IP addresses for 216.30.120.128

Network ID: 216.30.120.128 =

11011000.00011110.01111000.10000000

11011000.00011110.01111000.10000001 = 216.30.120.129
11011000.00011110.01111000.10000010 = 216.30.120.130
11011000.00011110.01111000.10000011 = 216.30.120.131
11011000.00011110.01111000.10000100 = 216.30.120.132

....

11011000.00011110.01111000.10111011 = 216.30.120.187
11011000.00011110.01111000.10111100 = 216.30.120.188
11011000.00011110.01111000.10111101 = 216.30.120.189
11011000.00011110.01111000.10111110 = 216.30.120.190

PART II

that subnetting has reduced our original complement of 256 unique IP addresses to only 124. Here's why:

256   (IP addresses to start)

−128   (The two subnets that would be all zeroes or all ones)

−4   (Two host numbers in each subnet that would be all zeroes or all ones)

=124   (Usable IP addresses)

Wow! Subnetting sure costs you a lot of IP addresses! No wonder most systems let you cheat the official subnetting rules and use subnets that contain all zeroes or all ones! If your systems allow it (Windows, NetWare, and Linux do, although you may need to tweak them), and if your router allows it (most do, but your router person may have to configure some special settings), you don't have to lose all these IP addresses. But remember, for the test, follow all the rules strictly.

Let's now plug some real values into our example network. Note that we had the router person update the router table for each subnet (see Figure 11-25).

Figure 11-25
Working subnet router settings

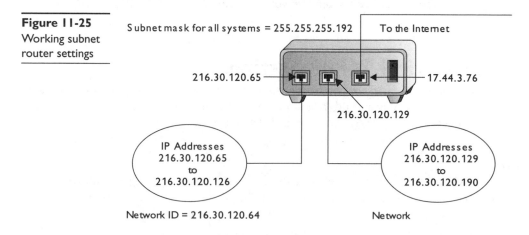

Subnet mask for all systems = 255.255.255.192

To the Internet

216.30.120.65

216.30.120.129

17.44.3.76

IP Addresses
216.30.120.65
to
216.30.120.126

IP Addresses
216.30.120.129
to
216.30.120.190

Network ID = 216.30.120.64

Network

Special IP Addresses

The folks who invented TCP/IP created a number of special IP addresses you need to know about. The first special address is 127.0.0.1, the famous loopback address. When you tell a device to send data to 127.0.0.1, you're telling that device to send the packets to itself. The loopback address has a number of uses; one of the most common is to use it with the **PING** command. We use the command **PING 127.0.0.1** to test a NIC's capability to send and receive packets.

NOTE Even though by convention we use 127.0.0.1 as the loopback address, the entire 127.0.0.0/8 subnet is reserved for loopback! You can use any address in the 127.0.0.0/8 subnet as a loopback address.

Lots of folks use TCP/IP in networks that either aren't connected to the Internet or that want to hide their computers from the rest of Internet. Certain groups of IP addresses, known as private IP addresses, are available to help in these situations. All routers are designed to destroy private IP addresses so they can never be used on the Internet, making them a handy way to hide systems! Anyone can use these private IP addresses, but they're useless for systems that need to access the Internet—unless you use one of those mysterious NAT things to which I just referred. (Bet you're dying to learn about NATs now!) For the moment, however, let's just look at the ranges of addresses that are designated private IP addresses:

- 10.0.0.0 through 10.255.255.255 (1 Class A license)
- 172.16.0.0 through 172.31.255.255 (16 Class B licenses)
- 192.168.0.0 through 192.168.255.255 (256 Class C licenses)

We refer to all other IP addresses as public IP addresses.

TIP Make sure you can quickly tell the difference between a private and a public IP address for the Network+ exam!

Other Critical TCP/IP Settings

You now understand the three most important settings on every TCP/IP computer: the IP address, the default gateway, and the subnet mask. But most computers on a TCP/IP network will need a few more critical settings. Let's take a look at DNS, WINS, and DHCP.

DNS

Anyone who's ever used a web browser is used to seeing Internet addresses like www.totalsem.com, ftp.microsoft.com, and so on; these invariably end with .com, .org,

.net, or some other three-character name (or two-character country code, like .uk for the United Kingdom). Now just a minute here—haven't we spent the last several pages explaining how every computer on the Internet has a unique IP address that distinguishes it from every other computer on the Internet? What's with this name business all of a sudden? Well, the folks who invented the Internet decided early on that it was way too painful for human beings to refer to computer systems using dotted decimal notation. There had to be some sort of Internet-naming convention that allowed people to refer to systems by human-friendly names, rather than cryptic but computer-friendly numbers. They couldn't just do away with the numbers, however, unless they were planning to teach the computers to read English, so they developed a procedure called *name resolution*. The idea was to have a list of IP addresses matched up with corresponding human-friendly names, that any computer on the Internet could use to translate a computer name into an IP address.

The original IP specification implemented name resolution using a special text file called *HOSTS*. A copy of this file was stored on every computer system on the Internet. The HOSTS file contained a list of IP addresses for every computer on the Internet, matched to the corresponding system names. Remember, not only was the Internet a lot smaller then, there weren't yet rules about how to compose Internet names, like they must end in .com or .org, or start with www or ftp. Anyone could name their computer pretty much anything they wanted (there were a few restrictions on length and allowable characters) as long as nobody else had snagged the name first. Part of an old HOSTS file might look something like this:

    192.168.2.1   fred

    201.32.16.4   school2

    123.21.44.16   server

If your system wanted to access the system called fred, it looked up the name fred in its HOSTS file, and then used the corresponding IP address to contact fred. Every HOSTS file on every system on the Internet was updated every night at 2 A.M. This worked fine when the Internet was still the province of a few university geeks and some military guys, but when the Internet grew to about 5,000 systems, it became impractical to make every system use and update a HOSTS file. This motivated the creation of the *Domain Name Service (DNS)* concept.

Believe it or not, the HOSTS file is still alive and well in every computer. You can find the HOSTS file in the \WINDOWS folder in Windows 9*x*, in the \WINNT\ SYSTEM32\DRIVERS\ETC folder in Windows NT/2000/2003, and in \WINDOWS\ SYSTEM32\DRIVERS\ETC in Windows XP. It's just a text file that you can open with any text editor. Here are a few lines from the default HOSTS file that comes with Windows. See the # signs? Those are remark symbols that designate lines as comments rather than code—take them off and Windows will read the lines and act on them. While all operating systems continue to support the HOSTS file, it is rarely used in the day-to-day workings of most TCP/IP systems.

```
# Additionally, comments (such as these) may be inserted on individual
# lines or following the machine name denoted by a '#' symbol.
#
# For example:
#
#        102.54.94.97        rhino.acme.com            # source server
#         38.25.63.10        x.acme.com                # x client host
127.0.0.1             localhost
```

How DNS Works

The Internet guys, faced with the task of replacing HOSTS, first came up with the idea of creating one super computer that did nothing but resolve names for all the other computers on the Internet. Problem: even now, no computer is big enough or powerful enough to handle the job alone. So, they fell back on that time-tested bureaucratic solution: delegation! The top-dog DNS system would delegate parts of the job to subsidiary DNS systems, who, in turn, would delegate part of their work to other systems, and so on, potentially without end. These systems run a special DNS server program, and are called, amazingly enough, DNS servers. This is all peachy, but it raises another issue: you need some way to decide how to divvy up the work. Toward this end, they created a naming system designed to facilitate delegation. The top dog DNS server is a bunch of powerful computers dispersed around the world and working as a team, known collectively as the DNS root. The Internet name of this computer team is "."—that's right, just "dot." Sure, it's weird, but it's quick to type, and they had to start somewhere! DNS root has the complete definitive name resolution table, but most name-resolution work is delegated to other DNS servers. Just below the DNS root in the hierarchy is a set of DNS servers that handle what are known as the top-level domain names. These are the famous COM, ORG, NET, EDU, GOV, MIL, and INT. (Even these are getting full—you may have seen news stories about new additions to this top-level domain list.) These top-level DNS servers delegate to thousands of second-level DNS servers; they handle the millions of names like totalsem.com and whitehouse.gov that have been created within each of the top-level domains.

These domain names must be registered for Internet use with an organization called ICANN (http://www.icann.org). They are arranged in the familiar "second level.top level" domain name format, where the top level is COM, ORG, NET, and so on, and the second level is the name of the individual entity registering the domain name. For example, in the domain name microsoft.com, "microsoft" is the second-level part and "com" is the top-level part. As we just learned, the Internet maintains a group of powerful and busy DNS servers that resolve the top-level parts of domain names. The second-level parts of domain names are resolved by the owners of those domain names, or by an ISP.

A DNS network may also have subdomains. The subdomain names are added to the left of the domain name. Let's use our standard example: the MHTechEd network, which has the domain name mhteched.com, may have subdomains with names like north.mhteched.com and south.mhteched.com. The owner of the second-level domain, MHTechEd in our example, maintains any subdomains on its own DNS servers or its ISP's DNS servers. Subdomains may also contain a further layer of subdomains (for example, bravo.north.mhteched.com), but this is rare, and usually is handled by in-house DNS servers where it does exist.

Every system on the Internet also has a host name added on to the left of its domain name, such as "www" for a web server or perhaps "domain1" for a domain controller in a Windows network. A *fully qualified domain name (FQDN)* contains the complete DNS name of a system, from its host name to the top-level domain name. I have a system in my office with an FQDN of vpn.totalsem.com that handles my virtual private network. I also have a system with the FQDN of www.totalsem.com that runs my web site. How about that—seems you've been using FQDNs for years and didn't even know it.

A system will have its own list of domain names, stored either in its HOSTS file or in a cache. When a system needs to resolve a domain name to an IP address and it doesn't have this information, it queries the DNS server listed in its DNS server settings. If the DNS server cannot resolve the name, the DNS server asks the root server. The root server then redirects your DNS server to a top-level DNS server. The top-level DNS server, in turn, points you to a second-level DNS server that will resolve the domain name. We'll look at how DNS works in much more detail in Chapter 14; right now, let's see how you configure a Windows client system to use DNS.

You configure DNS in Windows using the TCP/IP Properties dialog box. Figure 11-26 shows the DNS settings for my system. Note that I have more than one DNS server setting; the second one is a backup in case the first one isn't working. Two DNS settings is not a rule, however, so don't worry if your system shows only one DNS server setting, or perhaps more than two. You can check your current DNS server settings in Windows using either the **WINIPCFG** or the **IPCONFIG** command.

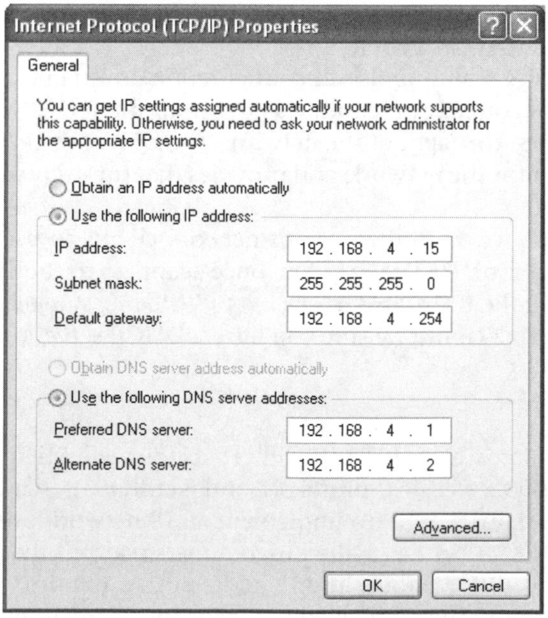

Figure 11-26
DNS settings in
Windows XP

That's pretty much all we need to talk about right now. What you need to know about DNS for the Network+ exam is how to set up the DNS server for your system if given the configuration information. In Chapter 14, "Going Large with TCP/IP," we look at DNS in more detail, including what it takes to make a DNS server!

DHCP

Before you read this, you must promise not to hit me, okay? So far we've discussed four items that must be configured for every system in an IP network: the IP address, the default gateway, the subnet mask, and the DNS server. Does this sound like a bit of a hassle? Imagine being informed by some network muckety-muck that your organization is changing its DNS servers, requiring you to reset the DNS server settings on every system in the network. Doesn't sound like too much fun, eh?

Fortunately for you, there's something called the *Dynamic Host Configuration Protocol (DHCP)*. DHCP enables individual client machines on an IP network to configure all of their IP settings (IP address, subnet mask, DNS, and more) automatically. DHCP requires a special system running a special program called a DHCP server. Autoconfiguration has been a boon to networks that change a lot (like mine), systems that travel around (like laptops), and dial-up systems. DHCP is extremely popular and heavily used in almost all IP networks.

 TIP DHCP is used mainly by Windows networks. There's another autoconfiguration protocol called BOOTP that is used for diskless workstations. They both work basically the same way.

How Does DHCP Work?

All of this DHCP automatic self-configuration doesn't let administrators completely off the hook, of course. Somebody has to set up the DHCP server before it can make the magic happen throughout the network. The DHCP server stores all of the necessary IP information for the network, and provides that information to clients as they boot into the network.

You also have to configure your network clients to use DHCP. Configuring a Windows system for DHCP is easy. Yes, once again, go to the TCP/IP Properties dialog box. This time, set the IP Address to *Obtain An IP Address Automatically*, and you're ready to go (see Figure 11-27). Just be sure you have a DHCP server on your network!

WINS

Years ago, Microsoft and TCP/IP didn't mix too well. Microsoft networks leaned heavily on the NetBIOS/NetBEUI protocols, and NetBIOS used a completely different naming convention than TCP/IP. To implement an IP network protocol in Windows NT while still using NetBIOS names, the programmers realized that NT needed some way to resolve NT's NetBIOS names into IP addresses. At the time, Microsoft didn't foresee the impact of the Internet; it seemed to make more sense to ignore DNS, because dropping

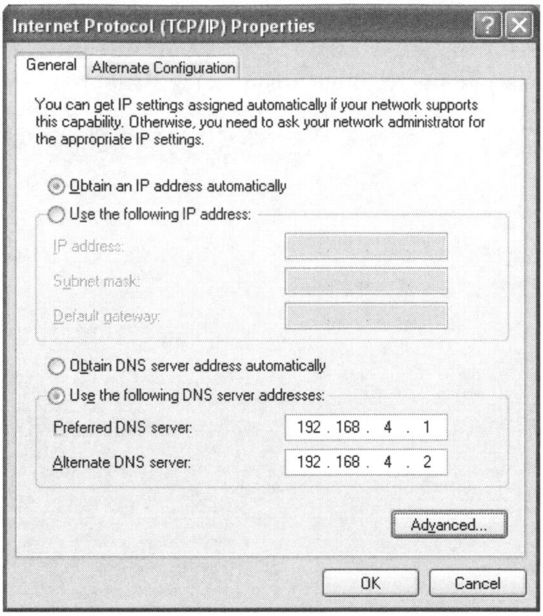

Figure 11-27
Configuring a
Windows XP
system for DHCP

Internet Protocol (TCP/IP) Properties

General | Alternate Configuration

You can get IP settings assigned automatically if your network supports
this capability. Otherwise, you need to ask your network administrator for
the appropriate IP settings.

○ O̲btain an IP address automatically
○ Use the following IP address:
IP address:
Subnet mask:
Default gateway:

○ O̲btain DNS server address automatically
◉ Use the following DNS server addresses:
Preferred DNS server: 192 . 168 . 4 . 1
A̲lternate DNS server: 192 . 168 . 4 . 2

[Ad̲vanced...]

[OK]   [Cancel]

PART II

NetBIOS would require a major redesign of Windows NT; instead, they came up with an equivalent that used the already existing NetBIOS functions.

NOTE Windows 2000/XP/2003 systems no longer need NetBIOS; they now use DNS, although they can support WINS if needed. Windows 9x and NT systems, however, still need WINS to use NETBIOS names across routed networks!

But why make a naming system that resolves IP addresses to NetBIOS names? As we saw in the previous chapter, name resolution in Windows has always depended on individual hosts broadcasting to the network their desire to use a particular NetBIOS name. Broadcasting was the problem! Routers do not allow broadcasting in an IP environment. Microsoft solved this dilemma with the creation of the *Windows Internet Naming Service (WINS)*.

WINS is a hierarchical naming system, similar to DNS in many ways. Just as DNS depends on DNS servers, WINS revolves around special WINS server software. A WINS server tracks all of the requests for NetBIOS names on a Windows TCP/IP network. When computers first log on to a WINS network, they register with the WINS server, and the server puts the client's NetBIOS name and IP address into its WINS database. Any system on the network can query the WINS server for NetBIOS name resolution.

Happily for network techs, Microsoft automated many aspects of WINS, making the actual setup and configuration of WINS almost trivially easy. Setting up WINS on a Windows client requires little more than a quick trip to the WINS Configuration tab

you guess?—the TCP/IP Properties dialog box, where you can select Use DHCP
NS resolution (see Figure 11-28). There are other setup options as well, which we
 in Chapter 14, "Going Large with TCP/IP."

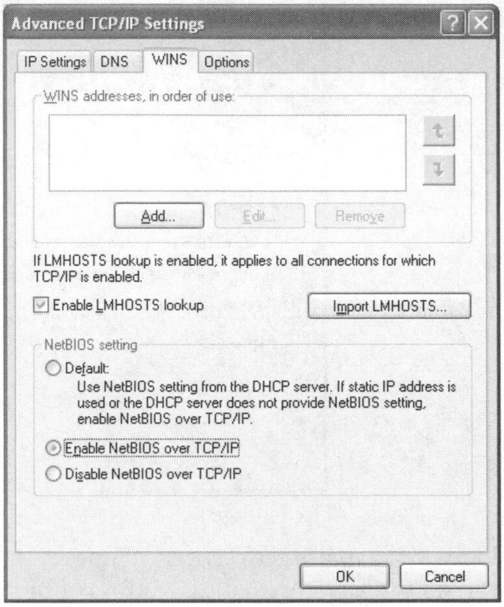

Figure 11-28
WINS settings
in Windows XP

The toughest part about DNS, WINS, and DHCP is the potential to confuse what each
one does, so here's a quick review to help you remember each one's job.

- **DNS** A TCP protocol that resolves domain names (for example,
  www.totalsem.com) into actual IP addresses
- **WINS** A Windows-only protocol used to resolve NetBIOS names into IP
  addresses
- **DHCP** A protocol that automatically configures a system's IP information
  for end users

You may have noticed that DNS, WINS, and DHCP all require a server. Be careful with
this terminology. In this context, server does not mean a physical computer—it means a
program that handles DNS, DHCP, or WINS requests from client computers. It's fairly
common, especially on smaller networks, for one server system to run all three of these
server programs simultaneously.

IP Ports

The term TCP/IP is a bit of a misnomer. It implies that TCP is the only type of data that IP
packets transport. In reality, while TCP is certainly the most common type of data found

in IP packets, it's certainly not the only one. IP supports a number of different types of data, each one used for a very specific purpose. Let's take a moment to look at TCP and two other important IP data types—UDP and ICMP—and see what they do.

TCP

Most folks who work in a network environment, especially a network with systems running Microsoft Windows, think that a network's main function is to share folders and printers. Back when the Internet was young, however, the folks who designed TCP/IP didn't think exactly in those terms. They looked at a network as a way to share terminals (remember this discussion from earlier in the book?), exchange e-mail, and perform other functions unrelated to our concept of networks as a way to share files and printers. But lucky for us, they also realized they would probably be using TCP/IP to share things they hadn't yet invented, so they designed it with a degree of flexibility that enables you and me today to share files, surf the Web, listen to streaming media, and play Everquest online with a thousand of our closest buddies at once. This is TCP's reason for being.

The inventors of TCP/IP assign a special number called a port to each separate network function, such as e-mail, web browsing, even online games like Everquest. This port number is placed inside every IP packet and is used by the sending and receiving systems to figure out which application to give the packet to. Possibly the most famous TCP port of all is good old port 80. If a packet comes into a computer with the port number 80 embedded in it, the system knows that the packet needs to go to your web browser. Packets sent to port 80 use a special protocol called HyperText Transfer Protocol (HTTP).

Port 80 Is for HTTP

UDP

If you get a chance, take a look at the link light on your NIC when you first start your system. You'll notice that the light is flickering away, showing that some kind of communication is taking place. Granted, not all of that communication is for your system, but trust me, a lot of it is—and you haven't even started your e-mail or opened a web browser! Clearly your PC is talking on the network even though you haven't asked it to do anything! Don't worry—this is a good thing. TCP/IP does lots of boring maintenance-type stuff in the background that you neither need nor want to care about. Most of these maintenance communications are simple things like an ARP request, or any one of about 500 other little maintenance jobs that TCP/IP handles for you automatically.

While these things are important, they do not require all the TCP information in an IP packet. Knowing this, the folks who designed TCP/IP created a much simpler protocol called *User Datagram Protocol (UDP)*. UDP transmits much less information than TCP. UDP packets are both simpler and smaller than TCP packets, and do most of the behind-the-scenes work in a TCP/IP network. UDP packets are what is called connectionless—that is, they don't worry about confirming that a packet reached its destination. TCP packets, in contrast, are connection-oriented—in other words, they must create a connection between the sending and receiving systems to ensure that the packet reaches its destination successfully. Important functions like e-mail will never use UDP.

...lder applications, most prominently TFTP (Trivial FTP), use UDP to transfer ...but even TFTP is quite rare today; UDP is almost completely relegated to impor-...but behind-the-scenes jobs on the network.

ICMP

...pplications that use the *Internet Control Message Protocol (ICMP)* are even simpler than UDP applications. ICMP messages consist of a single packet and are connectionless; like UDP. ICMP packets determine connectivity between two hosts. As such, they carry only a tiny set of responses, such as *echo reply*, *protocol unreachable*, or *host unreachable*. In a way, ICMP is simply a way to see things at the IP level. ICMP packets don't transfer data *per se*, but rather tell you how the IP packets between any two hosts are doing. The most famous ICMP application is PING.

NOTE There is another type of IP data called IGMP (Internet Group Management Protocol). IGMP is used to take advantage of multicasting—broadcasting a series of packets to very specific systems. IGMP is used for some videoconferencing and other applications.

Table 11-1 shows a list of the most common of all the TCP and UDP ports and their uses. Keep in mind that Table 11-1 shows only the most common ones—there are liter-ally hundreds more than these! For the Network+ exam, at least be sure you memorize this table.

Here are brief explanations of these ports, most of which I'll revisit in detail in later chapters.

HTTP (Port 80)
Web servers use *HyperText Transfer Protocol (HTTP)* to send web pages to clients running web browsers such as Internet Explorer or Mozilla Firefox.

FTP (Ports 20 and 21)
File Transfer Protocol (FTP) transfers data files between servers and clients. All implemen-tations of TCP/IP support FTP file transfers, making FTP an excellent choice for transfer-ring files between machines running different operating systems (Windows to UNIX, UNIX to Macintosh, and so on). FTP uses port 21 for control messages and sends the data using port 20. FTP servers can require users to log in before downloading or up-loading files. Most operating systems include a command-line FTP utility.

SFTP (Port 22)
FTP has one rather ugly aspect: by default, FTP transfers are not encrypted. Anyone clever enough to monitor an FTP session can intercept the username, password, and data. Se-cure FTP encrypts everything moving between the server and the client, so that the username, password, and data are safe from prying eyes.

Port Number	Service	Description
20	FTP DATA	File Transfer Protocol – Data, used for transferring files
21	FTP	File Transfer Protocol – Control, used for transferring files
23	TELNET	Telnet, used to gain "remote control" over another machine on the network
25	SMTP	Simple Mail Transfer Protocol, used for transferring e-mail between e-mail servers
69	TFTP	Trivial File Transfer Protocol, used for transferring files without a secure login
80	HTTP	HyperText Transfer Protocol, used for transferring HTML (HyperText Markup Language) files, i.e., web pages
110	POP3	Post Office Protocol version 3, used for transferring e-mail from an e-mail server to an e-mail client
119	NNTP	Network News Transfer Protocol, used to transfer Usenet newsgroup messages from a news server to a newsreader program
123	NTP	Network Time Protocol, used to synchronize the time of a server or workstation to another server
137	NETBIOS-NS	NetBIOS Name Service, used by Microsoft Networking
138	NETBIOS-DG	NetBIOS Datagram Service, used for transporting data by Microsoft Networking
139	NETBIOS-SS	NetBIOS Session Service, used by Microsoft Networking
161	SNMP	Simple Network Management Protocol, used to monitor network devices remotely
389	LDAP	Lightweight Directory Access Protocol, used to communicate with network directories/databases
443	HTTPS	HyperText Transfer Protocol with Secure Sockets Layer (SSL), used to transfer secure HTML files

Table 11-1   Common TCP and UDP ports

TFTP (Port 69)

Trivial File Transfer Protocol (TFTP) transfers files between servers and clients. Unlike FTP, TFTP requires no user login. Devices that need an operating system, but have no local hard disk (for example, diskless workstations and routers), often use TFTP to download their operating systems.

SMTP (Port 25)

Simple Mail Transfer Protocol (SMTP) sends e-mail messages between clients and servers or between servers. From the end user's perspective, SMTP handles outgoing mail only.

POP3 (Port 110)

Post Office Protocol version 3 (POP3) enables e-mail client software (for example, Outlook Express, Eudora, Netscape Mail) to retrieve e-mail from a mail server. POP3 does not send e-mail; SMTP handles that function.

SNMP (Port 161)

Simple Network Management Protocol (SNMP) enables network management applications to remotely monitor other devices on the network.

Telnet (Port 23)

Telnet enables a user to log in remotely and execute text-based commands on a remote host. Although any operating system can run a Telnet server, techs typically use Telnet to log in to UNIX-based systems.

NetBIOS (Ports 137, 138, 139)

Networks using NetBIOS over TCP/IP use ports 137, 138, and 139 for name resolution and other NetBIOS-specific tasks.

In most cases, you will never have to deal with ports. When you install an e-mail program, for example, your system will automatically assume that all packets coming on ports 110 and 25 are e-mail and will send them to the e-mail application. You don't have to do anything special to configure the port values—they just work. In later chapters, we will discuss configuring TCP/IP applications, and we'll see that, in some cases, you may have to change port numbers, but for now just be sure to memorize the port numbers in Table 11-1.

 TIP Although CompTIA claims to be vendor-neutral; TCP/IP questions on the Network+ exam generally assume that the client system uses a Microsoft Windows operating system.

NTP (Port 123)

Network Time Protocol (NTP) is a UDP protocol that has only one job: to announce the time. Think of it as the Big Ben of TCP/IP.

LDAP (Port 389)

The Lightweight Directory Access Protocol (LDAP) is the common language used to communicate with network directories. See Chapter 12, "Network Operating Systems," for more details on the many types of directories used by network operating systems.

IPv6

One of the big problems with TCP/IP stems from the fact that we seem to be running out of IP addresses. In theory, the 32-bit IP address under the current *IP version 4* specification (we officially call it *IPv4*) allows for 2^{32} or over 4 billion addresses. However, due to many restrictions, only about 1.7 billion are available, and many of those are wasted by organizations that take more IP addresses than they need. As a result, the Internet Engineering Task Force (IETF) developed a new IP addressing scheme, called *IP version 6*, abbreviated *IPv6* (first known as IP Next Generation [IPng]), that is expected to gradually replace IPv4 in coming years. IPv6 extends the 32-bit IP address to 128 bits, allowing up to 3.4×10^{38} addresses! Probably enough to last us for awhile, eh?

Remember that the IPv4 addresses are written as 197.169.94.82 using four octets. Well, IPv6 has now changed all that. IPv6 addresses are written like this:

FEDC:BA98:7654:3210:0800:200C:00CF:1234

IPv6 uses a colon as a separator, instead of the period used in IPv4's dotted decimal format. Each group is a hexadecimal number between 0000 and FFFF. As a refresher for those who don't play with hex regularly, one hexadecimal character (for example, *F*) represents four bits, so four hexadecimal characters make a 16-bit group. When writing IPv6 addresses, leading zeroes can be dropped from a group, so 00CF becomes simply CF, and 0000 becomes just 0. To write IPv6 addresses containing strings of zeroes, you can use a pair of colons (::) to represent a string of consecutive 16-bit groups with a value of zero. For example, using the :: rule you can write the IPv6 address FEDC:0000:0000:0000:00CF:0000:BA98:1234 as FEDC::CF:0:BA98:1234. Notice that I

IPv6	:: rule applied to IPv6 address	Function
1080:0:0:0:8:800:200C:417A	1080::8:800:200C:417A	Unicast address
0:0:0:0:0:0:0:1	::1	Loopback address
0:0:0:0:0:0:0:0	::	Unspecified address

Table 11-2   IPv6 Reserved Addresses and Their Function

could not use a second :: to represent the third-to-last group of four zeroes—only one :: per address! There's a good reason for this rule. If more than one :: was used, how could you tell how many sets of zeroes were in each group? Table 11-2 shows some of the reserved IPv6 addresses.

NOTE   The unspecified address (all zeroes) can never be used and neither can an address that contains all ones.

Chapter Review

Questions

1. A host is

    A. Any server on a TCP/IP network

    B. Any device on a TCP/IP network that can send or receive data packets

    C. A device on a TCP/IP network that forwards data packets to other networks

    D. A device on a TCP/IP network that resolves names to IP addresses

2. Before a TCP/IP host can communicate with another host on a different network, which of the following settings must it have configured correctly? (Select all that apply.)

    A. IP address

    B. Subnet mask

    C. DNS server

    D. Default gateway

3. What port number does HTTP use?

    A. 443

    B. 110

    C. 80

    D. 43

4. The binary number 11000101 has the decimal equivalent of

    A. 197

    B. 169

    C. 94

    D. 82

5. What is the loopback address for IPv4?

    A. 127.0.0.1

    B. 0:0:0:0:0:0:0:0

    C. ::1

    D. 0:0:0:0:0:0:0:1

6. The protocol that enables network management applications to monitor devices remotely is known as

    A. SNMP

    B. SMTP

   C. POP3

   D. TFTP

7. John is running Windows 98. He wants to find out his MAC address and IP address. What utility can John use to provide this information?

   A. ARP

   B. WINIPCFG

   C. IPCONFIG

   D. MACIP

8. Mike is running Windows 2000. He wants to find out his MAC address and IP address. What utility can Mike use to provide this information?

   A. ARP

   B. WINIPCFG

   C. IPCONFIG

   D. MACIP

9. Scott's system wants to send data to Roger's system. Scott's system knows Roger's IP address, but it doesn't know the MAC address, which it needs. What does the system use to request a MAC address for a known IP address?

   A. ARP

   B. WINIPCFG

   C. IPCONFIG

   D. MACIP

10. The IP address 192.23.45.123 has a default subnet mask of

   A. 255.0.0.0

   B. 255.255.0.0

   C. 255.255.255.0

   D. 255.255.255.255

Answers

1. **B.** Any device on a TCP/IP network that can send or receive data packets is called a host.

2. **A, B, D.** A host on a TCP/IP network must have its IP address, subnet mask, and default gateway correctly configured before it can communicate with hosts on other networks.

3. **C.** HyperText Transfer Protocol (HTTP) uses port 80.

4. **A.** The binary number 11000101 has the decimal equivalent of 197.

5. **A.** The loopback address for IPv4 is 127.0.0.1.

6. **A.** Simple Network Management Protocol (SNMP) enables network management applications to monitor devices remotely.

7. **B.** On a Windows 98 system, the WINIPCFG utility gives the MAC address and IP address currently used by that system.

8. **C.** On a Windows 2000 system, the IPCONFIG utility gives the MAC address and IP address currently used by that system.

9. **A.** The sending system sends out an address resolution protocol (ARP) request to get the MAC address for a known IP address.

10. **C.** The IP address 192.23.45.123 is in Class C and has the default subnet mask of 255.255.255.0.

## CHAPTER 12

Network Operating Systems

The Network+ Certification exam expects you to know how to

- 3.1   Identify the basic capabilities (for example: client support, interoperability, authentication, file and print services, application support and security) of the following server operating systems to access network resources: UNIX/Linux/Mac OS X Server, NetWare, Windows, AppleShare IP (Internet Protocol)
- 3.2   Identify the basic capabilities needed for client workstations to connect to and use network resources (for example: media, network protocols, and peer and server services)
- 3.4   Given a remote connectivity scenario [comprising] a protocol, an authentication scheme, and physical connectivity, configure the connection. Includes connection to the following servers: UNIX/Linux/Mac OS X Server, NetWare, Windows, AppleShare IP

To achieve these goals, you must be able to

- Define the concepts of resource-, server-, and organization-based network models and place any operating system into the proper model
- Describe in detail how different operating systems perform networking
- Configure a Windows client to connect to any version of a Windows server.

Fifteen years ago, operating systems and network operating systems were two very different things. Back then, operating systems (like the old DOS and the first versions of Windows) were stand-alone, designed only for running applications—word processors, games, spreadsheets, and so forth. Operating systems didn't come with any built-in networking software. If you wanted to make one of these old operating systems run on a network, you had to install third-party networking programs. At the same time, if you wanted to make a server system for all your little DOS and Windows computers to connect to, you had to buy special (and usually expensive) *network operating system (NOS)* software—a special operating system designed from the ground up to act as a server in a network. Manufacturers packaged the operating system and network operating system versions of their software differently.

Today the old line between an operating system and a network operating system no longer exists. With one glaring exception, every operating system today comes complete with all the networking software needed to enable any system to share resources and access shared resources. Even though operating systems and network operating systems are one in the same, different operating systems perform networking in very different ways. For example, Windows 98 SE shares a folder very differently than Windows Server 2003—there is simply no way a tech can support these operating systems without a deep appreciation of those differences!

Let's transform the definition of the term "network operating system" into something that works for today's operating systems. The phrase *network operating system* refers to the network functions built into a particular operating system. For example, Windows XP is an operating system, but how Windows XP accesses another system's shared resources on a network is a function of Windows XP's network operating system components.

The amount of security provided for users and data is the single greatest issue that differentiates one network operating system from another. The word *security* encompasses a number of critical issues as you'll see in this chapter, such as how, or even if, users can log in. This chapter begins by carefully defining client and server and providing some comparisons to appreciate how different operating systems use networking security. This section defines terms such as user accounts, groups, domains, and other important terms and shows that every operating system in existence fits into one of three groupings that I call models. Once you have a grasp on these three models, we then turn to the most common operating systems in use today: Windows 9x/Me, Windows NT/2000/XP/2003, Linux, Novell NetWare, and Macintosh. Last, we go through the process of creating a network of Windows servers and Windows clients to appreciate some of the issues that come into play when building a network.

Historical/Conceptual

Categorizing Operating Systems

All network operating systems share the same fundamental goal: to enable users, the human beings who sit at the computers, to get work done by sharing resources. The routes to that goal vary, of course, depending on the nature of the work. Some network operating systems simply enable users to share folders and printers, while others supply users with access to one or more of literally hundreds of sophisticated shared resources such as web servers, e-mail servers, and DHCP servers. Before choosing the right network operating system for your network, you must define the types of resources you want to share, which systems will do the sharing, and the level of security you require. Understanding how the different operating systems fulfill those goals helps facilitate this decision making process.

Before we define network operating system models, it's important to clarify the difference between a client and a server. Chapter 2 defines a client and a server as software programs. In order for a computer to share a resource it must run some form of serving software and a system that wants to access that shared resource must run a client program. While this is absolutely correct, it contradicts other meanings of server. For many people, the term "server" refers to a great, big, heavy-duty computer, hidden in some equipment room, using a powerful CPU, lots of RAM, and stacks of hard drives, as shown in Figure 12-1. If this is a server, how can a server simply be a program as described earlier?

Figure 12-1
A typical server

The answer is that both definitions of server are accurate. Consider a web server. I have an old Windows 98 SE computer that runs a web server software called Microsoft Personal Web Server (PWS). Figure 12-2 shows the PWS Personal Web Manager screen running on that system. I use this system in my home network to keep a calendar that everyone in my family uses to keep track of the many activities taking place in our lives—a handy tool for a very busy family.

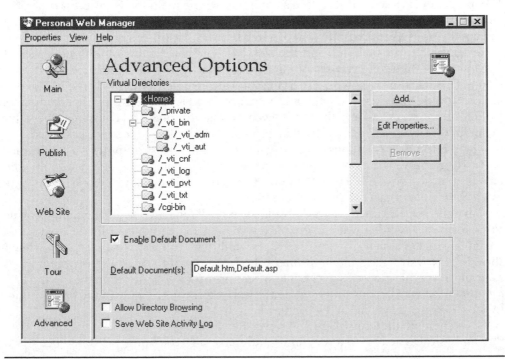

Figure 12-2   PWS running on an old Windows 98 system

This web server works perfectly for my little family, but if lots of people tried to access this web site, that little Windows 98 system's going to get pretty busy, isn't it? In fact, it would slow to a crawl. This is true for any computer running server software. Additionally, if my little server's hard drive crashes, no one will notice outside my family. Imagine the server that runs my company's web site—if that server's hard drive failed, many, many people would notice!

Server-class systems tend to have lots of RAM and powerful CPUs to support heavy use. They have big, redundant, hard drive arrays to keep the system running in case a drive dies. It's perfectly acceptable to call those big, powerful computers "servers" as long as you appreciate that a computer doesn't have to be big to be a server.

 NOTE There are cases where serving software demands server-class hardware. Some serving programs, such as the popular Microsoft Exchange Server, have substantial hardware requirements—my little Windows 98 box couldn't hope to run the latest version of Exchange!

While we're on the subject of servers, here's a quick question: If a server is any computer running serving software, can one computer run more than one serving program? Absolutely! In fact, that's the common way to use serving programs. My Windows 2003 server, for example, runs about 13 different serving programs at the same time.

Now that we've clarified the term "server," let's move to "client." As previously defined, a "client" is a program that is used to access resources shared by serving program. The term client is also used to define a computer whose main job is to access other system's shared resources, a computer that people sit at and use every day—the ones that run applications like Microsoft Word or a web browser. My office system, the one I use to write books, check e-mail and surf the Net, is a powerful Athlon 64 with gigabytes of RAM and hundreds of gigabytes of hard drive capacity, running Windows XP Professional. This machine has plenty of serving software installed, but I rarely use it. The vast majority of the time this computer only accesses shared resources from other computers (folders, printers, e-mail and the Web). Even though this powerful computer does a bit of serving—I share a single folder that someone might access once a week or so—its main job is to run applications I need to get my job done. This computer is a client computer. The term "workstation" is also used to define client computers. In general a *workstation* is a more powerful client system. The terms "client" and "workstation" are interchangeable from a networking standpoint.

Can a client system act as a server? Absolutely yes! All modern operating systems provide some form of serving software to enable a system to share folders or files. Can a server system also act as a client? In most cases, yes—although you'll see one exception when I show you Novell NetWare in a moment. Let's use my old Windows 98 system as an example. It's acting as a web server but I can still fire up a web browser on the PC and I access other servers' files or printers while the web server runs happily in the background. In most cases, one system can be both a client and a server.

Be careful with the terms client and server. Remember that either term may refer to either a physical system or to a program—and make sure you know the difference when you use these terms!

Test Specific

Why is it so important to understand this concept of server and client? It comes down to recognizing how different operating systems work. Every brand of operating system has very different ways of determining which systems can act as servers and which as clients. If you don't understand the differences in how Novell NetWare handles servers and clients as compared to Microsoft Windows XP, you could find yourself making a major mess by asking your NOS to do something it isn't designed to do!

Client/Server vs. Peer-to-Peer

Networking folks traditionally use the terms "client/server" and "peer-to-peer" to categorize network operating systems. Coined almost 20 years ago, these terms no longer work as an accurate tool for grouping today's complex and powerful operating systems. Even though they no longer do a good job in categorizing, their presence in the common networking vernacular (plus the fact these two terms are on the Network+ exam) motivate us to understand these terms. Let's look at how these two terms define the functionality of different network operating systems.

Client/Server

The earliest network operating systems used a *client/server* model. In that model, certain systems act as dedicated servers. Dedicated servers are called dedicated because that's all they do. You cannot go up to a dedicated server and run Word or Solitaire. Dedicated servers run powerful server network operating systems that offer up files, folders, web pages, and so on to the network's client systems. Client systems on a client/server network never function as servers. One client system can't access shared resources on another client system. Servers serve and clients access, and never the twain shall meet in client/server land! The classic example of this type of network operating system is the popular and powerful Novell NetWare. Figure 12-3 shows a typical client/server network. As far as the clients are concerned, the only system on the network is the server system. The clients cannot see each other nor can they share data with each other directly. They must save the data on the server so other systems can access it.

Figure 12-3
In a pure client/server network, the clients cannot access each other directly.

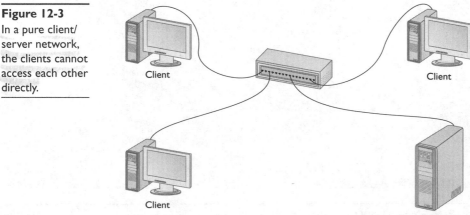

Client

Client

Client

Dedicated Server

Novell NetWare servers are true dedicated servers. You cannot go up to a Novell NetWare server and write yourself a resume; there is no Windows, there are no user applications. The only thing Novell NetWare servers know how to do is share their own resources, but they share those resources extremely well! Novell NetWare's operating system is totally different from Windows. It requires you to learn an entirely different set of installation, configuration, and administration commands. Figure 12-4 shows a screen from Novell NetWare. Don't let the passing resemblance to Windows fool you—it is a completely different operating system!

 TIP Fortunately, the Network+ exam does not expect you to know how to install, configure, or administer a NetWare server, or any other high-end NOS for that matter. Good thing, too, because if they did, this book would be about 5000 pages!

Peer-to-Peer

In a *peer-to-peer* network operating system, any system can act as a server or a client or both, depending on how you decide to configure it (see Figure 12-5). PCs on peer-to-peer networks frequently act as both clients and servers. One of the most common examples of a peer-to-peer network is the venerable Windows 9*x* series of operating systems.

At first glance, it would seem that peer-to-peer is the way to go—why create a network that doesn't allow the clients to see each other? Wouldn't it make more sense to give users the freedom to allow their systems to both share and access any resource? Good questions! Let's answer them by going back in time to around 1983.

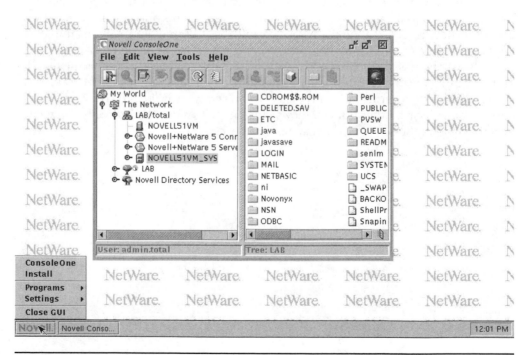

Figure 12-4 Novell NetWare—this isn't Windows!

Figure 12-5
In a pure peer-to-peer network, the clients may all act as servers.

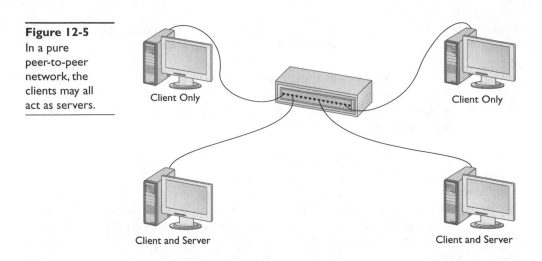

Client Only

Client Only

Client and Server

Client and Server

Back in the early 1980s, networking didn't really exist in the PC world. These were the days of the first processors, CPUs like the Intel 8088 and 80286. The demands of running a PC worked those poor CPUs to death. Then folks started to get the bright idea of adding networking to these systems. This was great in concept, but adding networking also meant adding lots of extra software, and networking software had to run continuously in the background while other activities were taking place. Those early systems had a very limited amount of processing power with which to tackle such networking challenges. Oh, and did I mention this was back in the days of DOS, the simplistic, single-tasking operating system of your forefathers? All the same, folks were determined to make 8088 systems running DOS handle networking. Clearly, this was going to take some doing!

The answer came in the form of client/server networking. Novell NetWare was invented back in the DOS days. Novell knew good and well that these little PCs didn't have the power to handle both networking and application software, so they put all the functionality in the server software and added the least possible amount of software to the client PCs in the form of special NetWare client software. A NetWare client was nothing more than a DOS—or eventually Windows—system with a little bit of extra software added so the client knew how to access the server's shared resources.

By keeping the server functionality separate from the client systems, the Novell folks made very powerful, dedicated servers without overwhelming the clients with tons of software. NetWare servers had (and still have) tremendous power and great security because the only thing they do is run serving software. In the early days of networking, client/server was king!

In time, CPU power advanced beyond those early CPUs, so Microsoft came up with a new answer to the resource sharing question: peer-to-peer networking. Although peer-to-peer networking appeared in the mid-1980s, it didn't really become popular until the introduction of Microsoft Windows for Workgroups in the early 1990s. Early versions of peer-to-peer network operating systems didn't have nearly the strength of Novell's client/server NOS, but they worked fairly well for small networks. They couldn't have the same security, reliability, and speed as NetWare running on the same hardware, for the simple reason that every system in a peer-to-peer network had to provide both server and client networking support, and still let users do things like run word processors.

 TIP The client/server model means dedicated servers with strong security. Clients can only see the server. In the peer-to-peer model, any system can be a client, server, or both, but at the cost of lower security and additional demands on the system resources of each peer.

For years, we divided all the operating systems into either the client/server or the peer-to-peer camps. The ability to pigeonhole all operating systems into these two network types made us happy and content. All was well with the networking world until Microsoft (who else?) came out with Windows NT in the early 1990s. Windows NT totally messed up the lovely division of networks into client/server and peer-to-peer, because an NT (and Windows 2000/2003 and Windows XP) system can be part of both a client/server network and a peer-to-peer network at the same time! A system running Windows NT gave you all the power and security of a dedicated server, while enabling that system to act as a client as well. Okay, it's actually not quite that simple, and I'll go into more detail in the next section, but the main point stands: NT messed up the entire client/server vs. peer-to-peer concept.

In my opinion, the terms "client/server" and "peer-to-peer" are no longer useful ways to organize different types of operating systems. Unfortunately, the terms peer-to-peer and client/server are still tossed around by network folks like dice at a craps table. So how do we manifest the concepts of client/server and peer-to-peer networking in a world that has outgrown these categories? The secret is in security.

Security

Network security involves protecting a network's users from their two greatest enemies: "bad guys" and themselves. When most people think about security issues, they immediately visualize some evil hacker attempting to break into a network and steal company secrets. For many organizations, especially those connected to the Internet, such threats are no joke. Network security, however, must also include controlling how users access the shared resources on their own network. *User-proofing* a network—preventing users from accidentally destroying data or granting access to unauthorized individuals—is a key part of network security.

 NOTE What you are about to learn is not on the Network+ exam, nor is it part of common network vernacular. It is my way of understanding networks, an idea I developed with my good friends Brian and Libby Schwarz a few years ago. Even though this concept is not directly on the Network+ exam, it will help you understand networking.

How do we secure our network shares? Well, that begs the question, "What aspects of the shared resource need to be secured?" Think about this for a second: If you're sharing a folder, what exactly do you want to protect? You could just stop anyone from doing anything to that folder—that's certainly secure—but you can slice the issue a lot more finely than just blocking everyone and everything. For example, you could set up security so users could read the files in a particular folder but not delete them. Or, slicing things even more finely, you could set it up so some users could edit files but not delete them. It's this fine level of detailed control that really makes a network powerful.

These security issues aren't limited to shared folders. Security comes into play with any type of resource you want to share. Every time you access a web site, you run headlong into security. I can set my web server up so some visitors can only view web pages, others can edit certain pages, and a very few others can do anything they want, including delete the entire site if necessary. I can secure my printers so that some people can print to a printer while others can not only print but also configure the printer remotely. The level of control that users can exercise on resources is called permissions or *rights*, depending on the brand of NOS you use. In the next chapter, I'll spend plenty of time discussing permissions and rights, types of protected resources, and how to share and secure them, but for now, what I want to discuss is the different approaches to how an NOS handles all this security—the security models.

Security Models

Odds are good you've heard of terms like "user accounts," "passwords," "groups," "domains," and the like. These terms are critical to understanding how a network secures resources. Don't worry if you don't understand any or all of them right now—I cover them all in detail in this chapter and the next. Whether you know these terms or not, do know this: each NOS uses these tools in different ways. This is what my security models concept is all about—it separates the different network operating systems by the way they secure the network's resources.

My scheme divides networks into three different security models, based on which part of the NOS handles the security: Resource, Server, and Organization. Think about this—some part of the NOS must keep track of who can do what on the network. Somewhere in the network, some system—or many systems—must store information that defines what resources are shared and how they are to be shared. Some part of the NOS must check this information whenever a client tries to access a shared resource to make sure that person is allowed to do whatever they are trying to do with that resource. My security models model identifies three parts of the NOS that do the dirty job of handling security. As I describe my three security models, I'll pause to define things like user accounts and groups. Let's get busy learning about the most basic type: resource-based security.

TIP   Even though the Network+ exam doesn't discuss my security models, this section of the chapter is crammed with critical definitions you need to understand for the exam.

Resource-Based Security Model

The simplest network operating systems use what I call resource-based security. In *resource-based network operating systems*, the individual resources themselves store the information about who can access the resource and what they can do (see Figure 12-6).

Figure 12-6

In resource-based network operating systems, the resources themselves store the security information.

Invoices   Inventory

Sales Promotions

This information is usually stored within some data structure that is part of the actual shared resource, although it can also be stored in some arbitrary part of the NOS itself. The important thing to understand is that there's no central storage facility for such information—each resource is in charge of its own security storage. The most common example of a resource-based NOS is the Microsoft Windows 9x series of operating systems. Most of what the traditional model calls peer-to-peer network operating systems belongs in my resource-based security model.

Storing security information within individual resources is a simple security solution, but one that can handle only simple security issues. As an example, let's take a look at my Windows 98 system. If I want to share a folder called C:\MHTechEDPersonnelRecords, I alternate-click (right-click) that folder and select Sharing. I click the Shared As radio button to see the folder's sharing properties (see Figure 12-7).

Note that I can choose from a whopping three levels of sharing. I can set up the folder so anyone who uses it gets full access to do anything they want; I can set it up so everyone gets only Read access, or I can set a password on the resource to control full vs. read-only access. These are your first examples of permissions/rights! Microsoft calls these network permissions.

While resource-based sharing works perfectly well as far as it goes, it has some serious limitations. First, unless I use a password, I have to give everyone who accesses this

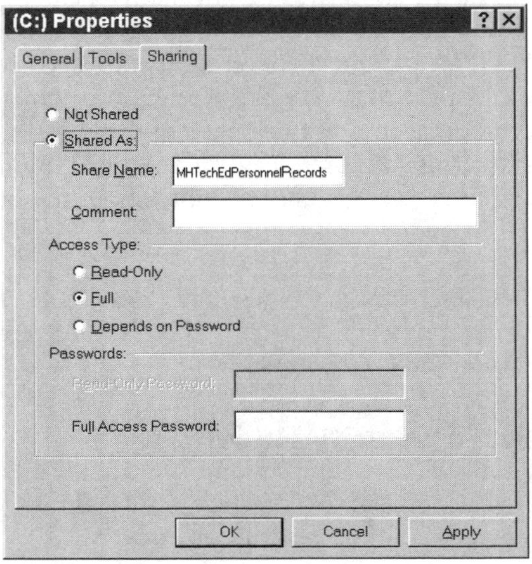

Figure 12-7

The Sharing folder in Windows 98

```
(C:) Properties                              ? X

General | Tools | Sharing

  ○ Not Shared
  ● Shared As

    Share Name:  MHTechEdPersonnelRecords

    Comment:

  Access Type:
    ○ Read-Only
    ● Full
    ○ Depends on Password

  Passwords:
    Read-Only Password:

    Full Access Password:


              OK        Cancel       Apply
```

folder the same level of access. What if I want some people to have full access and others just Read access? I can use a password, of course, but consider the problem from an administrator's standpoint: everyone with the same level of access has the same password. Suppose I want to change just one person's access—I have to change the password and then give the new password to everyone who needs access to that folder. This is not only wildly annoying, it's just asking for problems, because you're trusting those who know this one common password not to tell anyone else.

NOTE In a resource-based network operating system, each resource keeps track of its own permissions.

Now imagine there are 30 or 40 more shared folders and printers you need to protect this way—every one of those shared resources will get its own password! At this rate, a single system could use 60 to 70 different passwords! No problem, you say, if you make them all the same. Well, you could, but then how would you give different users different levels of access? But if you must have different passwords for different users of different resources, how can one lonely admin keep track of them all? Write it all down on a piece of paper? Make a spreadsheet? Let's face it, resource-based security may be fine for simple networks, but this is just not going to hack it in a more complex network.

Server-Based Security Model

A *server-based network* employs a central database on each server to track who gets what level of access to the resources on that server. Most folks give Novell the nod for inventing this security type since it first appeared in the early versions of NetWare. Since Novell had its own operating system, Novell could design every part of the dedicated server specifically to optimize its ability to handle sharing, including the file system. NetWare's file system is nothing like the old FAT16 or FAT32 file systems: Novell invented NetWare from the ground up to share folders. By creating its own file system, Novell could add resource sharing directly to the file system.

To access a shared resource on a NetWare server, you must have a user account. A *user account* contains lists of user rights that tell the network what the user can and cannot do on the network, including file system rights that determine which shared resources the user can access. Each user account also has a *password*. A person who wants to access the shared resources on the server must go through a process called logging onto the server. Figure 12-8 shows a classic example of how a person on a Windows system logs onto a NetWare server via the Novell Client for Windows. As soon as the person logs onto a NetWare server, all of the access privileges for every shared resource on the server are set for the duration of that session.

Server-based security makes life a lot easier from an administrative standpoint. Still, in a large organization, assigning specific rights to each user individually makes for an excessive workload for the network administrator. The solution: organize users with similar needs into *groups*. For example, Alice, the administrator of the network, assigns Greg, Bobby, and Peter's user accounts to the ACCOUNTING group and Jan's user

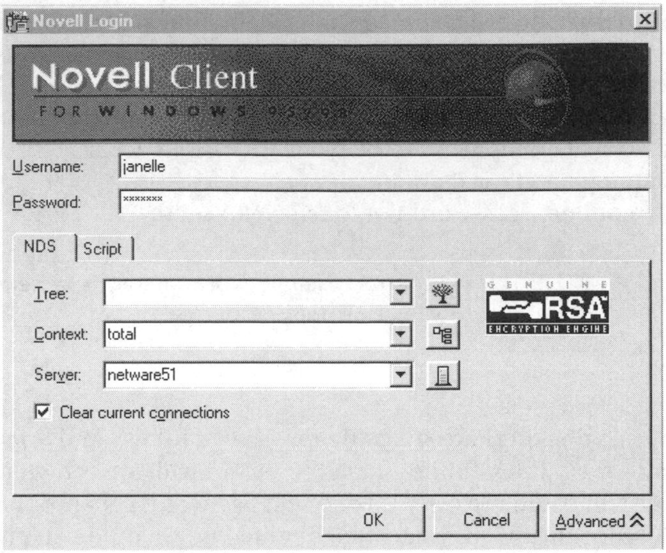

Figure 12-8
The NetWare
login screen

Novell Client
FOR WINDOWS 95/98

| Username: | janelle |
| Password: | ******* |

NDS | Script |

Tree: ▼ 🌲
Context: total ▼
Server: netware51 ▼

GENUINE
RSA
ENCRYPTION ENGINE

☑ Clear current connections

OK   Cancel   Advanced ≫

account to the SALES group. Alice then assigns the ACCOUNTING group permission to access the accounting database and any other appropriate resources. By virtue of their membership in ACCOUNTING, Greg, Bobby, and Peter's user accounts have access to the ACCOUNTING group's resources, without Alice having to touch the individual accounts. If the company hires more accountants, Alice simply creates new user accounts and adds them to the ACCOUNTING group. Alice creates groups for whatever different work specialties her company employs, and then assigns user accounts to the appropriate groups. In large organizations with hundreds of employees who have similar needs, the time and effort saved becomes significant.

In most instances, a user account's rights are cumulative, that is, a user receives the sum total of the rights granted to his individual user account and the rights granted to any of the groups to which he belongs. Greg, for example, belongs to both the MANAGERS and ACCOUNTANTS groups. Suppose Alice sets up a shared folder on a server and assigns the MANAGERS group the right to add files to the folder, the ACCOUNTANTS group the right to read (but not alter or delete) files in that folder, and Greg (as an individual) the right to modify files that already exist in that folder. To see what Greg can do, add up the rights: Greg can add files (MANAGERS), read files (ACCOUNTANTS), and modify files (Greg) in that directory because of his cumulative individual and group rights.

NOTE In a server-based network, every server keeps its own list of user accounts, groups, and permissions.

Server-based networks work great unless a network has more than one server. To use a server-based network with multiple servers, you must first have a user account on every server you want to use, and then you must log onto each one before you can use its resources. If your network only has a few servers, this isn't too much of a hassle for the user or the admin, but when the network has many servers, you've got an administrative nightmare once again.

Organization-Based Security Model

In an *organization-based network*, a single database acts as the logon point for all the shared resources of the network. This single source—I like to think of it as a database—stores at the minimum all of the user accounts and groups for the entire network. This database may reside on one computer, it may reside on one computer with one or more computers acting as a backup, or multiple computers might share complete copies of the database and constantly update each other through a process called *replication*. When a user logs on, that user's rights/permissions are checked against this database. A single logon defines the user's rights for every shared resourced on the network (see Figure 12-9). Different brands of network operating systems call this database by different names, but all of them work basically the same way.

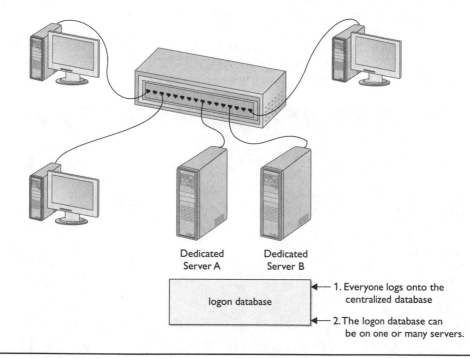

Dedicated Server A Dedicated Server B

logon database

1. Everyone logs onto the centralized database

2. The logon database can be on one or many servers.

Figure 12-9 Everyone authenticates through the logon database

Organization-based security model networks simplify network administration by replacing multiple logins to individual servers with a single login that works for all the servers on the network. All of the modern operating systems use some form of organization-based security model. In fact, both Microsoft and Novell now use an even more advanced type of database called a directory. A directory goes beyond just providing authentication for the user accounts—a directory literally maps out the entire network. A good directory implementation describes every system, every printer, every user, and every group on its network, providing a central repository of all that is the network in one big database.

Mixing Models

As you will soon see, every operating system fits nicely into one of these three security models. Some operating systems may fit into one or another model, depending on how they are configured. Do understand, however, that these models can and do work happily together in one physical network. For example, networked Windows 98 systems that operate in a resource-based mode when communicating among themselves can also communicate in a server-based mode with a NetWare server on the same physical network. Microsoft did an amazing job enabling Windows systems to act as clients in networks running multiple brands and models of servers. Better yet (but confusing to new techs), all this complexity is hidden from the user. Figure 12-10 shows a screenshot of My Network Places on a Windows XP system. There is a NetWare server, a Windows Server 2003, a Linux server, and a number of other Windows 2000 and XP systems. The NetWare and Linux servers look no different than a Windows system. If it weren't for the computer names, you wouldn't know one from the other.

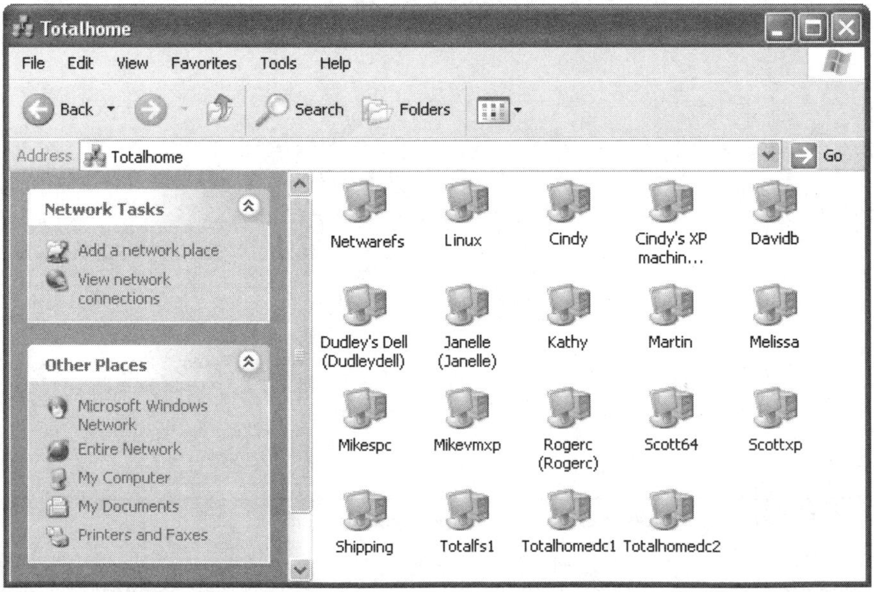

Figure 12-10   My Network Places

Client/Server and Peer-to-Peer Today

Okay, Mike, you say client/server and peer-to-peer no longer mean anything, but anyone who's into networking at all hears these terms now more than ever. So what do client/server and peer-to-peer mean in the context of today's networks?

Client/server and peer-to-peer have taken on new or updated definitions, and refer more to applications than to network operating systems. Consider e-mail for a moment. Most of us easily accept that for e-mail to work, you need an e-mail client like Microsoft Outlook Express. But you also need an e-mail server program like Microsoft Exchange to handle the e-mail requests from your e-mail client. Outlook Express is a *dedicated client*—you cannot use Outlook Express as a mail serving program. Likewise, you cannot use Microsoft Exchange as an e-mail client. Exchange is a *dedicated server* program.

Peer-to-peer applications act as both client and server. The best examples of these applications are the now infamous file-sharing programs based on special TCP/IP protocols. The applications, with names like LimeWire, BearShare, and Kazaa, act as both clients and servers, enabling a user both to share files and access shared files. Figure 12-11 shows one such program, Kazaa Lite, in the process of simultaneously uploading and downloading files.

The Dangers of Peer-to-Peer File Sharing

Peer-to-peer file sharing programs represent a creative use of TCP/IP protocols with powerful and useful implications and applications. On the other hand, the proven potential for abuse with these programs has made headline news around the world. So what's the big deal?

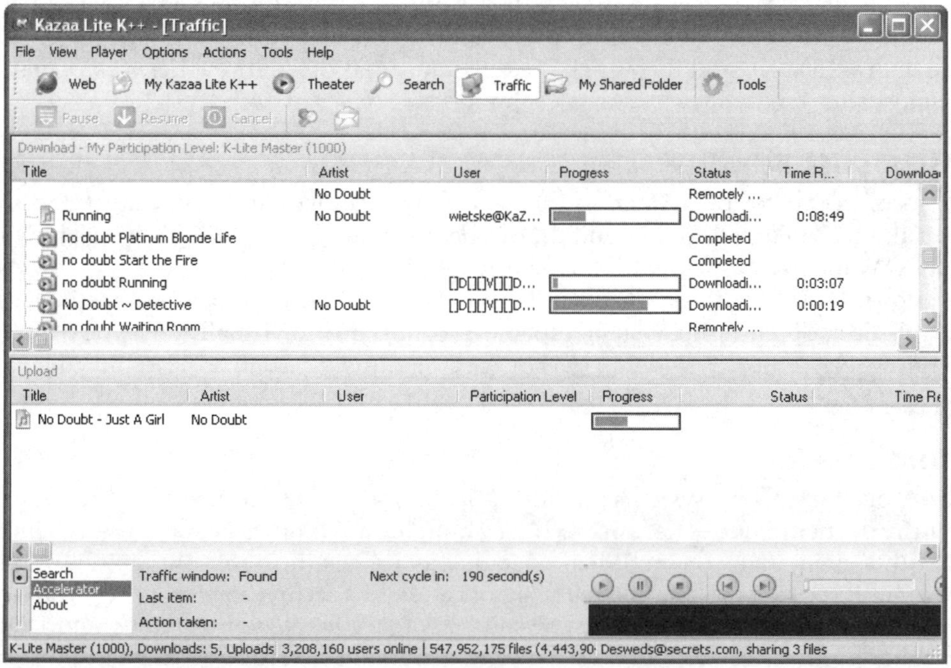

Figure 12-11   Kazaa Lite in action

On the plus side, peer-to-peer file sharing programs enable decentralized storage and distribution of many files. By storing on many serving systems, the loss of one or more of those systems means little in terms of the safety of the data being served. To bring a new system on line and get all the documents it needs for the user to be productive becomes a very simple operation.

On the negative side, many people have used peer-to-peer file sharing programs to flaunt intellectual property laws and steal substantial amounts of commercial music, videos, movies, and more. During the heyday of Napster and Kazaa, the theft was so commonplace that even otherwise upstanding citizens—who wouldn't dream of stealing a music CD from a record store—blithely stole hundreds of dollars of music every day!

To combat the loss of revenue, anti-piracy groups attacked in two ways. Some artists such as Madonna released bogus tracks onto the distributed networks. A search for a popular Madonna song, for example, will turn up a likely file; but when you click on it to play, you get Madonna calling you a dirty pirate (almost that plainly)! Second, record companies have gone after casual pirates through the legal system in the United States, suing people for revenue loss.

As a final word of caution, a lot of virus-infected files have made it into the distributed computing networks. This creates a dangerous situation for even legitimate uses and users of these networks. Use them at your own risk!

The Major Network Operating Systems

Microsoft, Novell, Apple and UNIX all provide strong network operating system solutions that address the goals of networking, including access to shared resources and security. Microsoft Windows dominates the client market (with some niche clients using Macintosh and Linux). Microsoft, Novell, Apple, and UNIX compete for the server NOS market. In this section, I'll cover all the different variations of these network operating systems, and discuss a few of the more important aspects of each.

Microsoft Windows

Microsoft competes for NOS market share with two distinct Windows product lines that I'll call: the *Windows 9x family* and the *Windows NT family*. The Windows 9x family includes Windows 95, 98, 98 SE, and Me. The Windows NT family includes Windows NT, Windows 2000, Windows XP, and Windows Server 2003. Windows 9x functions as a flexible desktop operating system, capable of connecting to virtually any type of server. Windows NT, 2000, XP, and 2003 in contrast, can function both as powerful client systems and as full-featured server network operating systems.

Windows 9x

Microsoft Windows 9x systems provide basic file and print sharing functions, but little security by themselves. A network tech can configure a Windows 9x system as a client, or as both a client and a server. When operating as a server, however, Windows 9x uses a share-level security model, making it significantly less secure than more sophisticated server operating systems like Windows NT, 2000, 2003, Novell NetWare, and UNIX. Overall, Windows 9x has very weak security. Neither passwords nor user accounts provide much, if any, security in a pure Windows 9x network.

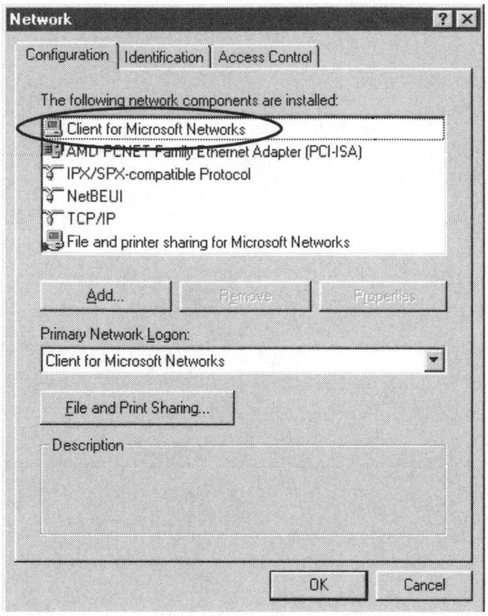

Figure 12-12
Client for
Microsoft
Networks
is installed.

A network composed of only Windows 9*x* systems will always use NetBIOS, either over NetBEUI or over TCP/IP. NetBIOS will manifest itself with the Client for Microsoft Networks, as shown in Figure 12-12. You don't have to worry about installing it, however—Windows installs Client for Microsoft Networks automatically when it detects a modem or a NIC.

Speaking of automatic installation, one of the more interesting aspects between different versions of Windows 9*x* comes in the default clients and protocols that Microsoft installs. Windows 95 installed support for NetWare networks and NetBEUI by default as shown in Figure 12-13. TCP/IP had to be installed manually.

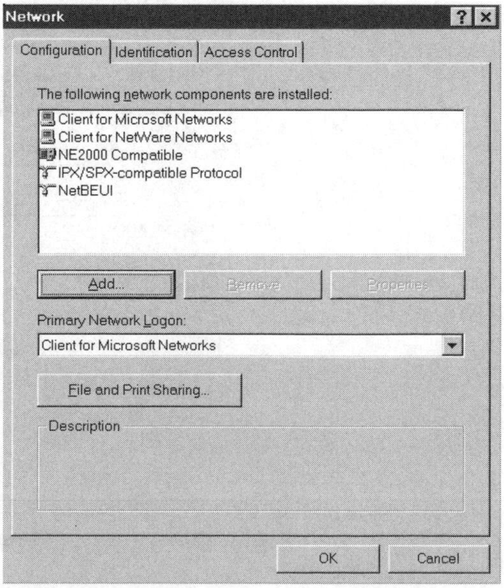

Figure 12-13
Windows 95
default Network
Properties

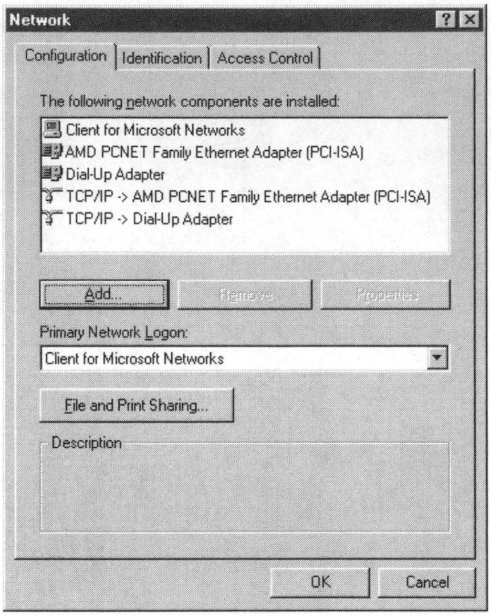

Figure 12-14
Windows 98
default Network
Properties

Starting with Windows 98, Microsoft stopped installing NetBEUI and NetWare support and instead went to only the Client for Microsoft Networks and TCP/IP, as shown in Figure 12-14. All versions of Windows 9x still support IPX/SPX and NetBEUI, but the protocols require manual installation.

Windows 9x systems receive their NetBIOS names at installation, but these can be changed in the Identification Tab of the Network Control Panel applet. Figure 12-15 shows this tab.

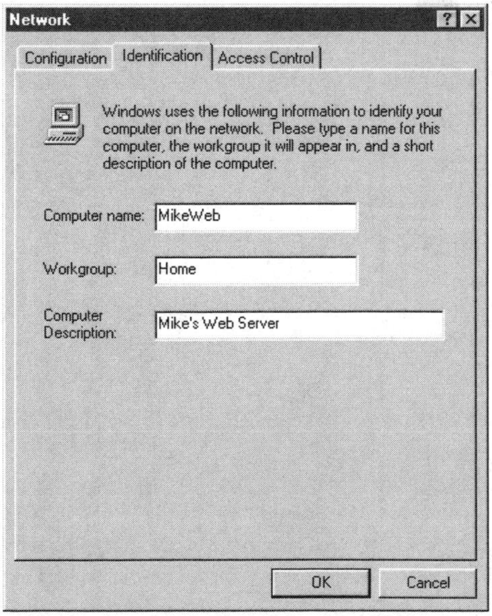

Figure 12-15
Windows 98
Identification Tab

Note the Workgroup setting in Figure 12-15. Windows 9*x* systems can be grouped into what are called *workgroups*. These workgroups have little purpose other than providing a way to organize slightly more complex networks. When you set up a Windows system, you give it a workgroup to join. Putting systems in workgroups makes it easier for other systems to find them in Network Neighborhood.

Again, workgroups don't really do anything other than organize. There's no security aspect to them that would stop an unauthorized user from accessing a workgroup or control what a user might do in a workgroup. Workgroups are actually a throwback to the early days of Microsoft networking, and have been replaced in more advanced Microsoft network operating systems with the much more powerful organization-based feature called a domain. Workgroups are still popular in Windows networks using a resource or server-based security model.

NOTE   All later versions of Windows support workgroups.

One very interesting issue commonly seen in pure Windows 9*x* environments is a little phenomena called a *browser election*. Because Windows 9*x* systems rely exclusively on NetBIOS, a single computer in the workgroup must be the keeper of all of the NetBIOS names. This computer is called the Browse Master or Master Browse Server. Any computer running NetBIOS can become the Browse Master; the process used by the computers in the network to determine the Browse Master is called a *browser election*. Browser elections take place whenever any computer cannot detect a Browse Master on the network. All NetBIOS computers announce their name on the network every 12 minutes, so any time any one of those computers cannot get a response from a Browse Master, a browser election takes place. A browser election slows down a Windows 9*x* network, sometimes quite dramatically, so you should reduce the occurrence of browser elections whenever possible.

The best way to remove this issue is to use a WINS server (see Chapter 14), but WINS only works with NetBIOS over TCP/IP. Another way to reduce browser elections, no matter what protocol NetBIOS is running on top of, is to go into the properties of the File and Printer Sharing for Microsoft Networks service. This service must be installed on a Windows 9*x* system for it to share folders and printers. Normally this is a service that is loaded and forgotten, but there is a handy setting in its properties that can substantially reduce browser elections. Figure 12-16 shows the File and printer sharing for Microsoft Networks Properties dialog box for a Windows 98 computer.

The File and Printer Sharing for Microsoft Networks Properties dialog box offers two settings: Browse Master—the one that's relevant here—and LM Announce. The Browse Master setting determines if this machine will attempt to become a Browse Master during an election. Turn this to Disabled for all the systems in your Windows 9*x* network except one—and on that machine set it to Enabled. The one machine with Browse Master set to Enabled will always be the Browse Master, eliminating any future browser elections. Be warned: this is a bit risky. Make sure that your designated Browse Master is always on the network. If that one machine ever goes off the network your computers won't be able to

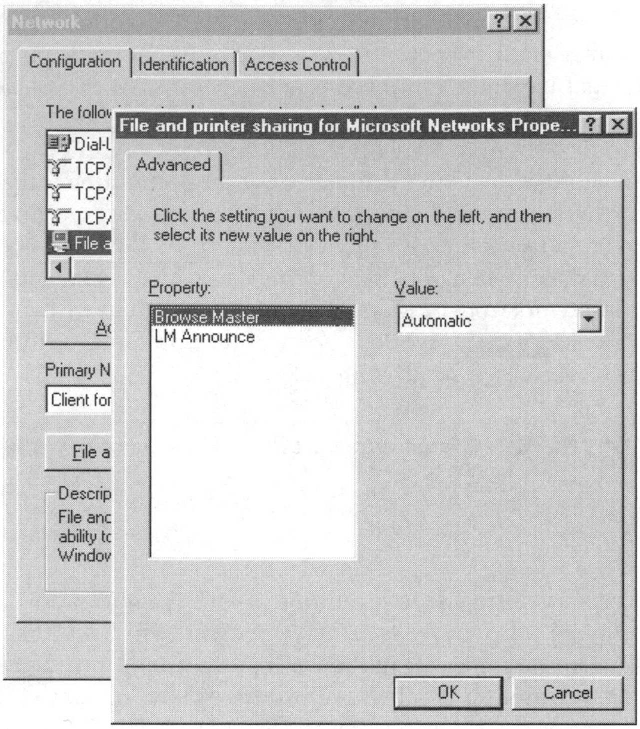

Figure 12-16
File and printer
sharing for
Microsoft
Networks
Properties

browse the network. If you want to play it safe, turn the Browse Master setting to Enabled on a second machine.

LM Announce is a virtually useless setting designed to enable a modern Windows system to work with any system running a very old form of Microsoft networking called LAN Manager. Unless you've got some ancient DOS machines in the corner, turn this setting to No.

NOTE The LM Announce setting can sometimes bite modern networkers when they least expect it. Ever have a Windows 9x system that never seems to shut down completely when you run Start | Shut Down? It's often due to the LM Announce setting set to Yes. Turn it to No and see if that fixes the problem!

The Windows 9x resource-based security model and complete dependence on NetBIOS makes it unacceptable for any but the smallest networks. Yet, a Windows 9x network, especially when running NetBEUI was so easy to set up that anyone could install a perfectly acceptable small network. Microsoft's ongoing desire to make the user's life as easy as possible had created a monster. NetBIOS made networking available to the world and Microsoft had to support it, even up to today's latest versions of Windows.

Windows 9x may not make a very robust network solution alone, but all versions of Windows 9x do an excellent job acting as clients in more advanced network operating systems running Windows NT, 2000, Server 2003, NetWare and UNIX. As we investigate these more powerful network operating systems, we'll return to Windows 9x to see what you need to do to make a Windows 9x system work with these network operating systems.

The Windows 9x line of products may have ceased production with the introduction of Windows XP, but given that the installed base of Windows 9x systems was in excess of 180 million copies late in 2001, you can rest assured that Windows 9x will continue to be an operating system you need to understand for years to come.

TIP You can technically still purchase older versions of Windows. But don't bother asking your local computer builder for a new system with Windows 98! These purchases are done through *channels*—that's Microspeak for calling Microsoft directly and begging.

Windows NT

When Microsoft developed Windows NT in the early 1990s, they chose to make two very different versions: Windows NT Workstation and Windows NT Server. Windows NT Workstation was marketed as the high-end desktop operating system and contained a number of underpinnings to give NT Workstation incredible network support. Windows NT Server had all the power of Windows NT Workstation, plus Microsoft added a number of server tools not found on NT Workstation such as DNS, WINS, and DHCP servers, as well as support for an organizational-based security model called a domain.

Windows NT Workstation

Windows NT Workstation offered the same user interface as Windows 95 but with greatly enhanced security and stability as compared to the weak Windows 9x security. First, Windows NT Workstation used a server-based security network model. If a user wanted to access anything on a Windows NT Workstation system, he or she had to have a user account and a password for that system. This was true whether you logged on at the machine or if you wanted to access a shared resource from another system. Windows NT workstation also used a new file system called NT File system (NTFS). NTFS gave tremendous control on how users and groups could use shared folders and files within shared folders. With NTFS, you could define permissions such as Modify (Change a file or the contents of a folder), List Contents (Define whether users or groups could see a file or the contents of a folder), and Read (Define whether users could open a file).

NOTE There were three versions of Windows NT: 3.1, 3.5 and 4.0. This section discusses the only popular version, NT 4.0. The 3.1 and 3.5 versions were very early and have disappeared from the market. When the Network+ exam talks about Windows NT, it means version 4.0.

Windows NT provides native support for NetBEUI and TCP/IP, as well as strong security by using robust user accounts. You cannot log onto a Windows NT system without a valid user account. Every Windows NT (as well as every Windows 2000, XP and 2003) operating system comes with a special "super user account" called *Administrator*. Anyone who logs in using the administrator account of a Windows NT, 2000, 2003 or XP system has complete and total control over the entire system. Clearly, very few people should ever have access to the administrator account!

NT User Accounts

Back in the days of Windows NT Workstation, creating a user account or a group meant a trip to the NT User Manager. Figure 12-17 shows a screen from User Manager in a newly installed NT Workstation system. Note the two preinstalled accounts: Administrator and Guest. The Guest account, which first appeared in Windows NT and continues in every version of Windows since, is a very basic account with very limited permissions.

At the bottom of the User Manager dialog box are the Windows built-in groups. Windows NT came with six built-in groups. Windows 2000, XP, and 2003 have seven such groups. In any Windows OS, you cannot delete these built-in groups.

- **Administrators** Any account that is a member of the Administrators group has complete administrator privileges. It is common for the primary user of a Windows 2000 or XP system to have his or her account in the Administrators group.

- **Power Users** Power users are almost as powerful as administrators, but they cannot install new devices or access other users' files or folders unless the files or folders specifically provide them access.

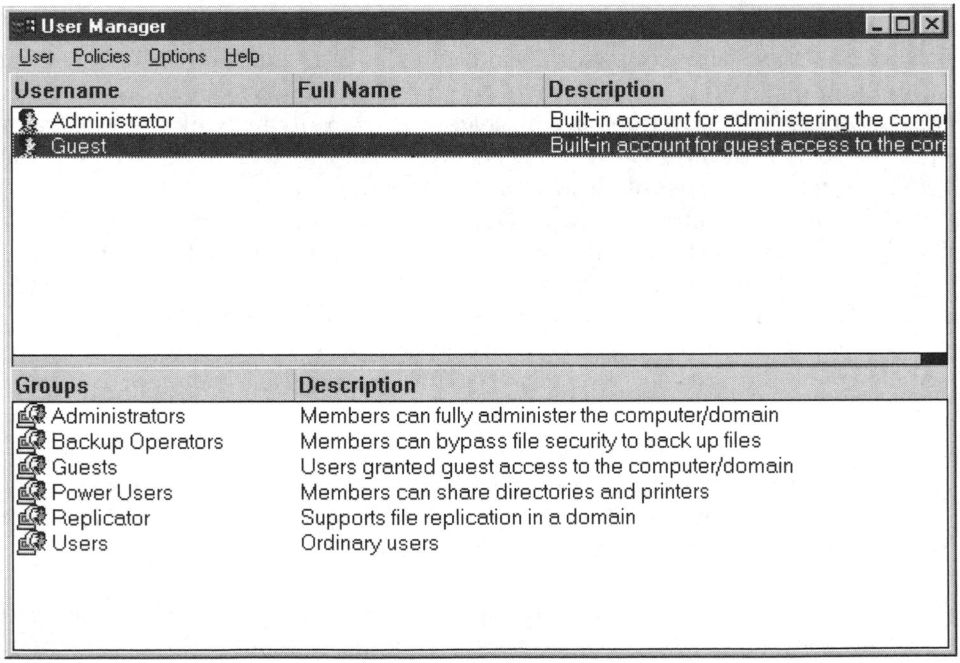

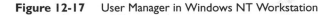

Figure 12-17   User Manager in Windows NT Workstation

- **Users**   Users cannot edit the Registry or access critical system files. They can create groups, but can manage only those groups they create.

- **Backup Operators**   Backup operators have the same rights as users, but they can run backup programs that access any file or folder—for backup purposes only.

- **Replicator**   Members of the Replicator group can replicate files and folders in a domain.

- **Guests**   Someone who does not have an account on the system can log on using the Guest account if the system has been set up to enable that feature. This group is used in certain network situations.

- **Everyone**   This account (which wasn't in Windows NT but appears in 2000, XP, and 2003) applies to any user that can log onto the system. You cannot edit this group.

Windows NT Workstation worked beautifully in a network environment except for one little nasty—every Windows NT Workstation system ran a server-based security model. This meant that if you wanted to access another Windows NT Workstation system, you had to have a user account on that other system. The accounts for each NT Workstation system are known as the *local user accounts*. Calling a user account a local account wasn't obvious in NT's User Manager for accounts, but NT Workstation also had local groups, which were far more obvious. Figure 12-18 shows the creation of a local group. Note how NT Workstation called the local groups "local groups," but only called the local users "users"—a strange aspect of NT that was corrected in later versions of Windows.

By default, all Windows systems use the login name and password you use when you first start a system to try to access network resources. Let's say you have a Windows NT Workstation system and you used the user name "Betsy" with the password "b3tsy232" when you logged in. If you then try to access another Windows NT Workstation system via Network Neighborhood, you'll be prompted for a login name and password for that system, unless that other system just happens to have an account with the user name "Betsy" with the password "b3tsy232!"

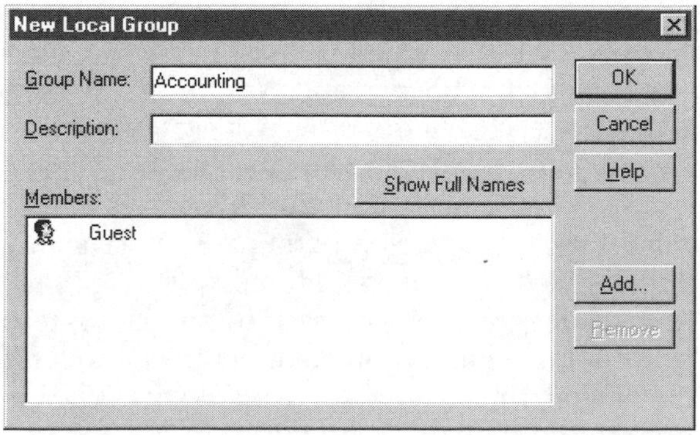

Figure 12-18
Creating a
local group in
Windows NT

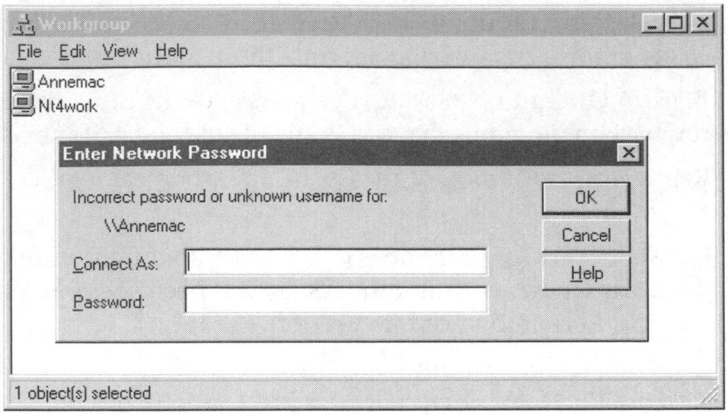

Figure 12-19
Prompting for
a logon on
another system

Note in Figure 12-19 that the Windows NT Workstation computer is part of a workgroup called Workgroup. A Windows NT (or 2000/2003 or XP) computer that's on a network must either be part of a workgroup or part of something far more powerful—a domain.

Windows NT Server

Windows NT Server has the ability to transform a group of individual Windows computers, each with its own local users and groups, into an organization-based model called a domain.

A *domain* functions like a workgroup, but has all the security centralized on a single server. In Windows NT Server, the system that held that central spot was called a primary domain controller (PDC). Any Windows NT network could have only a single PDC, but you could add one or more backup domain controller (BDC) computers also running Windows NT Server to provide some redundancy in case the PDC went down.

During the installation of Windows NT, you were prompted for what Microsoft called the *role* of the machine. A Windows NT Server system could just join a workgroup and handle its own local users and groups; it could create a new domain and act as the PDC of the domain; it could join an existing domain and act as a BDC; or it could join a domain, but not act as a PDC or BDC. Once the role of the server was defined, it could not easily be changed.

The creation of the Windows NT domain concept made for a bit of a problem when you had both Windows NT Server and Windows NT Workstation systems in the same domain. Remember, each Windows NT Workstation system has its own local users and groups. But when you created a domain, the PDC now had its own set of user names and accounts that were for the entire domain. This created a situation that still exists even today: dual sets of user accounts and groups. The users and groups created on the NT Server PDC were called *global users and groups*.

Figure 12-20 shows the problem: each computer has its own local users and groups, while the entire domain has its domain users and groups. Microsoft skirted this issue by creating a dual logon. In Windows NT—and every other version of Windows—you may either log onto the domain or log on locally.

Figure 12-20
Local and
Domain users
in the same
network

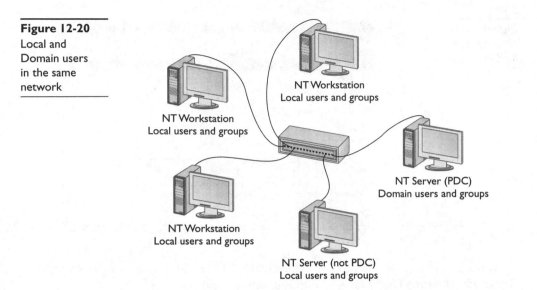

NT Workstation
Local users and groups

NT Workstation
Local users and groups

NT Server (PDC)
Domain users and groups

NT Workstation
Local users and groups

NT Server (not PDC)
Local users and groups

Figure 12-21 shows the logon screen of a Windows NT Workstation computer named NT4WORK before it joins a domain. Figure 12-22 shows the same system's logon screen after it joins a domain called TOTALHOME. Note that if the system is part of a domain, you are given the choice to log onto the domain or to just log on locally to the system.

One interesting point to note in Figure 12-22 is that both the local login and the domain login choice are listed under "Domain." Later versions of Windows would fix this!

Creating global users and groups in Windows NT Server required a different utility, called User Manager for Domains. User Manager for Domains was only found on Windows NT Server systems running as a PDC or BDC—if you wanted to create a global user

Figure 12-21
NT4WORK
before domain

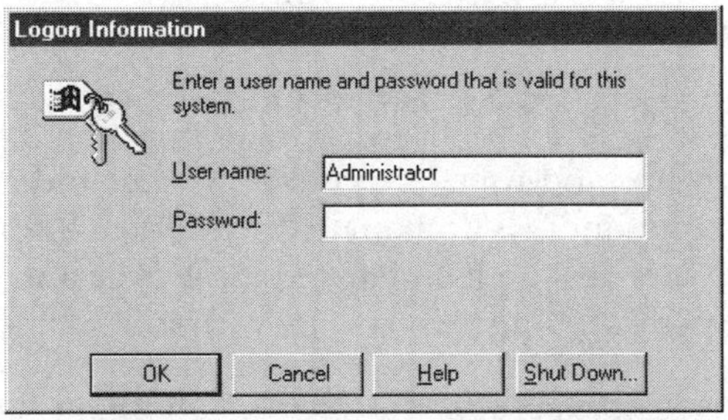

Logon Information

Enter a user name and password that is valid for this system.

User name: Administrator

Password:

OK   Cancel   Help   Shut Down...

Figure 12-22
NT4WORK
after joining
the domain
TOTALHOME

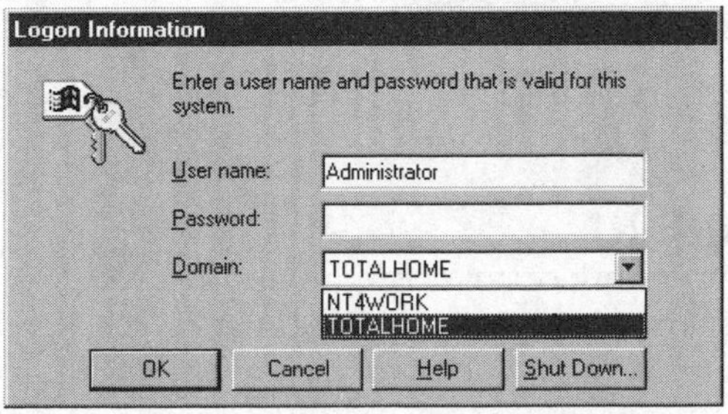

Logon Information

Enter a user name and password that is valid for this system.

User name: Administrator

Password:

Domain: TOTALHOME

NT4WORK
TOTALHOME

OK   Cancel   Help   Shut Down...

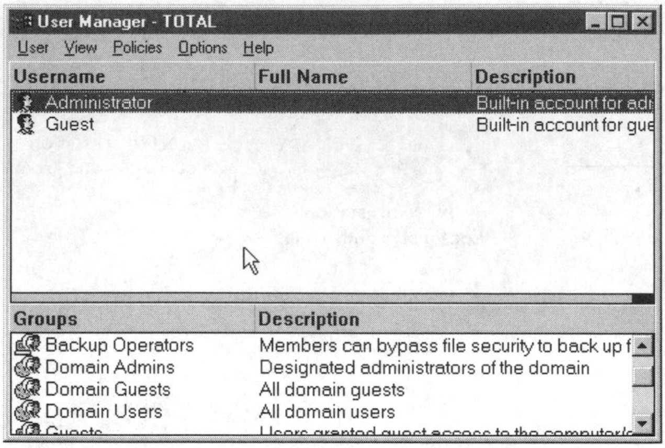

Figure 12-23
User Manager
for Domains

or group, you had to sit in front of a Windows NT PDC or BDC to create these accounts. Figure 12-23 shows User Manager for Domains.

At first glance, User Manager for Domains looks identical to User Manager in Windows NT Workstation. If you look down at the default groups, you'll notice that there are two sets of default accounts: one for the domain and one for the local computer. That's right—even the Windows NT Server systems that were part of the domain had local users and groups! The domain groups have a slightly different icon than the local groups. Windows NT has three built-in domain groups.

- **Domain Admins** Any account that is a member of this group has complete administrator privileges to the entire domain.
- **Domain Guests** Accounts assigned to this group are similar to local guest group accounts, but they span the entire domain.
- **Domain Users** This group includes all users who are part of the domain.

This dual-groups-and-users idea is still with us today in the latest versions of Windows. If you use a Windows domain with Windows 2000 Server or with Windows Server 2003, you'll always deal with global and local users and groups. To simplify working in this fashion, Microsoft long ago came up with some rules that are now in common use.

- Don't make local groups for users in a domain-based network. All users on the domain should have only global user accounts. Do not create local users or groups for people.
- Global users go into global groups. Make your groups (like ACCOUNTING or DALLAS) global groups.

Working with NT

Configuring a network on an existing Windows NT (Workstation or Server) PC meant a trip to the Network applet in the Control Panel. The Network applet enabled you to configure your network name, the domain or workgroup to which you wished to join the system, and all protocol and NIC settings (Figure 12-24).

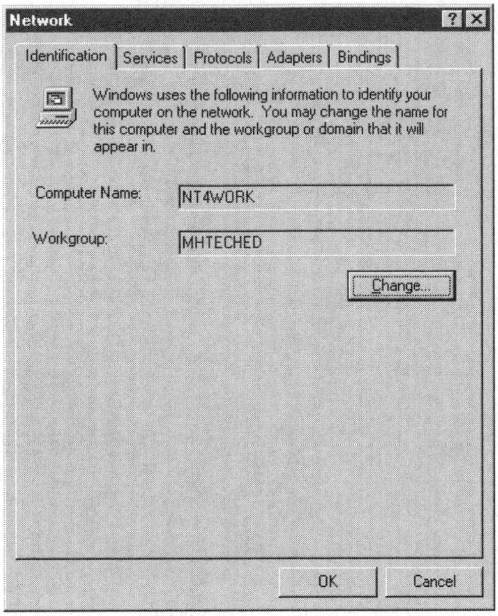

Figure 12-24
NT Network
applet dialog box

To change a computer's name, domain or workgroup membership, you clicked the Change button on the Identification tab (Figure 12-25). To add a computer to a domain, you also had to use the administrator account.

Adding, editing, or deleting a protocol required a trip to the Protocols tab. Figure 12-26 shows the TCP/IP Properties dialog box. Note that this copy of Windows NT also has the NetBEUI and IPX/SPX protocols installed.

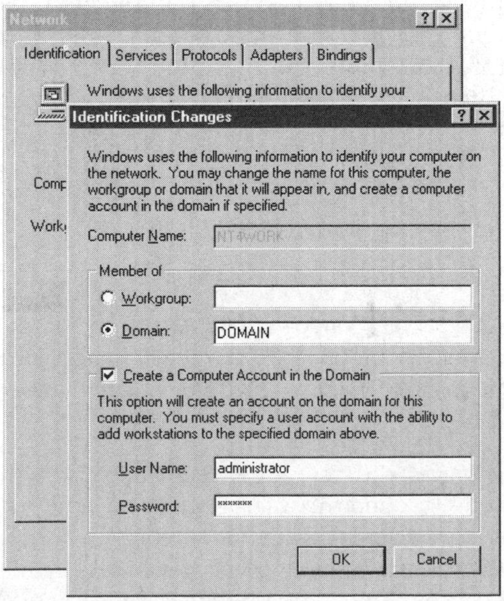

Figure 12-25
Changing
Identification
in NT

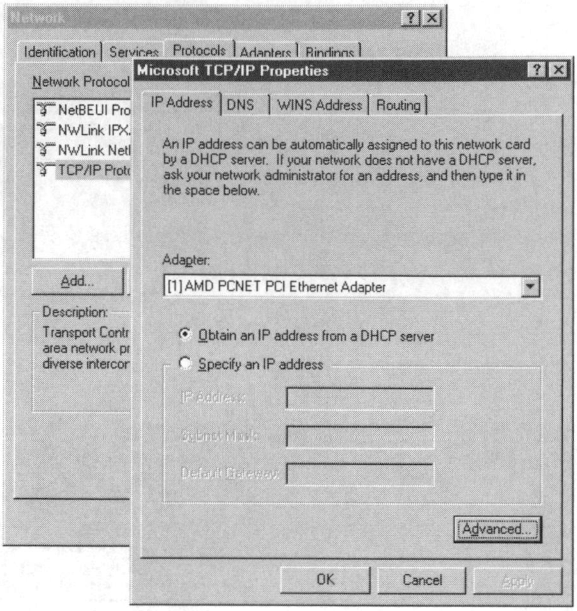

Figure 12-26
Changing IP
settings in NT

NOTE Windows NT does not have Device Manager! If you wanted to install, configure, or delete a NIC you had to go to the Network applet!

Windows 2000

Microsoft improved on the Windows NT family with the Windows 2000 generation of operating systems. Like NT, 2000 came out in a desktop and a server version, called Windows 2000 Professional and Windows 2000 Server. Windows 2000 combined the Windows 98 user interface with the underlying power of Windows NT. Windows 2000 was virtually identical to Windows NT in terms of networking, security and users, but had the more up-to-date features of Windows 98, like better driver support, Device Manager and Plug and Play. Windows 2000 only supported TCP/IP natively, although through extra configuration it supported NetBEUI, IPX/SPX, and AppleTalk.

TIP Windows 2000 Server came out in three different versions: Windows 2000 Server, Windows 2000 Advanced Server, and Windows 2000 Datacenter Server. For the specifics on the differences among these versions, head over to Microsoft's Windows 2000 site at http://www.microsoft.com/windows2000/default.asp.

Some of the biggest differences between 2000 and NT come in the networking arena. Microsoft, having watched the Internet grow around NT's NetBIOS-centric networking and tired of trying to come up with one method after another of keeping NetBIOS working in a world that was moving towards DNS in droves, totally redesigned their domains. The old NT NetBIOS domain names gave way to domains based on DNS names.

Even in a small network that's not part of the Internet, Windows 2000 domain names now have the dotted DNS naming scheme, such as *server.totalhome*. The last, and probably the biggest change in Windows networking came about with the introduction of a new super-domain called Active Directory. We discuss Active Directory shortly.

Windows 2000 Professional

Microsoft never liked being in the two operating system business, but by running the Windows 9*x* line alongside the Windows NT line of operating systems, that's exactly what they did. Microsoft didn't have much choice—NT had heavy hardware requirements and wasn't backward-compatible with a number of older Windows programs. Windows 9*x* was very much backward-compatible but was also showing its age in terms of outdated file systems (FAT), virtually non-existent security, and reliance on 16-bit code. Windows 9*x* needed replacing, but not at the cost of too many older systems.

Windows 2000 Professional was Microsoft's first attempt at replacing the old Windows 9*x* systems. Unlike NT, Windows 2000's use of Plug and Play, excellent hardware support, and an improved user interface made it a good replacement for many systems that used to run Windows 9*x*. Windows 2000 Professional still had heavy hardware requirements and couldn't totally displace Windows 9*x*. It would take Windows XP before Microsoft could officially declare Windows 9*x* obsolete.

For all of the improvements of Windows 2000, the OS retains many of the problems inherent to Windows networking. All Windows 2000 Professional systems still have local users. A group of Windows 2000 Professional computers will use a server-based organization model. If you log onto one Windows 2000 professional system and want to access another Windows 2000 Professional system via My Network Places, you'll need a separate local account on that system, just like we did in the Windows NT days.

The big change in networking comes when you add a Windows 2000 Server to your network and set up Active Directory!

Windows 2000 Server and Active Directory

Directory services are centralized storage areas for information about a network's resources, including users, applications, files, and printers. Directory services applications enable network administrators to centrally manage and share information about their networks' users and resources, and to centralize network security authority. Not until Windows 2000 did Microsoft finally create an NOS with directory services. Windows 2000's directory services are called Active Directory. All of the domain functions of Windows NT still work—they've just been incorporated into Active Directory. Just as in the NT days, a computer must be a member of either a workgroup or a domain. A single Active Directory consists of one or more domains. If you want a computer in the Active Directory, it will by default be in a domain.

 NOTE A single Active Directory consists of one or more domains.

Windows 2000 Server dumps the idea of PDCs and BDCs. Instead, all of the domain controllers (DCs) are equal. If you create a user on one DC, it will automatically replicate the new user information to all of the other DCs in the Active Directory. Active Directory domains are true DNS domains. In fact, all of the DNS data is built into the Active Directory itself.

When you install a Windows 2000 Server system, you eventually reach a screen that prompts you for the function that this server will perform. It will either be a domain controller, a member server (part of the domain but not a domain controller) or, if for some reason you didn't want to join a domain, a stand-alone server.

One of the most obvious places that Windows 2000 Server differs from Windows 2000 Professional is in the Administrative Tools. Windows 2000 Server includes every type of serving software necessary to run a Windows network, including DNS, WINS, and DHCP Servers. Figure 12-27 shows the standard Administrative Tools in Windows 2000 Professional. Compare that to a fairly typical set of Administrative Tools in Windows 2000 Server in Figure 12-28.

Figure 12-27
Administrative
Tools in
Windows 2000
Professional

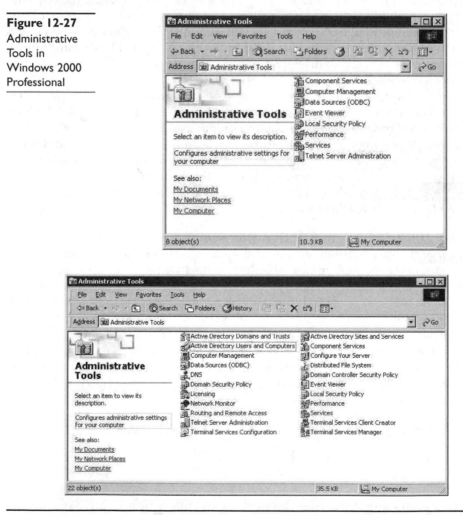

Figure 12-28   Administrative Tools in Windows 2000 server

There's no way to see the entire Active Directory, but there are some applications on Windows 2000 Server that give you a glimpse of parts of the Active Directory. Figure 12-29 shows the Active Directory Users and Computers utility. This handy program does many jobs, but it's most commonly used to create domain-level users and groups.

Note the name totalhome.local in Figure 12-26. Totalhome.local is a true DNS name—so why doesn't it end with ".com" or ".net" as we might expect? The ".local" shows that this domain is not open to the Internet. Of course any system on this domain may access the Internet, but none of these machines may act as an Internet web server, FTP server, or any other type of Internet server unless special security steps are taken.

Windows 2000 Server supports TCP/IP natively, but through extra configuration can support NetBEUI, IPX/SPX, and AppleTalk.

Working with 2000

One handy improvement in Windows 2000 over Windows NT is the consolidation of most all of the utilities you need into one handy tool called Computer Management. You can access this tool via your Control Panel, but most techs just alternate-click the My Computer icon and select the Manage menu option (Figure 12-30).

Computer Management is your one-stop shop for creating local user accounts and groups, accessing Device Manager, locating shared resources, and disk management. If you need to make any changes to your NICs, protocols, or network services, however, you still need to fire up your Network applet in the Control Panel. Windows 2000 calls this applet Network and Dial-up Connections (Figure 12-31).

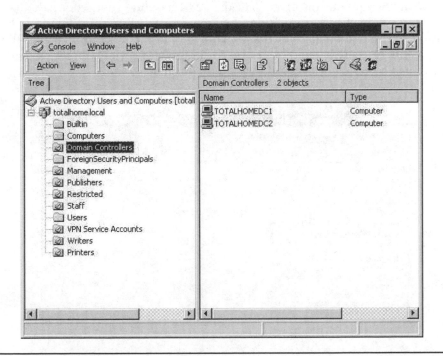

Figure 12-29   Active Directory users and groups

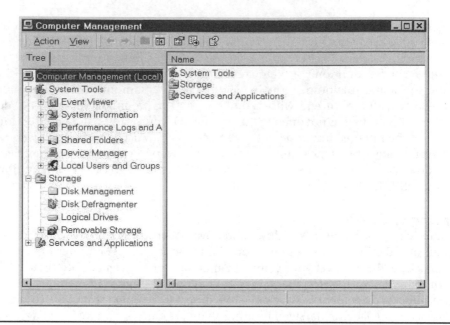

Figure 12-30   Computer Management in Windows 2000 Professional

Note that the computer displayed in Figure 12-31 has three connections: the 100BaseT is my main wired network connection; the Emergency dial-up connection is a backup dial-up I can use if my main network goes down; and the Bluetooth enables this machine to connect to any Bluetooth devices. The number of devices you see on a system is simply a matter of the number of devices in that system.

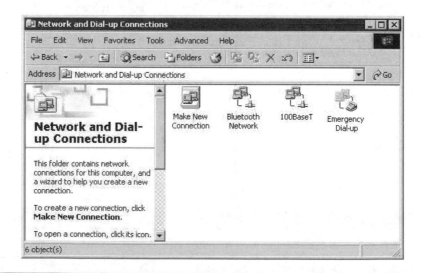

Figure 12-31   Network and Dial-up Connections

NOTE You can also access Network and Dial-up Connections directly from the Start menu by selecting Settings | Network and Dialup Connections.

Changing the name of your computer or changing the workgroup or domain membership is also very different in Windows 2000 compared to Windows 9*x* or Windows NT. Making any of these changes requires you to alternate-click on My Computer and select Properties to open your System Properties dialog box (alternatively you can select the System Control Panel applet). Click the Network Identification tab to see the current network settings, as shown in Figure 12-32.

You'll see two buttons: Network ID and Properties. Each of these buttons does the same job—change the computer name as well as the workgroup or domain membership. The Network ID button starts a handy wizard to walk you through the steps while the Properties button just brings up a dialog box to make the changes without a wizard (Figure 12-33).

Don't try changing the name of a Windows 2000 Server running as a domain controller this way! If you go over to your Network Identification screen on one of those machines, you'll see something like Figure 12-34, showing you that you cannot change the name of the Server system. Windows 2000 domain controllers are well named—they control the domains—so changing their names or domain membership takes a rather involved process. Note that this restriction applies only to 2000. Windows Server 2003 enables you to change the name of domain controllers.

In general, working with Windows 2000 in terms of network configuration is fairly straightforward—as long as you remember where to go to make those changes! The other nice part about knowing how to configure network settings in Windows 2000 is that it makes it easy to configure network settings in Windows XP—it's almost exactly the same.

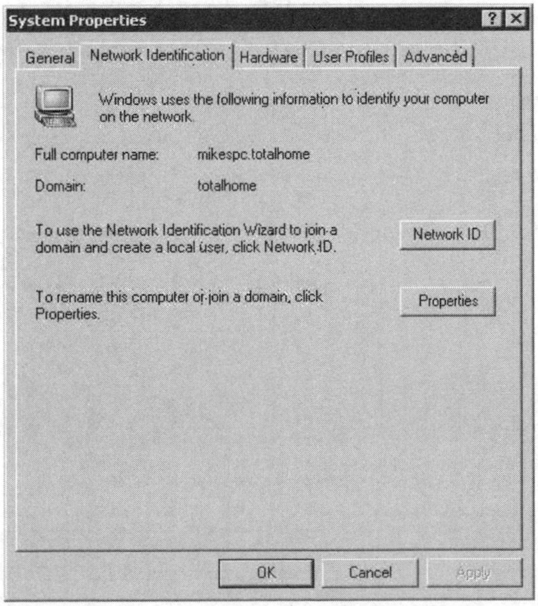

Figure 12-32
Network Identification tab in Windows 2000 Professional

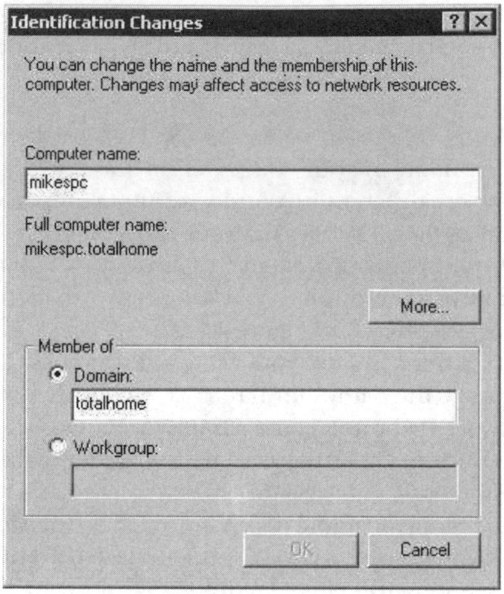

Figure 12-33

Network
Identification
Changes

Windows XP

Microsoft touts Windows XP as the unifying operating system, bringing together the power of NT/2000 with the backward compatibility of Windows 9x. This claim might be open to argument. Windows XP, underneath its slick user interface, slightly improved tools for backward compatibility with older programs, and a number of built-in tools like a CD burner and support for .zip files, is little more than a spiffed-up version of Windows 2000 Professional.

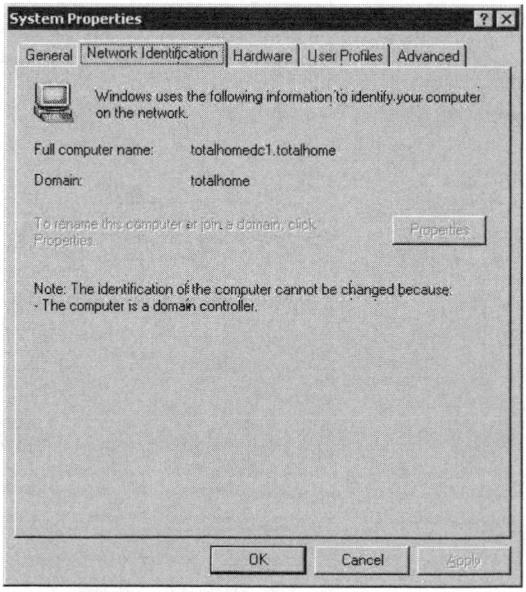

Figure 12-34

Network
Identification on
Windows 2000
domain controller

Windows XP has no Server version like we see with Windows NT and Windows 2000. There are however, two versions of Windows XP—Windows XP Home and Windows XP Professional, but these are both user versions. Windows XP Professional is designed to work in domain environments and has all the power and security of Windows 2000 Professional. There are no differences between Windows XP Professional and Windows 2000 Professional in terms of where you go to make any network configuration changes. To add, edit, or remove protocols and services, you go to your Network Connections Control Panel applet. Each network connection in Windows XP manifests as a separate icon, just as in Windows 2000. If you want to change the name of a system or change its workgroup or domain membership, you go to System properties. If you know how to configure a network in Windows 2000, then you know how to configure a network in Windows XP Professional, although a few names may be changed along the way. Let's say you want both a Windows 2000 and an XP Professional PC to join the MHTECHED.LOCAL domain. In both cases you select the System Control Panel applet. In Windows 2000 you click the Network Identification tab. In Windows XP you click the Computer Name tab (Figure 12-35).

Compare this figure to Figure 12-33 (earlier in this chapter); they are virtually identical. If you click on the Change button in XP you'll see that it is virtually identical to Windows 2000. Figure 12-36 puts these two dialog boxes next to each other for comparison.

Windows XP Home Edition, as its name implies, is a greatly simplified version of XP designed for home and small office users that do not need the same complex security features found in Windows XP Professional. In fact, Windows XP Home Edition is crippled so that it *cannot* join a Windows domain. If you access the Network Identification properties on a Windows XP home system, you'll see that there is no mention of a domain (see Figure 12-37).

Figure 12-35
Computer
Name tab in
System applet

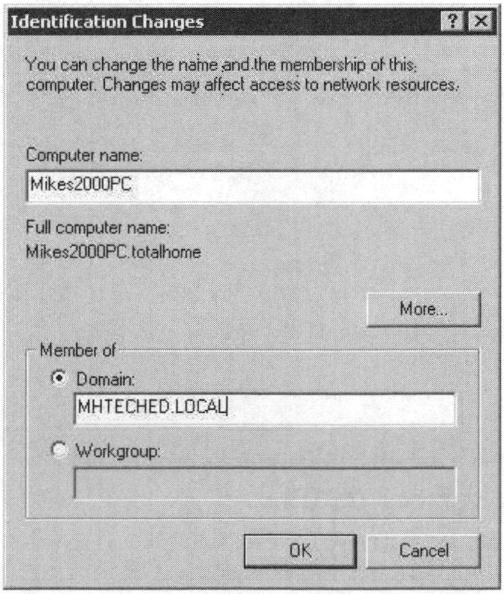

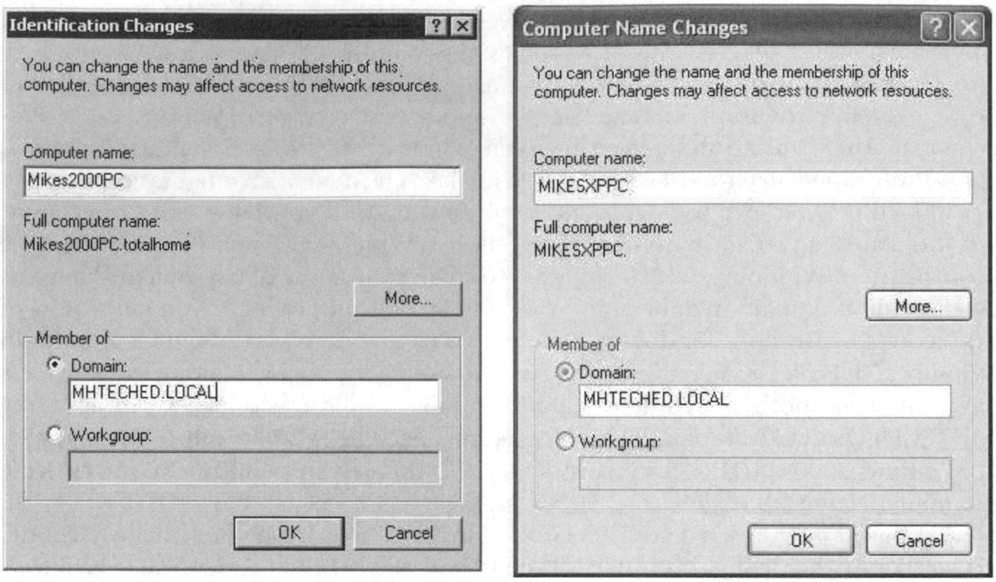

Figure 12-36   Networking's the same in Windows 2000 and Windows XP Professional.

Figure 12-37
No domain
in XP Home!

Windows Server 2003

Windows Server 2003 (note that we do not say Windows 2003 Server!) is Microsoft's current server version. Windows Server 2003 is virtually identical to Windows 2000 Server. With the exception of a few changes to the interface and some rather handy utilities, only advanced network technicians would notice the difference between these two network operating systems. Describing the differences is completely outside the scope of this book. Windows Server 2003 uses the same Active Directory, domain naming, services, and interfaces used in Windows 2000 Server.

User Profiles

All versions of Windows support the use of *user profiles*, which enhance both the usability and security of a network. A user profile is a collection of settings that corresponds to a specific user account and follows the user to any computer she uses on the network. User profiles enable users to customize their working environments. The server checks the user profiles to determine each user's wallpaper, desktop layout, and other environment preferences. Each time the user logs onto the network, the client system retrieves the profile and displays the OS accordingly. Here's an example.

Roger, Chris, and Cindy work different shifts and share the same Windows XP computer. When each of them logs onto the computer at the beginning of their respective shift, Windows XP loads the appropriate configuration from their profile. If the profiles exist on the local hard drive, they only affect that computer. But a savvy network administrator will store the profiles on a network server, enabling the profiles to follow the users regardless of where they sit. When Roger transfers to the day shift, he can use a different computer and still enjoy all of his customized settings. As much as Roger, Chris, and Cindy enjoy the benefits of user profiles, Martin, the network admin, likes them even more. Martin can use profiles to place restrictions on how Roger, Chris, and Cindy use their computers. When their boss, Dudley, complains that employees spend too much time playing Unreal Tournament 2004, Martin edits their profiles so they cannot run the Unreal Tournament program anymore. Martin can also restrict their use in other ways, to prevent them from doing the following:

- Running other programs
- Changing their desktop icons and wallpaper
- Loading new programs

User profiles offer a consistent look and feel to the end user, and control to the network administrator.

 TIP A profile is a set of configuration settings specific to an individual user. Profiles can be stored locally or on a server. Administrators can use profiles to place restrictions on what users can do with their computers.

Novell NetWare

The continued use of older versions testifies to the power and stability of Novell NetWare. Many organizations upgrade their client software, but continue to use their existing NetWare 3.*x* and 4.*x* servers, following those ancient words of wisdom: "If it ain't broke, don't fix it!" Network techs should familiarize themselves with four significant versions of NetWare: NetWare 3.*x*, NetWare 4.*x*, NetWare 5.*x*., and NetWare 6.*x*.

TIP The Network+ exam assumes all NetWare Networks use IPX/SPX unless specifically stated otherwise.

NetWare 3.x and the Bindery

NetWare 3.x offers solid file and print sharing capabilities using the IPX/SPX protocol suite, but lacks a centralized security database. Each NetWare 3.x server maintains its own security database, called the Bindery. When a user logs in, the NetWare server compares the user name and password to its Bindery database and then determines which resources it will share with the user. NetWare 3.x works best in networks that require only a single server, because each server maintains its own independent Bindery database (see Figure 12-38). A user accessing resources on three different servers must have three separate user accounts and passwords. NetWare 3.x's reliance on IPX/SPX also limits its use, as more and more networks move to TCP/IP as the protocol of choice.

 TIP Although it is possible to add TCP/IP support to a NetWare 3.x server, NetWare 3.x servers running TCP/IP rarely occur in the wild. For the purposes of the Network+ exam, assume that all NetWare 3.x servers use IPX/SPX as their sole networking protocol.

NetWare 4.x and NDS

NetWare 4.x built on the success of NetWare 3.x by adding two key features: Novell Directory Services (NDS) and TCP/IP encapsulation. The NDS feature organizes all user and resource information in a database referred to as the NDS tree. The NDS tree acts as

Figure 12-38
NetWare 3.x
servers maintain
separate Bindery
databases

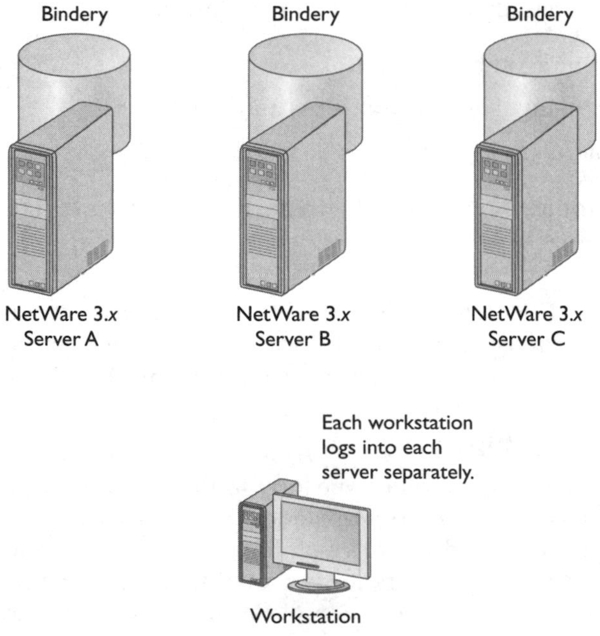

Bindery   Bindery   Bindery

NetWare 3.x   NetWare 3.x   NetWare 3.x
Server A   Server B   Server C

Each workstation
logs into each
server separately.

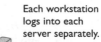

Workstation

Figure 12-39
Encapsulation
enables NetWare
4.*x* to use TCP/IP.

NetWare 4.*x* servers and clients can encapsulate IPX packets in TCP/IP packets.

NetWare 4.*x*
server

NetWare 4.*x*
client

a centralized security database, enabling users who log onto the directory to access all of their resources anywhere on the network. NDS has been around for quite a while and precedes Windows Active Directory by many years. NetWare 4.*x* also supports TCP/IP, enabling NetWare servers and clients to place IPX packets inside of TCP/IP packets, a process known as *encapsulation* (see Figure 12-39). Although NetWare's basic design assumes the use of IPX/SPX, encapsulation enables NetWare to use TCP/IP without a massive redesign. Unfortunately, encapsulation hurts performance by adding an additional layer of protocol information to each packet.

TIP Both NDS and Active Directory are based on a directory standard called X.500.

NetWare 5.*x*/6.*x*

NetWare 5.*x* and 6.*x* run TCP/IP natively, removing the need for TCP/IP encapsulation. Having native TCP/IP means that NetWare no longer needs to use IPX/SPX at all (although it can for backward compatibility). Because NetWare now speaks TCP/IP natively, it performs far more efficiently than NetWare 4.*x* when using TCP/IP.

For the Network+ exam, familiarize yourself with the protocols and security databases used by each version of NetWare, as shown in Table 12-1.

Novell calls its version of the Windows NT/2000/XP administrator account—an account that provides total and complete access to the system—the supervisor or admin account, depending on the version of NetWare. Make sure only a few administrators have access to the supervisor/admin account!

NetWare Version	Security Database	Protocol(s)
NetWare 3.*x*	Bindery	IPX/SPX
NetWare 4.*x*	NDS	IPX/SPX or TCP/IP
NetWare 5.*x*	NDS	IPX/SPX or TCP/IP
NetWare 6.*x*	NDS	IPX/SPX or TCP/IP

Table 12-1 NetWare Security Databases and Protocols

UNIX and Linux

As the importance of the Internet continues to grow, the *UNIX* operating system, long a mainstay of university and scientific computing, is becoming more important for the average network tech in the trenches. Originally, the Internet consisted of a few UNIX-based systems at a handful of universities spread around the world. The basic Internet protocols, like FTP, HTTP, DNS, and ARP, actually originated in the world of UNIX and were only later ported to other operating systems. UNIX comes in many versions, but they all share certain features. The flexibility of UNIX and the rise of open source variants like Linux and Free BSD make UNIX a network operating system that network techs ignore at their own peril.

Many Flavors

The wide variety of UNIX versions, commonly referred to in geek-land as *flavors*, arose because Bell Labs made UNIX available to universities, and allowed the universities to modify the operating system to meet their own needs. This freedom to adapt the operating system encouraged innovation, leading to the development of critical technologies such as TCP/IP-based networking, but it also resulted in many flavors of UNIX possessing significant differences. Today, major variations include Sun's Solaris, IBM's AIX UNIX, Hewlett-Packard's HP UNIX, and BSD. While all versions of UNIX share a similar look and feel, a program written for one flavor often requires significant revision before it can run on another. Fortunately, the typical network tech can safely leave the variations among UNIX flavors to the programmers. From the network tech's point of view, all versions of UNIX are more alike than different.

 TIP   The Network+ exam does not cover the differences between versions of UNIX/Linux.

Web Applications

Although it faces increasing competition from the Windows NT and NetWare families, UNIX remains the server of choice for providing Internet-based services such as web browsing and e-mail. The protocols used for Internet-based services mostly originated in UNIX versions, and many organizations that use NetWare or Windows for their file and print sharing needs still rely on UNIX for their Internet services.

Printing

For many years, the UNIX/Linux people used the protocol set LPR/LPD to handle printing chores. Clients used the line printer request (LPR) portion to submit a print job to a print server. The server ran the line printer daemon (LPD) protocol to handle those submissions.

The LPR/LPD printing system is quickly being replaced by the *Common UNIX Printing System (CUPS)*. CUPS addresses a number of limitations inherent to LPR/LPD and has made printing in UNIX and Linux far easier and flexible than in the past. The CUPS printing system is based on the Internet Printing Protocol (IPP) standard and includes substantial improvements over LPR/LPD. CUPS supports any printer language, although it's most commonly associated with the PostScript language. In fact, CUPS printer definition files all end with the PPD (Postscript Printer Definition) extension, even the ones that are used with non-PostScript printers. CUPS has built-in web-based support for printer connections and printer management and supports SAMBA and LPD printers. CUPS also supports most TCP/IP features such as encryption and proxies, and other features that LPD never knew how to handle.

The CUPS server program on UNIX /Linux systems is called—surprise—CUPS. On the client side you either run the CUPS service or use one of many different programs to access the CUPS server. On most UNIX/Linux distributions, CUPS is now hidden from users by some from of graphical printer configuration dialog box. For those die-hard command-line users who want to run CUPS from a command prompt, you use the **lp** or **lpr** command to send your CUPS print jobs to your CUPS server.

Open Source and Linux

If you haven't heard of Linux yet, you need to read the newspaper a little more often! Linus Torvalds, while a student, expressed his frustration over the high cost of most versions of UNIX by building his own. What makes this story special is that Torvalds licensed his UNIX clone, dubbed Linux, in a unique way. *Linux is an open source operating system*, distributed under the terms of the GNU General Public License (GPL), which means (among other things) that anyone who purchases a copy receives full access to its source code, the building blocks of the operating system. Free access to the source code gives software developers the power to modify the operating system to meet their needs. This has led to the rapid development of a wide variety of applications, including some of the most commonly used web and e-mail servers on the Internet. In most cases, both the Linux operating system and Linux applications are available for free download from the Internet, although vendors like SuSE and Caldera sell boxed versions, and charge for support services. For all intents and purposes, Linux is a full-featured clone of UNIX.

Does UNIX have a super account like Windows and NetWare? You bet it does! The all-powerful account in all versions of UNIX/Linux is called root. Again, giving someone the password to the root account gives them the ability to log onto a UNIX/Linux system with complete access to anything they want to do on that system. So give out the root password sparingly!

Mac OS

Apple Computer was one of the earliest adopters of network functions for its systems. In keeping with Apple's long-term attitude of "we can do it better," Apple implemented networking very differently from the other network operating systems. Adding to the confusion, over the years Apple has made a number of upgrades to the networking functions of the *Macintosh operating system*. All of these incremental changes make it difficult to give a brief overview of Macintosh networking without going way, way outside the scope of the Network+ exams. Instead, I'm going to concentrate on current Macintosh NOS functions, with a small nod to a few critical historical points that CompTIA wants you to know.

The key to the uniqueness of Macintosh networking in the early days is *AppleTalk*, Apple's do-it-all family of networking protocols. AppleTalk handles tasks ranging from Transport Layer packet creation to establishing sessions between systems to support for network applications. One can reasonably compare the functionality of AppleTalk with the territory covered by Microsoft's NetBIOS and NetBEUI (although any good Mac networking tech will probably cringe when I say that). Like NetBIOS, AppleTalk was designed primarily for file and printer sharing. Its naming conventions are very similar to what you see in NetBIOS, although AppleTalk supports very long system names. The practical limit for an AppleTalk name, however, is about 20 characters. Like NetBEUI, AppleTalk does not support routing and instead uses a NetBIOS-like broadcast function to enable systems to recognize each other. Macintosh systems also use a grouping function called *zones*. A zone works for the most part just like a Microsoft Workgroup. Zones do not provide any real network security and simply act as a tool for organization.

Not surprisingly, given its overwhelming popularity, all modern Macintosh systems implement TCP/IP, using a program called AppleShare IP. AppleShare IP's mission is to connect your Macintosh system to IP networks, including the Internet. Apple also makes Mac OS X Server, a full-blown server OS that includes tools to facilitate interconnectivity with Windows and Linux. It also greatly enhances network security, in particular by implementing groups and robust user accounts. So, networking in Macintosh involves two products: the basic networking functions of AppleShare IP, which are built into all Macintosh systems, and Mac Server.

Creating Servers and Clients

After choosing the best NOS for your network, you must install the operating system software on your networked systems. You will confront a number of critical issues at various steps during the installation process. While each operating system handles these issues differently, either you or the NOS must take care of each of them.

Network Interface

Every system on the network must have some device by which to access the network, called the *network interface*. In most cases, this will be a NIC or a modem. Fortunately, the world of Plug and Play (PnP) now predominates, and installing a NIC or modem has pretty much been reduced to plugging in the device and then kicking back while the NOS handles everything else for you. The only issue you need concern yourself with is making sure the device installed properly. That means knowing where in the operating system you go to check on this. In almost all versions of Windows, it means a trip to the good old Device Manager. Figure 12-40 shows a perfectly functioning NIC in the Windows 2000 Device Manager.

Other operating systems like Linux aren't nearly as pretty, but they're just as functional. Figure 12-41 shows someone running the **IFCONFIG** command and looking for eth0—the universal name for an Ethernet adapter in the UNIX/Linux world.

Figure 12-40
A functioning
NIC in the
Windows 2000
Device Manager

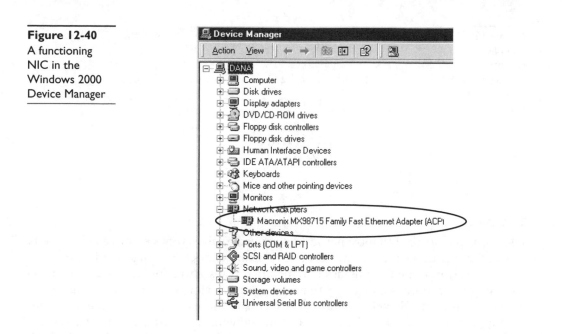

If a NIC isn't working correctly, you'll get some type of error information. Windows adds a pretty **X** or **?** to the graphic of the device, while Linux just gives you some text, but either way you can tell whether the NIC is working. Keep in mind that every operating system invariably provides more than one way to check the NIC. The two examples I gave aren't the only ways to check a NIC in either Windows or Linux—they're just the ones I use. Refer to Chapter 8 for more information on installing NICs.

Protocol

Every networked PC must run a software suite that enables the PC to communicate over the network, in other words, a *protocol*. Since everyone and their dog uses TCP/IP, you can bet that your NOS will invariably install TCP/IP as the default protocol, unless you're running something a tad older. This is a big deal in the Network+ exam's eyes—make sure you know the different protocols that install with the different network operating systems, including some of the older ones! I describe them all in this chapter.

Figure 12-41
Running
IFCONFIG
eth0 in Linux

```
[root@localhost /dev]# ifconfig eth0
eth0    Link encap:Ethernet HWaddr 00:40:F4:23:0C:51
        inet addr:192.168.4.19 Bcast:192.168.4.255 Mask:255.255.255.0
        UP BROADCAST RUNNING MTU:1500 Metric:1
        RX packets:14 errors:0 dropped:0 overruns:0 frame:0
        TX packets:14 errors:0 dropped:0 overruns:0 carrier:0
        collisions:0 txqueuelen:0
        Interrupt:10 Base address:0x1000

[root@localhost /dev]#
```

Figure 12-42
The Novell NetWare server displayed in My Network Places

Naming

Okay, this is a big one! In most networks you need to give every system, or at least every system that shares resources, a "friendly name," which is to say, one that isn't 192.168.43.2 or something else cryptic and hard to remember. You see this friendly name when you view shared network resources. In Windows, you can view shared resources using the ever-popular Network Neighborhood/My Network Places. (Novell NetWare also calls its application Network Neighborhood.) All network operating systems have some similar application. Figure 12-42 shows a Windows 2000 system's My Network Places displaying a Novell NetWare Server, called NETWARE51.

As I've said, organization-based networks name groups of computers for organizational purposes. Luckily, creating these group names is the realm of the folks who set up servers, an area Network+ doesn't expect you to know. However, if a network administrator tells you to set up a Windows 2000 client system, Network+ does expect you to understand organizational groups and group names, and it expects you to know how to assign a client to a group. Figure 12-43 shows five groups on my network. These groups are called domains because, well, that's what Microsoft decided to call its groups of computers. The domain names in this example are ones I created.

Different organization-based network operating systems use different names for these groups. Windows calls them domains. NetWare, meanwhile, calls them trees.

Server or Client

If you install Novell NetWare, it will automatically set up as a server. Other operating systems, such as Windows 98, automatically perform as clients. Windows 2000/XP/2003, Linux, and Macintosh computers run both as clients and servers. The trick is that some

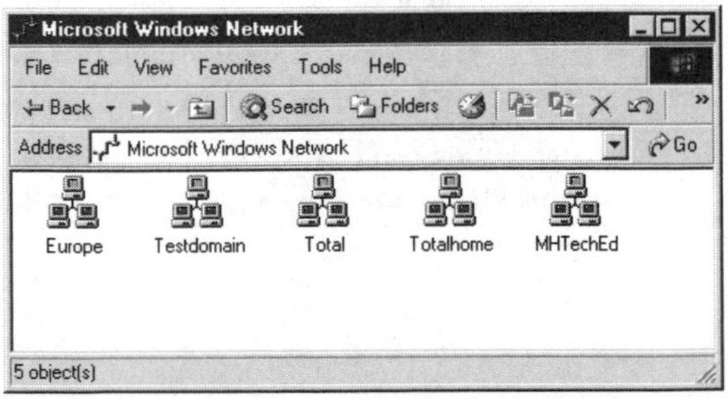

Figure 12-43
Domains in Mike's system

operating systems, particularly Windows 9x clients, when running in resource-based networks, require that you also set them up to act as servers. All this really means is you must turn on File and Print Sharing, so the Windows 9x systems can share.

Super User Accounts

All network operating systems require user accounts. Any NOS that requires this will come with a built-in, all-powerful user account that has total control of everything in the network. This account is called supervisor or admin in NetWare, Administrator in Windows NT/2000, and root in UNIX/Linux. When a system is first installed, you must set the password for this account. As you might imagine, this account's password is something you want only the most trusted people to know! Most operating systems require you to use this account, or an equivalent (you can usually make more accounts with the same power), to do most of the network administrative tasks. Most of the time the network admin herself will create user accounts; however, most network operating systems enable an administrator to delegate her power to create accounts to other user accounts—a nice way to delegate administrative work!

TIP As a security consideration, most network techs change the default name of the built-in administrator account. Why? Well, any potential hacker knows that there's an account called, for example, "Administrator" on a Windows server system. A valid user account name is half of the hack—now all they need to guess is the password! If you want to harden your server's security, you should also make them have to guess a valid user name. Some sneakier network techs even create a dummy account called "Administrator" that has no real power, except to act as an obstacle for hackers.

Groups

Most network operating systems have default groups. For example, Windows NT/2000 has a group called All Users. Anyone with a valid user account automatically becomes a part of this group. Your network admin will almost certainly have made such groups for your network.

Passwords

Passwords are now pretty common to all network operating systems, and the folks who give the Network+ exam want you to have a good general understanding of passwords.

Network security only works well when users keep their passwords secure. Passwords, for example, should never be written down where another user can find them, and users should never reveal their passwords to anyone, even the network administrator! In most cases, the administrator can reset a user's password without knowing the old one. Many users, however, remain unaware of this possibility and so fall prey to one of the oldest hacker tricks in the book: the fake tech support phone call. In a large organization, most users will not know every network support technician. A hacker can call up one of these hapless users and say, "This is Howie from tech support. We're upgrading the forward deflector array and we need your password so we can reset it when we're done." A shocking number of users will simply give out their password when asked over the phone. Getting humans to think is never easy, but it's a vital part of network security!

Educating network users about the proper care and feeding of their passwords is a critical part of any network security plan. First, teach users to pick good passwords. A good password cannot be guessed easily. They should never be based on any information about the user that a bad guy can obtain easily. For example, if Herman lives at 1313 Mockingbird Lane, is married to Lily, and has a pet named Spot, he should never use the following passwords:

- mockingbird
- dribgnikcom (mockingbird spelled backwards)
- lily
- ylil (lily spelled backwards)
- spot
- tops (spot spelled backwards)

Ideally, a password should not be a real word at all. Hackers probing a network often run password-guessing utilities that try common dictionary words at random. Network administrators can reduce the effectiveness of such password-guessing programs by requiring that all passwords be longer than six to eight characters. Hackers have a more difficult task guessing longer passwords because there are so many more possible combinations. The most secure passwords contain a combination of letters and numbers. Users hate them because they are also the hardest to remember. The following list contains strong passwords:

- gr78brk3
- tnk23wqk
- bob0tw2&

A good network administrator should assume that, given enough time, some users' passwords will become public knowledge. To limit the impact of these exposed passwords, a careful network administrator sets passwords to expire periodically, usually every 30 days at the most. If a password becomes public knowledge, the gap in network security will automatically close when the user changes his password. One of the most frustrating aspects of implementing passwords is the stream of support calls from users who can't log onto the network. If I only had a dollar for every time a user left on the CAPS LOCK key, or just didn't type in the password correctly!

 TIP A strong password should be at least eight characters, contain both letters and numbers, be changed on a regular schedule, and not be based on easily guessed information.

Most network operating systems also enable you to disable a user's account. A disabled user account is simply an account whose access has been disabled but that hasn't been removed from the system. Many network administrators will disable an account while a user is on extended leave or on temporary assignment. Of course, somebody is sure to hear about it when the user comes back and can't log on because their account is disabled! While the Network+ exam isn't interested in whether you know how to enable and disable user accounts for your particular NOS, you do need to know that they can be disabled.

As a person supporting networks, you must have a basic understanding of the different makes and models of network operating systems available today. Become familiar with the many variations of Novell, Microsoft, and Linux/UNIX products, and be sure you can explain the differences between client/server and peer-to-peer networking.

Chapter Review

Questions

1. Your network consists of a Novell NetWare 3 server and a UNIX system. Sally cannot access the server, so you go to My Network Places and discover that Sally has only the NetBEUI protocol installed. Which of the following protocols should you install to enable Sally to communicate with the NetWare server and the other systems using UNIX? (Select all that apply.)

   A. Banyan VINES

   B. TCP/IP

   C. IPX/SPX

   D. NetBEUI

2. Of the following NOS server programs, which one can only be a server and never a client?

   A. Novell NetWare

   B. Microsoft Windows 2000

   C. Microsoft Windows 98

   D. UNIX

3. What type of system accesses a resource?

   A. Mac

   B. Server

   C. Client

   D. Terminal

4. Novell NetWare, Windows NT/2000, and UNIX/Linux all have a built-in, all-powerful user account that has total control of anything on the network. Each NOS uses a different name for this all-powerful user. UNIX/Linux calls it a(n) _____; Windows NT/2000 calls it a(n) _____; and NetWare calls it either _____ or _____.

   A. Root, Administrator, Admin, Supervisor

   B. Supervisor, Root, Administrator, Admin

   C. Admin, Supervisor, Root, Administrator

   D. Administrator, Admin, Supervisor, Root

5. Your network is made up of ten Windows 98 systems, and you installed the TCP/IP protocol on all the systems. Now Melissa wants to share her hard drive. She goes to My Computer and alternate-clicks the C: drive, but Sharing is not listed as one of her choices. You know that her cable and NIC are working, and she can see everyone on the network. What could be the problem?

   A. IPX/SPX needs to be installed on Melissa's system.

   B. File and Print Sharing has not been installed on Melissa's system.

   C. Client for Microsoft Networks has not been installed on Melissa's system.

   D. Melissa is not running the sharing protocol.

6. May wants to allow Mary Jane and Peter to view and modify a database stored on her server. She wants Betty to be able to view the database but not modify it, and she wants Jonah to have no access to the database whatsoever. Each user should have his or her own password. What kind of security should May implement?

   A. High-level

   B. Share-level

   C. User-level

   D. SMTP-level

7. NetWare 3.*x* servers store user account and password information in a database called the

   A. Domain

   B. NDS tree

   C. Bindery

   D. Registry

8. You are running a Linux system on your network. In order for you to access root on this system, you need to know the

   A. Location of the directory

   B. Computer's name

    C. Password

    D. Root code

9. You are running a Windows 2000 server on your network. You need to make sure that the TCP/IP protocol suite, IPX/SPX protocol suite, and NetBEUI protocol suites are installed. Which of these protocols are found natively on Windows 2000? (Select all that apply.)

    A. NetBIOS

    B. NetBEUI

    C. TCP/IP

    D. IPX/SPX

10. When using a common security database, Novell NetWare servers must be organized into a(n)

    A. NDS tree

    B. Domain

    C. Ring

    D. Web

Answers

1. **B, C.** You need to make sure that Sally's system has the IPX/SPX protocol for the NetWare server and the TCP/IP protocol for the UNIX systems.

2. **A.** With the exception of Novell NetWare, every operating system capable of networking (Windows, UNIX/Linux, and Macintosh) allows systems to act as both servers and clients at the same time. Novell NetWare cannot act as both a server and a client on the same system.

3. **C.** A client is a system that accesses the shared resource.

4. **A.** UNIX/Linux calls its all-powerful user account Root; Windows NT/2000 calls it Administrator; and NetWare calls it either Admin or Supervisor.

5. **B.** Melissa must turn on File and Print Sharing before her Windows 98 system can function as a server and share her hard drive.

6. **C.** May should implement user-level security, which lets her assign different rights and permissions to each user, and give each user a unique password. Share-level security assigns a password to each resource, but would not fulfill May's needs because Mary Jane and Peter would use the same password to access the database. Simple Mail Transfer Protocol (SMTP) is an e-mail protocol that has nothing to do with securing files on a server. High-level security is a bogus term.

7. **C.** Each NetWare 3.*x* server has its own security database called the Bindery. NetWare 4.*x* and 5.*x* servers share a common NDS database, and Windows NT servers share a domain database. The Registry is a central hierarchical database used in Windows 95, 98, NT, and 2000 to store information necessary to configure the system for one or more users, applications, and hardware devices.

8. **C.** You need to know the password to the root account to log onto a UNIX/ Linux system with complete access to that system.

9. **C, D.** TCP/IP and IPX/SPX are native on a Windows 2000 system. NetBEUI comes with 2000, but you must install it.

10. **A.** Novell NetWare servers use Novell Directory Services when sharing a common security database. Servers sharing that database exist within an NDS tree.

PART III

Beyond the Basic LAN

## CHAPTER 13

Sharing Resources

The Network+ Certification exam expects you to know how to

- 3.1   Identify the basic capabilities (for example: client support, interoperability, authentication, file and print services, application support, and security) of the following server operating systems to access network resources: UNIX/Linux/ Mac OS X Server, NetWare, Windows
- 3.2   Identify the basic capabilities needed for client workstations to connect to and use network resources (for example: media, network protocols, and peer and server services)

To achieve these goals, you must be able to

- Understand the naming of shared resources using Universal Naming Convention (UNC) and Universal Resource Locater (URL)
- Learn about permissions for Windows 9*x*, Windows NT, Windows 2000/2003, Windows XP, NetWare 3.*x*, NetWare 4.*x*/5.*x*/6.*x*
- Understand sharing resources as it applies to the preceding operating systems
- Understand accessing shared resources

In every functional network, server systems share resources and client systems access those shared resources. This chapter looks at the different ways the common network operating systems enable servers to share resources, concentrating on folder and printer sharing in the different versions of Microsoft Windows, Novell NetWare, and Linux/UNIX. Then you'll see how to configure Windows 9*x*, 2000, and XP clients to access those shared resources. After all, an installed network of servers and client computers is useless without resources for the serving systems to share and the client systems to access!

The basic steps of making any resource sharable are pretty much the same whether you're sharing a folder on your C: drive to a small network or a huge web site to the entire Internet. To share a resource, you need to make it sharable and give it some name. How shared resources are named varies, depending on the operating system and the type of resource shared.

> # Historical/Conceptual

Resource Naming

Resource naming falls into one of two types: naming conventions invented by Novell and Microsoft, and the resource naming conventions we use for TCP/IP-based stuff. Windows and NetWare were sharing folders and files on their own internal LANs long before they moved out into the Internet world, and as a result have a different way to look at folder and printer sharing than what we might see on the Internet. Let's begin by understanding how Windows and NetWare name-shared resources.

Scott decides to share his C:\Half-Life folder on his Windows XP Professional system; how do his pals on the network know this resource is available for use? Let's assume that his system is running the correct protocol, is properly connected to the network, and his computer has the name Scottxp. That's half the battle, but a server name alone does not work. Each shared resource must also have a name.

The combination of server name and shared resource name gives people wanting to use the resource something to point at to select a specific resource. Windows clients use the Network Neighborhood/My Network Places tool to browse a network for available resources. Figure 13-1 shows the My Network Places folder on my PC. I can see all of the systems currently sharing resources, including Scott's PC (Scottxp). Double-clicking the Scottxp icon displays all the shared resources on his system, as shown in Figure 13-2.

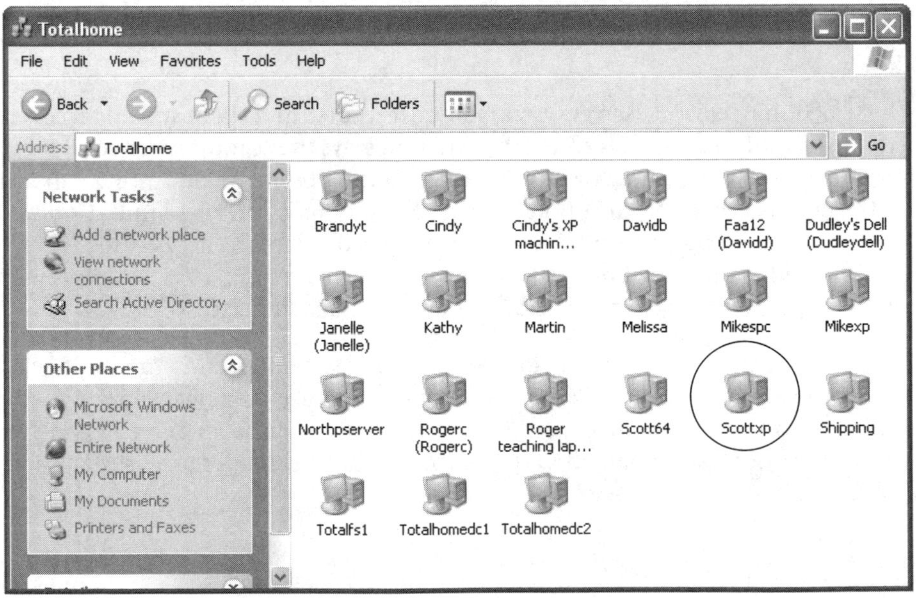

Figure 13-1   My Network Places showing Scott's PC

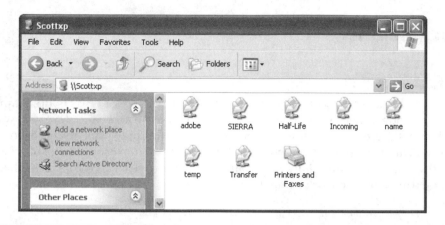

Figure 13-2   Shared folders on Scott's PC

NOTE   Windows 9x and NT call this folder Network Neighborhood; Windows Me, 2000, 2003, and XP call it My Network Places. For the remainder of this chapter, I'm going to keep things simple and call it My Network Places, regardless of the operating system.

You can easily see the Half-Life folder in Figure 13-2, because Scott chose to call his shared folder "Half-Life." That's not always the case. The name by which a resource is shared on a network does not have to be the same name as the actual resource. We call the name of the shared resource on the network the *network share name*. A shared resource's network name is not, and often cannot be, the same as its real name. Scott's shared C:\Half-Life folder has the network name Half-Life, but he could just as easily have called it "TIMMY" or "ScottGame" or just about anything else within the limits of the NetBIOS or DNS naming conventions. To access this folder, just double-click it; then, assuming no security restrictions prevent it, you can access the files and subfolders on this share.

NOTE   Using the term "NetBIOS naming conventions" often makes students' eyes roll back in their heads, especially when it means simply "normal" names, made with almost any combination of alphanumeric characters. You cannot use spaces or the following characters in names: \ / : * ? " ; |

Test Specific

UNC

Windows' My Network Places makes browsing through a network easy to do. Simply by clicking a group, serving system, or shared resource, you can access whatever you want—or at least whatever you're allowed to access. But networking hasn't always been about Windows client systems. Long ago, before Windows even existed, Microsoft championed the concept of the *Universal Naming Convention (UNC)*, which describes any shared resource in a network using this convention:

```
\\<server name>\<name of shared resource>
```

DOS programs (pre-Windows, remember?) accessed shared resources using commands typed at a command prompt. DOS systems needed UNC names to access shared resources. Let's say someone wanted to access Scott's C:\Half-Life folder. The UNC name you'd type to access his system would be \\Scottxp, and the UNC name for the shared folder would be \\Scottxp\Half-Life. If you were using the old DOS-based NOS called LAN Manager, you'd have to type strange commands at the C: prompt, like

```
NET use y:  \\Scottxp\\half-life
```

This command, in a process known as *mapping*, creates a Y: drive on the client system that's really the \\Scottxp\Half-Life share. All versions of Windows still support drive mapping. Fortunately, you no longer need to type strange commands at command prompts—although you still can if you want to! Just alternate-click (right-click) the folder in My Network Places and select Map Network Drive to get a wizard (in some versions of Windows); or open My Network Places in Windows XP and select Map Network Drive from the Tools menu to start the wizard (see Figure 13-3). Select a drive letter for the drive—and in Windows XP, browse to the shared folder—and the mapped share will appear like magic in your My Computer folder! Figure 13-4 shows the shared folder \\Scottxp\Half-Life mapped as the Y: drive on my system under My Computer. Windows XP is even nice enough to change the icon slightly and to list it separately from my local drives, so you know the folder is a *mapped drive*—can you see the difference?

Although Windows systems still support mapping, Windows applications can access shares directly by their UNC names, so you no longer need to map a shared folder to a drive letter. Even though mapping is not nearly as common as it once was, you'll still see it used in some networks, usually for security reasons or to support some older application that needs to access a drive letter and not a UNC name. Mapping, as well as a number of other share functions, simply would not work without UNC.

Make sure you can recognize a valid UNC name. They always begin with a double backslash (\\ ) followed by the name of the serving system, and then a single backslash (\ ) followed by the name of the shared resource.

Figure 13-3
The Map
Network Drive
wizard in
Windows XP

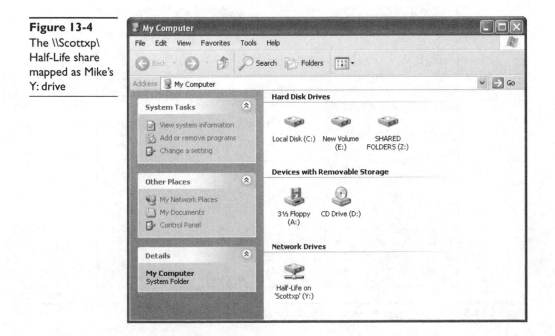

TIP Make sure you can tell a valid UNC name from an invalid one!

UNCs are not limited to shared folders and drives. You can also use a printer's UNC to connect to a shared printer. This process, similar to mapping, is called *capturing* a printer. A captured printer uses a local LPT port that connects to the networked printer. Like mapping, this is usually only done to support older programs that are not smart enough to know how to print directly to a UNC-named printer; it's quite rare today. Back in the

Figure 13-4
The \\Scottxp\
Half-Life share
mapped as Mike's
Y: drive

old days, we could capture a printer just like a shared folder, using the **NET** command in Windows:

```
NET use LPT1 \\Tim\Printer
```

 NOTE The CAPTURE command was the NetWare equivalent to the NET command in Windows.

Even though we rarely use these ancient commands to map folders and capture printers, UNCs are still very much part of the networking world, especially with Windows systems. Windows support for UNCs goes deep; almost any application in your system that has to do with locating a file or folder will read UNCs. Try opening either Internet Explorer or Windows Explorer and typing a known valid UNC name in the address area—the corresponding network folder will open. Figure 13-5 shows what happens when I type a UNC into the address bar of Internet Explorer.

URL

Although Microsoft developed UNC names to work with any shared resource, these days, they're mostly just used with folders and printers. Other shared resources like e-mail and web browsers use the more common, and more Internet-aware, *Universal Resource Locator (URL)* nomenclature. You'll learn more about URLs in Chapter 15, "TCP/IP and the Internet."

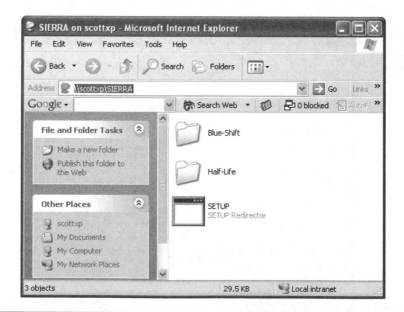

Figure 13-5   A UNC typed into the address bar of Internet Explorer

NOTE You will find that the *U* in URL can stand for either *uniform* or *universal*. While *universal* was the early choice, *uniform* is probably ahead in usage now. Neither one is "wrong" per se.

The rest of this chapter details how different network operating systems share resources, and then shows how to access those shared resources. We'll be messing with URLs like crazy, but before we do that, you need to understand the major concept of permissions.

Permissions

Once you've set up a resource for sharing and given it a network name, how do you control who gets to access it and what they can do to it? You know the answer to this one from Chapter 12, "Network Operating Systems," right? Permissions, of course! I touched on permissions—or *rights*, as they're called in Novell NetWare—in Chapter 12, but now it's time to go into them in more detail. I've included a bit of background here that'll sound familiar, but it could be a useful refresher if you've slept since reading the last chapter.

As you know, *permissions* are sets of attributes network administrators assign to resources to define what users and groups can do with them (the resources, not the admin!). A fairly typical permission used in all network operating systems is a permission assigned to folders called *execute*. The execute permission, as its name implies, enables the user or group that has it to execute, or run, any programs in that folder.

 NOTE The execute permission in a Linux/UNIX environment enables you to view the contents of a directory, as well as run programs in that directory.

Types of permissions vary, depending on the resource being shared. If I share a printer, I certainly don't need a permission called execute, although I do admit wishing I could have executed a few troublesome dot-matrix printers in the past! Instead, printers usually have permissions like manage printer that let certain users or groups reset the printer or start and stop print jobs.

There are many, many more permission types than the two I described here. I just wanted you to get an idea of what a couple looked like. One of the most fascinating aspects of permissions is the different ways network operating systems utilize them. Let's look at the more common network operating systems and appreciate how they use permissions.

Dueling Security Models

The first thing to understand here is that Windows 9*x* is a freak of nature when it comes to networking and permissions. It does permissions one way, and all the other operating systems we'll be discussing do them another (better) way. It all boils down to the difference between the resource-based security model, and the server- and organization-based models. The server- and organization-based models have two layers of security in between a user and the resource he wants to access, while the resource-based model has only one.

As you'll recall from Chapter 12, "Network Operating Systems," in the server and organization models, all users must log on before they can access shared resources. In the server-based model, users log into each server for access to the resources it controls; in the organization-based model, users log in once for access to the entire network. Either way, after a user has logged on successfully, that user account receives an electronic key it can show to serving systems on the network when it wants access to specific resources.

Hillary works for a super-secret spy agency. When she walks in the front door, she shows the badge to a guard to prove that it's okay to let her in. The guard then gives her a special electronic card with a secret code on it. The code specifies where she can go and what she can do during that particular visit. Every time Hillary wants to access a particular area, a security device checks her card to see what permissions she has. The type and extent of her access to the resources in that area will be determined by the specific permissions encoded on her card. What I've just described is a two-layer security model: First, you must get in the door of the building (log onto the network); second, you must have the necessary permissions to access the various resources inside (see Figure 13-6).

Figure 13-6
Two layer security:
log onto the
network and have
permissions.

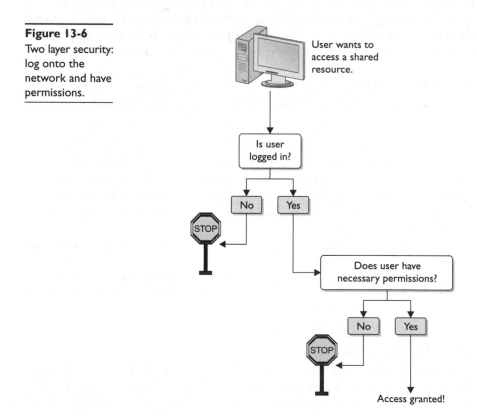

In resource-based security models, there's only one layer of security. Returning to my hypothetical situation, it would be as if there were no guard at the door—absolutely anyone could walk in to the building without anyone knowing who they were or when they came and went. The only security barrier between them and any particular area in the building would be the door to that area, which would either be locked, unlocked, or protected by a password code.

Windows 9x Permissions

All Windows 9x systems use the resource-based security model. The only security options are Full (the door is open—do what you want), Read-Only (you can look, but not touch), and Depends On Password (Full access requires a password). Interestingly, Windows 9x doesn't have a No Access option. Think about it—there's no point in having a resource nobody can access ever, but because 9x doesn't have real user accounts, it does not know who's knocking at the door. Your only choices with Windows 9x are (a) let everyone in to do whatever they want; (b) let everyone in, but only let them look; or (c) let everyone in to look, but only those who know the password can do whatever they want.

Additionally, these permissions, called *share permissions*, only control the access of other users on the network with whom you share your resource; they have no impact on you (or anyone else) sitting at the computer whose resource is being shared. These Windows 9x permissions are prehistoric in networking terms; they date from the days of LANMan 1.0 (the first NOS for PCs), before anybody could imagine a need for more than this basic amount of security.

Clearly, they were wrong about that. Gone are the days when computer security meant locking the computer room door! Today's networks have to be secured against all enemies, foreign and domestic. Network administrators need to be able to keep track of who can use their networks, and in what specific ways, regardless of whether the person is sitting at the serving system itself or dialing in from a country half-way around the world. Truly useful security also requires a more powerful and flexible set of permissions. Modern network operating systems like Windows NT/2000/2003/XP and Novell NetWare implement robustly featured user accounts, as you'll recall from Chapter 12, "Network Operating Systems." User accounts enable a network admin not only to control initial access to the network, but also to fine-tune any user's access to every resource being shared.

TIP Windows 9x does have user accounts, but those accounts exist only to enable a user on a Windows 9x client on a network to log into a Windows NT/ 2000/2003 server. The user account login provides absolutely no protection for the local machine itself. I'll let you in on a secret: you can just press the ESC key at the logon screen and Windows 9x will shrug its shoulders and let you have full access to its local resources.

PART III

Windows NT Permissions

If Windows 9x is a freak of nature, Windows NT has multiple personalities. Windows NT can handle security in two completely different ways.

Windows NT file and folder permissions are based on the powerful NT file system (NTFS) file format. When you format a partition in Windows NT, you can choose from two file formats: the old FAT partition used by Windows 9x systems, or NTFS. Figure 13-7 shows the Windows NT Disk Administrator tool—note the two NTFS partitions and one FAT partition. You don't have to use NTFS to format an NT volume, but if you choose not to format a partition on a Windows NT system with NTFS, you will lose all of the security that NTFS provides. You will be reduced to the Windows 9x share permissions just described. Of course, pretty much everyone uses NTFS on their Windows NT/2000/2003/XP systems nowadays!

NOTE   Windows 2000, 2003, and XP can use three different file systems: FAT, FAT32, and NTFS. Just as with FAT, FAT32 offers no security benefits to the system and thus should be avoided in most circumstances. Everything discussed in this section about NT's use of NTFS also holds true for Windows 2000, 2003, and XP.

NTFS embeds the powerful NTFS permissions into each shared resource. This does *not* mean that the resource itself handles security. That job goes either to the individual NT serving system or to the NT domain, depending on how the NT network is configured. This is a critical point and one that is often lost on folks new to more advanced network operating systems. If the network isn't running any copies of Windows NT Server, Windows 2000 Server, or Windows Server 2003, each system on the network must act as its own server; this means users must have an account on each system they want to access (see Figure 13-8).

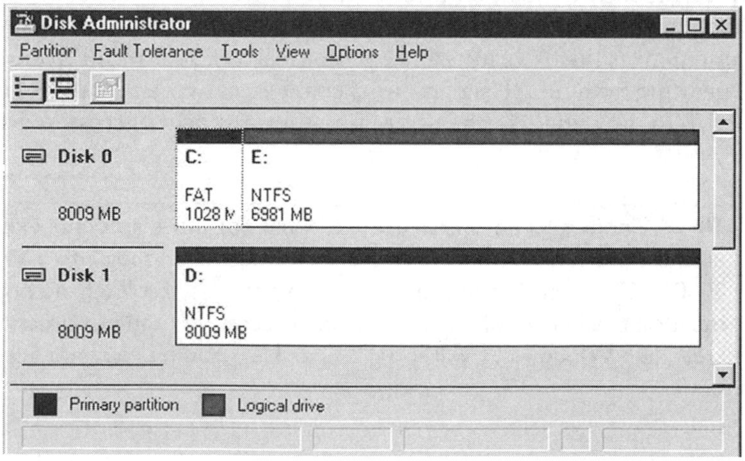

Figure 13-7   The Windows NT Disk Administrator tool

Computer A has to log onto B to access B's shares,
C for C's shares, and D for D's shares—what a hassle!

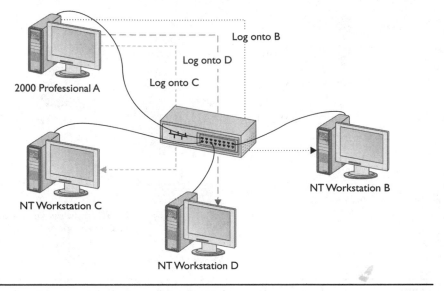

Figure 13-8   Logging onto each sharing system separately

Once you install a copy of Windows NT Server, Windows 2000 Server, or Windows Server 2003 and implement a domain, each user gets a domain user account that gives them access to the network in one quick logon (see Figure 13-9). In a domain-based network, no one has a local user account—all users get domain user accounts that must be set up by a special program on the Windows NT, 2000, or 2003 server system. Local accounts still exist in a Windows NT, 2000, or 2003 domain-based network (except for domain controllers, which have no local user accounts), but are rarely used except for perhaps an occasional maintenance function. To log on locally to a system that uses a domain, you must perform a special local logon. In fact, the Windows NT/2000/XP logon gives you the ability to log into the domain or just to the local system (see Figure 13-10). We log into a local system only to perform maintenance.

Table 13-1 lists Microsoft's standard *NTFS permissions* for files and folders under Windows NT. These standard permissions are groupings of what Microsoft calls special permissions that have names like Execute, Read, and Write. These special permissions are rarely accessed directly in most NT environments, but you can find these permissions in a resource's Properties. Figure 13-11 shows the special permissions for a folder.

The beauty of NTFS is that it doesn't matter to the serving system if you log in locally, log in over the network, or log into a domain. NTFS permissions work the same way whether the NT/2000/2003/XP system is on a network or running as a stand-alone system. If only one Windows NT, 2000, 2003, or XP system existed in the universe, you would still need a user account and NTFS permissions to access anything on the system.

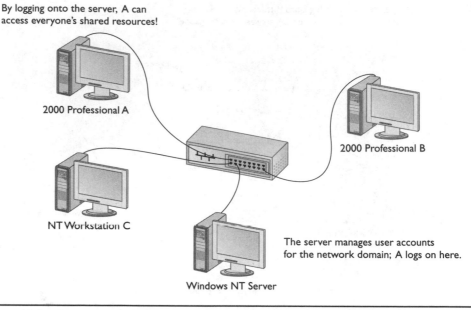

By logging onto the server, A can access everyone's shared resources!

2000 Professional A

2000 Professional B

NT Workstation C

The server manages user accounts for the network domain; A logs on here.

Windows NT Server

Figure 13-9   Logging onto the server does it all!

To differentiate these permissions from the share permissions, we call them NTFS permissions or local permissions.

So how can NTFS be used in a network? Simple! NTFS resources can store information on any user account. The account can be local just to that system, or if the system is part of a Windows NT/2000/2003 domain, it can be a domain user account. The only difference is whether the local system handles the user account logons, or the domain does—either way, it doesn't matter to NTFS!

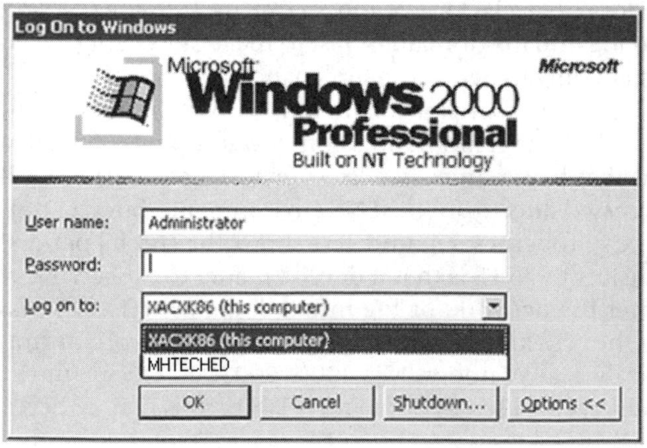

Figure 13-10
The Windows 2000 logon screen showing both local and domain logon options

Log On to Windows

Microsoft
Windows 2000
Professional
Built on NT Technology

Microsoft

User name: Administrator

Password: |

Log on to: XACXK86 (this computer)

XACXK86 (this computer)
MHTECHED

OK   Cancel   Shutdown...   Options <<

Permission	Folders?	Files?	What Does It Allow?
No Access	Yes	Yes	Denies all access to the file or folder. Users can see the file or folder, but cannot access it in any way.
List	Yes	No	Users can only see the contents of the folder and go to subfolders.
Read	Yes	Yes	Users can read files and folders, open files and subfolders, but cannot change any files.
Add	Yes	No	Users can add files or subfolders to the folder, but cannot open or change any files.
Add & Read	Yes	No	Users can read and add files or subfolders to the folder. Users can also open files in the folder.
Change	Yes	Yes	Users can do anything but delete the file or folder. They cannot change permissions on any files or subfolders.
Full Control	Yes	Yes	Users can do anything they want.

Table 13-1   NTFS Permissions for Files and Folders Under Windows NT

Figure 13-11
NTFS special permissions for a folder in a Windows NT system

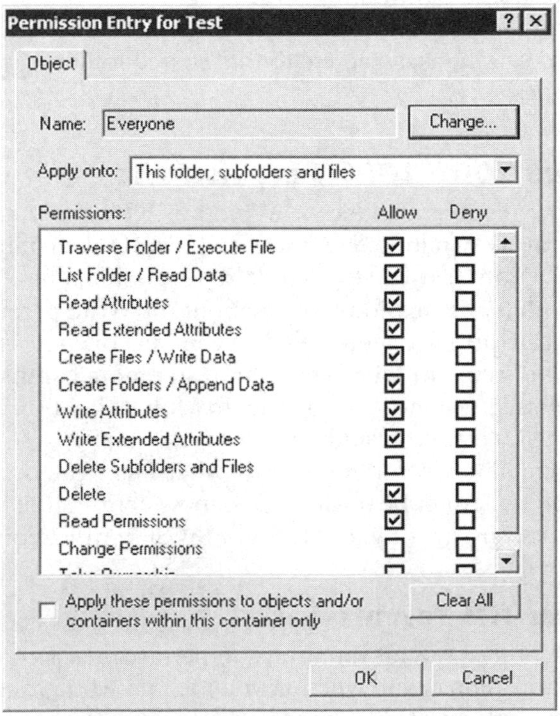

Whoa! Wait a minute, Mike! Are you telling me that Windows NT/2000/2003/XP systems have two different types of user accounts? Yup, that's right! You get two types: local users and domain users. (Actually, there are more than two, but we don't need to cover that here.) To use domains, however, you have to buy a special server version of Windows, such as Windows NT Server, Windows 2000 Server, or Windows Server 2003.

All of this security is invisible to the network user as long as he has a good user account and the necessary NTFS permissions. This process is not unique to Windows networks—NetWare and Linux networks use the same two-step security method.

Share vs. NTFS Permissions

When you have a folder stored on NTFS-formatted hard drives in a networked PC, that folder has one or two levels of permissions that apply whenever a user tries to access it: NTFS permissions and (if the folder is shared and the user accesses the folder over the network) share permissions. The question always comes up at this point: what wins if the two sets of permissions are in conflict?

In the case of a conflict between share and NTFS permissions, the most restrictive permission always applies. Suppose John has a folder called Incoming on his NTFS drive, shared as INCOMING on the network. He sets the NTFS permission for the folder to Read-Only for Everyone, and changes the share permission to *Full Control*. When Mary accesses that folder over the network and tries to add a file, imagine her surprise when she gets only Read-Only access to that folder!

The reverse scenario would be true as well. If John changed the NTFS permission to Full Control for Mary's account, but changed the network share permissions to Read, Mary would get only Read access to that shared folder. The most restrictive permission always applies.

Windows 2000/2003 Permissions

From the permissions standpoint, Windows 2000 and 2003 work pretty much exactly the same way as Windows NT; however, if you look at Table 13-2, you will find a few subtle distinctions between the standard permission types. Take a good look at the Windows 2000/2003 permissions. What about the Write permission—why would anyone want that? You can add or edit a file, but you can't open it? That sounds crazy! Actually, it makes a lot of sense to folks who administer more complex networks. Imagine a network full of users who need to add files to a folder, but by the same token, we don't want them to see files others are adding. Trust me, it happens. NTFS permissions give administrators incredible control over exactly what a user can or cannot do to a file or folder, even though it may not be obvious how these permissions work. If you want to get into NTFS permissions, go for your MCSA or MCSE certification!

Windows XP Permissions

Windows XP offers several variations on permissions according to the version you use, Home or Professional, and whether you log into workgroup or a domain. Windows XP Home offers only *simple file sharing*, which gives users the capability to share a folder,

Permission	Folders?	Files?	What Does It Allow?
Deny Access	Yes	Yes	Denies all access to the file or folder. Users can see the file or folder but cannot access it in any way.
List Folder Contents	Yes	No	Users can only see the contents of the folder and go to subfolders.
Read	Yes	Yes	Users can read files and folders, and open files and subfolders but cannot change any files.
Write	Yes	Yes	Users can add files or subfolders to the folder but cannot open or change any files or subfolders.
Read & Execute	Yes	Yes	Users can read and add files or subfolders to the folder. Users can also open files in the folder.
Modify	Yes	Yes	Users can do anything but delete the file or folder. They cannot change permissions on any files or subfolders.
Full Control	Yes	Yes	Users can do anything they want.

Table 13-2   Windows 2000/2003 Standard Permission Types

and then decide if anyone accessing that folder on the network can change the files. Note the fairly self-explanatory pair of check boxes under the Network Sharing And Security section of Figure 13-12.

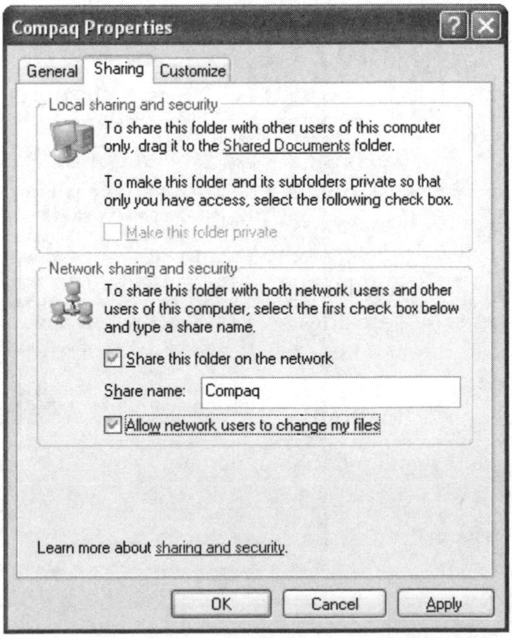

Figure 13-12
Simple file sharing in Windows XP Home

PART III

NOTE You can log into a domain only with Windows XP Professional, not with XP Home.

Even with NTFS, Windows XP Home offers no file or folder-level security once you share a folder over the network. It functions essentially like a less-secure version of Windows 9*x*, even lacking the capability to password-protect a shared folder!

Windows XP Professional in a workgroup environment by default uses simple file sharing, just like Windows XP Home, but you can disable this feature of dubious merit if you choose. Open Folder Options (either through the Control Panel applet of that name or select Tools | Folder Options | View tab in My Computer) and scroll all the way to the last option. Deselect the check box next to Use Simple File Sharing (Recommended) to disable (Figure 13-13).

Once you've disabled simple file sharing, Windows XP Professional offers the full range of sharing and security options available to Windows 2000 and Windows Server 2003. There's no difference. One thing to note, though, is that you need to be logged in with an Administrator account to change the file sharing in Folder Options *successfully*. Limited user accounts in Windows XP Professional can *appear* to change the sharing options, but Windows ignores the action. The box will remain unchecked, but Limited Users *cannot make network shares* in Windows XP!

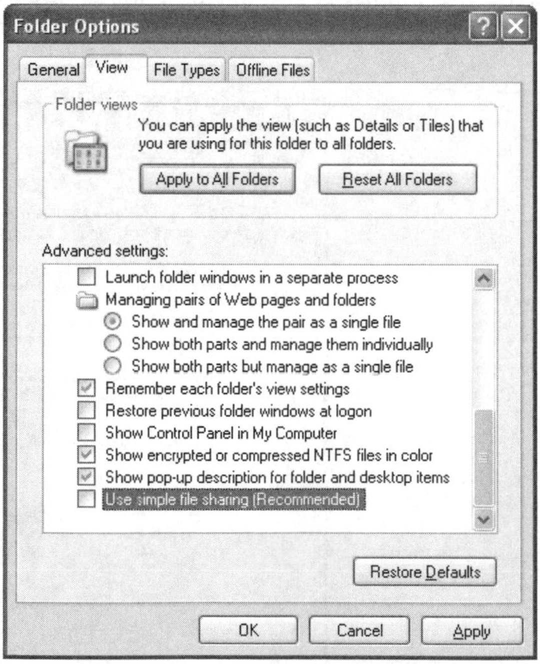

Figure 13-13
Disabling simple file sharing in Windows XP Professional

   Windows XP Professional machine connected to a domain has only the option of full file sharing, à la Windows 2000 or Windows Server 2003. You can change the option in Folder Options, but Windows will ignore the selection completely. You have no simple file sharing when connected to a domain, even if you log into the PC locally.

NetWare 3.x Rights

Novell NetWare 3.x was the first NOS to adopt more advanced permissions. Novell calls its permissions rights. Unlike Windows' NTFS, each Novell NetWare 3.x server stores this information in its own *Bindery* (see Chapter 12, "Network Operating Systems").

   Table 13-3 shows the NetWare 3.12 rights. Compare these to the Windows NT and 2000/2003 permissions. At first, they may seem quite different, but if you take your time and compare them, you'll see they're almost exactly the same.

NetWare 4.x/5.x/6.x

NetWare 4.x/5.x/6.x dispense with the Bindery, replacing it with *NetWare Directory Services (NDS)*. NDS controls access to network resources using network-wide permissions, rather than the file server–specific permissions used by NetWare 3.x's Bindery. NetWare 5.x introduced a new file format called *Novell Storage Services (NSS)*. From the standpoint of sharing files and folders, NetWare has never changed from its original permissions. Isn't it nice when you can count on something to stay the same? Microsoft, are you listening? Hello? Oh well, let's move on.

Right	Folders?	Files?	What Does It Allow?
Read	Yes	Yes	Users can read files and folders, and open files and subfolders, but cannot change any files.
Write	Yes	Yes	Users can open and write to files.
Create	Yes	Yes	Users can add files or subfolders and can open or change any files.
Erase	Yes	Yes	Users can delete any file or subfolder.
Modify	Yes	Yes	Users can change the attributes of or rename files or subfolders.
File Scan	Yes	Yes	Users can see the file or the contents of the folder.
Access Control	Yes	Yes	Users can modify other users' and groups' rights to this file or folder.
Supervisory	Yes	Yes	Users can do anything they want.

Table 13-3   NetWare 3.12 Rights

UNIX/Linux

The concept of permissions can get confusing when switching between Linux and Windows. *UNIX/Linux* systems do have local file and folder permissions like NetWare and NT/2000, but they look quite different than the ones we've just seen. They do share one common feature with Windows, however: permissions are the same for both networked and local users. File-serving programs like FTP use the local permissions to handle network access permissions.

Unlike NetWare and Windows, UNIX/Linux provides only three permissions (see Table 13-4). Because they lack the more detailed permissions available in NetWare and Windows, most network administrators don't like to use UNIX/Linux systems for pure file sharing. I realize in saying this I'm risking an avalanche of indignant e-mail from the million or so UNIX/Linux users out there, but what can I do? When I'm right, I'm right! (I just won't have any friends.)

Sharing Is Sharing

For all the differences in names and functions among the different types of permissions, the bottom line is they all perform roughly the same functions: enabling those who administer networks to control the level of access to shared files and folders. Keep in mind that permissions are not at all limited to just files and folders—pretty much any shared resource on any network will have some type of permissions to assign to users and groups. Still, files and folders are the things we love to share the most, and once you appreciate the variations in the ways different network operating systems share files and folders, sharing other resources like printers will seem pretty anticlimactic!

Now that you've got a grip on permissions, let's put this knowledge to work and start sharing some files and folders. Oh, and by the way, let's go ahead and start sharing some printers too, while we are at it!

Sharing Resources

Sharing a resource involves three distinct steps. First, make sure your system is capable of sharing. Second, you need to share the resource and name it. Third, you need to set permissions on that shared resource.

Let's get one thing settled right now: No network NOS enables you to share individual files. Sure, you can share entire volumes or you can share folders in those volumes, but you cannot share a file! Don't confuse the capability to place permissions on a file with sharing a file. Just because you can't share a file doesn't mean you can't place per-

Permission	Folders?	Files?	What Does It Allow?
Read	Yes	Yes	Users can read files and folders, and open files and subfolders, but cannot change any files.
Write	Yes	Yes	Users can open and write to files.
Execute	Yes	Yes	Users can execute the file

Table 13-4   UNIX/Linux Permissions

missions on it. Sharing is a network function; permissions are unique to a resource. When you share a folder, you apply permissions to the shared folder, which are then attributed to the files and subfolders in that shared folder. This subtle difference can cause confusion in the unwary.

Sharing Folders

Because sharing folders is the area of biggest interest to most techs, let's start with them. We'll look at the network operating systems just discussed and see what you need to do to set up a resource for sharing. This is going to look a bit redundant—but who cares? The process never changes. Once you know what you have to do, all that remains are the specific details of how to create a share on a particular NOS.

Windows 9x

Remember when I said the first step in sharing a resource is to ensure that your system is capable of sharing? Well, every NOS discussed in this book is preset to share resources automatically, except Windows 9x. All Windows 9x systems require you to install and activate a special service called File and Print Sharing. To install this service on a Windows 9x system, access the Network Neighborhood Properties dialog box (see Figure 13-14). You can also access these settings by running the Network applet in the Control Panel. Make sure you know how to get to the Network settings in a Windows 9x client—we're going to be doing this a lot over the rest of the book! Do you see the File And Print Sharing button? Click it to see the sharing options (see Figure 13-15).

Figure 13-14
The Network Neighborhood Properties dialog box showing the system's network settings

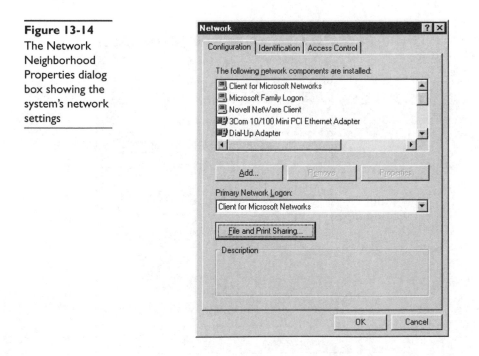

PART III

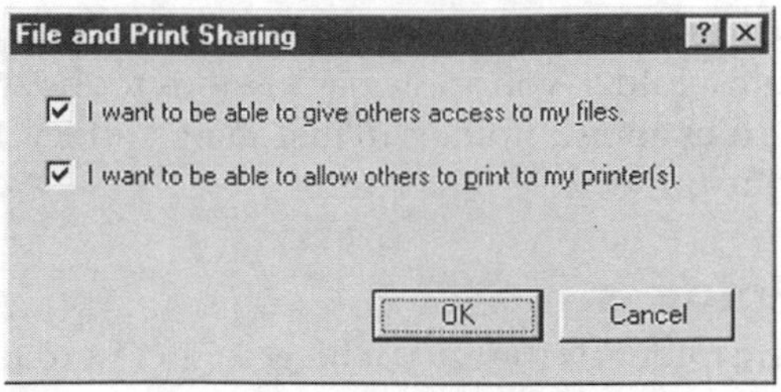

Figure 13-15
The File and Print
Sharing options

This is pretty simple stuff here. If you want to share your files and folders, click the *I want to be able to give others access to my files* check box. Let's see if you get the idea. What should you check to allow others to access your printers? Hey! You are a genius! Once you've checked the boxes you want, click OK, and be ready with your installation CD—Windows will want it. And you can pretty well count on a reboot, too (hey, it's Windows). But that's it! You've completed the first step in sharing a resource: making sure the system is configured to share by installing the *File and Printer Sharing service*. A *service* is any program that runs on Windows, which you don't normally see. Your Windows 9*x* system may look the same as before, but trust me, a new set of programs is now running, even if you can't see them. We're all done setting up systems to share. You won't see this step again because all the other network operating systems do this automatically. Hooray!

Let's assume you've installed the File and Printer Sharing service on your system (see Figure 13-16). You can go back to Network properties to see if it's there. Once this is installed, you're ready to start sharing some files and folders! Wheeee!

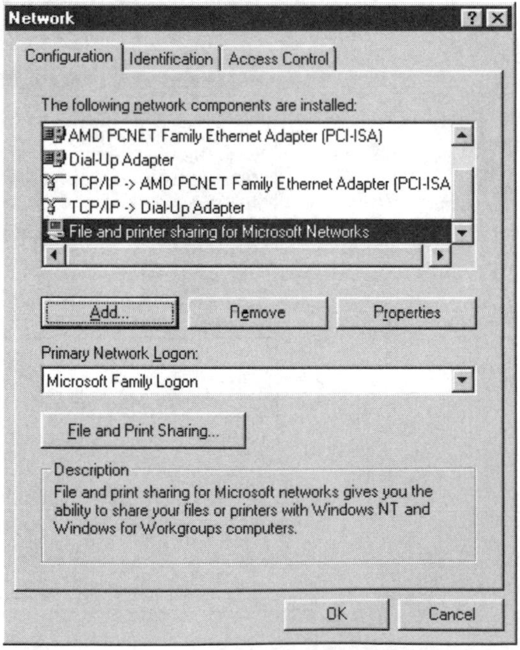

Figure 13-16
File and Printer
Sharing installed

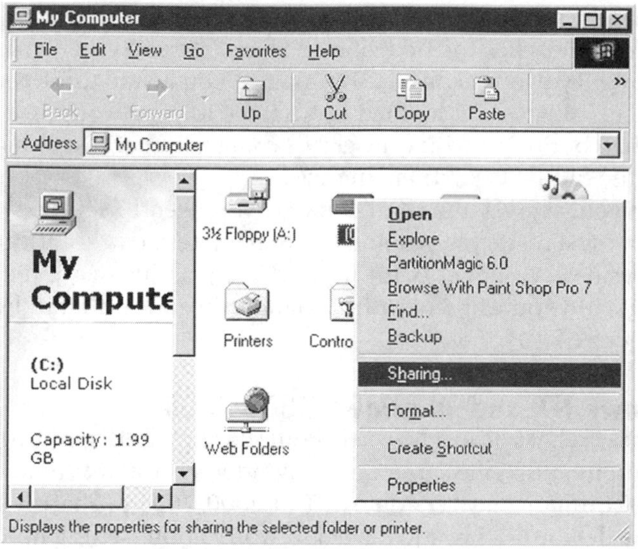

Figure 13-17
Selecting Sharing
in My Computer

Windows 9x lets you share folders and entire hard drives—whatever you're sharing, you configure it in the exact same way. Just use My Computer or Windows Explorer to select the resource you want to share, alternate-click the resource and select Sharing (see Figure 13-17).

If you don't see the Sharing menu option, you've either forgotten to add the File and Print Sharing service, or you didn't select the *I want to be able to give others access to my files* check box. Go ahead and select Sharing to see the dialog box in Figure 13-18.

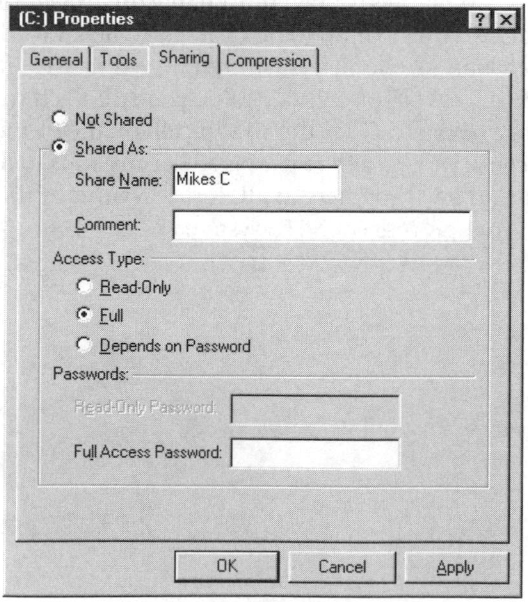

Figure 13-18
The Sharing tab

Remember seeing this dialog box earlier when we looked at how networks share? Well, this time, click the box labeled Shared As and enter a name. Because this is Windows 9x and you are using NetBIOS names, you would think the name could be up to 15 characters long, as you learned in Chapter 10, "Network Protocols." Yeah, well, you'd think that, but try it—you only get 12 characters, because Windows 9x systems are limited to the old DOS 8.3 filename size.

After you've given the share a name, you need to set the share permissions for this share. In most cases, you wouldn't be that interested in security (or you'd be using something besides Windows 9x for networking!), so just leave the permissions set to Full. Click OK and you will see the little hand icon appear that indicates a resource is shared (see Figure 13-19).

Windows NT and Windows 2000/2003

Remember what you just learned about sharing a folder or drive in Windows 9x? Well, it works pretty much the same way in Windows NT and Windows 2000/2003. You don't need to configure any version of NT or 2000/2003 to share—they are preconfigured to share by default—so you just need to worry about setting up the share. Just as you did with Windows 9x, select the drive or folder you want to share, alternate-click and select Sharing in NT or Sharing and Security in 2000/2003 to see the sharing dialog box. Figure 13-20 shows this box in Windows NT, while Figure 13-21 shows the same box in Windows 2000. They look basically the same.

If you don't see the Sharing menu option, it means you are not a member of the Administrators (NT/2000/2003) or the Power Users (2000/2003) group. A user account that is a member of the *Power Users* group has the capability to do many of the basic administrator functions; this is a handy way to give other users the ability to do things like share folders, without making them members of the all-powerful Administrators group.

Just like with Windows 9x, you must name the shared folder. Windows NT and 2000/2003 allow share names of up to 80 characters. Be aware, however, that any shares with names longer than 12 characters will not be visible to Windows 9x systems.

Even in Windows NT and 2000/2003, you still need to set share permissions before you can share a resource. Click the Sharing tab on the Properties dialog box of the shared resource. Because we're going to use NTFS permissions to do the actual security work, we don't need to do anything here at all. Just leave this at the default full-control settings; that's the normal process on NTFS systems.

Figure 13-19
A shared folder
showing the hand
icon

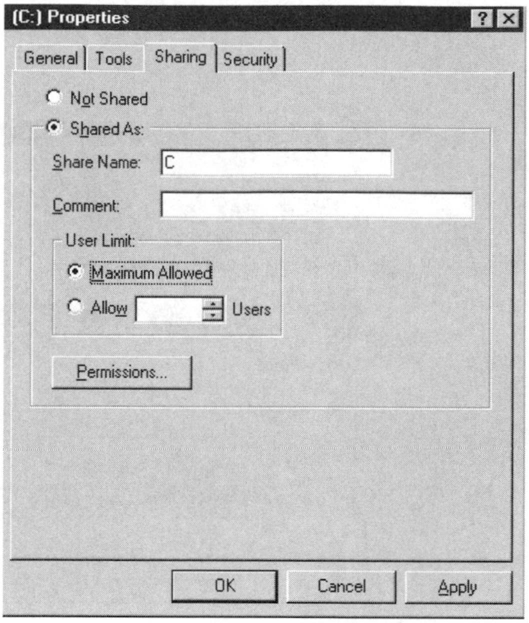

Figure 13-20
The Windows
NT Sharing tab

Now let's have some fun and start playing with NTFS permissions! In Windows NT, click the Security tab, and then click the Permissions button (see Figure 13-22). In Windows 2000/2003, just click the Security tab to see the NTFS settings (see Figure 13-23).

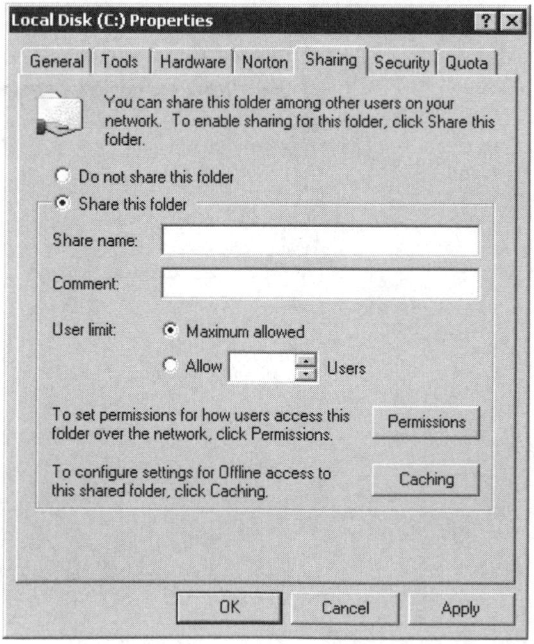

Figure 13-21
The Windows
2000 Sharing tab

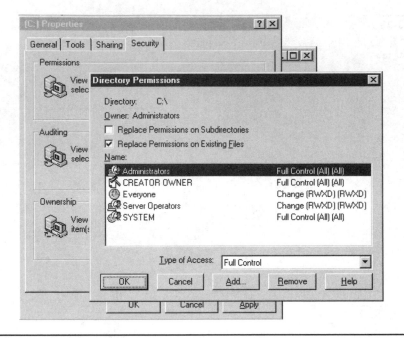

Figure 13-22 Windows NT permissions

Figure 13-23
Windows 2000
NTFS settings

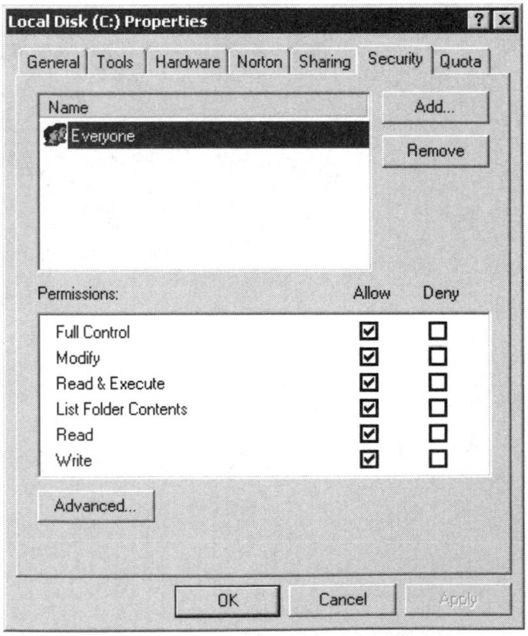

By default, everyone has complete access to a new share in Windows NT/2000/2003. All network operating systems start a new share with some default permissions applied to everyone, so your first job is to start limiting who gets access. Let's concentrate on Windows 2000/2003 for a moment because Windows NT does all this in roughly the same fashion. Let's say we only want the Accounting group to be able to read documents, and we want Mike Meyers to have full control. Microsoft does a nice job of making this easy to set up. Start by clicking Add to see a list of users and groups. Find the Mike Meyers user account in the Accounting group in the list (see Figure 13-24). Pretty much all network operating systems let you add multiple users and/or groups in one shot.

Click OK to return to the Security tab. You'll see Mike Meyers is now listed. Take a look at the default permissions. Like most other network operating systems, Windows 2000/2003 provides only Read & Execute, List Folder Contents, and Read permissions by default. We'll need to click Full Control to let Mike Meyers do whatever he wants. The Accounting group's default settings are just fine for what we want, so we'll leave them alone.

Oops! You can't leave yet! Remember the Everyone group? It has full control! As long as that's the case, everyone has full access—better change access to the defaults (Read & Execute, List Folder Contents, and Read) for the Everyone group before you exit (see Figure 13-25).

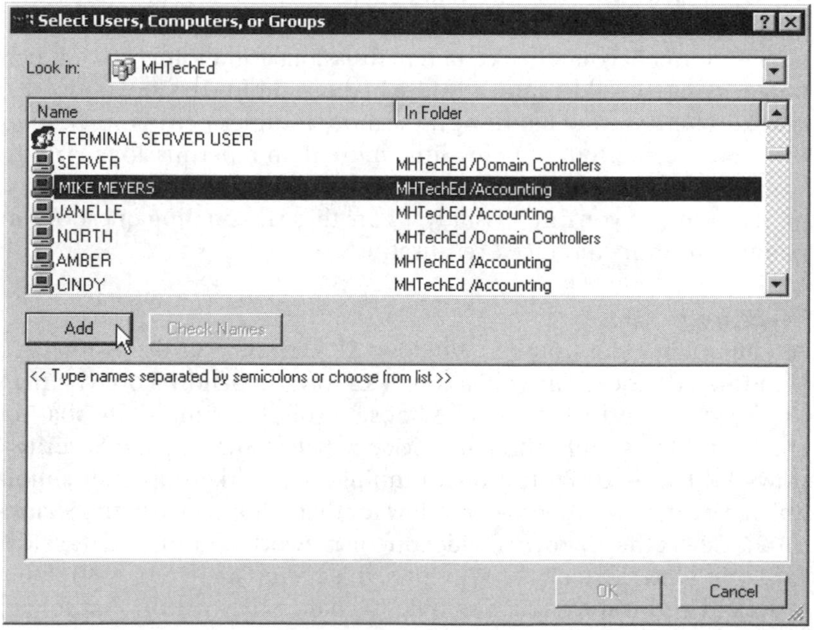

Figure 13-24
Finding Mike
Meyers and
Accounting
in the list

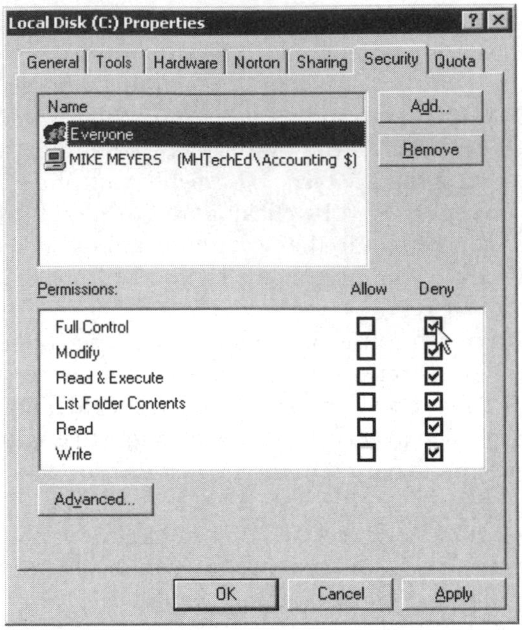

Figure 13-25
The Everyone group is denied access.

Hey, this brings up an interesting issue: What if a user account is a member of two different groups, and these two groups have different permissions for the same folder? Or what if a user account has certain permissions for a folder—what permissions do they have for any subfolders and any files in those subfolders? All network operating systems have different ways of handling these more complex permissions issues—you could easily make a career out of being little more than a permissions expert. Luckily, the Network+ exam isn't too interested in more than a basic understanding of the existence of permissions, so you can blissfully ignore these fascinating questions until you decide to go for your more advanced certifications.

Windows XP

As you might guess from the Windows XP permissions discussion earlier in the chapter, Windows XP does sharing in a couple of ways, depending on whether you use Home or Professional, and whether you choose to disable simple file sharing in the latter. To share a folder, simply alternate-click and select Sharing and Security. If you have Windows XP Home or Professional running in a workgroup with simple file sharing enabled, you get the Properties window for that folder, open at the Sharing tab, as in Figure 13-26. Select the Share this folder on the network option, and then assign a share name. Like other later versions of Windows, this name can be up to 80 characters and include spaces. If you want users to be able to change files within that folder, select the Allow Network Users To Change My Files option.

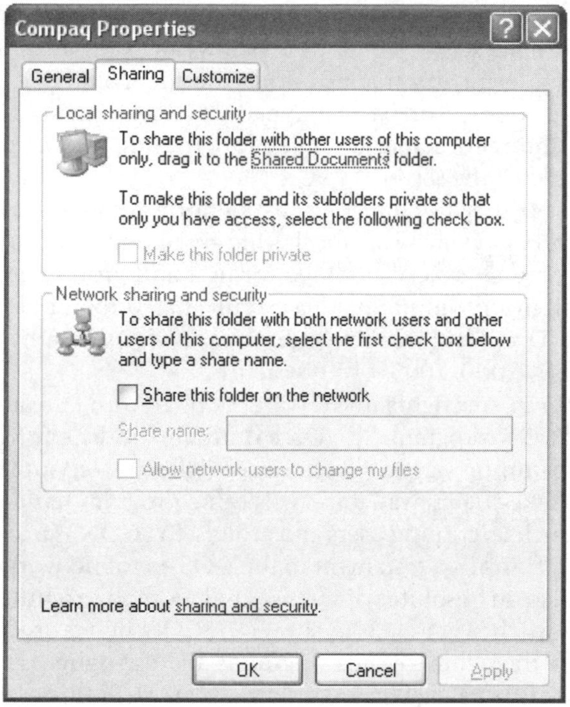

Figure 13-26

Simple file sharing in action

With simple file sharing disabled or if you run Windows XP Professional in a domain, you can share a folder or other resource precisely as you would in Windows 2000 and Windows Server 2003.

NetWare 3.x

The first thing to appreciate about Novell networks is that NetWare servers do not use the classic drive letters you see on Windows systems. When you look at a NetWare server, you see drive volumes with names like SYS: and VOL:. The SYS: volume is roughly equivalent to the Windows C: drive—by default, the SYS: volume stores all of the critical programs that make up the NetWare NOS itself.

You never sit down and work directly at a NetWare server, one of the features that distinguishes NetWare servers rather dramatically from Windows servers! You instead use client machines to access the server and do administrative work remotely. NetWare comes with a series of utilities that you run remotely on the server to perform almost every network task, including creating users/groups and setting rights to shared folders. These utilities are located by default in a special folder called \public on the SYS: drive on the server but most NetWare administrators will move this folder to a more secure area.

How can users access these programs if they can't see volumes with weird names like SYS:? The answer lies in special mapping that is automatically done for any system that needs to access a NetWare server. Every NetWare client has a special drive pre-mapped to a drive letter—in the case of Windows systems, this drive is usually called the F: drive, but that can easily be changed. When a Windows PC loaded with the correct NetWare client software boots up, this F: drive is automatically mapped, whether or not the client is logged into the server. Figure 13-27 shows an example of this mapped drive on a Windows system. Using this mapped drive, the client system can run utilities without even logging into the network. The mapped drive also acts as a public folder where certain files and utilities are made available to all, regardless of the level of rights that client has to other areas of the server.

There is no specific step you must perform to start sharing folders in NetWare. All folders on all drives are ready for sharing—you only need to set up the trustee rights. The term *trustee rights* is NetWare lingo for user and group permissions to a shared folder. Any user or group with rights to a certain shared folder is said to have trustee rights to that folder. Don't let these terms throw you—it's the same as setting permissions on a Windows NT, 2000, 2003, or XP system!

We set up trustee rights in NetWare 3.*x* by running the ancient, but completely functional, *SYSCON* program. There are other methods, but SYSCON is the most famous and most common way to set up trustee rights in NetWare 3.*x*. SYSCON does far more than just make shares available—this same program handles a number of administrative tasks, such as creating users and groups. SYSCON is a text mode utility that runs at a command prompt—a testament to the DOS era of networking. While SYSCON is powerful, it is also an absolute pain to use, and more than a little practice is required to get it to work properly. Figure 13-28 shows SYSCON being used to set up trustee rights to a folder. Note the names of the two groups and the rights assigned to them. You can't tell which is the trustee, right? That's okay—it's RWCEMF, on the right side. Go back to the permissions section of this chapter and check the NetWare rights table to see which rights are assigned to the users in this example.

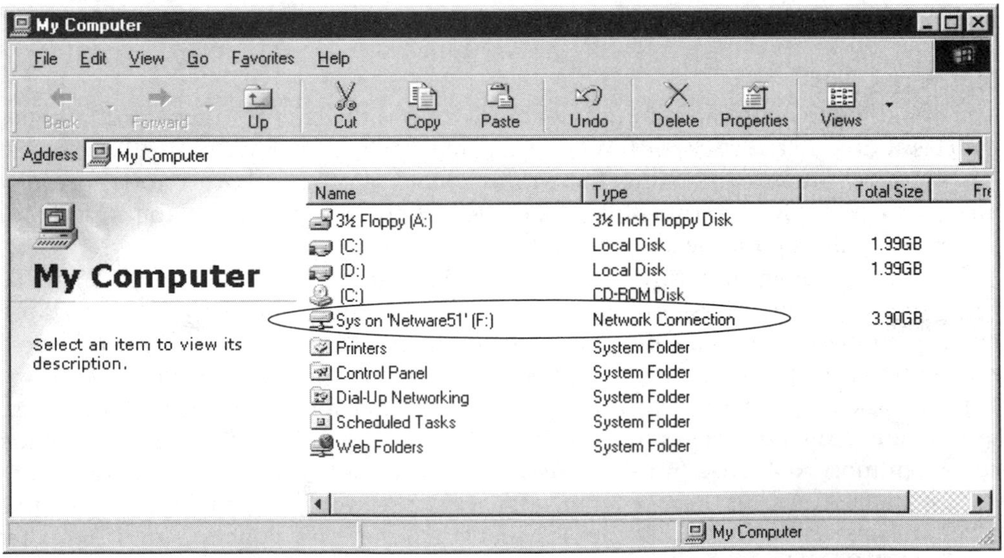

Figure 13-27   A mapped NetWare drive on a Windows system

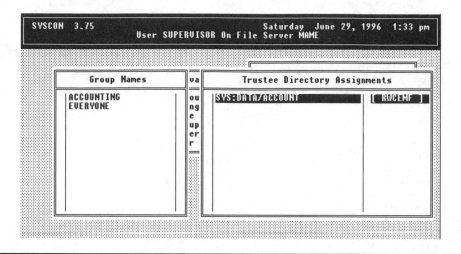

Figure 13-28   SYSCON in action

NetWare 4.*x*/5.*x*/6.*x*

NetWare 4.*x*/5.*x*/6.*x* work basically the same way as NetWare 3.*x*—but happily, the tools you have for assigning trustee rights have improved dramatically. The current tool we use to assign trustee rights is NWADMIN. Unlike the old SYSCON, *NWADMIN* is a Windows-based application that lets you click the folder you want to share and easily assign trustee rights. Figure 13-29 shows NWADMIN in action, configuring trustee rights for a shared folder.

Sharing Folders in UNIX/Linux

There are no standard graphical tools for sharing files in UNIX/Linux—each Linux distribution uses their own tools. UNIX/Linux systems do not have a sharing option that easily fits into the paradigm of Windows and NetWare systems. UNIX/Linux systems share files across a network in a variety of ways. These include File Transfer Protocol (FTP), Network File System (NFS), and Samba. FTP, as discussed in Chapter 11, "TCP/IP," enables two TCP/IP hosts to transfer files across a network. All implementations of TCP/IP support FTP, making it an excellent choice for moving files from a UNIX host to a machine running another operating system such as Windows 9*x*, Windows NT, a different flavor of UNIX, or even a Macintosh.

Network File System (NFS) enables a UNIX system to treat files and directories on another UNIX host as though they were local files. Let's say Fred needs to access the /mark /projects/current directory on Mark's UNIX system, named MARK1. Fred mounts the /mark/projects/current/ directory to his own file system as /markstuff/, adding it to his local directory structure. As far as any program on Fred's UNIX machine can tell, the files in the /markstuff/ directory are local files. NFS enables his UNIX machine to share files transparently by adding network directories to its local directory structure. Unfortunately, Windows-based machines don't get to play, because they don't come with an

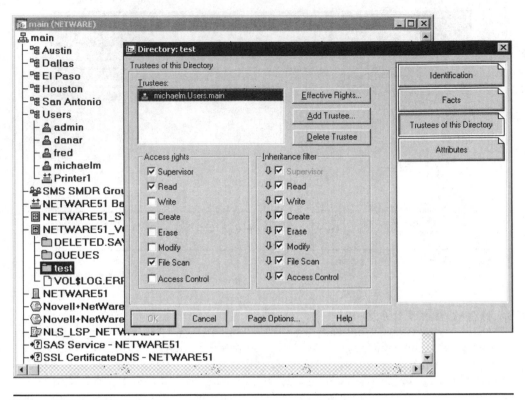

Figure 13-29   NWADMIN in action

NFS client. Although some fine third-party NFS tools are available for Windows, most of us just use FTP or Samba for Windows-to-UNIX/Linux file transfers.

UNIX systems, however, can also pretend to be Microsoft clients and servers using Samba, which enables UNIX systems to communicate using Server Message Blocks (SMBs). To a Windows-based system running Client for Microsoft Networks, a UNIX system running Samba looks just like a Microsoft server (see Figure 13-30). We'll see more of Samba, NFS, and FTP in later chapters.

Sharing Folders in Macintosh

Pre-OS X Macintosh systems have rudimentary networking functions, similar to Windows 9x networking. Unlike a Windows 9x system, a Macintosh is ready to share folders immediately. To share a folder on a Macintosh, you select the folder, click File/Get Info, and click the *Share this item and its contents* check box. Like Windows 9x, you only have three share permissions, which Apple calls Read & Write, Read Only, and interestingly enough, Write Only (see Figure 13-31). A shared folder manifests itself with a different icon, as shown in Figure 13-32. Unfortunately, these shares are only good for Mac-to-Mac communication—we'll see how to get Mac to talk to Windows clients in Chapter 18, "Interconnecting Network Operating Systems."

Figure 13-30
A UNIX system
running Samba
looks just like a
Microsoft server.

TIP The introduction of OS X has fundamentally changed the way Macs
share files and folders. With OS X, the sharing functions are now basically
identical to UNIX/Linux.

Follow the Steps

Regardless of the NOS, the steps you take to share a folder are basically the same. First,
you make sure the system is capable of sharing—this is done for you in all but Windows
9x systems. Second, you decide what you want to share, and make that folder available
for sharing. Finally, you set whatever share/permissions/rights you want the share to
have. Remember these three steps and sharing a folder is always easy!

Figure 13-31
Sharing a folder
on a Macintosh

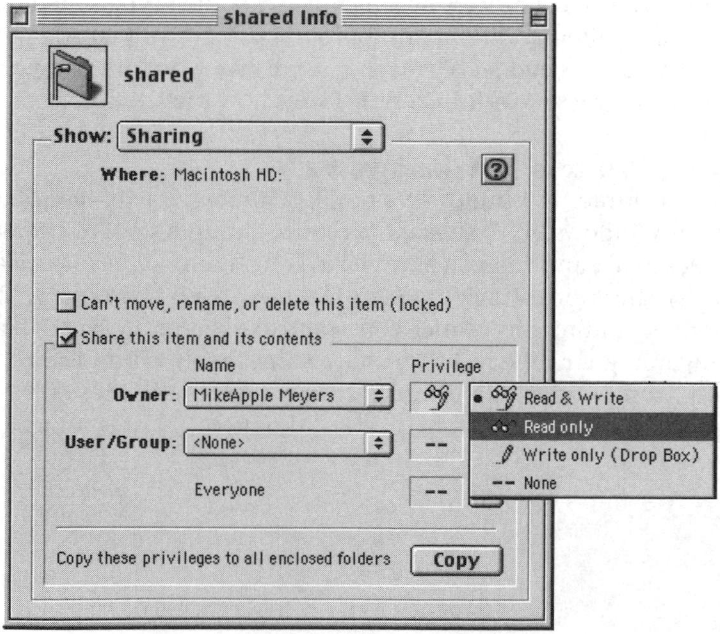

Figure 13-32
A shared folder
on a Macintosh

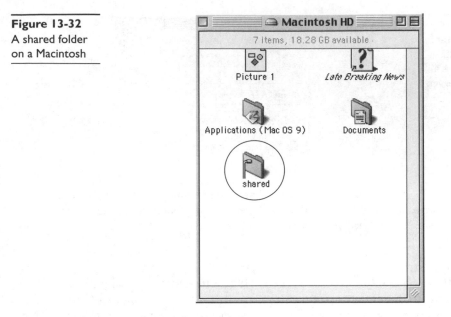

Sharing Printers

The process of sharing printers is similar to the folder sharing process—you must make sure the system is capable of sharing a printer, give the printer a share name, and set permissions. The actual process by which network operating systems share printers varies dramatically, although the sharing process doesn't vary nearly as much between versions of Windows and NetWare. This means we won't have to go into quite the same level of detail we saw with folders. Let's see how they do it!

Sharing Printers in Windows 9x

Sharing a printer in Windows 9x requires almost exactly the same steps as sharing a folder in Windows 9x. First, make sure the sharing system has added the File and Print Sharing service, and that you have clicked the *I want to be able to allow others to print to my printer(s)* check box. Having done those steps, you share the printer by opening My Computer, finding the printer you want to share and—yup, that's right!—selecting Sharing and giving the printer a share name, as shown in Figure 13-33. Windows 9x has no form of permissions for shared printers, but it does at least allow you to set a password for the network share. Like all network shares, this password only affects network users.

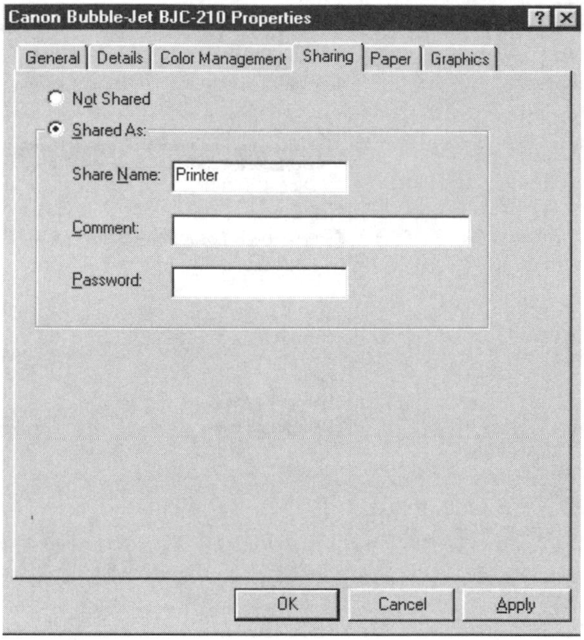

Figure 13-33
Sharing a printer
in Windows 9x

Sharing Printers in Windows NT/2000/2003/XP

Windows NT/2000/2003/XP share a printer exactly like Windows 9x, but they do provide more substantial permissions. A Windows NT/20002003/XP system provides three levels of print permissions: Print, Manage Printer, and Manage Documents. The Print permission enables users and groups to print to the printer. Manage Printer lets users control the printer properties, and Manage Documents gives users the right to delete, pause, and restart print jobs. Like folder permissions, these settings are found on the Security tab of the printer's Properties dialog box. Figure 13-34 shows the Printer sharing Security tab in Windows 2000.

Sharing Printers in NetWare

Novell NetWare has a bit of a problem with printers. While Windows NT/2000 can allow any system to act as a printer server, Novell NetWare can only control printers installed on a NetWare Server. Unfortunately, printers don't tend to hang around servers—they're installed around the network at user systems or as stand-alone network printers. Novell realized this long ago and developed complex, but powerful, methods for print serving; these print methods break away from the only-servers-serve attitude, instead allowing any system on any NetWare Network to act as a print server. All versions of Novell NetWare share basically the same two methods. The first is to allow a NetWare server to act as a print server. The second is to configure a client system to act as a print server. Novell allows virtually any type of OS client to act as a NetWare print server. This includes all versions of Windows, UNIX/Linux, and Macintosh computers, although

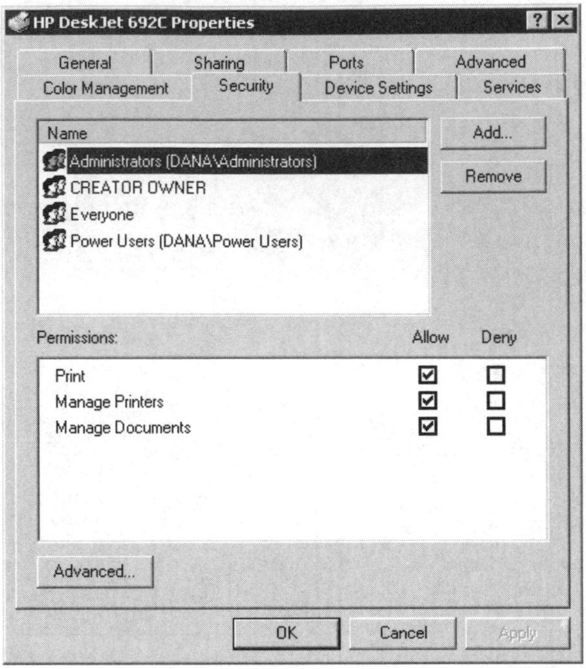

Figure 13-34
The Windows
2000 Printer
Properties
Security tab

you will need to install special NetWare printer server software on them to enable this to happen.

Sharing Printers in UNIX/Linux

Once again, UNIX/Linux does not have the same concept of actively sharing a printer that we saw in both Windows and NetWare. Instead, Linux systems typically use one of two methods: Samba or LPD/LPR. LPD/LPR consists of two TCP/IP functions: *Line Printer Daemon (LPD)* and *Line Printer Remote (LPR)*. The LPD program works as the server and runs on the system sharing the printer. Meanwhile, LPR runs on any system wanting to access a printer under the control of LPD. As a matter of fact, almost every operating system capable of supporting TCP/IP also includes the LPD and LPR programs, or at least something similar enough to support them. Go to a command prompt in Windows, type **lpr**, and press ENTER—it's almost certainly there!

Accessing Shared Resources

Once a folder or printer has been shared by a serving system, the next step is for the client systems to access that device and start to use it. The steps involved in accessing a shared resource usually include browsing to locate the shared resource, and then connecting to it to make it seem as though it were a local resource; neither of these steps is completely necessary in all situations, however.

In this section, we will concentrate exclusively on Windows client systems. That's about as much as the Network+ test wants to you to know. We'll save most of the UNIX/Linux connection issues for other chapters.

Accessing Files in Windows

You can access a shared resource in Windows in literally about six different ways, but the most common method is to browse through My Network Places to locate the shared resource you desire. Tim wants to store some files in a folder on the server. He talks to the person who shared the folder on the server, who tells him to use the timstuff share on the server. Tim uses My Network Places to locate the share, as shown in Figure 13-35. Once he has found the share, Tim has some choices. He can just leave the share open in My Network Places and use it like any other folder, but this has a downside: he'll have to do this every time he uses the share. Being a clever fellow, Tim instead decides to map the shared folder and give it a drive letter, checking the box that orders the share to reconnect at logon. We call this a *persistent connection* (see Figure 13-36). Any time you map a drive, only to have it disappear after a reboot, you can be pretty sure you did not make a persistent connection.

Keep in mind that Windows doesn't care what type of server is providing this share. As long as you have the right user account with the right permissions, you'll be able to treat a share the same way, whether it comes from a Windows NT Server system, a Linux box, or a NetWare server. All shared folders manifest the same way (see Figure 13-37).

PART III

Figure 13-35
Finding the share in My Network Places

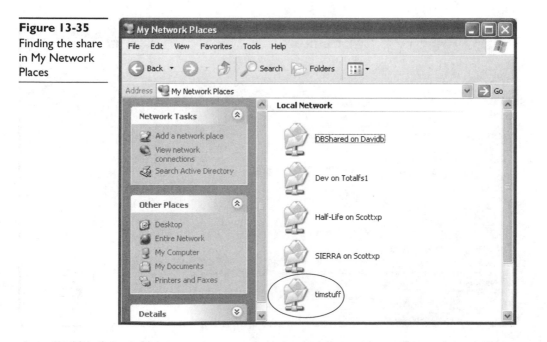

Figure 13-36
Setting a
persistent
connection

Beginning with Windows 95, you could create a desktop shortcut to a network share as an alternative to mapping the share to a drive letter. Just right-click and drag the shared folder to the desktop to create a shortcut. Windows 2000 added the Network Place concept. Basically just a shortcut, a Network Place points to a shared folder, but it is not limited just to shared folders—you can make a web site, an ftp site, almost anything you can share, a Network Place. The usual way to create these shortcuts is to open the My Network Places folder and select Add Network Place (see Figure 13-38).

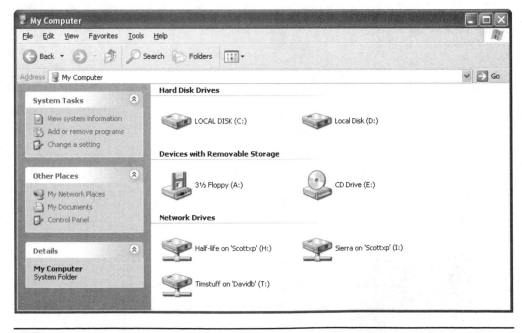

Figure 13-37   All shared folders look alike.

Figure 13-38
The Add
Network Place
Wizard in My
Network Places

Add Network Place Wizard

Welcome to the Add Network Place Wizard

This wizard helps you sign up for a service that offers online storage space. You can use this space to store, organize, and share your documents and pictures using only a Web browser and Internet connection.

You can also use this wizard to create a shortcut to a Web site, an FTP site, or other network location.

To continue, click Next.

< Back   Next >   Cancel

Accessing Shared Printers in Windows

One aspect of printers not shared by folders is that your system needs printer drivers to send print jobs. Back in the old days, we would capture the printer to an LPT port, and then install the printer drivers onto our local systems. We would then tell the printer to install to the captured port. Today, Windows makes all of this much easier—when we access a network printer, the printer drivers install automatically on the local system, a big benefit of Windows networking! NetWare has a similar feature.

Troubleshooting Shared Resources

Almost all problems with sharing or accessing shared resources stem from some mistake in the process of creating the share, as opposed to a problem with the shared resource itself. In fact, most of what appear to be sharing errors have nothing to do with the sharing process—they are lower-level errors like severed cables, incorrectly installed protocols, or attempts to access the wrong system. For the moment, let's assume none of these is the culprit, and look at some of the classic sharing errors that do take place on a network. We'll divide the most classic errors into two groups: sharing errors and access errors.

Sharing Errors

Sharing errors are problems that take place as you try to share a resource. Whenever I have a sharing error, I make a point to mentally review the steps required to create a share. Usually I realize that I skipped a step or failed to do a step properly.

The most frequent mistake people make is not sharing the right resource. This isn't exactly a sharing error, but it happens so often that I simply must mention it. One folder that folks like to share on a Windows system is the Desktop. That makes sense—I love to dump junk on my Desktop, and then tell others to "Get it off my Desktop!" The problem with Windows Desktops is that many people don't know where they are located. Do you remember? On a Windows 9x system, you'll find the Desktop in \Windows\Desktop. Windows NT and Windows 2000 make life more difficult, because they create a separate Desktop for each user. In Windows NT, each user's Desktop is hidden under the \WINNT\PROFILES folder. To find the Desktop of my Windows 2000 system, you have to dig down to \Documents and Settings\michaelm\Desktop. Desktops are not the only folders people have a problem finding to share. You can mess up sharing a folder in zillions of ways, so the wise user will double-check each folder before they start sharing it!

The other sharing issue that will bust you on more advanced network operating systems like Windows NT, 2000, and NetWare stems from permissions. The complexities of permissions make it way too easy to give someone insufficient permissions, preventing them from doing what they need to do on that share. Getting this right requires a bit of patience on your part as you experiment with different permission combinations to find the one that will let the user do what they need to do without unnecessarily sacrificing security.

Finally, watch out for share name incompatibilities. You can make a share in Windows XP called "This is the share Mike made on 12-1-04. Please use freely, but send me an e-mail when you do!" but many other systems, especially Windows 9x systems, won't be able to see it. Always think about the other systems on your network before you create share names!

Access Errors

As with sharing errors, almost all *access errors* are due to configuration problems, not some corrupt piece of software. The single biggest error flows directly from permissions: if you can't access a shared resource in the way you think you should be able to, ask the person who controls the share to give you the permissions you need. It's not uncommon to hear a conversation like this:

"Hey Alison, I can't make any changes to the Accounting database!"

"Yeah, well, you're not supposed to be able to! You don't have the right permissions!"

"Okay, well, either I make these changes or the boss is gonna yell at me—can you change my permissions?"

"Okay, gimme a sec."

"Thanks!"

I know some folks in more formal offices will laugh at this, because they have rigid procedures for changing permissions, but the basic process is still the same. Check to be sure you have the permissions you need. The fact that you had the right permissions yesterday is no guarantee that some network guru isn't going to change them today. Always assume permission problems first!

Chapter Review

Questions

1. Which of the following operating systems can use the file and folder permissions based on NTFS?

    A. NetWare

    B. Windows 2000

    C. Linux

    D. Windows 98

2. Your network consists of a NetWare server and a mixture of Windows 98 systems and Windows NT workstations. You add a Windows NT server to the network. All systems have the TCP/IP protocol suite installed. Samantha is unable to access a shared file on the NT server, but she is able to print from the shared printer. What could be the problem?

    A. Samantha's system and the Windows NT server are not connected to the same hub.

    B. Client for NetWare Networks has not been installed on Samantha's system.

    C. Client for Microsoft Networks has not been installed on Samantha's system.

    D. You have not given Samantha permission to access the shared file on the NT server.

3. Chris needs to work on a folder on the Desktop of your Windows 98 system. He is unable to access the folder, and you realize that you haven't shared the folder. You alternate-click the folder, but you don't get the Sharing option. What has happened?c

    A. Chris hasn't been given the correct permissions to access the folder on your Desktop.

    B. At the logon screen, you clicked Cancel instead of entering a password.

    C. You did not install File and Printer Sharing services on your system.

    D. The server is down.

4. The office's expensive laser printer is connected to Karen's Windows 98 system. Previously, other users have been able to print from that printer with no problem, but today they can't access it. What could be the problem?

    A. At the logon screen, Karen clicked Cancel instead of entering a password to log onto the network.

    B. File and Print Sharing services have not been installed on Karen's system.

C. The server is down.

D. Karen's system doesn't have the proper permissions set so other users can use the printer.

5. James is running a Windows 2000 system. He has shared his C: drive, but no one is able to access it. What could be causing this problem?

A. He needs to be the Administrator before he can share the drive.

B. He is set up as a Power User, and Power Users can't set permissions.

C. After he shares a device, he still needs to go into Security and set its permissions.

D. Everyone else's system has a problem. Only James' system is set up correctly.

6. Which of the following client systems can act as a printer server on a Novell NetWare network? (Select all that apply.)

A. UNIX/Linux

B. Macintosh

C. Windows 9x and 2000

D. NetWare Server

7. For client systems to act as a printer server on a Novell NetWare network, each of the client systems must have the NetWare printer server software installed.

A. True

B. False

8. To share printers on a UNIX/Linux network, which two printing services must be installed?

A. EPP

B. PPT

C. LPD

D. LPR

9. When we access a network printer, we don't need printer drivers.

A. True

B. False

10. Joe does a lot of work in a specific network folder, so he decided to map the folder as a network drive. The next morning when he booted up his system, the mapped network drive wasn't there. What happened?

A. You must map a network drive each day.

B. He didn't have the correct permissions to map a network drive.

C. The server was turned off, so the mapped network drive didn't appear.

D. He forgot to check the box to have the share reconnect at each logon.

Answers

1. **B.** Of the answers offered, only Windows 2000 uses NT File System (NTFS).

2. **D.** Samantha does not have permission to access the shared file on the NT server.

3. **C.** You did not install File and Printer Sharing services on your system.

4. **A.** Karen bypassed signing onto the network by clicking Cancel instead of entering a password at the logon screen. Windows 98 doesn't have permissions. Previously, the users have been able to use the printer, so the File and Print Sharing service is installed.

5. **C.** After a resource is shared in 2000, you still need to go to the Security tab and set permissions before others can access the resource. James must already be signed on as an Administrator or Power User because he was able to share the resource. A Power User can share resources.

6. **A, B, C, D.** All four answers are correct. With NetWare, each of these choices can act as a print server.

7. **A.** True. For client systems to act as a printer server on a Novell NetWare network, each of the client systems must have NetWare printer server software installed.

8. **C, D.** The LPD program works on the server and runs on the systems sharing the printer. LPR runs on any system wanting to access a printer under the control of LPD.

9. **B.** False. When you access a printer, you still need printer drivers, but Windows takes care of this automatically, so you don't have to worry about it.

10. **D.** Joe should have checked the box to have the mapped network drive reconnect at logon. If the server had been down, the mapped drive would have had a big red *X* across it.

Going Large with TCP/IP

The Network+ Certification exam expects you to know how to

- **2.9** Identify and differentiate between the following IP (Internet Protocol) addressing methods: static, dynamic, self-assigned (APIPA – Automatic Private Internet Protocol Addressing)
- **2.13** Identify the purpose of network services and protocols (for example: DNS – Domain Name Service, WINS – Windows Internet Naming Service)
- **4.1** Given a troubleshooting scenario, select the appropriate network utility from the following: ping, netstat, nbtstat, ipconfig/ifconfig, tracert/traceroute, winipcfg, nslookup/dig
- **4.2** Given output from a network diagnostic utility (for example: those utilities listed in objective 4.1), identify the utility and interpret the output
- **4.6** Given a scenario, determine the impact of modifying, adding, or removing network services (for example: DHCP – Dynamic Host Configuration Protocol, DNS – Domain Name Service, and WINS – Windows Internet Naming Service) for network resources and users

To achieve these goals, you must be able to

- Understand DNS in detail
- Learn about troubleshooting DNS
- Understand DHCP in detail
- Learn about troubleshooting DHCP
- Understand WINS in detail
- Learn about troubleshooting WINS
- Understand diagnosing TCP/IP networks

Well, no sooner do you think you're done with TCP/IP than I grab you by the collar and we're right back into it harder than ever! You didn't *really* think we were finished with TCP/IP yet, did you? I promise no more subnetting, but we do need to look more at some critical tools we use to make TCP/IP networks function, particularly large ones. In fact, we're going to work with the largest of all networks, the Internet itself.

In this chapter, you'll take an in-depth tour of DNS, WINS, and DHCP. Sure, I know you know how to set up your Windows clients for these fellas—if someone tells you what to enter in those TCP/IP Network Properties boxes, you know where to type them in. But now we're going to look at these in far more detail. In fact, we'll go a good bit beyond Network+ by looking at some real DNS, WINS, and DHCP servers! At the end of this chapter, we'll dive into the many software utilities (including some you've already seen, but in far more depth) and use them to diagnose and fix a number of the most common problems that occur in TCP/IP networks. You'll definitely want to know that part for the Network+ exam!

Odds are good you've got a system that is connected—or at least can connect—to the Internet. If I were you, I'd be firing that system up, because the vast majority of the programs you're going to learn about here come free with every operating system made. Finding them may be a challenge on some systems, but don't worry—I'll show you where they all hang out.

Historical/Conceptual

DNS

Chapter 11, "TCP/IP," gave you a brief, client-centric overview of DNS. Let's now go a bit deeper into DNS and take some time to appreciate how it works, see a DNS server in action, and then explore some of the neat tools you can use to diagnose DNS problems. We're going to revisit a few things, like HOSTS files and domain names, but we'll be looking at them in a more practical way—really getting into them, and even having a little fun.

DNS in Detail

In Chapter 11, you saw that DNS uses a hierarchical naming system and that it needs a magic box called a *DNS server* to resolve fully qualified domain names (FQDNs) to IP addresses. But how does this *really* work? More important, if you're having a problem, how can you determine if DNS is the culprit? If it is, what can you do about it without having to become an expert on DNS servers? Conveniently, it turns out that if you're having a DNS problem, it's probably not because of the DNS server crashing or some other problem over which you have no control. Instead, it's usually due to problems with the client systems, or another problem that you most certainly can control—*if* you understand DNS and know your DNS diagnostic tools.

DNS Organization

What does *hierarchical* mean in terms of DNS? Well, the DNS *hierarchical name space* is an imaginary tree structure of all possible names that could be used within a single system. By contrast, NetBIOS names use a *flat name space*—basically just one big undivided list containing all names, with no grouping whatsoever. In a flat name space, all names must be absolutely unique—no two machines can ever share the same name under any circumstances. A flat name space works fine on a small, isolated network, but not so well for a large organization with many interconnected networks. To avoid naming conflicts, all its administrators would need to keep track of all the names used throughout the entire corporate network.

> **TIP** NetBIOS names use a flat name space. Try making two computers in a Windows network with the same name and watch the errors appear.

A hierarchical name space offers a better solution, permitting a great deal more flexibility by enabling administrators to give networked systems longer, more fully descriptive names. The personal names people use every day are an example of a hierarchical name space. Most people address our town postman, Ron Samuels, simply as Ron. When his name comes up in conversation, people usually refer to him as Ron. The town troublemaker, Ron Falwell, and Mayor Jones's son, Ron, who went off to Toledo, obviously share first names with the postman. In some conversations, people need to distinguish between the good Ron, the bad Ron, and the Ron in Toledo (who may or may not be the ugly Ron). They could use a medieval style of address, and refer to the Rons as Ron the Postman, Ron the Blackguard, and Ron of Toledo, or they could use the modern Western style of address and add their surnames: "That Ron Samuels—he is such a card!" "That Ron Falwell is one bad apple." "That Ron Jones was the homeliest child I ever saw." You might visualize this as the People name space, illustrated in Figure 14-1. Adding the surname creates what you might fancifully call a *Fully Qualified Person Name*—enough information to prevent confusion among the various people named Ron.

A name space most of you are already familiar with is the hierarchical file name space used by hard drive volumes. Hard drives formatted using one of the popular file formats, like FAT, NTFS, or Linux's EXT3, use a hierarchical name space; you can create as many files named DATA.TXT as you want, as long as you store them in different parts of

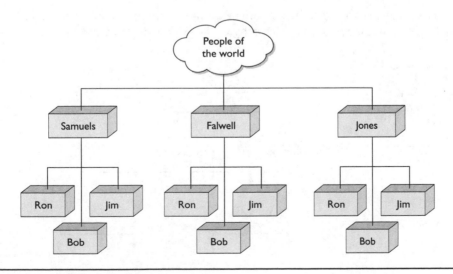

Figure 14-1 People name space

the file tree. In the example shown in Figure 14-2, two different files named DATA.TXT can exist simultaneously on the same system, but only if they are placed in different directories, such as C:\PROGRAM1\CURRENT\DATA.TXT and C:\PROGRAM1\BACKUP\ DATA.TXT. Although both files have the same basic filename—DATA.TXT—their fully qualified names are different: C:\PROGRAM1\CURRENT\DATA.TXT and C:\PROGRAM1\ BACKUP\DATA.TXT. Additionally, multiple subfolders can use the same name. There's no problem with having two folders using the name DATA, as long as they reside in different folders. Any Windows file system will happily let you create both C:\PROGRAM1\ DATA and C:\PROGRAM2\DATA folders. We like this because we often want to give the same name to multiple folders doing the same job for different applications.

In contrast, imagine what would happen if your computer's file system didn't support folders/directories. It would be as if Windows had to store all the files on your hard drive in the root directory! This is a classic example of a flat name space. Because all your files would be living together in one directory, each one would have to have a unique name. Naming files would be a nightmare! Software vendors would have to avoid sensible descriptive names like README.TXT, because they would almost certainly have been used already. You'd probably have to do what the Internet does for IP addresses: An organization of some sort would assign names out of the limited pool of possible file names. With a hierarchical name space, on the other hand, which is what all file systems use (thank goodness!), naming is much simpler. Lots of programs can have files called README.TXT, because each program can have its own folder and subfolders.

NOTE As hard as this may be to believe, some early file systems used a flat naming space. Back in the late 1970s and early 1980s, operating systems such as CPM and the early versions of DOS did not have the capability to use directories, creating a flat name space where all files resided on a single drive.

The DNS name space works in a manner extremely similar to your computer's file system. The DNS name space is a hierarchy of *DNS domains* and individual computer

Figure 14-2
Two DATA.TXT files in different directories on the same system

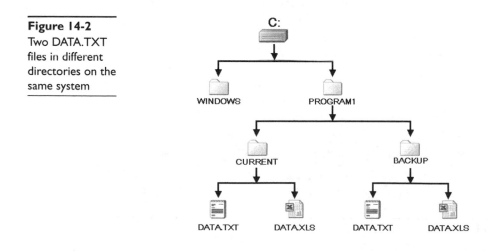

names organized into a tree-like structure that we call, rather appropriately, a *tree*. Each domain is like a folder—a domain is not a single computer, but rather a holding space into which you can add computer names. At the top of a *DNS tree* is the root. The *root* is the holding area to which all domains connect, just as the root directory in your file system is the holding area for all your folders. Individual computer names—more commonly called *host names* in the DNS naming convention—fit into domains. In the PC, you can place files directly into the root directory. The DNS world also enables us to add computer names to the root, but with the exception of a few special computers (described in a moment), this is rarely done. Each domain can have subdomains, just as the folders on your PC's file system can have subfolders. You separate each domain from its subdomains with a period. Characters for DNS domain names and host names are limited to uppercase and lowercase letters (A–Z, a–z), numbers (0–9), and the hyphen (-). No other characters may be used.

> **NOTE** Even though you may use uppercase or lowercase, DNS does not differentiate between them.

Figure 14-3 shows a sample DNS tree for a small TCP/IP network that is not attached to the Internet. In this case, there is only one domain: ABCDEF. Each computer on the network has a host name, as shown in the figure.

When you write out the complete path to a file stored on your PC, the naming convention starts with the root directory on the left, followed by the first folder, then any subfolders (in order), and finally, the name of the file—for example, c:\sounds\thunder\mynewcobra.wav. DNS naming convention is *exactly the opposite*. A complete DNS name, including the host name and all of its domains (in order), is called a *fully qualified domain name (FQDN)*, and it's written out with the root on the far right, followed by the names of the domains (in order) added to the left of the root, and the host name on the

Figure 14-3
Small DNS tree

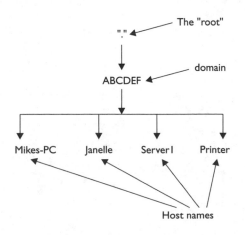

PART III

far left. The previous Figure 14-3 shows the FQDNs for two systems in the ABCDEF domain. Note the period for the root is on the far *right* of each FQDN!

> Mikes-PC.ABCDEF.
> Janelle.ABCDEF.

Given that every FQDN will always have a period on the end to signify the root, it is commonplace to drop the final period when writing out FQDNs. To make the two example FQDNs fit into common parlance, therefore, you'd skip the last period:

> Mikes-PC.ABCDEF
> Janelle.ABCDEF

If you're used to seeing DNS names on the Internet, you're probably wondering about the lack of ".com," ".net," or other common DNS domain names. Those conventions are needed for computers that are visible on the Internet, such as web servers, but they're not required on a private TCP/IP network. As long as I make a point never to make these computers visible on the Internet, I can use any naming convention I want!

Let's look at another DNS namespace example, but make it a bit more complex. This network is not on the Internet, so I can use any domain I want. The network has two domains: Houston and Dallas, as shown in Figure 14-4. Note that each domain has a computer called Server1.

Because the network has two different domains, it can have two systems (one on each domain) with the same host name, just as you can have two files with the same name in different folders on your PC. Now, let's add some subdomains to the DNS tree, so that it looks like Figure 14-5.

We write out the FQDN from left to right, starting with the host name and moving up to the top of the DNS tree, adding all domains until we get to the top of the DNS tree.

> Mikes-PC.Support.Houston
> Tom.Server1.Houston
> Janelle.Sales.Dallas
> Server1.Dallas

Figure 14-4
Two DNS
domains

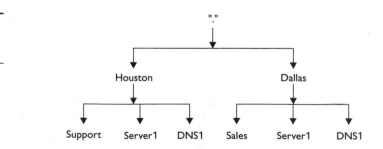

Figure 14-5
Subdomains
added

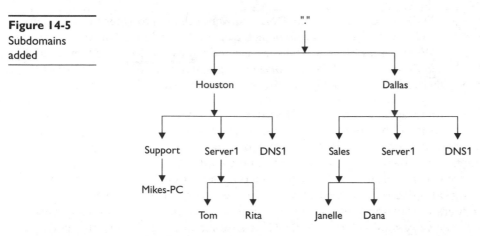

PART II

> **NOTE** The DNS naming convention allows for DNS names up to 255 characters, including the separating periods.

So where does this naming convention reside and how does it work? Here's where the analogy to the PC's file system breaks down completely. DNS does not have a single hard drive to store a directory structure, like you have on a PC. Rather, we store the DNS information on systems running DNS server software. When a system needs to know the IP address for a specific FQDN, it queries the DNS server listed in its TCP/IP configuration. On a simple network, like the one shown back in Figure 14-3, there is usually one DNS server for the entire network. This single DNS server has a list of all the host names on the domain and their corresponding IP address. It's known as the *authoritative DNS server* for the domain. Folks who administer complex networks assign different domains to different DNS servers to keep a single server from being swamped by DNS requests. A single DNS server may act as the authoritative DNS sever for one domain or many domains—DNS is very flexible.

But what if more than one DNS server is in control of different domains? How does an FQDN get resolved if your DNS server is not authoritative for a particular FQDN? Let's refer to Figure 14-5 for the answer. Let's say Mikes-PC.Support.Houston needs the IP address of Server1.Dallas. The network has two DNS servers: DNS1.Houston and DNS1.Dallas. DNS1.Dallas is the authoritative server for all of the Dallas domains and DNS1.Houston is in charge of all the Houston domains. DNS1.Houston is also the root server for the entire network. This means that the Houston server has a listing for every domain in the Dallas domain structure. This does *not* mean it knows the IP address for every system in the Dallas network! It only knows that if any system asks for an IP address from the Dallas side, it will tell that system the IP address of the Dallas server. The requesting system will then ask the Dallas DNS server for the IP address of the system it needs. That's the beauty of DNS root servers—they don't know the IP addresses for all of the computers, but they know where to send the requests!

NOTE In the early days of DNS, you were required to enter the host name and IP address of every system on the network into your DNS server manually. While you can still do that if you want, today most DNS servers take advantage of Dynamic DNS (DDNS). *DDNS* enables systems to register their host names with their DNS server automatically, eliminating the need to enter them manually.

The Internet most certainly uses a DNS tree. Not only does it use a DNS tree, but the folks who designed the Internet created a specific naming convention using the now-famous first-level domain names we've come to know and love: .com, .net, and so forth. The Internet also has a root. The DNS root for the entire Internet consists of 13 powerful DNS servers scattered all over the world. The Internet root is 13 "logical" servers—each single logical server is many DNS servers acting as one monstrous server.

The hierarchical aspect of DNS has a number of benefits. For example, the vast majority of web servers are called www. If DNS used a flat name space, only the first organization that created a server with the name www could use it. Because DNS naming appends domain names to the server names, however, the servers www.totalsem.com and www.microsoft.com can both exist simultaneously. DNS names like www.microsoft.com must fit within a worldwide hierarchical name space, meaning that no two machines should ever have the same fully qualified name.

TIP Just because most web servers are named www doesn't mean they must be named www! Naming a web server www is etiquette, not a requirement!

Figure 14-6 shows the host named *accounting* with a fully qualified domain name of *accounting.texas.microsoft.com*.

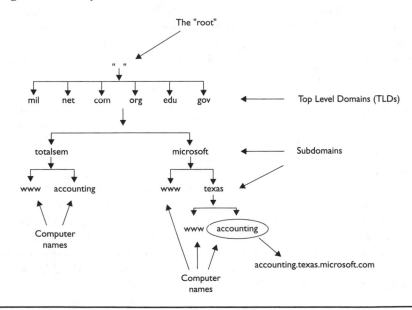

Figure 14-6   DNS domain *texas.microsoft.com* containing the host *accounting*

NOTE Technically, the texas.microsoft.com domain shown in Figure 14-6 is a subdomain of microsoft.com. Don't be surprised to see the terms "domain" and "subdomain" used interchangeably, as it's a common practice.

Name Resolution

You don't have to use DNS to access the Internet, but it sure makes life a lot easier! Programs like Internet Explorer accept names such as www.microsoft.com as a convenience to the end user, but utilize the IP address that corresponds to that name to create a connection. If you know the IP address of the system you want to talk to, you don't need DNS at all. Figure 14-7 shows Internet Explorer displaying the same web page when given the straight IP address as it does when given the DNS name www.microsoft.com. In theory, if you knew the IP addresses of all the systems you wanted to access, you could turn off DNS completely. I guess you could also start a fire using a bow and drill too, but most people wouldn't make a habit of it if there were a more efficient alternative, which in this case, DNS definitely is! I have no trouble keeping hundreds of DNS names in my head, but IP addresses? Forget it! Without DNS, I might as well not even try to use the Internet, and I'd wager that's true of most people.

When you type in a web address, Internet Explorer must resolve that name to the web server's IP address to make a connection to that web server. It can resolve the name in three ways: by broadcasting, by consulting a locally stored text file we discussed earlier, called HOSTS, or by contacting a DNS server.

To *broadcast* for name resolution, the host sends a message to all the machines on the network, saying something like, "Hey! If your name is JOESCOMPUTER, please respond with your IP address." All the networked hosts receive that packet, but only JOESCOMPUTER responds with an IP address. Broadcasting works fine for small networks, but it is limited because it cannot provide name resolution across routers. Routers do not forward broadcast messages to other networks, as illustrated in Figure 14-8.

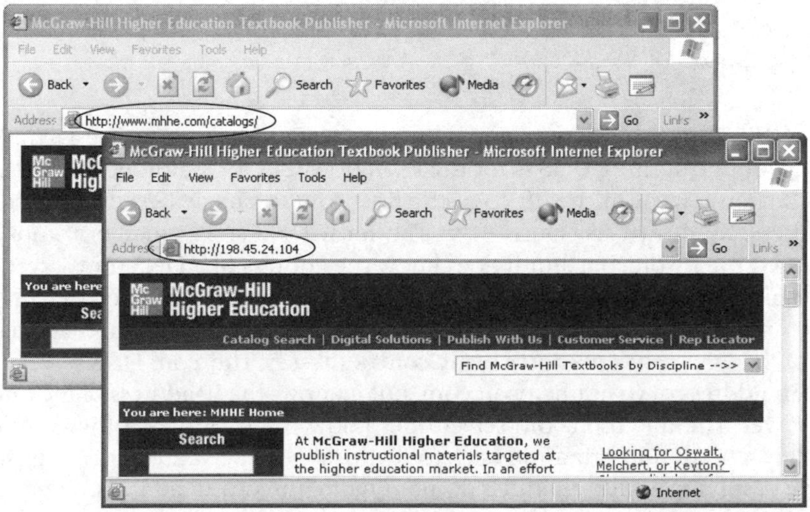

Figure 14-7
Sockets-based applications like Internet Explorer can accept IP addresses or DNS names.

Figure 14-8
Name resolution by broadcast does not work across routers because routers do not forward broadcasts.

2. The router hears the broadcast but doesn't forward it.

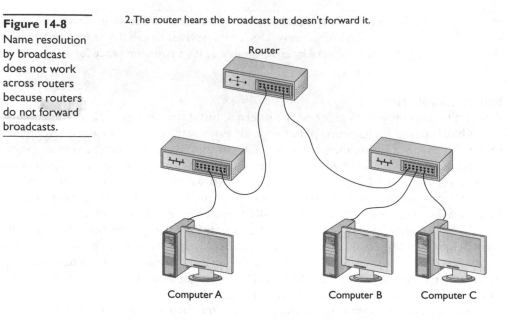

Router

Computer A   Computer B   Computer C

1. Computer A broadcasts a request for computer B's IP address.

As discussed earlier, a HOSTS file functions like a little black book, listing the names and addresses of machines on a network, just like a little black book lists the names and phone numbers of people. A typical HOSTS file would look like this:

```
109.54.94.197      stephen.totalsem.com
138.125.163.17     roger.totalsem.com
127.0.0.1          localhost
```

NOTE   Notice that the name "localhost" appears in the HOSTS file as an alias for the loopback address, 127.0.0.1.

The final way to resolve a name to an IP address is to use DNS. We've seen what a wonderful thing DNS is for the user; now let's look at how it does the job. To resolve the name www.microsoft.com, the host contacts its DNS server and requests the IP address, as shown in Figure 14-9. The local DNS server may not know the address for www.microsoft.com, but it does know the address of a DNS root server. The root servers, maintained by InterNIC, know all the addresses of the top-level domain DNS servers. The root servers don't know the address of www.microsoft.com, but they do know the address of the DNS server in charge of all .com addresses. The .com DNS server also doesn't know the address of www.microsoft.com, but it knows the IP address of the microsoft.com DNS server. The microsoft.com server does know the IP address of www.microsoft.com, and can send that information back to the local DNS server. Figure 14-10 shows the process of resolving a fully qualified domain name into an IP address.

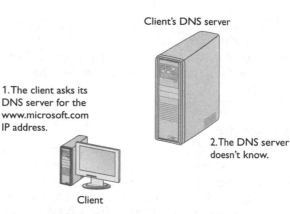

Figure 14-9
A host contacts its DNS server.

Client's DNS server

1. The client asks its DNS server for the www.microsoft.com IP address.

2. The DNS server doesn't know.

Client

No single machine needs to know every DNS name, as long as every machine knows who to ask for more information. The distributed, decentralized nature of the DNS database provides a great deal of flexibility and freedom to network administrators using DNS. DNS still requires an administrator to type in each name and address, just as they do with a HOSTS file. There are two key advantages, however, to maintaining this information in a DNS database, compared to maintaining the same information in the form of HOSTS files. First, because the database is centralized on the DNS server, an adminis-

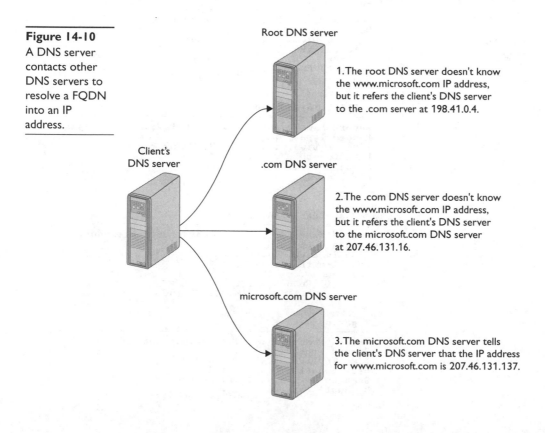

Figure 14-10
A DNS server contacts other DNS servers to resolve a FQDN into an IP address.

Root DNS server

1. The root DNS server doesn't know the www.microsoft.com IP address, but it refers the client's DNS server to the .com server at 198.41.0.4.

Client's DNS server

.com DNS server

2. The .com DNS server doesn't know the www.microsoft.com IP address, but it refers the client's DNS server to the microsoft.com DNS server at 207.46.131.16.

microsoft.com DNS server

3. The microsoft.com DNS server tells the client's DNS server that the IP address for www.microsoft.com is 207.46.131.137.

PART III

trator can add new entries just once, rather than walking around the network to add new entries to each machine. Second, the database is distributed, meaning that no single administrator must maintain a database that knows about every other machine in the world. A DNS server simply has to know about the other DNS servers where it can go for more information.

The DNS Cache

Most web browsers and Windows 2000/2003/XP systems keep track of DNS via a cache, logically called the *DNS resolver cache*. After a web browser or a Windows 2000/XP system has made a DNS request, it keeps that IP address in its own personal DNS cache. If you want to see the DNS cache on a Windows 2000, 2003, or XP system, use the IPCONFIG utility—run the command **IPCONFIG /DISPLAYDNS** at a command prompt. Internet Explorer and Netscape Navigator also have DNS caches, but you need a third-party utility to see their contents. IPCONFIG /DISPLAYDNS creates a rather messy, long output, so be ready to do some scrolling. Figure 14-11 shows just a small bit of the typical output from IPCONFIG /DISPLAYDNS. You can then erase this cache using the **IPCONFIG /FLUSHDNS** command. Remember this command—you'll need it in just a moment! For now, let's take a look at a real DNS server running on a Windows 2000 Server system.

Figure 14-11

Some output from the IPCONFIG / DISPLAYDNS command

```
ns.jump.net.
-----------------------------------------------------------
    Record Name . . . . . : ns.jump.net
    Record Type . . . . . : 1
    Time To Live  . . . . : 74548
    Data Length . . . . . : 4
    Section . . . . . . . : Answer
    A (Host) Record . . . :
                          204.238.120.5


1.0.0.127.in-addr.arpa.
-----------------------------------------------------------
    Record Name . . . . . : 1.0.0.127.in-addr.arpa
    Record Type . . . . . : 12
    Time To Live  . . . . : 31279767
    Data Length . . . . . : 4
    Section . . . . . . . : Answer
    PTR Record  . . . . . :
                          localhost


sca03.sec.dns.exodus.net.
-----------------------------------------------------------
    Record Name . . . . . : sca03.sec.dns.exodus.net
    Record Type . . . . . : 1
    Time To Live  . . . . : 70340
    Data Length . . . . . : 4
    Section . . . . . . . : Answer
    A (Host) Record . . . :
                          216.32.126.150


ns2.got.net.
-----------------------------------------------------------
    Record Name . . . . . : ns2.got.net
    Record Type . . . . . : 1
    Time To Live  . . . . : 67469
    Data Length . . . . . : 4
    Section . . . . . . . : Answer
    A (Host) Record . . . :
                          207.111.232.23
```

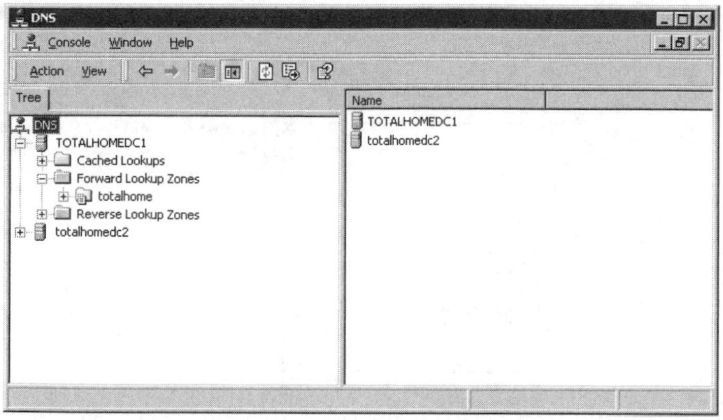

Figure 14-12
Mike's Windows 2000 DNS servers with the tree expanded under TOTALHOMEDC1

DNS Servers

We've been talking about DNS servers for so long, I feel I'd be untrue to my vision of an All-In-One book unless we took at least a quick peek at a DNS server in action. Lots of network operating systems come with built-in DNS server software, including Windows NT, 2000 and 2003 Server, NetWare 5.x and 6.x, and just about every version of UNIX/Linux. There are also a number of third-party DNS server programs for virtually any operating system. I'm going to use the DNS server program that comes with Microsoft Windows 2000 Server primarily because (1) it takes the prettiest screen snapshots and (2) it's the one I use here at the office. You start the DNS server by selecting Administrative Tools | DNS from the Start menu. When you first open the DNS server, there's not much to see other than the name of the server itself; in this case, Figure 14-12 shows two servers, imaginatively named TOTALHOMEDC1 and totalhomedc2.

> **NOTE** The most popular DNS server tool used in UNIX/Linux systems is called BIND.

When you open up the tree beneath a DNS server, the first folder you'll see is called Cached Lookups. Every DNS server keeps a list of *cached lookups*—that is, all the IP addresses it has already resolved—so it won't have to re-resolve a FQDN name it has already checked. There is a limit to the size of the cache, of course, and you can also set a limit on how long the DNS server holds cache entries. Windows does a nice job of separating these cached addresses by placing all cached lookups in little folders that share the first name of the top-level domain with subfolders that use the second-level domain. This sure makes it easy to see where folks have been web browsing! (See Figure 14-13.)

Now to the actual DNS serving work. Basically, there are two types of DNS servers. Authoritative DNS servers hold the IP addresses and names of systems for a particular domain or domains in special storage areas called *Forward Lookup Zones*. In Figure 14-14, the record called SOA (Start of Authority) in the folder totalhome indicates that my

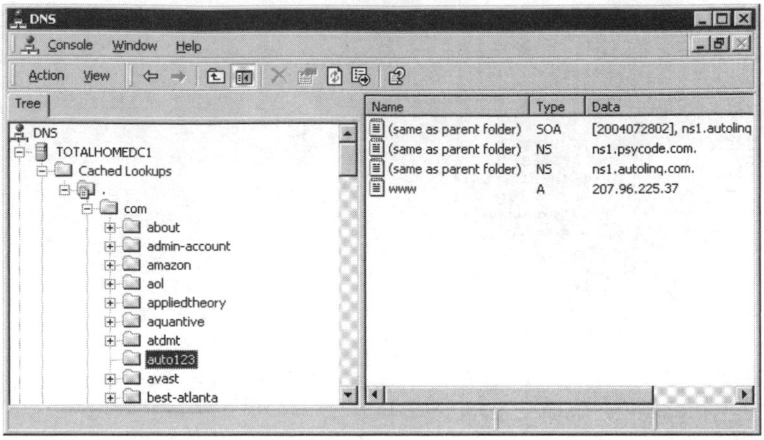

Figure 14-13   Cached Lookups

server is the authoritative server for a domain called totalhome. The totalhome domain is an internal DNS domain (none of the computers in the domain act as any type of Internet servers), so I don't have to keep with the official Internet naming structures like adding a ".com" to the end of totalhome. You can even see a few of the systems in that domain (note to hackers: these are fake, so don't bother). A tech looking at this would know that totalhomedc1.totalhome is the authoritative server for the totalhome domain. The NS records are all of the DNS servers for totalhome. Note that totalhome has two DNS servers: totalhomedc1 and totalhomedc2. Two DNS servers ensures that if one

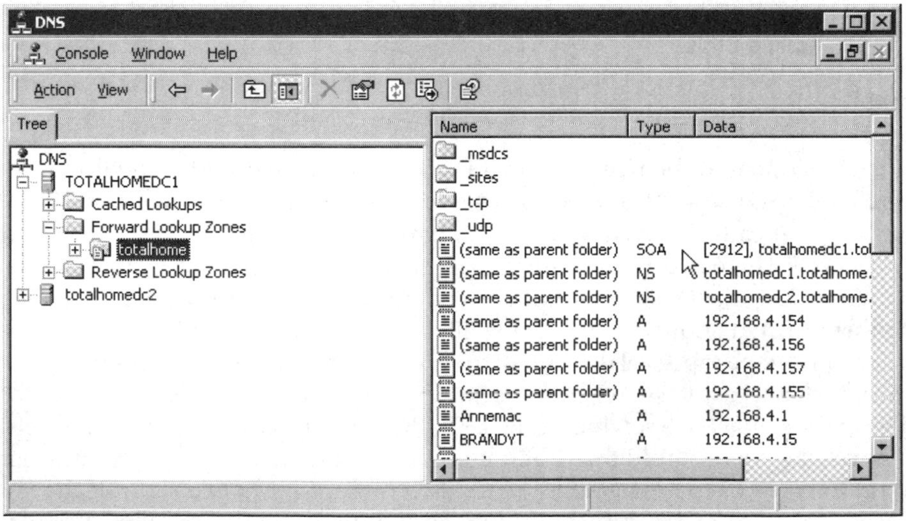

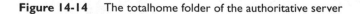

Figure 14-14   The totalhome folder of the authoritative server

fails, the totalhome domain will continue to have a DNS server. The *A* records in the folder are the IP addresses and names of all the systems on the totalhome domain.

The second type of DNS servers are *cache-only*. *Cache-only DNS servers* do not have any forward lookup zones. They will resolve names of systems on the Internet for the network, but are not responsible for telling other DNS servers the names of any clients. This is fairly common for DNS servers in smaller networks that still use NetBIOS. Internally, they use NetBIOS broadcasts to resolve each other's names, but then call on a cache-only DNS server when resolving names out on the Internet.

The other folder you can see in Figure 14-14 is called *Reverse Lookup Zones*. This rather strange setting enables a system to determine a FQDN by knowing the IP address; that is, it does the exact reverse of what DNS normally does! A few low-level functions and some security programs use reverse lookup zones, so DNS servers provide them.

Troubleshooting DNS

As I mentioned earlier, most DNS problems result from a problem with the client systems. This is because DNS servers rarely go down, and if they do, most clients have a secondary DNS server setting that lets them continue to work properly. DNS servers have been known to fail, however, so it's important to know when the problem is the client system, and when you can complain to the person in charge of your DNS server. All of the tools you're about to see come with every operating system that supports TCP/IP, with the exception of the IPCONFIG commands, which I'll mention when we get to them.

So how do you know when to suspect DNS as a problem on your network? Well, just about everything you do on an IP network depends on DNS to find the right system to talk to for whatever job the application does. E-mail clients use DNS to find their e-mail servers, FTP clients use DNS for their servers, web browsers use DNS to find web servers, and so on. The first clue is usually a user calling you and saying they're getting a "server not found" error. Server not found errors look different on different applications, but you can count on something in there that says "server not found." Figure 14-15 shows how this error appears in a web browser and in an e-mail client.

Before you start testing, you need to eliminate any DNS caches on the local system. If you're running Windows 2000 or Windows XP, run the IPCONFIG /FLUSHDNS command now. In addition, most web browsers also have caches, so you can't use a web browser for any testing. In such cases, it's time to turn to the PING command!

PING is your best friend when you're testing DNS. Run PING from a command prompt, followed by the name of a well-known web site, such as www.microsoft.com. Watch the output carefully to see if you get an IP address. You may get a "request timed out" message, but that's fine; you just want to see if DNS is resolving FQDN names into IP addresses (see Figure 14-16).

Figure 14-15
"Server not found" errors in web browsers and e-mail clients

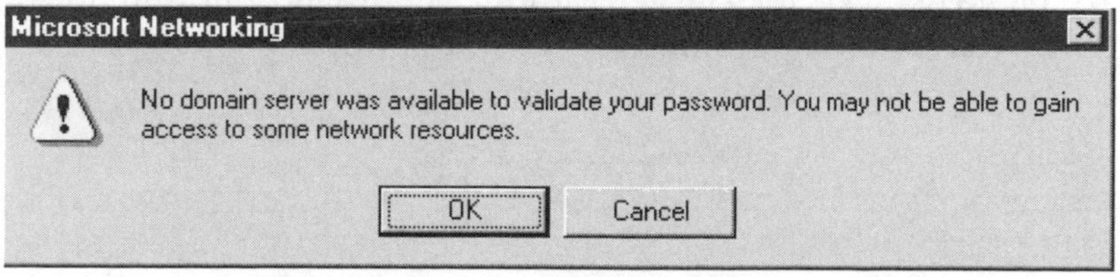

Microsoft Networking

No domain server was available to validate your password. You may not be able to gain access to some network resources.

OK   Cancel

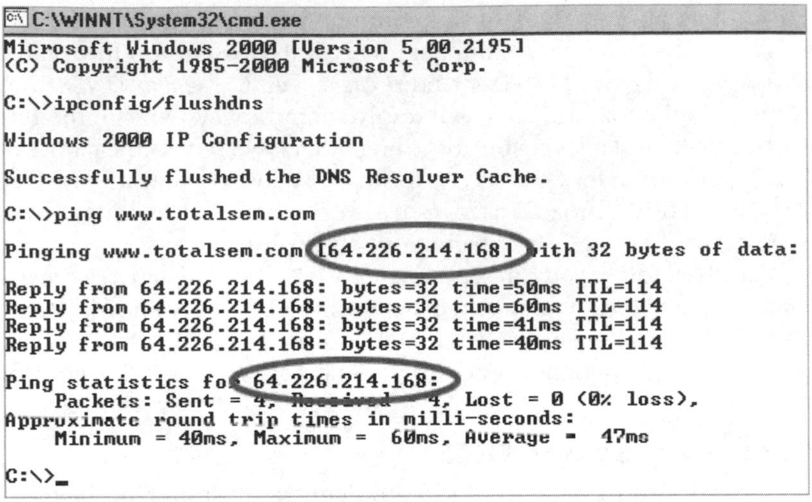

Figure 14-16

Pinging www
.totalsem.com

```
C:\WINNT\System32\cmd.exe
Microsoft Windows 2000 [Version 5.00.2195]
(C) Copyright 1985-2000 Microsoft Corp.

C:\>ipconfig/flushdns

Windows 2000 IP Configuration

Successfully flushed the DNS Resolver Cache.

C:\>ping www.totalsem.com

Pinging www.totalsem.com [64.226.214.168] with 32 bytes of data:

Reply from 64.226.214.168: bytes=32 time=50ms TTL=114
Reply from 64.226.214.168: bytes=32 time=60ms TTL=114
Reply from 64.226.214.168: bytes=32 time=41ms TTL=114
Reply from 64.226.214.168: bytes=32 time=40ms TTL=114

Ping statistics for 64.226.214.168:
    Packets: Sent = 4, Received = 4, Lost = 0 (0% loss),
Approximate round trip times in milli-seconds:
    Minimum = 40ms, Maximum = 60ms, Average = 47ms

C:\>_
```

If you get a "server not found" error, you need to ping again using just an IP address. Most network techs keep the IP address of a known server in their heads. If you don't have one memorized, try 205.161.6.57. If PING works with the IP address but not with the web site name, you know you've got a DNS problem.

Once you've determined there's a DNS problem, check to make sure your system has the correct DNS server entry. Again, this information is something you should keep around. I can tell you the DNS server IP address for every Internet link I own—two in the office, one at the house, plus two dialups I use on the road. You don't have to memorize the IP addresses, but you should have all the critical IP information written down. If that isn't the problem, run IPCONFIG (or WINIPCFG from the Start | Run dialog box) to see if those DNS settings are the same as the ones in the server; if they aren't, you may need to refresh your DHCP settings. I'll show you how to do that next.

If you have the correct DNS settings for your DNS server and the DNS settings in IPCONFIG/WINIPCFG match those settings, you can assume the problem is with the DNS server itself. There's a popular command for working with DNS servers called NSLOOKUP (name server lookup). NSLOOKUP comes with Windows (except 9x), Linux, and NetWare. It's a handy tool that advanced techs use to query the functions of DNS servers.

NSLOOKUP is an amazingly complex program that you run from a command prompt. With NSLOOKUP, you can (assuming you have the permission) query all types of information from a DNS server and change how your system uses DNS. While most of these commands are far outside the scope of Network+, there are a few places where NSLOOKUP makes for a great basic tool. For instance, just running NSLOOKUP alone shows you some output similar to the text shown here:

```
C:\>nslookup
Default Server:  totalhomedc2.totalhome
Address:  192.168.4.155

>
```

NOTE NSLOOKUP has its own prompt. To get back to a command prompt, type **exit** and press ENTER.

Running NSLOOKUP gives me the IP address and the name of my default DNS server. If I got an error at this point—perhaps a "server not found" error"—I would know that either my primary DNS server is down or I might not have the correct DNS server information in my DNS settings. I can attach to any DNS server by typing **server**, followed by the IP address or the domain name of the DNS server.

```
> server totalhomedc1
Default Server:  totalhomedc1.totalhome
Addresses:  192.168.4.157, 192.168.4.156
```

This new server has two IP addresses—it probably has two NICs, to ensure that there's a backup in case one NIC fails. If I get an error on one DNS server, I use NSLOOKUP to check for another DNS server. I can then switch to that server in my TCP/IP settings as a temporary fix until my DNS server comes back up.

Those using UNIX/Linux have an extra DNS tool called *dig*—short for *domain information groper*. Dig is very similar to NSLOOKUP, but it runs non-interactively. In NSLOOKUP, you're in the command until you type **exit**; NSLOOKUP even has its own prompt. The dig tool, on the other hand, is not interactive—you ask it a question, it answers the question, and it puts you back at a command prompt, with nothing to exit. When you run dig, you tend to get a large amount of information. The following is a sample of a dig command run from a Linux prompt.

```
[mike@localhost]$dig -x 13.65.14.4
 ; <<>> DiG 8.2 <<>> -x
;; res options: init recurs defnam dnsrch
;; got answer:
;; ->>HEADER<<- opcode: QUERY, status: NOERROR, id: 4
;; flags: qr aa rd ra; QUERY: 1, ANSWER: 1, AUTHORITY: 2, ADDITIONAL: 2
;; QUERY SECTION:
;;      4.14.65.13.in-addr.arpa, type = ANY, class = IN
;; ANSWER SECTION:
4.14.65.13.in-addr.arpa.  4H IN PTR  server3.houston.totalsem.com.
;; AUTHORITY SECTION:
65.14.4.in-addr.arpa.  4H IN NS  kernel.risc.uni-linz.ac.at.
65.14.4.in-addr.arpa.  4H IN NS  kludge.risc.uni-linz.ac.at.
;; ADDITIONAL SECTION:
kernel.risc.uni-linz.ac.at.  4H IN A  193.170.37.225
kludge.risc.uni-linz.ac.at.  4H IN A  193.170.37.224
;; Total query time: 1 msec
;; FROM: kernel to SERVER: default -- 127.0.0.1
;; WHEN: Thu Feb 10 18:03:41 2000
;; MSG SIZE  sent: 44  rcvd: 180
[mike@localhost]$
```

PART III

DHCP

Earlier, you saw that *Dynamic Host Configuration Protocol (DHCP)* could somehow magically take all your TCP/IP setup blues away by enabling any system to get all its necessary TCP/IP settings automatically from a DHCP server. In this section, we take a look at a DHCP server, consider some of the configuration issues, and then review some basic DHCP troubleshooting techniques.

DHCP in Detail

DHCP enables TCP/IP client autoconfiguration. The DHCP server stores IP information and disperses it to the client systems on the network. At first glance, you might think that DHCP gives out only IP addresses—but in fact, it can give out all types of IP information: IP addresses, default gateways, DNS servers, and so on. While DHCP is useful, it's important to note that the network's client systems aren't required to use DHCP. It's no problem at all if some systems on the network get their IP information from the DHCP server, while others use static IP information. Finally, a system can use DHCP to obtain some IP information, and use static IP information for other purposes—there's no rule that a single system must use only DHCP or static IP information.

The beauty of DHCP is that it massively reduces the administration of a TCP/IP network. If you need to change the IP address of your default gateway, you could find yourself facing hours of work in a network where all the systems have static IP information. If you have DHCP set up to provide IP information dynamically, on the other hand, the DHCP would update all those PCs for you.

DHCP Servers

DHCP Servers are common. You'll find a DHCP server built into NetWare, Linux, and Windows server versions, as well as in most routers. For an example, I'll show you the DHCP server that comes with Windows 2000 Server. At first glance, you might think you're looking at the DNS server program, because you only see the name of the server running the DHCP server program (see Figure 14-17).

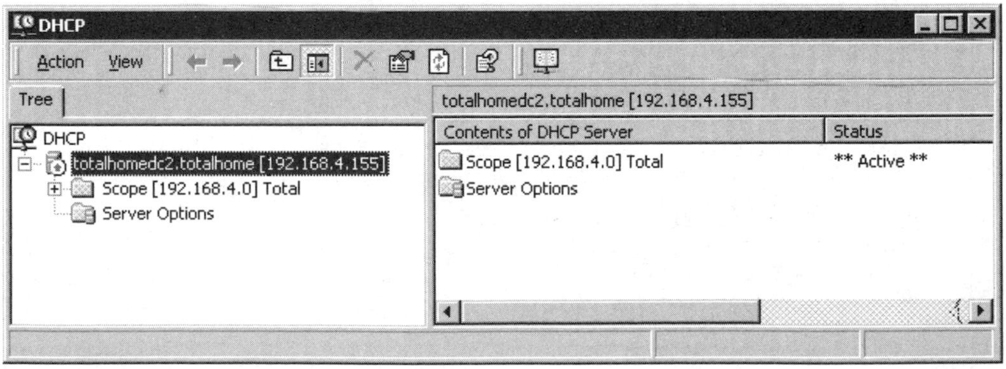

Figure 14-17   The Windows 2000 DHCP server program

If you click the name of the DHCP server, you'll see the cornerstone of DHCP: the DHCP scope. A *DHCP scope* is the pool of IP addresses that a DHCP server may allocate to clients requesting IP addresses, or other IP information like DNS server addresses. This DHCP server has a pool of IP addresses running from 192.168.4.1 up to 192.168.4.250 (see Figure 14-18). It passes out these IP addresses in order as they are requested; so the first system that asks for an IP address gets 192.168.4.1, the second one gets 192.168.4.2, and so on.

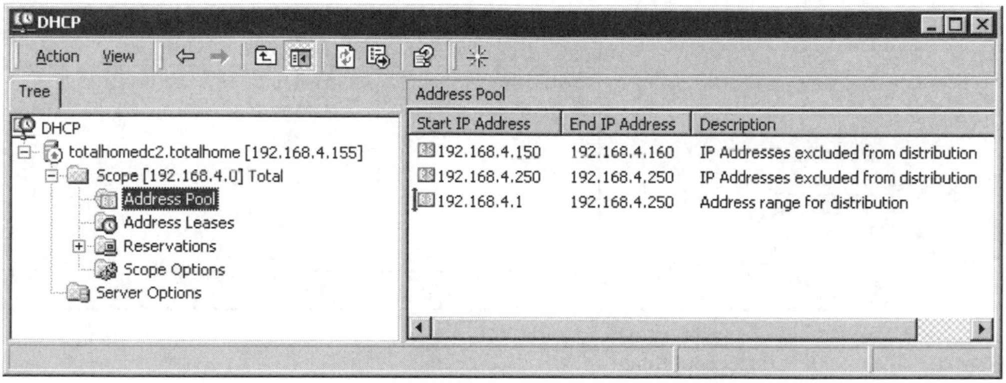

Figure 14-18   DHCP scope—a pool of IP addresses

When a system requests DHCP IP information, the DHCP server creates a *DHCP lease* for the requested IP information; this means the client may use these settings for a certain amount of time. Windows 2000 and 2003 set the lease duration to eight days by default (NT set it to three days). To see the systems currently leasing DHCP IP addresses, look under Address Leases in DHCP (see Figure 14-19).

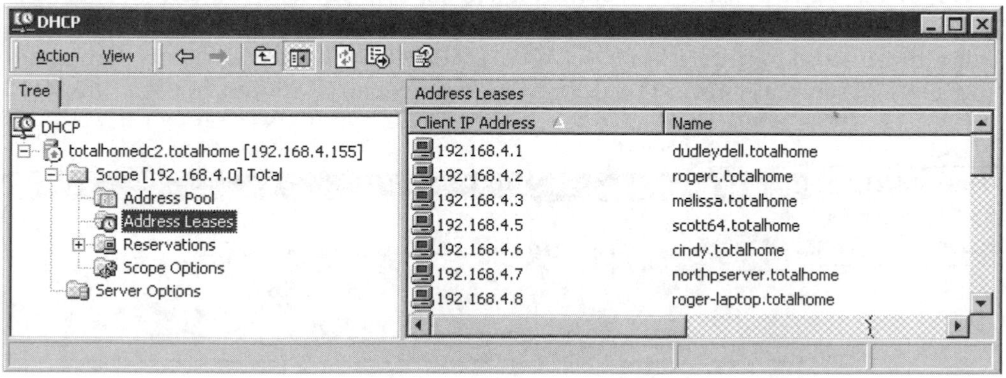

Figure 14-19   Address leases showing currently leased DHCP IP addresses

Remember that DHCP does more than just provide dynamic IP addresses. DHCP is great at dispensing all sorts of IP information your system might need. Figure 14-20 shows these DHCP scope options, and that I have the options for Default Gateway (Router), DNS server, and domain information activated, as well as my WINS server. All this information is passed to DHCP clients when they get their dynamic IP addresses.

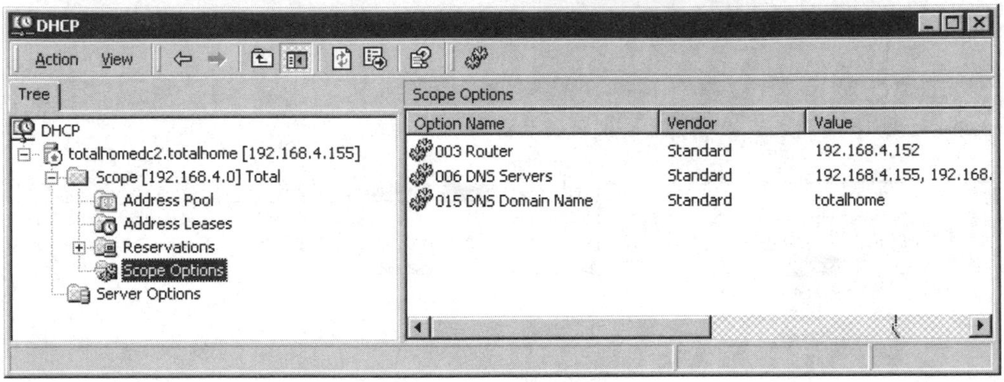

Figure 14-20   DHCP scope options

Troubleshooting DHCP

DHCP is a highly automated process that requires little configuration from the client side. This makes DHCP problems rare indeed. Once a system connects to a DHCP server and gets its dynamic IP information, it will run on those settings until the end of its lease period or until it reboots. If the DHCP client can't find a DHCP server to start or renew a lease, you'll get an error pointing to a DHCP problem. On reboot, you'll see something like the error shown in Figure 14-21.

Any Windows 98 and later Windows client that is configured for DHCP, but unable to access a DHCP server, will always default to a special IP address starting with 169.254. This is the *Automatic Private IP Address (APIPA)*. APIPA enables DHCP clients that cannot find a DHCP server a chance at working by giving them an IP address in the 169.254/16

Figure 14-21
No DHCP server present

network. Without APIPA, a DHCP client simply will not get an IP address and will not function. If you think DHCP access is a problem, use IPCONFIG or WINIPCFG to check if your system is using an APIPA address. If you do this check and get a 169.254.*x.x* IP address, run the **IPCONFIG /RENEW** command, or click the Renew button in the WINIPCFG dialog box. If you get an error like the one shown in Figure 14-22, you're not getting to the DHCP server. Make sure you're connected to the network, and then contact the person in charge of the DHCP server.

Figure 14-22
Unsuccessful
RENEW
command error:
DHCP Server
Unavailable:
Renewing adapter

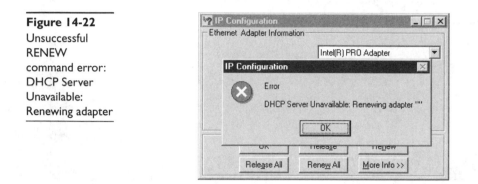

PART III

The one time DHCP will make some mistakes is during the initial setup. If you fail to provide the correct DNS server to your DHCP clients, they won't be able to resolve IP addresses. If you give them a pool of IP addresses that is not part of your network ID, they may not even be able to see other systems on the network. These aren't DHCP problems; they're regular IP configuration errors that happen to involve DHCP, which happily disperses them to all your networked systems.

Release or Renew?

WINIPCFG and IPCONFIG both come with the handy *release* and *renew* options. When do you release and when do you renew? This one's simple: if you know you're changing to a *new* DHCP server, first release, and then renew. If you know you're sticking with the same DHCP server, just renew. Linux users don't have the handy release and renew options, so they have to turn the NIC off and back on again to get the same result. To do this, run the **IFCONFIG eth0 down** command (*eth0* is what Linux names your NIC; if you have multiple NICs, the second would be *eth1*, and so on), and then the **IFCONFIG eth0 up** command. When the NIC comes back on, it will automatically try to renew the DHCP lease (see Figure 14-23).

```
[root@localhost /root]# ifconfig eth0 down
[root@localhost /root]# ifconfig eth0 up
[root@localhost /root]# ifconfig eth0
eth0      Link encap:Ethernet  HWaddr 00:A0:C9:98:12:F4
          inet addr:192.168.4.3  Bcast:192.168.4.255  Mask:255.255.255.0
          UP BROADCAST RUNNING MULTICAST  MTU:1500  Metric:1
          RX packets:149896 errors:0 dropped:0 overruns:0 frame:0
          TX packets:14026 errors:0 dropped:0 overruns:4 carrier:0
          collisions:2 txqueuelen:100
          Interrupt:5 Base address:0xd800

[root@localhost /root]#
```

Figure 14-23   Renewing a DHCP lease in Linux using the IFCONFIG up command

WINS

Remember *Windows Internet Naming Service (WINS)*? It resolves NetBIOS names to IP addresses. WINS drives many network types absolutely crazy, because it's one of those services that most networks simply don't need. Because only Windows networks run NetBIOS, WINS only operates in pure or nearly pure Windows networks. A Windows network must be running both IP and NetBIOS to need WINS, and even in those cases, you may not need WINS, because NetBIOS clients broadcast over a single segment. The latest versions of Windows—2000 and XP—have dumped native support for WINS, instead relying completely on DNS, except when running in networks with Windows 9*x* or NT systems. Bottom line? If you've never seen a WINS server before, this may be your only chance.

 TIP   Even though WINS is fading away, the Network+ exam still expects you to know it!

WINS in Detail

Let's review what we know about NetBIOS. In a simple NetBIOS network—no matter what protocol you're running—a NetBIOS system claims a NetBIOS name for itself simply by broadcasting out to the rest of the network (Figure 14-24). As long as no other sys-

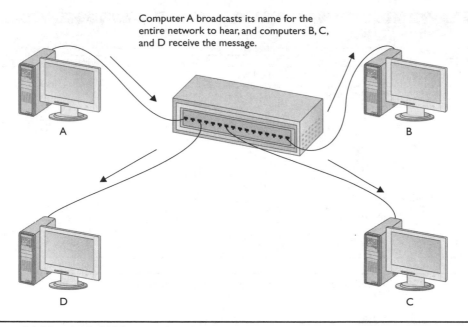

Computer A broadcasts its name for the entire network to hear, and computers B, C, and D receive the message.

Figure 14-24   A NetBIOS system broadcasting its name

tem is already using that name, it works just fine. Of course, broadcasting can be a bit of a problem for routers and such, but remember that this example presumes a single network on the same wire, so it's okay in this context.

Remember that NetBIOS was invented way back in the early 1980s. Microsoft had a big investment in NetBIOS, and had to support a large installed base of systems, so even after NetBEUI (the network protocol NetBIOS was designed for) began to lose market share to TCP/IP, Microsoft had to continue to support NetBIOS or incur the wrath of millions of customers. What happened next seems in retrospect more a comedy than the machinations of the most powerful software company in the world. Microsoft did something that should not have been possible: they redesigned NetBIOS to work with TCP/IP. Let's look at some of the strategies and techniques they used to make NetBIOS and TCP/IP coexist on the same network.

One early strategy Microsoft came up with to reduce the overhead from NetBIOS broadcasts was to use a special text file called LMHOSTS. LMHOSTS contains a list of the NetBIOS names and corresponding TCP/IP names of the host systems on the network. Sound familiar? Well, it should—the LMHOSTS file works exactly the same way as the DNS HOSTS file. Although Microsoft still supports LMHOSTS file usage, and every Windows system has an LMHOSTS file for backward compatibility, networks that still need NetBIOS support will usually run WINS servers. WINS servers let NetBIOS hosts register their names with just the one server, eliminating the need for broadcasting and thereby reducing NetBIOS overhead substantially. Figure 14-25 shows the copy of the WINS server that comes with Windows 2000 Server. Note that the PCs on this network have registered their names with the WINS server.

Record Name	Type	IP Address	State	Static	Owner
-__MSBROWSE__-	[01h] Other	192.168.4.11	Released		192.168.4.150
__VMWARE_US...	[03h] Messenger	192.168.4.20	Active		192.168.4.150
ADMIN	[03h] Messenger	192.168.4.19	Tombstoned		192.168.4.150
ADMINISTRATOR	[03h] Messenger	192.168.4.20	Active		192.168.4.150
AMBERK	[00h] WorkStation	192.168.4.8	Active		192.168.4.150
AMBERK	[03h] Messenger	192.168.4.8	Active		192.168.4.150
AMBERK	[20h] File Server	192.168.4.8	Active		192.168.4.150
BFUTURE	[03h] Messenger	192.168.4.59	Released		192.168.4.150
CARY	[00h] WorkStation	192.168.4.10	Active		192.168.4.150
CARY	[03h] Messenger	192.168.4.10	Active		192.168.4.150
CARY	[20h] File Server	192.168.4.10	Active		192.168.4.150
CARYD	[03h] Messenger	192.168.4.10	Active		192.168.4.150
CDOBA	[00h] WorkStation	192.168.4.11	Released		192.168.4.150
CHRIS	[00h] WorkStation	192.168.4.11	Released		192.168.4.150

Figure 14-25 The WINS server that comes with Windows 2000 Server

 NOTE You can find an LMHOSTS.SAM file on your Windows system. Use Notepad to open the file and inspect its contents.

There are only two good reasons to use a WINS server: (1) to reduce overhead from broadcasts; and (2) to enable NetBIOS name resolution across routers. What does a WINS server have to do with routers, you ask? Just this: the WINS server enables NetBIOS to function in a routed network. IP routers are programmed to *kill* all broadcasts, remember? While newer Windows clients will just register directly with the WINS server, older (pre-Win95) Windows systems will still try to broadcast. To get around this problem, you can configure a system to act as a *WINS relay agent,* forwarding WINS broadcasts to a WINS server on the other side of the router (see Figure 14-26).

The bottom line with WINS servers is this: larger or routed networks that run NetBIOS still need them. As long as Windows NT and Windows 9x systems are out there running NetBIOS, don't be surprised to find that some system somewhere is running a WINS server.

Configuring WINS Clients

You don't need to do much to get a Windows client to use WINS. In fact, you only need to configure the IP address of a WINS server in its WINS settings under Network Properties. From now on, the Windows system will look for a WINS server to register its NetBIOS name. If it finds a WINS server, it will register its NetBIOS name to the WINS server; if it doesn't, it will automatically start broadcasting its NetBIOS name. You can

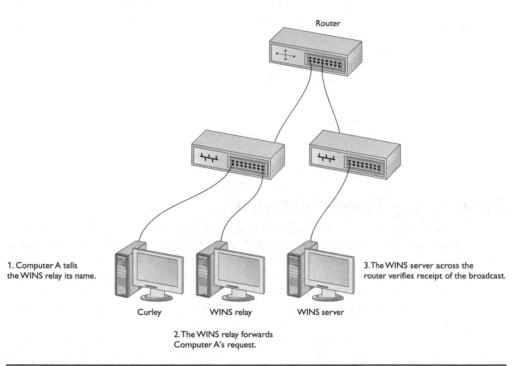

1. Computer A tells the WINS relay its name.

3. The WINS server across the router verifies receipt of the broadcast.

Curley

WINS relay

WINS server

2. The WINS relay forwards Computer A's request.

Figure 14-26   A WINS relay agent forwarding broadcasts across a router

add WINS information to DHCP if necessary, so unless you're running static IPs, you may never have to enter anything into your Windows clients to get WINS to work.

Troubleshooting WINS

Most WINS problems are not WINS problems at all. They are NetBIOS problems. By far, the most common problem is having two systems share the same name. In that case, you get a pretty clear error. It looks different in different versions of Windows, but it usually says about the same thing: another system has this name. How do you fix it? Change the name of the system!

The program we turn to for help with NetBIOS problems is called *NBTSTAT*. NBTSTAT will do a number of jobs, depending on the switches you add to the end of the command. The -c switch, for example, tells NBTSTAT to check the current NetBIOS name cache (yup, NetBIOS caches names just like some systems cache DNS names). The NetBIOS name cache contains the NetBIOS names and corresponding IP addresses that have been resolved by a particular host. You can use NBTSTAT to see if the WINS server has supplied inaccurate addresses to a WINS client. Here's an example of the **NBTSTAT -c** command and its results:

```
C:\ >NBTSTAT -c

Node IpAddress: [192.168.43.5] Scope Id: []
                 NetBIOS Remote Cache Name Table

    Name            Type      Host Address    Life [sec]
    -------------------------------------------------------
    WRITERS    <1B>  UNIQUE    192.168.43.13      420
    SCOTT      <20>  UNIQUE    192.168.43.3       420
    VENUSPDC   <00>  UNIQUE    192.168.43.13      120
    MIKE       <20>  UNIQUE    192.168.43.2       420
    NOTES01    <20>  UNIQUE    192.168.43.4       420
```

Diagnosing TCP/IP Networks

I've dedicated an entire chapter to network diagnostic procedures, but TCP/IP has a few little extras that I want to talk about here. TCP/IP is a pretty tough little protocol, and in good networks, it runs like a top for years without problems. Most of the TCP/IP problems you'll see come from improper configuration, so I'm going to assume you've run into problems with a new TCP/IP install, and we'll look at some classic screw-ups common in this situation. I want to concentrate on making sure you can ping anyone you want to ping.

I've done thousands of IP installations over the years, and I'm proud to say that, in most cases, they worked right the first time. My users jumped on the newly configured systems, fired up their Network Neighborhoods, e-mail software, and web browsers, and were last seen typing away, smiling from ear to ear. But I'd be a liar if I didn't also admit that plenty of setups didn't work so well. Let's start with the hypothetical case of a user who can't see something on the network. You get a call: "Help!" they cry. The first troubleshooting point to remember here: it doesn't matter *what* they can't see. It doesn't matter if they can't see other systems in Network Neighborhood, or they can't see the home page on their browser, because you go through the same steps in any event.

Remember to use common sense and more than one brain cell at a time wherever possible. If the problem system can't ping by DNS name, but all the other systems can, is the DNS server down? Of course not! If something—*anything*—doesn't work on one system, *always* try it on another one to determine if the problem is specific to one system or affects the entire network.

One thing I always do is check the network connections and protocols. We're going to cover those topics in greater detail later in the book, so, for now, we'll assume our problem systems are properly connected and have good protocols installed. Here are some steps to take:

1. *Diagnose the NIC.* First, use PING with the loopback address to determine if the system can send and receive packets. Specifically, type **PING 127.0.0.1** or **PING LOCALHOST** (remember the HOSTS file?). If you're not getting a good response, your NIC has a problem! Check your NIC's driver and replace it if necessary.

2. *Diagnose locally.* If the card's okay, diagnose locally by pinging a few neighboring systems, both by IP address and DNS name. If you're using NetBIOS, use the **NET VIEW** command to see if the other local systems are visible (see Figure 14-27).

Figure 14-27
NET VIEW shows other local systems.

```
C:\>net view
Servers available in workgroup WHEEBO.
Server name              Remark

\\JANELLE
\\DANA
\\HIATT
\\AMBER
The command was completed successfully.

C:\>net view \\Dana
Shared resources at \\DANA

Sharename       Type           Comment

C               Disk
Dana's F        Disk
HP Something    Print          HP DeskJet 692C
TS              Disk
ZIP 100MB       Disk
The command was completed successfully.

C:\>
```

If you can't ping by DNS, check your DNS settings. If you can't see the network using NET VIEW, you may have a problem with your NetBIOS settings.

If you're having a problem pinging locally, make sure you have the right IP address and subnet mask. Oh, if I had a nickel for every time I entered those incorrectly! If you're on DHCP, try renewing the lease—sometimes that will do the trick. If DHCP fails, call the person in charge of the server.

TIP A good testing trick is to use the NET SEND command to try sending messages to other systems. Not all versions of Windows support NET SEND, however.

At this point, another little handy program comes into play called *NETSTAT*. NETSTAT offers a number of options. The two handiest ways to run NETSTAT are with no options at all, and with the –s option. Running NETSTAT with no options will show you all the current connections to your system. Look for a connection here that isn't working with an application—that's often a clue to an application problem, such as a broken application or a sneaky application running in the background. Figure 14-28 shows a NETSTAT program running.

Figure 14-28
NETSTAT

```
Microsoft Windows 2000 [Version 5.00.2195]
(C) Copyright 1985-2000 Microsoft Corp.

C:\>netstat

Active Connections

  Proto  Local Address          Foreign Address        State
  TCP    dana:microsoft-ds      CHRISD:2546            ESTABLISHED
  TCP    dana:3832              UPN:1376               ESTABLISHED
  TCP    dana:3837              UPN:1376               ESTABLISHED
  TCP    dana:4164              AMBERK:microsoft-ds    ESTABLISHED
  TCP    dana:4168              server.totalhome:microsoft-ds  ESTABLISHED
  TCP    dana:4235              UPN:netbios-ssn        TIME_WAIT
  TCP    dana:4237              UPN:microsoft-ds       TIME_WAIT

C:\>_
```

Running NETSTAT with the –s option displays several statistics that can help you diagnose problems. For example, if the display shows you are sending but not receiving, you almost certainly have a bad cable with a broken receive wire.

3. *Diagnose to the gateway.* If you can't get out to the Internet, check to see if you can ping the router. Remember, the router has two interfaces, so try both: first the local interface (the one on your subnet), and then the one to the Internet. You *do* have both of those IP addresses memorized, don't you? You should! If you can't ping the router, either it's down, or you're not connected to it. If you can only ping the near side, something in the router itself is messed up.

4. *Diagnose to the Internet.* If you can ping the router, it's time to try to ping something on the Internet. If you can't ping one address, try another—it's always possible that the first place you try to ping is down. If you still can't get through, you can try to locate the problem using the *TRACERT* (trace route) command. TRACERT will mark out the entire route the ping packet traveled between you and whatever you were trying to ping, and even better, it will tell you where the problem lies (see Figure 14-29).

```
C:\>tracert 216.115.108.243

Tracing route to img3.yahoo.com [216.115.108.243]
over a maximum of 30 hops:

  1     30 ms     30 ms     30 ms  houston-interface-static-01.redback.jump.net [21
6.30.120.1]
  2     20 ms     20 ms     20 ms  hou-core-01-f1-0-0.jump.net [206.196.64.1]
  3     20 ms     30 ms     30 ms  gigabitethernet5-0-178.hsipaccess2.Houston1.Leve
l3.net [209.247.109.113]
  4     20 ms     20 ms     20 ms  ge-6-0-1.mp1.Houston1.Level3.net [209.247.11.185
]
  5     60 ms     71 ms     60 ms  so-3-0-0.mp2.SanJose1.Level3.net [64.159.1.130]

  6     60 ms     70 ms     60 ms  gigabitethernet10-2.ipcolo4.SanJose1.Level3.net
[64.159.2.170]
  7      *         *         *     Request timed out.
  8     80 ms     90 ms     90 ms  ge-3-3-0.msr1.pao.yahoo.com [216.115.101.42]
  9     80 ms     90 ms    100 ms  vl20.bas1.snv.yahoo.com [216.115.100.225]
 10      *        90 ms     90 ms  img3.yahoo.com [216.115.108.243]

Trace complete.

C:\>
```

Figure 14-29   Simple TRACERT

Chapter Review

Questions

1. NetBIOS uses what type of name space?

    A. Hierarchical name space

    B. People name space

    C. DNS name space

    D. Flat name space

2. The DNS root directory is represented by what symbol?

    A. . (dot)

    B. / (forward slash)

    C. \ (back slash)

    D. $ (dollar sign)

3. What command do you use to see the DNS cache on a Windows 2000 system?

    A. WINIPCFG /SHOWDNS

    B. IPCONFIG /SHOWDNS

    C. IPCONFIG /DISPLAYDNS

    D. WINIPCFG /DISPLAYDNS

4. What do you call the pool of IP addresses that a DHCP server may allocate to client systems?

    A. DHCP pool

    B. DHCP scope

    C. DHCP array

    D. DHCP lease

5. What folder in the DHCS program lists the systems currently leasing DHCP IP addresses?

    A. Reservations

    B. Address Pool

    C. Address Leases

    D. Current Addresses

6. The users on your network haven't been able to connect to the server for 30 minutes. You check and reboot the server, but it's unable to ping either its own loopback address or any of your client systems. What should you do?

    A. Restart the DHCP server.

    B. Restart the DNS server.

    C. Replace the NIC on the server, because it has failed.

    D. Have your users ping the server.

7. What are the two reasons to use a WINS server?

    A. To reduce overhead from broadcasts

    B. To facilitate broadcast of NetBIOS names

    C. To support Windows XP systems on IP networks

    D. To enable NetBIOS name resolution across routers

8. What command do you use to check the current NetBIOS name cache?

    A. NETSTAT –n

    B. NETSTAT –c

    C. NBTSTAT –n

    D. NBTSTAT –c

9. A user calls to say she can't see the other systems on the network when she looks in Network Neighborhood. You are not using NetBIOS. What are your first two troubleshooting steps?

    A. Ping the address of a known web site.

    B. Ping the loopback address to test her NIC.

    C. Ping several neighboring systems using both DNS names and IP addresses.

    D. Ping the IP addresses of the router.

10. When troubleshooting a network using NetBIOS, what command do you use to see if the other local systems are visible?

    A. NBTSTAT

    B. NET VIEW

    C. NBT VIEW

    D. VIEW LOCAL

Answers

1. **D.** NetBIOS uses a flat name space, while DNS servers use a hierarchical name space.

2. **A.** The DNS root directory is represented by a dot (.).

3. **C.** To see the DNS cache on a Windows 2000 or XP system, run the command **IPCONFIG /DISPLAYDNS** at a command prompt.

4. **B.** A DHCP scope is the pool of IP addresses that a DHCP server may allocate to client systems.

5. **C.** The Address Leases folder in the DHCS program lists the systems currently leasing DHCP IP addresses. The Address Pool folder lists the range of available IP addresses.

6. **C.** You should replace the server's NIC, because it's bad. It doesn't need either DNS or DHCP to ping its loopback address. Having the users ping the server is also pointless, as you already know they can't connect to it.

7. **A, D.** Two reasons to use a WINS server are to reduce overhead from broadcasts and to enable NetBIOS name resolution across routers. WINS servers eliminate the need for broadcasting NetBIOS names. They are needed by Windows 9*x* and NT systems running on IP networks; WINS is not even native to Windows 2000 and XP.

8. **D.** You use the **NBTSTAT –c** command to check the current NetBIOS name cache.

9. **B, C.** Your first two troubleshooting steps are to ping the loopback address—to check the client's NIC—and to ping neighboring systems. If the NIC and the local network check out, then you might try pinging the router and a web site, but those are later steps.

10. **B.** When troubleshooting a network using NetBIOS, use the **NET VIEW** command to see if the other local systems are visible.

PART III

TCP/IP and the Internet

The Network+ Certification exam expects you to know how to
- 1.6   Identify the purposes, features, and functions of the following network components: routers, gateways, firewalls
- 2.10   Define the purpose, function, and use of the following protocols used in the TCP/IP (Transmission Control Protocol/Internet Protocol) suite: FTP, TFTP, SMTP, HTTP, HTTPS, POP3/IMAP4, Telnet
- 2.13   Identify the purpose of network services and protocols (for example: NAT – Network Address Translation)
- 3.6   Identify the purpose, benefits, and characteristics of using a proxy service

To achieve these goals, you must be able to
- Explain how routers work using routing tables
- Define static and dynamic routers, and name different dynamic routing standards
- Explain network address translation (NAT) and proxy serving
- Define FTP, TFTP, SMTP, HTTP, HTTPS, POP3/IMAP4, and Telnet

The Internet uses TCP/IP to enable computers—and people—from all over the world to communicate. You've seen TCP/IP in operation on lesser networks in previous chapters and have by now a good understanding of how the protocol suite works. This chapter enables you to apply that knowledge to the grandest network of all, the Internet. The chapter starts with an in-depth look into the machines that form the backbone of the Internet—routers—and then explores the many tools that make the Internet run, such as network address translation (NAT), proxy servers, HTTP, FTP, e-mail, Telnet, and SSH (Secure Shell).

Test Specific

Real World Routers

Routers, routers, routers! The word "router" invariably seems to send chills down the spines of folks just starting out in the networking world as they contemplate these magic boxes that create all the connections that make up the Internet. Although I've referenced routers in numerous spots—you've even had a peek at a routing table—you need to know more. We know a *router* directs incoming network protocol packets from one LAN

Figure 15-1   Routers

to another based on OSI Network layer information stored in the incoming packets—in the case of TCP/IP that means IP addresses. Routers determine where packets must go via their routing tables. To route these packets, a router by definition must have at least two interfaces, although some routers have three or more, depending on the needs of the network. If you think about it for a moment, a router acts a lot like a switch, except it works on the OSI Network layer (Layer 3), while a typical switch works on the OSI Data Link layer (Layer 2). That's why you hear a lot of network folks call a regular switch a *layer 2 switch* and a router a *layer 3 switch*. Be comfortable using both terms, as techs tend to use them interchangeably, even in the same sentence (see Figure 15-1).

Routers come in a dizzying variety of shapes, sizes, and functions. You find little routers used in homes and small businesses, like the handy-dandy Linksys router I use at my house (see Figure 15-2), and mid-sized routers used to connect a couple of buildings. At the top end are the massive backbone routers that literally make the big connections on the Internet (see Figure 15-3).

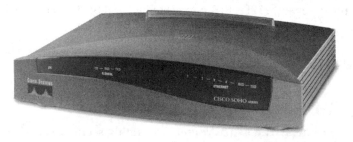

Figure 15-2   Little router

Figure 15-3 Big routers

You don't necessarily need special hardware to have a router. Pretty much every modern operating system enables you to turn a PC into a router by adding an extra NIC, modem, or some other device to connect to another LAN. Figure 15-4 shows a screen shot from my old router, a beat-up Pentium 166 system with two NICs, no hard drive or CD-ROM drive, running a handy little Linux-based router program—called Coyote Linux (www.coyotelinux.com)—completely from the floppy drive.

```
        Coyote Linux Gateway -- configuration menu

    1 ) Network settings          4) Change system password

    2 ) System settings
    3 ) Package settings

    c) Show running configuration   b) Back-up configuration

                                    h) Help
q) quit
------------------------------------------------------------
    Selection:
```

Figure 15-4 Coyote Linux configuration screen

The vast majority of routers seen in the small- to medium-sized networks act as nothing more than a tool to link your LAN to the Internet via your local ISP. In almost all cases, these routers, whether a special box or just a PC in the network, will have two interfaces: a NIC that connects to your LAN and some other connection that links to a regular phone line, a more advanced telephone connection like ISDN, ADSL, or T1, or maybe a cable modem. Whatever the connection type, these two-interface-only routers are extremely common.

People often describe the Internet as a network of computers, but there's a strong argument to call the Internet a network of routers. Because the Internet is a world-wide network, the most important connections—often called *backbones*—are the long distance connections between cities. When a piece of fiber-optic cable runs from, say, Houston to Chicago, the ends of that connection go to powerful routers like the ones displayed in Figure 15-3, not to computers! Add a few thousand more connections like the one running between Houston and Chicago, and then you see the Internet—a massive network of routers, spanning the entire globe.

 NOTE In terms of basic function, there's not much difference between a powerful, high-end router and a small SOHO router other than the amount of traffic they can handle.

We can divide all routers into one of two functions. A regular router is typically a device that only connects to other routers. A *gateway* or *gateway router* connects individual LANs to a larger network—usually the Internet. Gateway routers also have extra functions built into them to protect the LAN or to support individual computers that a regular router doesn't. We'll see some of these gateway functions in this chapter.

People often become confused when they hear the terms gateway and default gateway, and in truth, the terms are often synonymous. The term *default gateway* can refer to the hardware router (as in, "that box is my default gateway to the Internet"), but you'll also find it specifically referred to as the *IP address* of the router interface that connects to your LAN, called the *local side* or the *local interface* of your router (see Figure 15-5). The distinction is not of critical importance, but just be aware of different uses of the term when a fellow tech starts talking.

The Network+ exam doesn't expect you to know how to configure a router, but you should be familiar with some of the ways those who do configure routers do it. To use an analogy, if this were an exam about automobiles, you wouldn't actually have to drive a car, but you would need to be able to explain how drivers steer and brake. Get it? A key basic feature of the router is the *routing table*. All routers have a built-in routing table that tells them how to send packets. Where does this routing table information come from? Let's look at how routing tables get created.

Static Routes

In the bleak old days of the Internet, routing tables were composed entirely of static entries. In other words, somebody who really understood routers (and subnetting) had to type this information into the routing table. The router person would link into the

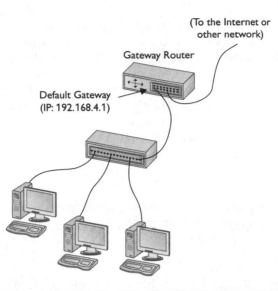

Figure 15-5   A default gateway

router using a serial cable or something called Telnet (see the "Telnet" section later in this chapter) and type in a command to add or remove static routes from the routing table. Would you like to see a routing table? If you're sitting at a Windows or UNIX/Linux system, get to a prompt and type in one of these two commands: NETSTAT—NR or ROUTE PRINT. Both of these commands result in basically the same output as shown in Figure 15-6.

```
Microsoft(R) Windows DOS
(C)Copyright Microsoft Corp 1990-1999.

C:\>route print
===========================================================================
Interface List
0x1 ........................... MS TCP Loopback interface
0x1000003 ...00 80 ad 7b 48 39 ...... PCI Bus Master Adapter
===========================================================================
===========================================================================
Active Routes:
Network Destination        Netmask          Gateway        Interface  Metric
          0.0.0.0          0.0.0.0    192.168.4.152   192.168.4.15       1
        127.0.0.0        255.0.0.0        127.0.0.1       127.0.0.1       1
      192.168.4.0    255.255.255.0     192.168.4.15    192.168.4.15       1
     192.168.4.15  255.255.255.255        127.0.0.1       127.0.0.1       1
    192.168.4.255  255.255.255.255     192.168.4.15    192.168.4.15       1
        224.0.0.0        224.0.0.0     192.168.4.15    192.168.4.15       1
  255.255.255.255  255.255.255.255     192.168.4.15    192.168.4.15       1
Default Gateway:      192.168.4.152
===========================================================================
Persistent Routes:
  None

C:\>_
```

Figure 15-6   ROUTE PRINT output

Every IP client has a routing table. Does that mean that every IP client is a router? Well, sort of. IP clients are routers in the sense that they need to know how to address their outgoing packets. An IP client refers to its routing table when it sends packets. Now, you may be thinking that it seems kind of silly for a client to have a routing table when it only has one interface—I mean, where else is it going to send these packets? Two exceptions should make the need for a routing table clear. First, some packets—such as loopback—don't go beyond the PC. The host needs to know *not* to send loopback packets out, but rather to loop them back. Second, a single host may have multiple NICs, with each NIC assigned a different job. The best way to see this is to take a few moments to understand how to read a routing table, using Figure 15-6 as our guide.

NOTE   The routing table examples used here are from a Windows system. All routing tables—from the one in your Windows PC, to the one in a Linux system, to the routing table in a hardware router—are virtually identical.

Routing tables typically consist of a number of routes, each listed as a single line in the routing table. Each route consists of five columns of information needed to determine where a packet is to go on the network: the Network Destination, Netmask, Gateway, Interface, and Metric.

- **Network Destination**   This is the IP address of the outgoing packet and refers to either a single address or a network ID.

- **Netmask**   The netmask is similar to a subnet mask and is compared to the Network destination to determine where the packet is sent. Zeroes in the netmask mean any value is acceptable. Ones mean the value must be exact. Default netmask usually use the classfull 0 and 255 values but they can also use classless values. Remember your subnetting rules if you see values other than 0 or 255 in the netmask!

- **Gateway**   This determines the gateway for a packet. On an IP client, this is commonly either the true default gateway for the network, the loopback, or the IP address of the client's NIC.

- **Interface**   This determines through which NIC to send out the packet. On an IP client, this is either the loopback or the NIC's IP address.

- **Metric**   This determines the number of hops to the destination. A *hop* is the number of local networks the packet must move through. In most cases, this is just 1: the client's local network.

Great, let's now look at each line in Figure 15-6 and see how the routing table works for a client system. In a routing table, the least restrictive route is listed first, followed by more and more restrictive routes with the most restrictive routes at the bottom of the list. Let me explain.

Here's the first line in the routing table (with column headers added to each route for clarity):

Network Destination	Netmask	Gateway	Interface	Metric
0.0.0.0	0.0.0.0	192.168.4.152	192.168.4.27	1

The network destination of all zeroes means no restriction on the IP address. The netmask of all zeroes means no restriction on the netmask. Your machine interprets this entry to mean that every packet goes out on interface 192.168.4.27 (the client's NIC) via gateway 192.168.4.152, which is in this local network (Metric of 1). In other words, send everything out to the gateway. This is great except for the fact that you'll have other options further down in the routing table. The best way to think of how the routing table works is to think that every packet goes through every route of the routing table until it finds the "best fit" for the route it needs. Even though the first route defines a default route for any packet, other routes further down the list might be more detailed. (As we go further into the list this will make more sense.) As you read the next line, think of the word "except" as you read it. Here's the next line:

Network Destination	Netmask	Gateway	Interface	Metric
127.0.0.0	255.0.0.0	127.0.0.1	127.0.0.1	1

So, this provides the first "except" clause: "Except if the packet is addressed for the 127.0.0.0/8 network." In that case, send it out to the 127.0.0.1 interface (the loopback) using the loopback as the gateway. This packet won't use a gateway; the routing table says this by using the client's loopback address rather than the true gateway. Any packet that starts with 127 will loop back. Next line!

Network Destination	Netmask	Gateway	Interface	Metric
192.168.4.0	255.255.255.0	192.168.4.27	192.168.4.27	1

Here's the next except clause: "Except if the IP address is in the network ID of 192.168.4/24." In that case, send the packet out on the client's NIC without using the gateway. This is a local address. When you (or when DHCP) enter the IP address and the subnet mask into you system, you are just updating the routing table! Neat, eh? Next line!

Network Destination	Netmask	Gateway	Interface	Metric
192.168.4.27	255.255.255.255	127.0.0.1	127.0.0.1	1

Here's the next except clause: "Except if the destination address is exactly for 192.168.4.27." In that case just loopback! Next line!

Network Destination	Netmask	Gateway	Interface	Metric
192.168.4.255	255.255.255.255	192.168.4.27	192.168.4.27	1

Here's the next except clause: "Except if the destination address is specifically for 192.168.4.255 (the broadcast address for the local network)." In that case, send it out the NIC without using a gateway. Next line!

Network Destination	Netmask	Gateway	Interface	Metric
224.0.0.0	224.0.0.0	192.168.4.27	192.168.4.27	1

PART III

Here's the next except clause: "Except if the packet is a multicast packet." In that case send it out to the local network through the NIC without a gateway. Programs that generate multicast packets are uncommon but they do have their niches. Symantec's Ghost drive imaging software is one example of a program that uses multicast addresses. Next line!

```
Network Destination        Netmask         Gateway        Interface  Metric
    255.255.255.255  255.255.255.255     192.168.4.27    192.168.4.27       1
```

And the final except clause: "Except if the destination address is exactly for 255.255.255.255 (another broadcast address for the network)." In that case send it out the NIC without using a gateway.

Keep in mind that there's nothing to stop a client from having more than one NIC. I often put a second NIC in my system when I want to test some network thingy without trashing my real network. In that case, my routing table is going to look a lot more complex, as you can see in Figure 15-7. Just look at the Interface column. You'll see I now have two IP addresses: 192.168.4.27 and 203.14.12.1, one for each NIC. Without the routing table, my system wouldn't know which NIC to use to send packets.

By the same token, a regular IP client is not a router in that both NICs are completely separated on the routing table. If you look at the routing table, you won't see any rows that say to send anything with a network destination of network ID 192.168.4.27 to Interface 203.14.12.1. If this were a router you would see rows that instructed the system how to route data from one interface to the other and trust me, there are none here. So, even though IP clients do have routing tables, they don't route by default in the classic sense of moving packets from one network to another. They do route in the sense that it is the routing table that decides whether to send a packet to the gateway or just to keep it on the local network (although nothing stops you from turning the client into a router).

```
C:\>route print
===========================================================================
Interface List
0x1 ........................... MS TCP Loopback interface
0x1000003 ...00 a0 c9 98 97 7f ...... Intel(R) PRO/100+ PCI Adapter
0x3000005 ...00 50 56 c0 00 01 ...... VMware Virtual Ethernet Adapter
===========================================================================
===========================================================================
Active Routes:
Network Destination        Netmask         Gateway        Interface  Metric
        0.0.0.0          0.0.0.0     192.168.4.152    192.168.4.27       1
      127.0.0.0        255.0.0.0       127.0.0.1       127.0.0.1       1
    192.168.4.0    255.255.255.0     192.168.4.27    192.168.4.27       1
   192.168.4.27  255.255.255.255       127.0.0.1       127.0.0.1       1
  192.168.4.255  255.255.255.255     192.168.4.27    192.168.4.27       1
    203.14.12.0    255.255.255.0     203.14.12.1     203.14.12.1       1
    203.14.12.1  255.255.255.255       127.0.0.1       127.0.0.1       1
  203.14.12.255  255.255.255.255     203.14.12.1     203.14.12.1       1
      224.0.0.0        224.0.0.0     192.168.4.27    192.168.4.27       1
      224.0.0.0        224.0.0.0     203.14.12.1     203.14.12.1       1
255.255.255.255  255.255.255.255     192.168.4.27    192.168.4.27       1
Default Gateway:       192.168.4.152
===========================================================================
Persistent Routes:
  None

C:\>
```

Figure 15-7   Routing table for Mike's PC with two NICs

The question now becomes this: Where did this routing table come from? Was it entered statically? Thank goodness no! Your system generates this table at boot based on your IP information. Static IP addresses are rarely used in client systems unless something unique is taking place. Remember the subnetting scenario discussed in Chapter 11, "TCP/IP," where you had to configure the routing table to split one subnet into two? That would be one situation that would require you to do this—but leave that to the router gurus!

SNMP

One big question I often receive from someone new to routers is "How do I access the router to make changes? For example, how can I add a static route to a router?" The oldest way is using a terminal. Heavy duty routers come with special configuration ports, usually serial ports. You connect a PC to that port, and then use a terminal program to connect to the router. Cisco's IOS routing software is a classic example. These interfaces are text-based and challenging to use but powerful. Lower-end routers will use a web-based interface like the one shown in Figure 15-8.

A *static route* tells a router a specific path to use to reach another network. In a small network, you could tell the router which IP to use for Internet traffic, for example, and which to use for internal traffic.

You can use a powerful protocol called *Simple Network Management Protocol (SNMP)* to track the status of routers. SNMP gives smart devices—routers, switches, and individual PCs—the capability to report their status and to allow administrators to make changes. SNMP-capable devices are common on all but the lowest echelon of networking hardware.

Most small- to medium-sized routers today do not use static routing—that would be entirely too cumbersome for hard working router administrators! Rather, they use some sort of dynamic routing. Let's go there now.

Dynamic Routing

Early on in the life of the Internet it became painfully clear that routers using only static IPs were incapable of handling the demands of anything but a network where nothing changed. If a new router was introduced to the network, it was useless until humans could get in and update not only the new router but also all of the new router's neighbors. While this might have worked when the number of routers on the Internet was small, it simply did not work as the number began to grow past a few dozen.

Furthermore, neither TCP/IP nor the Internet was ever designed to run on only static routers. When DARPA first created the entire concept of TCP/IP and the Internet, they were tasked by the U.S. military to create a network that could survive having any single part disappear under a mushroom cloud. In reality, the Internet invented routers more than routers invented the Internet. The Internet's designers visualized a mesh of routers, each having at least three connections, to provide a large level of redundancy in the case of multiple connection failures. They never realized just how large this mesh of routers would someday become!

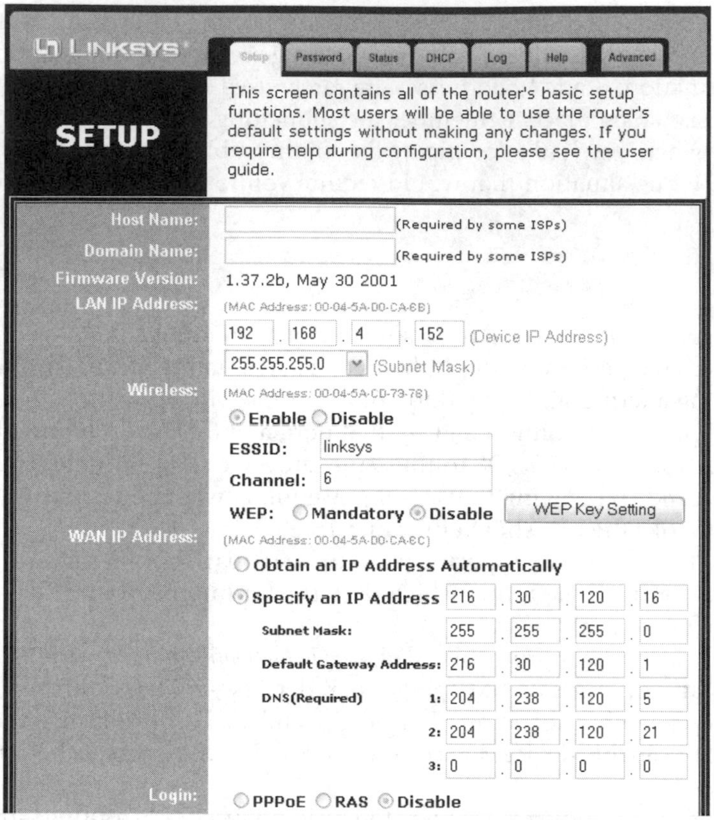

Figure 15-8 Linksys router web interface

All these routers needed to be able to communicate with each other in such a way that they could detect changes to the network and redirect routes to new interfaces without human intervention. Certainly, a router would initially have a few routes listed on its routing table, but once the router started operating, it would need to update the table. The answer: *dynamic routing*.

Like every other aspect of the Internet and TCP/IP, dynamic routing methods have grown in number and complexity over the years. The variety of these methods—with fun acronyms and initials such as RIP, OSPF, BGP, and IGRP—has reached a point where we categorize them into two types: interior routing methods and exterior routing methods. Interior routing methods are used primarily in routed private networks and smaller Internet ISPs. The main Internet backbone and large ISPs use exterior gateway routing methods. Let's check them out.

The oldest of all routing methods is called *Routing Information Protocol (RIP)*. Developed in the late 1970s and early 1980s, RIP stood alone as the only routing method for many years. RIP uses a *distance vector algorithm*—basically just a nice way to say that neighboring routers share their routing tables. RIP is now only used as an interior routing protocol, having long been kicked off the more critical Internet routers. RIP has a number of shortcomings. In particular, RIP routers do not respond rapidly to changes and tend to flood the network with information as they update. Regardless of these shortcomings, you can count on any router knowing how to do RIP. Most interior routers still use RIP, but it is slowly being replaced by OSPF.

TIP Among its many shortcomings, one item in particular prevents RIP from use on the Internet: it can handle a maximum of only 16 hops.

The *Open Shortest Path First (OSPF)* methodology is a much newer and far better way to update routers dynamically. OSPF routers use a *link state* algorithm: routers constantly monitor their neighbors with tiny messages—called *hellos*—and share more detailed information—called *link state advertisements*. If a connection is lost or created, the routers share only the changed information with their neighboring routers. A RIP router sends routing information at a set interval, even if there is no change.

Knowing that an exterior gateway protocol is used on the Internet backbone, and that there's only one Internet, you shouldn't be too surprised to learn that the Internet uses only one exterior gateway routing protocol: *Border Gateway Protocol (BGP)*. BGP has also been around for quite some time, but it has gone through a number of iterations. The current one is BGP-4. BGP works using a distance vector methodology like RIP, but once the routers have initially exchanged routing tables, they only pass changes in their tables, rather than entire tables, dramatically reducing router traffic.

NOTE I couldn't discuss routing methods without at least mentioning Interior Gateway Routing Protocol (IGRP) and its successor, Enhanced Interior Gateway Routing Protocol (EIGRP). Cisco developed these protocols to work in enterprise-wide routing environments. If Cisco had its way, EIGRP would replace BGP-4 as the primary Internet protocol!

In addition to routing protocols, most routers offer extra features such as the capability to read an incoming IP packet and send it along on another port to another destination based on network ID and subnet mask. Although these are not "official" router functions, these processes—called natural address translation (NAT) and proxy serving—have become closely associated with routers, in particular gateway routers that connect local networks to the Internet. Let's look at both of these router-like features in detail and see how they are used to connect to the Internet.

Connecting to the Internet

If you're going to connect your local TCP/IP network to the Internet or to any other TCP/IP network, you're going to need a gateway router. Now, a router in the sense of a device that connects two different IP network is a marvel of technology, but it also has some limitations. First of all, every computer on the local network must have a legitimate Internet IP address. This is not always the best idea. Second, there just aren't that many

IP addresses available and getting enough IP addresses for every computer in your network might be rather expensive. Finally, "real" IP addresses mean your computers are exposed to hacking from outside your network.

Real IP addresses are not the only problem with routers. Another issue comes in the form of TCP/UDP ports. Routers, or at least the classic routers we've discussed so far, ignore port numbers. But hackers can take advantage of ports to do mean and nasty things to your computers.

The answer to both of these issues is to hide IP addresses and/or ports. The best place to go about this hiding business is at the interface between your local network and the larger network, that is, at the router. Most every router now has extra tools to do exactly this type of hiding. Two technologies that handle the majority of these hiding chores are called NAT and proxy server.

NAT

The Internet has a real problem with IP addresses, or rather a lack of IP addresses. Not only is it difficult to get public IP addresses for every system in your network, but most ISPs charge you for them. Additionally, any system using a public IP address is susceptible to hacking, requiring the use of protection devices called firewalls (see the firewall discussion in Chapter 17, "Protecting Your Network"). *Network address translation (NAT)* was created in an effort to reduce the demand for public IP addresses, and to provide more security to systems.

Network address translation is a process whereby a NAT program running on a system or a router translates a system's IP address into a different IP address before it's sent out to a larger network. A network using NAT will provide its systems with private IP addresses—192.168.1.*x* addresses are the most popular, but other private IP addresses work equally well. The system running the NAT software will have two interfaces, one connected to the internal network and the other connected to the larger network. The NAT program takes packets from the client systems bound for the larger network and translates their internal private IP addresses to its own public IP address, enabling many systems to share that single IP address (see Figure 15-9).

When a system sends a packet destined for another system on the Internet, it includes the destination IP address, the destination port, and its own IP address. It also includes an arbitrarily generated origination port number that will usually be used as the incoming port number for the return data of the session. The NAT uses the origination port number of the outgoing IP packet, recording that port number along with the internal IP address of the sending system into its own internal table. The NAT then replaces the sending system's IP address with its own IP address and sends the packet out to the Internet. When the packet returns from the larger network, the NAT refers to its internal table of IP addresses and port numbers to determine which system should receive the incoming packet (see Figure 15-10).

NAT is not the perfect solution for everything. It works well for networks where the clients access the Internet but are not themselves accessed by systems on the Internet. You don't place web servers as NAT clients, for example, because systems outside the

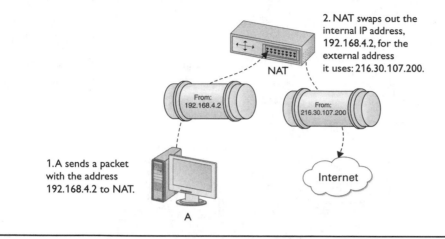

Figure 15-9 NAT swapping private and public IP addresses with wild abandon

network typically cannot access systems on the NAT. If you want a browser to be able to access your web server, you place the web server *outside* the NAT-controller area. Figure 15-11 shows a typical placement for a web server in a NAT network.

As more and more gateway routers have appeared in small networks, some folks wanted to place web servers and other servers inside the protected network, yet also make those servers accessible for folks across the Internet. As a result, many routers now come with a special feature called *port forwarding*. A router with port forwarding enables you to direct incoming traffic based on port number (like port 80 for HTTP) to a specific computer in your network. This computer will have a private address, but the router will forward packets with that specific port number to that one system.

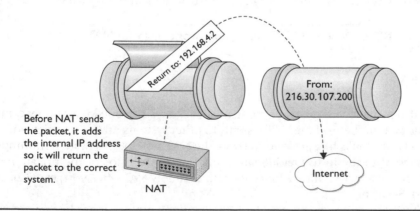

Figure 15-10 NAT adding more information

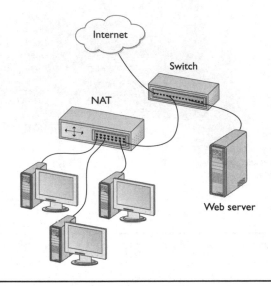

Figure 15-11   Typical placement of a web server in a NAT network

There are an amazing number of ways to implement NAT. You can use the NAT functions built into the OS (nearly every operating system comes with NAT capabilities) or you can buy a third-party NAT program to make any system with two interfaces a NAT server. You can even buy a router with built-in NAT. Many operating systems come with NAT programs, but in many cases you simply do not see them—they just work! Many of the popular gateway routers come with DHCP and NAT built into the same box. Even my little Linksys router (refer to Figure 15-8) has NAT built in. I just give it an IP address and a subnet mask for its internal interface and it automatically translates any IP address from my network. There simply aren't any NAT settings in many cases!

NOTE   Not all TCP/IP applications work well with NAT.

NAT also provides a strong defense against hacking since outsiders simply cannot see any of the systems behind the NAT system. To other systems on the Internet, your entire private network looks like just one system—the NAT system. Any system running a NAT gets labeled with the term *firewall,* since it acts as a protector of the private network. You'll learn that a firewall means much more than simply NAT when you get to Chapter 17, "Network Security."

NAT has become extremely popular for networking. In fact, it has become so popular that the long-anticipated day when the world runs out of IP addresses has thus far failed to materialize due to the dominance of networks using NAT (combined with dumping class licenses for CSLIDs—refer to Chapter 11, "TCP/IP," to refresh yourself on CSLID). A NAT's capability to enable multiple systems to share a single IP address, combined with strong protection against hacking, have made NATs as common as servers in most networks.

Proxy Server

A *proxy server* also hides your internal computers from outside networks but uses a totally different method. While a NAT translates incoming and outgoing IP addresses by switching out its own IP address for each system's IP address, a proxy server receives and sends encapsulated packets from specific applications. Proxy servers commonly translate the TCP port number to another port number. Because of this encapsulation and port translation, applications like web browsers and e-mail clients must be *proxy aware*—that is, they must be able to (a) know the IP address of the proxy server so they can encapsulate packets and (b) change their standard ports to whatever the proxy server uses. For example, HTTP uses TCP port 80 by default, but we can change the proxy server to accept only certain TCP port numbers, like port 88 for HTTP requests from clients. When the proxy server receives those requests, it will change the client system's IP address to its own, change the port back to 80, and then send the request out to the Internet (see Figure 15-12).

Proxy servers can dramatically improve performance for groups of users. This is because a proxy server can *cache* requests from users, greatly reducing network traffic. Most businesses access a few web sites frequently. Proxy servers can hold on to the information resulting from user requests for a prespecified amount of time, eliminating the need to reaccess that information from the remote site that contains the HTML document.

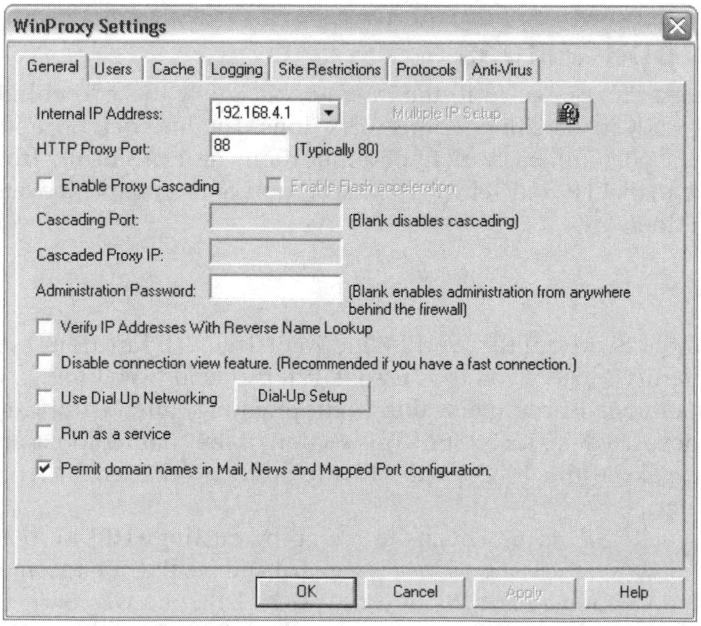

Figure 15-12 A proxy server at work

Proxy servers can also be used to filter requests. This can further secure a network by limiting the types of web sites and Internet resources its users can access. For instance, you can use a proxy server to block certain web sites (like BestBuy.com and Amazon.com) if you find that your employees spend work time shopping for music online.

So What's the Big Difference Between NAT and a Proxy, Anyway?

As you know by now, both proxies and NAT mask IP addresses, enabling a network to have a set of internal private IP addresses that use one public IP address to communicate with the Internet. The difference between using proxies and NAT is where they operate in the network structure. Proxies work at the application level, which means the relevant applications must know how to interact with a proxy, whereas NAT works at the router level, providing transparent Internet access to users.

Think of a proxy server as an old-time telephone operator in a hotel. Just as the hotel operator receives incoming calls for hotel guests and forwards them to the proper room, a proxy server takes incoming requests for Internet services (such as FTP) and forwards them to the actual applications that perform those services. Conversely, just as a guest needing an outside line would go through the hotel operator, a network user needing an Internet service goes through the proxy to the Internet. Because proxies provide replacement connections and act as gateways, they are sometimes known as *application-level gateways*.

Now that we know *how* information travels outside of your network, let's take a look at the information your users have been trying so hard to find.

TCP/IP Applications

Once you have a PC connected to the Internet, but safely tucked behind a protective router, you're ready to get some serious work done. The Internet, or more specifically, TCP/IP, offers a phenomenal variety of applications and protocols, from the World Wide Web to e-mail, FTP, and Telnet. The last section of this chapter covers these topics in detail. Let's do it!

The Web

Where would we be without the World Wide Web? The Web functions as the graphical face for the Internet. Most of you have used it, firing up your web browser to surf to one cool site after another, learning new things, clicking links, often ending up somewhere completely unexpected . . . it's all fun! This section of the chapter looks at the Web and the tools that make it function, specifically the protocols that enable communication over the Internet.

You can find an HTML document on the Internet by entering a URL in your web browser. A *URL*, short for *Uniform Resource Locator*, is a global address that all documents and other resources on the Web must have. When you type the URL of a web page, such as http://www.mhteched.com, you are telling the browser which TCP/IP application to use and typing the address by which your browser locates the HTML document on a remote computer.

HTTP

HTTP is short for *HyperText Transfer Protocol*. It is the underlying protocol used by the World Wide Web, and it runs by default on TCP/IP port 80. Notice the HTTP at the beginning of the URL in Figure 15-13. The HTTP at the beginning of the URL defines how messages are formatted and transmitted, and what actions web servers and browsers should take in response to various commands. When you enter a URL in your browser, it sends an HTTP command to the web server directing it to find and return the requested web page.

HTTP has a general weakness in its handling of web pages: it relays commands executed by users without reference to any commands previously executed. The problem with this is that web designers continue to design more complex and truly interactive web pages. HTTP is pretty dumb when it comes to remembering what people have done on a web site. Luckily for web designers everywhere, other technologies exist to help HTTP relay commands and thus support more interactive, intelligent web sites. These technologies include JavaScript, Active Server Pages, and cookies.

Publishing Web Pages

Once you've designed and created a web document, you can share it with the rest of the world. Sharing a page on the World Wide Web is quite an easy matter. Once the web document is finished, you need to find a server that will host the site. Most ISPs provide web servers of their own, or you can find relatively inexpensive web hosting elsewhere. The price of web hosting usually depends on the services and drive space offered. You can typically find a good web host for around $10 a month.

One option that has been available for a while is free web hosting. Usually the services are not too bad, but you will run across a few limitations. Nearly all free web hosts will insist on the right to place ads on your web page. This is not as much of an issue if you are posting a vanity or fan web page, but if you are doing any sort of business with your web site, this can be most annoying to your customers. The worst sort of free web host services place pop-up ads over your web page. Beyond annoying!

Once you have selected your web host, you need to select your domain name. Domain names have to be registered through InterNIC; this enables your web site name to be resolved to the IP address of the server that has your web site. Fortunately, registering your domain name is a breeze. Most web hosts will offer to register your domain name for you (for a nominal fee). The cost of registering your domain name is usually about $10 a year.

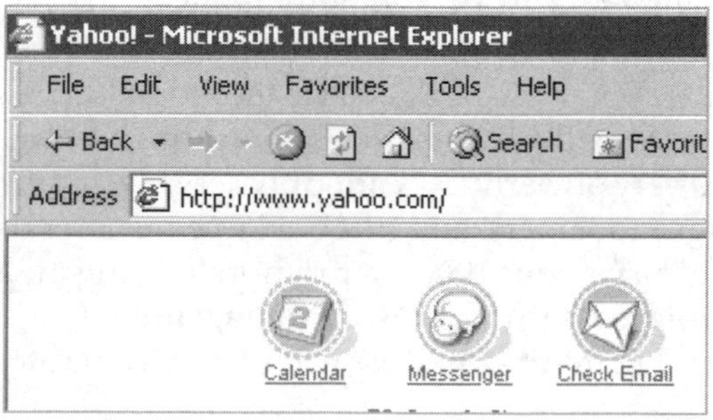

Figure 15-13
A run-of-the-mill URL

The trickiest aspect of registering your domain name is finding a domain name that has not already been taken. The last time I checked, the Web had about 11 million registered domain names, and that number has undoubtedly climbed steadily since. Many web sites that offer registration for domain names (such as www.register.com) offer a search that will check to see whether a name has already been registered.

Once you have your domain name registered and your web hosting covered, it's time to upload your web page to the web server. What's a web server? I'm glad you asked!

Web Servers and Web Clients

A web server is a computer that delivers (or *serves up*) web pages. Every web server has at least one static IP address and at least one domain name. For example, if you enter the URL www.mhteched.com/index.html, your browser sends a request to the server named www whose domain name is mhteched.com. The server then fetches the page named index.html and sends it to your browser. A web server *must* have a static IP address, because once you register your domain name, browsers must be able to resolve that domain name to a steady, unchanging IP address.

You can turn any computer into a web server by installing server software and connecting the machine to the Internet, but you need to consider the operating system and web server program you'll use to serve your web site. Windows 95/98/Me operating systems make poor web servers, for example, due to their poor support for multiple connections. More than ten connections to a Windows 98 or Me system can cause the system to lock up and Microsoft strongly recommends against using 95/98/Me as an operating system for your web server. Web serving programs vary greatly in their capabilities. If you use a program called Personal Web Server (PWS), you'll serve a maximum of one web site out to a limited number of users. The Windows NT Workstation OS has similar limitations. The Windows 2000 Professional OS can run a light version of Microsoft's Internet Information Server (IIS), but as with Personal Web Server it can only host one web site and has a ten-connection limit. You can, however, use more powerful, third-party, web server programs such as Apache and get around this limit.

Windows 2000 Server, Windows Server 2003, and UNIX/Linux-based operating systems can serve as full-blown web servers. This means they can host multiple web sites with multiple domain names, as well as multiple FTP and newsgroup servers. The two most popular web server software applications are Apache and Microsoft's Internet Information Server (IIS). As of this writing, Apache serves about 60 percent of the web sites on the Internet. Apache is incredibly popular because it's full-featured and powerful, runs on multiple operating systems (including Windows), and best of all, it's *free!* Better yet, you can add on different GUIs such as WebAdmin or Comanche that make administering Apache a breeze. Figure 15-14 illustrates the wonderful simplicity that is Comanche.

Microsoft's IIS is both easy to use (although complex to configure and secure properly) and very powerful. IIS not only serves web pages, it also can create FTP servers and newsgroup servers, and offers a large number of administrative options. You can even administer your IIS server remotely using an administrative web page. The IIS console runs from the Microsoft Management Console, and it's simple to use, as you can see in Figure 15-15. Alas, IIS is only available on Windows-based systems.

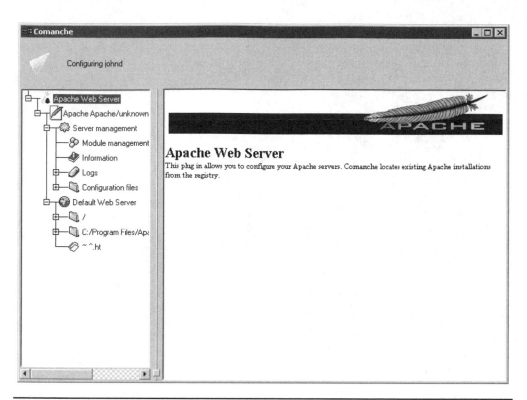

Figure 15-14 The Comanche GUI

There are many other web server solutions to choose from besides Apache and IIS, however, including Netscape Enterprise, iPlanet Web Server, and Enterprise for NetWare.

Web clients are the programs we use to surf the Internet. A user uses a client program (an Internet *browser*) to read web pages and interact with the Internet. Most browsers can handle multiple functions, from reading HTML documents to offering FTP services and even serving as an e-mail or newsgroup reader. The two biggest Internet browsers out there are Microsoft's *Internet Explorer* and Netscape's *Netscape Navigator*. Both are full-featured browsers that offer nearly identical services. Another fine Internet browser is Mozilla's *Firefox*. Firefox offers many options for the more experienced Internet surfer, and accesses information from the Internet quickly. The best thing about all of these browsers is that they're free!

Secure Sockets Layer and HTTPS

Because the Web has blossomed into a major economic player, the concern over security has become a near panic. In the early days of e-commerce, people feared that a simple credit card transaction on a less-than-secure web site could transform their dreams of

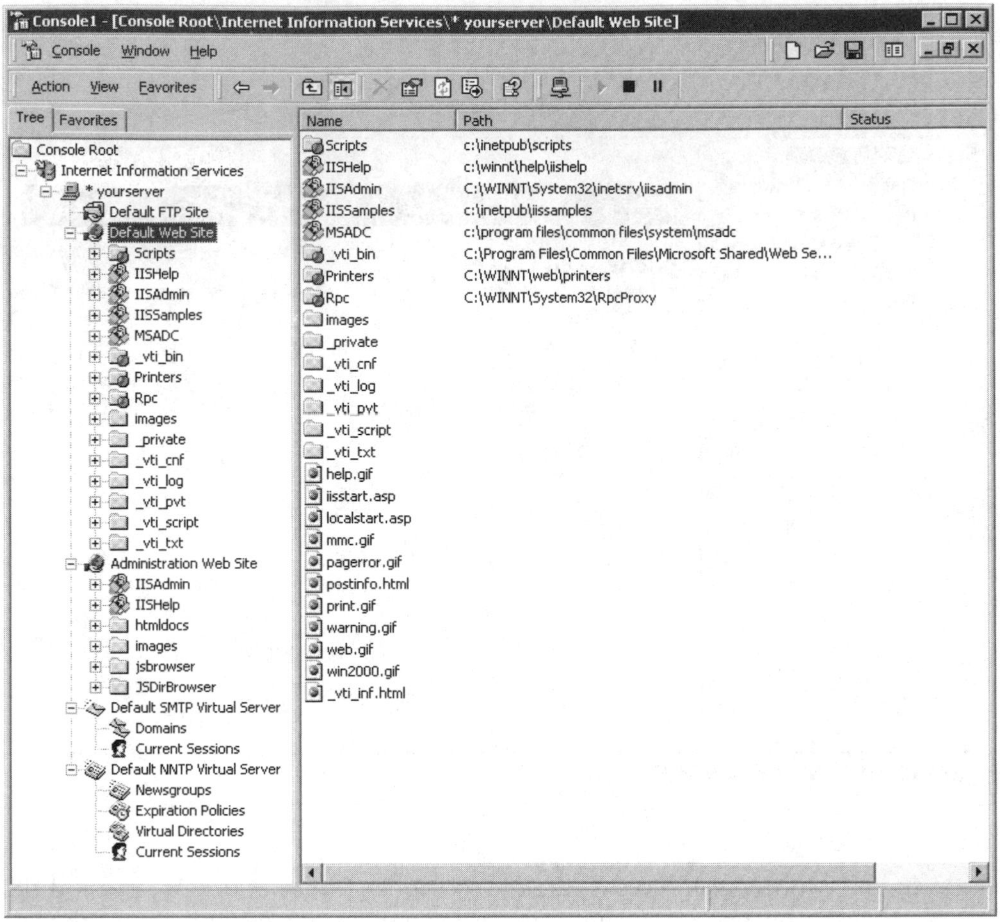

Figure 15-15   The IIS console

easy online buying into a nightmare of being robbed blind and ending up living in a re-frigerator box.

I can safely say that it was *never* as bad as all that. And nowadays, there are a number of safeguards on the Internet that can protect your purchase *and* your anonymity. One such safeguard is called *Secure Sockets Layer (SSL)*.

SSL is a protocol developed by Netscape for transmitting private documents over the Internet. SSL works by using a public key to encrypt sensitive data. This encrypted data is sent over an SSL connection, and then decrypted at the receiving end using a private key. Both Netscape Navigator and Internet Explorer support SSL, and many web sites use the protocol to obtain confidential user information, such as credit card numbers. One way to tell if a site is using SSL is by looking at the URL. By convention, URLs that use an SSL connection start with *https* instead of *http*. *HTTPS* stands for *HyperText Transport Protocol with SSL*.

Configuring a Web Browser

Configuring your web browser to run on the Internet is a simple process. In the case of Windows, an Internet Connection Wizard walks you through all the steps you need to get Internet Explorer to surf the Web with ease. Netscape Navigator and Firefox are much the same. You need to make sure your TCP/IP settings are correct.

Two things you can control on your browser are the number of cookies the browser uses and the caching of web pages. Each browser has its own particular way of accessing the user configuration areas. In Netscape Navigator, the preferences are set in Edit | Preferences. In Internet Explorer, go to Tools | Internet Options. (See Figure 15-16.)

Troubleshooting

If you're having problems connecting to the Internet, one of the first things to try is *pinging* a domain using the PING command at a command prompt. This command will tell you if there are connectivity problems.

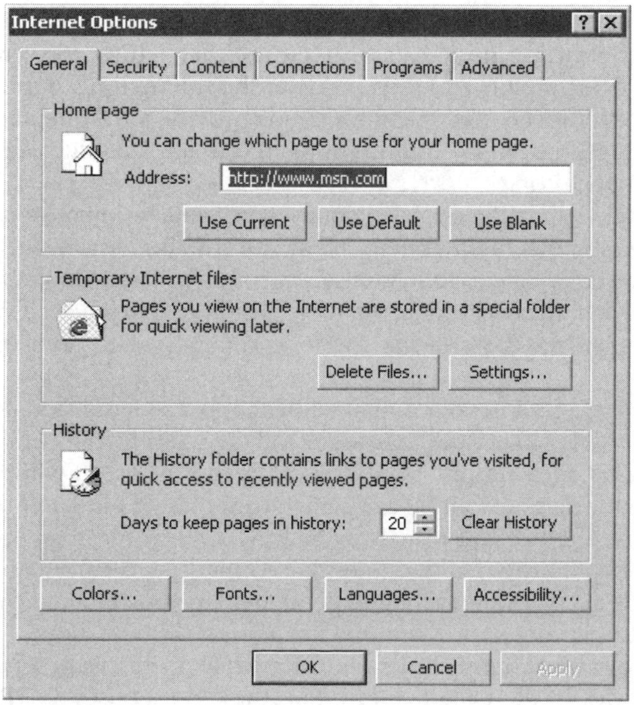

Figure 15-16   Internet Options in Internet Explorer

When using your browser to see if there are connectivity issues, either call up a web site you have not accessed for a long time, or reload the page once or twice, because browsers are usually set to cache frequently accessed web pages, which can therefore appear even when your Internet access isn't working.

Whether you are using a dial-up modem or a cable modem (to a lesser degree), your connection is likely to slow down during peak usage times on the Internet when masses of people are trying to access the same information at once. Lunchtime, suppertime, and evenings are popular times for surfing and checking e-mail. If you must join the crowd, you may have to be patient.

When buying on the Internet from a secured web page using SSL, be careful to follow the instructions exactly about not over-clicking buttons. Occasionally, information travels a little more slowly over an SSL connection than over a regular unsecured connection, due to the time it takes to encrypt and decrypt the information. If you keep clicking the order button over and over again, you may be sending in order after order to the server. However, if you don't mind paying for the same item 50 times, go right ahead!

Now that we've taken a look at the World Wide Web, it's time to learn about the second most popular feature of the Internet: e-mail.

E-mail

E-mail, short for *electronic mail,* has been a major part of the Internet revolution, and not just because it has streamlined the junk mail industry. E-mail provides an extremely quick way for people to communicate with one another, letting you send messages and attachments (like documents and pictures) over the Internet. It's normally offered as a free service by ISPs. Most e-mail client programs provide a rudimentary text editor for composing messages, but many can be configured to let you edit your messages using more sophisticated editors.

When you create an e-mail message, you must specify the recipient's e-mail address, consisting of the user's name and a domain name: for instance, MyName@Mhteched.com. When you send an e-mail message, it travels from router to router until it finds the domain in question. Then your message is directed to the specific user to whom it's addressed. If you want to, you can also send the same message to several users at the same time. This is called *broadcasting.*

When a message is sent to your e-mail address, it is normally stored in an electronic mailbox on your ISP's server until you come and get it. Some ISPs limit the amount of time they keep messages around, so always check this aspect of your user agreement! Most e-mail client programs can be configured to signal you in some way when a new message has arrived. Once you read an e-mail message, you can archive it, forward it, print it, or delete it. Many e-mail programs are configured to automatically delete messages from the ISP's server when you download them to your local machine, but you can usually change this configuration option to suit your circumstances.

E-mail programs use a number of application-level protocols to send and receive information. Specifically, the e-mail you find on the Internet uses SMTP to send e-mail, and either POP3 or IMAP to receive e-mail.

SMTP, POP3, and IMAP, Oh My!

The previous discussion might lead you to think e-mail is directly connected with the World Wide Web, but in fact, the two are quite separate and different. HTML pages use the HTTP protocol, whereas e-mail is sent and received using a number of different protocols. The following is a list of the different protocols that the Internet uses to transfer and receive mail.

SMTP   The *Simple Mail Transfer Protocol (SMTP)* is used to send e-mail. SMTP travels over TCP/IP port 25, and is used by clients to send messages. You need to specify the POP or IMAP server as well as the SMTP server when you configure your e-mail application, of course. Otherwise, you could send but not receive e-mail!

POP3   *POP3* is the protocol that receives the e-mail from the server. It stands for *Post Office Protocol version 3,* and uses TCP/IP port 110. Most e-mail clients use this protocol, although some use IMAP.

IMAP   IMAP is an alternative to POP3. *IMAP* stands for *Internet Message Access Protocol,* and like POP3, it retrieves e-mail from an e-mail server. IMAP uses TCP/IP port 143. The latest version, *IMAP4,* supports some features that are not supported in POP3. For example, IMAP4 enables you to search through messages on the mail server to find specific keywords, and select the messages you want to download onto your machine.

Other Internet protocols include Extended Simple Mail Transfer Protocol (ESMTP), Authenticated Post Office Protocol (APOP), Multipurpose Internet Mail Extensions (MIME), and Directory Access Protocol (DAP). Many mail servers are also adding S/MIME, SSL, or RSA support for message encryption; and Lightweight Directory Access Protocol (LDAP) support to access operating system directory information about mail users.

Alternatives to SMTP, POP3, and IMAP

While SMTP and POP3 or IMAP are by far the most common and most traditional tools for doing e-mail, two other options have wide popularity: web-based e-mail and proprietary solutions. Web-based mail, as the name implies, requires a web interface. From a web browser, you simply surf to the web-mail server, log in, and access your e-mail. The cool part is that you can do it from anywhere in the world where you find a web browser and an Internet hookup! You get the benefit of e-mail without even needing to own a computer. Some of the more popular web-based services are Microsoft's MSN Hotmail and Yahoo! Mail.

The key benefits of web-based are as follows:

- You can access your e-mail from anywhere.
- They're free.
- They're handy for throw-away accounts (like when you're required to give an e-mail address to download something, but you know you're going to get spammed if you do).

PART III

Many traditional SMTP/POP/IMAP accounts also provide web interfaces, but you should not confuse them with web mail services. Web-based e-mail services are only available through the web (although some will also give you SMTP/POP access at an extra charge).

The best example of proprietary e-mail is the popular America Online (AOL). When you subscribe to the AOL service, you are in a sense accessing the Internet through a gated community—you see the Internet, but using the America Online interface. Figure 15-17 shows a typical AOL client installed on a Windows system.

> **NOTE** If you have an AOL account, you can also access your e-mail through a web-based interface, just like with Hotmail or Yahoo! Mail, from any computer connected to the Internet.

E-mail Servers and E-mail Clients

To give you a clearer idea of how the whole enchilada works, I'm now going to describe an e-mail server and an e-mail client.

E-mail Server Many people have heard of web servers and know what they do, but for some reason e-mail servers remain a mystery. This is odd, because e-mail servers are nearly as prevalent on the Internet as web servers. E-mail is used daily by millions of people, both within private networks and on the Internet. This means that e-mail servers are a vital part of any large network.

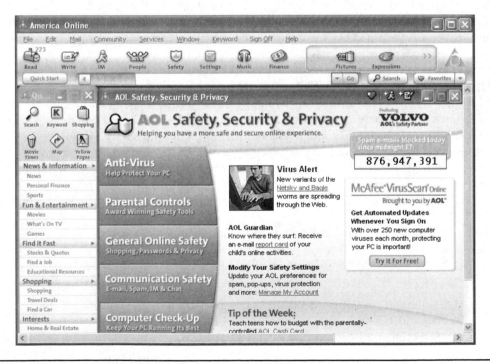

Figure 15-17 Typical AOL interface

E-mail servers accept incoming mail and sort out the mail for recipients into mailboxes. These *mailboxes* are special separate holding areas for each user's e-mail. An e-mail server works much like a post office, sorting and arranging incoming messages, and kicking back those messages that have no known recipient.

Perhaps one reason e-mail servers are so little understood is that they're difficult to manage. E-mail servers store user lists, user rights, and messages, and are constantly involved in Internet traffic and resources. Setting up and administering an e-mail server takes a lot of planning, although it's getting easier. Most e-mail server software runs in a GUI interface, but even the command-line-based interface of e-mail servers is becoming more intuitive.

E-mail Client   An *e-mail client* is a program that runs on a computer and enables you to send, receive, and organize e-mail. The e-mail client program communicates with the e-mail server and downloads the messages from the e-mail server to the client computer.

Configuring an E-mail Client   Configuring a client is an easy matter. You need the POP3 or IMAP address and the SMTP address for the e-mail server. The SMTP address for MHTechEd, for example, is mail.mhteched.com. Besides the e-mail server addresses, you must also enter the user name and password of the e-mail account the client will be managing. The user name will usually be part of the e-mail address. For example, the user name for the e-mail address ghengizsam@mhteched.com will probably be ghengizsam.

Troubleshooting E-mail

If you encounter a problem with an SMTP or POP3 name, it's likely you have a problem with the DNS not recognizing the name of the mail server you have entered. Figure 15-18 shows you the error screen in Microsoft Outlook resulting from a bad SMTP connection. In this case, you can check to see if there is a problem with the mail server. Because an SMTP or POP3 name is a name resolved in DNS, how can you check to see if that server is online? You can ping it. Ping the mail server to see if you can find it online. If it is not responding to the ping, you have your answer right there.

Another common problem is a bad password. A mail server is like any other server: you need permission to access its resources. If you can't get access, your password may not be correct. Most e-mail client programs will prompt a dialog box to appear if your e-mail password is set incorrectly, as seen in Figure 15-19.

FTP

File Transfer Protocol (FTP) is the protocol used on the Internet for transferring files. Although HTTP can be used to transfer files as well, the transfer is often not as reliable or as fast as with FTP. In addition, FTP can do the transfer with security and data integrity. FTP uses TCP/IP ports 21 and 20 by default, although you can often change the port number for security reasons.

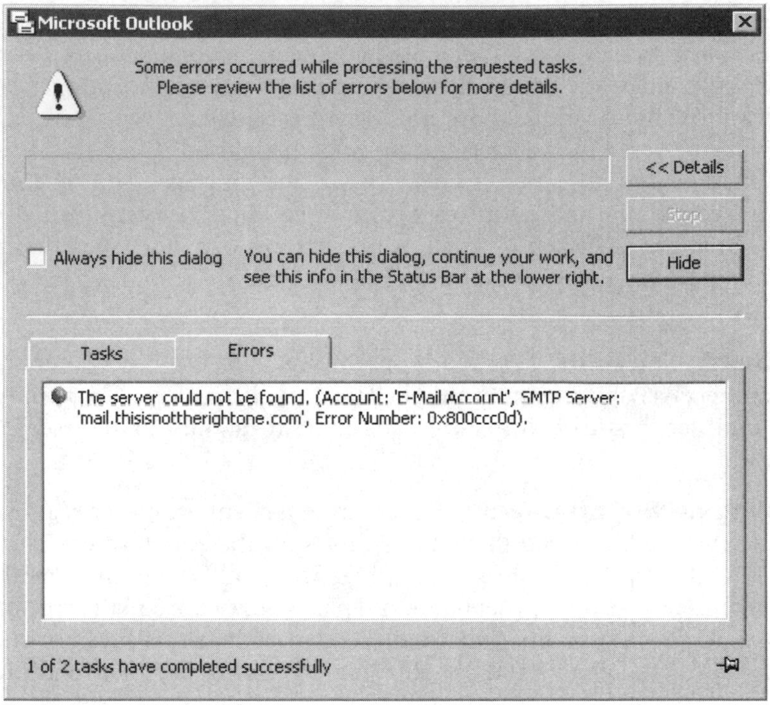

Figure 15-18   Bad SMTP!

FTP sites are either anonymous sites, meaning that anyone can log on, or secured sites, meaning that you must have a user name and password to be able to transfer files. A single FTP site can offer both anonymous access and protected access, but you'll see different resources depending on which way you log in.

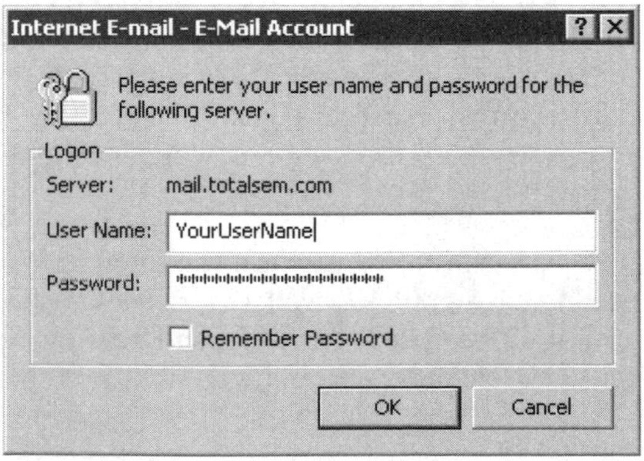

Figure 15-19   What was my password again?

FTP Servers and FTP Clients

Like many Internet applications, FTP uses a client and server arrangement. The FTP server does all the real work of storing the files, keeping everything secure, and transferring the files. The client logs onto the FTP server (either from a web site, a command line, or a special FTP application) and downloads the requested files onto the local hard drive.

FTP Servers   Most web servers come with their own internal FTP server software, enabling you to set up an FTP server with a minimum of fuss. These bundled versions of FTP server are robust, but do not provide all the options one might want. Luckily for you, many specialized FTP server software applications provide a full array of options for the administrator.

One aspect of FTP servers you should be aware of concerns FTP passwords. Although it may sound like a good idea to set up a secure, user-only FTP server, in the end this is *less* secure than an anonymous FTP server. How can this be? The problem is that FTP passwords are unencrypted (that is, they are sent over the Internet as plain text). Suppose you are an administrator setting up an FTP server for a company. You decide to extend user rights and login permissions to your FTP server so your company employees may access and download some important programs. When a remote user enters a user name and password to log onto the FTP server—the *same* data they use to log on and off the network—they send this data in *clear text* to the FTP server. Anyone who happens to be eavesdropping on the *network* can intercept this user name and password and use it to log onto the network as if they were an authorized user. This, as you can see, is very, *very* bad for security! In the end, it's safer just to set up a general FTP server with anonymous access, and then change the ports it uses. That way only people you authorize to know about the FTP server can find out which port their FTP client software must use to access the data. This is still not foolproof—someone taking the trouble to tap into your dial-up line can retrieve the FTP port information, and then log in anonymously—but it certainly deters casual mischief.

Another thing to check when deciding on an FTP server setup is the number of clients you want to support. Most anonymous FTP sites limit the number of users who may download at any one time to around 500. This protects you from a sudden influx of users flooding your server and eating up all your Internet bandwidth.

FTP Clients   FTP clients, as noted before, can access an FTP server through a web site, a command line, or a special FTP application. Usually special FTP applications offer the most choices for accessing and using an FTP site.

Configuring an FTP Client   Using an FTP client to upload content is a simple process. To transfer files via FTP, you must have an FTP client installed on your PC. Most FTP sites require a user name of *some* sort to log in, even if the FTP server allows anonymous logins. In the case of anonymous FTP, it's common for the user name to be anonymous and the password to be your e-mail address. You must also know the host name of the FTP server. This name is an IP address, which is resolved to a host name using DNS. The MHTechEd FTP server, for example, is ftp.mhteched.com.

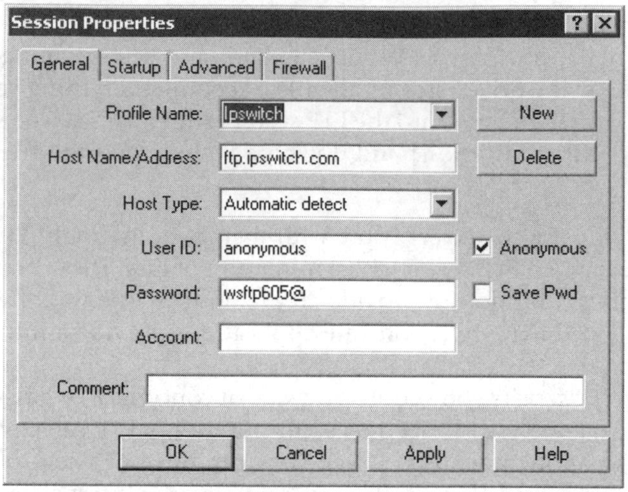

Figure 15-20   FTP login using WS_FTP LE

When you first start up an FTP client program, a dialog box will appear in which you can enter this information (as shown in Figure 15-20). After you log in, you will have access to the files on the FTP server's hard drive. One pane will display the contents of your hard drive, and the other will show you the FTP site's hard drive (see Figure 15-21).

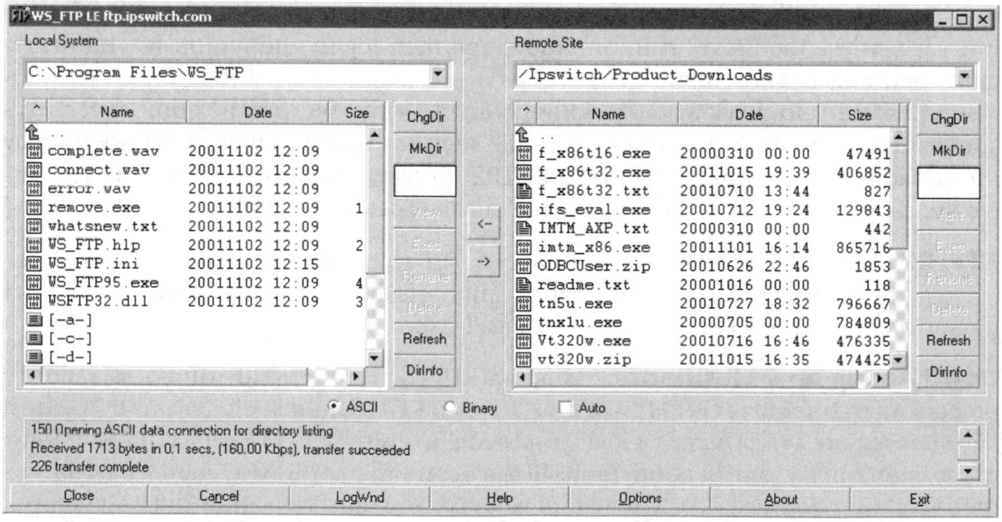

Figure 15-21   Downloading fun with WS_FTP LE!

Your FTP client should let you select which file transfer mode you want to use, either ASCII or binary. *ASCII* mode is used to transfer text files, while *binary* mode is used to transfer binary files, like programs and graphics. Most FTP clients have an Automatic transfer mode option, which automatically detects which transfer mode is correct for each file.

Troubleshooting FTP

If you can't connect to an FTP site, first make sure you have an *active* dial-up or direct Internet connection. FTP programs are not automatic dialers. If your connection closes after a certain number of minutes of inactivity, you have run afoul of the FTP server. This is a feature for system administrators: you can set an FTP server to boot out users who have been inactive for some number of minutes or hours. This is particularly important on anonymous FTP servers that have a limit regarding how many users can be on simultaneously. Most FTP sites will close a connection after a few minutes of inactivity. If the files you transfer are corrupted, the most likely problem is the transfer mode you (often unwittingly, by not changing a previous selection) chose. If you try to transfer a binary file in ASCII mode, you can damage the file. Check to make sure you have selected the proper mode, and do so manually if you think Automatic mode is not working correctly.

Telnet

Telnet is a terminal emulation program for TCP/IP networks that runs on TCP/IP port 23. Telnet enables you to connect to a server and run commands on that server as if you were sitting right in front of it. This way, you can remotely administer a server and communicate with other servers on your network. As you can imagine, this is sort of risky. If you can remotely control a computer, what is to stop others from doing the same? Thankfully, Telnet does not just allow *anyone* to log on and wreak havoc with your network. You must enter a special user name and password to run Telnet.

Telnet is mostly used nowadays to control web servers remotely. This is rather important because web servers often need extra care and attention. Suppose you're the administrator for your company's web server. You are sitting at home when you get a call. There is a problem with your company's web page: a hacker has broken into your web server and replaced the web page with a picture of someone . . . ah . . . *fabricly challenged*. You can use Telnet to connect remotely to the web server and remove the offending page, and then run processes and administer the web server without ever having left your comfy chair. A wonderful capability for the overworked system admin!

Telnet Servers and Clients

A Telnet server enables users to log onto a host computer and perform tasks as if they're working on the remote computer itself. Users can access the host through the Telnet server from anywhere in the world using a Telnet client. When you create a Telnet server, you can also create a web page that handles server management. Most web server software will do this for you. For instance, IIS enables you to manage an IIS web server via a secured web page.

A Telnet client is the computer from which you log onto the remote server. To use Telnet from the client, you must have the proper permissions. If you do not have a web site that will handle the remote connection for you, you can select from a number of terminal emulators that enable you to operate from a GUI.

Configuring a Telnet Client

When you configure a Telnet client, you must provide the host name, your user logon name, and the password. As I mentioned previously, you must have permission to access the server to use Telnet.

Host Name   A *host name* is the name or IP address of the computer to which you want to connect. For instance, you might connect to a web server with the host name websrv.mhteched.com.

Login Name   The user *login name* you give Telnet should be the same login name you'd use if you logged into the server at its location. Some computers, usually university libraries with online catalogs, have open systems that enable you to log in with Telnet. These sites will either display a banner before the login prompt that tells you what login name to use, or they'll require no login name at all.

Password   As with the login name, you use the same password for a Telnet login that you'd use to log into the server directly. It's that simple. Computers with open access will either tell you what password to use when they tell you what login name to use, or they'll require no login name/password at all.

SSH and the Death of Telnet

Telnet has seen long and heavy use in the TCP world from the earliest days of the Internet, but it suffers from a serious flaw—it has no security. Telnet passwords as well as data are transmitted in clear text and are thus easily hacked. To that end, a new (well, newer) TCP application has now replaced Telnet on most real-world servers: *Secure Shell*, better known by its initials, *SSH*. In terms of what is does, SSH is extremely similar to Telnet in that it creates a terminal connection to a remote host. Every aspect of SSH, however, including both login and data transmittal, are encrypted. SSH also uses TCP port 22 instead of Telnet's port 23. Figure 15-22 shows the popular Windows SSH tool, Cygwin, running on a Windows system.

SSH has come into vogue for many other traditionally unsecured applications such as FTP. Secure FTP (SFTP) is FTP running over an encrypted SSH connection. SFTP typically uses SSH's port 22, although many SFTP servers may change this to a non-standard port such as 199. SSH even works with some rather offbeat protocols such as Secure Copy Protocol (SCP), a secure replacement for the ancient command line RCP (remote copy program) that allows for file transfer between two systems.

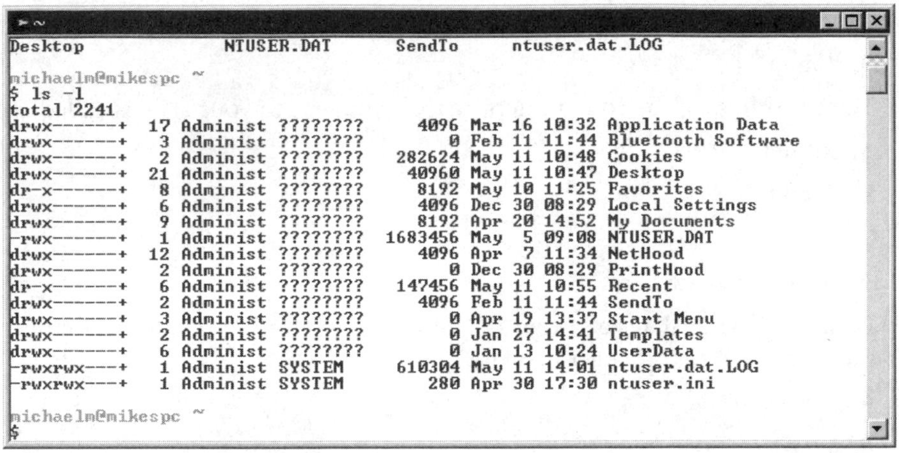

```
 ~
Desktop          NTUSER.DAT      SendTo      ntuser.dat.LOG

michaelm@mikespc ~
$ ls -l
total 2241
drwx------+  17 Administ ????????    4096 Mar 16 10:32 Application Data
drwx------+   3 Administ ????????       0 Feb 11 11:44 Bluetooth Software
drwx------+   2 Administ ????????  282624 May 11 10:48 Cookies
drwx------+  21 Administ ????????   40960 May 11 10:47 Desktop
dr-x------+   8 Administ ????????    8192 May 10 11:25 Favorites
drwx------+   6 Administ ????????    4096 Dec 30 08:29 Local Settings
drwx------+   9 Administ ????????    8192 Apr 20 14:52 My Documents
-rwx------+   1 Administ ???????? 1683456 May  5 09:08 NTUSER.DAT
drwx------+  12 Administ ????????    4096 Apr  7 11:34 NetHood
drwx------+   2 Administ ????????       0 Dec 30 08:29 PrintHood
dr-x------+   6 Administ ????????  147456 May 11 10:55 Recent
drwx------+   2 Administ ????????    4096 Feb 11 11:44 SendTo
drwx------+   3 Administ ????????       0 Apr 19 13:37 Start Menu
drwx------+   2 Administ ????????       0 Jan 27 14:41 Templates
drwx------+   6 Administ ????????       0 Jan 13 10:24 UserData
-rwxrwx---+   1 Administ SYSTEM    610304 May 11 14:01 ntuser.dat.LOG
-rwxrwx---+   1 Administ SYSTEM       280 Apr 30 17:30 ntuser.ini

michaelm@mikespc ~
$
```

Figure 15-22 The Cygwin program

Chapter Review

Questions

1. What device directs incoming network protocol packets from one LAN to another based on OSI Network layer information stored in the incoming packets?

    A. Hub

    B. Switch

    C. Bridge

    D. Router

2. To route packets, a router must have at least _____ interfaces.

    A. One

    B. Two

    C. Three

    D. Four

3. What device connects two LANs that use different hardware?

    A. Gateway

    B. Switch

    C. Bridge

    D. Router

4. The IP address of the router interface that connects to your LAN is called a(n):

    A. Subnet mask

    B. IP address

    C. DNS

    D. Default gateway

5. What device translates a system's IP address into another IP address before sending it out to the larger network?

    A. A firewall

    B. A NAT

    C. A router

    D. A proxy server

6. What device, acting at the Application level, translates a port number to a different port number to add more security to the system?

    A. A firewall

    B. A NAT

    C. A router

    D. A proxy server

7. The protocol developed by Netscape for transmitting private documents over the Internet is known as

    A. SSS

    B. SSA

    C. SSL

    D. NSSL

8. Which of the following are key benefits of web-based mail? (Select all that apply.)

    A. You can use a third-party application, like Microsoft Outlook, to download your e-mail.

    B. You can access your e-mail from anywhere in the world from a computer with a browser and an Internet connection.

    C. They are completely spam-free.

    D. They're great for making throw-away accounts.

9. An SSL URL connection starts with

    A. HTTP

    B. WWW

C. FTP

D. HTTPS

10. Joe likes to surf the Web instead of doing his work. He calls you and tells you he can't connect to the Internet. Which of the following would be one of the first utilities you would use to diagnose his problem?

A. NBSTAT

B. TRACEROUTE

C. ROUTE PRINT

D. PING

Answers

1. **D.** Routers direct incoming network protocol packets from one LAN to another based on OSI Network layer information stored in the incoming packets.

2. **B.** To route these packets, a router by definition must have at least two interfaces, although some routers have three or more depending on the needs of the network.

3. **A.** A gateway, in contrast to a regular router, connects two LANs that use different hardware. You wouldn't refer to a router that connects two Ethernet LANs, for example, as a gateway. A router that connects an Ethernet LAN to a DSL router or to a Token Ring LAN is an example of a gateway.

4. **D.** The default gateway is the IP address of the router interface that connects to your LAN. That interface is called the local side or the local interface on your router.

5. **B.** A NAT translates a system's IP address into another IP address before sending it out to the larger network. NATs work at the Network layer.

6. **D.** Proxy servers translate port numbers to a different port number to add more security to the system. Proxy servers work at the Application layer.

7. **C.** Secure Sockets Layer (SSL) is a protocol developed by Netscape for transmitting private documents over the Internet. SSL works by using a public key to encrypt sensitive data.

8. **B, D.** You can access a web-based e-mail account from any browser on any machine connected to the Internet. These accounts are great for making throw-away e-mail addresses.

9. **D.** URLs that use an SSL connection start with HTTPS instead of HTTP.

10. **D.** One of the first things to try is the PING utility; type **PING** at a command prompt. Pinging is a great way to discover connectivity problems.

Remote Connectivity

The Network+ Certification exam expects you to know how to

- 1.6   Identify the purpose, features, and functions of the following network components: CSU/DSU (Channel Service Unit/Data Service Unit), NICs, ISDN adapters, modems
- 2.14   Identify the basic characteristics (for example, speed, capacity, media) of the following WAN technologies: packet switching, circuit switching, ISDN, FDDI, T1/E1/J1, T3/E3/J3, OCx (Optical Carrier), X.25
- 2.15   Identify the basic characteristics of the following Internet access technologies: xDSL (Digital Subscriber Line), broadband cable (cable modem), POTS/PSTN (Plain Old Telephone Service/Public Switched Telephone Network), satellite
- 2.16   Define the function of the following remote access protocols and services: RAS (Remote Access Service), PPP (Point-to-Point Protocol), SLIP (Serial Line Internet Protocol), PPPoE (Point-to-Point Protocol over Ethernet), PPTP (Point-to-Point Tunneling Protocol), VPN (Virtual Private Network)
- 2.17   Identify the following security protocols and describe their purpose and function: L2TP
- 2.18   Identify authentication protocols (for example: CHAP—Challenge Handshake Authentication Protocol, MS-CHAP—Microsoft Challenge Handshake Authentication Protocol, PAP—Password Authentication Protocol, RADIUS—Remote Authentication Dial-In User Service, Kerberos, and EAP—Extensible Authentication Protocol)
- 3.8   Identify the main characteristics of VLANs (Virtual Local Area Networks)
- 3.9   Identify the main characteristics and purpose of extranets and intranets
- 4.4   Given a troubleshooting scenario involving a client accessing remote network services, identify the cause of the problem (for example: file services, print services, authentication failure, protocol configuration, physical connectivity, and SOHO—Small Office/Home Office—router)

To achieve these goals, you must be able to

- Describe the different types of SOHO connections such as dial-up, ADSL, and cable modems
- Describe the different types of higher-capacity connections such as T1/T3, OC-1/OC-3, Frame Relay, and ATM, commonly used for WAN connectivity
- Explain how to set up and use clients and servers for remote access
- Troubleshoot basic remote access problems

Long before the Internet came into popular use, network users and developers desired to take a single system or group of systems and connect them to another network. Connecting individual computers and LANs into other individual computers and LANs gives us the ability to share more resources and to communicate more readily among more computers. Making these interconnections is a challenge, requiring specialized long-distance media, hardware that can convert data from one format to another, unique security functions, and software that understands how to make interconnected systems work together. This chapter begins by inspecting the many remote connection media options, from good old telephone lines to advanced fiber-optic carriers, and even satellites. There are so many ways to make remote connections that this section is broken into two parts. The first part, "SOHO LAN Connections," deals with the types of remote connections more commonly seen in small offices and the home. This includes dial-up, DSL, and cable modems. The next section, "WAN Connections," goes into the big pipes—the high-capacity, dedicated connections more commonly seen in the corporate environment.

Once you've seen the transmission options, the chapter goes into the types of remote connection you can make. It's easy to think everything connects to the Internet, but there are a number of situations that have nothing to do with the Internet. What if a person wants to connect his or her laptop to the home office's network in Texas from a café in Paris? (And who wouldn't?) At the end of that section, we'll look at some of the more common problems that take place with remote connectivity and learn how to deal with these problems.

Test Specific

SOHO LAN Connections

For many years the only viable connection available to small office and home office (SOHO) users was your telephone via the classic dial-up connection. Dial-up is still the most popular way to get a single computer connected to another network, but today you have a number of excellent options that provide high-speed connectivity at low prices. All of these methods enable you to connect a local area network (LAN) to the Internet through a single PC. Let's look at these options, starting with the oldest and most well-known, your telephone line.

Telephone Options

There are many different types of telephone lines available, but all the choices break down into two groups: dedicated and dial-up. *Dedicated* telephone *lines* are always off the hook (that is, they never hang up on each other). A true dedicated line does not have a phone number. In essence, the telephone company creates a permanent, hard-wired connection between the two locations, rendering a phone number superfluous. *Dial-up lines,* by contrast, have phone numbers; they must dial each other up to make a connection. When they're finished communicating, they hang up. Telephone companies hate it, but many locations use dial-up lines in a dedicated manner. If a dial-up connection is made and the two ends never disconnect, you have basically the same function as a dedicated line. But it is still a dial-up connection, even if the two sides rarely disconnect. Two technologies make up the overwhelming majority of dial-up connections—PSTN and ISDN.

Public Switched Telephone Network

The oldest, slowest, and most common phone connection is the *Public Switched Telephone Network (PSTN)*. PSTN is also known as *Plain Old Telephone Service* (seriously!—you see it all the time with the acronym *POTS*). PSTN is just a regular phone line, the same line that runs into everybody's home telephone jacks from the central office of your local exchange carrier (LEC—the telephone company that provides local connections).

Because PSTN was designed long before computers were common, it was designed to work with only one type of data: sound. Here's how it works. The telephone's microphone takes the sound of your voice and translates it into an electrical analog waveform. The telephone then sends that signal through the PSTN line to the phone on the other end of the connection. That phone translates the signal into sound on the other end using its speaker. The important word here is *analog*. The telephone microphone converts the sounds into electrical waveforms that cycle 2400 times a second. An individual cycle is known as a *baud*. The number of bauds per second is called the *baud rate*. Pretty much all phone companies' PSTN lines have a baud rate of 2400. PSTN uses a connector called RJ-11. It's the classic connector you see on all telephones (see Figure 16-1).

When you connect your modem to a phone jack, the line then runs to a special box known as the *network interface (NI)* or *demarc* (short for demarcation point). The term "network interface" is more commonly used to describe the small box on the side of your home that accepts the incoming lines from the telephone company, and then splits them to the different wall outlets. *Demarc* is more commonly used to describe large connections used in businesses. The terms are interchangeable and always describe the interface between the lines the telephone company is responsible for and the lines for which you are responsible.

Computers, as you know, don't speak analog—only digital (ones and zeros) will do. In addition, the digital signal goes in and out of your computer in eight bits at a time. To connect over phone lines, they need a device that converts the 8-bit wide digital signals from the computer into serial (1-bit wide) digital data, and then convert (modulate) the data into analog waveforms that can travel across PSTN lines. This same device must

Figure 16-1

RJ-11 connectors (top and side views)

demodulate the analog signals from the PSTN wall jack into 8-bit wide sets of ones and zeros the computer can understand. The device that converts the analog data to digital and back is called a *MOdulator DEModulator* (*modem*). There are two types of modems seen in the PC world: internal and external. Internal modems are two devices: a UART (Universal Asynchronous Receiver/Transmitter) and a modem. The UART takes the 8-bit wide digital data and converts it into bit-wide digital data and hands it to the modem for conversion to analog data. The process is reversed for incoming data. External modems do not have a UART and instead connect to a serial port or a USB port. These ports have built-in UART functions (see Figure 16-2).

Baud vs. Bits per Second

Modems utilize phone lines to transmit data, not just voice, at various speeds. These speeds cause a world of confusion and problems for computer people. This is where a little bit of knowledge becomes dangerous. Standard modems you can buy for your home computer normally transmit data at speeds up to 56 Kbps. That's 56 kilobits per second, *not* 56 kilo-baud! Many people confuse the terms *baud* and *bits per second*. This confusion arises because the baud rate and bps are the same for modems until the data transfer rate surpasses 2400 baud.

A PSTN phone line takes analog samples of sound 2400 times a second. This standard was determined a long time ago as an acceptable rate for sending voice traffic over phone lines. Although 2400-baud analog signals are in fact fine for voice communication, they are a big problem for computers trying to send data as computers only work

Figure 16-2

Typical internal modem

with digital signals. The job of the modem is to take the digital signals it receives from the computer and send them out over the phone line in an analog form, using the baud cycles from the phone system. The earliest modems—often erroneously called 300-baud modems—used four analog bauds just to send one bit of data. As you should already have realized, they weren't 300-baud modems at all—they were 300 *bps* modems; however, the name baud kind of stuck for describing modem speeds.

As technology progressed, modems became faster and faster. To get past the 2,400 baud limit, modems would modulate the 2,400 baud signal twice in each cycle, thereby transmitting 4,800 bits per second. To get 9,600 bps, the modem would modulate the signal four times per cycle. All PSTN modem speeds are always a multiple of 2,400. Look at the following classic modem speeds:

- $2,400 \times 1 = 2,400$ bps
- $2,400 \times 2 = 4,800$ bps
- $2,400 \times 4 = 9,600$ bps
- $2,400 \times 6 = 14,400$ bps
- $2,400 \times 8 = 19,200$ bps
- $2,400 \times 12 = 28,800$ bps
- $2,400 \times 24 = 57,600$ bps (56 Kbps)

So, if someone comes up to you and asks, "Is that a 56K baud modem?" you can look them straight in the eye and say, "No, it's a 2,400-baud modem. But its bits per second rate is 57,600!" You'll be technically correct, but soon you will have no friends.

V Standards

For two modems to communicate with each other at their fastest rate, they must modulate signals in the same fashion. The two modems must also negotiate with, or *query*, each other to determine the fastest speed they share. The modem manufacturers themselves originally standardized these processes as a set of proprietary protocols. The downside to these protocols was that unless you had two modems from the same manufacturer, modems often would not work together. In response, a European standards body called the CCITT established standards for modems. These standards, known generically as the V standards, define the speeds at which modems can modulate. The most common of these speed standards are as follows:

- V.22   1,200 bps
- V.22bis   2,400 bps
- V.32   9,600 bps
- V.32bis   14,400 bps
- V.34   28,000 bps
- V.90   57,600 bps
- V.92   57,600 bps

The current modem standard now on the market is the *V.92 standard*. V.92 has the same download speed as the V.90, but upstream rates increase to as much as 48 Kbps. If your modem is having trouble getting 56 Kbps rates with V.90 in your area, you will not notice an improvement. V.92 also offers a Quick Connect feature, which implements faster handshaking to cut connection delays. Finally, the V.92 standard offers a Modem On Hold feature, which enables the modem to stay connected while you take an incoming call-waiting call or even initiate an outgoing voice call. This feature only works if the V.92 server modem is configured to enable it.

 TIP Know your V standards!

In addition to speed standards, the CCITT, now known simply as ITU, has established standards controlling how modems compress data and perform error checking when they communicate. These standards are as follows:

- V.42   Error Checking
- V.42bis   Data Compression
- V.44   Data Compression

- MNP5   Both error checking and data compression

The beauty of these standards is that you don't need to do anything special to enjoy their benefits. If you want 56 Kbps data transfers, for example, you simply need to ensure that the modems in the local system and the remote system both support the V.90 standard. Assuming you have good line quality, the connections will run at or at least close to 56 Kbps.

 TIP Some people get confused by the concept of port speed vs. modem speed. All versions of Windows give you the opportunity to set the port speed. *Port speed* is the speed at which the data travels between the serial port (really the UART) and the modem, not between the local and remote modems (that's the modem speed). As a rule, always set the port speed to the highest setting available (this should be 115,200 bps, assuming your UART is a 16500 or better).

Installing a PSTN Connection

Installing a PSTN connection in a Windows computer is a two-step process. First you install a modem, and then you create a connection. Installing a modem in a Windows system is virtually automatic. Modem technologies haven't changed much in the last few years, so any Windows 98 SE client or later almost certainly has a driver you need built into the operating system. Even though Windows probably has a functional driver, you should still use the driver supplied with the modem to take advantage of extra features such as faxing or answering machine functions. Like any newly installed device, a quick trip to Device Manager to confirm that Windows sees the device is always a good idea (Figure 16-3).

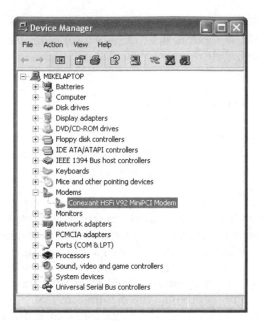

Figure 16-3
Properly working modem in Device Manager

Once a modem has been installed you can then begin to create connections (and the upcoming "Using Remote Access" section shows you how to make these connections). But before a connection can be made, we have one more issue to deal with. How does one modem know where one packet ends and another begins? Sure, the V standards will get the data from one modem to another, but how do the modems know how to send an IP packet on a serial line in such a way that it makes it intact to the other side? The answer to this issue lies in two Data-Link layer protocols for dial-up connections called SLIP and PPP.

SLIP

Serial Line Internet Protocol (SLIP) was the network community's first effort to make a Data Link protocol for telephony, and it shows. About the only thing good you can say about SLIP is that it worked—barely. SLIP had a number of major limitations. First, it only supported TCP/IP. If you had a NetBEUI or IPX network, you were out of luck. Second, SLIP could not use DHCP, so any system that used SLIP required a static IP address. This wasn't too much of an issue in the early days of the Internet, but as the Internet became more popular, no Internet provider wanted an IP address tied up when you weren't online. As if this were not enough, SLIP provided no error checking and instead relied on the hardware making the connection to do any error correction. SLIP also did not natively support compression, which meant that there was no way to streamline your network protocol. There were later versions, such as CSLIP (or Compressed SLIP), which supported a little bit of compression, but it did not fit the bill. Perhaps worst of all (at least from a security standpoint), SLIP transmitted all authentication passwords as clear text. That's right; there was no encryption on the password. To make matters even more interesting, you usually had to create a script to log on to a server using SLIP. So aside from no security, no support for protocols other than TCP/IP, no compression, no compatibility with DHCP, and a pain-in-the-rear login system, SLIP was not such a bad protocol.

SLIP continues to be supported by most remote access programs, primarily as a backward-compatibility option. But time and technology have moved away from SLIP and into the brighter, better days of PPP.

PPP

SLIP's many shortcomings motivated the creation of an improved Data Link protocol called *Point-to-Point Protocol (PPP)*. PPP addressed all of the shortcomings of SLIP, and has totally replaced SLIP in all but the oldest connections. Although PPP has many powerful features, two stand out. PPP supports IPX and NetBEUI as well as IP, and it supports dynamic IP addresses. All remote access software comes with the PPP protocol, so PPP *is* the one to use!

How do you choose your dial-up protocol? Windows uses a handy tool called Dial-up Networking that enables you to create connections for your modem to dial. Go to the Modems Control Panel applet in Windows 9*x* or the Network Connections in Windows XP. (Note that Windows 2000 calls the section the Network and Dial-up Connections.) A single modem might have multiple connections (my laptop has about ten that I use in different towns) so each connection manifests itself as a separate icon. It's here where you set up the number to dial, the dial-up protocol, any special dialing properties, account numbers, and passwords. You'll see dial-up networking in detail in the "Remote Access Options" section later in this chapter.

ISDN

There are many pieces to a PSTN telephone connection. First, there's the phone line that runs from your phone out to a network interface box (the little box on the side of your house), and into a central switch. The *central switch* is the device that interconnects multiple individual local connections into the larger telephone network. A central switch will connect to long-distance carriers via high-capacity *trunk lines* and will also connect to other nearby central switches. Central switches are usually rather large and require their own building, called, obviously enough, a central office (CO). Metropolitan areas have a large number of central offices. Houston, Texas, for example, has nearly 100 offices in the general metro area. Before 1970, the entire phone system was analog, but phone companies upgraded their trunk lines to digital systems during the late 1970s and 1980s. Nowadays, the entire telephone system, with the exception of the line from your phone to the central office, is digital.

During this upgrade period, customers continued to demand higher throughput from their phone lines. The old PSTN was not expected to produce more than 28.8 Kbps (56K modems, which were a *big* surprise to the phone companies, didn't appear until 1995). Needless to say, the phone companies were motivated to come up with a way to generate higher capacities. Their answer was fairly straightforward: make the entire phone system digital. By adding special equipment at the central office and the user's location, phone companies can achieve a throughput of up to 64 Kbps per line (see the following) over the same copper wires already used by PSTN lines. This process of sending telephone transmission across fully digital lines end-to-end is called *Integrated Services Digital Network (ISDN)* service.

NOTE ISDN also supports voice, but requires special ISDN telephones.

ISDN service consists of two types of channels: Bearer or B channels and Delta or D channels. *B channels* carry data and voice information at 64 Kbps, while *D channels* carry setup and configuration information, as well as data, at 16 Kbps. Most providers of ISDN let the user choose either one or two B channels. The more common setup is two B/one D, usually called a *Basic Rate Interface (BRI)* setup. A BRI setup uses only one physical line, but each B channel sends 64 Kbps, doubling the throughput total to 128 Kbps. Far less common but still available in some areas is ISDN PRI. ISDN PRI only provides a single B channel for a total throughput of 64 Kbps. ISDN connects much faster than PSTN, eliminating that long, annoying, modem mating call you get with PSTN. The monthly cost per B channel is slightly more than a PSTN line, and there is usually a fairly steep initial cost for the installation and equipment. The other limitation is that not everyone can get ISDN. You usually need to be within about 18,000 feet of a central office to use ISDN.

NOTE ISDN uses only PPP, not SLIP!

The physical connections for ISDN bear some similarity to PSTN modems. An ISDN wall socket is usually something that looks like a standard RJ-45 network jack. This line runs to your demarc. In home installations most telephone companies will install a second demarc separate from your PSTN demarc. The most common interface for your computer is a device called a *terminal adapter (TA)*. TAs look like regular modems, and like modems, come in external and internal variants. You can even get TAs that also function as hubs, enabling your system to support a direct LAN connection (see Figure 16-4).

TIP A single channel is often referred to as a DS0 channel.

When you install an ISDN TA, you must configure the other ISDN telephone number you want to call and a special number called the Service Profile ID (SPID). Your Internet service provider (ISP) provides the telephone number and the telephone company gives you the SPID. (In many cases the telephone company is also the ISP.) Figure 16-5 shows a typical installation screen for an internal ISDN TA. Note that each channel has a phone number in this case. Once installed an external ISDN TA looks like another modem in Device Manager.

Figure 16-4
An ISDN terminal
adapter with hub

ISDN continues to soldier on in today's networking world, but has for the most part been replaced by faster and cheaper methods such as DSL and cable modems. Nevertheless, every major telephone company still provides ISDN. ISDN is often the only option for users in locations where other high-speed connection options don't exist.

DSL

Digital Subscriber Line (DSL) is a fully digital, dedicated (no phone number) connection provided by a number of telephone companies. DSL represented the next great leap forward past ISDN for telephone lines. A DSL connection manifests as just another PSTN connection, using the same RJ11 jack as any regular phone line. DSL comes in two versions, *Symmetric DSL (SDSL)* and *Asymmetric DSL (ADSL)*. SDSL lines provide the same upload and download speeds, making them excellent for those who send as much data as they receive, although SDSL is relatively expensive. ADSL uses different upload and

Figure 16-5
ISDN TA
configuration
screen

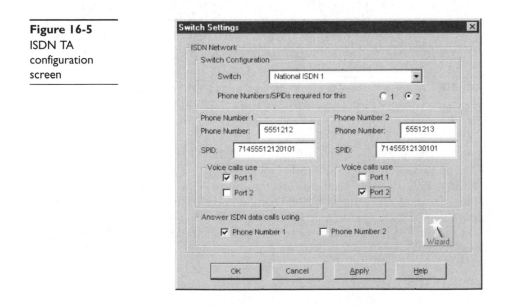

download speeds. ADSL download speeds are much faster than the upload speeds. Most SOHO users are primarily concerned with fast *downloads* for things like web pages, and can tolerate slower upload speeds. ADSL is always much cheaper than SDSL.

> **NOTE** These speeds are just for Houston, Texas! Your local providers may offer different speed options.

SDSL

SDSL provides equal upload and download speed and in theory provides speeds up to 9 Mbps, although the vast majority of ISPs provide packages ranging from 192 Kbps to 1.5 Mbps. A recent tour of some major DSL providers in the author's home town, Houston, Texas, revealed the following SDSL speed options:

- 192 Kbps
- 384 Kbps
- 768 Kbps
- 1.1 Mbps
- 1.5 Mbps

As you might imagine, the pricing for the faster services was higher than the lower packages!

ADSL

ADSL provides a theoretical maximum download speeds up to 9 Mbps and upload speeds up to 1 Mbps over PSTN lines. However, all ADSL suppliers "throttle" their ADSL speeds and provide different levels of service. Real-world ADSL download speeds vary from 384 Kbps to 3 Mbps and upload speeds go from as low as 64 Kbps to around 384 Kbps. Touring the same DSL providers in Houston, Texas, I found the following speed options:

- 384 Kbps Down/128 Kbps Up
- 1.5 Mbps Down/128 Kbps Up
- 1.5 Mbps Down/384 Kbps Up

DSL Features

The only real difference between ADSL and SDSL is speed. Everything else—equipment and distance limits—is the same.

One nice aspect of DSL is that you don't have to run new phone lines. The same DSL line you use for data can simultaneously transmit your voice calls. The only downside to DSL is that you can't use it unless your ISP specifically supports DSL. Many ISPs currently support DSL, so most customers have a wide array of choices.

Both versions of DSL have the same central office-to-end-user distance restrictions as ISDN—around 18,000 feet from your demarc to the central office. At the central office your DSL provider has a device called a DSL Access Multiplexer (DSLAM) that connects multiple customers to the Internet.

NOTE No DSL provider guarantees any particular transmission speed and will only provide service as a "best efforts" contract—a nice way to say that DSL lines are notorious for substantial variations in throughput. This is true, even of ISPs that lease the lines from the same telephone service.

Installing DSL

DSL operates using your pre-existing telephone lines (assuming they are up to spec). This is wonderful, but also presents a technical challenge. For DSL and your run-of-the-mill POTS line to coexist, you need to filter out the DSL signal on the POTS line. A DSL line has three information channels: a high-speed downstream channel, a medium-speed duplex channel, and a POTS channel. Segregating the two DSL channels from the POTS channel guarantees that your POTS line will continue to operate even if the DSL fails. This is accomplished by inserting a filter on each POTS line, or a splitter mechanism that allows all three channels to flow to the DSL modem, but sends only the POTS channel down the POTS line. The DSL company should provide you with a few POTS filters for your telephones. If you need more, most computer/electronics stores stock DSL POTS filters.

TIP If you install a telephone onto a line in your home with DSL and you forget to add a filter, don't panic. You won't destroy anything, although you won't get a dial tone either! Just insert a DSL POTS filter and the telephone will work.

The most common DSL installation consists of a *DSL modem* connected to a telephone wall jack, and to a standard NIC in your computer (see Figure 16-6). A DSL modem is not an actual modem—it's more like an ISDN terminal adapter—but the term stuck, and even the manufacturers of the devices now call them DSL modems.

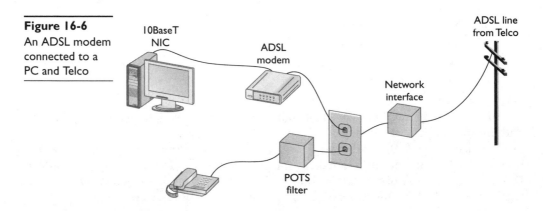

Figure 16-6
An ADSL modem connected to a PC and Telco

10BaseT NIC

ADSL modem

Network interface

ADSL line from Telco

POTS filter

NOTE The one potentially costly aspect of ADSL service is the ISP link. Many ISPs add a significant surcharge to use ADSL. Before you choose ADSL, make sure that your ISP provides ADSL links at a reasonable price. Most telephone companies bundle ISP services with their ADSL service for a low cost.

Many offices use DSL. In my office we use a special DSL line (we use a digital phone system so the DSL must be separate) that runs directly into our equipment room (Figure 16-7).

This DSL line runs into our DSL modem via a standard phone line with RJ-11 connectors. The DSL modem connects to our gateway router with a CAT 5e patch cable, which in turn connects to the company's hub. Figure 16-8 shows an ADSL modem and a router, giving an idea of the configuration in our office.

Home users often connect the DSL modem directly to their PC's NIC. Either way, there is nothing to do in terms of installing DSL equipment on an individual system—just make sure you have a NIC that works with your DSL modem (almost all do). The person who installs your DSL will test the DSL line, install the DSL modem, connect it to your system, and verify that it all works. The one issue you may run into with DSL is something called *PPP over Ethernet (PPPoE)*.

The first generation of DSL providers used *bridged connection*—once the DSL line was running it was the same as if you snapped an Ethernet cable into your NIC—you were on the network. Those were good days for DSL. You just plugged your DSL modem into your NIC and, assuming your IP settings were whatever the DSL folks told you to use, you were running.

The DSL providers didn't like that too much. There was no control—no way to monitor who was using the DSL modem. As a result, the DSL folks started to use PPPoE, a protocol that was originally designed to encapsulate PPP frames into Ethernet frames. The DSL people adopted it to make stronger controls over your DSL connection. In particular, you could no longer simply connect, you now had to logon with an account and a password to make the DSL connection. PPPoE is now predominant on DSL. If you get a DSL line, you must add software to your PC to enable you to logon to your DSL network. If you have Windows XP, you have built in support. Many SOHO routers come with built in PPPoE support, enabling you to enter your user name and password into the router itself.

While most DSL providers will gladly configure a single system for DSL, no DSL provider will configure a gateway router for free—some DSL companies even try to prevent more than one machine from using a single DSL connection. Many companies sell SOHO routers with all the necessary DSL support—including PPPoE.

Figure 16-7
DSL line into equipment room

Figure 16-8
DSL connection
with router

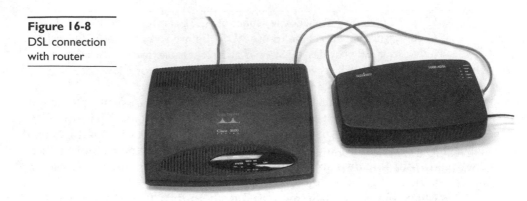

Cable Modems

The big competition for ADSL comes from the cable companies. Almost every house in America has a coax cable running into it for cable TV. In a moment of genius, the cable industry realized if they could put the Home Shopping Network and the History Channel into every home, why not provide Internet access? The entire infrastructure of the cabling industry had to undergo some major changes to deal with issues like bidirectional communication, but most cities in the United States now provide cable modem service. Cable modems are well on their way to becoming as common as cable TV boxes, or at least such is the dream of the cable companies.

NOTE DSL and cable modem are collectively called *broadband* connections.

The single most impressive aspect of cable modems is their phenomenal top speeds. These speeds vary from cable company to cable company, but most advertise speeds in the (are you sitting down?) *10 to 27 megabits per second* range! Okay, now that you've heard this exciting news, don't get too excited, because there is a catch: You have to *share* that massive throughput with all of your neighbors who also have cable modems. The problem: as more people in the neighborhood connect, the throughput of any individual modem drops. How significant is this drop? Some early installations showed that the throughput of a heavily used cable line can drop to *under* 100 Kbps! The cable modem providers are aware of this and now do a good job of keeping any single neighborhood from getting too many systems and causing these terrible drops in service. Today most cable modems provide a throughput speed of 1 to 3 Mbps downloading and 500 Kbps uploading, though some service providers limit upstream access speeds to 256 Kbps or less.

NOTE Unlike DSL, most cable companies do provide a guaranteed minimum speed.

A cable modem installation consists of a cable modem connected to a cable outlet. The cable modem gets its own cable outlet, separate from the one that goes to the television. It's the same cable line, just split from the main line as if you were adding a second cable outlet for another television. As with ADSL, cable modems connect to PCs using a standard NIC (see Figure 16-9).

It's hard to tell a cable modem from a DSL modem! The only difference, other than the fact that one will have "cable modem" printed on it while the other will say "DSL modem" is that the cable modem has a coax and an RJ-45 connecter while the DSL modem has an RJ-11 and an RJ-45 connector.

Cable modems have proven themselves to be reliable and fast and have surpassed DSL as the broadband connection of choice in homes. Cable companies are also aggressively marketing to business customers with high-speed packages, making cable a viable option for businesses.

Satellite

Living in the countryside may have its charms, but it makes it tough to get high-speed Internet access. For those too far away to get anything else, satellite may be your only option. Satellite access comes in two types: one-way and two-way. *One-way* means that you download from satellite but you must use a PSTN connection for uploads. *Two-way* means the satellite service handles both the uploading and downloading.

Satellite isn't as fast as DSL or cable modems, but it's still faster than PSTN. Both one-way and two-way satellite connections provide around 500 Kbps download and 50 Kbps upload. Satellite requires a small satellite antenna, identical to the ones used for satellite television. This antenna connects to a satellite modem, which in turn connects to your PC or your network (Figure 16-10).

TIP   Neither cable modems nor satellite use PPP, PPPoE, or anything else that begins with three Ps.

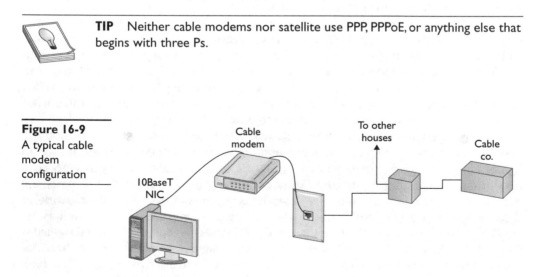

Figure 16-9
A typical cable modem configuration

Figure 16-10
Satellite setup

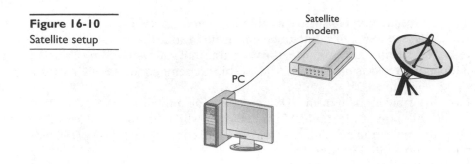

Which Connection?

With so many connection options for homes and small offices, making a decision is often a challenge. Your first question is availability: which services are available in your area? The second question is how much bandwidth do you need? This is a question of great argument. Most services will be more than glad to increase service levels if you find a certain level is too slow. I usually advise clients to start with a relatively slow level, and then increase if necessary. After all, it's hard to go slower once you've tasted the higher speeds, but relatively painless to go faster!

WAN Connections

A *wide area network (WAN)* is a computer network that spans a relatively large geographical area. Typically, a WAN consists of two or more LANs connected together over a distance. Computers in a WAN often connect through a public network, such as the telephone system. They can also connect through leased lines or satellites. The largest WAN in existence is—can you guess?—the Internet.

As I hope you realize by now, mystical packet gnomes do not magically whisk information from one LAN to another. Packets travel over a variety of connection media. Because a large quantity of information needs to travel between LANs in a speedy and reliable fashion, WAN backbone connections are faster and *far* more expensive than any SOHO connection. You're not going to find a typical home user connecting her computer to an ATM or a T3 connection (we'll discuss these in a moment); those are for businesses and universities that have many computers connecting to other LANs across the globe.

WAN connections come with a rather hairy hodgepodge of terms, so it's best to think about WAN connections using the OSI seven-layer model. All WAN connections are digital and use some form of data packets, so there's a strong analogy between WAN connections and LAN connections. All WAN connections consist of three distinct parts: the physical link, the signal method, and the switching protocol. The *physical link* works at the Physical layer of OSI, and is simply the cabling and the connections, as well as the equipment on each end of the link that sends and reads the signal. The *signal method* is roughly the Data Link layer and deals with how the signals propagate across the WAN connection. The *switching protocol* is the framing method and also works at the Data Link layer, defining the ways each WAN device is addressed and defines the packets used.

We can break all WAN connections in two groups: copper carriers and fiber carriers. Both copper and fiber have their own unique physical links and signal methods but share the same switching protocols. Let's look at copper and fiber connections, and then see the switching protocols they share.

Copper Carriers: T1 and T3

Taking an analog voice signal and moving it across hundreds or thousands of miles has always been a challenge for the telephone industry. One way to make voice transmission easier is to convert it from analog to digital. Digital signals are easier to create, can accept more degradation over distance than analog, and allow for the idea of packetizing the information to allow multiple conversations to take place over the same line at the same time. Digitizing voice for long-distance communication can be traced back to the 1930s, but it wasn't until the introduction of the T1 technology that we saw widespread use of digital voice communication across the United States.

T1 has several meanings. First, it refers to a high-speed digital networking technology called a T1 connection. Second, the term *T1 line* refers to the specific, shielded, two-pair cabling that connects the two ends of a T1 connection (Figure 16-11). Two wires are for sending data and two wires for receiving data. At either end of a T1 line you'll find an un-assuming box called a Channel Service Unit/Digital Service Unit (CSU/DSU). The CSU/DSU has a second connection that goes from the phone company (where the boxes reside) to a customer's equipment (usually a router). A T1 connection is point-to-point—you cannot have more than two CSU/DSUs on a single T1 line.

T1 uses a special signaling method called DS1. *DS1* uses a relatively primitive frame—the frame doesn't need to be complex because with point to point there's no addressing necessary. Further, error checking is handled at higher layers, not at the Physical layer, which means the frame does not need the added complexity.

Each DS1 frame has 25 pieces: a framing bit and 24 data channels. Each data channel can hold 8 bits of data; the framing bit and data channels combine to make 193 bits per DS1 frame. These frames are transmitted 8000 times/sec, making a total throughput of 1.544 Mbps (Figure 16-12). DS1 defines, therefore, a data transfer speed of 1.544 Mbps, split into 24 64-Kbps *channels*. Each channel can carry a separate signal, or channels can be configured (with the right CSU) to work together. This process of having frames that carry a bit of every channel in every frame sent on a regular interval is called *time division multiplexing*.

Figure 16-11
T1 cable

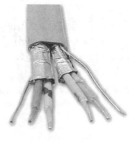

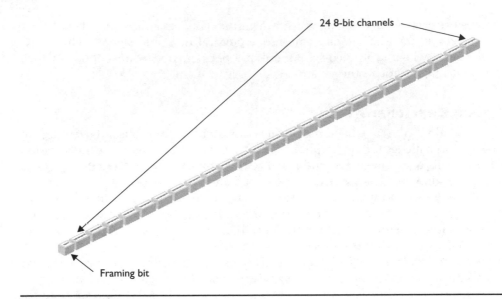

24 8-bit channels

Framing bit

Figure 16-12   DSI frame

 TIP   If you're handy with math in your head or with a calculator, you might immediately question the accuracy of the numbers involved in describing T1 speeds. After all, 193 bits × 8,000 seconds = 1,544,000 bits per second, or 1.544 million bits per second. You normally wouldn't use the abbreviation Mbps for *million* bits per second, right? Sadly, that's exactly the case here. When reading the signaling speeds regarding T1 and other WAN technologies (such as SONET, discussed in the following), think "millions" and "billions" of bits per second when you see Mbps and Gbps!

An analogy I like to use in class for T1 technology is that of a conveyor belt in a milk-bottling factory. At regular intervals, big crates with 24 bottles come rolling down the belt. When they reach the filling machine, the bottles get filled with milk and the crate keeps rolling down to the other end where two machines take over: the labeling and sorting machines. The labeling machine plucks out the bottles and applies a label to each, appropriate to the contents. The sorting machine sorts the bottles into cases of each type.

This is pretty simple if the filling machine uses only one type of milk. All 24 bottles fill with whole milk; all are labeled as whole milk; and all go into the case marked "Whole Milk." Once enough bottles come in with the milk, the case gets completed, and you have a product.

That's pretty much how an Ethernet packet works, right? The whole packet is used for a single set of data, and then multiple packets get put together at the end to make your data transfer complete.

The cool thing about the DS1 frame, though, is that you don't have to use the whole frame for a single set of data. With the right CSU/DSU at either end, you can specify which channels go with a specific thread of data. Sloshing back into the analogy . . . the milk company produces four types of milk: whole milk, lowfat milk, chocolate milk, and strawberry milk. The strawberry milk is seasonal; the whole milk sells the most, followed by chocolate, and then lowfat.

To accommodate the different products, the factory master designates channels 1–10 for whole milk, 11–18 for chocolate milk, 19–22 for lowfat milk, and 23–24 for strawberry. Now the labeling and sorting machines are going to have to work for a living! When a crate reaches the filling machine, the bottles get filled with the various types of milk, and then the crate trundles on down the belt. The labeling machine knows the numbering system, so it labels bottles 1–10 as whole milk, 11–18 as chocolate, and so on. The sorting machine also knows the system and has four cases at hand, one for each product. As the bottles arrive, it places them into the appropriate cases. Now notice that the cases will fill at different rates of speed. It'll take a while for the strawberry case to fill, especially compared to the whole milk, because only two channels in each crate carry strawberry.

What happens if the cows temporarily stop producing chocolate milk? Will the whole factory need to be reordered so the filling machine's eight chocolate dispensers can dispense some other kind of milk? The answer at this factory is no. The crates continue to roll down the conveyor belt at regular intervals. The filling machine fills the bottles in channels 1–10 with whole milk, leaves the bottles in channels 11–18 empty, and puts lowfat and strawberry in channels 19–22 and 23–24, respectively.

DS1 and T1 work the same way! The frame just keeps jetting down the line, even if some of the channels contain no data. The CSU/DSU at the other end collects the data streams and keeps them separate. To paraphrase the immortal words of Professor Egon, "Never cross the streams." Otherwise you'd lose data!

To bring the milk bottling factory analogy completely into the realm of networking and T1 connections, keep in mind that there would be two conveyor belts running in opposite directions. Milk flows in; milk flows out. You can both send and receive on T1 connections.

A T1 line is a dedicated phone connection that you lease, usually on a monthly basis, from the telephone company. It has no telephone number and it's always connected. An entire T1 bundle can be expensive, so many telephone companies let you buy just some of these individual channels. This is known as *fractional T1 access*.

NOTE Each 64K channel in a DS1 signal is called a DS0. ISDN B lines are DS0 channels.

A *T3 line* is a dedicated telephone connection supporting a data rate of about 43 Mbps. A T3 line consists of 672 individual channels, each of which supports 64 Kbps. T3 lines (sometimes referred to as DS3 lines) are used mainly by ISPs connecting to the Internet backbone, and by the backbone itself.

Similar to the North American T1 line, *E1* is the European format for digital transmission. An E1 line carries signals at 2 Mbps (32 channels at 64 Kbps), compared to the T1's 1.544 Mbps (24 channels at 64 Kbps). Both E1 and T1 lines may be interconnected for international use. There are also E3 lines, which are similar to T3 lines, with a bandwidth of 45 Mbps. Japan also has its own digital transmission formats: J-1 is identical to T1 in every way with the exception of a few signaling differences, while J-3 provides 480 channels with a throughput of 32 Mbps.

A CSU/DSU, as mentioned earlier, connects a leased T1 or T3 line from the telephone company to a customer's equipment. A CSU/DSU has (at least) two connectors, one that goes to the T1/T3 line running out of your demarc/NI and another connection that goes to your router. It performs line encoding and conditioning functions, and often has a loopback function for testing. Although CSU/DSUs look a lot like modems, they are not modems, because they don't modulate/demodulate. All they do is interface between a T1 or T3 line and a router. Many newer routers have CSU/DSUs built into them. Figure 16-13 shows the back of a Cisco router with two T1 interfaces. Two interfaces on one router is quite common, the dual links providing redundancy if one link goes down.

The CSU part of a CSU/DSU is designed to protect the T1 or T3 line and the user equipment from lightning strikes and other types of electrical interference. It also stores statistics and has capabilities for loopback testing. The DSU part supplies timing to each user port, taking the incoming user data signals and converting the input signal into the specified line code, and then framing the format for transmission over the provided line.

Fiber Carriers: SONET/SDH and OC

In the early 1980s, fiber-optic cabling became the primary tool for long distance communication all over the world, but the major telephone carriers had four different, virtually incompatible transmission standards—not a good thing. In an incredible moment of corporate cooperation, in 1987, all of the primary fiber-optic carriers decided to drop their own standards and move to a new international standard called *Synchronous Optical Network (SONET)* in the United States and *Synchronous Digital Hierarchy (SDH)* in Europe.

Figure 16-13
Cisco router with two WAN connections (photo courtesy of Cisco Corp.)

NOTE Students often wonder why two separate names exist for the same technology. In reality, SONET and SDH vary a little in their signaling and frame type, but routers and other magic boxes on the Internet handle the interoperability between the standards. The American National Standards Institute (ANSI) publishes the standard as SONET; the International Telecommunications Union (ITU) publishes the standard as SDH, but includes SONET signaling. For simplicity sake and because SONET is the more common term in the United States, this book uses SONET as the generic term for this technology.

SONET is the primary standard for connecting fiber-optic transmission systems. There is a high level of comparison of SONET to network standards like Ethernet or Token Ring because SONET defines interface standards at the Physical and Data Link layers of the OSI seven-layer model. The physical aspect of SONET is partially covered by the Optical Carrier standards, but it also defines a ring-based topology that most SONET adopters now use. SONET does not require a ring, but a SONET ring has extra survivability in case of line loss. As a result, most of the big, long-distance optical pipes for the world's telecommunications networks are SONET rings.

TIP SONET is one of the most important standards for making all of our WAN interconnections—and it's also the least likely standard you'll ever see because it's hidden away from all but the biggest networks.

The real beauty of SONET lies in its multiplexing capabilities. A single SONET ring can combine multiple DS1, DS3, even European E1 signals and package them into one big SONET frame for transmission down the line. Clearly, for SONET to handle such large data rates it needs high-capacity fiber optics—and that's where the optical carrier standards come into play!

The *Optical Carrier (OC)* specification is used to denote the optical data carrying capacity (in Mbps) of fiber-optic cables in networks conforming to the SONET standard. The OC standard is an escalating series of speeds, designed to meet the needs of medium-to-large corporations. SONET establishes OCs from 51.8 Mbps (OC-1) to 13.2 Gbps (OC-256).

SONET uses the *Synchronous Transport Signal (STS)* signal method. The STS consists of two parts: the STS *payload* (which carries data), and the STS *overhead* (which carries the signaling and protocol information). When we talk about STS, we add a number to the end of "STS" to designate the speed of the signal. For example, STS-1 is the 51.85 Mbps signal that runs on an OC-1 line. STS-3 runs at 155.52 Mbps on OC-3 lines, and so on.

Table 16-1 describes the most common optical carriers.

Packet Switching

All of these impressive connections that start with Ts and Os are powerful, but they are not in and of themselves a complete WAN solution. These WAN connections make up the entire mesh of long-range connections we call the Internet, but these same connec-

PART III

Table 16-1	SONET Optical Level	Line Speed	Signal Method
Optical Carriers	OC-1	51.85 Mbps	STS-1
	OC-3	155.52 Mbps	STS-3
	OC-12	622.08 Mbps	STS-12
	OC-24	1.244 Gbps	STS-24
	OC-48	2.488 Gbps	STS-48
	OC-192	9.955 Gbps	STS-192
	OC-256	13.22 Gbps	STS-256
	OC-768	39.82 Gbps	STS-768

tions also carry voice and other types of data as well as TCP/IP packets. All of these connections are point to point, so we need to add another level of devices to enable us to connect multiple T1s, T3s, or OC connections together to make that mesh. That's where packet switching comes into play.

Around the same time the ARPANET folks came up with the idea of routers, the telephone industry was moving from an analog system to a digital one where long-distance (and later, local) conversations were moved using packets of data. Packets, as you know from what you've learned about networking, need some form of addressing scheme to get from one location to another. The telephone industry came up with its own types of packets that run on ISDN, T1/T3, and OC lines to get data from one CO to another. These packet-switching protocols are functionally identical to routable network protocols such as IPX/SPX and TCP/IP. One of these packet-switching protocols—ATM—started as a high-speed LAN protocol but is not used by the telephone industry.

X.25

X.25 Packet Switched networks enable remote devices to communicate with each other across high-speed digital links without the expense of individual leased lines. X.25 encompasses the first three layers of the OSI seven-layer architecture, and gives you a virtual high-quality digital network at low cost. It is inexpensive because you share the infrastructure with other people who use the service. In most parts of the world, users pay for X.25 by way of a fixed monthly connection fee combined with a charge for the amount of data passed through the X.25 connection.

X.25 is considerably slower than the other WAN communications discussed here, but it's still out there. The big reason, aside from its continued large presence in Europe, is that X.25 is used by Automatic Teller Machines (ATMs) in the United States. So, oddly enough, X.25 *is* used with ATM, just not the ATM you're about to learn about! X.25 has been around since the mid-1970s, so it's thoroughly debugged and stable. You literally never encounter data errors on modern X.25 networks.

Frame Relay

Frame Relay is an extremely efficient data-transmission technique used to send digital information such as voice, data, LAN, and WAN traffic quickly and cost-efficiently to many destinations from one port. It is especially effective for the off-again/on-again traffic typical of most LAN applications. Frame Relay switches packets end-to-end much faster than X.25, but without any guarantee of data integrity at all. The network delivers the frames whether the CRC check matches or not. You can't even count on it to deliver all the frames, because it will discard frames whenever there is network congestion. In practice, however, a Frame Relay network delivers data quite reliably. Unlike the analog communication lines that were originally used for X.25, the modern digital lines that use Frame relay have very low error rates.

Frame Relay is extremely popular. If you decide to go with a T1 line in the United States, what you're getting is a T1 line running Frame Relay, although some companies are now moving away from Frame Relay and moving toward ATM as their packet-switching solution.

ATM

Most people think an ATM is an automatic teller machine, and so it is, but not in this case. ATM is short for *Asynchronous Transfer Mode*. ATM was originally designed as a high-speed LAN networking technology. While ATM only saw limited success in the LAN world, ATM has become extremely popular in the WAN world. Most of the SONET rings that move voice and data all over the world use ATM for packet switching. *ATM* integrates voice, video, and data on one connection, using short and fixed-length packets called *cells* to transfer information. Every cell sent with the same source and destination travels over the same route, giving ATM the potential to remove the performance bottlenecks that exist in today's LANs and WANs. The key problem ATM addresses is that data and audio/video transmissions have different transfer requirements. Data can tolerate a delay in transfer, but not signal loss. Audio and video transmissions, on the other hand, can tolerate signal loss but not delay. Because ATM transfers information in cells of one set size (53 bytes long), it is scalable and can handle both types of transfers well. ATM transfer speeds range from 155.52 to 622.08 Mbps and beyond.

Using Remote Access

Because most businesses are no longer limited to a simple little shop like you would find in a Dickens novel, there is a great need for people to be able to access files and resources over a great distance. Enter remote access. *Remote access* uses WAN and LAN connections to enable a computer user to log on to a network from the other side of a city, a state, or even the globe. As people travel, information has to remain accessible. Remote access enables users to dial into a server at the business location and log in to the network as if they were in the same building as the company. The only problem with remote access is that there are so many ways to do it! The four most common forms of remote access are as follows:

- **Dial-up to the Internet**   Using a dial-up connection to connect to your ISP

- **Private dial-up**   Using a dial-up connection to connect to your private network

- **Virtual private network**   Using an Internet connection to connect to a private network

- **Dedicated connection**   Using a non-dial-up connection to another private network or the Internet

In this section we look at configuring these four types of connections in a Windows environment. After seeing how to configure these types of remote connections, we move into observing some security issues common to every type of remote connections. Last, we'll see how to use Windows Internet Connection Sharing with any of these remote access options to enable a network of computers to use a single connection for remote access.

 NOTE *Extranet* is one of those terms that you'll see more in books than in the day-to-day workings of networks and network techs. So, what is an extranet? Whenever you allow authorized remote users to access some part of your private network, you have created an extranet.

Dial-up to the Internet

Dialing up to the Internet is the oldest, cheapest, and the most common way for home and small office users to connect to the Internet. Dial-up requires you to have some method to create a connection to your ISP. This connection needs information to work. At the very least, you'll need:

- The telephone number to dial
- The modem to use (you might have more than one!)
- User name and password (provided to you by the ISP)
- Type of connection (PPP or SLIP)
- IP information (provided to you by the ISP)

Also keep in mind that you might have more than one dial-up connection. Your operating system needs a way to create and store multiple connections for you to choose from depending on which dial-up connection you want to make at a given moment.

Every version of Microsoft Windows since Windows 95 comes with some tool to help you set up your dial-up connections. This tool has had many names. It's called *Dial-Up Networking* (*DUN*) in Windows NT and 9*x* (Figure 16-14) and treats dial-up connections

Figure 16-14
DUN in
Windows 98

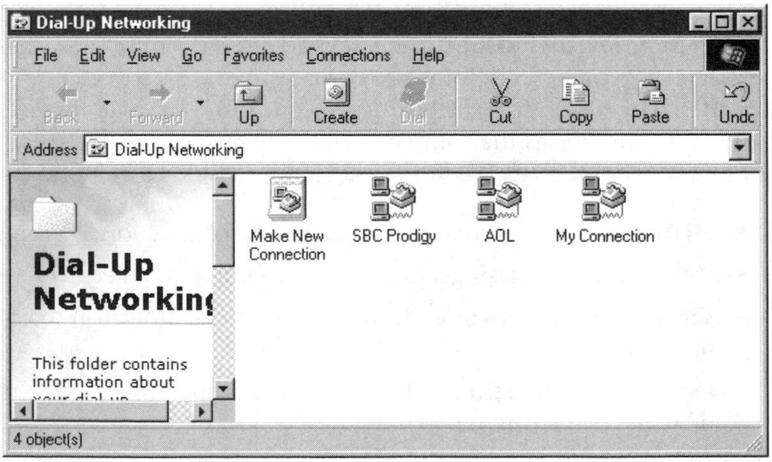

> **Dial-Up Networking**
> File Edit View Go Favorites Connections Help
>
> Back Forward Up Create Dial Cut Copy Paste Undo
>
> Address Dial-Up Networking
>
> **Dial-Up Networking**
> This folder contains information about your dial-up
>
> Make New Connection   SBC Prodigy   AOL   My Connection
>
> 4 object(s)

separately from other network connections. Windows 2000 calls it Network and Dial-up Connections; Windows XP calls it Network Connections, combining dial-up connections into the same dialog box as your other network connections (Figure 16-15). Whatever the name, this tool is what you use to create dial-up connections.

TIP Two issues to remember. First, even though all of these programs have different names, they are accessed the same way: Start | Programs | Accessories | Communications | *<name of program>*. Second, make sure you are comfortable with the different names for the different versions of Windows.

All these tools have a Make New Connection (or *Create a new connection* option in Windows XP) icon that starts a utility (a *wizard* in Microsoft parlance) to help you make the connections you need. Every version of Windows has a slightly different wizard. Even though these wizards may each have their own look, they all do the same thing—make new connections. Figure 16-16 shows the Windows 98 wizard in action. Note that it only configures dial-up connections. If you want to make any other type of connection, you need to head over to the Network Neighborhood Properties dialog box.

The New Connection Wizard in Windows XP (Figure 16-17) is for more than just dial-up connections. This one wizard handles every type of remote connection you might want to make, not just dial-up connections. We'll see this wizard again as we move into other remote connection options.

Each Windows dial-up wizard has a different look and feel, but we can watch the creation of two dial-up connections—one in Windows 98 and one in Windows XP—to get a pretty good grasp of the scope of how to do this. Let's start with Windows 98.

Figure 16-15
Network Connections in Windows XP Professional

Figure 16-16
Windows 98
DUN Wizard in
action

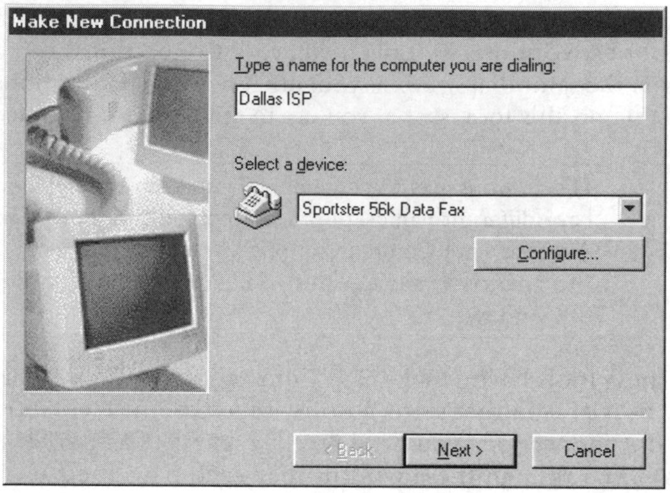

Dial-up in Windows 98

Creating a dial-up connection in Windows 98 is simple—possibly too simple as you often need to go back into a connection after it's created by the wizard to add information. The previous Figure 16-16 just showed you the first screen in the DUN wizard in Windows 98, asking for a name for the connection and the modem to use. Always give your connections a good descriptive name so you can tell them apart. Clicking the Next button (Figure 16-18) brings you to the second and last screen (other than the Finish screen) of the wizard where it prompts you for a phone number and country code (for those who like to make expensive remote connections)!

Figure 16-17
Windows XP
Professional New
Connection
Wizard in action

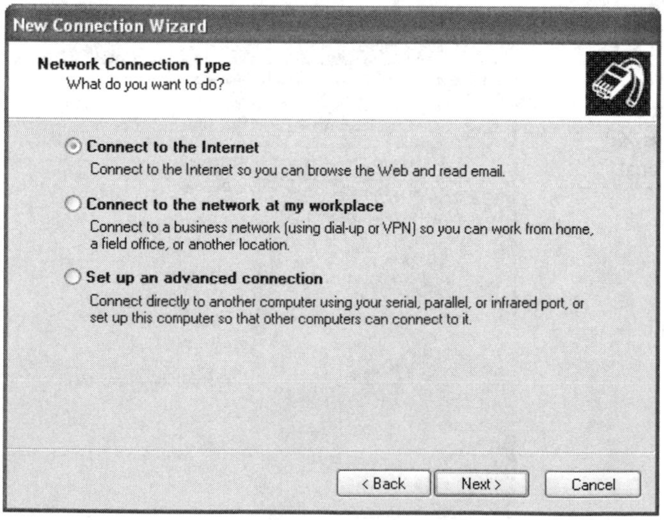

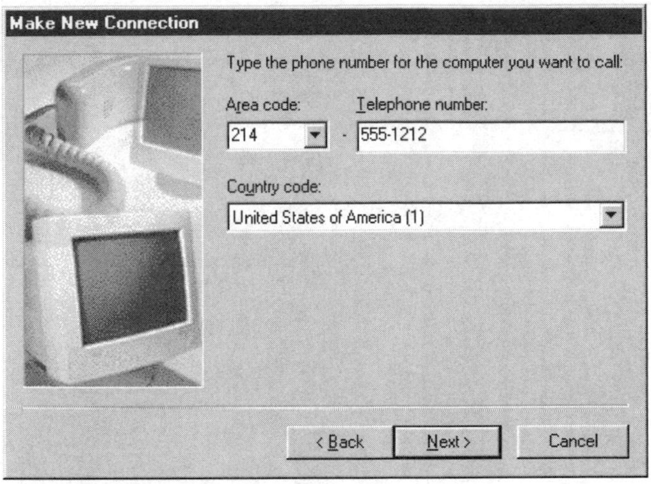

Figure 16-18
Prompting for telephone number

That's pretty much it for the Windows 98 DUN wizard. So where is the SLIP/PPP selection? Where do you enter the user name and password? Where do you enter IP information? This is where the age of the old Windows 98 wizard shows—you need to go to other places to complete the process. The user name and password are saved the first time you dial the connection. Figure 16-19 shows the Connect To dialog box when you select a connection the first time. Here you enter the user name, password, and dialing location—we'll discuss dialing locations in a moment. You can also change the phone number here.

To make other changes to a dial-up connection's settings in Windows 98, you'll need to head to the connections' Properties dialog box. To change a connection's properties, just alternate-click the connection and select Properties to see a dialog box like the one shown in Figure 16-20. The General tab enables you to make changes to the phone number and the modem you want to use as well as other settings.

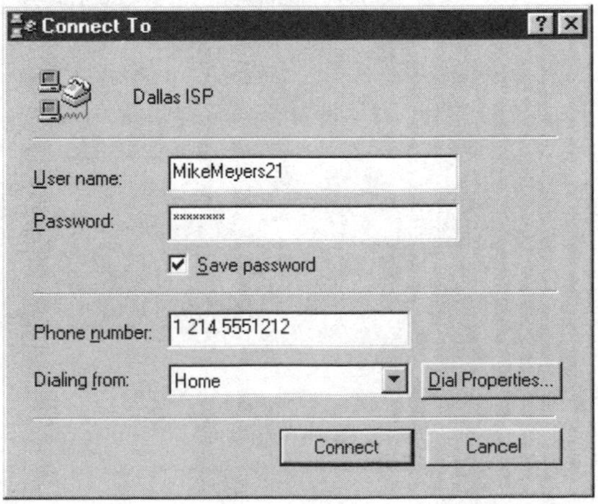

Figure 16-19
Connect To
dialog box

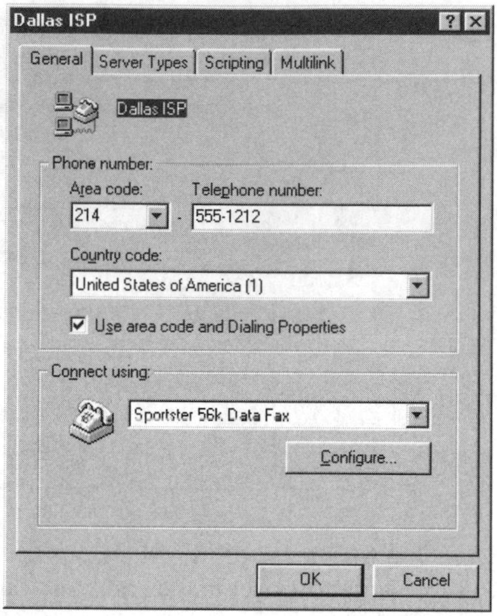

Figure 16-20
Connection
Properties
General tab

The most heavily visited tab in this dialog box is the Server Types tab (Figure 16-21). If you're having a problem with a Windows 98 dial-up connection, this is probably your first place to check. This is where you select the type of connection: PPP, SLIP, and other types; but given that Windows 98 defaults to PPP, you're usually in good shape.

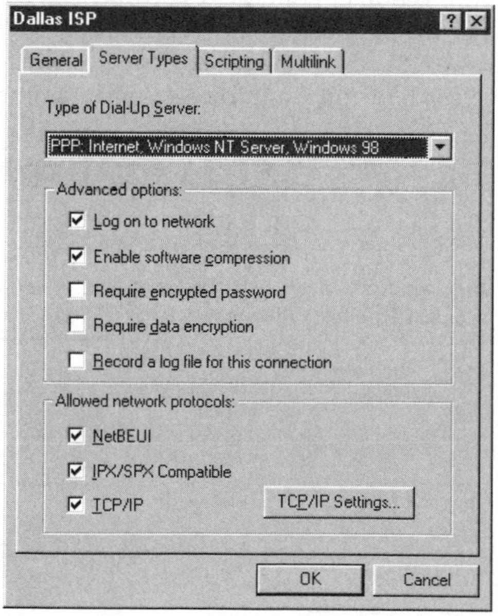

Figure 16-21
Connection
Properties Server
Types tab

How you need to set up the Advanced options differs for every ISP, although the defaults of *log on to network* and *Enable software compression* work for most ISPs. The *Allowed network protocols* section defines what protocols to load for this connection. By default, Windows 98 loads NetBEUI, IPS/SPX, and TCP/IP. This is not good because running NetBEUI in particular will expose your system to hacking. Be sure to turn off NetBEUI and IPX/SPX! Your connection is set up for DHCP by default, but if you needed to configure TCP/IP settings like the IP address or DNS server, you click on the TCP/IP Settings button.

NOTE The Scripting and Multilink tabs are rarely used. The Scripting tab runs script files to support older connections and the Multilink tab enables two modems to work together as one connection. Multilink requires ISP support and few ISPs offer this option.

Once you've made these settings, you're ready to start dialing. Keep in mind that your best source for information on configuring a dial-up connection (and this is true for all versions of Windows) is your ISP. Every ISP has good-to-superb support to show you how to configure these settings properly. Let's do this again, but this time use Windows XP Professional.

Windows XP Dial-up

The Windows XP New Connection Wizard shows how Microsoft has matured the dial-up process. You'll find more screens and more questions, reflecting more robust and sophisticated dial-up connections. This is an intelligent wizard that can change based on how you're connected to the network (domain vs. workgroup) and other settings. Way back in Figure 16-17 you saw the first screen of XP's New Connection Wizard. Note that it has three settings. Now look at Figure 16-22—it has a fourth setting called *Set up a home or small office network*. The computer in Figure 16-17 is part of a domain so the wizard assumes you don't want to set up a home or small office network—a pretty safe assumption!

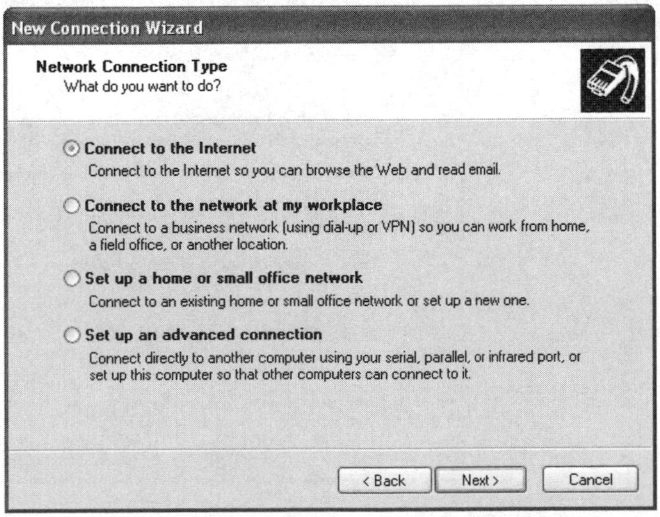

Figure 16-22
New Connection Wizard in Windows XP

New Connection Wizard

Network Connection Type
What do you want to do?

◉ **Connect to the Internet**
Connect to the Internet so you can browse the Web and read email.

○ **Connect to the network at my workplace**
Connect to a business network (using dial-up or VPN) so you can work from home, a field office, or another location.

○ **Set up a home or small office network**
Connect to an existing home or small office network or set up a new one.

○ **Set up an advanced connection**
Connect directly to another computer using your serial, parallel, or infrared port, or set up this computer so that other computers can connect to it.

[< Back] [Next >] [Cancel]

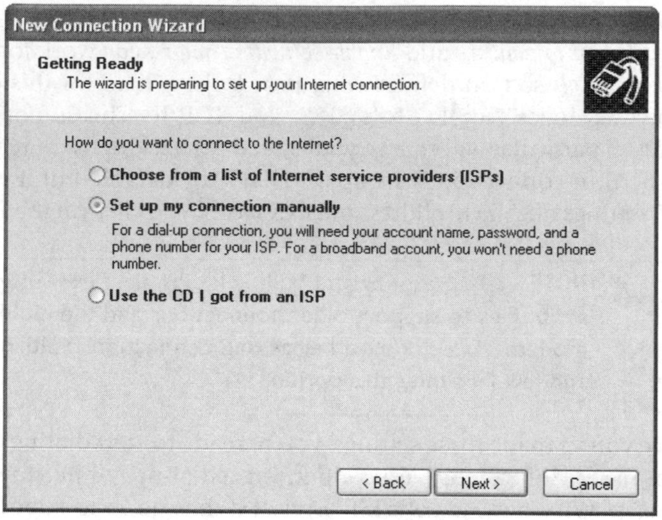

Figure 16-23

Selecting a manual connection setup

Either way, you're going to configure a dial-up connection to the Internet, so just se-lect the *Connect to the Internet* radio button and click Next to see Figure 16-23. Given that most people who connect to the Internet aren't astute like us, Microsoft gives the user the choice for more automated setups for common ISPs, either built into Windows (can you say MSN?) or via CDs provided by the ISP. Because we *are* astute techs, select *Set up my connection manually* (Figure 16-24), click Next, and choose how you want to connect to the Internet.

Ah ha! While the obvious choice is *Connect using a dial-up modem*, as Figure 16-24 shows, note the other choices—these will be handy when you configure a dedicated connection later.

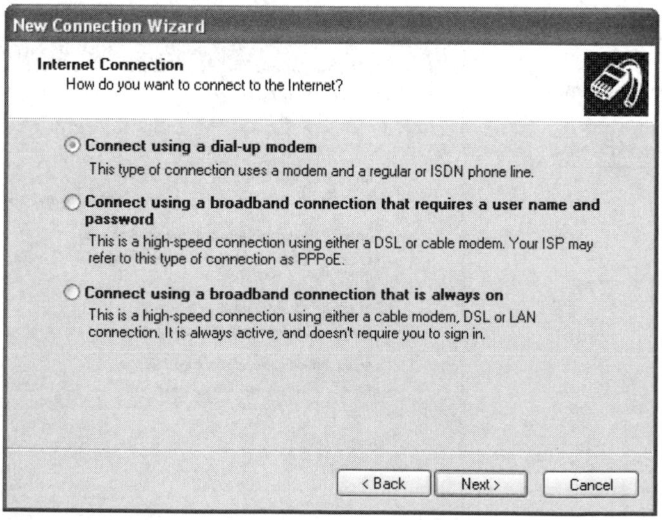

Figure 16-24

Connection type

The next two screens are simple. Just click Next and the wizard prompts for the name of the ISP; click Next again and it prompts for the phone number. The screen after that (Figure 16-25) asks for the user account and password. It also has three check boxes. The first enables anyone on this computer to use the same user account and password—this is handy when multiple people use the same dial-up connection to access the Internet. The second check box defines this as the default Internet connection. My laptop has an 802.11 NIC that I use as my default, so I turn this off. The third and last check box turns on Internet Connection Firewall (ICF)—Windows XP's built-in protection software for computers connecting to the Internet. Chapter 17, "Protecting Your Network," covers ICF and other firewalls in some detail.

When you click Next the wizard is done (after a few Finish dialog boxes) and a new connection shows up in Network Connections. If any settings for this connection need adjusting, you go into the connection properties, just as you did in Windows 98. Figure 16-26 shows the Properties dialog box for a dial-up connection to MHTechEd.

The Properties dialog box for a dial-up connection in Windows XP is similar to the one in Windows 98, but adds a number of extras. The General tab enables you to change telephone numbers, modem, and something called Dialing Rules. Dialing Rules are the same thing as dialing locations in Windows 98 and we'll discuss them in the next section. The Options tab provides general options like *Display progress while connecting* or the number of times to redial. The Security tab determines how to log on—how you set this varies among ISPs. (Log on is covered in more detail in the "Private Dial-up" section later in this chapter.) The Networking tab is where you go to set SLIP/PPP and edit TCP/IP settings. The Advanced tab is covered in the next chapter.

As you can see, configuring a dial-up connection isn't difficult in any version of Windows. The only real challenge is remembering what you need to configure—usually your ISP has the answer for you—and getting comfortable with the differences in wizards.

Both of the dial-up connection installations you just saw required a dialing location (Windows 98) or a Dialing Rule (Windows XP). Let's see what that's all about.

Figure 16-25
Internet Account
Information

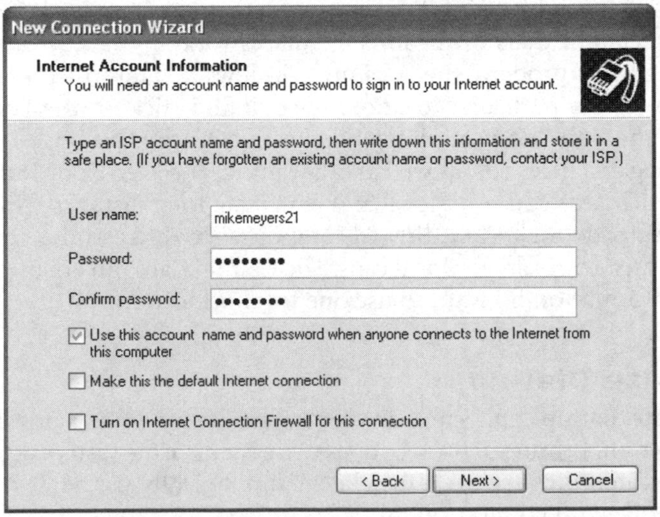

Figure 16-26
Dial-up
connection
Properties
dialog box

Dialing Rules

A dialing location/Dialing Rules (we'll use the term "Dialing Rules") is the set of rules that tells the modem how to dial from your current location. Do you need to dial a 9 first to get a dial tone? Do you need to use area codes to make a local call? Do you need to disable call waiting? Do you want to use a calling card? That's where the Dialing Rules are important. Every version of Windows has a Control Panel applet to help you configure these options. In Windows 98 and NT the applet is called Telephony. In Windows 2000 and XP the applet is called Phone and Modem Options. Whatever the name, this applet gives you the ability to configure your modem to dial from any location. Dialing Rules aren't terribly helpful to a computer that stays in one place, but are important for a computer that dials from different places (like my laptop). Figure 16-27 shows the Dialing Rules property sheet for my Windows XP laptop—I travel a lot!

To set up a particular location, select it and click on the Edit button. Figure 16-28 shows the Edit Location dialog box for my Office location. Note the options for local and long distance calls, as well as call waiting. The Area Code Rules tab enables me to select which area codes are local and which are long distance—in Houston we must dial the area code for local calls and long distance calls, so the computer needs to know which area codes are for local calls. The Calling Card tab enables me to enter my calling card information if I want to use one for this location.

Private Dial-up

A private dial-up connection connects a remote system to a private network via a dial-up connection. Private dial-up requires two systems. One system acts as a *remote access server (RAS)*. The other system is the client running DUN (or whatever your version of Windows calls your connection tool).

Figure 16-27
Dialing Rules in
Windows XP

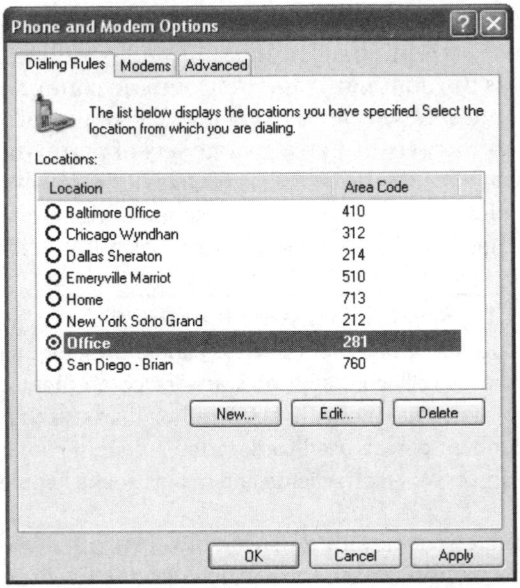

Phone and Modem Options

Dialing Rules | Modems | Advanced

The list below displays the locations you have specified. Select the location from which you are dialing.

Locations:

Location	Area Code
○ Baltimore Office	410
○ Chicago Wyndhan	312
○ Dallas Sheraton	214
○ Emeryville Marriot	510
○ Home	713
○ New York Soho Grand	212
⊙ Office	281
○ San Diego - Brian	760

New... | Edit... | Delete

OK | Cancel | Apply

In Windows a RAS is a server dedicated to handling users who are not directly connected to a LAN but who need to access file and print services on the LAN from a remote location. For example, when a user dials into a network from home using an analog modem or an ISDN connection, she is dialing into a RAS. Once the user is authenticated, she can access shared drives and printers as if her computer were physically connected to the office LAN.

Figure 16-28
Edit Location
dialog box in
Windows XP

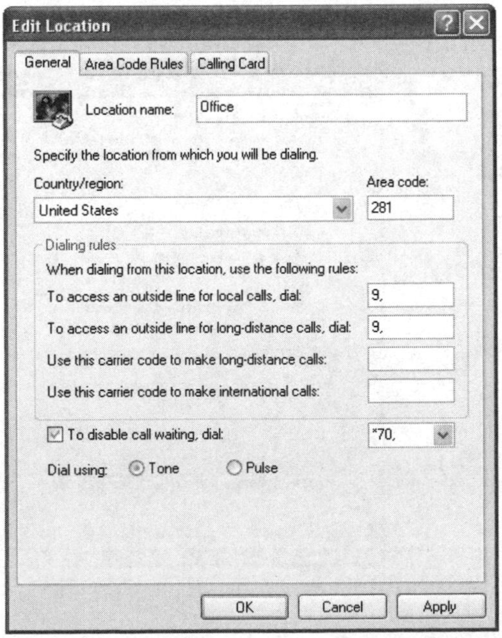

Edit Location

General | Area Code Rules | Calling Card

Location name: Office

Specify the location from which you will be dialing.

Country/region: Area code:
United States   281

Dialing rules
When dialing from this location, use the following rules:

To access an outside line for local calls, dial: 9,
To access an outside line for long-distance calls, dial: 9,
Use this carrier code to make long-distance calls:
Use this carrier code to make international calls:

☑ To disable call waiting, dial: *70,

Dial using: ⊙ Tone   ○ Pulse

OK | Cancel | Apply

PART III

You must set up a server system in your LAN as a RAS server. That system becomes your RAS server, accepting incoming calls and handling password authentication. Because TCP/IP is the dominant (and best) remote connection protocol, you must ensure that your remote access server is using the TCP/IP protocol for its network communications. Many remote servers have separate sets of permissions for dial-in users and local users. You must also configure the server to set the dial-in user's rights and permissions. Configuring a RAS system is outside the scope of this book but it is important for you to properly configure a Windows system to act as a RAS client!

TIP *Remote access server* is a catchall phrase. It refers to both the hardware component (servers built to handle the unique stresses of a large number of clients calling in) and the software component of a remote access solution. Most techs call RAS "razz," rather than use the initials, "R-A-S." This creates a seemingly redundant phrase used to describe a system running RAS: "RAS server." This helps distinguish servers from clients and makes geeks happier.

Creating the client side of a private dial-up connection is identical to setting up a dial-up connection to the Internet. All versions of Windows provide a wizard (Figures 16-29, 16-30) that prompts for the name of the connection, the telephone number, and so forth and creates a new dial-up connection. This new connection resides in the same folder as your other dial-up connections. The only difference is that instead of having an ISP tell you what IP settings, account name, and password to use, the person who sets up the RAS server tells you this information. The one area that gets interesting in a private dial-up compared to dialing up to an ISP is how the remote user authenticates to the RAS.

Figure 16-29
Windows XP
New Connection
Wizard prompting
for connection

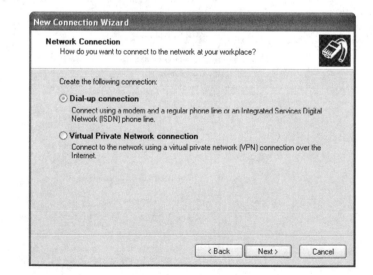

Figure 16-30
Windows XP
New Connection
Wizard prompting
for connection
type

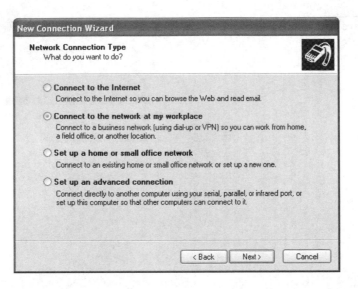

Authentication

When a computer logs into a server in a LAN, the user name and password must travel along the wires of the network to the serving system. In early networks, this data was transmitted "in the clear." The user name and password were transmitted on the wires in plain text, what most network techs refer to as *clear text*. Over the years, NOS makers came up with methods to encrypt the user name and password to prevent hackers from intercepting this important information. Because NOS makers control software development of both their client and their server software, for the most part they created their own proprietary encryption protocols.

In today's increasingly interconnected and diverse networking environment, there is a motivation to enable different network operating systems to authenticate any client system from any other NOS. Modern network operating systems use standardized authentication protocols based on encryption methods like MIT's Kerberos, enabling multiple brands of servers to authenticate multiple brands of clients. These LAN encryptions are usually transparent and work quite nicely even in mixed networks.

The need for good authentication was especially critical in dial-up environments. Given that any modem configured to accept incoming calls was effectively open to the public, the powers that be developed a blanket protocol called Remote Authentication Dial-In User Service (RADIUS). A RADIUS server keeps track of all authorized dial-in users and their passwords, effectively locking out any unauthorized remote access attempts. Unfortunately, RADIUS doesn't include specifics for *how* to do this, leaving the details to various vendors who have created their own access tools over the years.

Today there are so many different remote access tools—based on UNIX/Linux, NetWare, and Windows serving programs—that most remote access systems and clients have to support a variety of different authentication protocols. All Windows clients come with good support for all of the common authentication protocols. Let's take a look at a Windows XP connection, learn about some of the most common authentication protocols, and see where to configure them.

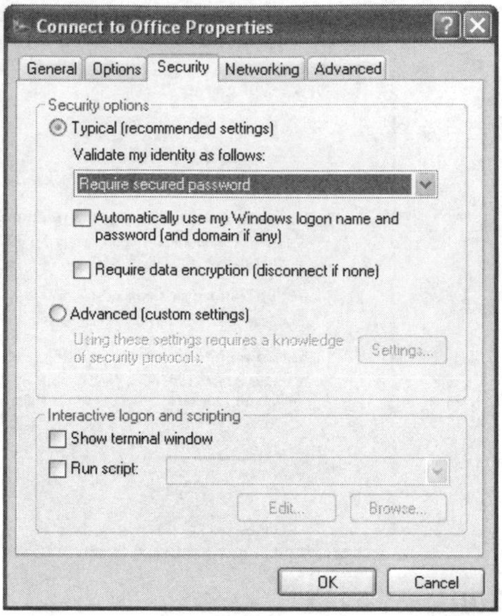

Figure 16-31
Security tab in
Windows XP

In the "Dial-up to the Internet" section earlier in this chapter, you saw the Properties dialog box for a Windows XP dial-up connection. Let's go back to the Properties dialog box, this time concentrating on the Security tab. The Security tab is the primary tool used to configure authentication for private dial-up clients (Figure 16-31).

The Security options area is where you configure an authentication protocol. To see them, select the Advanced radio button, and then click the Settings button to display the authentication protocols Windows supports. Figure 16-32 shows the Advanced Security Settings dialog box.

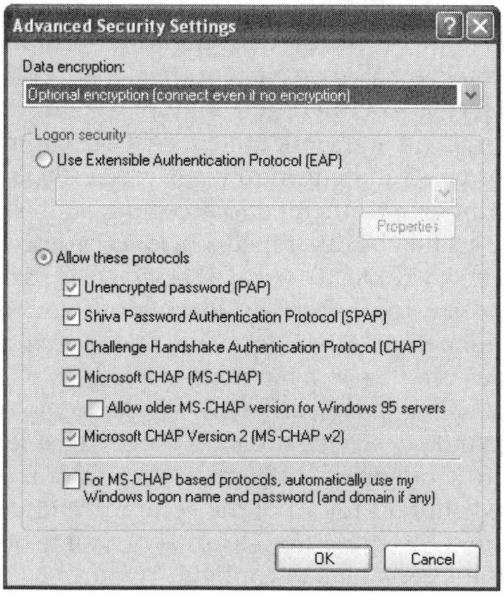

Figure 16-32
Authentication
protocols available
in Windows XP

Here is a quick list of the more common authentication protocols and their uses.

- **PAP**   Password Authentication Protocol (PAP) is the oldest and most basic form of authentication. It's also the least safe, because it sends all passwords in clear text. No NOS uses PAP for a client system's login, but almost all network operating systems that provide remote access service will support PAP.

- **SPAP**   Shiva is the brand name for a family of popular remote access servers. The Shiva Password Authentication Protocol is a unique encrypted protocol used to enable Windows clients to connect to these servers.

- **CHAP**   Challenge Handshake Authentication Protocol (CHAP) is the most common remote access protocol. CHAP has the serving system challenge the remote client, which must provide an encrypted password.

- **MS-CHAP**   MS-CHAP is Microsoft's variation of the CHAP protocol. It uses a slightly more advanced encryption protocol. MS-CHAP V2 is yet another improvement on MS-CHAP.

- **EAP**   All the previous protocols use encryptions generated by either the server, the client, or both. While this is good encryption, there is nothing unique about the encryption to identify the system that created it. That's where the Extensible Authentication Protocol (EAP) shines. EAP uses a special device—like a smart card—or special, unique data called certificates to create the encryption and to identify the source of the encryption.

Note in Figure 16-32 that multiple protocols are checked. This enables the client dial-up connection to try a number of authentication protocols until it finds one that the RAS server system will accept. In the real world, the person who sets up the RAS server will tell you which authentication to use and you then turn off all of the other protocols.

Data Encryption

Encryption methods don't stop at the authentication level. There are a number of ways to encrypt network *data* as well. The choice of encryption method is dictated to a large degree by the method used by the communicating systems to connect. Many networks consist of multiple networks linked together by some sort of private connection, usually some kind of telephone line like ISDN or T1. Microsoft's encryption method of choice for this type of network is called *IPSec* (derived from IP security). IPSec provides transparent encryption between the server and the client.

VPNs

Many networks forego the idea of using private long-distance lines to connect a client to a RAS and instead use the Internet itself as a way to connect LANs both to individual systems and to each other. The obvious danger with this is the complete exposure of all network data to the Internet. This has led to the development of encryption methods designed to protect data moving between systems. A network employing encryption to use the Internet as if it were a private network is referred to as a *virtual private network (VPN)*.

Figure 16-33
VPN packet

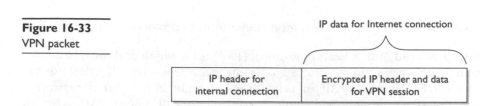

IP data for Internet connection

IP header for internal connection	Encrypted IP header and data for VPN session

A VPN connection consists of two items: a regular connection to the Internet (dial-up or dedicated) and an encrypted IP session that runs within the Internet connection. The regular Internet connection uses the IP address allocated to it from the ISP. The encrypted connection uses IP addresses of the private network. Figure 16-33 diagrams a typical VPN packet between a LAN and a remote client.

You can make a VPN through dedicated hardware or through a software solution. Figure 16-34 shows a Linksys VPN router. This VPN router connects to another identical router at another location to make a VPN connection. Hardware solutions are attractive in that they are fast and there is little or nothing to do at the actual client—the VPN is just your Internet connection. Hardware VPN solutions are a popular method to connect a desktop client to a private LAN or to connect two LANs.

Software VPNs have one big advantage—there is no hardware for the clients to haul around, making it the obvious choice for laptop users who want to connect to a home or office LAN. A software VPN solution manifests on the client as a separate remote connection, as shown in Figure 16-35. Windows 9*x* had no real support for VPNs, requiring you to use special software. Windows 2000/2003 and XP have excellent wizards to help you configure a VPN client. Creating a VPN client requires that you have the IP address of the device on your private LAN that can accept your VPN request and create a VPN connection.

If you look closely at Figure 16-35 you'll see the term "PPTP." *Point-to-Point Tunneling Protocol (PPTP)* is the Microsoft VPN encryption protocol. Cisco uses its own VPN encryption protocol called *Layer 2 Tunneling Protocol (L2TP)*. Microsoft went proprietary with Windows NT—you couldn't find a place to choose between these two protocols and had to use PPTP. Later versions of Windows use both PPTP and L2TP.

Figure 16-34
A Linksys VPN
router

Figure 16-35
VPN connection
in Windows XP

Dedicated Connection

Dedicated connections are remote connections that never disconnect. Dedicated connections can be broken into two groups: dedicated private connections between two locations and dedicated connections to the Internet. Dedicated private connections manifest themselves as two locations interconnected by a (usually high-speed) connection such as a T1 line (Figure 16-36).

Each end of the T1 line goes into a router (after going through a CSU/DSU, of course!). Note that this connection does not use the Internet in any way—it is not a VPN connection! Dedicated connections of this type are expensive and are only used by organizations that need the high bandwidth these connections provide. These connections are invisible to the individual computers on each network. There is no special remote connection configuration of the individual systems, although there may be some configuration of DHCP, DNS, and WINS servers to insure that the network runs optimally.

Dedicated connections to the Internet are common today. Cable modems and DSL have made dedicated connections to the Internet inexpensive and very popular. In most cases there is nothing to configure in these dedicated connections but many cable and DSL providers give you a CD-ROM disc that installs testing software, PPPoE login support, and little extras such as e-mail clients and software firewalls (consult Chapter 17, "Protecting Your Network," for information on software firewalls). Figures 16-37 and 16-38 show an ADSL install program for Windows 98 from my ISP, SBC/Prodigy. This program enables you to connect by entering your PPPoE information for your ADSL connection. Once started, these programs usually stay running in the system tray until your next reboot.

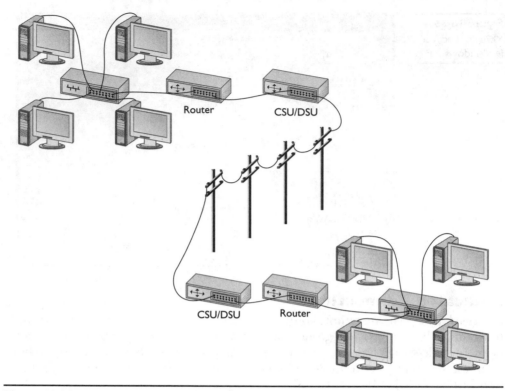

Figure 16-36   Dedicated private connection

Windows XP is the first version of Windows to come with broadband support wizards. When you run the Windows XP New Connection Wizard and select *Connect to the Internet | Set up my connection manually,* you get the screen shown in Figure 16-39. Note the two broadband options: one for a connection that needs a user name and another for a broadband connection that does not.

Figure 16-37
DSL connections

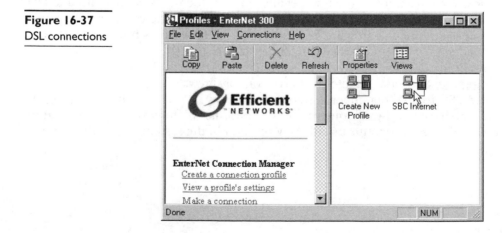

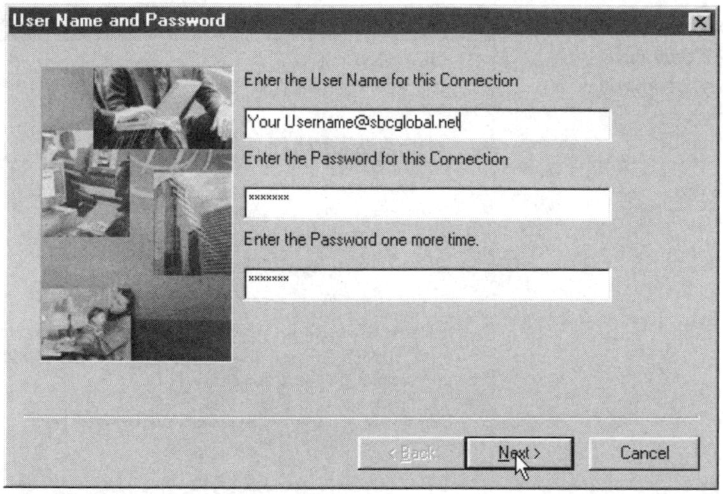

Figure 16-38
PPPoE
information

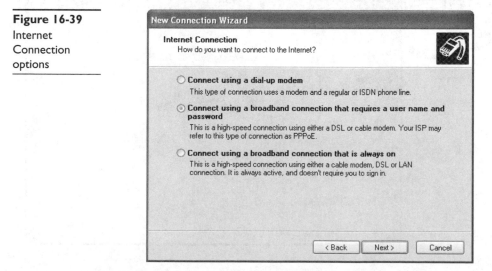

If you choose to create a connection that the Windows wizard describes as "always on," the wizard doesn't do anything other than tell you that your connection should already be working. This makes sense because your cable modem or non-PPPoE DSL simply uses your NIC. If you choose *Connect using a broadband connection that requires a user name and password*, however, then you'll see a dialog box asking for a connection name followed by the dialog box shown in Figure 16-40, prompting for a user name and password. Once this connection is created it shows up in Network Connections (Figure 16-41).

Internet Connection Sharing

All of these types of remote connections have shown a single remote system connecting to either the Internet or to a private network. What if you have a small LAN with a dial-up or dedicated remote Internet connection on one system and you want all the other PCs in the LAN to connect to the Internet? That's the job of Internet Connection Sharing.

Figure 16-39
Internet
Connection
options

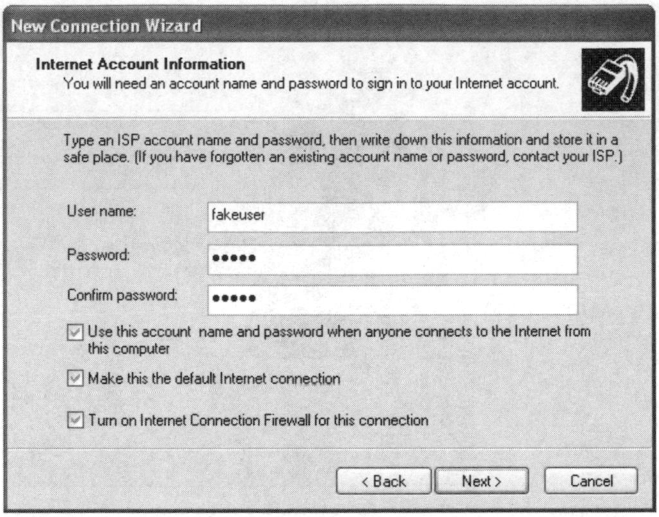

Figure 16-40
New Connection
Wizard prompting
for PPPoE
information

Internet Connection Sharing (ICS) is Microsoft's term to describe the technique of allowing more than one computer to access the Internet simultaneously using a single Internet connection on a single system. When you use ICS, you connect an entire LAN to the Internet using one computer. This connection to the Internet may be via modem, cable modem, ADSL, ISDN, leased line, or T1. In most cases, ICS uses *Network Address Translation (NAT)* to achieve this sharing.

NOTE ICS is only for sharing Internet connections. It is not designed to support connecting to another private network.

Figure 16-41
PPPoE
connection in
Windows XP

There are many benefits to using ICS. For starters, having only one Internet account reduces costs. ICS also protects your data by putting your computers behind a firewall, and by enabling administrators to control user access to Internet services and resources. If you have multiple computers on a LAN, you can use ICS to allow different computers on the LAN to perform different tasks simultaneously. For example, one person can send and receive e-mail messages, while another person downloads a file, and another person browses the Internet. ICS uses DHCP and DNS to configure TCP/IP information automatically for clients in the LAN. Any IP-attached device can connect to the LAN, including older Windows clients and non-Windows-based clients, without any additional client software.

ICS has the following components:

- **DHCP Allocator**   Assigns the IP address, gateway, and name server on the local network.
- **DNS Proxy**   Resolves names on behalf of local network clients and forwards queries.
- **Network Address Translation (NAT)**   Maps a set of private addresses to a set of public addresses. NAT tracks private-source IP addresses and public-destination IP addresses for outbound data flows. It changes the IP address information and edits the required IP header information dynamically.
- **Auto-dial**   Automatically dials connections.
- **Application Programming Interfaces (APIs)**   Used by programs for configuration, status, and dial control.

Configuring ICS is simple. You turn on ICS on one system and it works (Figure 16-42). An ICS system must have two connections: an Internet connection via an ISP, and a NIC that connects to the rest of the network. ICS doesn't have to use dial-up. Any computer connected to the ISP via dial-up modem, cable modem, DSL modem, or over even a T1 line can use ICS. The location of ICS varies on different versions of Windows but usually is located under the modem's properties.

Troubleshooting Remote Access

Troubleshooting remote access connections might seem at first to be a bit of a challenge, given the different physical connection options as well as the type of remote access you are using. In reality, troubleshooting remote access is usually easy if you first realize that all remote access connections share a number of common areas. Let's see what every remote access connection has in common and see how to use these common issues to troubleshoot.

NOTE   These remote issues are not in any particular order.

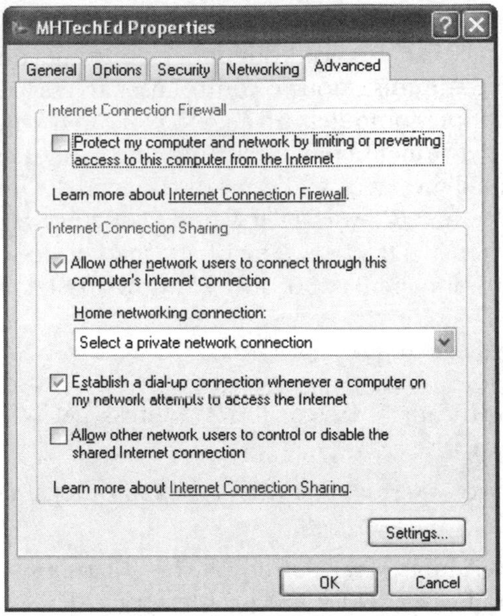

Figure 16-42
ICS in
Windows XP

Is the Physical Remote Connection Running?

The physical connection is the signal that runs between your PC and your other connection. These are the telephone lines (PSTN, DSL, T1) or coaxial cables (cable modems) as well as the signal they carry. If a connection works one day but doesn't work the next odds are good nothing has changed on your remote client. If a remote access connection suddenly quits working you need to determine if the physical remote connection is available. The trick is how to do this—and that varies by the type of connection.

If it's a PSTN line, this simply means to check for a dial tone. Lack of a dial tone usually means the modem is unplugged from the phone jack or a telephone in another room was left off the hook.

Cable and DSL connections are virtually identical in terms of verifying their physical connections—the secret is the LEDs on the cable or DSL modem. Figure 16-43 shows drawings of two sets of LEDs, the left from my cable modem and the right from my DSL modem. There are two LEDs of interest that help determine if the connection is up. The most important is the one that says "Cable" or "ADSL." These LEDs are on when your cable or DSL modem has a connection to whatever device is on the other end to make this connection work. If those LEDs are not on, you don't have a connection.

Most DSL and cable providers go down from time to time—if those LEDs are off, you'll need to try to reset the connection. How this is done varies; some devices have a reset button and some have to be turned off and then turned back on to reset. During the reset the test LED comes on. The test LED flickers and blinks, eventually turning off after the connection is reestablished. The test LED is also used by your cable or DSL provider's telephone support staff if you call in with problems.

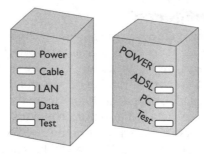

Figure 16-43
Cable (left) and
DSL (right) LEDs

Most cable and DSL tech support people use the term "cycle the modem" when they want you to unplug the modem for 10–30 seconds and plug it back in. You'll find the need to cycle the modem if you change hardware; for example, if you swap out NICs or add a broadband router to the mix.

> **NOTE** Every DSL and cable modem is different. Some have more and some have fewer LEDS than the ones described here.

If the DSL or cable modem fails to work after a reset, your provider will come onsite for diagnostics and repair armed with handy testers with funny names such as a Bit Error Rate (BERT) tester or a SNR (Signal to Noise Ratio) tester. Based on their findings, they will repair internal lines (you pay for this) or external lines (they pay for that) to ensure a good connection.

If you use T1 or other higher-end connections, the CSU/DSU is the place to check for your connection. Every CSU/DSU has an LED that confirms a connection to the far CSU/DSC. If this LED shows no connection, call your local exchange carrier to have them perform a "loopback" or "loop" test of their line. Additionally, all CSU/DSUs have some form of self-test to verify that the connection to the other CSU/DSU is in good order. This self-test is handy for making sure the wire running from the demarc to the CSU/DSU is in good shape. It is common for you to run this program yourself—a good reason to keep the CSU/DSU manual handy!

Is Your Hardware Running?

Your own hardware is almost always overlooked. Is your modem/NIC working? Do you have a good connection to your cable modem or DSL modem? Is the DSL or cable modem working properly? Take advantage of Device Manager to test internal devices and use any testing programs at your disposal if available for your device. One of the best times to learn about testing programs is at installation. Don't be afraid to ask the install techs what testing if any they provide. The testing tools vary widely between technologies and providers so ask the people who know best—the install and repair techs.

Are You Configured?

Improper configuration is the single biggest reason for remote connection failures. Configurations take place at so many levels. Start with hardware configuration. Some devices—cable modems are a great example—have no user configuration. Other devices such as ISDN modems have a number of configurations such as the SPID number. The best idea here is to perform what I call the "mental reinstall:" going through the process of installation to see what configurations come up.

Configuration doesn't stop with the hardware. Connections have plenty of configurations. Are you running PPP or SLIP? Do you have the right telephone number? Do the dialing rules work properly? What are the TCP/IP settings for this connection? One of the nice aspects to connections is that you can make as many as you want. If I think a connection is improperly configured, I just make another one. Of course I keep the old connection to compare and check!

Is the Server Awake?

The term "server" here has two meanings. The first meaning has to do with private connections and VPNs. In these cases the connection itself must have some device on the other end to make a connection. If the RAS or VPN server isn't functioning, you won't make a connection. There's only one way to test this—call someone at the other location. If no one's there you have no way to confirm whether the server is up and running.

The second meaning to the word "server" is more in the vein of Internet connections. All Internet connections need the usual assortment of DNS, DHCP, and other such servers running to connect. Testing TCP/IP on a remote connection is no different than on a LAN. Use the tools and techniques you learned about in Chapter 14, "Going Large with TCP/IP," to make sure your Internet servers are working.

Chapter Review

Questions

1. Which of the following is *not* a Data Link protocol for telephone lines? (Select all that apply.)

   A. SLIP

   B. IP

   C. PPP

   D. PPTP

2. Which of the following provides the fastest throughput?

   A. PSTN

   B. ISDN BRI

    C. ISDN PRI

    D. POTS

3. The popular Microsoft remote access client is called

    A. RAS

    B. Dial-Up Networking

    C. Dial-Up Server

    D. Microsoft Client for Networks

4. Thor is concerned that e-mail sent from his laptop to the RAS system in his home office could be read by others. What does he need to use?

    A. A password

    B. Encryption

    C. A login name

    D. SMTP

5. BRI ISDN uses

    A. One B channel and 24 D channels

    B. 24 B channels and one D channel

    C. One B channel and two D channels

    D. Two B channels and one D channel

6. The V.90 standard defines a modem speed of

    A. 56 Kbps

    B. 33.6K baud

    C. 28.8 Kbps

    D. 2400 baud

7. Which of the following V standards defines error checking?

    A. V.42

    B. V.42bis

    C. V.34

    D. MNP 8

8. The ISDN equivalent of a modem is called a

    A. Terminal point

    B. Network interface device

    C. Terminal adapter

    D. Network adapter

PART III

9. Which of the following are benefits of ISDN over PSTN? (Select all that apply.)

    A. ISDN is more widely available.

    B. ISDN is faster.

    C. ISDN connects more quickly.

    D. ISDN is cheaper.

10. Generally, how close do you need to be to a central office to use ISDN?

    A. 1,800 feet

    B. 1,800 meters

    C. 18,000 feet

    D. 18,000 meters

Answers

1. **B, D.** SLIP and PPP are Data Link protocols for telephone lines.

2. **C.** ISDN PRI has a throughput of 1.5 Mbps. The next fastest is ISDN BRI at 128 Kbps.

3. **B.** The popular Microsoft remote access client is called Dial-Up Networking. RAS is remote access server software.

4. **B.** Thor needs to use some form of encryption.

5. **D.** BRI ISDN uses two B channels and one D channel.

6. **A.** The V.90 standard defines a 56-Kbps modem speed.

7. **A.** The V.42 standard defines modem error checking.

8. **C.** The ISDN equivalent of a modem is called a terminal adapter.

9. **B, C.** ISDN is faster than PSTN and connects more quickly.

10. **C.** You generally need to be within 18,000 feet of a central office to take advantage of ISDN.

Protecting Your Network

The Network+ Certification exam expects you to know how to

- 2.17   Identify the following security protocols and describe their purpose and function: IPSec, SSL
- 3.5   Identify the purpose, benefits, and characteristics of using a firewall
- 3.6   Identify the purpose, benefits, and characteristics of using a proxy service
- 3.7   Given a connectivity scenario, determine the impact on network functionality of a particular security implementation (for example, port blocking/filtering, authentication, encryption)
- 3.8 Identify the main characteristics of VLANs (Virtual Local Area Networks)
- 3.9 Identify the main characteristics and purpose of extranets and intranets

To achieve these goals, you must be able to

- Define the various types of network threats and how they are caused
- Explain how firewalls, NAT, port filtering, packet filtering, encryption, and authentication protect a network from threats
- Explain how to implement these levels of protection on different types of networks

The very nature of networking makes networks vulnerable to a dizzying array of threats. By definition, a network must allow for multiple users to access serving systems, but at the same time we must protect the network from harm. Who are the people causing this harm?

The news may be full of tales about *hackers* and other malicious people with nothing better to do than lurk around the Internet and trash the peace-loving systems of good folks like us, but in reality hackers are only one of many serious *network threats*. You will learn how to protect your networks from hackers, but first I want you to appreciate that the average network faces plenty of threats from the folks who are *authorized* to use it! Users with good intentions are far more likely to cause you trouble than any hacker. So, the first order of business is to stop and think about the types of threats that face the average network. After we define the threats, we can discuss the many tools and methods used to protect our precious networks from intentional harm.

NOTE Be aware that in some circles, the term "hacker" describes folks who love the challenge of overcoming obstacles and perceived limitations—and that's a positive thing! To distinguish these good hackers from the bad guys that we hear so much about, folks who consider themselves good hackers have coined the term "cracker" to describe the bad guys who abuse computer systems. Sadly, the mainstream press continues to use the term "hacker" instead of "cracker," and we will follow that common usage going forward.

Historical/Conceptual

Defining Network Threats

What is a threat? What makes something bad for our network? In my opinion, anything that prevents users from accessing the resources they need to get work done is a threat. Clearly that includes the evil hacker who reformats the server's hard drive, but it also includes things like bad configurations, screwed up permissions, viruses, and unintentional corruption of data by users. To make the security task more manageable, I like to sort these possibilities into two groups: internal threats and external threats.

Internal Threats

Internal threats are all the things our own users do to networks to keep them from sharing resources properly. Internal threats may not be as intriguing as external threats, but they are far more likely to bring a network to its knees, and they're the ones we need to be most vigilant to prevent. Here are the most common internal threats:

- Unauthorized access
- Data destruction
- Administrative access
- System crash/hardware failure
- Virus

Let's look at each one of these threats in turn.

Unauthorized Access

The most common of all network threats, unauthorized access, occurs when a user accesses resources in an unauthorized way. The unauthorized access itself does no actual damage to data; the person is usually just accessing data in a way that he or she shouldn't—such as reading employee personnel files or notes from the last board of directors meeting. Not all unauthorized access is malicious—usually this problem arises when users who are randomly poking around in the network discover that they can access resources in a fashion the administrators did not intend. Once a user has unauthorized access to a resource, they might just see more than they should; or worse, it can lead to data destruction. Our job is to protect these users from themselves.

Data Destruction

An extension of unauthorized access, accidental data destruction means more than just intentionally or accidentally erasing or corrupting data. Consider the case where users are authorized to access certain data, but what they do to that data goes beyond what they are authorized to do. A good example is the person who legitimately accesses a Microsoft Access product database to modify the product descriptions, only to discover he can change the prices of the products, too. This type of threat is particularly dangerous where users are not clearly informed about the extent to which they are authorized to make changes. A fellow tech once told me about a user who managed to mangle an important database due to someone giving them incorrect access. When confronted, the user said: "If I wasn't allowed to change it, the system wouldn't let me do it!" Many users believe that systems are configured in a paternalistic way that wouldn't allow them to do anything inappropriate. As a result, users will often assume they're authorized to make any changes they believe are necessary when working on a piece of data they know they're authorized to access.

Administrative Access

Throughout this book you've seen that every *network operating system (NOS)* is packed with administrative tools and functionality. We need these tools to get all kinds of work done, but by the same token we need to work hard to keep these capabilities out of the reach of those who don't need them. Clearly giving regular users Administrator/Supervisor/root access is a bad idea, but far more subtle problems can arise. I once gave a user Manage Documents permission for a busy laser printer in a Windows 2003 network. She quickly realized she could pause other users' print jobs and send her print jobs to the beginning of the print queue—nice for her but not so nice for her coworkers. Protecting administrative programs and functions from access and abuse by users is a real challenge, and one that requires an extensive knowledge of the NOS and of users' motivations.

System Crash/Hardware Failure

Like any technology, computers can and will fail—usually when you can least afford for it to happen. Hard drives crash, servers lock up, the power fails—it's all part of the joy of working in the networking business. We need to create redundancy in areas prone to failure (like installing backup power in case of electrical failure) and perform those all-important data backups. Chapter 19, "The Perfect Server," goes into detail about these and other issues involved in creating a stable and reliable server.

Virus

Networks are without a doubt the fastest and most efficient vehicles for transferring computer viruses among systems. News reports focus attention on the many virus attacks from the Internet, but a huge number of viruses still come from users who bring in programs on floppy disks, writeable CDs, and USB drives. We could treat viruses as an external threat as well, but instead of repeating myself, I'm going to cover internal and external issues of computer virus protection in Chapter 19, "The Perfect Server," including both the various methods of virus infection, and what you need to do to prevent virus infection of your networked systems.

External Threats

External threats come in two different forms. First, an outsider can manipulate your people to gain access to your network, a process called *social engineering*. Second, a hacker at a remote location can use technical exploits of your network to gain access. The mechanics of gaining access differs dramatically between the two threats, but both result in the same problems for you. Let's take a look.

Social Engineering

The vast majority of attacks against your network come under the heading of *social engineering*—the process of using or manipulating people inside the networking environment to gain access to that network from the outside. The term "social engineering" covers the many ways humans can use other humans to gain unauthorized information. This unauthorized information may be a network login, a credit card number, company customer data—almost anything you might imagine that one person or organization may not want a person outside of that organization to access.

Social engineering attacks aren't hacking—at least in the classic sense of the word—although the goals are the same. Social engineering is where people attack an organization through the people in the organization or physically access the organization to get the information they need. Here are a few of the more classic types of social engineering attacks.

 NOTE It's common for these attacks to be used together, so if you discover one of them being used against your organization, it's a good idea to look for others.

Infiltration Hackers can physically enter your building under the guise of someone who might have legitimate reason for being there, such as cleaning personnel, repair technicians, or messengers. They then snoop around desks, looking for whatever they can. They might talk with people inside the organization, gathering names, office numbers, department names—little things in and of themselves, but powerful tools when combined later with other social engineering attacks.

Telephone Scams *Telephone scams* are probably the most common social engineering attacks. In this case the attacker makes a phone call to someone in the organization to gain information. The attacker attempts to come across as someone in the organization and uses this to get the desired information. Probably one of the most famous of all of these scams is the "I forgot my user name and password" scam. In this gambit, the attacker first learns the account name of a legitimate person in the organization, usually using the infiltration method. The attacker then calls someone in the organization, usually the help desk, in an attempt to gather information, in this case a password.

> **Hacker:** "Hi, this is John Anderson in accounting. I forgot my password. Can you reset it please?"
> **Help Desk:** "Sure, what's your user name?"
> **Hacker:** "j_w_Anderson"
> **Help Desk:** "OK, I reset it to e34rd3"

Certainly telephone scams aren't limited to attempts to get network access. There are documented telephone scams against organizations aimed at getting cash, blackmail material, or other valuables.

Dumpster Diving   *Dumpster diving* is the generic term for anytime a hacker goes through your refuse, looking for information. The amount of sensitive information that makes it into any organization's trash bin boggles the mind! Years ago, I worked with an IT security guru who gave me and a few other IT people a tour of our office's trash. In one 20-minute tour of the personal wastebaskets of one office area, we had enough information to access the network easily, as well as to seriously embarrass more than a few people. When it comes to getting information, trash is the place to look!

Physical Theft   I once had a fellow network geek challenge me to try to bring down his newly installed network. He had just installed a powerful and expensive *firewall* router and was convinced that I couldn't get to a test server he added to his network just for me to try to access. After a few attempts to hack in over the Internet, I saw that I wasn't going to get anywhere that way. So I jumped in my car and drove to his office, having first outfitted myself in a techy looking jumpsuit and an ancient ID badge I just happened to have in my sock drawer. I smiled sweetly at the receptionist, and walked right by my friend's office (I noticed he was smugly monitoring incoming IP traffic using some neato packet-sniffing program) to his new server. I quickly pulled the wires out of the back of his precious server, picked it up, and walked out the door. The receptionist was too busy trying to figure out why her e-mail wasn't working to notice me as I whisked by her carrying the 65-pound server box. I stopped in the hall and called him from my cell phone.

> **Me (cheerily):** "Dude, I got all your data!"
> **Him (not cheerily):** "You rebooted my server! How did you do it?"
> **Me (smiling):** "I didn't reboot it—go over and look at it!"
> **Him (really mad now):** "YOU <EXPLETIVE> THIEF! YOU STOLE MY SERVER!"
> **Me (cordially):** "Why, yes. Yes, I did. Give me two days to hack your password in the comfort of my home, and I'll see everything! Bye!"

I immediately walked back in and handed him back the test server. It was fun. The moral here is simple—never forget that the best network software security measures can be rendered useless if you fail to physically protect your systems!

Hacking

Ah, here's the part I know you want to talk about—those infamous network threats from outside, the lawless hacker working out of his basement somewhere on another continent, using satellite uplinks to punch into networks using sophisticated Internet worms and other arcane geek weapons. Given Hollywood's influence from popular high-tech movies, many people assume that hacking is a sexy, exciting business, full of suspense and beautiful people. I hate to break this to those of you inclined to such a view, but the world of hackers is a pathetic sideshow of punk kids, Internet newbies, and a few otherwise normal folks with some extra networking knowledge who for one reason or another find a motivation to try to get into areas of public and private networks where they have no business. Hacking isn't sexy—it's a felony.

The secret to preventing hacking is to understand the motivations of hackers. I divide hackers into four groups, each with different motivations: inspectors, interceptors, controllers, and flooders.

Inspector

An *inspector* is a person who wants to poke around on your serving systems like a regular user. This person looks for vulnerabilities in your Internet access, permissions, passwords, and other methods to gain access to your network. The inspector's motivation ranges from the casual—a person who notices open doors into your network—to the serious—hackers looking for specific data. This is the type of hacker most of us visualize when we think of hacking.

Interceptor

An *interceptor* doesn't try to hack into systems. This person just monitors your network traffic looking for intercept information. Once an interceptor finds the traffic he wants, he may read or redirect the traffic for a number of nefarious purposes, such as the classic "man in the middle" attack. (In this type of attack, the hacker changes intercepted data to make it appear that he is one of the people who's supposed to be in on the conversation.) The interceptor is often collecting passwords for later invasion of a network.

Controller

A *controller* wants to take and keep control of one particular aspect of your system. One of the controller's favorite gambits is taking control of SMTP servers and using them for other purposes—usually spamming. Other popular targets are FTP and web servers. Possibly the most nefarious of all controller type attacks are known as *zombie attacks*. To launch a *zombie attack*, a hacker infects a large number of systems with a Trojan horse of some type. The bad guy then uses these systems to perform a large-scale attack on other systems, making it difficult if not impossible to trace the attack to the bad guy.

Flooder

Flooding attacks, more commonly called *denial of service (DoS) attacks*, are the work of hackers whose only interest is in bringing a network to its knees. This is accomplished by flooding the network with so many requests that it becomes overwhelmed and ceases functioning. These attacks are most commonly performed on web sites and mail servers, but virtually any part of a network can be attacked via some DoS method. The zombie attack I mentioned earlier is a common type of flooding.

Test Specific

Protecting from Internal Threats

The vast majority of protective strategies related to internal threats are based on policies rather than technology. Even the smallest network will have a number of user accounts and groups scattered about with different levels of rights/permissions. Every time you give a user access to a resource, you create potential loopholes that can leave your network vulnerable to unauthorized accesses, data destruction, and other administrative nightmares. To protect your network from internal threats, you need to implement the right controls over passwords, user accounts, permissions, and policies. Let's start with probably the most abused of all these areas: passwords.

Passwords

Passwords are the ultimate key to protecting your network. A user account with a valid password will get you into any system. Even if the user account only has limited permissions, you still have a security breach. Remember: for a hacker, just getting into the network is half the battle.

Protect your passwords. Never give out passwords over the phone. If a user loses a password, an administrator should reset the password to a complex combination of letters and numbers, and then allow the user to change the password to something they want. All of the stronger network operating systems have this capability. Windows 2000 Server, for example, provides a setting called *User must change password at next logon*, as shown in Figure 17-1.

Make your users choose good passwords. I once attended a network security seminar, and the speaker had everyone stand up. She then began to ask questions about our passwords—if we responded positively to the question we were to sit down. She began to ask questions like "Do you use the name of your spouse as a password?" and "Do you use your pet's name?"

By the time she was done asking about 15 questions, only 6 people out of some 300 were still standing! The reality is that most of us choose passwords that are amazingly easy to hack. Make sure you use strong passwords: at least six to eight characters in length, including letters, numbers, and punctuation symbols.

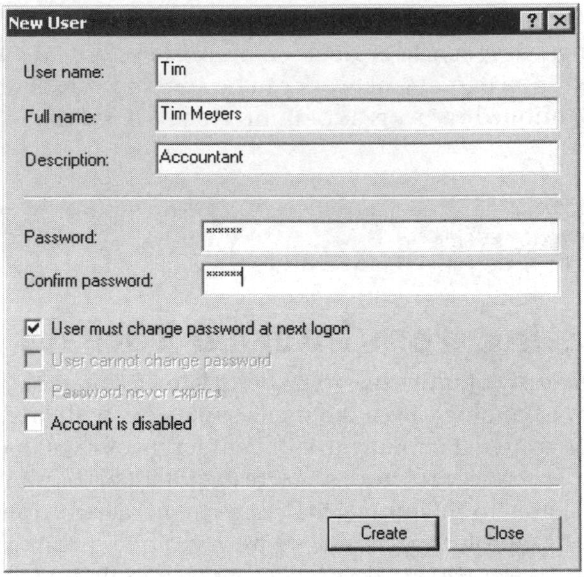

Figure 17-1
Windows 2000 Server's User must change password at next logon setting

New User

User name: Tim

Full name: Tim Meyers

Description: Accountant

Password: ××××××

Confirm password: ××××××

☑ User must change password at next logon
☐ User cannot change password
☐ Password never expires
☐ Account is disabled

Create   Close

 TIP Using non-alphanumeric characters makes any password much more difficult to crack for two reasons. First, adding non-alphanumeric characters forces the hacker to consider many more possible characters than just letters and numbers. Second, most password crackers use combinations of common words and numbers to try to hack a password. Because non-alphanumeric characters don't fit into common words or numbers, including a character such as an exclamation point will defeat these common-word hacks. Not all serving systems let you use characters such as @, $, %, or \, however, so you need to experiment to see if a particular server will accept them.

Once you've forced your users to choose strong passwords, you should make them change passwords at regular intervals. While this concept sounds good on paper, and for the Network+ exam you should remember that regular password changing is a good idea, in the real world it is a hard policy to maintain. For starters, users tend to forget passwords when they change a lot. One way to remember passwords if your organization forces you to change them is to use a numbering system. I worked at a company that required me to change my password at the beginning of each month, so I did something simple. I took a root password—let's say it was "m3y3rs5"—and simply added a number to the end representing the current month. So when June rolled around, for example, I would change my password to "m3y3rs56." It worked pretty well!

No matter how well your password implantation goes, using passwords always creates administrative problems. First, users forget passwords and someone (usually you) have to access their account and reset their passwords. Second, users will write passwords down, giving hackers an easy way into the network if those bits of paper fall into the wrong hands. If you've got the cash, there are two alternatives to passwords: smart devices and biometrics.

Smart devices are credit cards, USB keys, or other small devices that you insert into your PC in lieu of entering a password. They work extremely well and are incredibly difficult to bypass. They do have the downside in that you might lose them.

If you want to go seriously space-age, then biometrics are the way to go. *Biometric devices* scan fingerprints, retinas, or even the sound of the user's voice to provide a foolproof replacement for both passwords and smart devices. Biometrics have been around for quite a while, but were relegated to extremely high-security networks due to their high cost (thousand of dollars per device). That price has dropped substantially, making biometrics worthy of consideration for some networks.

User Account Control

Access to user accounts should be restricted to the assigned individuals, and those accounts should have permission to access only the resources they need, no more. Tight control of user accounts is critical to preventing unauthorized access. Disabling unused accounts is an important part of this strategy, but good user account control goes far deeper than that. One of your best tools for user account control is groups. Instead of giving permissions/rights to individual user accounts, give them to groups; this makes keeping track of the permissions assigned to individual user accounts much easier. Figure 17-2 shows me giving permissions to a group for a folder in Windows 2000. Once a group is created and its permissions set, you can then add user accounts to that group as needed. Any user account that becomes a member of a group automatically gets the permissions assigned to that group. Figure 17-3 shows me adding a user to a newly created group in the same Windows 2000 system.

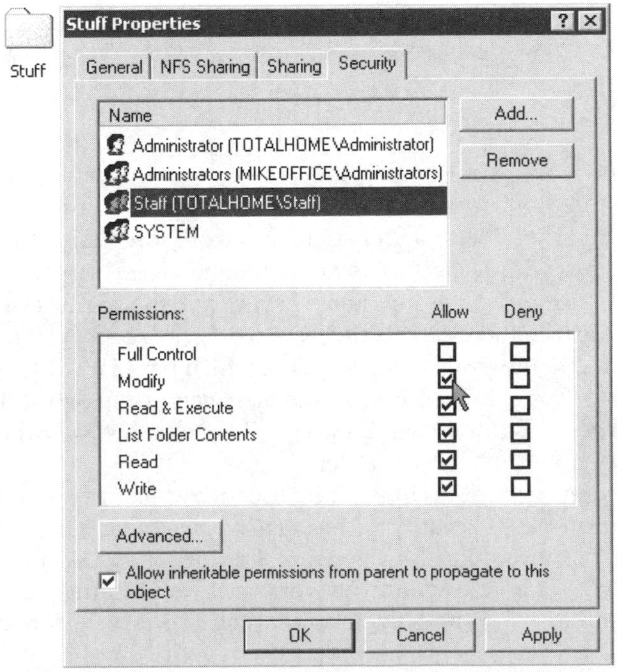

Figure 17-2
Giving a group permissions for a folder in Windows 2000

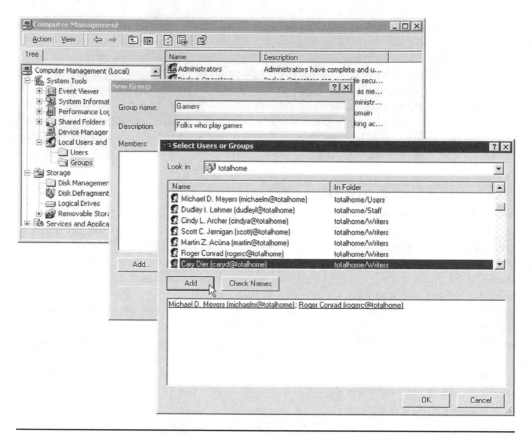

Figure 17-3   Adding a user to a newly created group in Windows 2000

Groups are a great way to get increased complexity without increasing the administrative burden on network administrators, because all network operating systems combine permissions. When a user is a member of more than one group, which permissions does he have with respect to any particular resource? In all network operating systems, the permissions of the groups are *combined*, and the result is what we call the *effective permissions* the user has to access the resource. Let's use an example from Windows 2000. If Timmy is a member of the Sales group, which has List Folder Contents permission to a folder, and he is also a member of the Managers group, which has Read and Execute permissions to the same folder, Timmy will have both List Folder Contents *and* Read and Execute permissions to that folder.

Another great tool for organizing user accounts in network operating systems using organization-based security is the *organizational unit (OU)*. Organizational-based network operating systems like NetWare 4.*x*/5.*x*/6.*x* and Windows 2000 Server/Windows Server 2003 store the entire network structure—computers, groups, printers, users, shared resources—as one big directory tree. This is great for administration, but having all your groups in one big directory tree can become unwieldy when networks grow past a certain size. Large organizations tend to be geographically dispersed and organizationally complex. For example, most large companies don't just have *an* accounting organization, they have *many* accounting organizations serving different locations and different organizations. Organizational units are a tool to help network administrators group the groups. An OU usually does not get rights or permissions; it is only a storage area for users and groups. Figure 17-4 shows the Dallas OU, containing the Sales and Accounting groups, on a Windows 2000 Server system.

Figure 17-4
Dallas organizational unit containing Sales and Accounting groups

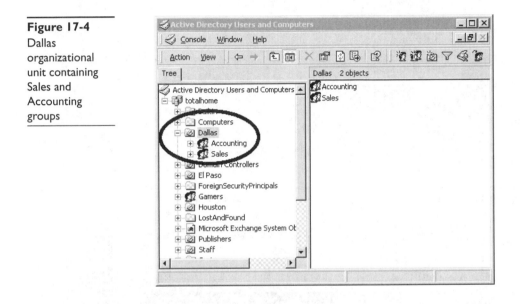

Both Windows and NetWare network operating systems provide powerful applications that enable you to see and manipulate various parts of the network tree. Figure 17-5 shows me using the NetWare 5.*x* NWADMIN application to add users to the Accounting group in the directory tree. Figure 17-6 shows the same activity in the equivalent Windows 2000 Server tool, called Active Directory Users and Computers. These are pretty similar interfaces for such different network operating systems.

Watch out for *default* user accounts and groups—they can become secret backdoors to your network! All network operating systems have a default Everyone group and it can easily be used to sneak into shared resources. This Everyone group, as its name implies, literally includes anyone who connects to that resource. Windows 2000 gives full control to the Everyone group by default, while NetWare gives the Everyone group no access—make sure you know this when working with these operating systems!

All of the default groups—Everyone, Guest, Users—define broad groups of users. Never use them unless you intend to permit all those folks to access a resource. If you use one of the default groups, remember to configure them with the proper rights/permissions to prevent users from doing things you don't want them to do with a shared resource!

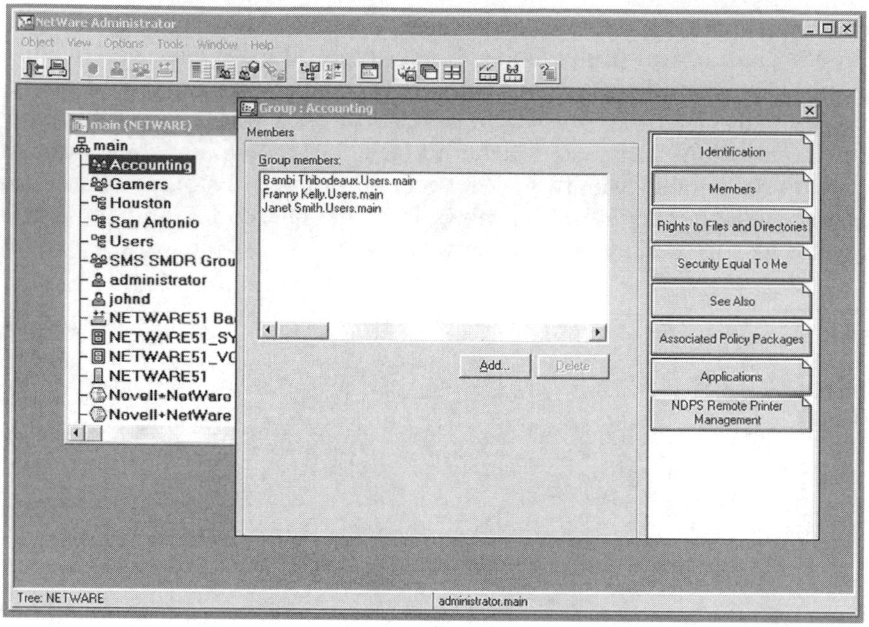

Figure 17-5   Adding users to a group in NetWare 5.*x* NWADMIN

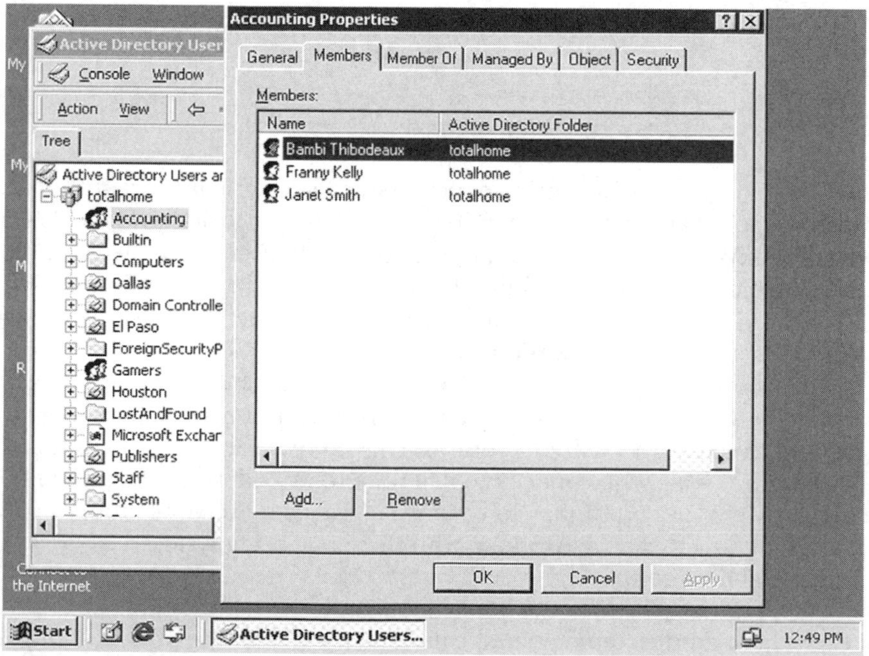

Figure 17-6   Adding users to a group in Windows 2000 Server's Active Directory Users and Computers

All of these groups and organizational units only do one thing for you: They let you keep track of your user accounts. That way you know they are only available for those who need them, and they only access the resources you want them to use. Before we move on, let me add one more tool to your kit: diligence. Managing user accounts is a thankless and difficult task, but one that you must stay on top of if you want to keep your network secure. Most organizations integrate the creation, disabling/enabling, and deletion of user accounts with the work of their human resources folks. Whenever a person joins, quits, or moves, the network admin is always one of the first to know!

Careful Use of Permissions

I have to admit that I gave most of this part away in the previous section when I discussed groups. The administration of rights/permissions can become incredibly complex even with judicious use of groups and organizational units. You now know what happens when a user account has multiple sets of rights/permissions to the same resource, but what happens if the user has one set of rights to a folder, and a different set of rights to one of its subfolders? This brings up a phenomenon called *inheritance*. We won't get into the many ways different network operating systems handle inherited permissions. Lucky for you, Network+ doesn't expect you to understand all the nuances of combined or inherited permissions—just be aware that they exist. However, those who go on to get more advanced certifications such as the CNE or MCSE will become extremely familiar with the many complex permutations of permissions.

Policies

While rights/permissions control how users access shared resources, there are a number of other functions it would be useful to control that are outside the scope of resources. For example, do you want users to be able to access a command prompt at their Windows system? Do you want users to be able to install software? Would you like to control what systems or what time of day a user can log in? All network operating systems provide you with some capability to control these and literally hundreds of other security parameters, under what both Windows and NetWare call *policies*. I like to think of policies as permissions for activities as opposed to true permissions, which control access to resources. The actual process of performing and using policies varies not only from NOS to NOS, but even among different versions of a single NOS. In concept, however, they all work the same way.

A policy is usually applied to a user account, a computer, a group, or an OU—again this depends on the make and model of NOS. Let's use the example of a network composed of Windows 2000 Professional systems with a Windows 2000 Server system. Every Windows 2000 system has its own local policies program, which enables policies to be placed on that system only. Figure 17-7 shows the tool we use to set local policies on an individual system, called *Local Security Settings*, being used to deny the user account Danar the capability to log on locally.

Local policies work great for individual systems, but they can be a pain to configure if you want to apply the same settings to more than one PC on your network. If you want

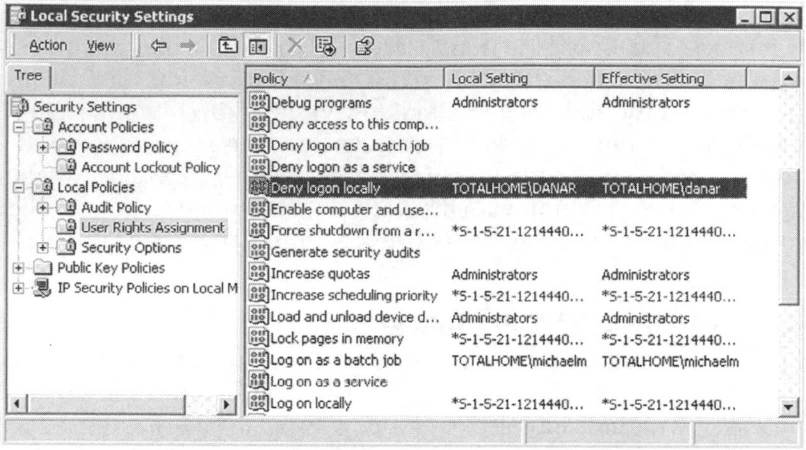

Figure 17-7
Local Security
Settings

to apply policy settings *en masse*, then you need to step up to Windows Active Directory domain-based *Group Policy*. Using Group Policy, you can exercise deity-like—Microsoft prefers to use the term *granular*—control over your network clients.

Want to set default wallpaper for every PC in your domain? Group Policy can do that. Want to make certain tools inaccessible to everyone except authorized users? Group Policy can do that too. Want to control access to the Internet, redirect home folders, run scripts, deploy software, or just remind folks that unauthorized access to the network will get them nowhere fast? Group Policy is the answer.

In a Windows 2000 Server or Server 2003 AD domain environment, you apply Group Policy settings to your network in bundles called a *Group Policy Objects (GPOs)*. These GPOs can be linked to the entire domain, to OUs, or to *sites*, which are units that represent PCs (usually Windows 2000 Server or Server 2003 domain controllers) connected to logical IP subnets. For example, Figure 17-8 shows me using the Active Directory Users and Computers console to apply to the Writers OU in my domain a GPO that enables disk quota management. By applying this Group Policy setting, I can set limits to the amount of disk space that members of the Writers OU are allowed to use. *That should keep my editor from storing too many of his Irish folk music MP3s on the server!*

That's just one simple example of the types of settings you can configure using Group Policy. There are literally hundreds of "tweaks" you can apply through Group Policy, from the great to the small, but don't worry too much about familiarizing yourself with each and every one. Group Policy settings are a big topic in the Microsoft Certified Systems Administrator (MCSA) and Microsoft Certified Systems Engineer (MCSE) certification tracks, but for the purposes of the CompTIA Network+ exam, you simply have to be comfortable with the concept behind Group Policy.

For many years NetWare didn't do a lot with policies. NetWare was content to add some of their own policies to the Windows policy list—a pretty smart way to handle things, given that NetWare wasn't that interested in the goings-on of client systems. Later versions of NetWare began to include a number of tools that made policies more important to NetWare networks, and Novell created a tool called ZENworks. ZENworks has its

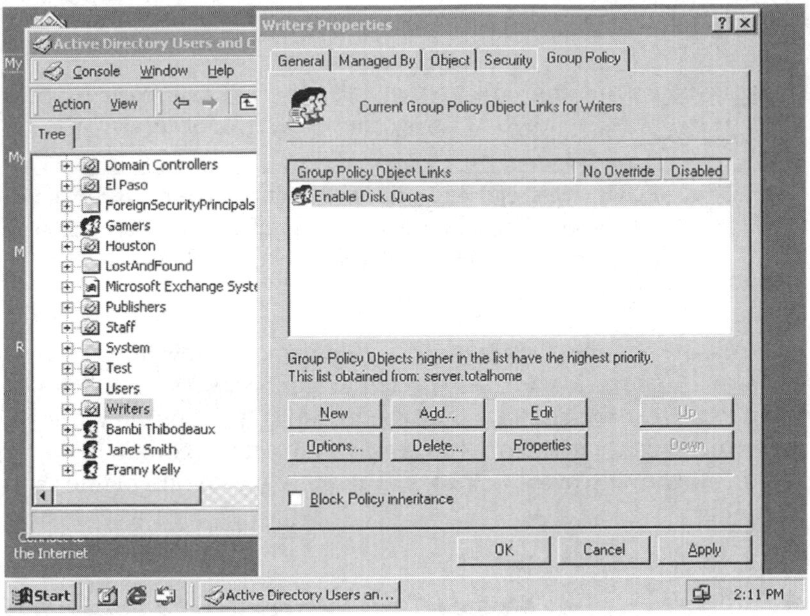

Figure 17-8
Applying a GPO
using Active
Directory Users
and Computers

own set of policies to address issues that Windows policies do not cover. This tool does much more than just create NetWare policies; for example, ZENworks is Novell's tool for network-based software installation.

Linux doesn't provide a single application that you open to set up policies, like Windows does. In fact, Linux doesn't even use the name policies. Instead, Linux relies on individual applications to set up policies for whatever they're doing. This is in keeping with the Linux paradigm of having lots of little programs that do one thing well, as opposed to the Windows paradigm of having one program try to be all things for all applications. For the Network+ exam, you can safely say that Linux does not have policies. Certainly not in the Microsoft sense of the word!

Although I could never name every possible policy you can enable on a Windows system, here's a list of some of those more commonly used:

- **Prevent Registry Edits**   If you try to edit the Registry, you get a failure message.

- **Prevent Access to the Command Prompt**   This policy keeps users from getting to the command prompt by turning off the **Run** command and the MS-DOS Prompt shortcut.

- **Log on Locally**   This policy defines who may log on to the system locally.

- **Shut Down System**   This policy defines who may shut down the system.

- **Minimum Password Length**   This policy forces a minimum password length.

- **Account Lockout Threshold**   This policy sets the maximum number of logon attempts a person can make before they are locked out of the account.

- **Disable Windows Installer**   This policy prevents users from installing software.

- **Printer Browsing**   This policy enables users to browse for printers on the network, as opposed to using only assigned printers.

 NOTE   One of the big improvements of Windows Server 2003 over Windows 2000 Server is in the use of policies. Server 2003 has many new policies that provide more powerful control over users.

While the Network+ exam doesn't expect you to know how to implement policies on any type of network, you are expected to understand that policies exist, especially on Windows networks, and that they can do amazing things in terms of controlling what users can do on their systems. If you ever try to get to a command prompt on a Windows system, only to discover the **Run** command is grayed out, blame it on a policy, not the computer!

Protecting a Network from External Threats

So far, I've stressed that internal threats are far more likely to cause network failures than external threats, but in no way am I suggesting you should take external threats lightly. Hacking has reached epidemic proportions as the Internet has expanded beyond the wildest fantasies of network pioneers, and easy access to hacking tools and information has made virtually any 13-year-old with a modem and time on his hands a serious threat to your network.

Securing networks from external threats is an ever-evolving competition between hackers and security people to find vulnerabilities in networking software and hardware. It can be a horse race—hackers finding and exploiting network vulnerabilities, neck and neck with security experts creating fixes. Newly discovered vulnerabilities always make the news, but the vast majority of intrusions are not due to a hacker discovering a new vulnerability and using it. In almost all cases, hackers take advantage of well-known vulnerabilities that network administrators have simply failed to fix. These well-known vulnerabilities are what we'll concentrate on in this section.

Physical Protection

Most techs consider installing firewalls and instituting policies a critical step in securing your network. No doubt these issues are important, but you can't consider a network secure unless you provide some physical protection to your network. I separate physical protection into two different areas: protection of servers and protection of clients.

Server protection is easy. Lock up your servers to prevent physical access by any unauthorized person. Large organizations have special server rooms, complete with card-key locks and tracking of anyone who enters or exits. Smaller organizations will at least have a locked closet. While you're locking up your servers, don't forget about any network switches! Hackers can access networks by plugging into a switch, so don't leave any switches available to them.

Physical server protection doesn't stop with a locked door. One of the most common mistakes made by techs is walking away from a server while still logged in. Always log off your server when not in use! As a backup, add a password-protected screen saver.

It's difficult to lock up all of your client systems, but you should have your users performing some physical security. First, all users should use screensaver passwords. Hackers will take advantage of unattended systems to get access to networks. Second, make users aware of the potential for dumpster diving and make paper shredders available. Last, tell users to mind their work areas. It's amazing how many users leave passwords available. I can go into any office, open a few desk drawers, and will invariably find little yellow sticky notes with user names and passwords. If users must write down passwords, tell them to put them in locked drawers!

Firewalls

I always fear the moment when technical terms move beyond the technical people and start to find use in the nontechnical world. The moment any technical term becomes part of the common vernacular, you can bet that its true meaning will become obscured, because without a technical background people are reduced to simplistic descriptions of what is invariably a far more complex idea. I submit the term *firewall* as a perfect example of this phenomenon. Most people with some level of computer knowledge think of a firewall as some sort of thing-a-ma-bob that protects an internal network from unauthorized access to and from the Internet at large. That type of definition might work for your VP as you explain why you need to get a firewall, but as techs, we need a deeper understanding.

Firewalls protect networks using a number of methods, such as hiding IP addresses and blocking TCP/IP ports. Any device that uses any or all of the techniques discussed next is by definition a firewall. Let's look at the protection methods, and then turn to implementation in the last section of this chapter.

Hiding the IPs

The first and most common technique for protecting a network is to hide the real IP addresses of the internal network systems from the Internet. If a hacker gets a real IP address, he can then begin to probe that system, looking for vulnerabilities. If you can prevent a hacker from getting an IP address to probe, you've stopped most hacking techniques cold. You already know how to hide IP addresses: either via a *Network Address Translation (NAT)* or a proxy server. Choosing between a NAT and a proxy server requires some analysis, because each has its advantages and disadvantages. NATs only translate IP addresses. This means a NAT has no interest in the TCP port or the information and it can work fairly quickly. A proxy server can change the port numbers as well as hide the IP addresses; this adds an extra level of security but at the cost of slower throughput because this involves more work by the system. For this reason, many networks only use NATs.

One problem we run into when discussing proxy servers and NAT is that proxy-serving programs also provide address translation—but using a completely different method then a NAT. At first you may say, "Well, if a proxy server changes the port number as well as the IP address, isn't a proxy server always better?" A proxy server certainly provides more protection than a router that only performs NAT, but it comes with a significant overhead cost. Proxy servers tend to slow down network access—plus, if you ever change your proxy server's IP address, you'll have to go to every network-aware application on every system on your network and update the proxy server settings. For these reasons, most networks have abandoned proxy serving in favor of routers with NAT.

 TIP Most Windows clients now have such powerful caches that a proxy server's caching capability doesn't provide substantial improvement in web page access.

Now you know another reason why most routers have built-in NATs. Not only do NATs reduce the need for true IANA-supplied public IP addresses, but they also do a great job protecting networks from hackers (see Figure 17-9).

Port Filtering

The second most common firewall tool is *port filtering*, also called *port blocking*. Hackers will often try less commonly used port numbers to get into a network. Port filtering simply means preventing the passage of any TCP or UDP packets through any ports other than the ones prescribed by the system administrator. Port filtering is effective, but it requires some serious configuration to work properly. The question is always, "Which ports do I allow into the network?" No one has problems with the well-known ports like 80 (HTTP), 20/21 (FTP), 25 (SMTP), and 110 (POP), but there are a large number of lesser-known ports that networks often want opened.

I recently installed port filtering on my personal firewall and everything worked great—until I decided to play the popular game Half-Life on the Internet. I simply could not connect to the Internet servers, until I discovered that Half-Life required TCP ports

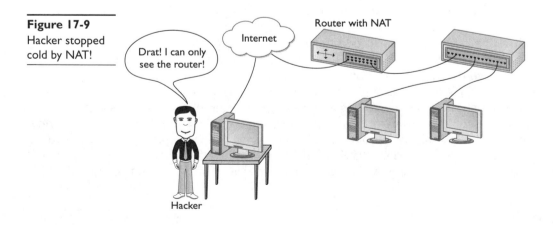

Figure 17-9
Hacker stopped
cold by NAT!

Drat! I can only
see the router!

Internet

Router with NAT

Hacker

27010 and 27015 to work over the Internet. After reconfiguring my port filter I was able to play Half-Life, but when I tried to talk to my friends using Microsoft NetMeeting, I couldn't log on to a NetMeeting server! Want to guess where the problem lay? Yup, I needed to open ports 389, 522, 1503, 1720, and 1731! How did I figure this out? I didn't know which ports to open, but I suspected that my problem was in the port arena so I fired up my web browser (thank goodness that worked!) and went to the Microsoft NetMeeting web site, which told me which ports I needed to open. This constant opening and closing of ports is one of the prices you pay for the protection of port filtering, but it sure stops hackers if they can't use strange ports to gain access!

Most routers that provide port blocking manifest it in one of two ways. The first way is to have port filtering close *all* ports until you open them explicitly. The other port filtering method is to leave all ports open unless you explicitly close them. The gotcha here is that most types of IP sessions require *dynamic port* usage. For example, when my system makes a query for a web page on HTTP port 80, the web server and my system establish a session using a *different* port to send the web pages to my system. Figure 17-10 shows the results of running NETSTAT with the –n switch while I have a number of web pages open—note the TCP ports used for the incoming web pages (the Local Address column). Dynamic ports can cause some problems for older (much older) port filtering systems, but almost all of today's port filtering systems are aware of this issue and handle it automatically.

Port filters have many different interfaces. On my little gateway router, the port filtering uses a pretty, web-based interface shown in Figure 17-11. Linux systems use either IPTABLES or NETFILTER for their firewall work. Like most Linux tools, these programs are rather dull to look at directly and require substantial skill manipulating text files to do your filtering chores. Most Linux distributions come with handy graphical tools, however, to make the job much easier. Figure 17-12 shows the firewall configuration screen from the popular YaST utility, found on the SUSE Linux distribution.

```
Microsoft Windows 2000 [Version 5.00.2195]
(C) Copyright 1985-1999 Microsoft Corp.

C:\>netstat -n

Active Connections

  Proto  Local Address          Foreign Address        State
  TCP    192.168.4.10:1707      207.46.144.86:80       ESTABLISHED
  TCP    192.168.4.10:1710      207.46.238.24:80       ESTABLISHED
  TCP    192.168.4.10:1711      207.46.144.86:80       ESTABLISHED
  TCP    192.168.4.10:1712      207.46.144.86:80       ESTABLISHED
  TCP    192.168.4.10:1713      207.46.144.86:80       ESTABLISHED
  TCP    192.168.4.10:1741      216.239.33.100:80      CLOSE_WAIT

C:\>
```

Figure 17-10 The netstat –n command showing HTTP connections

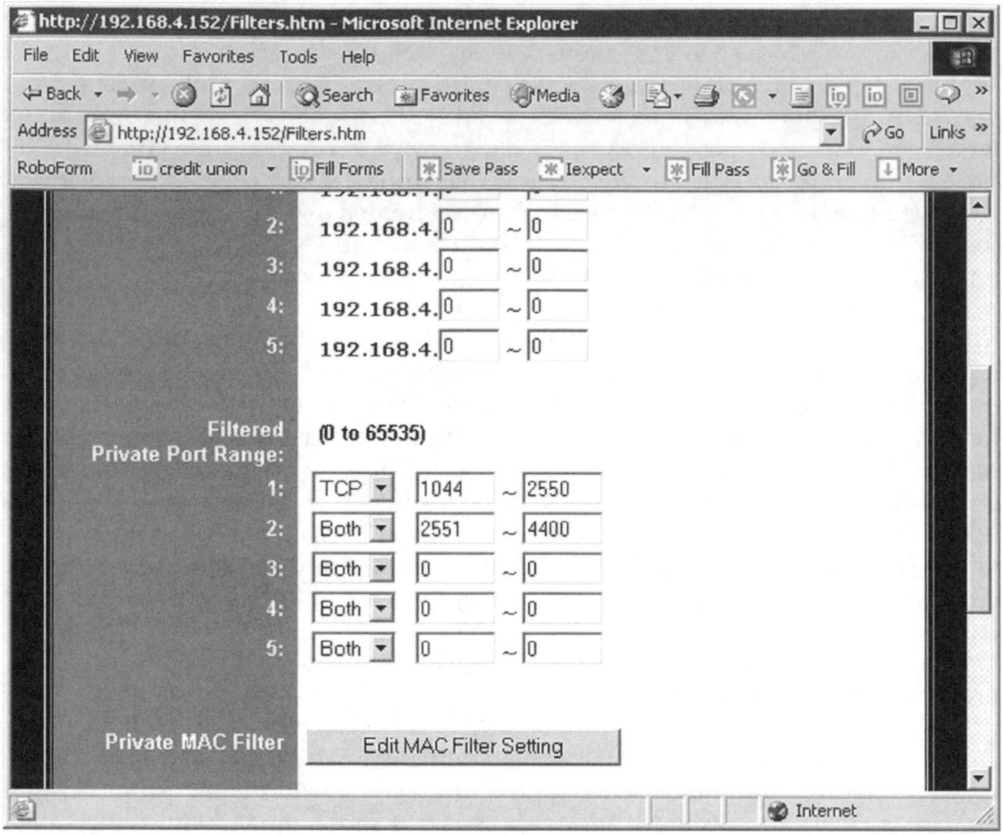

Figure 17-11 Web-based port-filtering interface

So, can one router have both a NAT and port filtering? You bet it can! Most gateway routers come with both—you just need to take the time to configure them and make them work!

TIP The Network+ exam expects you to know that NAT, proxy servers, and port filters are typical firewall functions!

Packet Filtering
Port filtering deals only with port numbers; it completely disregards IP addresses. If an IP packet comes in with a filtered port number, the packet is blocked, regardless of the IP address. *Packet filtering* works in the same way, except it only looks at the IP addresses. *Packet filters,* also known as *IP filters,* will block any incoming or outgoing packet from a

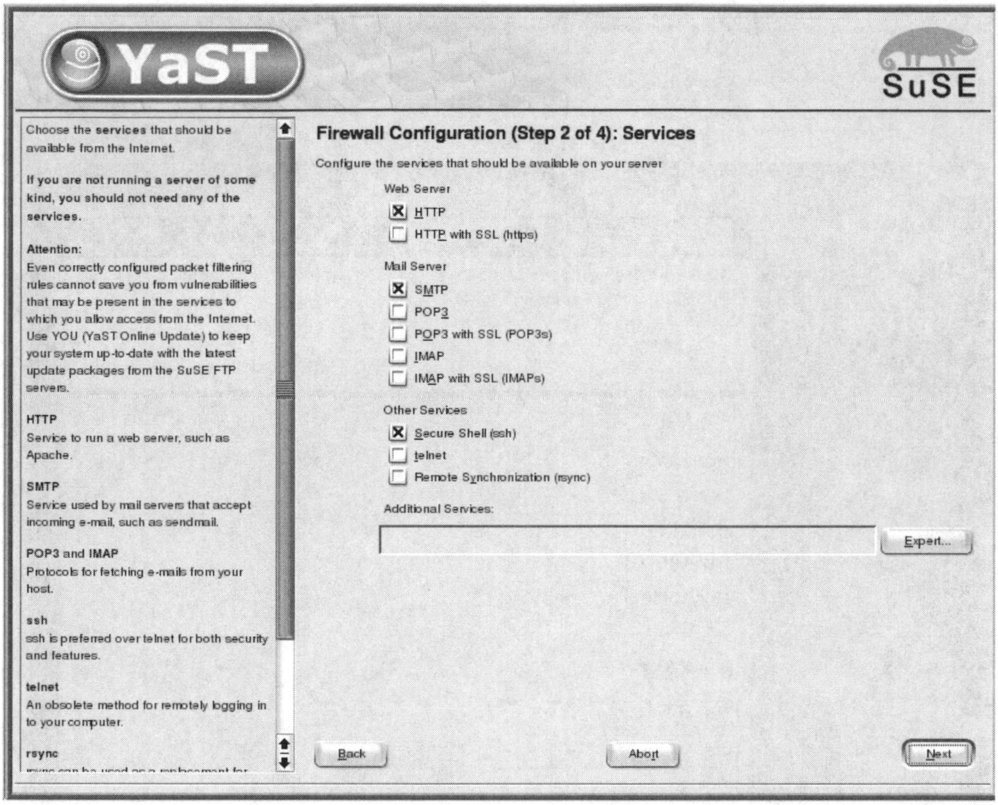

Figure 17-12   The YaST configuration program

particular IP address or range of IP addresses. Packet filters are far better at blocking outgoing IP addresses, because the network administrator knows and can specify the IP addresses of the internal systems. Blocking outgoing packets is a good way to prevent users on certain systems from accessing the Internet. Figure 17-13 shows a configuration page from a router designed to block different ranges of IP addresses and port numbers.

Encryption

Firewalls do a great job controlling traffic coming into or out of a network from the Internet, but they do nothing to stop interceptor hackers who monitor traffic on the public Internet looking for vulnerabilities. Once a packet is on the Internet itself, anyone with the right equipment can intercept and inspect it. Inspected packets are a cornucopia of passwords, account names, and other tidbits that hackers can use to intrude into your network. Because we can't stop hackers from inspecting these packets, we must turn to *encryption* to make them unreadable.

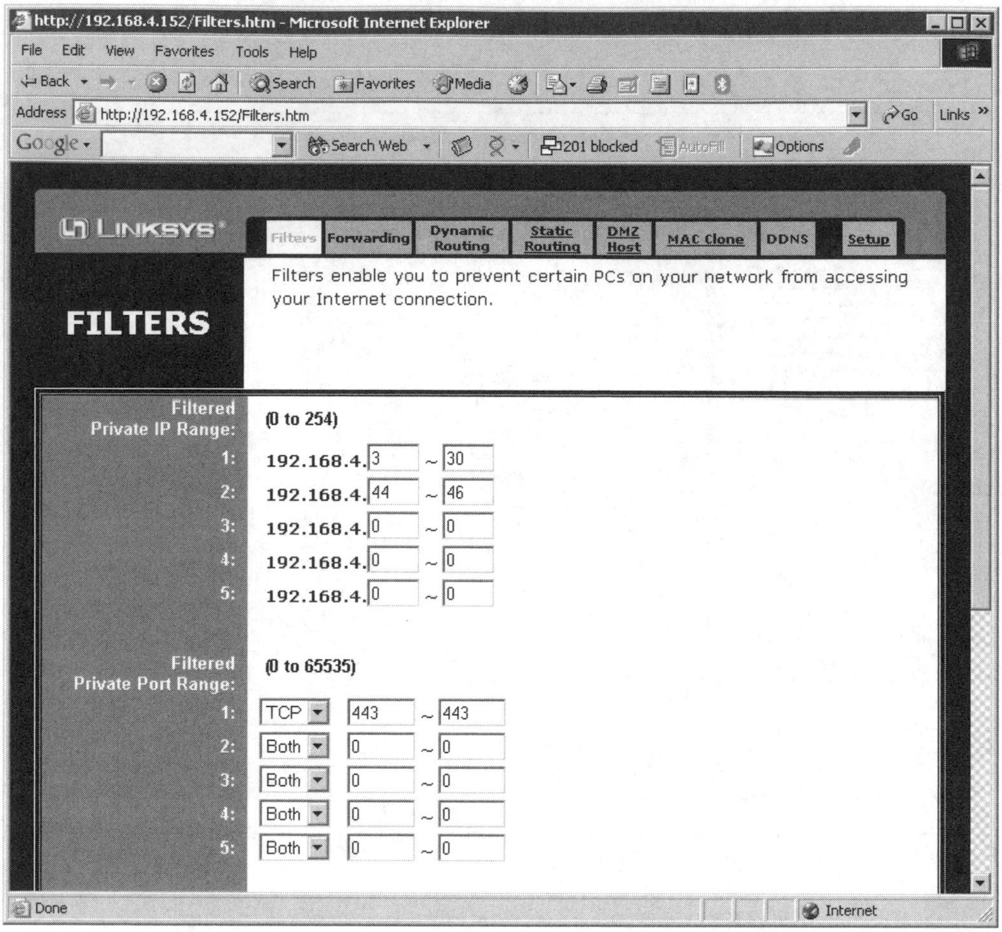

Figure 17-13 Blocking IP addresses

Network encryption occurs at many different levels and is in no way limited to Internet-based activities. Not only are there many levels of network encryption, but each encryption level provides multiple standards and options, making encryption one of the most complicated of all networking issues. You need to understand where encryption comes into play, what options are available, and what you can use to protect your network.

Authentication

Throughout this book, I've used examples where users type in user names and passwords to gain access to networks. But have you ever considered the process that takes place each time this *authentication* is requested? If you're thinking that when a user types in a user name and password, that information is sent to a server of some sort to be authenticated, you're right—but do you know how the user name and password get to the serving system? That's where encryption becomes important in authentication.

In a local network, encryption is usually handled by the NOS. Because NOS makers usually control software development of both the client and the server, they can create their own proprietary encryptions. However, in today's increasingly interconnected and diverse networking environment, there is a motivation to enable different network operating systems to authenticate any client system from any other NOS. Modern network operating systems like Windows NT/2000/XP/2003 and NetWare 4.*x*/5.*x*/6.*x* use standard authentication encryptions like MIT's *Kerberos*, enabling multiple brands of servers to authenticate multiple brands of clients. These LAN encryptions are usually transparent and work quite nicely even in mixed networks.

Unfortunately, this uniformity falls away as you begin to add remote access authentications. There are so many different remote access tools, based on UNIX/Linux, NetWare, and Windows serving programs, that most remote access systems have to support a variety of different authentication methods.

PAP Password Authentication Protocol (PAP) is the oldest and most basic form of authentication. It's also the least safe, because it sends all passwords in clear text. No NOS uses PAP for a client system's login, but almost all network operating systems that provide remote access service will support PAP for backward compatibility with a host of older programs (like Telnet) that only use PAP.

CHAP Challenge Handshake Authentication Protocol (CHAP) is the most common remote access protocol. CHAP has the serving system challenge the remote client. A *challenge* is where the host system asks the remote client some secret—usually a password— that the remote client must then respond with for the host to allow the connection.

MS-CHAP MS-CHAP is Microsoft's variation of the CHAP protocol. It uses a slightly more advanced encryption protocol.

Configuring Dial-Up Encryption

It's the server not the client that controls the choice of dial-up encryption. Microsoft clients can handle a broad selection of authentication encryption methods, including no authentication at all. On the rare occasion when you have to change your client's default encryption settings for a dial-up connection, you'll need to journey deep into the bowels of its properties. Figure 17-14 shows the Windows 2000 dialog box where you configure encryption, called Advanced Security Settings. The person who controls the server's configuration will tell you which encryption method to select here.

Data Encryption

Encryption methods don't stop at the authentication level. There are a number of ways to encrypt network *data* as well. The choice of encryption method is dictated to a large degree by the method used by the communicating systems to connect. Many networks consist of multiple networks linked together by some sort of private connection, usually some kind of telephone line like ISDN or T1. Microsoft's encryption method of choice for this type of network is called *IPSec* (derived from *IP security*). IPSec provides transparent encryption between the server and the client. IPSec will also work in VPNs, but other encryption methods are more commonly used in those situations.

Figure 17-14

Setting dial-up encryption in the Windows 2000 Advanced Security Settings dialog box

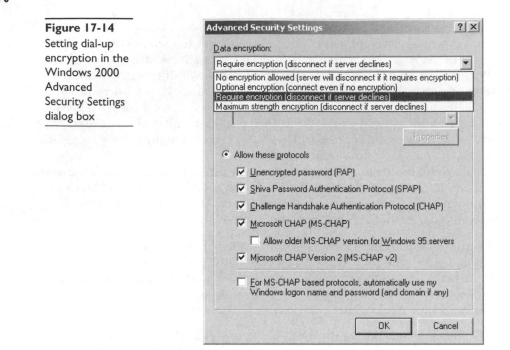

Application Encryption

When it comes to encryption, even TCP/IP applications can get into the swing of things. The most famous of all application encryptions is Netscape's *Secure Sockets Layer (SSL)* security protocol, which is used to create secure web sites. Microsoft incorporates SSL into its more far-reaching HTTPS (HTTP over SSL) protocol. These protocols make it possible to create the secure web sites we use to make purchases over the Internet. HTTPS web sites can be identified by the *HTTPS://* included in their URL (see Figure 17-15).

Public Keys and Certificates

Did you ever use one of those "secret decoder rings" when you were young? I thought secret decoder rings were a thing of the past, until I recently saw my daughter playing with one she got from a box of breakfast cereal. A secret decoder ring uses an encryption algorithm to exchange each letter of the alphabet for another, enabling you to turn readable text into a coded message or vice versa. For example, your decoder ring might exchange each letter in the alphabet for the letter three steps away—which would transform the statement "I HAVE A SECRET" into something like "F EXSB X PBZOBQ." In this case, moving the letters of the alphabet three positions is the algorithm, and the secret decoder ring is the key we use to encrypt and decrypt.

Encryption in the world of electronic data works in much the same way. Incredibly complex algorithms use a special string of numbers and letters, known as a key, to encrypt and decrypt anything from Word documents to the data areas of IP packets. Given enough time, most people could break the simple, three-letter algorithm used in our

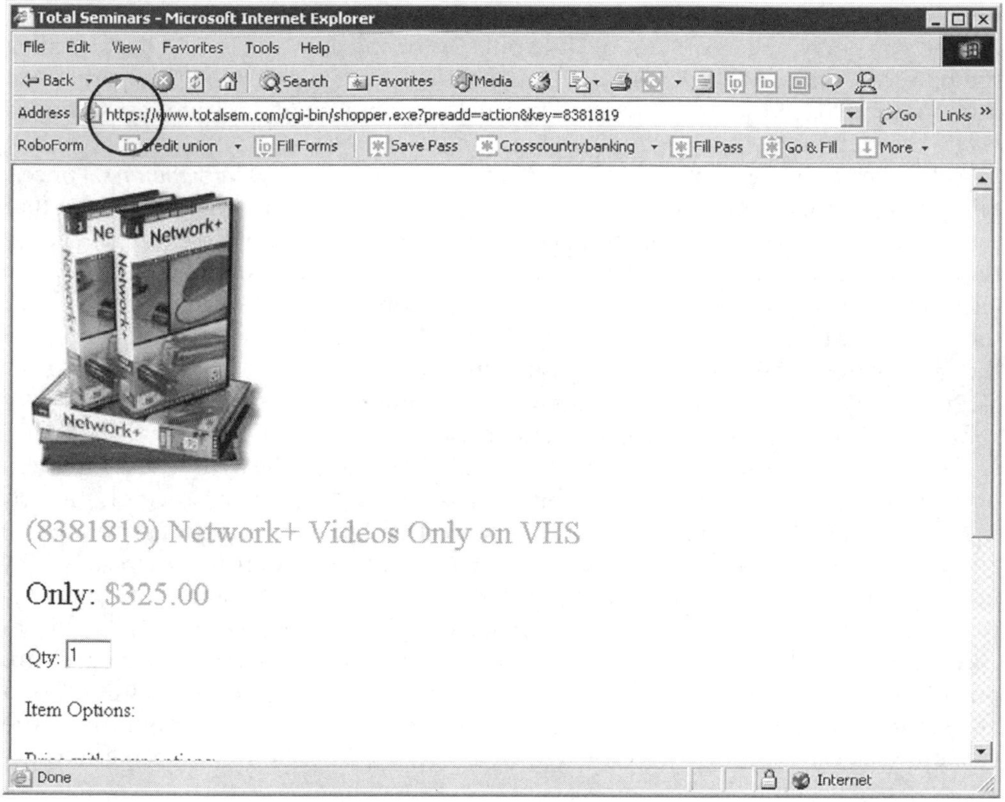

Figure 17-15   A secure web site

first example—we call this *weak encryption*. The best encryption algorithms used in computing are for all practical purposes impossible to crack, and are thus known as *strong encryption*.

> **TIP**   The length of the key is an indicator of the strength of the algorithm. Most encryption methods will mention the size of their key in bits. 128-bit is considered the safest practical key size.

Even the strongest encryption is easily broken if someone can get the key. Early encryption techniques used what is called *symmetric key*. Symmetric key means the same key is used both to encrypt and to decrypt. This leads to the obvious question: "How do you get the key to the other person without anyone else getting it?" Simply sending it over the network is risky—a hacker might intercept it. If the key is stolen from either system the encryption is also compromised.

To avoid this single-key issue, most strong encryption uses an *asymmetric key* methodology. The asymmetric approach uses two keys: a public key and a private key. The encryption algorithms are designed so that anything encrypted with the public key can only be decrypted with the private key. You send out the public key to anyone you want to send you encrypted information. Since only the private key can decrypt data, stealing the public key is useless. Of course, if you want two-way encryption, each party must send the other its public key. We refer to this method of public and private keys simply as *public key* encryption.

Public key provides another big benefit beyond encryption: *digital signatures*. For certain types of transactions, you don't need encryption, but you *would* like to know that the data is actually coming from the person or source that you think is sending it. A digital signature is a string of characters created by running an algorithm on the private key and a special value of the data called a *hash*. The person receiving the signature then uses the public key to generate what's called a *digest* and compares the two values. If they are the same, you can be certain that they came from the person holding the private key!

Public key has one weak spot. Let's say you're about to go to a secure web site to buy some great textbooks. Part of SSL's security comes from the use of public keys. Secure web sites will send you a public key for that web site to handle the transaction. But then, how can you know this truly is the public key, and not a forged key placed on the web site by a hacker? This is the third interesting aspect of Public keys: digital certificates.

Digital certificates are public keys signed with the digital signature from a trusted third party called a certificate authority (CA). Web sites pay these CAs hundreds of dollars per year just for the CA to sign the web site's digital certificates. The predominate CA for secure web sites is Verisign (www.verisign.com). Certificates are interesting in that they are one of the few parts of the HTTPS protocol that you can actually see if you want. Go to any secure web site and look for the small lock icon that appears at the bottom of the web browser. Click the lock to see the certificate. Figure 17-16 shows a typical certificate.

Figure 17-16
Certificate details

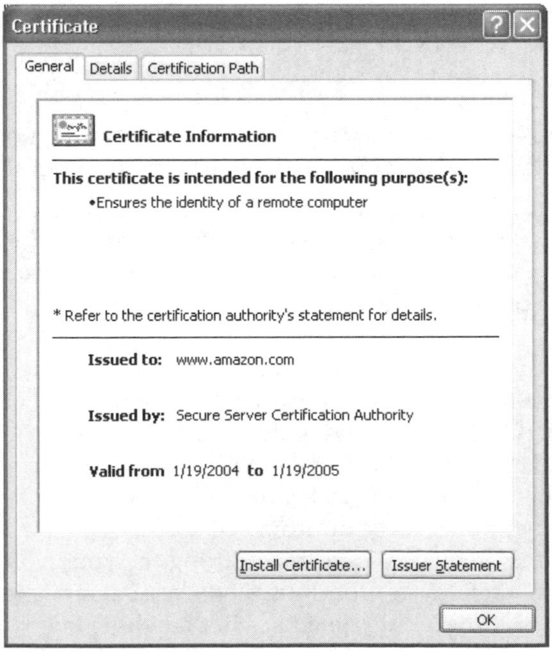

VLAN

The best place for a hacker to access a system is right at the system itself. The second best place to access a system is by sitting at another computer on the same collision domain. When two computers sit on the same collision domain, the hacker has no concerns about firewalls and other tools that we use to protect our systems from outside threats. When you place a number of systems on a single switch, they will by design have total access to one another—they are after all on the same collision domain. In most cases, this is fine. We want all systems on a single collision domain to have easy access to each other. More secure environments or environments that want to cut down on broadcast traffic, however, may find themselves wanting to reorganize their networks into multiple collision domains.

Chopping a single collision domain into multiple domains is usually a pricey and somewhat complex process. In most cases, a network on a single collision domain is probably already well-established. You have a single switch (or a few switches chained together) in a single equipment room with horizontal cable connections to each system. Breaking this network into multiple pieces requires you to add routers between the switches—and if you don't have multiple switches, you had better go buy some! The cost of routers and the sheer amount of configuration involved in this process motivated the networking industry in the mid-1990s to come up with an alternative method of organizing networks. That solution was called a *Virtual LAN (VLAN)*.

Simply put, a VLAN is a LAN that—using smart, VLAN-capable switches—can place some systems (or any systems, on the more expensive VLANs) on whatever collision domain you want. The simplest manifestation of VLAN comes in the form of small, eight-port switches; at the press of a button, these switches can split the single eight-port collision domain into two four-port domains (Figure 17-17).

NOTE VLANs are great for security, but they're also a great solution for reducing network traffic and for administration of networks.

Figure 17-17
Simple VLAN

Single collision domain

Two collision domains

With a VLAN, it's as though you take a single switch and with the press of a button turn it into two separate switches! So how would computers on different sides of this VLAN communicate? Well, with this particular VLAN, they wouldn't—unless you could figure out a way to place a router in between the two collision domains! More complex VLAN boxes have built-in functions to enable the two collision domains to connect. Some have a built-in router; others use proprietary methods involving MAC addresses or some electronics that can tell one port on the VLAN switch from another.

The VLAN boxes that identify each port enable you to combine the ports into any grouping of collision domains. A 48-port VLAN box can create a collision domain, for example, with ports 2 and 46. These boxes provide excellent control over network splitting and configuration, although at a hefty price tag. Figure 17-18 shows the configuration screen for a high-end Cisco VLAN box. Note the number of VLANs on the left-hand side. In this case, two of the ports on slot 3, port 15 and port 25, are configured for VLAN-1.

What's a slot? Well, this VLAN box is so large that it uses slots: open spaces on the box that accept many different types of ports on modules called *blades*. You can insert a blade of switched ports into these slots, for example, and create a huge VLAN configuration!

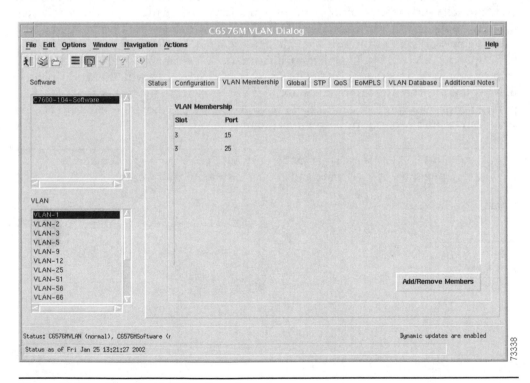

Figure 17-18 Complex VLAN configuration

NOTE When VLAN switches get complex enough to configure individual ports, many of the folks who make these boxes don't like to call them switches because they do so much more than mere switches. Some manufacturers call them routers; others stick with switches. I've used the word "box" as a generic label.

The ultimate in VLANs comes when you have multiple VLAN boxes that work together to make complex collision domains that span physical boxes. Figure 17-19 shows just this type of VLAN setup. Note how even though there are three VLAN boxes, different systems connected to different boxes can all be members of the same collision domain. In this example, there are three collision domains: VLAN-1, VLAN-2, and VLAN-3.

Figure 17-19
Very complex
VLAN

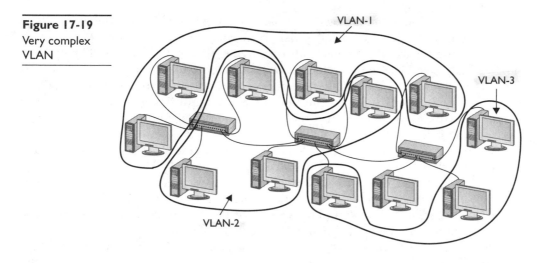

VLANs are also handy in situations where you have a large number of systems with static IP information that you don't want to change, for example an ISP running hundreds of web servers. If a system must be physically moved, it's easy to reconfigure the VLAN to keep the system in its original network ID, enabling the system to keep all of its IP information.

Implementing External Network Security

Now that you understand how to protect your networks from external threats, let's take a look at a few common implementations of network protection. I've chosen three typical setups: a single home system connected to the Internet, a small office network, and a large organizational network.

Personal Connections

Back in the days of dial-up connections, the concept of protection from external threats wasn't very interesting. The concept of dial-up alone was more than enough protection for most users. First, systems using dial-up connections were by definition only periodically on the Internet, making them tough for hackers to detect. Second, all dial-up connections use DHCP-assigned IP addresses, so even if a hacker could access a dial-up user during one session, that dial-up user would almost certainly have a different IP address the next time they accessed the Internet. As long as they have installed a good anti-virus program, dial-up users have nothing to fear from hackers.

The onset of high-speed, always-connected Internet links has changed the security picture completely. The user who dumps his or her dial-up connection for ADSL or a cable modem immediately becomes a prime target for hackers. Even though most ADSL and cable modems use DHCP links, the lease time for these addresses is more than long enough to give even the casual hacker all the time they need to poke around in the systems.

One of the first items on the agenda of Windows users with high-bandwidth connections is to turn off File and Print Sharing. Because NetBIOS can run over IP, sharing a folder or printer makes it available to anyone on the Internet unless your ISP helps you out by filtering NetBIOS traffic. Some hacker groups run port scanner programs looking for systems with File and Print Sharing enabled and post these IP addresses to public sites (no, I will not tell you where to find them!). When I first got my cable modem about two years ago, I absentmindedly clicked Network Neighborhood and discovered that four of my fellow cable users had their systems shared, and two of them were sharing printers! Being a good neighbor and not a hacker, I made sure they changed their erroneous ways!

Although you can buy a firewall system to place between your system and the Internet, most single users prefer to employ a personal software firewall program like BlackICE Defender or ZoneAlarm Pro (see Figure 17-20). These personal firewall programs are quite powerful, and have the added benefit of being easy to use—plus, many of them are free! These days, there's no excuse for an individual Internet user not to use a personal firewall.

Every version of Windows comes with the handy Internet connection sharing (ICS) but ICS alone doesn't provide any level of support other than NAT. Starting with Windows XP we now have *Internet Connection Firewall (ICF)*. ICF works with ICS to provide basic firewall protection for your network. ICF is often used without ICS to provide protection for single machines connected to the Internet. Figure 17-21 shows the Advanced tab of the NIC's properties dialog box to turn on ICF.

Figure 17-20
ZoneAlarm Pro

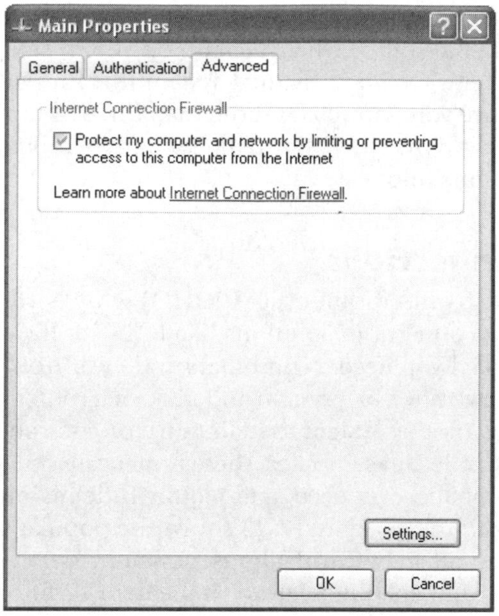

Figure 17-21
Advanced tab
for ICF

By default ICF blocks all incoming IP packets that attempt to initiate a session. This is great for networks that only use the Internet to browse the Web or grab e-mail, but will cause problems in circumstances where you want to provide any type of Internet server on your network. To open well-known TCP ports, click the Settings button (see Figure 17-22).

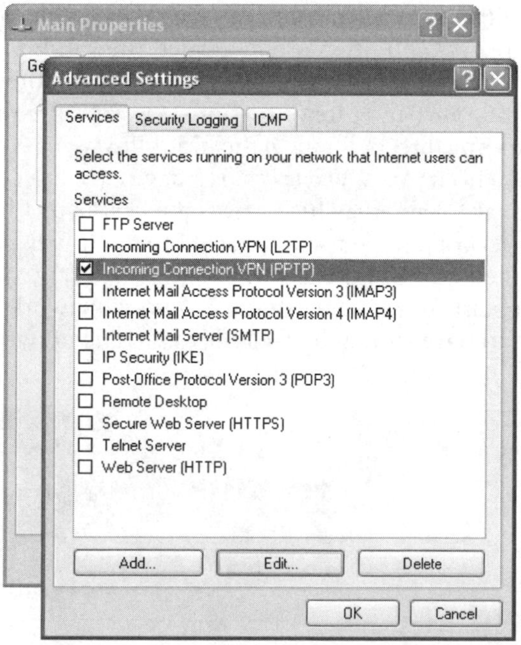

Figure 17-22
Opening a VPN
port in ICF

Products such as ZoneAlarm and ICF do a fine job protecting a single machine or a small network. But software firewalls run on your system, taking CPU processing away form your system. On an individual system this firewall overhead doesn't strain your system, but once you start to add more than three or four systems or if you need to add advanced functions like a VPN, you'll need a more robust solution. That's where SOHO connections come into play.

SOHO Connections

The typical small office/home office (SOHO) setup is a few networked systems sharing a single Internet connection. Solutions like ICS with ICF will work, but if you want reliability and speed you need a combination firewall/router. You have two choices here: you can drop two NICs in a system and make it a router (expensive, challenging to configure, and yet another system to maintain), or you can buy a SOHO firewall/gateway router like my little Linksys router. These routers are cheap, provide all the firewall functions you'll probably ever need, and require little maintenance. There are a number of great brands out there. Figure 17-23 shows the popular Cisco SOHO 70 series router.

These routers all do NAT with almost no setup. As your needs grow, these SOHO routers grow with you, enabling you to implement IP filtering, port blocking, and many other handy extras. Plus, as your network grows, you can use these same small routers to support separate DNS, DHCP, and WINS servers, although the configuration can become challenging.

Large Network Connections

Large networks need heavy-duty protection that not only protects from external threats, but does so without undue restriction on the overall throughput of the network. To do this, large networks will often use dedicated firewall boxes, which usually sit between the gateway router and the protected network. These firewalls are designed to filter IP traffic (including NAT and proxy functions), as well as to provide high-end tools to track and stop incoming threats. Some of the firewall systems even contain a rather interesting feature called a honey pot. A *honey pot* is a device (or a set of functions within a firewall) that creates a fake network, which seems attackable to a hacker. Instead of trying to access the real network, hackers are attracted to the honey pot, which does nothing more than record their actions and keep them away from the true network.

Once you start to add components to your network like web and e-mail servers, you're going to have to step up to a more serious network protection configuration.

Figure 17-23
Cisco SOHO 70
series router

Because web and e-mail servers must have exposure to the Internet, you will need to create what we call a *demilitarized zone (DMZ)*. A DMZ is a lightly protected or unprotected network positioned between your firewall and the Internet. There are a number of ways to configure this; Figure 17-24 shows one classic example.

Figure 17-24
A DMZ
configuration

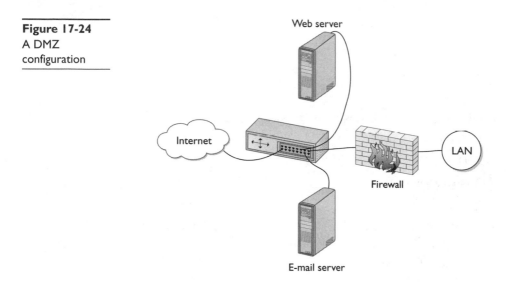

The private, protected network is called an *intranet*. Compare this term to the term *extranet* you learned in the last chapter and make sure you understand the difference!

Chapter Review

Questions

1. Which two encryption applications work together to make secure web sites for online purchases?

   A. HTTP

   B. VPN

   C. HTTPS

   D. SSL

2. Which three basic technologies are used with firewalls?

   A. Proxy servers

   B. Packet filtering

   C. Dynamic routing

   D. Network Address Translation (NAT)

3. What is the most common technique for protecting a network?

   A. Port filtering

   B. Hiding IP addresses

   C. Packet filtering

   D. Encryption

4. Most routers have built-in proxy servers.

   A. True

   B. False

5. Which two of the following methods can you use to hide IP addresses?

   A. Static IP addresses

   B. DHCP

   C. Proxy server

   D. NAT

6. Which of the following blocks IP packets using any port other than the ones prescribed by the system administrator?

   A. Hiding IP addresses

   B. Port filtering

   C. Packet filtering

   D. Encryption

7. Which of the following blocks any incoming or outgoing packets from a particular IP address or range of IP addresses?

   A. Hiding IP addresses

   B. Port filtering

   C. Packet filtering

   D. Encryption

8. Firewalls cannot stop which type of hacker?

   A. Inspector

   B. Interceptor

   C. Controller

   D. Flooder

9. Which method prevents hackers from reading packets intercepted on the Internet?

   A. Hiding IP addresses

   B. Port filtering

    C. Packet filtering

    D. Encryption

10. Of the following choices, which two are encryption methods?

    A. L2TP

    B. PPTP

    C. VPN

    D. SLIP

Answers

1. **C, D.** HTTP secure (HTTPS) and Secure Sockets Layer (SSL) are used to create secure web sites.

2. **A, B, D.** Proxy servers, packet filtering, and network address translation are the basic technologies used with firewalls.

3. **B.** Hiding IP addresses is the most common technique for protecting a network.

4. **B.** False. Most routers have built-in NATs, not built-in proxy servers.

5. **C, D.** Both a proxy server and a NAT can hide IP addresses.

6. **B.** Port filtering blocks IP packets using any ports other than the ones prescribed by the system administrator.

7. **C.** Packet filtering blocks any incoming or outgoing packets from a particular IP address or range of IP addresses.

8. **B.** Firewalls can do nothing to stop interceptor hackers who monitor traffic on the public Internet looking for vulnerabilities.

9. **D.** Encryption prevents hackers from reading packets intercepted on the Internet.

10. **A, B.** L2TP is a Cisco encryption method, and PPTP is a Microsoft encryption method.

Interconnecting Network Operating Systems

The Network+ Certification exam expects you to know how to

- 2.13 Identify the purpose of network services and protocols (for example: NFS—Network File System, AFP—Apple File Protocol, LPD—Line Printer Daemon)
- 2.16 Define the function of the following remote access protocols and services: RDP (Remote Desktop Protocol)
- 3.4 Given a remote connectivity scenario [comprising] a protocol, an authentication scheme, and physical connectivity, configure the connection. Includes connection to the following servers: UNIX/Linux/MAC OS X Server, NetWare, Windows, AppleShare IP (Internet Protocol)
- 4.5 Given a troubleshooting scenario between a client and the following server environments, identify the cause of a stated problem: UNIX/Linux/Mac OS X Server, NetWare, Windows, AppleShare IP

To achieve these goals, you must be able to

- Understand the interconnection issues of Windows 9x, NT, 2000, XP, and 2003 with other network operating systems
- Learn the interconnection issues of NetWare relating to other network operating systems
- Explain the interconnection issues of Macintosh with other network operating systems
- Describe the interconnection issues of UNIX/Linux with other network operating systems

Many real-world networks blend systems running many different operating systems. If you came to my office today, for example, you'd find the following systems running with these operating systems:

- One Windows Server 2003 (new file server)
- Two Windows 2000 Servers (domain controllers)
- One Novell NetWare 5 Server (file server)
- One Novell NetWare 6 Server (file server)

- One Fedora Linux (testing system)
- One SuSE Linux (Samba server)
- Ten Windows XP Professional (workstations)
- Three Windows 2000 Professional (workstations)
- Two Windows XP Home (laptops)
- Two Macs running OS X (graphics workstations)
- Five systems running different versions of Windows 9x (testing systems)

While Total Seminars may have a more heterogeneous network than most real-world offices, it's more common than not to walk into a network and find many different operating systems all at work. The challenge you face is to make these different operating systems share their resources!

The widespread adoption of TCP/IP makes today's world a world of interoperability. As long as one uses TCP/IP applications such as WWW, FTP, and SMTP/POP e-mail, it doesn't matter what brand name of network operating system (NOS) is running on either the server or the client. I use the Safari web browser on my Macintosh laptop, for example, and have no problem accessing a web page on a Windows 2003 system running the Internet Information Services (IIS) web server program. My old Windows 98 system running the WSFTP_LE FTP client application easily transfers files to and from a Fedora Linux computer running the WU-FTP FTP server program. With TCP/IP applications, the NOS is unimportant and invisible.

Historical/Conceptual

This wasn't always the case with networking. In the days before all these wonderful, universal TCP/IP applications, each NOS had its own, usually proprietary method of enabling clients to access shared resources on servers—in particular shared folders and printers. To connect to a particular NOS server you had to have the same brand of client. Interoperability wasn't something that folks at Novell, Apple, or Microsoft seriously considered or even desired. Microsoft would be thrilled if every server and client system ran only Windows. The Novell folks would love for every server in the world to run NetWare; and the Apple people know that *everyone* should own a Mac.

The odd men out in this "we don't want to work with anyone else" attitude were the makers of the UNIX and later Linux operating systems. All versions of UNIX/Linux use TCP/IP at their core and as a result all versions of UNIX/Linux run TCP/IP applications. Long before the Internet dominated the world, UNIX LANs happily used TCP/IP applications to share folders and printers. Many of these applications (with names such as NFS and LPD) were adopted by Microsoft, Novell, and Apple into their network operating systems and became some of the first methods of interoperability among different network operating systems.

One issue that all the NOS makers learned early on was that interoperability makes their network operating systems more attractive to potential purchasers. No one wants to adopt a new NOS that requires them to replace all of their clients or even get rid of their current servers. By creating methods that enabled one brand of client-access shared resources on another brand of server, NOS makers could enable a new adopter to transition from one NOS to another. As a result, every NOS now has some method to enable their servers or clients to access shared folders and printers on other network operating systems.

This chapter provides an overview of the many ways different network operating systems interconnect to share folders and printers. There's no way you can expect to memorize all the steps necessary to make every type of NOS share every type of possible resource with every type of NOS client that's available. There are just way too many NOS combinations out there! Entire books are written on topics such as "Making NetWare Servers Share Folders with Windows Clients." To make this chapter more manageable, I've selected the network operating systems that we most commonly use to act as servers: Microsoft Windows, Novell NetWare, Apple Macintosh, and UNIX/Linux; and the three most common client systems: Windows, UNIX/Linux, and Macintosh. In each section, I'll discuss how one type of server connects to each type of client. Because this chapter is about interconnections among different network operating systems, I'm not going to include Linux clients when I discuss connecting to Linux servers, Macintosh clients when discussing Macintosh servers, or Windows clients in the Windows servers section. Also, because NetWare is a server-only NOS, I will cover all three client types when we cover NetWare servers.

So, what exactly are the serving systems we want to discuss? Clearly we need to cover Windows NT, 2000/2003, and Windows XP. I'll also discuss connecting to Windows 9*x* systems—don't forget they can share folders and printers, too! Next up: NetWare 3.*x*, followed by NetWare 4.*x*/5.*x*/6.*x* servers. The interconnectivity methods of NetWare 3.*x* are quite different from those of NetWare 4.*x*/5.*x*/6.*x*. Macintosh serving systems are next-to-last, followed, finally, by UNIX/Linux. It's a tall order, but an interesting one, too! Let's get started.

Test Specific

Connecting to Windows

The easiest way to get a non-Windows operating system like Macintosh or UNIX/Linux to connect to a Windows computer is to make that non-Windows system look like another Windows computer to the system you are trying to access. The challenge to this is that Windows systems themselves have evolved over the years so the method used to connect a Macintosh to access a Windows 98 SE system's shared folder is different from the way you connect that same Macintosh to a Windows Server 2003 system running Active Directory. But Windows is the predominant operating system, so the latest versions of both Macintosh and UNIX/Linux systems come with plenty of software enabling them to make most of these connections easily. Sadly, not everyone owns the latest versions of these operating systems, so we'll need to look at a few of the methods that older Macs and UNIX/Linux systems used to connect to Windows.

For a non-Windows computer to act like a Windows computer it needs to run the same network protocol, use the same naming convention, and work with the security functions of the version of Windows it wants to access. A Windows 9x system will use NetBEUI or TCP/IP, while most other versions of Windows use TCP/IP. Windows NT and 9x use NetBIOS, while later versions use DNS.

Connecting Macintosh to Windows 9x Shared Resources

Connecting a Macintosh to a Windows 9x system differs depending on whether you're using a Mac with OS X or if you use an earlier Mac operating system. For many years, Apple relied on third-party programs to do the interconnections between Mac and Windows. Starting with the OS X 10.1 operation system, Macintosh computers use the same tools and methods to connect to Windows that all UNIX/Linux systems currently use: namely Samba, which we'll discuss in the UNIX/Linux section following this one. The OS X operating system is so different from its predecessors that it makes more sense to not even think of it as a Macintosh OS but rather as a UNIX/Linux OS. So let's talk about the pre-OS X days in this section and discuss the OS X Macs under the Connecting UNIX/Linux systems to Windows 9x system section next.

The first area where you will get in trouble connecting Macs to any Windows system is in network protocol. Many older Macs use the AppleTalk protocol, while Windows 9x systems use NetBEUI or TCP/IP.

 TIP Later Macintoshes all use TCP/IP, but the Network+ exam seems not to know this—if the test says Macintosh, assume AppleTalk!

Communication between Macintosh and Windows systems is further complicated by the fact that Macs and PCs use different higher-level protocols, too. Macintosh systems use the AppleTalk protocol for roughly the same jobs NetBIOS handles in Windows systems. So, even when your Macintosh and Windows systems are both using TCP/IP, you still have two different protocols handling the sessions, network naming conventions, and other important jobs. Windows 9x systems do not come with the AppleTalk protocol, and Macintoshes don't come with NetBIOS, so you're not going to get a Windows 9x client to talk to a Macintosh without some extra software. No problem! Now that all newer Macintosh systems support TCP/IP, a number of third-party vendors sell excellent programs that enable Macintosh computers to access shared folders and printers on Windows 9x systems. Figure 18-1 shows the popular interconnectivity program *PC MACLAN* running on a Windows system.

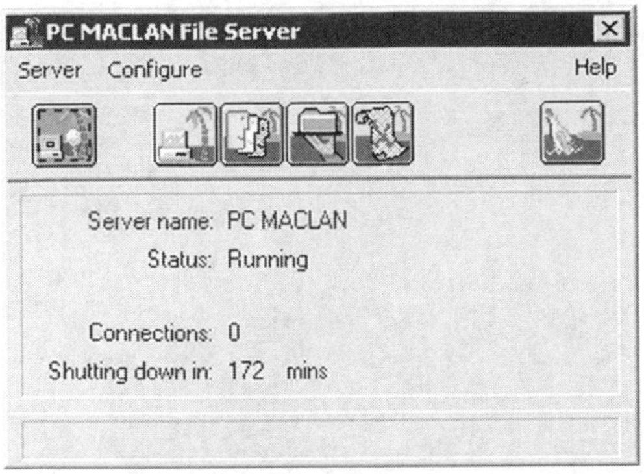

Figure 18-1
PC MACLAN
running on a
Windows system

Another program to connect Mac to Windows is called DAVE. Unlike PCMACLAN, DAVE is a two-way product: it enables Windows computers to access shared resources on Macs and Macs to access shared resources on Windows. We'll see more of DAVE in the "Connecting to Macintosh" section later in this chapter.

Connecting UNIX/Linux Systems to Windows 9x Systems

Connecting UNIX/Linux systems to Windows 9x systems for native access to shared folders requires you to run a program called Samba on the UNIX/Linux system. *Samba* makes the UNIX/Linux box look like just another Windows 9x system to the Windows server. Once you've got Samba running on the UNIX/Linux box, it will have access to the Windows system's shared folders. Samba is also used to connect Windows machines to shared folders and printers on UNIX/Linux and Mac OS X systems, as you'll see later in this chapter.

Like most UNIX/Linux applications, Samba isn't interesting to look at—it runs in the background and doesn't even have an interface. All Samba's configuration is stored in text files on each UNIX/Linux system. The primary configuration file for Samba is the smb.conf file. This file stores basic information such as the NetBIOS name for the UNIX/Linux system and the workgroup or domain to join. Here's a small bit of a typical smb.conf file:

Learning how to configure Samba is challenging—if you head over to your local technical bookstore, you'll see that the thickest books are the ones on configuring Samba. Fortunately, there are third-party tools that help automate this process, such as the popular SWAT program (Figure 18-2).

Shared Windows folders manifest themselves as drives that must then be mounted in UNIX/Linux. The most common tool is called smbmount. Many UNIX/Linux distributions now have programs similar to My Network Places or Windows Explorer that display mounted Samba drives (Figure 18-3).

Macintosh computers running OS X also use Samba, but Apple does a great job of automating the process. Figure 18-4 shows a Macintosh system accessing shared folders on a Windows system.

PART III

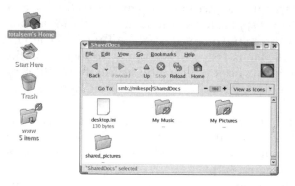

Figure 18-2   SWAT running on Linux

Figure 18-3   Shared Windows folders on Linux system

Figure 18-4   Mac OS X connecting to Windows system

Connecting to Windows Workstations (NT/2000/XP)

There's not much difference in how you connect a Macintosh or UNIX/Linux system to a Windows NT Workstation, Windows 2000 Professional, or Windows XP system than to a Windows 9x system. The tools just described are still used but unlike Windows 9x, you'll need a local account on any Windows system you want to access. Figure 18-5 shows a Macintosh system prompting for a username and password to access a shared folder on Windows XP.

Connecting to Windows Server Systems

The Windows Server platforms—Windows NT Server, Windows 2000 Server, and Windows Server 2003—all support Macintosh and UNIX/Linux systems natively. *Native support* means that the Windows server will act like Macintosh or UNIX/Linux systems—you don't have to make the Macs or UNIX/Linux computers act like Windows machines. This support is manifested via special services that you install into your Windows server. You may also use the Macintosh and UNIX/Linux program mentioned earlier, but you'll run into a big problem if you want those machines to join a domain or an Active Directory.

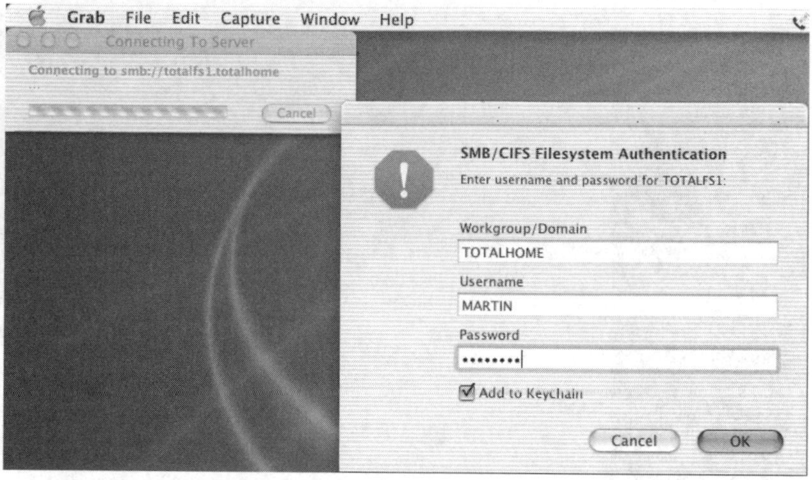

Figure 18-5
Prompting for
username and
password

> Grab File Edit Capture Window Help
>
> Connecting To Server
>
> Connecting to smb://totalfs1.totalhome
>
> [Cancel]
>
> **SMB/CIFS Filesystem Authentication**
>
> Enter username and password for TOTALFS1:
>
> Workgroup/Domain
> TOTALHOME
>
> Username
> MARTIN
>
> Password
> ••••••••
>
> ☑ Add to Keychain
>
> [Cancel] [OK]

Windows domains and Active Directory cause a bit of a headache for Macintosh and UNIX/Linux systems. The services Microsoft provides to support Macintosh and UNIX/Linux clients create separate folders on the Windows server that are not part of the domain or Active Directory. This effectively treats Macintosh and UNIX/Linux systems as separate entities, and excludes them from accessing the same shared folders as the Windows systems on the domain or Active Directory. The tools that Macintosh and UNIX/Linux use to access Windows shared resources do support domains, but there's no program yet that enables a Macintosh or UNIX/Linux system to join an Active Directory—with the lone exception of DAVE for Macintosh. Given that we've already seen the tools Macs and UNIX/Linux systems use to connect to Windows, let's concentrate on the services provided by Microsoft as we see how to connect to Windows server systems.

Connecting Macintosh to Windows Server Shared Resources

Windows NT, 2000, and 2003 Server come with both an AppleTalk protocol and two services: *File Services for Macintosh (FSM)* and *Print Services for Macintosh (PSM)*. With AppleTalk protocol support, File Services for Macintosh and Print Services for Macintosh, Windows NT, 2000, and 2003 Server have all the functionality they need to provide seamless interconnectivity for Macintosh computers running pre-Mac OS X operating system versions. Systems running OS X usually don't bother with these Microsoft services because the tools that come with OS X are preinstalled, faster, and easier to use than FSM and PSM.

 TIP The Windows NT version of FSM, called File Server for Macintosh service, must run with AppleTalk. Later versions will work with TCP/IP.

FSM and PSM are installed as services from the Windows Components section of the Add/Remove programs applet (see Figure 18-6). There's nothing to configure, you just click the check box. The configuration work comes into play when you create shared folders.

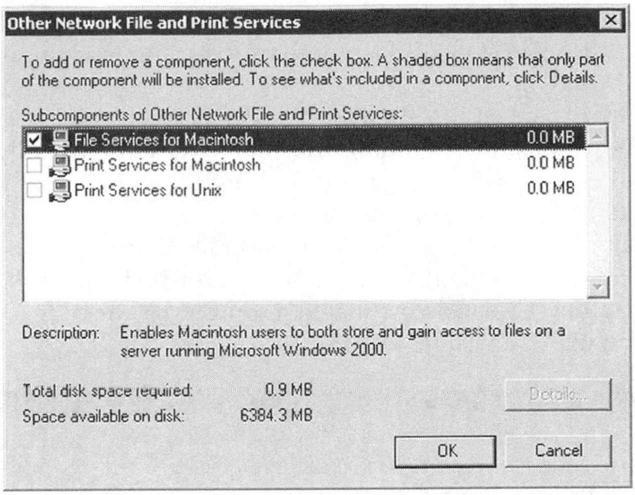

Figure 18-6
Installing File Services for Macintosh on a Windows 2000 system

Once you've installed the File Services for Macintosh, you need to create a special volume that will store the files you want the Microsoft clients to access. When you create a share on the Windows server, you must specify that it is to be shared by Macintosh clients (see Figure 18-7). All the Macintosh systems will also need to have valid user accounts on the Windows server.

Using Print Services for Macintosh is even easier than FSM. Just make sure that the system sharing the printer is running AppleTalk to support Macintosh systems. Once the service is running, Macintosh systems will see the server's shared printers in their Chooser program.

Connecting UNIX/Linux Systems to Windows Server Shared Resources

The primary method to get any UNIX/Linux system to access a shared resource on a Windows system is Samba. Samba's inability to have a UNIX/Linux system join an Active

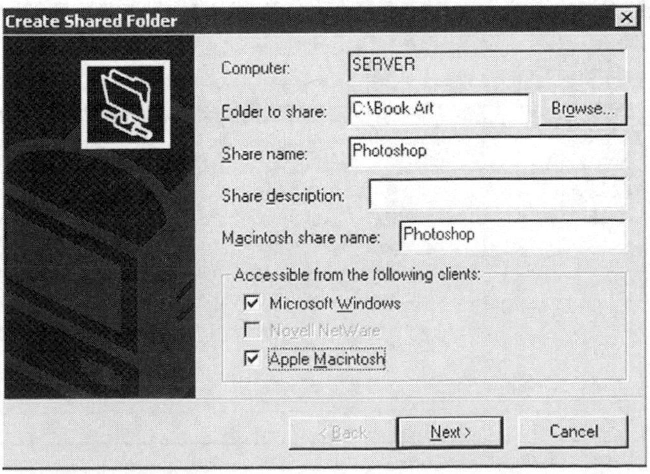

Figure 18-7
Creating a new share for Macintosh systems on a Windows server

Directory isn't too much of a problem for most users. Remember, having a computer join an Active Directory is different than accessing shared resources in an Active Directory environment.

For many years Microsoft has provided a product called *Services for UNIX (SFU)*. SFU is a UNIX subsystem for Windows that manifests itself primarily as a UNIX-style shell, as shown in Figure 18-8. SFU has been around for a number of years, but was only available as an add-on, and at additional cost.

SFU also includes many of the standard TCP/IP applications for file and print sharing such as NFS, FTP, and LPD (Figure 18-9). So while Microsoft doesn't push FSU as an interoperability tool to access shared resources, it's the only option other than running Samba on the UNIX/Linux systems.

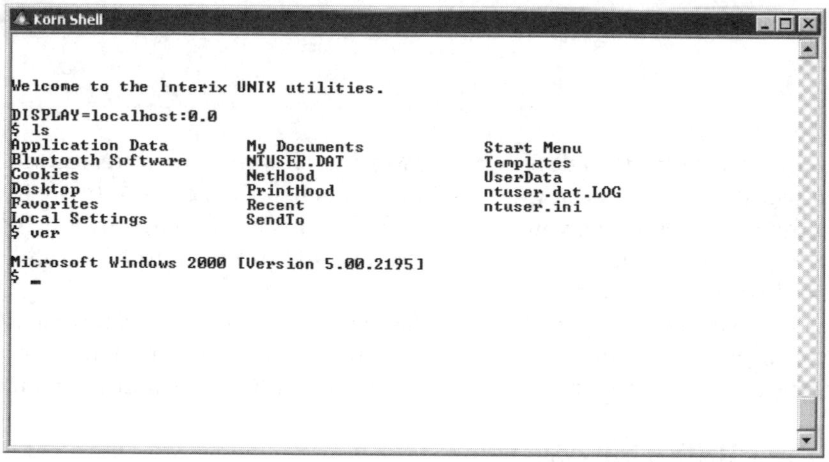

Figure 18-8 SFU running in Windows 2000

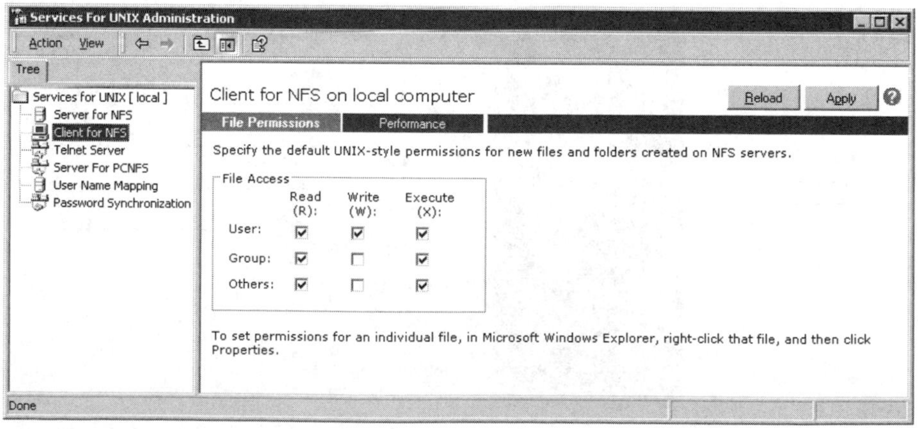

Figure 18-9 NFS Client configuration in SFU

Connecting to NetWare

If there's one NOS that makes interconnectivity a snap, it's Novell NetWare—or at least NetWare 4.*x*/5.*x*/6.*x*. Because NetWare is purely a server NOS, it must, by definition, perform interconnectivity every time you use it: there's no such thing as a NetWare client operating system. Windows, Macintosh, and UNIX/Linux systems must all use some form of *NetWare client software* to connect to a NetWare server, and Novell has, by necessity, created excellent client software for all of them. You can download the clients directly from Novell's web site, http://www.novell.com/download.

Connecting Windows Systems to NetWare

Novell has made client software for every Microsoft operating system including the ancient DOS of the 1980s. Over time, Novell has continued to evolve the NetWare client software: going graphical with the onset of Windows, supporting mixed environments of NetWare and Windows servers, and constantly updating to use the latest features of NetWare. As of this writing, the latest NetWare clients were version 4.9 for Windows NT/2000/XP and version 3.4 for Windows 9*x*. Figure 18-10 shows the logon screen from a modern NetWare client running on Windows XP.

Novell called the first client written for Windows 95, *Client32. Client32* is long obsolete, but the name has stuck as the common term for any Windows NetWare client provided by Novell. The latest versions of Client32 are powerful, providing support for IPX/SPX, the old NetWare 3.*x* binderies, and the more modern NetWare 4.*x*/5.*x*/6.*x* NDS trees. In addition, anyone running Client32 has complete control over the entire NetWare network—assuming of course they have the supervisor/admin rights! Figure 18-11 shows a NetWare client accessing the NDS tree of a small NetWare 6 network.

Microsoft has never been happy with NetWare clients taking over the login and other functions and for many years has supplied its own client with Windows. This client is

Figure 18-10
NetWare
client logon

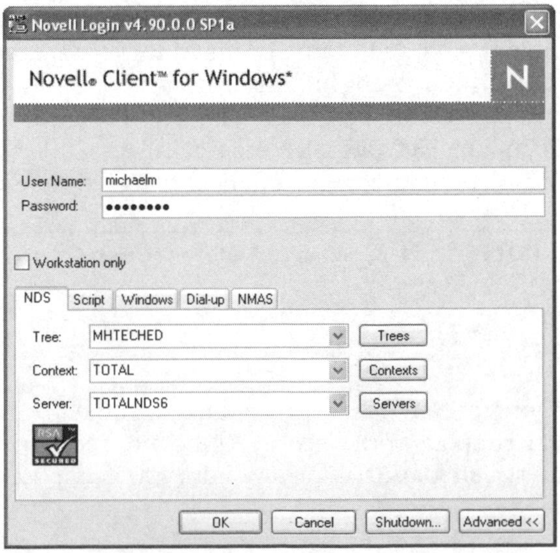

Figure 18-11
NDS tree from
NetWare client

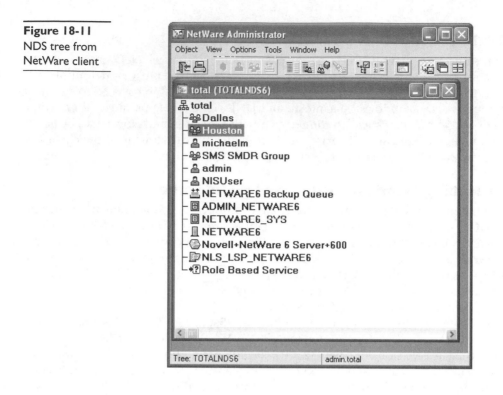

called Microsoft *Client for NetWare Networks* in Windows 9*x* and *Client Service for NetWare (CSNW)* in Windows NT, 2000, and XP (Figure 18-12). The Microsoft client comes with Windows but is not installed by default. (Windows 95 is the only exception to this.)

The Microsoft Client for NetWare Networks is weak compared to Novell's Client32. It enables a Windows 9*x* client to connect to resources on a NetWare server but little else. The Microsoft Client for NetWare Networks has two key weaknesses. First, it requires the IPX/SPX-compatible protocol and cannot connect to NetWare servers using TCP/IP. As Novell joins the rest of the networking industry in its headlong stampede toward TCP/IP, Windows 9*x* clients running the Microsoft Client for NetWare Networks get left behind. Second, the Microsoft Client for NetWare Networks does not understand *Novell Directory Services (NDS)*, NetWare's default security, and the directory systems for NetWare 4, 5, and 6.

NOTE Later versions of NetWare use the term *eDirectory* in place of NDS.

Client Service for NetWare is more robust than the Microsoft Client for NetWare Networks in that it supports both NetWare 3 binderies and NDS trees. Figure 18-13 shows the configuration screen for CSNW on a Windows XP computer. Note the two radio buttons

Figure 18-12
Client Service
for NetWare

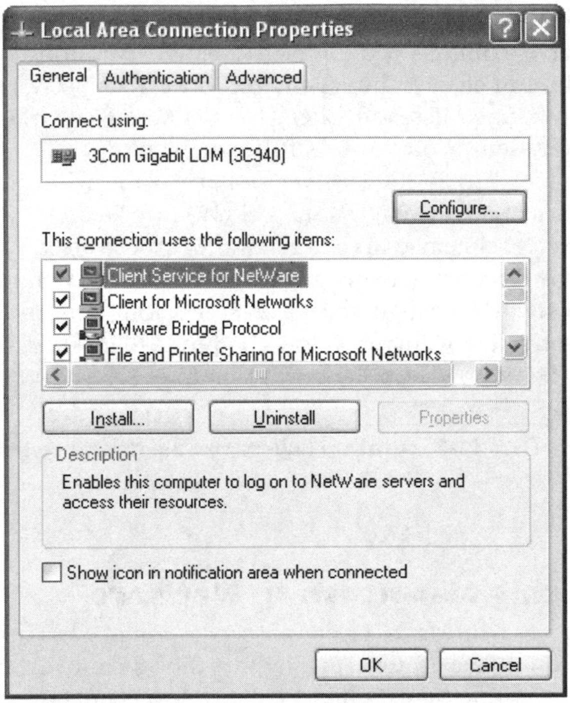

Figure 18-13
CSNW
configuration

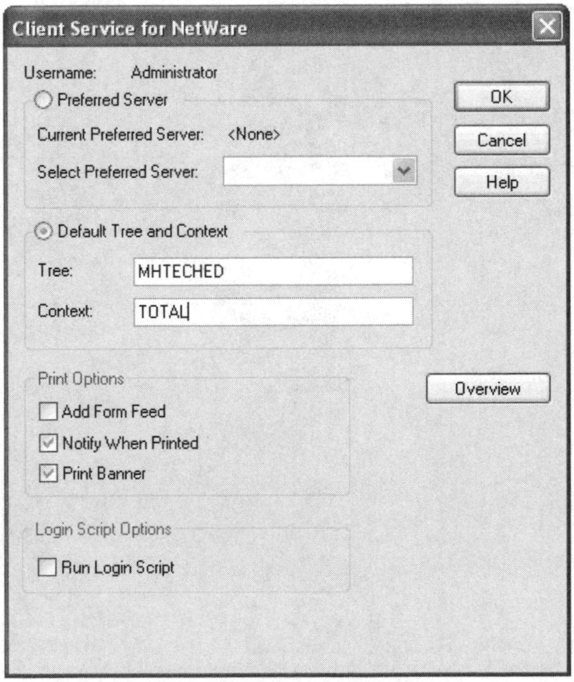

at the top. Choosing the Preferred Server radio button and entering the name of a NetWare server connects you to a NetWare Bindery. Choosing the Default Tree and Context radio button enables the system to connect to a NetWare NDS tree.

CSNW, like the Microsoft Client for NetWare Networks, only supports IPX/SPX. If your NetWare servers only run TCP/IP, you won't use CSNW.

Windows NT/2000/2003 Server systems come with an interesting little program called *Gateway Services for NetWare (GSNW)* (see Figure 18-14). GSNW enables a single Windows Server system to act as a gateway to a NetWare network. The gateway computer logs in to the NetWare network and enables all of the Windows computers to access the NetWare network through the gateway without running a NetWare client. GSNW sounds great, but in reality it is slow and prone to lockups. GSNW is also dependent on IPX/SPX. GSNW is not supplied with Windows Server 2003.

 TIP Make sure you understand the difference between CSNW and GSNW!

Connecting Macintosh to NetWare

To connect a Macintosh to a NetWare server, you need to install the *Macintosh Client for NetWare* on the Mac. Figure 18-15 shows the Macintosh Client for NetWare. Once the Macintosh NetWare client is installed, the OS has full access to the shared resources on

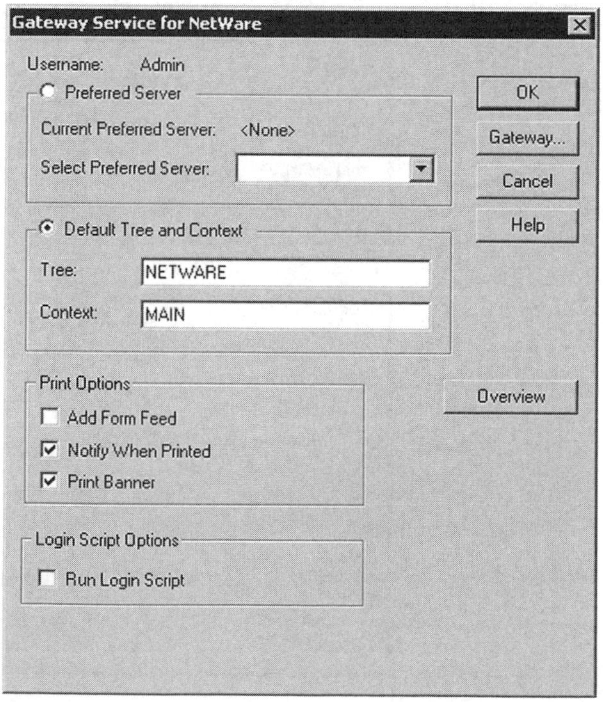

Figure 18-14
Configuring GSNW on a Windows 2000 server

Gateway Service for NetWare

Username: Admin
○ Preferred Server
  Current Preferred Server: <None>
  Select Preferred Server: [▼]

● Default Tree and Context
  Tree: [NETWARE]
  Context: [MAIN]

Print Options
  ☐ Add Form Feed
  ☑ Notify When Printed
  ☑ Print Banner

Login Script Options
  ☐ Run Login Script

[OK]
[Gateway...]
[Cancel]
[Help]

[Overview]

Figure 18-15
Macintosh Client
for NetWare

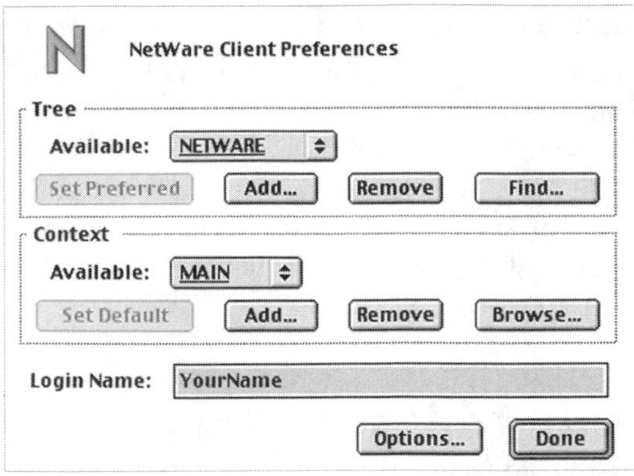

NetWare Client Preferences

Tree
Available: NETWARE ▼

Set Preferred   Add...   Remove   Find...

Context
Available: MAIN ▼

Set Default   Add...   Remove   Browse...

Login Name: YourName

Options...   Done

the NetWare server, both folders and printers. Figure 18-16 shows a shared folder on a NetWare server being accessed from a Macintosh client. One interesting aspect unique to the Macintosh client is that it's the only one you have to pay to use because Novell stopped making Macintosh clients in the mid 1990s. A third-party vendor called ProSoft (www.prosoft.com) now makes the Macintosh NetWare client software. Both the Windows (any version) and UNIX/Linux clients are available free from Novell.

NetWare client software (of all sorts) can't do its job unless the client system runs the correct protocol. Modern clients all use TCP/IP, but there are many older clients still in use in the world. Fortunately, Novell provides IPX drivers for all network client systems to support the occasional NetWare network that still uses IPX as its network protocol. But whether your network runs IPX or IP, the NetWare client will work perfectly for Windows, Macintosh, or UNIX/Linux systems.

NOTE   To download Novell client software, go to:
http://www.novell.com/download.

Figure 18-16
Macintosh client
accessing shared
folder on
NetWare server

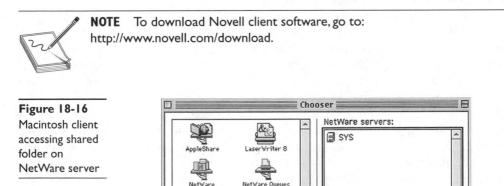

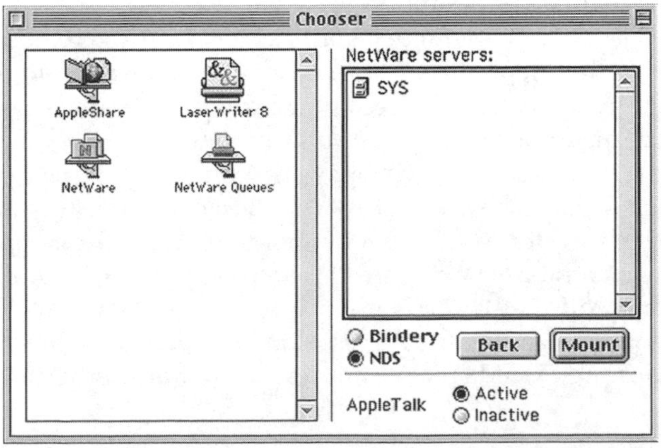

Native File Access

NetWare versions 5.1 and 6 support a fascinating technology that Novell calls Native File Access. *Native File Access* is a series of programs run on NetWare Servers that make the shared NetWare folders look like the native format for Windows and Macintosh computers. Native File Access removes the need to install a NetWare client on each computer—the NetWare servers and shared folders look like Windows systems to Windows clients and Macintosh systems to Mac clients! Native File Access is gaining in popularity with NetWare users.

Connecting to Macintosh

Even though modern Macintosh operating systems all use IP as their network protocol, Apple still relies on the venerable AppleTalk for higher-level network functions, just as Windows 9*x* still relies on NetBIOS even though most Windows 9*x* systems now use IP. This means that any time you have a Macintosh system talking to any other type of system, you must have some form of software on one end or the other that translates the AppleTalk information (like network names) into something the client NOS can understand.

Once again, the evolution of OS X over its predecessors makes a big difference in how other operating systems connect to Macintosh computers. OS X runs Samba by default so Windows systems automatically see Macs on their network. UNIX/Linux systems can connect to a Mac via Samba or by using TCP/IP applications like NFS or FTP. In the next section, we'll look at pre-OS X Macs.

Connecting Windows Systems to Macintosh Serving Systems

The most common way to get a Macintosh system to share its resources with Windows and UNIX/Linux systems is via the AppleShare IP program. *AppleShare IP* has built-in server message block (SMB) support, making it something like a Samba for Macintosh. AppleShare also provides printing support to clients running the TCP/IP LPR program or the more modern CUPS. Conveniently, this is no problem because both Windows and UNIX/Linux clients support LPR.

AppleShare IP is powerful but is an extra cost item and requires fairly serious Macintosh hardware to run. AppleShare IP also includes a web server, an FTP server, and other items that might be more than you need just to connect to a Macintosh or two in a smaller network. For smaller jobs, many networks use the DAVE program from Thursby Software. *DAVE* runs on a Macintosh, enabling any Windows systems to access shared folders and printers on Macintosh systems. DAVE has the added benefit of not requiring the Windows system to run any form of client software—the DAVE software runs only on the Macintosh. Figure 18-17 shows a DAVE-shared Macintosh as seen by a Windows client system.

I should add that DAVE is not just for Mac-to-Windows sharing. It works equally well to enable Mac clients to access shared folders on Windows systems. A number of companies provide Mac-to-Windows and Windows-to-Mac interconnectivity tools.

Figure 18-17
A DAVE-shared
Macintosh named
Imac as seen by
Windows

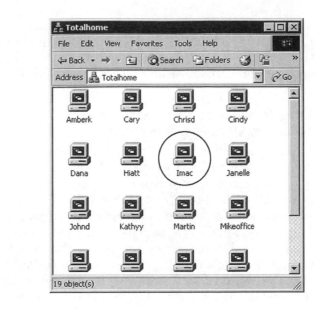

If you're interested in getting Mac and Windows systems to work together, check out www.macwindows.com.

Connecting UNIX/Linux Systems to Macintosh Sharing Systems

Until the advent of the *Mac OS X* operating system, Macintosh systems lacked a truly handy way for UNIX/Linux systems to connect to shared folders on Macintosh systems. Macintosh systems have used various NFS server programs, which worked moderately well. UNIX/Linux systems can use their built-in NFS-based tools to access NFS shares on Macintosh systems. With the introduction of the UNIX-based OS X, Macintosh systems now share the same UNIX NFS as pure UNIX/Linux systems. UNIX/Linux systems use CUPS as well as good old LPR/LPD to share printers.

TIP Apple has a full-blown, UNIX-based server operating system called Mac OS X Server. It has complete, native support for Macintosh, UNIX/Linux, and Windows clients, including DNS and DHCP, File and Printer Sharing, and more. It has a built-in VPN, NAT, web server, mail server, QuickTime streaming media server, and more. Apple definitely did the Mac OS X Server right! For more information on Mac OS X Server, go straight to the source: www.apple.com.

Connecting to UNIX/Linux

UNIX/Linux systems rely on Samba or NFS to enable non-UNIX/Linux client systems to access their resources. Samba is popular because you only have to configure the UNIX/Linux system for its resources to be visible to all Windows clients. However, you must do the Samba configuration on each UNIX/Linux system. This is fine as long as you only have a few UNIX/Linux servers and are using Windows clients, but if you have lots of UNIX/Linux systems, or if you're using Macintosh clients, you need some other options.

Connecting Windows Systems to UNIX/Linux Sharing Systems

To reduce network congestion and to make configuration easier, Microsoft provides *Microsoft Windows Services for UNIX (MWSU)*. This group of services, really just a toolbox of NFS programs, can access any type of NFS volume, including any from a UNIX/Linux system. MWSU is an add-on product that will run on any Windows NT or Windows 2000 system. To enable a Windows 9*x* system to access a UNIX/Linux folder, you need to find a good third-party NFS client program. Figure 18-18 shows the OMNI NFS client program from Xlink Technology running on a Windows 9*x* system.

One interesting part of MWSU is the *Gateway Services for UNIX*. As with Gateway Services for NetWare, MWSU enables a Windows NT/2000 Server system to act as a gateway connecting a Windows network and UNIX/Linux serving systems. None of the Windows systems need to run an NFS client program, and all of the UNIX/Linux servers appear to the Windows systems as though they're Windows servers.

Connecting Macintosh Systems to UNIX/Linux Sharing Systems

Okay, I've covered almost all of the possible NOS interconnectivity combinations. The last combination I need to cover is connecting Macintosh systems to shared resources on UNIX/Linux systems. You should be able to tell me the answer at this point—can you? Remember that Mac OS X has full NFS support for file sharing and

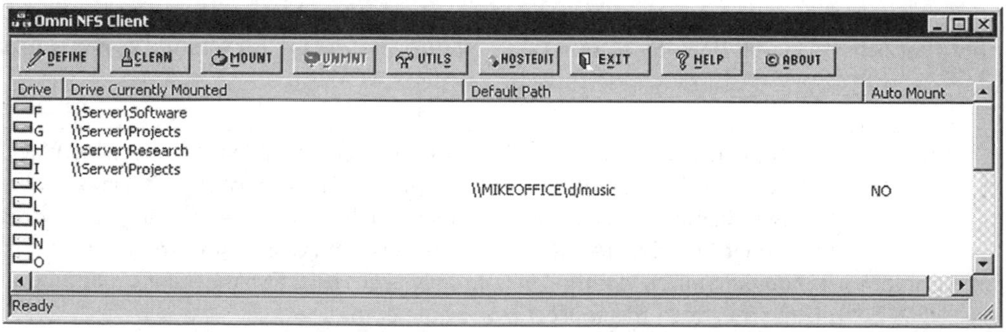

Figure 18-18 The OMNI NFS client running on a Windows 9*x* system

LPD/LPR support for accessing shared printers. But I can't end this chapter without at least one more peek at some fun third-party software. Many UNIX/Linux servers that need to provide access to Macintosh systems use a little program called Netatalk. *Netatalk* creates AppleTalk-compliant folder and printer shares on UNIX/Linux systems. While Netatalk itself is a text-based program, many folks use it with a graphical front end like the *AppleTalk Configurator* (see Figure 18-19).

When All Else Fails, Terminal Emulate!

Terminal emulation has been a part of TCP/IP from its earliest days, in the form of good old Telnet. Because it dates from pre-GUI days, Telnet is a text-based utility, and all modern operating systems are graphical. Citrix Corporation made the first (arguably) popular (also arguably) terminal emulation product—the *Winframe/MetaFrame* products (Figure 18-20). Citrix isn't free, but it runs on any operating system and is a mature and dependable product.

In keeping with the GUI world we live in today, many operating systems come equipped with some type of graphical terminal emulator. Some, like Windows and Linux, include built-in emulators like the handy Windows 2000 *Terminal Services* (see Figure 18-21).

All Microsoft remote access products run on the Remote Desktop Protocol (RDP). RDP, developed by Citrix and licensed by Microsoft, provides a protocol for everyone who wants to make a program to connect to a Windows system. RDP typically runs on TCP port 3389.

Unfortunately, Terminal Services only works in the Windows environment; however, a number of third parties make absolutely amazing terminal-emulation programs that

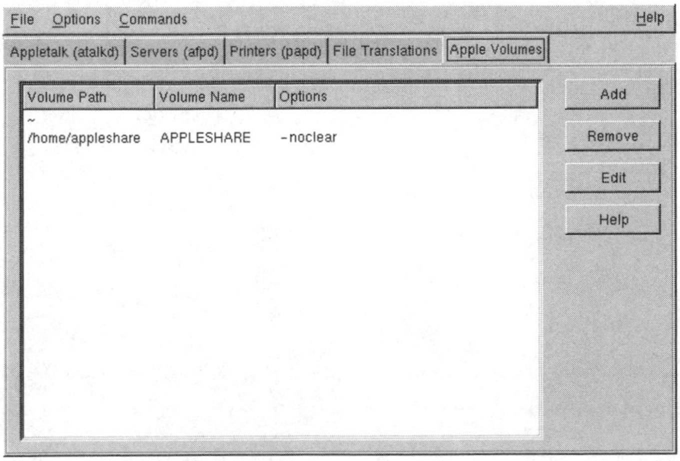

Figure 18-19
The AppleTalk Configurator graphical front end

Figure 18-20
Citrix in action

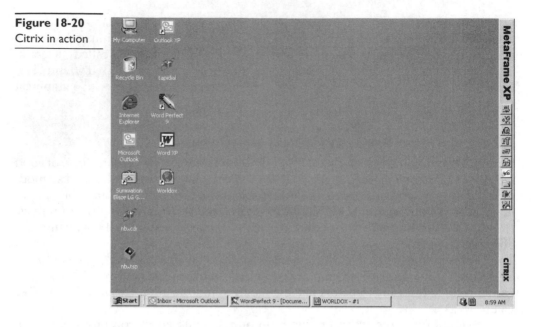

run on any operating system. One of the best of these is *VNC*, which stands for virtual network computing (see Figure 18-22). VNC doesn't let you share folders or printers, because it is only a terminal emulator. But it runs on almost every client NOS, is solid as a rock, and even runs from a web browser. Why bother sharing if you can literally be at the screen? Oh, and did I mention that VNC is free?

Figure 18-21
Windows 2000
Terminal Services
in action

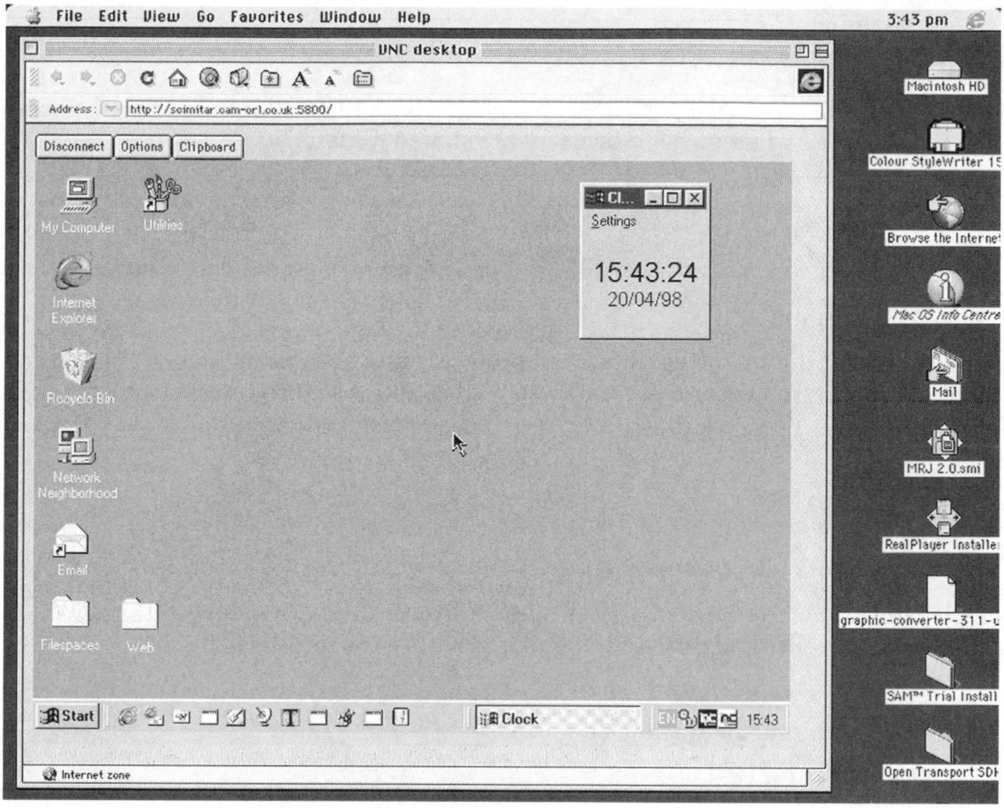

Figure 18-22 The VNC desktop

Chapter Review

Questions

1. The universal adoption of what protocol suite has made the concept of interconnectivity between network operating systems much easier?

   A. TCP/IP

   B. IPX/SPX

   C. Samba

   D. AppleTalk

2. What protocol suite has Macintosh historically used?

   A. TCP/IP

   B. IPX/SPX

    C. Samba

    D. AppleTalk

3. What program makes a UNIX/Linux system look like a Windows 9*x* system, and enables it to access a Windows system's shared folders?

    A. TCP/IP

    B. IPX/SPX

    C. Samba

    D. AppleTalk

4. Which of the following file system protocols must be installed on a Windows 9*x* system for that system to share its folders like a UNIX/Linux system?

    A. NT file system (NTFS)

    B. FAT32

    C. Samba

    D. Network File System (NFS)

5. Which of the following services must be installed on a Windows NT or 2000 server for files and printers to be shared with a Macintosh client?

    A. File and Print Sharing

    B. File Sharing for Macintosh

    C. Services for UNIX

    D. Client Services for NetWare

6. Which of the following services must be installed on a Windows NT or 2000 server for files and printers to be shared with a UNIX/Linux client?

    A. File and Print Sharing

    B. File Sharing for Macintosh

    C. Services for UNIX

    D. Client Services for NetWare

7. What client software must be installed on a Macintosh client system to enable it to connect to a NetWare server?

    A. File and Print Sharing

    B. File Sharing for Macintosh

    C. Services for UNIX

    D. Macintosh Client for NetWare

8. When you connect a Windows or UNIX/Linux system to a Macintosh server, what program is used to share the Mac resources?

   A. Macintosh Client for NetWare

   B. File Sharing for Macintosh

   C. AppleShare IP

   D. Client Services for NetWare

9. What program can you install on a Macintosh serving system in a smaller network, where you don't need all the extras that come with AppleShare IP, to enable a Windows system to access shared resources on that Mac?

   A. TCP/IP

   B. DAVE

   C. WIN2MAC

   D. File Sharing for Macintosh

10. Windows 2000 has a built-in terminal emulator. What is it called?

    A. Windows 2000 Terminal Services

    B. Windows 2000 Terminal Emulator

    C. Windows 2000 Telnet

    D. Windows 2000 Emulation Services

Answers

1. **A.** The universal adoption of TCP/IP has made interconnectivity much easier than it was in the days when different networks ran IPX/SPX, NetBEUI, AppleTalk, and other network protocols.

2. **D.** Many older Macs use the AppleTalk protocol, and most Windows systems use NetBEUI or TCP/IP. Later Macs all use TCP/IP, but for the Network+ exam, assume AppleTalk for all Macintosh questions unless the question specifies otherwise.

3. **C.** Samba makes a UNIX/Linux system look like a Windows 9x system, and enables it to access a Windows system's shared folders.

4. **D.** The NFS protocol is the closest thing the TCP world has to Windows' folder sharing functions. Installing an NFS server program on a Windows 9x system will enable it to share its folders just like a UNIX/Linux system.

5. **B.** With File Sharing for Macintosh and AppleTalk protocol support, Windows NT Server and Windows 2000 Server have everything they need to provide Macintosh clients with seamless interconnectivity to Windows NT/2000 serving systems.

PART III

6. **C.** Microsoft provides a product called Services for UNIX (SFU) to enable NT and 2000 serving systems to share their resources with UNIX/Linux clients, but it comes as an add-on, and at additional cost.

7. **D.** A Macintosh client needs Macintosh Client for NetWare software to connect to a NetWare server.

8. **C.** The AppleShare IP program enables a Macintosh serving system to share its resources with Windows and UNIX/Linux clients. AppleShare IP has built-in SMB support, making it something like a Samba for Macintosh. AppleShare also provides printing support, but only to clients running the TCP/IP LPR program—which isn't a problem because Windows and UNIX/Linux clients both support LPR.

9. **B.** In a smaller network, where you don't need all the extras that come with AppleShare IP, you can install a program called DAVE on a Macintosh serving system, enabling Windows clients to access shared folders and printers on the Mac.

10. **A.** Windows' built-in terminal emulator is called Windows 2000 Terminal Services.

## CHAPTER 19

The Perfect Server

The Network+ Certification exam expects you to know how to

- 3.10   Identify the purpose, benefits, and characteristics of using antivirus software
- 3.11   Identify the purpose and characteristics of fault tolerance: power, link redundancy, storage, services
- 3.12   Identify the purpose and characteristics of disaster recovery: hot and cold spares

To achieve these goals, you must be able to

- Identify methods and hardware used for protecting data
- Describe server-specific hardware used for boosting speed
- Explain methods and hardware used for server reliability

The job of networking demands fundamental hardware differences between a PC that connects to a network and a PC that does not connect to a network. Arguably, the designers of the Personal Computer never considered the PC as a device to participate in a network. You can't blame them. The original PC simply didn't pack the necessary firepower to function in any but the most primitive of networks. The first PCs used tiny (less than 10 megabyte) hard drives—or only floppy drives—and the 4.77-MHz Intel 8088 simply could not handle the many calculations demanded by even the most basic network operating systems. The mainframe-centric world of IBM created the PC to work primarily as an individual computer, a stand-alone system, or to perform as a dumb terminal for mainframe access.

Historical/Conceptual

While networks were not part of the original PC concept, the ongoing improvements in the power and phenomenal flexibly of PCs enabled them to move easily from a world of individual, stand-alone systems into the interactive world of connected, networked machines. Even though any stand-alone PC transforms nicely into a networked machine, the different jobs of a stand-alone versus a networked machine require significantly different hardware in each. What are these requirements? What hardware does a networked PC need that a stand-alone PC can live without? The network functions themselves supply the answers (see Figure 19-1).

A networked PC has four significant functions. First, it must connect to the network. This connection usually runs through a cable of some type, but wireless networks are becoming more common.

Figure 19-1
Networked
PCs need
more hardware.

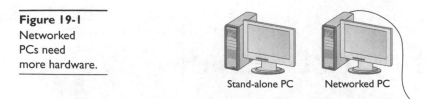

Stand-alone PC   Networked PC

Second, if the PC shares data, the PC needs to protect that shared data by creating more than one copy of the data. The data is usually copied with multiple storage devices—almost always hard drives—that work together to create multiple copies of data.

Third, and again only if the PC shares data, it needs specialized hardware that enables it to share the data as quickly as possible. A sharing PC often uses a number of different hardware technologies to increase the speed with which it shares its resources. A good example of a speed technology is a specialized network card that enables faster data access.

The fourth and last function unique to a network PC is reliability. The shared resources of the network must be available whenever another system accesses them. The networked PC must use special hardware to prevent a sharing system from failing to provide their shared resources. We're not talking about more hard drives here; we've already covered that! Reliability means methods to make sure the PC doesn't stop working due to a failed component. These hardware devices manifest themselves in items such as redundant power supplies or air conditioning units. Together or separately, every network PC has at least one of these four functions (see Figure 19-2).

The process of deciding which functions appear in a network PC is determined by the job of that particular system. The biggest line of demarcation is between systems that share resources (servers) and systems that only access the server's shared resources (workstations). The hardware requirements for a workstation and a server differ fundamentally. The only specialized function of a workstation is connecting to the network via a network interface card (NIC). Workstations do not share resources, so they have little need for reliability, speed, and data protection beyond that already built into any stand-alone PC.

Servers, on the other hand, use all of the functions creating the need for highly specialized systems full of specialized hardware to provide most, if not all, of these four network functions. The incorporation of the specialized hardware in a PC is what makes what we call a *server system*. The incorporation of these extra features makes a server stand out compared to a workstation. Servers are often designed as rack mounts to fit into an equipment rack or are large, floor-mounted units (see Figure 19-3).

Figure 19-2
The four network
functions

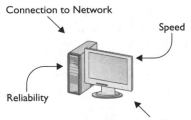

Connection to Network

Speed

Reliability

Protection of Data

Figure 19-3
A typical network server (Courtesy of International Business Machines Corporation. Unauthorized use not permitted.)

Keep in mind that there is no requirement for a serving system to have the extra hardware. Virtually any PC can act as a serving system—as long as you are willing to put up with lack of reliability, slower response times, and the higher potential for data loss. Equally, in peer-to-peer networks, some, most, or all of the systems act as servers. It's usually logistically impractical and financially imprudent to give every user in a peer-to-peer network a powerful server system (although if you did, you'd be extremely popular!). A good network person considers the network functions of a particular system to determine which ones the system needs. They then balance the needed network functions against cost, time, and support needs to determine what hardware a particular system requires (see Figure 19-4).

Figure 19-4
Balancing needs versus expense

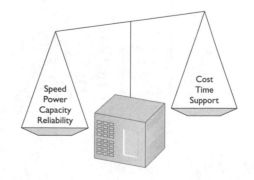

Test Specific

Server PCs need extra hardware or software to provide data safety, speed, and reliability. In this chapter, we first define conceptually each of these functions and then explore how servers utilize the wide variety of hardware, software, and organization solutions used in today's networks to fulfill the needs of these functions.

Protection of Data—Fault Tolerance

The single most important part of most networks is the *shared data*. The main motivation for networks is the ability for many users to access shared data. This shared data might be as trivial as pre-made forms or as critical as accounts receivable information. The sudden loss of data in their networks would cripple most organizations. Computers can be replaced and new employees hired, but the data is what makes most organizations function. Certainly, any good network must include a solid backup plan, but restoring backups takes time and effort. Unless the data is being continually backed up, the backups will always be a little dated. Backups are a last-resort option. Businesses have failed after the loss of data—even with relatively good backups. The shared data of a network should have better protection than the fallback of laboriously having to restore potentially dated backups! A good network must have a method of protecting data such that if a hard drive fails, a network technician can bring the data instantly, or at least quickly, back online. This requires some sort of instant backup or automatic copy of the data stored on a second drive. The capability of a server to respond to a hardware failure while continuing to operate is called *fault tolerance*.

Okay, so you need to come up with a way to make data redundant on the serving system. How do you do this? Well, first of all, you could install some fancy hard drive controller that reads and writes data to two hard drives simultaneously (see Figure 19-5). This would ensure that the data on each drive was always identical. One drive would be the primary drive, while the other drive, called the *mirror* drive, would not be used unless the primary drive failed. This process of reading and writing data at the same time to two drives is called *drive mirroring*.

Figure 19-5
Mirrored drives

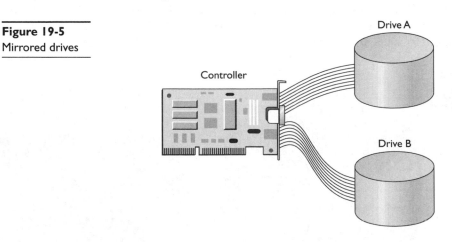

Controller

Drive A

Drive B

Figure 19-6
Duplexing drives

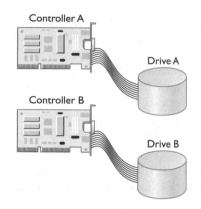

Controller A

Controller B

Drive A

Drive B

PART III

If you want to make data safe, you can use two separate controllers for each drive. With two drives, each on a separate controller, the system will continue to operate, even if the primary drive's controller stops working. This super-drive mirroring technique is called *drive duplexing* (see Figure 19-6) and is much faster than drive mirroring because one controller does not write each piece of data twice.

Even though drive duplexing is faster than drive mirroring, they both are slower than the classic one drive, one controller setup. The third and most common way to create redundant data is by a method called *disk striping with parity*. *Disk striping* (without parity) spreads the data among multiple (at least two) drives. Disk striping by itself provides no redundancy. If you save a small Microsoft Word file, for example, the file is split into multiple pieces; half of the pieces go on one drive and half on the other (see Figure 19-7).

The one and only advantage of disk striping is speed—it is a fast way to read and write to hard drives. But if either drive fails, *all* data is lost. Disk striping is not something we ever want to do—unless you simply need all the speed you can get and don't care about data.

NOTE A number of popular technical web sites have tested two striped drives against a single drive to see if striping provides any increase in data throughput. In every case, the amount of increase in data throughput with two striped drives was negligible as compared to a single drive. *Disk striping by itself is not a recommended practice.*

Figure 19-7
Disk striping

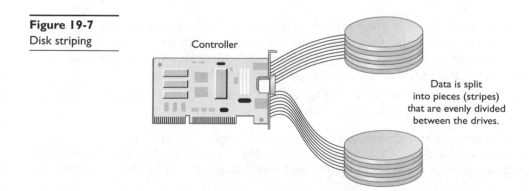

Controller

Data is split
into pieces (stripes)
that are evenly divided
between the drives.

Disk striping with parity, in contrast, protects data. Disk striping with parity adds an extra drive, called a *parity drive*, that stores information that can be used to rebuild data should one of the data drives fail. Let's look at that same Microsoft Word document used earlier. The data is still stored on the two data drives, but this time a calculation is done on the data from each equivalent location on the data drives to create parity information on the parity drive. This parity data is created by a simple, but accurate calculation. It's similar to dividing two numbers and storing the result of the division. The calculation is not important; the fact that the parity data can be used to rebuild either drive is, however.

 NOTE Modern implementations of disk striping with parity spread the parity information and the data across all three drives, as you'll see in the next section on RAID.

Disk striping with parity must have at least three drives, but it's common to see more than three. Unfortunately, the more drives used, the higher the chance one might fail. Disk striping with parity can only recover data if one drive fails. If two drives fail, you're heading for the backup tapes!

Disk striping with parity combines the best of disk mirroring and plain disk striping. It protects data and is quite fast. In fact, the majority of network servers use a type of disk striping with parity.

RAID

The many different techniques of using multiple drives for data protection and increasing speeds were organized by a couple of sharp guys at Berkeley back in the 1980s. This organization was presented under the name *Random Array of Inexpensive Disks (RAID)* or *Random Array of Independent Disks*. There are seven official levels of RAID, numbered 0 through 6, which are as follows:

- **RAID 0** Disk striping
- **RAID 1** Disk mirroring and disk duplexing
- **RAID 2** Disk striping with multiple parity drives. Unused, ignore it.
- **RAID 3 and RAID 4** Disk striping with parity. The differences between the two are trivial.
- **RAID 5** Disk striping with parity, where parity information is placed on all drives. This method combines data redundancy with a performance boost (or at least no performance hit like you see with RAID 1). RAID 5 is the most common RAID implementation on server machines.
- **RAID 6** RAID 5 with the added capability of asynchronous and cached data transmission. Think of it as a Super RAID 5.

A lot of modern motherboards come with RAID controllers built in and sporting one or two non-traditional RAID modes called RAID 0+1 and RAID 10. Both methods purport to offer RAID 5 data redundancy and performance, but this claim is problematic.

Both modes require four physical drives, rather than the three needed in a RAID 5 array. RAID 0+1 mirrors two sets of striped drives. RAID 10 stripes two sets of mirrored drives. The implementations are pretty much flip sides of the same coin.

The only problems with these nontraditional RAID modes are the quantity of drives required—four hard drives is quite an investment, even at today's prices—and the performance does not equal a good RAID 5 array. On the other hand, if you've got the drives, power for the drives, and a built-in controller, why not? RAID 5 controllers generally cost a lot more than a controller that can do RAID 0+1 or RAID 10, and both of the nontraditional RAID modes are better than RAID 0 or RAID 1 for data redundancy and performance combined.

No network tech worth her salt says things like "We're implementing disk striping with parity." Use the RAID level. Say, "We're implementing RAID 5." It's more accurate and impressive to the folks in Accounting!

Drive Technologies

Talking about RAID levels is like singing about Einstein's Theory of Brownian Motion. You may sound good, but that doesn't mean you know what you are talking about! Remember that RAID levels are a general framework; they describe methods to provide data redundancy and enhance the speed of data throughput to and from groups of hard drives. They do not say *how* to implement these methods. There are literally thousands of different methods to set up RAID. The method used depends largely on the desired level of RAID, the operating system used, and the thickness of your wallet. Before we delve into these solutions, however, let's do a quick run-through of the three leading hard drive technologies—parallel ATA, serial ATA, and SCSI—to make a few terms more clear.

PATA If you peek into most desktop PCs, you will find hard drives based on the ultra-popular *Parallel Advanced Technology Attachment (PATA)* standard. PATA drives are always internal—inside the PC, which is designed traditionally to use up to four PATA drives. PATA drives can be identified by their unique 40-pin ribbon cable connection (see Figure 19-8). The cables are either 40-wire (for the older drives) or 80-wire (for newer drives). Figure 19-9 shows the two ribbon cables.

Figure 19-8
PATA connection
on hard drive

PART III

Figure 19-9
PATA cables

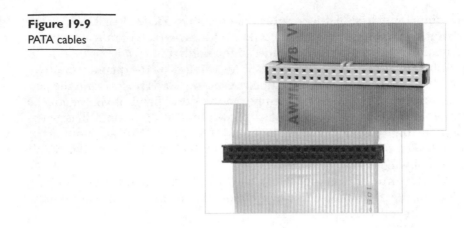

NOTE You will often hear PATA drives referred to by their older technology names, such as Integrated Device Electronics (IDE) and Enhanced Integrated Device Electronics (EIDE). Although we old techs can argue about the distinctions, they're pretty irrelevant to the modern network tech. All three terms—PATA, IDE, and EIDE—are used synonymously.

TIP the Network+ exam uses the term "IDE" to describe all PATA drives.

The price, performance, and ease of installation explain the tremendous popularity of PATA drives. PATA can accept any type of storage device, including CD- and DVD-media drives, tape backups, and removable drives. Even with the capability to handle diverse devices, the PC cannot handle more than the maximum of four PATA devices without special additional hardware. My new high-end motherboard, for example, has a total of four PATA connections, two of which are standard connections, and two of which are RAID-capable. Each connection can handle two drives, so I can theoretically put eight PATA drives on this system. Plus, it has two additional hard drive connectors that utilize the current drive technology to which every one is turning, serial ATA.

SATA For all its longevity as the mass storage interface of choice for the PC, parallel ATA has problems. First, the flat ribbon cables impede airflow and can be a pain to insert properly. Second, the cables have a limited length, only 18 inches. Third, *hot swapping* isn't possible with PATA drives—that is, you can't add or remove such a drive with the system running. You have to shut down completely before installing or replacing a drive. Finally, the technology has simply reached the limits of what it can do in terms of throughput.

Serial ATA (SATA) addresses these issues. SATA creates a point-to-point connection between the SATA device—hard drive, CD-ROM, CD-RW, DVD-ROM, DVD-RW, and so on—and the SATA controller. At a glance, SATA devices look identical to standard PATA devices. Take a closer look at the cable and power connectors, however, and you'll see significant differences (Figure 19-10). Because SATA devices send data serially instead of in parallel, the SATA interface needs far fewer physical wires—seven instead of the eighty wires that is typical of PATA—resulting in much thinner cabling. This might not seem significant, but the benefit is that thinner cabling means better cable control and better airflow through the PC case resulting in better cooling.

Further, the maximum SATA device cable length is more than twice that of an IDE cable—one meter (39.4 inches) instead of 18 inches. Again, this might not seem like a big deal, unless you've struggled to connect a PATA hard drive installed into the top bay of a full-tower case to a controller located all the way at the bottom!

SATA devices are *hot-swappable*, meaning that they can be plugged into or removed from the PC without having to shut down. This makes SATA a natural fit for RAID technology on operating systems that support it.

The big news, however, is in data throughput. As the name implies, SATA devices transfer data in serial bursts instead of parallel, as PATA devices do. Typically, you don't think of serial devices as being faster than parallel, but in this case, that's exactly the case. A SATA device's single stream of data moves much faster than the multiple streams of data coming from a parallel IDE device—theoretically up to 30 times faster!

SATA devices currently have a rated maximum data burst throughput rate of 150 Mbps. Granted, this isn't much of an immediate gain over current PATA speeds, but the SATA technology specification calls for eventual throughput speeds of up to 600 Mbps! Obviously the potential for greatly improved performance is the biggest draw to SATA.

Installing SATA hard drives is even easier than PATA devices because there's no master, slave, or cable select configuration to mess with. In fact, there are no jumper settings to worry about at all, as SATA only supports a single device per controller channel. Simply connect the power and plug the controller cable in as shown in Figure 19-11—the operating system automatically detects the drive and it's ready to go! The keying on SATA controller and power cables makes it impossible to install either incorrectly.

Figure 19-10
SATA hard drive data (left) and power (right) connections

Figure 19-11
Properly
connected
SATA cables

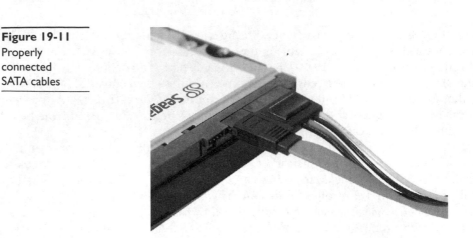

SCSI *Small Computer System Interface (SCSI)* accomplishes much the same goals as EIDE—making hard drives and other devices available to the PC. SCSI, however, is not a hard drive technology. Think instead of SCSI as a mininetwork that connects many different types of devices. Virtually any kind of storage device you can imagine comes in a SCSI version, but SCSI hard drives are the most common type of SCSI storage device. SCSI manifests itself in PCs via a card called a *host adapter*. This host adapter then connects to SCSI devices in a daisy-chain (see Figure 19-12). An installed set of SCSI devices is called a *SCSI chain*.

Figure 19-12
A SCSI chain

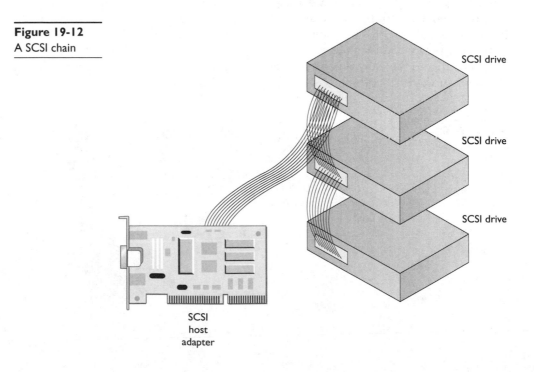

SCSI drive

SCSI drive

SCSI drive

SCSI
host
adapter

Each SCSI device on the SCSI chain must have a unique SCSI ID. Older SCSI devices are numbered 0 through 7, with 7 usually reserved for the host adapter itself. More advanced versions of SCSI can support up to 16 devices (including the host adapter).

SCSI devices can be internal or external. Better host adapters come with an internal and an external connector, enabling both types of devices to exist on the same SCSI chain. Figure 19-13 shows a SCSI chain with both internal and external devices. Note that each device gets a unique SCSI ID.

SCSI Connections   Fortunately, the Network+ exam isn't interested in your ability to configure SCSI. It does, however, demand you know the many connections unique to SCSI devices. No other class of device has as many connections as SCSI. This is because SCSI has been in existence for a long time and has gone through four distinct standard upgrades, fostering many variations within each standard over the years.

SCSI connections differ for internal and external SCSI devices. There are two types of internal SCSI connections, both of which are inserted into a ribbon cable, just like PATA: the 50-pin narrow connection and the 68-pin wide SCSI. Figure 19-14 shows a typical 50-pin narrow connection with a ribbon cable attached. Figure 19-15 shows a 68-pin connection.

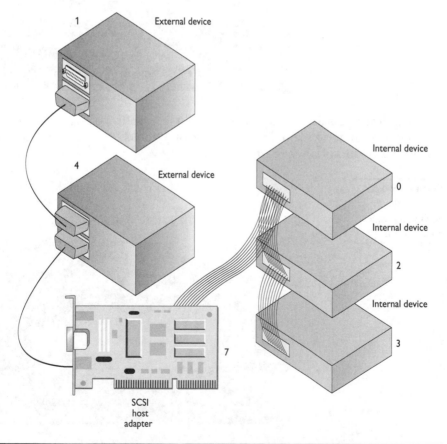

Figure 19-13   A typical SCSI chain with internal and external devices

Figure 19-14
The 50-pin narrow SCSI connection

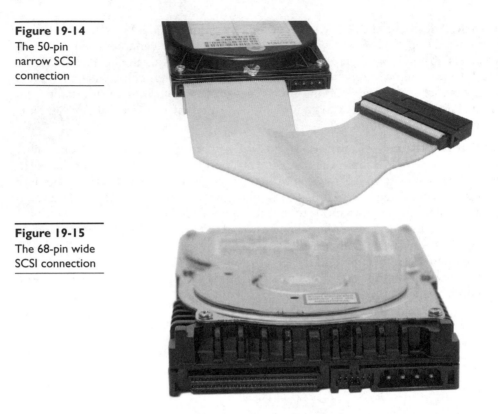

Figure 19-15
The 68-pin wide SCSI connection

The oldest external SCSI connection is a 50-pin Centronics. Although dated, a large number of SCSI devices still use this connector. It looks like a slightly longer version of the printer Centronics (see Figure 19-16).

Figure 19-16
Two 50-pin SCSI Centronics connections

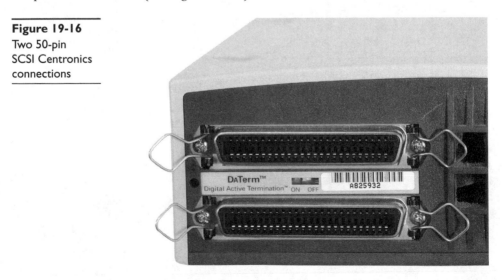

Figure 19-17
Parallel and SCSI
connections—
both DB-25s

The ports may look the same, but they are completely different.

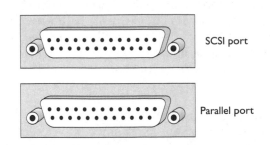

SCSI port

Parallel port

Many host adapters use a female DB-25 connector. Apple has been using female DB-25 connectors for SCSI on its computers for many years, but they are fairly new to PCs. This Apple-style SCSI connector is identical to a PC parallel port (see Figure 19-17), which is unfortunate because they are not electrically compatible. If you plug your printer into the SCSI port, or a SCSI device into the printer, it definitely will not work—and in some cases may damage devices!

Most modern SCSI devices now come with the special, SCSI-only, high-density DB connectors. High-density DB connectors look like regular DBs at first, but have much thinner and more densely packed pins. High-density DB connectors come in 50- and 68-pin versions, the former being the more common of the two (see Figure 19-18).

They All Work!   PATA, SATA, and SCSI drives work beautifully for RAID implementations. People who are new to RAID immediately assume that RAID requires some special, expensive stack of SCSI drives. Such is not the case. You certainly can spend the money on fancy RAID boxes, but you do not have to go that route. You can easily implement RAID using nothing but inexpensive PATA drives and cheap, sometimes free software. Furthermore, RAID can use combinations of PATA, SATA, and SCSI (although trying to keep track of combinations of drives is not recommended!). In fact, PATA and SATA RAID arrays have lately become so stable that they rival the security that only SCSI used to promise. The only real distinction nowadays is a difference in access speed and price.

Figure 19-18
The high-density
DB-50

Most people prefer SCSI drives for RAID, because they tend to be faster than PATA drives and you can put more drives into a system (7 to 15, rather than the 4 in PATA). The only drawback with SCSI is cost—hard drives are more expensive and you often must purchase a host adapter as well. When speed outweighs cost as a factor in what type of hard drive technology to use in a RAID array, SCSI implementations win out. Finally, if you need serious speed and extra bells and whistles, you can install any number of expensive "stack of SCSI drives" solutions.

RAID Implementations

All RAID implementations break down into either hardware or software methods. *Software RAID* means to use the regular drives on your system, and then to use software, usually the operating system, to create the RAID arrays. The operating system itself is in charge of running the array. Each hard drive in the array is visible to the operating system. If you go into Disk Management in Windows, for example, you'll see every drive in the array. Software RAID is often used when price takes priority over performance and is not popular for real-world servers.

Hardware RAID means to use dedicated RAID controllers to create the RAID arrays. Hardware RAID uses either a CMOS-like configuration or proprietary configuration software to set up the array. Once the array is configured, the RAID controller handles the running of the RAID array. The individual drives in hardware RAID arrays are invisible to the operating system. If you use a hardware RAID array and go into Disk Management in Windows, for example, you'll see the RAID array as a single drive. Hardware is used when you need speed along with data redundancy.

The most famous software implementation of RAID is the built-in RAID software that comes with Windows NT Server/2000 Server/Server 2003. The NT Disk Administrator and 2000/2003 Disk Management can configure drives for RAID 0, 1, or 5, and they work with PATA, SATA, and SCSI drives (see Figure 19-19). Windows 2000 and XP Professional only support RAID 0.

You can use Disk Management in Windows 2000 and XP Professional only to create RAID 0 on Windows 2000 and XP Professional machines. If you start Disk Management on a Windows 2000 or XP Professional machine and attach to (choose to manage) a Windows 2000 Server or Server 2003 system, you can create a RAID 1 or RAID 5 array on that server machine remotely.

The one great downside of RAID stems from the fact that with the exception of RAID 0, every version of RAID sacrifices total storage capacity for safety. Take RAID 1 for example. If you have two 160-GB drives in your system not running as RAID, you'll have a total storage capacity of 320 GB. If you then mirror those two drives, each drive stores an identical copy of the same data, reducing your total storage capacity to only 160 GB.

More advanced RAID versions suffer from the same loss of capacity for the sake of safety. Let's say you have three 100 GB drives, making a total storage capacity of 300 GB. If you make those three drives into a RAID 5 array, one third of the total capacity is used for parity data, reducing the total storage capacity down to 200 GB.

Windows NT/2000/2003 are not the only software RAID games in town. There are a number of third-party software programs available that can be used with other operating systems. There are even third-party software RAID solutions for NT that add a number of extra features above what the Disk Administrator or Disk Management provide.

```
Computer Management                                          _ □ ×
 Action   View   ⇦ ⇨  ⬜ 🔲  ⬜   🔄

Tree │                          Volume        Layout    Type      File System
                                 Emergency Backup (D:)  Mirror    Dynamic   NTFS
 Computer Management (TOTALFS1.TOTALHOME)  Free Space (F:)  Partition  Basic  NTFS
 ⊟ System Tools                  OS (C:)       Partition  Basic     NTFS
   ⊞ Event Viewer                Paging (E:)   Partition  Basic     NTFS
   ⊞ System Information          VERITAS (H:)  Partition  Basic     CDFS
   ⊞ Performance Logs and Alerts
   ⊞ Shared Folders
     Device Manager
   ⊞ Local Users and Groups
 ⊟ Storage
     Disk Management
     Disk Defragmenter
     Logical Drives
   ⊞ Removable Storage
 ⊞ Services and Applications

                        Disk 0      OS (C:)   Paging (E:  Free Space
                        Basic       4.99 GB NTF 5.00 GB NTF 8.64 GB NTFS
                        18.64 GB    Healthy (Sy Healthy (Pa Healthy
                        Online

                        Disk 1      Emergency Backup  (D:)
                        Dynamic     128.00 GB NTFS
                        128.00 GB   Healthy
                        Online

                        Disk 2      Emergency Backup  (D:)
                        Dynamic     128.00 GB NTFS
                        128.00 GB   Healthy
                        Online

                        ■ Primary Partition ■ Mirrored Volume
```

Figure 19-19   Disk Management at work

Most techs and administrators prefer hardware RAID. Software RAID works for small RAID solutions, but tends to run quite slowly and usually requires shutting down the PC to reconfigure and replace drives. When you *really* need to keep going, when you need RAID that doesn't even let the users know there was ever a problem, hardware RAID is the only answer. Because most organizations fit into this latter category, most RAID in the real world is hardware-based. There are a large number of hardware RAID solutions, and almost all these solutions rely on SCSI. SCSI can do one thing that PATA still cannot do—assuming that you have the right type of host adapter, you can yank a bad SCSI drive off of a SCSI chain and replace it with another one without even rebooting the server. This hot-swapping process is common in hardware RAID (see Figure 19-20). SATA, as noted earlier, can do hot swapping very nicely, thank you!

Figure 19-20
Hot swapping
a drive

Okay, now that you have an idea of how to RAID, the next big question is "What do you want to RAID?" Granted, RAID 5 is popular but most techs when first exposed to RAID simply assume that they'll drop at least three drives into a server and make one big RAID 5 array. This solution will work, but the demands of the different types of data on a server often require a more refined and complicated approach.

One standard trick often performed with RAID is to separate the operating system itself from the data. The operating system files are neither unique nor do they change often compared to your data. If you lose the operating system you can simply reinstall it, assuming your server can afford to go down the amount of time necessary for reinstalling the operating system. In these cases, you put the operating system files on a non-RAID partition. If you want to get the operating system up more quickly, hold the operating system files on a mirrored partition. Most RAID mirroring solutions require an operating system reboot, but at least you'll be up in a minute or two as compared to the one hour (or more) rebuilding the operating system from scratch.

Another area to consider are swap files and temporary files. These files take up massive amounts of space and are useless if your system crashes. Many server admins place these files on a totally separate, non-RAID drive. There are exceptions to this, but those exceptions are usually operating system– or application-specific. One big exception is the "server that must never go down." In this case, the operating system, complete with the swap and temporary files, usually sits on its own separate RAID 5 or better array.

On most servers, the important data of your business has its own separate RAID 5 array. The low cost of today's RAID 5 solutions makes RAID almost a given on any server holding any data that's important to you or your organization.

RAID provides data redundancy. Implementing RAID requires that you decide the level of RAID you want to use and whether you want to go the hardware or software route. For the exam, make sure you can quote the different levels of RAID—and know your hard-drive connections. You'll fly through those questions without any difficulty!

NAS

If there's one thing no network ever seems to get enough of, it's space for file storage. For many years, the way we increased file storage space was to add more and larger capacity hard drives to our servers. This works well and is still a way to increase file storage space on many networks. But as networks grow, the burden of increased file *handling* begins to take its toll on the servers. This problem is exacerbated by the fact that most servers are already doing a lot of other jobs, such as name resolution, authentication, and e-mail serving—all of them critical jobs that we need servers to do to make our networks run. Over the years, I've seen a trend to spread these many jobs out to different servers. In my network, for example, I have one system that handles DNS, another that takes care of DHCP and WINS, and a third that handles authentication. However, all of these systems are also tasked with providing file sharing. What if we had a server that did absolutely nothing but file sharing?

This is one of many situations where *network attached storage (NAS)* is handy. NAS is a prebuilt system, usually running Linux with Samba and/or NFS, which you snap into your network to provide quick and easy storage with little or no setup involved. An NAS is a server, but it doesn't come with all of the extras programs you'll find on most server systems. Instead, it's optimized to share folders or tape backups. A true NAS doesn't have a monitor, keyboard, or mouse. Configuration is handled through programs run from another system or a web interface. An NAS is usually much cheaper and much faster than a traditional server with the same storage capacity. Figure 19-21 shows a common brand of NAS, a Snap Server from the company Snap Appliance.

Most NAS devices have DHCP enabled and will run right out of the box. Even though they can run with no or little configuration, all NAS devices come with the capability to create security groups, user names, and passwords. It's common to keep a NAS in a Windows environment on its own domain—early NAS systems had to be on their own domain—but most will now join an existing domain or even an Active Directory.

The important issue to remember here is that an NAS is a standalone system running an operating system, usually Linux. It has a regular NIC and runs TCP/IP. The NAS server runs using either NFS or Samba to enable other systems to access its shared folders. This is important because NAS is often confused with something far more complex called a SAN.

SAN

A *storage area network (SAN)* system is a group of computers connected to an array of hard drives using an advanced serial technology such as SCSI fibre channel, a high-speed interface that functions similarly to SCSI interfaces. Designed for multiple-drive systems that can afford to have little or no downtime, Fibre Channel enables hot swapping of drives, RAID, and cable distances of up to 30 meters (!) between a device and the Host Bus Adapter (HBA). These capabilities (and many more), combined with data throughput speeds of up to 100 Mbps, put Fibre Channel in a class by itself.

All of the systems in the SAN may or may not have their own internal hard drives. In a SAN, each system connects to a Fibre Channel switch via a special NIC called a *host bus adapter (HBA)*. Figure 19-22 shows a Fibre Channel HBA. Note that the Fibre Channel HBA is virtually identical to a fiber-optic NIC.

The power of the SAN is in the disk array. One of the great aspects about Fibre Channel SCSI is that there is no practical limit to the number of drives in a single array. It's common to see a single Fibre Channel array with over one hundred drives. Figure 19-23 shows just such an array. This flexibility enables users of SANs to look at a single array as

Figure 19-21
Snap Server 2200

Figure 19-22
Fibre Channel
HBA

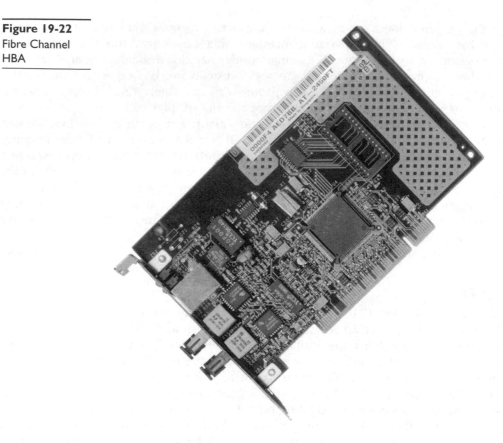

one huge "glob" of hard drive that they can then take chunks out of and partition and format in any way they want. These partitions can be RAID or *Just a Bunch of Disks (JBOD)*. (No, I am not making this up! That is a real term!) Users can then attach or detach drives from their systems using the standard disk manipulation tools, such as Disk Management in Windows XP.

SANs are fast and can handle vast amounts of data, but they are also incredibly expensive. Odds are good that you could go your entire tech life and never see a SAN.

Tape Backup

Various RAID solutions provide data redundancy to a certain degree, but to secure your server data fully, nothing beats a tape backup. If the RAID solution works properly, that tape backup can happily collect dust on an offsite shelf somewhere. In the event of a catastrophe such as a hardware crash or a flood in the server room, only that tape can save the day.

Figure 19-23
Fibre Channel
SAN array

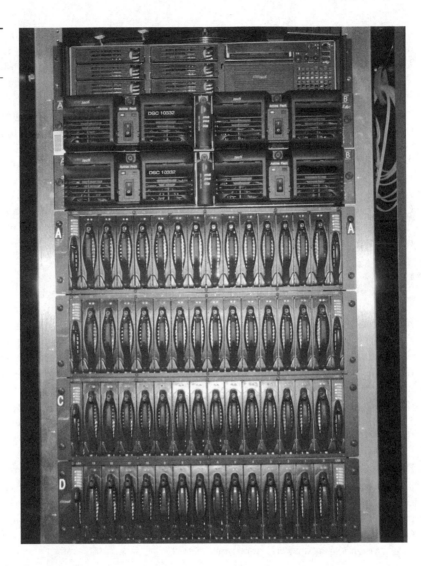

Magnetic tape is the oldest of all methods for storing data with computers. Who has not seen an episode of the old TV shows like "Time Tunnel" or "Voyage to the Bottom of the Sea" and watched the old reel-to-reel tapes spinning merrily in the background? The reel-to-reels are gone, replaced by hard drives; tapes are now relegated to the world of backup. Nothing can beat magnetic tape's capability to store phenomenal amounts of data cheaply and safely.

Every properly designed network uses a tape backup, so every network tech must learn to use them. The type of tape backup implemented varies from network to network, as do the methods for backing up data. This section covers the types of tape backup; refer to Chapter 20, "Zen and the Art of Network Support," for the methods.

There are a dizzying number of tape backup options, each with different advantages and disadvantages. They basically break down into three major groups: QIC, DAT, and DLT. All of the groups similarly use *cartridge tapes*—square tapes like fat audio cassettes—but the physical cartridge size, capacity, recording method, tape length, and speed vary enormously.

All tape backup solutions can back up data in compressed format. How much any data might compress varies on the type of data getting compressed. Tape manufacturers will advertise their capacities based on an assumption of 50 percent compression. When you see a tape that will store 30 GB, for example, that probably means it will store 15 GB of uncompressed data. Most manufacturers now advertise their capacities in both uncompressed and compressed values. A recent tape I purchased advertised itself as 10/20 GB—10 GB uncompressed and 20 compressed. Be advised, however, that the compressed value is just a guess! Without knowing the data that's being compressed, there's no way to know the compressed value!

QIC

Quarter-inch tape (QIC) is an old standard and rarely used in any but the smallest of networks. QIC was one of the first standards used for PC backups, but it has gone through many evolutions in an attempt to keep up with the demand for increased capacities over the years. The earliest versions of QIC could store about 40 megabytes—fine for the days when tiny hard drives were the rule, but unacceptable today. There have been a number of increases in QIC capacities, as high as two gigabytes, but QIC has fallen out as a desired tape standard. Imation Corporation created an improved QIC format called *Travan* that is quite popular, again on smaller networks, with capacities of up to 8 gigabytes. Under the Travan banner, QIC lives on as a tape backup option. Older QIC/Travan drives used a floppy connection, but EIDE or SCSI connections are more common today.

DAT

Digital audio tape (DAT) was the first tape system to use a totally digital recording method. *DAT* was originally designed to record digital audio and video, but it has easily moved into the tape-backup world. DAT tapes have much higher storage capacities than QIC/Travan tapes—up to 24 gigabytes—and are popular for medium-sized networks. DAT drives use a SCSI connection.

DLT

Digital linear tape (DLT) is quickly becoming the tape backup standard of choice. It's a relatively new standard that has massive data capacity (up to 70 gigabytes), is fast, incredibly reliable, and quite expensive compared to earlier technologies. When the data is critical, however, the price of the tape backup is considered insignificant. DLT drives use a SCSI connection.

Data Redundancy Is the Key

Data redundancy provides networks with one of the most important things they need—security. Improper preparation for the day a server hard drive dies leads to many quickly prepared résumés for the suddenly out-of-work network technician. When the data is important enough (and when *isn't* it?), providing data redundancy via RAID solutions is required for the properly designed network.

Speed

A system providing a resource to a network has a tough job. It needs to be able to handle thousands, millions, even billions of transactions over the network to provide that shared resource to other systems. All of this work can bring a standard desktop PC to its knees. Anyone who has taken a regular desktop PC, shared a folder or a printer, and watched their PC act as though it just shifted into first gear can attest to the fact that sharing resources is a drain on a PC. Systems that share resources, and especially dedicated servers, require more powerful, faster hardware to be able to respond to the needs of the network.

There are a number of methods for making a serving system faster. Making a good server isn't just a matter of buying faster or multiple CPUs. You can't just dump in tons of the fastest RAM. Fast CPUs and RAM are important, but there are two other critical areas that tend to be ignored—a good server needs fast NICs and fast drives.

Fast NICs

The first place to look when you think of making a server faster is the NIC. Placing the same NIC in your server that you place in your workstations is like putting a garden hose on a fire hydrant—it just isn't designed to handle the job. There are a number of methods for making the NIC better suited to the task. You can increase the megabits (the data throughput), make the NIC smarter and pickier, and make it do more than one thing at a time. A lot of this was covered in detail in Chapter 6, "Modern Ethernet," so let's simply do the high points here.

Increase the Megabits

Most networks are a mix of 10BaseT, 100BaseT, and 1000BaseT. With autodetecting NICs and switches, different speed devices can communicate; sometimes a little bit of NIC organization or rearranging can work wonders to speed up a network—especially when it comes to your server. The trick is to have the server part of the network run at a faster speed than the rest of the network. If you have a 10BaseT network, you can purchase a switch that has a couple of 100 megabit ports. Put a 100BaseT NIC in the server and connect it to one of the 100BaseT connectors on the switch. The server runs at 100 Mbps while the workstations run at 10 Mbps (see Figure 19-24). This optimizes the server speed and, because the server does most of the work in the network, optimizes your network as well.

Smarter NICs

Many NICs still need the CPU to handle most of the network job, but several companies make powerful NICs with onboard processors that take most of the work away from the CPU. Every NIC manufacturer has a different method to provide this support and those methods are way outside the scope of this book. From a network person's standpoint,

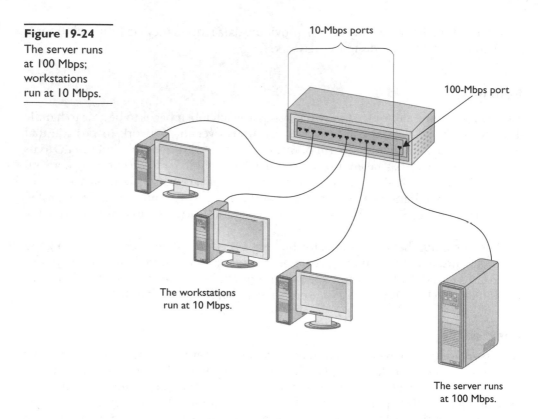

Figure 19-24 The server runs at 100 Mbps; workstations run at 10 Mbps.

10-Mbps ports

100-Mbps port

The workstations run at 10 Mbps.

The server runs at 100 Mbps.

just buy a special server NIC, plug that sucker in, and enjoy the benefits of faster response times.

Full-Duplex NICs

Most network technologies consist of send and receive wires, and most NICs can handle only sending or receiving at a given moment. Full-duplex NICs can both send and receive data at the same time, which practically doubles the speed of the network card. Make sure your server NICs are full-duplex, but be warned that you may need to upgrade the server's hub to take advantage of full-duplex!

Making the NIC better is one of the easiest upgrades to a server as it usually means simply yanking out an inferior NIC and replacing it with something better. At worst, you may have to replace a hub or a switch. Make your NIC better and you'll see the results.

Make the Drives Faster

The other big way to increase a server's speed is to make the process of getting the data to and from the shared drives faster. There are two big options here. First is to get fast drives. Using run-of-the-mill PATA drives in a busy serving system is not smart. Try using high-performance SCSI drives on a fast controller. It makes a big difference. Second, use RAID 5. Because you probably need it for data protection anyway, you'll also enjoy the speed.

It's Not Just Hardware

The demands of networking require servers to have better hardware than your run-of-the-mill, stand-alone PC. Improving CPUs, adding RAM, using powerful NICs, and running fast hard drives all work together to make your serving PC more powerful. But hardware is not the only answer. Good maintenance, such as defragging and setting up good disk caches, also plays an important role. Many times, slow resource access is due to poor network design and is not the fault of the serving system. Be careful about throwing hardware at the slow access issues; it can often be a big waste of money!

Reliability

The last network function, primarily for serving systems, is reliability. The shared resource must be there when the user needs it. *Reliability* is achieved by providing a secure environment for the server and by adding redundant hardware to compensate for failed components. There is a nasty tendency to mistake reliability for data protection. Don't confuse the two. All the pretty RAID systems aren't going to do you any good if somebody steals the server. Tape backups are useless if the power supply dies. Clearly, other technologies are needed to keep the serving system reliable. There is no logical order to explaining these technologies and safeguards, so we will cover them in no particular order.

NOTE The disaster recovery folks like to use terms like *hot spares* and *cold spares* when discussing any type of redundant equipment, but these terms work especially well for PCs. A hot spare is any redundant device that will instantly take over if the primary device fails. A cold spare is a redundant device that is onsite and ready to go, but is normally turned off.

Good Power

All of the components in the PC run on DC current electrical power. Without clean, steady, DC power, the components stop working. There are a number of steps that electrical power must take between the power company and those components. At any given moment, if one of those steps fails to do its part, the PC no longer works. You can take several actions to safeguard your hardware to make sure this doesn't happen, starting with the power company.

Electrical power in the United States is a wonderful commodity. Electrical service is pretty reliable, and the electricity is generally of high quality. Most folks in the United States can count on a good electrical service 98 percent of the time. It's that other 2 percent that will get you! Electrical power sometimes stops (power outages) and sometimes goes bad (electrical spikes and sags). Additionally, techs (and nontechs alike) can screw up perfectly good electricity on their own by overloading circuits with too much equipment. You can protect the servers from problems of power outages, electrical spikes, and overloaded circuits with several important technologies—dedicated circuits, surge suppressors, UPSes, and backup power.

Dedicated Circuits

A *dedicated circuit* is a circuit that runs from the breaker box to only certain outlets. In most homes and offices, a circuit might have many jobs. The circuit that runs your PC might also run the office water cooler and the big laser printer. Using too many devices on one circuit causes the power to sag, which might cause your computer to do nothing, lock up, or spontaneously reboot. It all depends on how lucky you are at that moment! Dedicated circuits keep this from happening. In most cases, dedicated circuits have outlets with bright orange faceplates to let you know that they are dedicated. This will (theoretically) prevent some uninformed person from plugging a photocopier into the circuit.

Surge Suppressors

It almost sounds silly to talk about suppressors these days, doesn't it? Does anyone really need to be convinced that all PCs, both network and stand-alone, need surge suppressors? An electrical surge—a sudden increase in the voltage on a circuit—can (and will) destroy an unprotected computer. Translation: every computer should plug into a surge suppressor!

UPS

An uninterruptible power supply (UPS) is standard equipment for servers. Any good UPS will also provide excellent surge suppression as well as support for power sags. Most only offer a few minutes of power, but it's enough to enable the server to shut down cleanly. All servers will have a UPS.

Backup Power

When you want serious reliability, get a backup power supply. Many server systems come with two power supplies. If either power supply fails, you can replace it without even turning off the system. But if the power from the power company goes out, you'll need a true backup system. There are a number of small battery-based backup systems that will provide a few hours of protection. If you want something that will last for a few days, however, you will need a gasoline/diesel backup system.

The Computer Virus

Ah, would that the only problem you faced was with faulty power. But alas, this is not the case. There are a large number of computer viruses and malicious code just waiting to infect your network. So what do you do when you think your computer has caught a code? In this chapter, you will find out.

The words "I think your machine has a virus" can send shudders down the back of even the most competent technician. The thought of megabytes of critical data being wiped away by the work of some evil programmer is at best annoying—and at worst a serious financial disaster.

So, where do viruses come from? Just like many human viruses, they live in host bodies—in this case, computers. Your computer can only catch one if it interacts with other computers, or with programs or data from an infected computer. Problem is, these days almost everyone's computer (aside from folks like the CIA) is connected to the Internet, and thereby to many, many other computers. Also, many viruses are spread through the sharing of programs or information on floppy disks or CD-ROMs.

How do you know if you've caught a virus? You feel sluggish, start sneezing and coughing, want to sleep—or in this case, the computer equivalents of those symptoms might be as follows: your computer seems unusually sluggish, generates strange error messages or other odd emissions, or possibly even locks up and refuses to function entirely. All these are classic symptoms, but you cannot assume your computer is virus-free just because it seems fine. Some viruses do their work in secret, as we shall discuss shortly.

The secret to avoiding viruses is to understand how they work. A *virus* is a program that has two functions: (1) *proliferate* (make more copies of itself) and (2) *activate* (at some signal, count, date, and so on, do something—usually something bad like delete the boot sector). A virus does not have to do damage to be a virus. Some of the first viruses written were harmless and downright amusing. Without going into too much of the nitty-gritty, there are only five typical types of viruses—boot sector, executable, macro, worm, and Trojan—plus a sixth type that is a combination of any two other viruses—bimodal/bipartite.

Boot Sector

A *boot sector virus* changes the code in the master boot record (MBR) of the hard drive. Once the machine is booted, the viruses reside in memory, attempting to infect the MBRs of other drives by spreading themselves to removable media, connecting to network machines, and creating whatever havoc they are designed to do by the programmer.

Executable

An *executable virus* resides in executable files. These viruses are literally extensions of executables and are unable to exist by themselves. Once the infected executable file is run, the virus loads into memory, adding copies of itself to other EXEs that are subsequently run, and again doing whatever evil that the virus was designed to do.

Macro

A *macro virus* is a specially written application macro. Although they are not truly programs, they perform the same functions as regular viruses. These viruses will autostart when the particular application is run and will then attempt to make more copies of themselves—some will even try to find other copies of the same application across a network to propagate.

Trojan

Trojans are true, freestanding programs that do something other than what the person who runs the program thinks they will do. An example of a *Trojan virus* would be a program that a person thinks is a game but that is a CMOS eraser. Some Trojans are quite sophisticated. It might be a game that works perfectly well, but when the user quits the game, it causes some type of damage.

Bimodal/Bipartite

A *bimodal or bipartite virus* uses both boot-sector and executable functions.

Worm

A *worm* is a network-aware virus that spreads through applications such as e-mail and web browsers. *E-mail worms* are currently the greatest single virus threat. These worms propagate by reading e-mail address books and sending copies of themselves to everybody. Most will mask their origin by using a false e-mail address as the sender.

Antivirus Programs

The only way to protect your PC permanently from getting a virus is to disconnect from the Internet and never permit any potentially infected software to touch your precious computer. Because neither scenario is likely these days, you need to use a specialized antivirus program to help stave off the inevitable virus assaults.

An antivirus program protects your PC in two ways. It can be both sword and shield, working in an active seek-and-destroy mode and in a passive sentry mode. When ordered to seek and destroy, the program will scan the computer's boot sector and files for viruses, and if it finds any, present you with the available options for removing or disabling them. Antivirus programs can also operate as virus shields that passively monitor your computer's activity, checking for viruses only when certain events occur, such as a program executing or a file being downloaded.

Antivirus programs use different techniques to combat different types of viruses. They detect boot-sector viruses simply by comparing the drive's boot sector to a standard boot sector. This works because most boot sectors are basically the same. Some antivirus programs make a backup copy of the boot sector. If they detect a virus, the programs will use that backup copy to replace the infected boot sector. Executable viruses are a little more difficult to find because they can be on any file in the drive. To detect executable viruses, the antivirus program uses a library of signatures. A *signature* is a code pattern of a known virus. The antivirus program compares an executable file to its library of signatures. There have been instances where a perfectly clean program coincidentally held a virus signature. Usually the antivirus program's creator will provide a patch to prevent further alarms. Antivirus programs detect macro viruses through the presence of virus signatures or of certain macro commands that indicate a known macro virus. Now that we understand the types of viruses and how antivirus programs try to protect against them, let's review a few terms that are often used when describing certain traits of viruses.

Polymorphics/Polymorphs

A *polymorph virus* attempts to change its signature to prevent detection by antivirus programs, usually by continually scrambling a bit of useless code. Fortunately, the scrambling code itself can be identified and used as the signature—once the antivirus makers become aware of the virus. One technique sometimes used to combat unknown polymorphs is to have the antivirus program create a checksum on every file in the drive. A *checksum* in this context is a number generated by the software based on the contents of the file rather than the name, date, or size of that file. The algorithms for creating these checksums vary among different antivirus programs (they are also usually kept secret to help prevent virus makers from coming up with ways to beat them). Every time a program is run, the antivirus program calculates a new checksum and compares it with the earlier calculation. If the checksums are different, it is a sure sign of a virus.

Stealth

The term "stealth" is more of a concept than an actual virus function. Most *stealth virus* programs are boot sector viruses that use various methods to hide from antivirus software. One popular stealth virus will hook on to a little-known but often-used software interrupt, running only when that interrupt runs. Others make copies of innocent-looking files.

Virus Prevention Tips

The secret to preventing damage from a virus attack is to keep from getting one in the first place. As discussed earlier, all good antivirus programs include a virus shield that will automatically scan floppies, downloads, and so on (see Figure 19-25).

Use your antivirus shield. It is also a good idea to scan a PC daily for possible virus attacks. All antivirus programs include terminate-and-stay resident programs (TSRs) that will run every time the PC is booted. Last but not least, know where software has come from before you load it. While the chance of commercial, shrink-wrapped software having a virus is virtually nil (there have been a couple of well-publicized exceptions), that illegal copy of Unreal Tournament you borrowed from a local hacker should definitely be inspected with care.

Get into the habit of keeping around an antivirus floppy disk—a bootable, write-protected floppy with a copy of an antivirus program. If you suspect a virus, use the diskette, even if your antivirus program claims to have eliminated it. Turn off the PC and reboot it from the antivirus diskette. Run your antivirus program's most comprehensive virus scan. Then check all removable media that were exposed to the system, and any other machine that may have received data from it, or that is networked to the cleaned machine. A virus can often go for months before anyone knows of its presence.

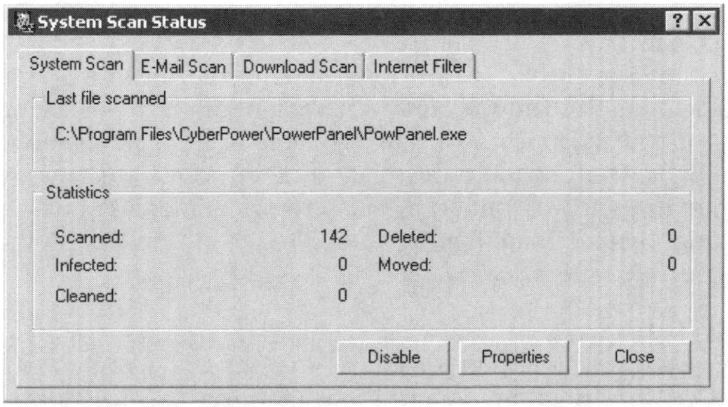

Figure 19-25
A virus shield
in action

Environment

Keep the server room locked at all times. Get a card lock or a combination lock door-knob and make sure that only the right people have access. Keep the humidity low, but not too low—around 40 percent is about right for most electronics. Keep the room a little on the cool side—right around 68 degrees is just about perfect, although most PCs can handle about 80 to 85 degrees before overheating becomes a problem. Check with the system's manufacturer for their recommendations.

Redundant Components

Many components inside the system can be made redundant. It is common to find servers with redundant power supplies where a power supply can be removed without even shutting down the PC. You can buy NICs that work together in the same PC, covering for one or the other if one dies—there are even NICs that can be replaced without rebooting the PC! Placing hard drives on separate controllers—like the drive duplexing discussed earlier in this chapter—provides excellent redundancy.

Last, there are methods for making the entire server redundant. For instance, there are a number of methods where two or more servers can be mirrored, providing the ultimate in reliability (assuming the cost is bearable)!

How Much Reliability Do You Need?

Reliability is like any security system—expensive, boring, a pain to administer, and you never have enough when you need it. Measure the cost of being down vs. the cost of reliability to make your decision. You might be surprised to find that it's a lot cheaper to be safe than sorry.

Putting Them All Together

Now that you've got a grasp on the many hardware and software features that make up a server, what's the right server for your needs? As much as I'd love to give you a checklist of every possible issue and the right type of hardware or software to use to deal with that issue, the complexities and continuing new features of networking make such a checklist impossible to create. But that doesn't leave you to nothing but a guess. Here are a few issues to consider and some guidelines to help you get the server you need to your network.

Function

What is this server going to do? Understanding the function of a server is the first step toward defining the hardware and software it needs. Is this server only going to support a small in-house web server or is this going to be a file server supporting a massive database? Equally important to the function is the number of systems accessing that server. How many users will connect to that server at a time? What type of data will they be requesting? By understanding the server's function, you can get the following questions answered.

Fault Tolerance

Servers with complete fault tolerance—the "server that can never go down"—are expensive. Certainly, there are organizations that need this level of fault tolerance but that doesn't mean every server needs dual power supplies, hot-swappable RAID 5, and redundant NICs. Look at the data and visualize the effect on your organization if the server were to go down. Ask others in the organization and make your judgment.

On the same token, don't go cheap on the basics. There's no excuse for a server not to use a good UPS with plenty of standby power.

CPU/RAM

Should you get a server with a single AMD Athlon XP or go for the one with the dual Itaniums? Should you go with 1 GB of RAM or 16 GB? Choosing the CPU and RAM depends on the serving applications of your server and the number of users accessing that system. Check the web sites of whoever makes the server applications—they all provide guidance on how much RAM their applications need.

Speaking of applications, dual CPUs are useless unless you have applications that take advantage of them. Many server applications do take advantage of multiple processors but not all do so. Again, check with the application maker before spending the big cash on multiprocessor systems!

Scalability

Sure, the server may work well now, but what happens as needs expand? Can you add more RAM? Can you add drives? Don't limit yourself to the single server—could you add another server to take away some of the workload as needs increase?

Nothing's Perfect

There is no such thing as the *perfect* server. Certainly every network PC needs to connect to the network, but data protection, speed, and reliability are functions that vary tremendously depending on network size, types of data and applications, the existing network cabling system, demands of growth, and of course, your pocketbook. The Network+ exam does not assume you can build the perfect network PC, but it does expect you to have a feel for the options you have. When it comes time to build or buy that system, you can act as an advocate for your network, to ensure that you get as close to that perfect network PC as possible.

Chapter Review

Questions

1. Of the following, which is the most important to consider when determining the amount of RAM to install in a server?

   A. The NIC

   B. The network protocol

   C. The applications

   D. The Service Pack

2. A computer virus can be categorized as which of the following? (Select all that apply.)

   A. Always destructive

   B. Self-replicating

   C. Self-activating

   D. Self-destructive

3. Which of the following is an improvement of SATA over PATA?

   A. Three drives per cable

   B. Maximum of 16 drives on a system

   C. No more master/slave jumpers

   D. Drives spin more slowly

4. Which is the most common RAID implementation on servers?

   A. RAID 0

   B. RAID 1

   C. RAID 3

   D. RAID 5

5. How many drives attach to a single PATA cable?

   A. 1

   B. 2

   C. 4

   D. Unlimited

6. If Janet mirrors two 100-GB drives, what will be her effective total capacity?

   A. 100 GB

   B. 166 GB

   C. 200 GB

   D. Depends on the RAID level

7. Which term describes the practice of using multiple controllers when mirroring?

   A. Multiplexing

   B. Distributing

   C. Duplexing

   D. Omniplexing

8. Which of the following terms defines a storage technology?

   A. PCI

   B. AGP

C. MATA

D. SATA

9. Disk mirroring is under which level of RAID?

A. RAID 0

B. RAID 1

C. RAID 2

D. RAID 3

10. Which of the following connectors are used with SCSI? (Select all that apply.)

A. 50-pin Centronics

B. 36-pin Centronics

C. Female DB-15

D. Female DB-25

Answers

1. **C.** The applications running on the server are the most important consideration.

2. **B, C.** For a program to be considered a virus, it must be self-replicating and self-activating.

3. **C.** SATA eliminates the need for master/slave jumpers.

4. **D.** RAID 5 is the most common RAID implementation on servers.

5. **B.** PATA allows for a maximum of two drives per cable.

6. **A.** Each drive stores the same data, making an effective storage capacity of 100 GB.

7. **C.** Duplexing is the mirroring method in which each mirrored drive uses its own controller.

8. **D.** Of the answers listed, only SATA is a storage technology.

9. **B.** Disk mirroring is under RAID 1.

10. **A, D.** Both 50-pin Centronics and female DB-25 connectors are used with SCSI.

## CHAPTER 20

Zen and the Art of Network Support

The Network+ Certification exam expects you to know how to

- 3.12   Identify the purpose and characteristics of disaster recovery: backup/restore, offsite storage, and hot, warm, and cold sites
- 4.8   Given a network troubleshooting scenario involving an infrastructure (for example: wired or wireless) problem, identify the cause of a stated problem (for example: bad media, interference, network hardware or environment)
- 4.9   Given a network problem scenario, select an appropriate course of action based on a logical troubleshooting strategy. This strategy can include the following steps:
  1. Identify the symptoms and potential causes
  2. Identify the affected area
  3. Establish what has changed
  4. Select the most probable cause
  5. plement an action plan and solution including potential effects
  6. Test the result
  7. Identify the results and effects of the solution
  8. Document the solution and process

To achieve these goals, you must be able to

- Describe typical troubleshooting tools
- Explain the troubleshooting process
- Understand backups
- Explain baselines
- Understand troubleshooting models
- Understand Mike's Four-Layer Model
- Look at troubleshooting scenarios

Have you ever seen a tech who walks up to a network and seems to know all the answers, effortlessly typing in a few commands and magically making the system or network work? I've always been intrigued by how they do this. Observing such techs over the years, I've noticed that they tend to follow the same steps for similar problems—looking in the same places, typing the same commands, and so on. When someone performs a task the same way every time, I figure they're probably following a plan. They understand what tools they have to work with, and they know where to start and what to do second and third and fourth until they find the problem. This chapter's lofty goal is to consolidate my observations on how these "übertechs" fix networks. We'll look at the primary troubleshooting tools, formulate a troubleshooting plan, and learn where to look for different sorts of problems. At the end of the chapter, we'll apply this knowledge to some common troubleshooting scenarios.

Test Specific

Troubleshooting Tools

While working through the process of finding the cause of a problem, you will need to use many tools. Some of these tools are difficult to quantify—including things like asking questions, referring to your network baselines and documentation, and synthesizing your network knowledge. Other tools are easier to describe; these are the software and hardware tools that provide information about your network. Many of the tools that fall into this category have been described already, such as hardware or software loopback testing devices, utilities like PING and TRACERT, and hardware tools like tone locators. The trick is knowing when and how to use these tools to solve your network problems.

 NOTE No matter what the problem, always consider the safety of your data first. Ask yourself this question *before* you perform any troubleshooting action: "Can what I'm about to do potentially damage my data?"

"Touchy" Tools

The tools that are the most difficult to quantify, because they are mostly within you, are what I call *touchy tools*. An example of a touchy tool is asking questions of the person who has the problem. This is touchy because there's no predetermined set of questions to ask—your background knowledge and intuition must tell you which questions are the right ones. The *types* of questions you should ask can be grouped into a few categories:

- *Questions designed to find out exactly what steps the user took that may have caused the symptom.* This information can help you re-create the problem. In addition, these types of questions can provide insight into whether the problem was caused by user error or improper procedures. Note from the Geek Central Human Relations Department: be careful how you phrase these sorts of questions. An annoyed, "What did you do this time, you pinhead?!" tends to cause people to clam up. Your goal, remember, is to extract information.

- *Questions designed to find out exactly what any error messages said and the context of the error.* This information can be critical when you need to search manufacturers' knowledge bases and support lines.

- *Questions designed to find out what the user has tried to do to fix the problem.* This information can help you determine whether you are dealing with multiple layers of problems. Many users will try to fix things, but won't think to write down what they're doing. When at some point in the process they reach a standstill and can't get back to where they started, they will come crying to you for help. Be gentle! Your goal is to get the user to remember most, if not all, of the steps they tried, so you can backtrack to the original problem rather than troubleshooting a multilayered one.

Another touchy tool you can use is to compare the current situation to the baselines and documentation you created for your network. When users complain of slow connections or downloads, for example, you should compare the bandwidth and connection speeds from your baseline to what you are able to test while the problem exists. You may find that the difficulty lies more with the user's expectations than any real network problem. You can then decide whether to upgrade your systems and connectivity, or explain to your users the limitations of the network.

The most complicated touchy tool to describe and quantify is the network knowledge you have that you can apply to your network's problems. The Network+ exam contains many network troubleshooting questions that you should be able to answer, not from reading this chapter, but from reading the rest of the book. Troubleshooting often comes down to applying prior knowledge in a new way. You know, for example, that an IP address, a subnet mask, and a default gateway are all necessary if your network is to communicate with the Internet using the TCP/IP protocol. Edgar complains that he cannot connect his Windows XP client to the Internet. His hardware seems to be functioning correctly (link lights are on and he connects to the server) and the proxy server is up. At that point, you might check his TCP/IP configuration by using the IPCONFIG utility. If you notice that he has no default gateway, you have solved the problem. The knowledge to solve this problem came partially from understanding how to troubleshoot by eliminating possibilities, but it also came from your knowledge of the elements required to connect a machine to the Internet. As you prepare for the exam, and for administering your company's network, ask yourself how each thing you learn about networking could be applied toward troubleshooting the network. This prepares you for the time when you have to make that leap.

Hardware Tools

In Chapter 8, "Installing a Physical Network," you read about a few hardware tools you use when configuring your network. These *hardware tools* include cable testers, protocol analyzers, hardware loopback devices, and toners. These tools can also be used in *troubleshooting scenarios* to help you eliminate or narrow down the possible causes of certain problems. In addition, there are other pieces of hardware which, although they can't actively be used for troubleshooting, can provide clues to the problems you face.

A cable tester enables you to determine if a particular cable is bad. *Bad* can be defined in a variety of ways, but it essentially means that the cable is not delivering the data for whatever reason—perhaps the cable is broken, crimped badly, or sits too close to a heat or electrical source. In most troubleshooting situations, you will use other clues to determine if you have a hardware or software problem. Then, if you have narrowed down the problem to a hardware connectivity issue, a cable tester can help you determine if the cable is good or bad. Another option, if you are without one of these tools, is to replace the cables (one at a time) and test the connectivity. In the "I can't log on" scenario, for example, if you have determined that everyone else in the area can log on, and that this user can log on from another location, you have narrowed the problem to either a configuration or hardware issue. If all network activity is broken (in other words, nothing is available in Network Neighborhood or you cannot ping the default gateway), you may choose to test cables connecting the PC to the server. This is not the only option, but it is one variable that can be tested and eliminated.

Protocol analyzers come in both hardware and software flavors. Most of the hardware analyzers have an additional software component. These tools enable administrators to determine what types of traffic are flowing through their networks. Most analyzers translate the packets flowing over the network to provide destination, source, protocol, and some information about content. In a situation where you have a network slowdown, you might use a protocol analyzer to determine what types of packets are passing over your network, and where they are originating. In some cases, a dying network card can produce large numbers of spurious packets, which can be detected by using a protocol analyzer and noticing that all of the packets are coming from one location. Once you have narrowed your problem down to a particular machine, you can concentrate on that rather than blaming your servers, bandwidth, or other elements.

Software Tools

Throughout the book, you have read about *software tools* for configuring your network that can also be applied to troubleshooting. Because most of these have been described in previous chapters, I'll just review the basic purposes of these tools here. Key software *troubleshooting tools* include the following:

- **Software-based protocol or network analyzers**   These include applications such as the *Network Monitor (NetMon)* provided with most versions of Windows. Also called *packet sniffers,* such as the popular Ethereal, included with the CD in this book, *network analyzers* collect and analyze individual packets on a network to determine bottlenecks or security breaches. Use these tools when you have unexplained slowdowns on your network, to help determine which machines are sending packets. This enables you to determine if there is too much broadcasting in general, or if you are the victim of some more sinister event like a hacker attack.

- **System logs**   Applications like Windows NT/2000/XP/2003's Event Viewer create *system logs* that display any errors or problems that have occurred in your system. If a user repeatedly fails at his logon, for example, this might be recorded in the appropriate view in the Event Viewer tool. That information could be the clue you need to determine that the user is locked out, either because he forgot his password or because someone has been trying to hack into that account. Logs also provide information on services or components of the operating system that won't start or are receiving errors. This is a good way to troubleshoot system crashes on a particular machine.

- **Performance monitors**   Tools like the Performance Monitor mentioned earlier in this chapter can provide clues to the utilization pattern of a particular machine. When users complain of slowdowns or logon problems that can be traced to a specific system or server, this tool can often give you clues as to what's happening on that system that could be causing problems. For example, if a system is going to 100-percent memory utilization when a particular application is started, it may mean that you need more RAM, or perhaps that you need to put that application on a dedicated server. Use this tool for troubleshooting when you have tracked the problem to a particular machine, and now must determine where in that machine the bottleneck exists.

Your Toolbox

It always amazes me when a person calls and asks me what tools they need to become a network tech. My answer is always the same: just your brain—everything else will pretty much appear when you need it. There is no such thing as the correct network tech's toolbox, full of hardware and software tools you haul around to get networks fixed. I certainly don't haul around cable testers, toners, or Time Domain Reflectometers (TDRs). I may bring them along if I suspect a cabling problem, but I normally won't dump them in my backpack until *after* I suspect a problem.

Software tools all come with the network operating systems themselves. I don't need a floppy disk with PING, for example, because it's on every PC in the house! The software tools you need to fix a network are sitting there, ready for you to use. Your task is to know *how* to use them. It's the *know-how* you need to bring, and in most cases, little or nothing else!

My lack of dependence on a toolkit makes some customers unhappy—they just can't reconcile in their minds that I can get their networks up and running without some big toolbox. At times this has become so much of an issue that I have brought along a toolkit just to look good! Seriously! I call that box full of stuff my prop because it's of no more real use than a rubber stage sword.

Now that we're no longer obsessing on carrying the right tools, let's instead concentrate on the real toolbox—your brain. In an amazingly brazen act of self-confidence, I have taken the liberty of quantifying the many mental processes you should use when fixing networks into the following section.

PART III

The Troubleshooting Process

Troubleshooting is a dynamic, fluid process that requires you to make snap judgments and act on them to try and make the network go. Any attempt to cover every possible scenario would be futile at best, and probably also not in your best interests, because any reference that tried to list every troubleshooting problem would be obsolete the moment it was created. If an exhaustive listing of all network problems is impossible, then how do you decide what to do and in what order?

Before you touch a single console or cable, you should remember two basic rules: as the Greek/Roman physician Galen wisely admonished, "First, do no harm." If at all possible, don't make a network problem bigger than it was originally. This is a rule I've broken thousands of times, and you will too. But if we change the good doctor's phrase a bit, it's possible to formulate a rule you can live with: "First, do not trash the data!" My gosh, if I had a dollar for every megabyte of irreplaceable data I've destroyed, I'd be rich! I've learned my lesson, and you should learn from my mistakes: Always make good backups! The second rule is to create *baselines* (that is, data on how the network runs when nothing is broken). *Backups* enable you to rebuild a trashed system. Baselines enable you to compare your network's current performance to how it behaves when all is well. Both of these steps should precede *any* actual troubleshooting activity on your part.

Once you've done your backups and baselines, and it's time to start typing commands or yanking cable, you need a plan. You need to know what steps to take and in what order. These steps are pretty much universal to all network problems, and you should learn them well. You also need a guide to where you should look in the network for problems. For that job, I will gift you with what I modestly call *Mike's Four-Layer Model*. As in troubleshooting, so in this chapter—first, backups and baselines, and then you can start taking troubleshooting steps with my model to guide you.

Backups

Think about how much work you have done to create nice, stable servers, responsive workstations, and overall network wonderfulness. Imagine how many hours your users have spent creating data and storing it on those servers. Now imagine a virus deleting critical data or configuration files—not a good situation, for either your blood pressure or your job security. Simple common sense dictates that you create backups of your data. Repeatedly. Backups are useless unless they are current. Your users won't thank you for restoring a three-week-old copy of a file that gets updated daily. You should therefore create a backup schedule for your data that ensures it's backed up often enough that a useful copy can be restored easily. Your backup plan should include the following details:

- When the backups will occur and what the tape rotation schedule will be
- What types of backups will be done at each time
- Where the backups will be stored

Perhaps the most important details are the types of backups and the schedule, or strategy, for the backups.

Types of Backups

The goal of backing up data is to ensure that when a system dies, there will be an available, recent copy you can use to restore the system. You could simply back up the complete system at the end of each day—or whatever interval you feel is prudent to keep the backups fresh—but complete backups can be a tremendous waste of time and materials. Instead of backing up the entire system, take advantage of the fact that all the files won't be changed in any given period; much of the time you only need to back up what's changed since your last backup. Recognizing this, most backup software solutions have a series of options available beyond the old complete (usually called Full or Normal) backup.

The key to understanding backups other than the full backup is a little fellow called the Archive attribute. All files have little 1-bit storage areas called *attributes*. The most common attributes are Hidden (don't show the file in My Computer or when **DIR** is typed at the command line), System (it's a critical file for the system), Read-Only (can't erase it), and the archive bit. These attributes were first used in FAT-formatted drives in the DOS era, but they are still completely supported today by all file formats. The *archive bit* works basically like this: whenever a file is saved, the archive bit is turned on. Simply opening a file will affect the current state of the archive bit. Backup programs will usually turn off a file's archive bit when it's backed up. In theory, if a file's archive bit is turned off, it means there's a good backup of that file on some tape. If the archive bit is turned on, it means that the file has been changed since it was last backed up (see Figure 20-1).

NOTE Windows Explorer / My Computer in Windows XP by default does not show much about files in any view, even when you select Details from the View menu. The Details view is highly customizable, however, and can reveal a phenomenal amount and variety of information about files.

To customize your view, alternate-click (right-click) the column bar (the gray bar that says Name, Size, Type, Date Modified, and so forth) to look at the default choices. You'll see everything from Attributes, Owner, Author, and Title, to file-type specific information such as Genre, Duration, and Bit Rate (for music files). If the 15 default extra view options don't get your motor revving, selecting the More option brings up a menu offering 32 view options! For the purposes of this section, click the Attribute box to display file and folder attributes.

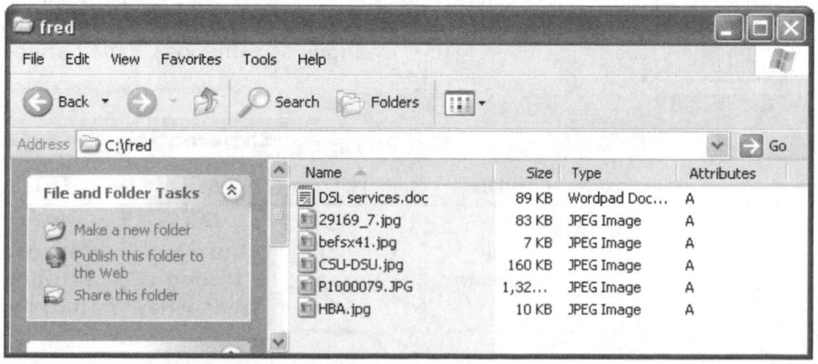

Figure 20-1

The archive bit

Archive bits are used to perform backups that are not full backups. The following backup types are most often supported:

- A *normal backup* is a full backup. Every file selected will be backed up, and the archive bit will be turned off for every file backed up. This is the standard "back it all up" option.

- A *copy backup* is identical to a normal backup, with the important distinction that the archive bits are *not* changed. This is used (although not often) for making extra copies of a previously completed backup.

- An *incremental backup* includes only files with the archive bit turned on. In other words, it copies only the files that have been changed since the last backup. This backup turns off the archive bits.

- A *differential backup* is identical to an incremental backups, except that it doesn't turn off the archive bits.

- A *daily backup*, also known as a *daily copy backup*, makes copies of all the files that have been changed that day. It does not change the archive bits.

 TIP Be sure you know the different types of backups, including which ones change the archive bits and which ones do not.

The motivation for having both the incremental and differential backups may not be clear at first glance—they seem so similar as to be basically the same. Incremental seems the better option at first. If a file is backed up, you would want to turn off the archive bit, right? Well, maybe. But there is one scenario where that might not be too attractive. Most backups do a big weekly normal backup, followed by daily incremental or differential backups at the end of every business day. Figure 20-2 shows the difference between incremental and differential backups.

Figure 20-2
Incremental vs. differential

Incremental

MON	TUE	WED	THU	FRI
Full Backup	All Tuesday Changes	All Wednesday Changes	All Thursday Changes	All Friday Changes

Differential

MON	TUE	WED	THU	FRI
Full Backup	All Changes Through Tuesday	All Changes Through Wednesday	All Changes Through Thursday	All Changes Through Friday

Notice that a differential backup is a cumulative backup. Because the archive bits are not set, it keeps backing up all changes since the last normal backup. This means the backup files will get progressively larger throughout the week (assuming a standard weekly normal backup). The incremental backup, by contrast, only backs up files changed since the last backup. Each incremental backup file will be relatively small and also totally different from the previous backup file. Let's assume that the system is wiped out on a Thursday morning. How can you restore the system to a useful state? If you're using an incremental backup, you will first have to restore the last weekly backup you ran on Monday, then the Tuesday backup, and then the Wednesday backup before the system is restored to its Thursday morning state. The longer the time between normal backups, the more incremental backups you must restore. Using the same scenario, but assuming you're doing differential instead of incremental backups, you'll only need the weekly backup, and then the Wednesday backup to restore your system. A differential backup will always require only two backups to restore a system (see Figure 20-3). Suddenly, the differential backup looks better than the incremental! On the other hand, one big benefit of incremental over differential is backup file size. Differential backup files will be massive compared to incremental ones.

Choosing between incremental backups and differential backups is only one factor in choosing how you back up your data. You must also consider your business, your data, your backup hardware, your operating systems, and other factors to create a backup strategy.

Backup Strategies

One of the issues you must address to successfully answer questions on backups and recoverability is how to choose strategies that meet your needs for doing backups and restores in your actual network environment. Your goal is to be able to back up, and then easily restore all the necessary information from all the necessary machines. This can include both servers and workstations. Decisions about backing up multiple machines can revolve around both hardware and time factors. Another issue to consider when

Figure 20-3
Restoring from backups

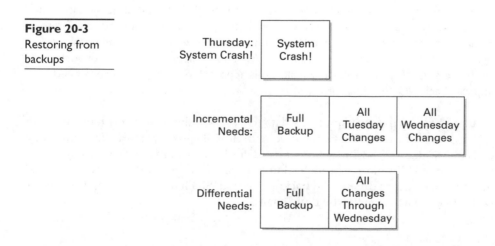

planning your backup strategy is what to do with the all-important tapes. Recognize that you are protecting your network not only against viruses and other computer-related disasters, but also against fire, flood, and man-made catastrophes. Let's look at a typical network and see how to create a backup strategy.

Shannen works at a small company that has never had any form of reliable backup. The network consists of a single Windows Server 2003 system that acts as a file server for the entire network. The file server stores an Access database—a single .MDB file—constantly updated during the course of the business day by almost every user on the network. Each of the client systems also stores a number of mission-critical Word documents.

Shannen first determines what data needs backing up. She needs to back up the entire server operating system—about 1.3 GB for the operating system and applications. The Access database is roughly 45 MB and hasn't grown much in the past year. She then goes through the many Word documents stored on each user's system, creates a directory called \Home on the file server with a subfolder for each user, and instructs the users to copy their Word documents to their individual subfolders. Combined, the Word documents take up roughly 100 MB.

This is an interesting side effect of backups. Creating a backup strategy often forces network administrators to change the way their network stores data. Shannen will also have to enforce a policy (lots of finger wagging and reminder e-mails) for users to save their work to the server. Perhaps a bit of training might also be in order!

Shannen didn't have to force the users to copy their data to the server just for backing up. Many companies sell superb, powerful backup software that will enable the administrator to back up multiple systems in almost any way he or she might imagine. A single backup job can back up entire systems or selectively back up only certain folders on each system. This type of online backup is popular today. You can even find companies that will back up your systems over the Internet for a monthly charge.

 TIP Ever wish you could back up your entire system? Sure, Windows has plenty of recovery tools, but they're not always perfect. Tools such as System Restore and the recovery console are useless if your hard drive dies. In some companies, entire systems are backed up using a number of products. These backups are often stored on optical media or on massive server drives on the network. Although full system backups can be complex to use and challenging on your network bandwidth, the ease of system recovery makes this approach popular for those "I need my computer back NOW!" situations.

Now that Shannen has a grasp on the data to back up, she turns her attention to her backup hardware. She has a DLT tape drive with 30-GB capacity tapes—far more than her needs of less than 2 GB with plenty of room for future expansion. This also tells her that a single tape will hold multiple backups—a handy thing to do to save on tapes! Shannen chooses to use a differential backup method. She'll need two tapes: one for the weekly full backup and one for the daily changes.

Shannen has two more issues to deal with: offsite backups and tape wear and tear. Backup strategies require some method of rotation of tapes to ensure that one backup is offsite in case of a serious disaster, to prolong tape life, and to retire older tapes. This is called a *tape rotation method* or a *tape backup scheme*. Shannen chooses to use a tape rotation method called Grandfather-Father-Son. This tried-and-true method has many variations, but the one Shannen uses works like this. The tape she uses for backup on the last Friday of each month is called the grandfather tape. She stores this tape offsite. The tape she uses every Friday (except the last Friday of the month) is the father tape and is also stored offsite. The tape used for the daily backup (except on Friday) is called the son. Shannen keeps these tapes onsite. If a fire wipes out the office, she'll have a complete server backup that is always less than a week old offsite.

Disaster Recovery

Backups are a critical part of a larger process called *disaster recovery*. Disaster recovery is not simply a computing issue. Disaster recovery is a corporate plan implanted to bring the entire organization back online in the case of a catastrophe. For example, what would happen to your organization if your offices were destroyed overnight? Backups are useless without a computer to take the restored data! Organizations that cannot risk this type of disaster will often have redundant locations called *backup sites*. Disaster recovery experts separate backup sites into three classes: hot, warm, and cold.

A hot site is a completely redundant site, filled with all the equipment used in the main corporate location: air-conditioners, desks, telephone, network—everything but the people to run your organization. Hot sites will often also have up-to-date copies of your systems.

A warm site has most of the hardware, but will not have up-to-date backups of systems. Warm sites enable corporations to get mission-critical jobs up and running quickly; less-critical jobs come online in the days that follow the disaster.

A cold site is a location without computers but that is ready to accept your systems. A corporation could designate a spare, unused office building as a cold site. In the face of a disaster, you'd have to install computers and restore off-site backups before getting mission-critical jobs functioning. But having a cold site at least takes the guesswork out of where you need to go in the chaos following a catastrophe.

Baselines

The best way to know when a problem is brewing is to know how things perform when all's well with the system. You need to establish a *baseline*: a log of performance indicators such as CPU usage, network utilization, and other values to give you a picture of your network and servers when they are working correctly. A major change in these values can point to problems on a server or the network as a whole. A common tool used to create a baseline on Windows systems is the Performance Monitor utility that comes with Windows NT/2000/XP/2003. Conveniently, all network operating systems come with similar tools, and you can also create baselines using most network management utilities.

Windows NT/2000/XP/2003—Performance Monitor

Administrators use *Performance Monitor* (also called *PerfMon*) to view the behavior of hardware and other resources on NT/2000/XP/2003 machines, either locally or remotely. PerfMon can monitor both real time and historical data about the performance of your systems. To access the Performance Monitor applet, choose Start | Programs | Administrative Tools | Performance Monitor from any Windows NT machine. On a Windows 2000 system, choose Start | Settings | Control Panel, and then double-click Administrative Tools, and double-click Performance.

Once you access PerfMon, you need to configure it to display data—but first you must understand the concepts of objects, counters, and views. An *object*, in Performance Monitor terms, is the component of your system you want to monitor, such as the processor or the memory. Each object has different measurable features, called *counters*. Counters, in other words, are the aspects of an object that you want to track. As you decide which object(s) to monitor, you must also select at least one counter for each object. Performance Monitor can organize and display selected counter information using a variety of *views*, each of which provides different types of information. The Log view, for example, enables you to store data about your system for later review. This is the view you use to create a baseline. Although it's the only one I'm going to discuss here, the other views—Chart, Alert, and Report—are useful for troubleshooting problems as they arise.

To access the Log view in Windows NT, either click the Log View button or choose View | Log. To add objects to the Log view, either click Add To (the plus sign) or choose Edit | Add To Log. In the Add To Log dialog box, first select the computer you want to monitor. You can choose either the local machine (the default) or a remote machine. To monitor a remote machine, type the Universal Naming Convention (UNC) name of the computer in question. To monitor a machine named HOUBDC1, for example, you would type **HOUBDC1** in the Computer field. You can also use the Select Computer button (at the right end of the Computer field) to view the available machines and select the one you want to monitor, as shown in Figure 20-4.

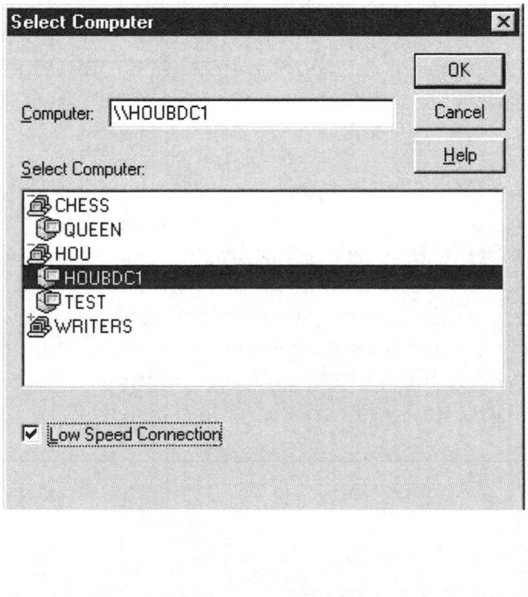

Figure 20-4
The Select
Computer
dialog box in
Performance
Monitor

Although it is usually easier to monitor a machine locally, it is often more accurate to monitor a machine remotely. PerfMon itself, as it runs on a machine, uses a certain amount of that system's resources to take the measurements and display the data graphically. You can corrupt your results by monitoring locally, especially when you need to troubleshoot problems with disk performance, memory and paging, or processor use. There are some cases where monitoring locally is preferred or required, however. If you are monitoring network access or networking protocol objects, for example, monitoring locally will affect the readings to a lesser degree than monitoring remotely. Similarly, you must monitor a system locally if you can't access that system over the network. Finally, when you monitor objects created by a specific application, such as Exchange, you should monitor locally, as the objects related to this application are only created locally and will not be available from another system.

Once you have selected a system to monitor, either locally or remotely, you must select the object to monitor. Select one or more objects to monitor from the list in the Object field. Note that the Log view is somewhat different from the other views, in that you only add *objects* to the view, not the specific counters for the objects, as shown in the Add To Log dialog box in Figure 20-5.

After you select the objects for the Performance Monitor to track and log, select Options | Log Options to save the data to a log file, and then start logging by clicking the Start Log button, as shown in Figure 20-6. This dialog box also gives you the opportunity to select the update method and time.

After you have configured the log to save to a particular file, you can see the log file name, status of the logging process, log interval, and file size of the log in the Performance Monitor dialog box. To stop collecting data in a log, open the Log Options dialog box again and click Stop Log. You can then choose to create a new Log file and begin logging again, if necessary. You can also view data from one of these saved log files by selecting Options | Data From. In the Data From... dialog box, shown in Figure 20-7, you can choose to continue obtaining data from the current activity, or obtain data from a particular log file.

When you choose to obtain data from a saved log, you go back to that frozen moment in time and add counters to the other views for the objects you chose to save in the log. In our Log options, for example, we chose to store data for the Logical Disk object. After

Figure 20-5
Add To Log in Performance Monitor

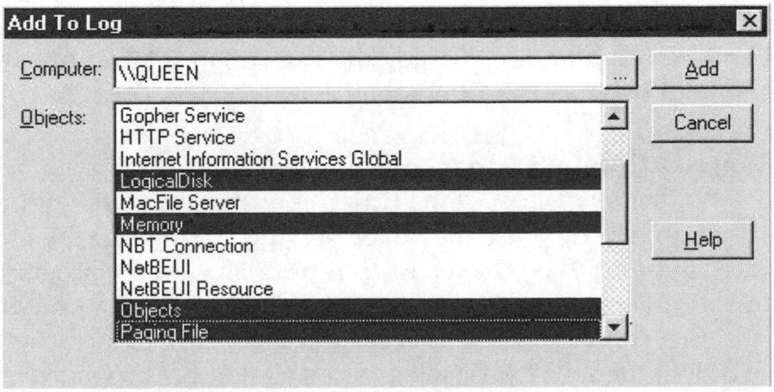

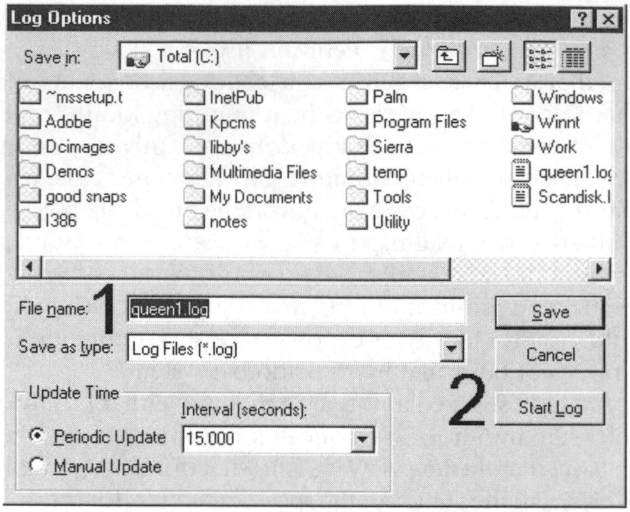

Figure 20-6

How to select a log file (1) and start logging (2) in Performance Monitor

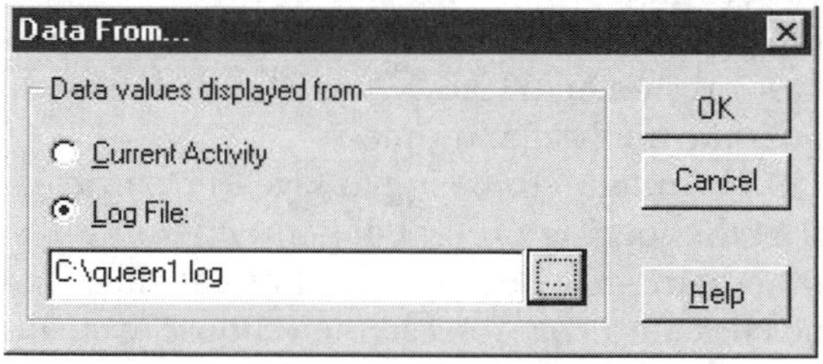

Figure 20-7

The Data From... dialog box in Performance Monitor

we've loaded that particular log file, we can change to the Chart view, add counters there for the Logical Disk object, and view a static chart for that moment in time (Figure 20-8). You may want to select a wide variety of objects to save while in Log view, so that when you open the log to display in any of the other views (Chart, Alert, and Report), you can add a wide range of counters.

The Performance Monitor utility described here is specific to Windows NT systems, but you should create baselines for whatever types of systems you have, and they should cover all aspects of your network. Be certain to create multiple baselines, to show the systems both at rest and in use, using the Performance Monitor as well as other systems management or network sniffer tools.

NetWare—Console Monitor

On a NetWare server, most of the critical information you might need to see and document to establish your baseline can be obtained by loading the *Console Monitor* application (see Figure 20-9) on the server itself. You can view the program remotely on a client PC, but it only runs on the server. Novell NetWare calls a program that runs on the server in this way a *NetWare Loadable Module (NLM)*. You issue the command **LOAD MONITOR** at the server's console prompt to start the program.

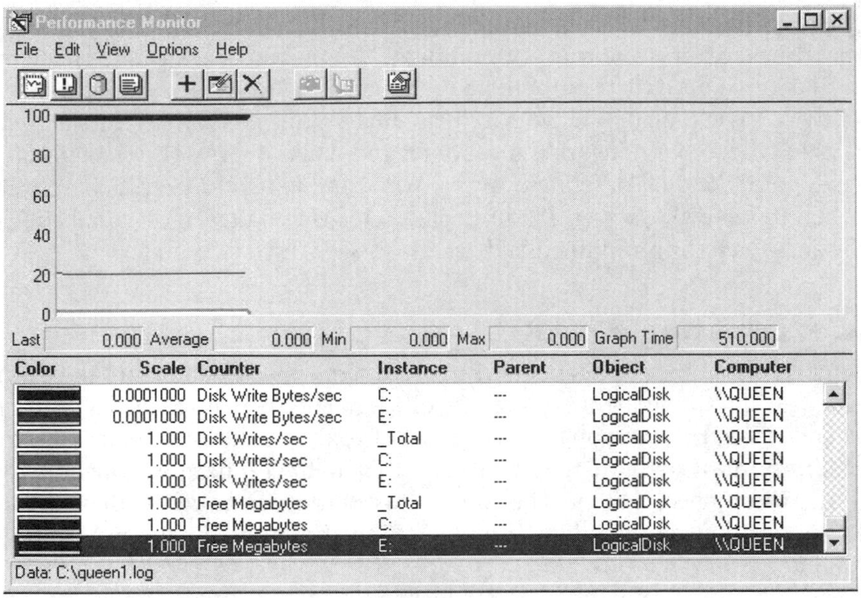
Performance Monitor
File Edit View Options Help
100
80
60
40
20
0
Last 0.000 Average 0.000 Min 0.000 Max 0.000 Graph Time 510.000
Color Scale Counter Instance Parent Object Computer
0.0001000 Disk Write Bytes/sec C: --- LogicalDisk \\QUEEN
0.0001000 Disk Write Bytes/sec E: --- LogicalDisk \\QUEEN
1.000 Disk Writes/sec _Total --- LogicalDisk \\QUEEN
1.000 Disk Writes/sec C: --- LogicalDisk \\QUEEN
1.000 Disk Writes/sec E: --- LogicalDisk \\QUEEN
1.000 Free Megabytes _Total --- LogicalDisk \\QUEEN
1.000 Free Megabytes C: --- LogicalDisk \\QUEEN
1.000 Free Megabytes E: --- LogicalDisk \\QUEEN
Data: C:\queen1.log

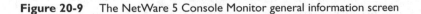

Figure 20-8 Viewing a static chart in Performance Monitor

The Console Monitor NLM can display a wide range of information, from memory use to individual statistics about the network interface cards (NICs) installed in the server. Many system managers leave Console Monitor running all the time so they can keep an eye on things. It can also be used to kick users off the server and see which files they're accessing!

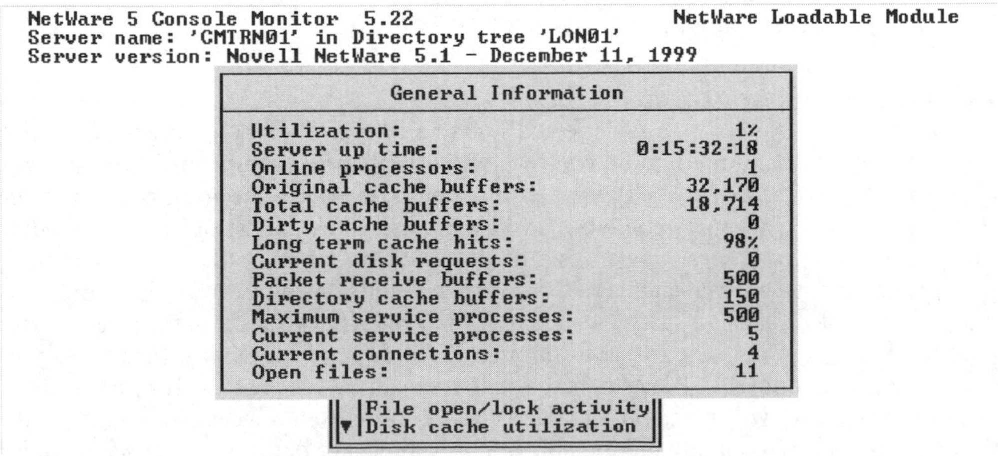
NetWare 5 Console Monitor 5.22
NetWare Loadable Module
Server name: 'CMTRN01' in Directory tree 'LON01'
Server version: Novell NetWare 5.1 - December 11, 1999
General Information
Utilization: 1%
Server up time: 0:15:32:18
Online processors: 1
Original cache buffers: 32,170
Total cache buffers: 18,714
Dirty cache buffers: 0
Long term cache hits: 98%
Current disk requests: 0
Packet receive buffers: 500
Directory cache buffers: 150
Maximum service processes: 500
Current service processes: 5
Current connections: 4
Open files: 11
File open/lock activity
Disk cache utilization

Figure 20-9 The NetWare 5 Console Monitor general information screen

Using Baselines

Using baselines requires a serious commitment. Not only do you need to create them in the first place, you need to monitor them continually to know when changes take place. Be careful not to be fooled by a bad baseline—make a number of baselines at first to get an idea as to when your network is most quiet and when it's most busy. Many administrators like to make dual baselines: one for when the network/server is at rest and another when the network/server is at its busiest. This is a matter of personal choice—try both the single baseline and the dual baseline to see which you prefer.

Troubleshooting Model

No matter how complex and fancy, any *troubleshooting model* can be broken down into simple steps. Having a sequence of steps to follow makes the entire *troubleshooting process* simpler and easier, because you have a clear set of goals to achieve in a specific sequence. The most important steps are the first three—they help you narrow down the cause of the problem to a specific item. The reason this matters so much is that figuring out what's wrong will also probably tell you how to fix the problem, and how to prevent it from happening in the future.

The basics of any troubleshooting model should include the following steps:

1. Establish the symptoms.
2. Isolate the cause of the problem (identify the scope of the problem).
3. Establish what has changed that might have caused the problem.
4. Identify the most probable cause.
5. Implement a solution.
6. Test the solution.
7. Recognize the potential effects of the solution.
8. Document the solution.

Establish the Symptoms

If you are working directly on the affected system and not relying on somebody on the other end of a telephone to guide you, you will establish the symptoms through your observation of what is (or isn't) happening. If you're troubleshooting over the telephone (always a joy, in my experience), you will need to ask questions based on what the user is telling you. These questions can be *close-ended*, which is to say there can only be a yes or no type answer, such as, "Can you see a light on the front of the monitor?" You can also ask *open-ended* questions, such as, "Tell me what you see on the screen." The type of question you use at any given moment will depend on what information you need, and on the knowledge level of the user. If, for example, the user seems to be technically oriented, you will probably be able to ask more close-ended questions, because they will know what you are talking about. If, on the other hand, the user seems to be confused about what's happening, open-ended questions will allow him to explain what is going on in his own words.

Isolate the Cause of the Problem

One of the first steps in trying to determine the cause of a problem is to understand the extent of the problem—is it specific to one user or is it network-wide? Sometimes this entails trying the task yourself, both from the user's machine and from your own or another machine.

For example, if a user is experiencing problems logging in to the network, you might need to go to that user's machine and try to use their user name to log in. This will tell you whether the problem is a user error of some kind, as well as enable you to see the symptoms of the problem yourself. Next, you probably want to try logging in with your own user name from that machine, or have the user try to log in from another machine. In some cases, you can ask other users in the area if they are experiencing the same problem, to see if the problem is affecting more than one user. Depending on the size of your network, you should find out if the problem is occurring in only one part of your company, or across the entire network.

What does all of this tell you? Essentially, it tells you how big the problem is. If nobody in an entire remote office can log in, you may be able to assume that the problem is the network link or router connecting that office to the server. If nobody in any office can log in, you may be able to assume that the server is down or not accepting logins. If only that one user in that one location can't log in, it may be a problem with that user, that machine, or that user's account.

 TIP   Eliminating variables is one of the first tools in your arsenal of diagnostic techniques.

Establish What Has Changed That Might Have Caused the Problem

After determining the extent of a problem, the next step is to eliminate all the extra variables, that is, all the incorrect possible causes of the problem. If you have determined that the problem is specific to that user on that machine, you have already learned a great deal. First, you have learned that this isn't a user account problem, because that user was able to log in from another machine. You have also determined that it isn't user error, because you've tried it yourself. By having other users at other machines successfully try the task, you eliminated the possibility that the server is down.

Ask Isolating Questions

The goal of this step is to isolate the problem to a specific item (hardware, software, user error, and so on), or to identify what has changed that might have caused the problem. You may not have to ask many questions before the problem is isolated, but it can sometimes take quite a bit of time and involve further work behind the scenes. Isolating questions are designed to home in on the likely cause of the problem. Here are some examples:

- "Tell me exactly what you were doing when the problem occurred."

- "Has anything been changed on the system recently?"
- "Has the system been moved recently?"

Notice the way I've tactfully avoided the word *you*, as in "Have *you* changed anything on the system recently?" This is a deliberate tactic to avoid any implied blame on the part of the user. Being nice never hurts, and it makes the whole troubleshooting process more friendly.

You should be asking some isolating questions *internally* of yourself, such as, "Was that machine involved in the software push last night?" or, "Didn't a tech visit that machine this morning?" Note that you will only be able to answer these questions if *your* documentation is up to scratch. Sometimes, isolating a problem may require you to check system and hardware logs (such as those stored by some routers and other network devices), so make sure you know how to do this.

Identify the Most Probable Cause

This step comes down to experience—or good use of the support tools at your disposal, such as your knowledge base. You need to select the most *probable* cause from all the *possible* causes, so the solution you choose fixes the problem the first time. This may not always happen, but whenever possible, you want to avoid spending a whole day stabbing in the dark while the problem snores softly to itself in some cozy, neglected corner of your network.

Implement a Solution

Once you think you have isolated the cause of the problem, you should decide what you think is the best way to fix it, and then try your solution, whether that's giving advice over the phone to a user, installing a replacement part, or adding a software patch. All the way through this step, try only one likely solution at a time. There's no point in installing several patches at once, because then you can't tell which one fixed the problem. Similarly, there's no point in replacing several items of hardware (such as a hard disk and its controller cable) at the same time because then you can't tell which part (or parts) was faulty. As you try each possibility, always *document* what you do and what results you get. This isn't just for a future problem, either—during a lengthy troubleshooting process, it's easy to forget exactly what you tried two hours before, or which thing you tried produced a particular result. Although it may take longer to be methodical, it will save time the next time—and it may enable you to pinpoint what needs to be done to stop the problem from recurring at all, thereby reducing future call volume to your support team—and as any support person will tell you, that's definitely worth the effort!

Test the Solution

This is the part everybody hates. Once you think you've fixed a problem, you should try to make it happen again. If you can't, great! But sometimes you will be able to re-create the problem, and then you know you haven't finished the job at hand. Many techs want to slide away quietly as soon as everything seems to be fine, but trust me on this, it won't impress your customer when their problem flares up again 30 seconds after you've left the building—not to mention that you get the joy of another two-hour car trip the next day to fix the same problem, for an even more unhappy client! In the scenario where you are providing support to someone else rather than working directly on the problem, you should make *them* try to re-create the problem. This will confirm whether they understand what you have been telling them, and will educate them at the same time, lessening the chance they'll call you back later and ask, "Can we just go through that one more time?"

Recognize the Potential Effects of the Solution

Okay, now that *you* have changed something on the system in the process of solving one problem, you must think about the wider repercussions of what you have done. If you've replaced a faulty NIC in a server, for instance, will the fact that the MAC address has changed (remember, it's built in to the NIC) affect anything else, such as the logon security controls, or your network management and inventory software? If you've installed a patch on a client PC, will this change the default protocol or any other default settings that may affect other functionality? If you've changed a user's security settings, will this affect their ability to access other network resources? This is part of testing your solution to make sure it works properly, but it also makes you think about the impact of your work on the system as a whole.

Document the Solution

It is *vital* that you document the problem, symptoms, and solutions of all support calls, for two reasons. First, you're creating a support database that will be a knowledge base for future reference, enabling everyone on the support team to identify new problems as they arise, and know how to deal with them quickly, without having to duplicate someone else's research efforts. Second, documentation enables you to track problem trends and anticipate future workloads, or even to identify a particular brand or model of an item, such as a printer or a NIC, that seems to be less reliable or that creates more work for you than others. Don't skip this step—it *really* is essential!

TIP Remember these problem analysis steps:
  Establish the symptoms
  Isolate the cause
  Establish what has changed
  Ask isolating questions
  Identify the most probable cause
  Implement a solution
  Recognize potential effects of the solution
  Document the solution

Troubleshooting as Art—Mike's Four-Layer Model

Troubleshooting is not something that can be definitively described in a nice neat list of ten easy steps. It is more of an art—an ability to become "one with the network" and intuit where the problems are hiding. The best troubleshooters are those who have a huge amount of knowledge about every element of the network—hardware, software, connections, and so on. These people can then synthesize all that knowledge into good guesses about where to start looking for problems. All of the previous steps give you a theoretical concept of where to look and how to proceed when troubleshooting your own network. The theory, however, is easier to implement in real life if you know where (and where not) to look within the network to find the problem.

The troubleshooting model does a great job of describing the steps necessary to get a network problem fixed, but it doesn't tell you where to look in the first place. So how do you figure out where to look for problems? Some might think to use the OSI seven-layer model, but while the OSI seven-layer model provides a superb tool for those who create network hardware and software, it doesn't do a lot for the folks who need to work on a network every day. Instead, I use a model that I modestly call Mike's Four-Layer Model. The Four-Layer Model concentrates on the main components of the hardware and software you need to deal with to make a networking system work, while ignoring the parts of the hardware and software over which you have no control. The core idea behind the four layers of my model is that you can access, change, remove, install, troubleshoot, and fix every layer—unlike most of the layers of the OSI seven-layer model.

The Four-Layer Model breaks all networks into—surprise!—four major areas: Hardware, Protocols, Network, and Shared Resources. No matter what specific networking hardware or software you use, every one of these four layers exists—although some network operating systems like to hide them! If you understand Mike's Four-Layer Model, you should have no problem fixing just about any network, any time. By using the Four-Layer Model when you have a problem with a network, you'll never find yourself saying, "I have no idea why this is happening to my network! What do I do?" Instead, you'll find yourself saying, "I know why this problem exists. I just need to figure out how to fix it!" Trust me, figuring out how to fix a known problem is a lot easier than trying to troubleshoot a mystery problem on your network.

NOTE   The layers of Mike's Four-Layer Model are
1. Hardware
2. Protocols
3. Network
4. Shared Resources

Mike's Four-Layer Model also *ignores the function of the layers* and concentrates instead on *what you need to do to make the layers function* (that is, what you do to verify that a particular layer works correctly or needs diagnosing). For example, if you've installed the hardware correctly, then the hardware layer works. To determine this, you run a certain type of test (like pinging another system), and if you're successful, you in essence check off the hardware layer as good and move on to the next one.

Some of my critics suggest that if diagnostic success is the goal, then my Four-Layer Model is by definition not a true model; they argue that it's nothing more than a diagnostic procedure. These people do have a point—if you get technical about it, my Four-

Layer Model *is* nothing more than a diagnostic procedure. Here's what I have to say to those critics: "Well, it's the best darn totally-universal, easy-to-understand, 100-percent-accurate, *practical* diagnostic procedure you'll ever meet! Six weeks after the Network+ exam, you'll probably have forgotten most of the seven OSI layers, but you'll never forget my model!" Why? Because you'll use it every day!

NOTE Mike's Four-Layer Model is in fact nothing more than this one tech's opinion of how best to fix a network. It is neither an industry standard nor that well-known—yet. It is not part of the Network+ test in any way, but it will help you on the test by providing a framework you can use to analyze the many scenario questions on the exam and quickly generate correct answers.

I once had a reader e-mail me about the Four-Layer Model. She said I should change its name to Mike's Four-Doors Model. Her suggestion for the name change came from the fact that the four layers of my model seemed to her like doorways to the innards of the network, rather than a true definition of all network functions. In a way, she was right—my model does not define all the functions of a network, like the OSI seven-layer model does. I ignore or blend most of the OSI layers into my model because I *want to deal with things I can touch in the network*. So, I guess the doorway analogy is a decent way to think about my model, but I'm too lazy to change all my work so I'm sticking to the name Four-Layer Model. Let's look at each of its layers.

Hardware
Hardware is probably the most self-explanatory of the four categories. This layer covers the many different ways data can be moved from one PC to another, from copper to fiber to wireless signals. It includes the Physical and Data Link components of the OSI model, but concentrates on the parts that make this all work, like hubs, cables, and connectors. It also includes items that the OSI model does not directly address, like NICs, device drivers for NICs, and how you install and test them.

Protocols
I should call this section "Network Protocols," but I don't want you confusing it with the next one. Protocols are the languages of networks. As you've learned, these languages have interesting names such as NetBIOS/NetBEUI, IPX/SPX, and the ever-popular TCP/IP. A *protocol* is a highly standardized language that handles most of the "invisible" functions on a network, like determining which computer is SERVER1, or disassembling and reassembling data passed over the network. Here we concern ourselves with installing and configuring the protocol so that a system can communicate with other systems on the network. We're not too interested in how this all works in great detail—the point here is that if you install the right protocol and configure it properly, it will work.

Network
Once you install the hardware and the protocol, you need to make two critical determinations. First, you need to decide which systems will share resources and which systems

will only access those shared resources. In other words, you must determine which systems will act as servers and which will act as clients, and then configure them accordingly. Second, you need to name the systems, so they can see each other, usually something like *Server1* or *Mike's PC*. In this layer, the concepts of client/server, peer-to-peer, and domain-based networks come into play. Different network operating systems use different methods to name their systems and to determine which systems share and which do not. This layer requires that you appreciate the differences among programs like Windows, NetWare, and Linux.

Shared Resources

The entire reason we network is to share resources, so this final layer encompasses all the steps required to enable a system to share a resource, and to allow and enable other systems access to that shared resource. This layer includes a number of steps, and unlike the earlier layers, these steps often need to be done fairly frequently, because by their nature, shared resources and the users who access them change pretty much continuously. This layer includes most of the day-to-day administration of networks and tends to be the place we spend the majority of our time.

Using the Four-Layer Model

The secret to using the Four-Layer Model to diagnose network problems is to use it to structure your analysis when problems occur, and to proceed through the layers as you diagnose the problem. Let me show you how I use it by giving you a scenario.

I recently replaced an ancient router that had an ISDN Internet connection, with a new SOHO gateway DSL router, in a Windows 2000 network. The Windows network had DNS, WINS, and DHCP servers for all the clients on the network. I configured the new router to use the same IP addresses as the old router. When I went to a system to test the setup, I popped right up on the Internet, no problem. I then fired up IPCONFIG and released and renewed the IP address to make sure the new router worked. I got a new IP address and everything looked okay. Then I decided to browse the network—and I couldn't see any other system! Not good. Time to use the Four-Layer Model.

 NOTE If you have Windows 9x/Me/XP, you can run the graphical utility WINIPCFG in place of IPCONFIG. It accomplishes the same goals, but like all good GUI tools, it gives you buttons to click instead of command strings to type. To run the application, go to Start | Run and type **winipcfg**; click the OK button and you're off!

First, the Physical layer—was I disconnected from the network, or was a piece of hardware broken? Not likely, given the fact that I could still get on the Internet. But I used PING to test the router—no problem. Then I pinged the server and didn't get an answer. Hmm, was there a cable problem between me and the server? I checked and saw good link lights all around. Plus, everyone else was still hitting the server just fine. Time to assume the Physical layer was okay.

On to the second layer, Protocol. I'm running TCP/IP, and it's unlikely I could get to the Internet if I had a problem there. But I still checked the system with IPCONFIG. Wait a minute! A quick look reveals that my IP address is 192.45.15.10, but the network ID I want is 192.168.4.0! This is weird—where did this strange IP address come from? Well, I set up the router for DHCP—maybe there's a problem with the DHCP server. The network admin checks and tells me it's up and running. I want to verify this so I go to another system and do a release/renew there. Lo and behold, suddenly IT has an IP address of 192.45.15.11! What's going on here? I ask myself the million-dollar question: "What has changed on this network that might have caused this?" The answer was easy: the only recent change to the network was the new router. A quick examination reveals the problem: The router was set up to do DHCP. I quickly shut off the router's DHCP, and then do another release/renew on the two systems with the bad IP addresses, and voilà, problem solved, and I'm on to the next job!

By using the Four-Layer Model, I could quickly remove physical issues from the possible problems and move on to examine protocol issues, where I found the problem. Try my Four-Layer Model for yourself—it works!

Troubleshooting Scenarios

I want to end this chapter and the book with some good troubleshooting scenarios. Take some time and think about these situations and how you would handle them. What questions would you ask? What tests would you do first? The Network+ exam absolutely *loves* to ask scenario questions. The knowledge from the previous chapters combined with the methods you've learned in this chapter should enable you to fix any network!

"I Can't Log In!"

One of the most complex troubleshooting issues is that one set of symptoms, in this case a user's inability to log in, can have many causes. Suppose Woody has called complaining that he cannot log in to the company's intranet. Tina Tech first tries accessing the intranet site from her workstation, and finds she has no problem. Tina might also want to have other users try to log in, or confirm that other users are not having the same problem. Next, Tina should have Woody try to log in from another machine. This will help Tina determine whether the problem lies with Woody's user account's capability to log in, or with Woody's Windows 98 workstation or connectivity.

If Woody is unable to log in from another machine, Tina should probably check to be sure Woody is using the correct login ID, password, and procedure when he logs in. On the other hand, if Woody is able to log in from another user's workstation, Tina should probably focus on determining whether Woody's workstation is working properly and connecting to the network. One step she could try here is pinging Woody's workstation. If Tina is able to ping Woody's machine successfully, she knows that the machine is up, the TCP/IP protocol is configured correctly, and the system is connected to the network. Tina might then check the configuration of the network client on Woody's workstation. If Tina is not able to ping the workstation, however, she might need to test the cables and NIC using cable testers or loopback devices, and verify that TCP/IP was correctly configured using WINIPCFG.

"I Can't Get to This Web Site!"

Reaching external web sites requires that a variety of components be configured correctly. Some of these components are within your company's internal control; many of them are not. When Fatima calls and tells Tina Tech that she cannot reach www.comptia.org, Tina's first step is to try to reach that site herself. In this case, Tina was also unable to get a response from the comptia.org site. One of her next steps is to ping the site, first by name, and then by IP address. In this case, she gets no response by name, but she does get a normal response when she pings the site by IP address. This immediately indicates to her that the problem is name resolution, in this case: DNS.

On the other hand, had Tina been unable to ping successfully using either the IP address or host name, she should consider two possibilities. First, if her company uses a firewall or proxy server to reach the Internet, she should ping that machine. This machine usually has the same IP address as the default gateway TCP/IP setting. If Tina can successfully ping her default gateway, she can be almost certain that the problem is not something she or her company has any control over. To verify this, Tina should attempt to reach some other external sites, both by pinging and using a web browser. If she can reach other sites successfully, the problem is most likely with the comptia.org site or the gateway.

"Our Web Server Is Sluggish!"

Slow response from a server can be related to a variety of things. Usually, however, the problem can be traced to a connection to the server, or to the server itself. When Wanda calls in from working at home and tells Tina Tech that she is getting a slow response from the company's web site, Tina Tech leaps into action. Tina tries to reach the offending server and is immediately connected; this indicates a connectivity problem for that user. She asks Wanda to execute a **TRACERT** command from her workstation to the slow server. This reveals to Tina that the slowdown stems from one of the intermediate steps through which Wanda's system connects to the server. Because of this, the problem is out of Tina's hands, unless she can offer a direct dial-up option for Wanda.

If Tina finds she cannot reach the offending server quickly when she tries from her workstation, then the problem may lie with the server itself. Tina checks the Change Log for the web server, to see if anyone has changed anything recently. She discovers a new anti-virus component was recently added, so she checks the vendor's web site to make sure there are no known problems or patches for that piece of software. She also uses the Performance Monitor to compare the server's current responses to the baseline that she previously recorded. This shows her that the bottleneck is related to excessive paging, indicating that the server may need more physical memory, or RAM.

"I Can't See Anything in Network Neighborhood!"

When a user is completely cut off from the network, the problem is usually limited to that user's workstation or network connection. When Tina gets a call from Johnny saying his Windows 98 machine is on, but that he can't log in and can't see any other machines on the company's TCP/IP network, Tina goes to Johnny's office to run some tests. The first test Tina runs is to ping an external machine. She doesn't expect it to work, but tests just to be certain. Next, she tries to ping Johnny's machine using either **ping localhost** or **ping 127.0.0.1** (remember the loopback address?). When this ping doesn't work, Tina guesses that the problem is in the TCP/IP configuration. To view the machine's TCP/IP configuration, Tina uses WINIPCFG, and notices the IP address is blank. After checking her network documentation to verify what IP address Johnny's machine should have, she adds the IP address and he is able to connect to the network.

If Tina's **ping 127.0.0.1** had worked, she would have had to assume the TCP/IP and networking configuration of Johnny's machine was correct. She should then check the hardware, using a network card utility to verify that the NIC itself is working correctly, and a cable tester to verify that the cable from Johnny's workstation is operating properly. In this case, the cable tester shows that the cable is bad, so she replaces the cable between Johnny's workstation and the patch panel, and he is able to connect.

Troubleshooting Is Fun!

The art of network troubleshooting can be a fun, frolicsome, and frequently frustrating feature of your network career. By applying a good troubleshooting methodology and constantly increasing your knowledge of networks, you too can develop into a great troubleshooting artist. This takes time, naturally, but stick with it. Begin the training. Use the Force. Learn new stuff, document problems and fixes, talk to other network techs about similar problems. Every bit of knowledge and experience you gain will make things that much easier for you when crunch time comes and a network disaster occurs—and as any experienced network tech can tell you, it will, even in the most robust network.

Chapter Review

Questions

1. You can't connect to your network server. Your system is configured to obtain an IP address automatically. You ran the **IPCONFIG** command to find your default gateway address, which is 192.168.4.152, and you successfully pinged your default gateway. **IPCONFIG** showed your IP address to be 192.168.4.15. You also were able to ping your IP address, but you still cannot connect to your server. What could be causing this problem?

   A. Your hub is malfunctioning.

   B. The cable connecting the hub to the DSL router is bad.

   C. The cable connecting the hub to your system is bad.

   D. The network's SDSL router is also running DHCP, causing a DHCP conflict.

2. This morning you have gotten many complaints about the network being sluggish. You are monitoring the network's performance and you notice it is having a high number of collisions. Which of the following could be contributing to this problem?

   A. Your network is connected with old CAT 3 cabling.

   B. There is a loose 50-ohm terminator on the network cabling.

   C. Your network hub has died.

   D. A BNC connector is connected incorrectly without the T-connector.

3. Your boss has decided he wants you to remove WINS from the network and use DNS instead. You have one network segment that has four addresses that are resolved by the WINS server. What is the best way to make this change and make sure your users can reach those addresses by host name?

   A. Add a WINS proxy to your network segment.

   B. Request that the addresses be added into DNS.

   C. Enter the four host names and addresses in the HOSTS file.

   D. Enter the four host names and addresses in the LMHOSTS file.

4. You removed an old NT workstation from your network that had been configured with static IP, and placed the old workstation in a closet. You have your network clients obtaining IP addresses automatically, and then you notice someone has hooked the old system back up to the network. Meanwhile, the old system and another workstation are experiencing problems getting online. What could be the cause of this?

   A. There is an IP address conflict.

   B. Your LMHOSTS file has become corrupt and is causing network problems.

   C. Your DNS server is down.

   D. The network printer is offline.

5. You have a NetWare network with some Windows 98 systems as workstations. You have installed TCP/IP on your workstation, and add a Windows NT server to the network. The NT server has several resources shared with the network, but not all the Windows 98 workstations can access the NT server's shares. Which of the following are possible reasons for this problem? (Select all that apply.)

   A. The cable connecting the server to the hub is broken.

   B. The Windows 98 workstations have not been given the needed permissions to access the NT server shares.

   C. The Windows 98 workstations do not have Client for NetWare Networks installed.

   D. The Windows 98 workstations do not have Client for Microsoft Networks installed.

6. Some, but not all of the NICs on your network need to be replaced, so you replace NICs in several of your old workstation systems. Afterward, the workstations with the new NICs can't log on to the server. Which of the following would be a logical step to take to diagnose the problem?

   A. Reboot all the systems on the network.

   B. Check to make sure the appropriate protocols have been installed properly for the new NICs.

   C. Check to see if the server NIC is connected properly.

   D. Test all the cables on the network.

7. The users on your network have been unable to connect to the server for the last ten minutes. You ping the server from several workstations but it times out. You then run the **IPCONFIG** command, revealing your IP address to be 169.254.1.16. You reboot the workstations, but they still can't connect to the server. Which of the following would be one of your first steps in diagnosing the problem?

   A. Reboot the DHCP server.

   B. Reboot the workstations again.

   C. Test all the network cables.

   D. Run a diagnostic test on all of the server NICs.

8. You are running a Token Ring network, and to increase capacity you've added a new MAU. Afterward, you discover your users can't connect to the LAN. Using a network analyzer, you test connectivity from the NICs to the RJ-45 plugs in the MAU. They appear correct, so what could be causing this problem?

   A. The MAU is set for full-duplex.

   B. CSU/DSU is disconnected.

   C. The Ring In and Ring Out ports are not configured correctly between the MAUs.

   D. You have the workstation cable connected to the wrong port on the hub.

9. Roger is in a hotel room in Virginia trying to access the network in the Houston office, but is having difficulties dialing in to the network. He unplugs the cable from the phone and plugs it into the modem, but gets no dial tone. What is the problem?

   A. The modem on his laptop does not support ISDN.

   B. The dial-up server is not responding.

   C. The wrong protocols are installed.

   D. The dial-up connections are not configured properly.

10. Two of the following devices work together to trace cable by sending an electrical signal along a wire at a particular frequency. One of them emits a sound when it distinguishes that frequency. The devices go by the nickname "Fox and Hound." Which two devices make up this diagnostic tool? (Select two of the following.)

A. Frequency locator

B. Tone generator

C. Frequency generator

D. Tone locator

Answers

1. **D.** The network's SDSL router is also running DHCP, causing a DHCP conflict. The other choices cannot be correct because the pings were successful.

2. **B.** The terminator is loose enough to cause reflection, making it appear that there are many collisions.

3. **B.** The best way to make this change and make sure your users can reach those addresses by host name is to request that the addresses be added into DNS.

4. **A.** The most likely answer is an IP address conflict. The old NT workstation is using one of the DHCP-assigned IP addresses, causing a conflict with the other problem workstation.

5. **B, D.** The two possible reasons for this problem are that the Windows 98 workstations have not been given the needed permissions to access the NT server shares, and that they don't have Client for Microsoft Networks installed. The server they can't access is not the NetWare server, so Client for NetWare Networks is irrelevant, and if the cable were broken, the Windows 98 workstations wouldn't be the only ones exhibiting the problem.

6. **B.** The logical step to take in diagnosing why the new NICs can't log on to the server is to make sure all the appropriate protocols have been installed. Because only the new NICs are affected, the problem isn't likely to be the server's NIC, and rebooting all the systems or checking all the cabling are both serious overkill.

7. **A.** The first thing to try is rebooting the DHCP server. You've already rebooted the workstations, and it's unlikely that all the server NICs or cables suddenly failed.

8. **C.** The problem could be that the Ring In and Ring Out ports are connected incorrectly.

9. **D.** Roger's dial-up connections are not configured properly. Neither the server nor any protocols have come into play yet.

10. **B, D.** The tone generator and tone locator work together to trace cables by sending an electrical signal along a wire at a particular frequency.

About the CD-ROM

The CD-ROM included with this book comes complete with Total Tester practice exam software, an electronic copy of the book and Session 1 of LearnKey's online training. The testing software is easy to install on any Windows 98/NT/2000/XP computer and must be installed to access the Total Tester practice exams. The electronic copy of the book is a series of Adobe Acrobat files. If you don't have Adobe Acrobat Reader it is available for installation on the CD. To install the LearnKey video training, simply click the **Install LearnKey Demo** link on the CD splash screen and follow the directions to install the software.

System Requirements

The Total Tester software requires Windows 98 or higher, Internet Explorer 5.0 or above, and 30MB of hard disk space for full installation. The LearnKey video training requires Windows Media Player, which will be automatically installed when you load the program.

Installing and Running Total Tester

If your computer CD-ROM drive is configured to auto run, the CD-ROM will automatically start up upon inserting the disk. If the auto run feature does not launch your CD, browse to the CD and Click the Launch.exe icon.

From the opening screen you may install Total Tester by pressing the **Install Network+ Practice Exams** button. This will begin the installation process, create a program group named "Total Seminars," and put an icon on your desktop. To run Total Tester use Start | Programs |Total Seminars or just double click the icon on your desktop.

To uninstall the Total Tester software go to Start | Settings | Control Panel | Add/Remove Programs and select the Network+ Total Tester program. Select Remove and windows will completely uninstall the software.

Total Tester

Total Tester provides you with a simulation of the actual exam. There are two full exams included that can be taken in either practice or final mode. Practice mode provides an assistance window with hints, references to the book, an explanation of the answer, and the ability to check your answers as you take the test. Both practice and final modes provide an overall grade and a grade broken down by certification objective. To take a test, first launch the program, select a suite from the menu at the top, then select an exam from the menu.

Accessing the Electronic Copy of the Book

To access the electronic copy of the book, first make sure you have a copy of Adobe Acrobat Reader. If you don't have Acrobat Reader installed on your system, you can install it from the CD-ROM by clicking the **Install Adobe Acrobat Reader** button. Once you have installed Acrobat Reader, click the **Electronic Book** button, which will take you to a list of each of the chapters of the book. Select a chapter to view and click the button to open and view the file.

LearnKey Online Training

The **Install LearnKey Demo** link will install the video software on your system. The installation will create a LearnKey group in your Programs menu and will put an icon on your desktop. To view the videos, launch the program and choose a user name and password. Make sure to take note of this information—you will need it each time you return to the video training. Once you log in, the video training will begin automatically. You can watch the training in sequence or navigate through the topics. The first session of this course is provided at no charge. The complete video training course may be purchased from Total Seminars at www.totalsem.com or by calling 800-446-6004.

Technical Support

For questions regarding the Total Tester software, visit www.totalsem.com, e-mail support@totalsem.com, or e-mail customer.service@mcgraw-hill.com. For customers outside the 50 United States, e-mail international_cs@mcgraw-hill.com.

LearnKey Technical Support

For technical problems with the software (installation, operation, removing installations) and for questions regarding LearnKey Online Training, e-mail techsupport@learnkey.com.

5-4-3 Rule   A general rule for approximating the correct size of a collision domain. In a collision domain, no two nodes may be separated by more than five segments, four repeaters, and three populated segments.

10Base2   An Ethernet LAN designed to run on common coax RG-58 cabling, almost exactly like the coax for cable television. It runs at 10 megabits per second and has a maximum segment length of 185 meters. Also known as *Thinnet* or *Thin Ethernet*. It uses baseband signaling and BNC connectors.

10Base5   The original Ethernet LAN, designed to run on specialized coax cabling. It runs at 10 megabits per second and has a maximum segment length of 500 meters. Also known as *Thicknet* or *Thick Ethernet*, 10Base5 uses baseband signaling running on RG-8 coaxial cable. It uses DIX connectors and external transceivers, known as *AUI connectors*.

10BaseFL   Fiber-optic implementation of Ethernet that runs at 10 megabits per second using baseband signaling. Maximum segment length is 2 kilometers.

10BaseT   An Ethernet LAN designed to run on UTP cabling, 10BaseT runs at 10 megabits per second. The maximum length for the cabling between the NIC and the hub (or the switch, the repeater, and so forth) is 100 meters. It uses baseband signaling.

16-Bit   Able to process 16 bits of data at a time.

24-Bit Color   Also referred to as *true color*, this uses 3 bytes per pixel to represent a color image in a PC. The 24 bits enable up to 16,777,216 colors to be stored and displayed.

100BaseFX   An Ethernet LAN designed to run on fiber-optic cabling. It runs at 100 megabits per second and uses baseband signaling.

100BaseT   A generic term for any Ethernet cabling system that is designed to run at 100 megabits per second on UTP cabling. It uses baseband signaling.

100BaseT4   This is an Ethernet LAN designed to run on UTP cabling. It runs at 100 megabits per second and uses four pairs of wires on CAT 3 or better cabling.

100BaseTX   This is an Ethernet LAN designed to run on UTP cabling. It runs at 100 megabits per second and uses two pairs of wires on CAT 5 cabling. It uses baseband signaling.

100BaseVG   Also called *100BaseVGAnyLAN*. Uses CAT 3 cabling and an access method called Demand Priority.

110-Punchdown   The most common connection used on the back of an RJ-45 jack.

110-Punchdown Tool   A specialized tool for connecting UTP wires to an RJ-45 jack.

286   Also called *80286*. Intel's second-generation processor. The 286 had a 16-bit external data bus and a 24-bit address bus. It was the first Intel processor to achieve protected mode.

386   Also called *80386DX*. Intel's third-generation processor. The 386 DX had a 32-bit external data bus and a 32-bit address bus.

386SX   Also called *80386SX*. This was a hybrid chip that combined the 32-bit functions and modes of the 80386DX with the 16-bit external data bus and the 24-bit address bus of the 80286.

486DX   Intel's fourth-generation CPU. Essentially, an 80386DX with a built-in cache and math coprocessor.

486DX/2, 486DX/3, 486DX/4   486 CPUs that operate externally at one speed and internally at a speed that is two, three, or four times faster. Although the internal speed can be more than two times as fast as the external speed, these CPUs are known collectively as *clock doublers*.

486SX   A 486DX without the functional math coprocessor.

586   This is an unofficial, generic term that describes the Intel Pentium family of CPUs, as well as comparable CPUs made by other manufacturers.

802.3 Ethernet   *See* Ethernet.

802.11   *See* IEEE 802.11.

802.11a   A wireless standard that operates in the frequency range of 5 GHz and offers throughput of up to 54 Mbps.

802.11b   The most popular wireless standard, 802.11b operates in the frequency range of 2.4 GHz and offers throughput of up to 11 Mbps.

802.11g   The newest wireless standard in general use, 802.11g operates in the frequency range of 2.4 GHz and offers throughput of up to 54 Mbps.

1000BaseT   Gigabit Ethernet. This is an Ethernet LAN designed to run on UTP cabling. It runs at 1000 megabits per second and uses two pairs of wires on CAT 5e or better cabling. It uses baseband signaling.

8086/8088   These were the first generation of Intel processors to be used in IBM PCs. The 8086 and 8088 were identical with the exception of the external data bus: the 8086 had a 16-bit bus, while the 8088 had an 8-bit bus.

8086 Mode   *See* Real Mode.

8237   This is the part number for the original DMA controller. Although long obsolete, the name is still often used in reference to DMA usage.

8259   This is the part number for the original IRQ controller. Although long obsolete, the name is still often used in reference to IRQ usage.

16450, 16550, 16550A, 16550AF, 16550AFN   These are incremental improvements in UARTs. The 16550AFN is considered the most sophisticated UART available today. Note: the 16450 should not be used with any modem faster than a 14.4 Kbps modem.

Access   The reading or writing of data. Also a verb meaning "to gain entry to data." Most commonly used in connection with information access via a user ID and qualified by an indication of the kinds of access permitted. For example, "read-only access" means that the contents of the file may be read, but not altered or erased.

Access Time   The time interval measured from the moment that data is requested to the moment it is received. Most commonly used in measuring the speed of storage devices.

Account   A registered set of rights and/or permissions to an individual computer or to a network of computers.

ACPI (Advanced Configuration and Power Interface)   A power management specification that far surpasses its predecessor, APM, by providing support for hot-swappable devices and better control of power modes.

Active Directory   A form of directory service used in networks with Windows 2000/2003 servers.

Active Matrix   A type of liquid crystal display that replaced the passive matrix technology used in early portable computer displays.

Activity Light   An LED on a NIC, hub, or switch that blinks rapidly to show data transfers over the network.

Address Bus   The wires leading from the CPU to the Northbridge that enable the CPU to address RAM. Also used by the CPU for I/O addressing.

Address Resolution Protocol (ARP)   A protocol in the TCP/IP suite used with the command-line utility of the same name to determine the MAC address that corresponds to a particular IP address.

Address Space   The total amount of memory addresses that an address bus can contain.

Ad-hoc Mode   Each wireless node in ad-hoc mode is in direct contact with every other node in a decentralized free-for-all. Wireless network ad-hoc mode is similar to the wired network *mesh topology*.

Administrative Tools   A group of Control Panel applets, including Computer Management, Event Viewer, and Performance, that enable you to handle routine administrative tasks in Windows 2000, Windows XP, and Windows Server 2003 systems.

Administrator   The person whose job it is to maintain a computer system or network.

Administrator Account   A user account that has unrestricted access to all system functions, services, and data. A default administrator account, such as the appropriately named Administrator account in Windows, is created when the NOS is installed on the PC.

ADSL (Asymmetric Digital Subscriber Line)   *See* Asymmetric Digital Subscriber Line (ADSL).

AGP (Accelerated Graphics Port)   A 32-bit expansion slot designed by Intel specifically for video, which runs at 66 MHz and yields a throughput of 254 megabytes per second, at least. Later versions (2*X*, 3*X*, 4*X*) give substantially higher throughput.

AIX (Advanced Interactive Executive)   IBM's version of UNIX, which runs on 386 or better PCs.

Algorithm   A set of rules for solving a problem in a given number of steps.

Alternating Current (AC)   A type of electricity where the flow of electrons alternates direction, back and forth, in a circuit.

ALU (Arithmetic Logic Unit)   The circuit that performs CPU math calculations and logic operations.

AMD (Advanced Micro Devices)   The manufacturer of chipsets and microprocessors. AMD produces CPUs for computers worldwide.

Amperes (Amps or A)   The unit of measure for amperage, or electrical current.

Amplifier   A device that strengthens electrical signals, enabling them to travel farther.

Analog   A type of device that uses a physical quantity, such as length or voltage, to represent the value of a number. By contrast, digital storage relies on a coding system of numeric units.

Analog Video   Picture signals represented by a number of smooth transitions between video levels. Television signals are analog, whereas digital video signals assign a finite set of levels. Because computer signals are digital, video must be converted into analog form before it can be shown on a computer screen. All modern CRTs use analog video standards based on the VGA standard. *See* VGA (Video Graphics Array).

ANDing   A Boolean logic function used by TCP/IP to determine if IP addresses are local or remote. In the ANDing process, IP addresses and subnet masks are reduced to their binary values and compared. Any combination of bits set to 1 ("on") yields a result of 1. Any other combination (e.g., 1 + 0, 0 + 1, or 0 + 0) yields a result of 0. *See* Boolean logic.

ANSI (American National Standards Institute)   The body responsible for standards, such as ASCII.

ANSI Character Set   The ANSI-standard character set that defines 256 characters. The first 128 are ASCII, and the second group of 128 contain math and language symbols.

Anti-Aliasing   In computer imaging, a blending effect that smoothes sharp contrasts between two regions, that is, jagged lines or different colors. This reduces the jagged edges of text or objects. In voice signal processing, it refers to the process of removing or smoothing out spurious frequencies from waveforms produced by converting digital signals back to analog.

API (Application Programming Interface)   A software definition that describes operating system calls for application software; conventions defining how a service is invoked.

APM (Advanced Power Management)   The BIOS routines that enable the CPU to selectively turn on and off selected peripherals.

AppleTalk   A network protocol suite invented to run on Apple computers. Modern Macintosh systems still support AppleTalk, but most Macintosh systems use TCP/IP rather than AppleTalk.

Application   A program designed to perform a job for the user of a PC. A word processor and a spreadsheet program are typical applications.

Application Layer   *See* OSI Seven-Layer Model.

Application Servers   Servers that provide clients access to software or other applications that run on the server only. Examples include web servers, e-mail servers, and database servers.

Archive   To copy programs and data on to a relatively inexpensive storage medium (disk, tape, and so forth) for long-term retention.

Archive Bit   An attribute of a file that shows whether the file has been backed up since the last change. Each time a file is opened, changed, or saved, the archive bit is turned on. Some types of backups will turn off this archive bit to indicate that a good backup of the file exists on tape.

ARCnet (Attached Resource Computer Network)   The original ARCnet standard defined a true star topology, in which both the physical and logical topology work as a star. ARCnet uses token passing to get frames from one system to another. ARCnet runs at 2.5 megabits per second.

Argument   A value supplied to a procedure, a macro, a subroutine, or a command that is required to evaluate that procedure, macro, subroutine, or command. Synonymous with *parameter*.

ARP (Address Resolution Protocol)   *See* Address Resolution Protocol (ARP).

ARPANET   The first practical network ever created. It was conceived by an organization called the Advanced Research Projects Agency (ARPA).

ASCII (American Standard Code for Information Interchange)
The industry standard 8-bit characters used to define text characters, consisting of 96 uppercase and lowercase letters, plus 32 nonprinting control characters, each of which is numbered. These numbers were designed to achieve uniformity among different computer devices for printing and the exchange of simple text documents.

Aspect Ratio   The ratio of width to height of an object. In television, this is usually a 4:3 ratio, except in the new HDTV standard, which is 16:9.

ASPI (Advanced SCSI Programming Interface)   A series of tight standards that enable SCSI devices to share a common set of highly compatible drivers.

Assembler   A program that converts symbolically coded programs into object-level, machine code. In an assembler program, unlike a compiler, there is a one-to-one correspondence between human-readable instructions and the machine-language code.

Asymmetric Digital Subscriber Line (ADSL)   A fully digital, dedicated connection to the telephone system that provides download speeds of up to 9 megabits per second and upload speeds of up to 1 megabit per second.

Asynchronous Communication   A type of communication in which the receiving devices must send an acknowledgement or ACK to the sending unit to verify a piece of data has been sent.

Asynchronous Transfer Mode (ATM)   A network technology that runs at speeds between 25 and 622 megabits per second using fiber-optic cabling or CAT 5 UTP.

AT (Advanced Technology)   The model name of the second-generation, 80286-based IBM computer. Many aspects of the AT, such as the BIOS, CMOS, and expansion bus, have become de facto standards in the PC industry.

ATA (AT Attachment)   A type of hard drive and controller. ATA was designed to replace the earlier ST506 and ESDI drives without requiring the replacement of the AT BIOS. These drives are more popularly known as IDE drives. *See* ST506, ESDI, and IDE. The ATA/33 standard has drive transfer speeds up to 33 MB/s; the ATA/66 up to 66 MB/s; the ATA/100 up to 100 MB/s; and the ATA/133 up to 133 MB/s.

ATAPI (AT Attachment Packet Interface)   A series of standards that enables mass storage devices other than hard drives to use the IDE/ATA controllers. Extremely popular with CD-media, DVD-media, and removable media drives like the Iomega Zip drive. *See also* EIDE.

AT Bus   The 16-bit expansion bus used in the IBM Personal Computer and the 32-bit bus of computers using the Intel 386 and 486 microprocessors.

Athlon   A family of fifth, sixth, and seventh generation CPUs produced by AMD. Includes the Athlon, Athlon XP, and Athlon 64.

ATM (Asynchronous Transfer Mode)   *See* Asynchronous Transfer Mode (ATM).

AUI Connector   An AUI or Attachment Unit Interface is the standard connector used with 10Base5 Ethernet. This is a 15-pin female DB connector, also known as *DIX.*

Authentication   A process that proves good data traffic truly came from where it says it originated by verifying the sending and receiving users and computers.

Authoritative DNS Servers   DNS servers that hold the IP addresses and names of systems for a particular domain or domains in special storage areas called *Forward Lookup Zones.*

AUTOEXEC.BAT   A batch file that DOS executes when you start or restart the system. AUTOEXEC.BAT is not necessary, but when you're running a computer to which you've attached several devices and several different software applications, the file is essential for efficient operation. AUTOEXEC.BAT files commonly include PATH statements that tell DOS where to find application programs and commands to install a mouse or operate your printer.

Automated System Recovery (ASR)   A utility included with Windows XP that enables a user to create a complete system backup.

Automatic Private IP Addressing (APIPA)   A feature of later Windows operating systems that enables TCP/IP clients to self-configure an IP address and subnet mask in the Class B Private IP range (169.254.*x.x*, with a subnet mask of 255.255.0.0) automatically when a DHCP server isn't available.

Automatic Skip Driver (ASD)   A utility for preventing "bad" drivers from running the next time that you boot your computer. This utility examines startup log files and removes problematic drivers from the boot process.

Backbone   A generalized term defining a primary network cabling and hardware systems that connect networks.

Background Processing   Users may use a terminal for one project and concurrently submit a job that is placed in a background queue that the computer will run as resources become available. Also refers to any processing in which a job runs without being connected to a terminal.

Backside Bus   The set of wires that connect the CPU to Level 2 cache. The backside bus first appeared in the Pentium Pro, and most modern CPUs have a special backside bus. Some buses, such as that in the later Celeron processors (300A and beyond), run at the full speed of the CPU, whereas others run at a fraction of this speed. Earlier Pentium IIs, for example, had backside buses running at half the speed of the processor. *See also* Frontside Bus and External Data Bus.

Back Up   To save important data in a secondary location as a safety precaution against the loss of the primary data.

Backward-Compatible   Compatible with earlier versions of a program or earlier models of a computer.

Bandwidth   A piece of the spectrum occupied by some form of signal, whether it is television, voice, fax data, and so forth. Signals require a certain size and location of band-width to be transmitted. The higher the bandwidth, the faster the signal transmission, thus allowing for a more complex signal such as audio or video. Because bandwidth is a limited space, when one user is occupying it, others must wait their turn. Bandwidth is also the capacity of a network to transmit a given amount of data during a given period.

Bank   The total number of SIMMs or DIMMs that can be simultaneously accessed by the chipset. This is determined by dividing the width of the data bus by the width of the RAM sticks.

Baseband   Digital signaling that has only one signal (a single signal) on the cable at a time. The signals must be in one of three states: one, zero, or idle.

Baseline   A measurement of a network's (or system's) performance when all elements are known to be working properly.

BASIC (Beginners All-Purpose Symbolic Instruction Code)   A commonly used personal-computer language first developed at Dartmouth during the 1960s and popularized by Microsoft.

Basic Disks   A hard disk drive partitioned in the classic way in Windows 2000/XP/ 2003, with a master boot record (MBR) and partition table.

Basic Rate Interface (BRI)   The basic ISDN configuration, which consists of two B channels (which can carry voice or data at rate of 64 Kbps) and one D channel (which carries setup and configuration information, as well as data, at 16 Kbps).

Basic Service Set (BSS)   In wireless networking, a single access point servicing a given area.

Baud   One analog cycle on a telephone line. In the early days of telephone data trans-mission, the baud rate was often analogous to bits-per-second. Due to advanced modu-lation of baud cycles as well as data compression, this is no longer true.

BBS (Bulletin Board System)   A term for dial-up online systems from which users can download software and graphics, send and receive e-mail, and exchange infor-mation. Usually run by individuals from their homes. Although once very popular, BBS sites are rapidly disappearing because of the popularity of the Internet.

Bimodal (Bipartite) Virus   A type of virus that combines the characteristics of boot sector and executable viruses.

Binary Numbers   A number system with a base of 2, unlike the number systems most of us use that have bases of 10 (decimal numbers), 12 (measurement in feet and inches), and 60 (time). Binary numbers are preferred for computers for precision and economy. Building an electronic circuit that can detect the difference between two states (on–off, 0–1) is easier and more inexpensive that one that could detect the differences among ten states (0–9).

Bindery   Security and account database used by default on Novell NetWare 3.*x* servers and available to NetWare 4.*x*, 5.*x*, and 6.*x* servers.

Binding   The process of determining which NICs use which protocols for which transactions. Every protocol installed on a system must be bound to one or more NICs, and every NIC must be bound to one or more specific protocols.

BIOS (Basic Input/Output System)   Classically, the software routines burned onto the system ROM of a PC. More commonly seen as any software that directly controls a particular piece of hardware. A set of programs encoded in read-only memory (ROM) on computers. These programs handle startup operations and the low-level control for hardware such as disk drives, the keyboard, and the monitor.

Bit (Binary Digit)   A single binary digit, typically represented by 1s and 0s. Any device that can be in an on or an off state.

Bluetooth   Bluetooth is a radio-frequency standard that creates a small wireless network between PCs and peripheral devices such as PDAs and printers, input devices like keyboards and mice, and consumer electronics like cell phones, home stereos, televisions, and home security systems. Bluetooth uses a spread-spectrum broadcasting method, switching among any of the 79 frequencies available in the 2.45-GHz range.

BNC Connector   Stands for *British Naval Connector* (or *Bayonet Connector*). A cylindrical-shaped connector used for 10Base2 coaxial cable. All BNC connectors have to be locked into place by rotating the locking ring 90 degrees.

Boolean logic   Boolean logic (named for the 19th-century mathematician George Boole) is a mathematical process in which all values are reduced to either true or false: or in binary, 1 or 0. The TCP/IP ANDing process is an example of Boolean logic.

Boot   To initiate an automatic routine that clears the memory, loads the operating system, and prepares the computer for use. The term *boot* is derived from the phrase "pull yourself up by your bootstraps." PCs must do that because RAM doesn't retain program instructions when the power is turned off. A "cold boot" occurs when the PC is physically switched on, while a "warm boot" enables the system to reset itself without putting a strain on the electronic circuitry. To perform a warm boot, you press the CTRL, ALT, and DELETE keys at the same time, a ritual commonly known as the "three-fingered salute."

BOOTP (Bootstrap Protocol)   This is a component of TCP/IP that allows computers to discover and receive an IP address from a DHCP server prior to booting the OS. Other items that may be discovered during the BOOTP process are the IP address of the default gateway for the subnet and the IP addresses of any name servers.

Boot Sector   The first sector on an IBM-PC hard drive or floppy disk, track 0. The bootup software in ROM tells the computer to load whatever program is found there. If a system disk is read, the program in the boot record directs the computer to the root directory to load MS-DOS. *See* ROM.

Boot Sector Virus   A type of virus that changes the code in the master boot record (MBR) of the hard drive. The virus resides in memory and attempts to infect the MBRs of other drives by spreading to removable media and networked machines.

Border Gateway Protocol (BGP)   An exterior gateway routing protocol that enables groups of routers to share routing information so that efficient, loop-free routes can be established.

bps (bits per second)   A measurement of how fast data is moved from one place to another. A 28.8 modem can move 28,800 bits per second.

Bridge   A device that connects two networks and passes traffic between them based only on the node address, so that traffic between nodes on one network does not appear on the other network. For example, an Ethernet bridge only looks at the Ethernet address. Bridges filter and forward packets based on MAC addresses and operate at Level 2 (the Data Link layer) of the OSI seven-layer model.

Broadband   Analog signaling that sends multiple signals over the cable at the same time. The best example of broadband signaling is cable television. The zero, one, and idle states (*see* Baseband) exist on multiple channels on the same cable.

Broadcast   A broadcast is a packet addressed to all machines. In TCP/IP, the general broadcast address is 255.255.255.255.

Broadcast Address   The address a NIC attaches to a frame when it wants every other NIC on the network to read it.

Browser   A software program specifically designed to retrieve, interpret, and display web pages.

Buffer   Electronic storage, usually DRAM, that holds data moving between two devices. Buffers are used anywhere there is a situation where one device may send or receive data faster or slower than the other device with which it is communicating. For example, the BUFFERS statement in DOS is used to set aside RAM for communication with hard drives.

Bug   A programming error that causes a program or a computer system to perform erratically, produce inconsistent results, or crash. This term was coined when a real bug was found in a circuit of one of the first ENIAC computers.

Building Entrance   The building entrance is where all the cables from the outside world (telephone lines, cables from other buildings, and so on) come into a building.

Bus   A series of wires connecting two or more separate electronic devices, enabling those devices to communicate.

Bus Topology   A network topology in which all computers connect to the network via a central bus cable.

Byte   Eight contiguous bits, the fundamental data unit of personal computers. Storing the equivalent of one character, the byte is also the basic unit of measurement for computer storage. Bytes are counted in powers of two.

CAB Files   Short for "cabinet files." These files are compressed and most commonly used during Microsoft operating system installation to store many smaller files, such as device drivers.

Cable Drop   A cable drop is the location where the cable comes out of the wall.

Cable Modem   High-speed home Internet access that runs through a coax cable laid by a cable company.

Cable Tester   A device that tests the continuity of cables. Some testers also test for electrical shorts, crossed wires, or other electrical characteristics.

Cache   A special area of RAM that stores the data most frequently accessed from the hard drive. Cache memory can optimize the use of your systems.

Cached-Lookup   The A list kept by a DNS server of IP addresses it has already re-solved, so it won't have to re-resolve a FQDN name it has already checked.

Cache Memory   A special section of fast memory chips set aside to store the infor-mation most frequently accessed from RAM.

Cache-Only DNS Servers (Caching-Only DNS Servers)   DNS servers that do not have any Forward Lookup Zones. They will resolve names of systems on the Internet for the network, but are not responsible for telling other DNS servers the names of any clients.

Capturing   A process by which a printer uses a local LPT port that connects to a net-worked printer is called *capturing a printer*. This is usually only done to support older programs that are not smart enough to know how to print directly to a UNC-named printer; it's quite rare today.

Card   Generic term for anything that you can snap into an expansion slot.

CAT 3   Category 3 wire, a TIA /EIA standard for UTP wiring that can operate at up to 16 megabits per second.

CAT 4   Category 4 wire, a TIA /EIA standard for UTP wiring that can operate at up to 20 megabits per second. This is not widely used, except in older Token Ring networks.

CAT 5 Category 5 wire, a TIA /EIA standard for UTP wiring that can operate at up to 100 megabits per second.

CAT 5e Category 5e wire, a TIA /EIA standard for UTP wiring with improved support for 100 megabits per second using two pairs, and support for 1000 megabits per second using four pairs.

CAT 6 Category 6 wire, a TIA /EIA standard for UTP wiring with improved support for 1000 megabits per second.

Category (CAT) Rating A variety of grades called *categories* help network install-ers get the right cable for the right network technology. CAT ratings are officially rated in megahertz (MHz), indicating the highest frequency bandwidth the cable can handle.

CD-R (Compact Disc—Recordable) An improvement on CD-ROM technology that allows for a single write onto the media.

CD-ROM (Compact Disc Read-Only Memory) A read-only compact storage disc for audio or video data. Recordable devices, such as CD-Rs and CD-RWs, are up-dated versions of the older CD-ROM players.

CD-RW (Compact Disc Read/Write) A technology that enables repeated writ-ing and erasing of data to a compact disc designed for such an activity (a CD-RW disc).

CHAP (Challenge Handshake Authentication Protocol) CHAP is the most common remote access protocol. It has the serving system challenge the remote client, which must provide an encrypted password.

Chat A multiparty, real-time text conversation. The Internet's most popular version is known as Internet Relay Chat (IRC), which many groups use to converse in real time with each other.

Checksum A simple error-detection method that adds a numerical value to each data packet, based on the number of data bits in the packet. The receiving node applies the same formula to the data and verifies that the numerical value is the same; if not, the data has been corrupted and must be re-sent.

Chipset Electronic chips that handle all of the fundamental functions of a PC, such as controlling the memory and handling device input/output, which in the original PC were handled by close to 30 different chips. Chipsets usually consist of one, two, or three separate chips to handle all of these functions.

CHS (Cylinder/Heads/Sectors per Track) The initials for the combination of the three critical geometries used to determine the size of a hard drive: cylinders, heads, and sectors per track.

CISC (Complex Instruction-Set Computing) A CPU design that enables the processor to handle more complex instructions from the software at the expense of speed. The Intel *x*86 series (386, 486, Pentium) for PCs are CISC processors.

Cladding   The exterior casing of a network cable. With fiber-optic cabling, the cladding makes the light reflect down the fiber.

Classful Subnet   A subnet that falls into a pre-defined subnet class; for example, 255.255.0.0 is a Class B subnet.

Classless Subnet   A subnet that does not fall into the common categories such as Class A, Class B, and Class C.

Client   A computer program that uses the services of another computer program; software that extracts information from a server. Your autodial phone is a client, and the phone company is its server. Also, a machine that accesses shared resources on a server.

Client/Server   A relationship in which client software obtains services from a server on behalf of a user.

Client/Server Application   An application that performs some or all of its processing on an application server rather than on the client. The client usually only receives the result of the processing.

Client/Server Network   A network that has dedicated server machines and client machines.

Clipboard   A temporary storage space from which captured data can be copied or pasted into other documents.

Clock   An electronic circuit using a quartz crystal to generate evenly spaced pulses at speeds of millions of cycles per second. The pulses are used to synchronize the flow of information through the computer's internal communication channels. Most of the chips on a PC synchronize to this clock. The speed of the clock's signal is called the *clock rate*.

Cluster   1. Groups of sectors organized by the operating system to store files. The number of sectors in a cluster is dependent on the size of the partition and the file system used. When an operating system stores files on disk, it writes those files into dozens or even hundreds of clusters. 2. A pair or group of computers that function as a single unit.

CMOS (Complimentary Metal-Oxide Semiconductor)   Originally, the type of non-volatile RAM that held information about the most basic parts of your PC such as hard drives, floppies, and amount of DRAM. Today, actual CMOS chips have been replaced by "Flash" -type non-volatile RAM. The information is the same, however, and is still called *CMOS*, even though it is now almost always stored on Flash RAM.

Coax   Short for coaxial. Cabling in which an internal conductor is surrounded by another, outer conductor, thus sharing the same axis.

Code   A set of symbols representing characters (for example, ASCII code) or instructions in a computer program (a programmer writes *source* code, which must be translated into *executable* or *machine* code for the computer to use). Used colloquially as a verb—*to code* is to write computer code—and as a noun, "He writes clean/sloppy/bad code."

Collision   The result of two nodes transmitting data packets at the same time on a multiple access network such as the Ethernet. Data packets that collide become corrupted and are unusable.

Collision Domain   A set of Ethernet segments that receive all traffic generated by any node within those segments. Repeaters, amplifiers, and hubs do not create separate collision domains, but bridges, routers, and switches do.

Collision Light   A light on some older hubs and NICs that flickers to indicate when a network collision is detected.

COM   1. In Microsoft operating systems, a device name that refers to the serial communications ports available on your computer. 2. When used as a program extension, .COM indicates an executable program file limited to 64K.

Command   A request, typed from a terminal or embedded in a file, to perform an operation or to execute a particular program.

COMMAND.COM   In DOS and Windows 9x, a file that contains the command processor. This file must be present on the startup disk for DOS to run. COMMAND.COM is usually located in the root directory of your hard drive. Windows NT, 2000, and XP use CMD.EXE instead of COMMAND.COM.

Command Processor   The part of the operating system that accepts input from the user and displays any messages, such as confirmation and error messages.

Common UNIX Printing System (CUPS)   A printing system based on the Internet Printing Protocol (IPP) standard that supports any printer language, although it is most commonly associated with the PostScript language.

Communications Program   A program that makes a computer act as a terminal to another computer. Communications programs usually provide for file transfer between microcomputers and mainframes.

Compression   The process of reducing the size of files, allowing them to be stored using less space and transmitted using less bandwidth. Different compression applications use different methods to reduce file size, such as removing blank spaces, redundant characters, and so on.

Computer   A device or system that is capable of carrying out a sequence of operations in a distinctly and explicitly defined manner. These operations are frequently numeric computations or data manipulations, but they also include data input and output. The capability to branch within sequences is its key feature.

Concentrator   A device that brings together at a common center connections to a particular kind of network (such as Ethernet), and implements that network internally.

CONFIG.SYS   An ASCII text file in the root directory that contains configuration commands. CONFIG.SYS enables the system to be set up to configure high, expanded, and extended memories by the loading of HIMEM.SYS and EMM386.EXE drivers, as well as drivers for non-standard peripheral components.

Connectionless Protocol   A protocol that does not establish and verify a connection between the hosts before sending data; it just sends the data and hopes for the best. This is faster than connection-oriented protocols. UDP is an example of a connectionless protocol.

Connectionless Session   A networking session in which packets are sent without first creating a connection-oriented session. Network protocols use connectionless sessions only for data that won't cause problems if it doesn't make it to the intended recipient.

Connection-Oriented Protocol   A protocol that establishes a connection between two hosts before transmitting data and verifies receipt before closing the connection between the hosts. TCP is an example of a connection-oriented protocol.

Contiguous   Adjacent; placed one next to the other.

Control Panel   A collection of Windows applets (small, specialized programs) that are used to configure various hardware, software, and services in a system.

Controller Card   A card adapter that connects devices, like a disk drive, to the main computer bus/motherboard.

Conventional Memory   In any IBM PC-compatible computer, the first 640KB of the computer's RAM.

Copy Backup   A type of backup similar to Normal or Full, in that all selected files on a system are backed up. This type of backup does *not* change the archive bit of the files being backed up.

CPU (Central Processing Unit)   The "brain" of the computer. The microprocessor that handles the primary calculations for the computer. Intel and American Micro Devices (AMD) are the largest CPU manufacturers, producing CPUs with names such as Pentium 4 and Athlon XP.

CRC (Cyclical Redundancy Check)   A mathematical method that is used to check for errors in long streams of transmitted data with high accuracy. Before data is sent, the main computer uses the data to calculate a CRC value from the data's contents. If the receiver calculates a different CRC value from the received data, the data was corrupted during transmission and is resent. Ethernet packets have a CRC code.

Crimpers   Also called *crimping tool*. The tool used to secure a connector, such as an RJ-45 connector, onto the end of a cable.

Cross-Linked Files   A file-storage error that occurs when the file allocation table indicates that two files claim the same disk cluster. These occur when the system is abnormally halted.

Crossover Cable   A special UTP cable used to connect hubs or to connect network cards without a hub. Crossover cables reverse the sending and receiving wire pairs from one end to the other.

Crossover Port   Special port in a hub that crosses the sending and receiving wires, thus removing the need for a crossover cable to connect the hubs. *See* Uplink Port.

Cross-Platform Support   This refers to standards created to enable terminals (or now operating systems) from different companies to interact with one another.

Crosstalk   Electrical signal interference between two cables that are in close proximity to each other.

CRT (Cathode Ray Tube)   The tube of a monitor in which rays of electrons are beamed onto a phosphorescent screen to produce images. Monitors are sometimes called *CRT Displays*.

CSMA/CA (Carrier Sense Multiple Access with Collision Avoidance)
This access method is used mainly on Apple networks and is also implemented on wireless networks. With CSMA/CA, before hosts send out data, they send out a signal that checks to make sure that the network is free of other signals. If data is detected on the wire, the hosts wait a random time period before trying again. If the wire is free, the data is sent out.

CSMA/CD (Carrier Sense Multiple Access with Collision Detection)
The access method Ethernet systems use in LAN technologies, enabling packets of data to flow through the network and ultimately reach address locations. Known as a *contention* protocol, hosts on CSMA/CD networks send out data without checking to see if the wire is free first. If a collision occurs, then both hosts wait a random time period before retransmitting the data.

CSU/DSU (Channel Service Unit/Data Service Unit)   A piece of equipment that connects a leased line from the telephone company to a customer's equipment (such as a router). It performs line encoding and conditioning functions, and it often has a loopback function for testing.

Cursor   A symbol on a display screen that indicates the position at which the next character entered will be displayed. The symbol often blinks so that it is more visible.

Cyrix   Company that made CPUs in direct competition with Intel and AMD. Now owned by VIA Technologies.

Daily Backup   Also called a *daily copy backup*, this backup type makes a copy of all files that have been changed on that day without changing the archive bits of those files.

Daisy-chain   A method of connecting together several devices along a bus and managing the signals for each device.

DAT (Digital Audio Tape)   Higher storage capacity tape recording system that uses digital recording methods. Used for digital audio and video as well as data backups.

Database   A collection of data that is organized in such as way that users can easily input and retrieve specific information. Users search databases via structured requests called *queries*. Examples of database programs include Microsoft Access, Microsoft SQL Server, dBase, and so on. *See* DBMS (Database Management System).

Datagram   Another term for *network packets* or *frames*. *See* Packets and Frames.

Data Link Control (DLC)   A network protocol used for many years to link PCs to mainframe computers. Because Hewlett-Packard adopted the DLC protocol for use by network printers, DLC enjoyed a much longer life than it probably should have—given the existence of so many alternatives. All versions of Windows, including Windows XP, still support DLC.

Data Link Layer   *See* OSI Seven-Layer Model.

DB-15   DB connector (female) used in 10Base5 networks. *See also* DIX and AUI.

DB Connectors   D-shaped connectors used for a variety of different connections in the PC and networking world. Can be either male or female, with a varying number of pins or sockets.

DBMS (Database Management System)   A systematic approach to storing, updating, securing, and retrieving information stored as data files. Each data file contains any number of *records*, which in turn store specific data items in different *fields*. For example, Microsoft Active Directory uses a database file (NTDS.DIT) to store user account records. Each user account record contains individual fields such as the user name, password, group membership, and so on.

Debug   To detect, trace, and eliminate errors in computer programs.

Dedicated Circuit   A circuit that runs from a breaker box to specific outlets.

Dedicated Server   A machine that does not use any client functions, only server functions.

Dedicated Telephone Line   A telephone line that is an always open, or connected, circuit. Dedicated telephone lines usually do not have numbers.

Default   A software function or operation that occurs automatically unless the user specifies something else.

Default Gateway   In a TCP/IP network, the nearest router to a particular host. This router's IP address is part of the necessary TCP/IP configuration for communicating with multiple networks using IP.

Defragmentation (DEFRAG)   A procedure in which all the files on a hard disk are rewritten on disk so that all parts of each file are written in contiguous clusters. The result is an improvement of up to 75 percent of the disk's speed during retrieval operations.

Denial of Service (DoS) Attacks   Also known as *flooding attacks*. DoS attacks flood the network with so many requests that it becomes overwhelmed and ceases functioning.

Deterministic   This means access to the wire is granted in a predictable way, rather than through a random process like CSMA/CD. Token passing is an example of a deterministic method to resolve which machine should have access to the wire at a given moment.

Device Driver   A subprogram to control communications between the computer and some peripheral hardware.

DHCP (Dynamic Host Configuration Protocol)   A service that enables a DHCP server to set TCP/IP settings automatically for a network's DHCP clients.

DHCP Lease   When a system requests DHCP IP information, the DHCP server creates a DHCP lease for the requested IP information, which allows the client to use these settings for a certain amount of time.

DHCP Scope   The pool of IP addresses that a DHCP server may allocate to clients requesting IP addresses, or other IP information like DNS server addresses.

Differential Backup   Similar to an incremental backup in that it backs up the files that have been changed since the last backup. This type of backup does not change the state of the archive bit.

Digital Certificate   A public encryption key signed with the digital signature from a trusted third party called a *certificate authority (CA)*. This key serves to validate the identity of its holder when that person or company sends data to other parties.

Digital Signature   A string of characters created from a private encryption key, which verifies a sender's identity to those who receive encrypted data or messages.

Digital Subscriber Line (DSL)   A high-speed Internet connection technology that uses a regular telephone line for connectivity. DSL comes in several varieties, including Asynchronous (ADSL) and Synchronous (SDSL), and many speeds. Typical home-user DSL connections are ADSL with a download speed of up to 1.5 Mbps and an upload speed of up to 384 Kbps.

DIMM (Dual In-Line Memory Module)   A type of DRAM packaging, similar to SIMMs with the distinction that each side of each tab inserted into the system performs a separate function. Comes in 72- and 144-pin Small Outline (SO) as well as 144-, 168-, and 184-pin versions.

Direct Cable Connection   A direct serial-to-serial, parallel-to-parallel, or infra-red-to-infrared port connection between two PCs.

Direct Current (DC)   A type of electricity where the flow of electrons is in a complete circle.

Directory   A logical container of files and other directories; synonymous with *folder*. Typically implemented as a file that contains pointers (directions) to files or other directories.

Directory Service   A distributed database that contains all user, group, and security information for a network structure such as a *domain*. Microsoft Active Directory, Novell NetWare Directory Service (NDS, later called eDirectory), and Banyan Vines are examples of directory services.

Direct-Sequence Spread-Spectrum (DSSS)   A spread-spectrum broadcasting method defined in the 802.11 standard that sends data out on different frequencies at the same time.

Disk Drive Controller   The circuitry that controls the physical operations of the floppy disks and/or hard disks connected to the computer.

Disk Management   A snap-in available with the Microsoft Management Console that allows a user to configure the various disks installed on a system; available from the Administrative Tools area of the Control Panel.

Disk Mirroring   Process by which data is written simultaneously to two or more disk drives. Read and write speed is decreased but redundancy, in case of catastrophe, is increased. Considered RAID level 1.

Disk Striping   Process by which data is spread among multiple (at least two) drives. It increases speed for both reads and writes of data. Considered RAID level 0, because it does *not* provide fault tolerance.

Disk Striping with Parity   Provides fault tolerance by writing data across multiple drives, and includes an additional drive, called a *parity drive*, that stores information to rebuild the data contained on the other drives. Disk Striping with Parity requires at least three physical disks: two for the data and a third for the parity drive. It provides data redundancy at RAID levels 3–5 with different options.

Display   A device that enables information, either textual or pictorial, to be seen but not permanently recorded. Sometimes called the *monitor*, the most widely used kind is the cathode-ray tube, or CRT; liquid crystal diode, or LCD, displays are also popular.

Distributed Coordination Function (DCF)   One of two methods of collision avoidance defined by the 802.11 standard and the only one currently implemented. DCF specifies much stricter rules for sending data onto the network media.

Dithering   A technique for smoothing out digitized images; using alternating colors in a pattern to produce perceived color detail.

DIX Connector (Digital, Intel, Xerox)   The DIX standard was the original implementation of Ethernet. The DIX connector is the standard connector used with 10Base5 Ethernet, also known as the *AUI*.

DLC   *See* Data Link Control (DLC).

DLL (Dynamic Link Library)   A file of executable functions or data that can be used by a Windows application. Typically, a DLL provides one or more particular functions, and a program accesses the functions by creating links to the DLL.

DLT (Digital Linear Tape)   Huge data capacity tapes used for tape backups.

DMA (Direct Memory Access)   A technique that some PC hardware devices use to transfer data to and from the memory without requiring the use of the CPU.

DMZ (Demilitarized Zone)   A lightly protected or unprotected network positioned between your firewall and the Internet.

DNS (Domain Name Service or System)   A TCP/IP name resolution service that resolves host names to IP addresses.

DNS Domain   A specific branch of the DNS name space. First-level DNS domains include .com, .gov, and .edu.

DNS Resolver Cache   A cache used by Windows workstation clients to keep track of previously resolved DNS information.

DNS Tree   A hierarchy of DNS domains and individual computer names organized into a tree-like structure. At the top of a DNS tree is the root.

Document   A medium and the data recorded on it for human use; for example, a report sheet or book. By extension, any record that has permanence and that can be read by a human or a machine.

Documentation   A collection of organized documents or the information recorded in documents. Also instructional material specifying the inputs, operations, and outputs of a computer program or system.

Domain   A term used to describe logical security boundaries that contain groupings of users, computers, or networks. In Microsoft networking, a domain is a group of computers and users that share a common account database and a common security policy. For the Internet, a domain is a group of computers that share a common element in their hierarchical name. Other types of domains also exist, such as collision domains.

Domain Controller   A Microsoft Windows NT/2000/2003 machine that stores the user and server account information for its domain in a central database. On a Windows NT domain controller, the database is called the *Security Accounts Manager,* or *SAM* database, and is stored as part of the registry. Windows 2000/2003 domain controllers store all account and security information in the *Active Directory* directory service.

Domain Users and Groups   Users and groups that are defined across an entire network domain.

DOS (Disk Operating System)   The set of programming that allows a program to interact with the computer. Examples of disk operating systems include Microsoft's MS-DOS, IBM's PC-DOS and OS/2, and Apple's MacOS System 7. Microsoft's Windows 3.1 was not technically an operating system because it still required MS-DOS to work, but it was often referred to as one. All modern versions of Windows (95/98/Me/NT/2000/XP/2003, Mac OS (9/X/X.2), and all versions of Linux are true disk operating systems.

DOSKEY A DOS utility that enables you to type more than one command on a line, store and retrieve previously used DOS commands, create stored macros, and customize all DOS commands.

DOS Prompt A letter representing the disk drive, followed by the greater-than sign (>), which together inform you that the operating system is ready to receive a command.

Dot-Matrix Printer A printer that creates each character from an array of dots. Pins striking a ribbon against the paper, one pin for each dot position, form the dots. The printer may be a serial printer (printing one character at a time) or a line printer.

Double Word A group of 32 binary digits. Four bytes.

Download The transfer of information from a remote computer system to the user's system. Opposite of upload.

Downstream Neighbor A receiving node in a Token Ring network is the downstream neighbor to the sending node.

DPI (Dots Per Inch) A measure of printer resolution that counts the dots the device can produce per linear inch.

DRAM (Dynamic Random Access Memory) The memory used to store data in most personal computers. DRAM stores each bit in a "cell" composed of a transistor and a capacitor. Because the capacitor in a DRAM cell can only hold a charge for a few milliseconds, DRAM must be continually refreshed, or rewritten, to retain its data.

Drive Duplexing The process of writing identical data to two hard drives on different controllers at the same time, to provide data redundancy.

Drive Mirroring The process of writing identical data to two hard drives on the same controller at the same time, to provide data redundancy.

DSL (Digital Subscriber Line) *See* Digital Subscriber Line (DSL).

DSP (Digital Signal Processor) A specialized microprocessor-like device that processes digital signals at the expense of other capabilities, much as the FPU is optimized for math functions. DSPs are used in such specialized hardware as high-speed modems, multimedia sound cards, MIDI equipment, and real-time video capture and compression.

Dumb Terminal A device that enables a user to access programs and data on mainframe computers. Dumb terminals resemble personal computers in that they have a monitor, keyboard, and possibly a mouse, but they are not stand-alone computing devices. All have some sort of networking device, such as a modem or network interface card (NIC).

Duplexing Also called *disk duplexing* or *drive duplexing*, duplexing is similar to mirroring, in that data is written to and read from two physical drives for fault tolerance.

In addition, separate controllers are used for each drive, for both additional fault tolerance and additional speed. Considered RAID level 1.

DVI (Digital Video Interface) While traditional CRT monitors are analog, LCD monitors are digital. DVI is the digital video interface that is most often seen on LCD flat-panel monitors.

Dynamic Link A method of linking data so that it is shared by two or more programs. When data is changed in one program, the data is likewise changed in the other.

Dynamic Link Library (DLL) *See* DLL (Dynamic Link Library).

Dynamic Routing Process by which routers in an internetwork automatically exchange information with all other routers, enabling them to build their own list of routes to various networks, called a *routing table*. Dynamic routing requires a dynamic routing protocol, such as OSPF or RIP.

Dynamic Routing Protocol A protocol that supports the building of automatic routing tables, such as OSPF (Open Shortest Path First) or RIP (Routing Information Protocol).

EDB (External Data Bus) The primary data highway of all computers. Everything in your computer is tied either directly or indirectly to the external data bus. *See also* Frontside Bus and Backside Bus.

EDO (Enhanced Data Out) An improvement on FPM DRAM in that more data can be read before the RAM must be refreshed.

EEPROM (Electrically Erasable Programmable Read-Only Memory) A type of ROM chip that can be erased and reprogrammed electrically. EEPROMs were the most common BIOS storage device until the advent of Flash ROM.

EIA/TIA (Electronics Industry Association/Telecommunications Industry Association) The standards body that defines most of the standards for computer network cabling. Most of these standards are defined under the EIA/TIA 568 standard. Also known as the TIA/EIA.

EIDE (Enhanced IDE) A marketing concept by Western Digital that consolidated four improvements for IDE drives. These improvements included support for drives with capacity beyond 504MB, four devices in a system, increase in drive throughput, and nonhard drive devices. *See* ATAPI, Parallel ATA, and PIO.

EISA (Enhanced ISA) An improved expansion bus, based on the ISA bus, with a top speed of 8.33 MHz, a 32-bit data path, and a high degree of self-configuration. Backward-compatible with legacy ISA cards.

E-mail (Electronic Mail) A service that enables users to communicate via written messages routed through the Internet. E-mail messages may contain HTML formatting and file *attachments*. E-mail applications include Microsoft Outlook, Pegasus, Eudora, and others. E-mail can be sent automatically to a large number of addresses, known as a *mailing list*.

E-mail Server   Also known as *mail server*. Server that accepts incoming mail, sorts the mail for recipients into mailboxes, and sends mail to other servers using the Simple Mail Transfer Protocol (SMTP) and Post Office Protocol (POP) e-mail protocols.

Emergency Repair Disk (ERD)   This disk saves critical boot files and partition information and is our main tool for fixing boot problems in Windows 2000/XP/2003.

EMI (Electro-Magnetic Interference)   An electrical interference from one device to another, resulting in poor performance in the device capabilities. This is similar to having static on your TV while running a hair dryer, or placing two monitors too close together and getting a "shaky" screen.

EMM386.EXE   An expanded memory emulator that enables DOS applications to use the extended memory as if it were expanded memory. EMM386.EXE also enables the user to load device drivers and programs into the upper memory area.

Encapsulation   The process of putting the packets from one protocol inside the packets of another protocol. An example of this is TCP/IP encapsulation in NetWare servers, which places IPX/SPX packets inside TCP/IP packets. This encapsulation enables Novell NetWare to use TCP/IP for transport while still allowing the network operating system to gain the data it needs from IPX/SPX.

Encryption   A method of securing messages by scrambling and encoding each packet as it is sent across an unsecured medium, such as the Internet. Each encryption level provides multiple standards and options.

EPROM (Erasable Programmable Read-Only Memory)   A special form of ROM that can be erased by high-intensity ultraviolet light, and then rewritten or reprogrammed.

Equipment Rack   A metal structure used in equipment rooms to secure network hardware devices and patch panels. Devices designed to fit in such a rack use a height measurement called *units*, or simply *U*.

Equipment Room   A central location for computer or telephone equipment and, most important, centralized cabling. All cables will usually run to the equipment room from the rest of the installation.

ESD (Electro-Static Discharge)   The movement of electrons from one body to another. ESD is a real menace to PCs as it can cause permanent damage to semiconductors.

ESDI (Enhanced Small Device Interface)   Second-generation hard drives, distinct from their predecessors, ST506, by greater data density and lack of dependence on CMOS settings. Completely obsolete.

Ethernet   Name coined by Xerox for the first standard of network cabling and protocols. Ethernet is based on a bus topology. The IEEE 802.3 subcommittee defines the current Ethernet specifications.

Event Viewer   A utility made available as an MMC snap-in in Windows 2000/XP/2003 that enables a user to monitor various system events, including network bandwidth usage and CPU utilization.

Executable Virus   Viruses that are literally extensions of executables and that are unable to exist by themselves. Once an infected executable file is run, the virus loads into memory, adding copies of itself to other EXEs that are subsequently run.

Expansion Bus   Set of wires going to the CPU, governed by the Expansion Bus Crystal, directly connected to expansion slots of varying types (ISA, PCI, AGP, and so forth). Depending on the type of slots, the expansion bus runs at a percentage of the main system speed (8.33–66 MHz).

Expansion Slot   A receptacle connected to the computer's expansion bus, designed to accept adapters.

Extended Basic Service Set (EBSS)   A single wireless access point servicing a given area that has been extended by adding more access points.

External Data Bus (EDB)   The primary data highway of all computers. Everything in your computer is tied either directly or indirectly to the external data bus. *See also* Frontside Bus and Backside Bus.

External Network Address   A number added to the MAC address of every computer on an IPX/SPX network, which defines every computer on the network; this is often referred to as a *network number*.

External Network Number   A special number, added to the MAC address of every computer on an IPX/SPX network, that provides each computer on the network with a unique identifier.

External Threats   Threats to your network through external means; examples include virus attacks and the exploitation of users, security holes in the OS, or the network hardware itself.

FAQ (Frequently Asked Questions)   Common abbreviation coined by BBS users and spread to Usenet and the Internet. This is a list of questions and answers that pertain to a particular topic, maintained so that users new to the group don't all bombard the group with similar questions. Examples are "What is the name of the actor who plays X on this show, and was he in anything else?" or "Can anyone list all of the books by this author in the order that they were published so that I can read them in that order?" The common answer to this type of question is "Read the FAQ!"

Fast Ethernet   Any of several flavors of Ethernet that operate at 100 megabits per second.

FAT (File Allocation Table)   A FAT is a hidden table of every cluster on a hard disk. The FAT records how files are stored in distinct clusters. The address of the first cluster of the file is stored in the directory file. In the FAT entry for the first cluster is the address of the second cluster used to store that file. In the entry for the second cluster for that file is the address for the third cluster, and so on. This table is the only way for DOS to know where to access files. There are two FATs created, mirror images of each other, in case one is destroyed or damaged.

FAT16   File allocation table that uses 16 bits for addressing clusters. Commonly used with DOS and Windows 95 systems.

FAT32   File allocation table that uses 32 bits for addressing clusters. Commonly used with Windows 98 and Windows Me systems. Some Windows 2000/XP systems also use FAT32, although most use the more robust NTFS.

Fault Tolerance   The capability of any system to continue functioning after some part of the system has failed. RAID is an example of a hardware device that provides fault tolerance.

FDDI (Fiber Distributed Data Interface)   A standard for transmitting data on optical fiber cables at a rate of around 100 million bps.

Federal Communications Commission (FCC)   In the United States, the FCC regulates public airwaves and rates PCs and other equipment according to the amount of radiation emitted.

Fiber Optics   A high-speed physical medium for transmitting data, which is made of high-purity glass fibers sealed within a flexible opaque tube. Much faster than conventional copper wire such as coaxial cable.

File   A collection of any form of data that is stored beyond the time of execution of a single job. A file may contain program instructions or data, which may be numerical, textual, or graphical information.

File and Print Sharing Service   A service running on Windows that enables the system to share its resources.

File Format   The type of file, such as picture or text; represented as a suffix at the end of the filename (text = TXT or .txt, and so forth).

File Fragmentation   The allocation of a file in a noncontiguous sector on a disk. Fragmentation occurs because of multiple deletions and write operations.

Filename   A name assigned to a file when the file is first written on a disk. Every file on a disk within the same folder must have a unique name. Prior to Windows 95, filenames were restricted to 11 characters—8 characters for the filename and 3 characters for the extension—hence, the so-called 8.3 naming convention. Starting with Windows 95, you may use up to 255 characters for filenames on a Windows machine. Macintosh filenames are limited to 31 characters. Filenames can contain nearly any character (including spaces). The list of forbidden characters varies according to operating system, but often include the following: \ / : * ? " < > |

File Server   A computer designated to store software, courseware, administrative tools, and other data on a local or wide area network. It "serves" this information to other computers via the network when users enter their personal access codes.

Fire Rating   Ratings developed by Underwriters Laboratories and the National Electrical Code (NEC) to define the risk of network cables burning and creating noxious fumes and smoke.

Firewall   A device or application that restricts traffic between a local network and the Internet based on the type of data transmitted.

FireWire   An IEEE 1394 standard to send wide-band signals over a thin connector system that plugs into TVs, VCRs, TV cameras, PCs, and so forth. This serial bus developed by Apple and Texas Instruments enables connection of 60 devices at speeds ranging from 100 to 800 megabits per second.

Flash ROM   A type of ROM technology that can be electrically reprogrammed while still in the PC. Flash is overwhelmingly the most common storage medium of BIOS in PCs today, because it can be upgraded without even having to open the computer on most systems.

Flat Name Space   A naming convention that gives each device only one name that must be unique. NetBIOS uses a flat name space. TCP/IP's DNS uses a hierarchical name space.

Floppy Disk   A removable and widely used data storage medium that uses a magnetically coated flexible disk of Mylar enclosed in a plastic envelope or case.

Font   A set of consistent size, shape, or style of printer characters, including alphabetic and numeric characters and other signs and symbols.

Forward Lookup Zones   Special storage areas that hold the IP addresses and names of systems for a particular domain or domains. Forward Lookup Zones are contained within authoritative DNS servers.

FPU (Floating Point Unit)   A formal term for the math coprocessor (also called a *numeric processor*). This is a specialized processor that handles certain calculations faster than the CPU. A math coprocessor calculates using floating point math (which allows for decimals), whereas the CPU can only deal with integers. Intel's 486 and Pentium chips and Motorola's PowerPC have an FPU built into the CPU chip, whereas earlier designs, such as Intel's 80387, needed a separate chip to be installed.

FQDN (Fully Qualified Domain Name)   The complete DNS name of a system, from its host name to the top-level domain name. For example, mikespc.houston.totalsem.com is an FQDN.

Frame   A defined series of binary data that is the basic container for a discrete amount of data moving across a network. Also commonly called a *packet*.

Frame Check Sequence (FCS)   A sequence of bits placed in a frame that is used to check the primary data for errors.

Frame Relay   An extremely efficient data transmission technique used to send digital information such as voice, data, LAN, and WAN traffic quickly and cost-efficiently to many destinations from one port. Frame relay switches packets end-to-end much faster than X.25 but with no guarantee of data integrity.

Freeware   Software that is distributed for free, with no licensing fee.

Frequency-Hopping Spread-Spectrum (FHSS)   A spread-spectrum broadcasting method defined in the 802.11 standard that sends data on one frequency at a time, constantly shifting (or *hopping*) frequencies.

Frontside Bus   Name for the wires that connect the CPU to the main system RAM. Generally runs at speeds of 66–533 MHz. Distinct from the expansion bus and the backside bus, even though the frontside bus shares wires with the former.

FRU (Field Replaceable Unit)   Any part of a PC that is considered to be replaceable "in the field," that is, a customer location. There is no official list of FRUs; it is usually a matter of policy by the repair center.

FTP (File Transfer Protocol)   A service that enables computers to transfer and store data files to and from FTP servers quickly using the FTP protocol. The FTP service is built into all modern network operating systems. Examples of third-party FTP clients include Cute FTP, WS-FTP, and LeechFTP.

Full Control   A standard NTFS permission that allows users full access over a file or folder.

Full-Duplex   Describes any device that can send and receive data simultaneously.

Function Key   A keyboard key that gives an instruction to a computer, as opposed to keys that produce letters, numbers, marks of punctuation, and so forth.

Gateway   1. A hardware or software setup that translates between two dissimilar protocols. For example, Prodigy has a gateway that translates among its internal, proprietary e-mail format, and Internet e-mail format. 2. Any mechanism for providing access to another system; for example, AOL might be called a *gateway* to the Internet. *See* Default Gateway.

GIF (Graphics Interchange Format)   A method of storing graphics developed for CompuServe in the early 1980s. Because GIF is a compressed format, it takes up much less disk space than conventional file formats and can, therefore, be transmitted faster over phone lines. GIF is a non-lossy format, meaning that no data is lost when an image is converted to GIF, but the format is limited to 8-bit graphics, or 256 colors.

Giga-   The prefix that generally refers to the quantity 1,073,741,824. One gigabyte would be 1,073,741,824 bytes. With frequencies, in contrast, giga- often refers to one billion. One gigahertz would be 1,000,000,000 hertz.

Gigabit Ethernet   *See* 1000BaseT.

Gigabyte   1024 megabytes.

Global Users and Groups   Users and groups that are defined for an entire Windows domain.

Gopher   A widely successful method of making menus of material available over the Internet. Gopher is a client/server-style program, which requires that the user have a Gopher Client program. Although Gopher spread rapidly across the globe in only a couple of years, it has been largely supplanted by HTTP, also known as the *World Wide Web*. Thousands of Gopher Servers are still on the Internet and they will probably be with us for awhile.

Graphic   A computer-generated picture produced on a computer screen or paper, ranging from simple line or bar graphs to colorful and detailed images.

Green PC   A computer system designed to operate in an energy-efficient manner.

Group Policy   A feature of Windows' Active Directory that enables an administrator to apply policy settings, such as desktop configuration or security settings, to network users *en masse*.

Group Policy Objects (GPOs)   A Group Policy Object (GPO) enables network administrators to define multiple rights and permissions to entire sets of users all at one time.

Groups   Collections of network users who share similar tasks and need similar permissions; defined to make administration tasks easier.

GroupWare   Software that serves the group and makes the group as a whole more productive and efficient in group tasks, for example Group Scheduling.

GUI (Graphical User Interface)   The method by which a computer and a user interact. Early interfaces were text-based; that is, the user "talked" to the computer by typing and the computer responded with text on a CRT. A GUI, on the other hand, enables the user to interact with the computer graphically, by manipulating icons that represent programs or documents with a mouse or other pointing device.

Half-Duplex   Any device that can only send or receive data at any given moment. Most Ethernet transmissions are half-duplex.

Handshaking   A procedure performed by modems, terminals, and computers to verify that communication has been correctly established.

Hang   When a computer freezes, so that it does not respond to keyboard commands, it is said to "hang" or to have "hung." Synonymous with *freeze* or *frozen*, and *halt* or *halted*.

Hang Time   The number of seconds a too-often-hung computer is airborne after you've thrown it out a second-story window.

Hard Drive   A data-recording system using solid disks of magnetic material turning at high speeds.

Hardware   Physical computer equipment such as electrical, electronic, magnetic, and mechanical devices. Anything in the computer world that you can hold in your hand. A floppy drive is hardware; Microsoft Word is not.

Hardware Abstraction Layer (HAL)   A part of the Windows NT/2000/XP/2003 operating system that separates system-specific device drivers from the system hardware.

Hardware Compatibility List (HCL)   A list that is maintained by Microsoft that names all the hardware that is supported by an operating system. This list is helpful to use when upgrading a system; with a quick glance, you can make sure that support is available for all the devices in a system before you begin the upgrade.

Hardware Profile   A list of devices that Windows automatically enables or disables in the Device Manager, depending on what devices the system detects.

Hardware Protocol   A hardware protocol defines many aspects of a network, from the packet type to the cabling and connectors used.

Hardware Tools   Physical tools used to configure a network, including cable testers, protocol analyzers, hardware loopback devices, and toners.

Hayes Command Set   A standardized set of instructions used to control modems. Examples are

- **AT**   Attention (used to start commands)
- **ATDT**   Attention Dial Tone
- **ATDP**   Attention Dial Pulse
- **ATH**   Attention Hang Up

Hex (Hexadecimal)   Hex symbols based on a numbering system of 16 (computer shorthand for binary numbers), using ten digits and six letters to condense 0s and 1s to binary numbers. Hex is represented by digits 0 through 9 and alpha *A* through *F*, so that 09h has a value of 9, and 0Ah has a value of 10.

Hierarchical Name Space   A naming scheme where the full name of each object includes its position within the hierarchy. An example of a hierarchical name is www.totalseminars.com, which includes not only the host name, but also the domain name. DNS uses a hierarchical name space scheme for Fully Qualified Domain Names (FQDNs).

High Resolution   Using a sufficient number of pixels in display monitors or dots per inch when printing, to produce well-defined text characters and smoothly defined curves in graphic images.

HIMEM.SYS A DOS device driver that configures extended memory and high memory so that programs conforming to XMS can access it.

HMA (High Memory Area) The first 64K of memory above 1 megabyte. Programs that conform to XMS can use HMA as a direct extension of conventional memory. Most of the portions of DOS that must be loaded into conventional memory can be loaded into the HMA.

Homepage The web page that your browser is set to use when it starts up or the main web page for a business, organization, or person. Also, the main page in any collection of web pages.

Home Radio Frequency (HomeRF) An implementation of the IEEE 802.11 wireless Ethernet standard that is intended for home use. Not for use in large business network environments.

Honey Pot An area of a network that an administrator sets up for the express purpose of attracting a computer hacker. If a hacker takes the bait, the network's important resources are unharmed and network personnel can analyze the attack to predict and protect against future attacks, making the network more secure.

Horizontal Cabling Cabling that connects the equipment room to the work area.

Host A single device (usually a computer) on a TCP/IP network that has an IP address; any device that can be the source or destination of a data packet. Also, in the mainframe world, a computer that is made available for use by multiple people simultaneously.

Host ID The portion of an IP address that defines a specific machine.

HOSTS File A static text file that resides on a computer and is used to resolve DNS host names to IP addresses. The HOSTS file is checked before the machine sends a name resolution request to a DNS name server. The HOSTS file has no extension.

HTML (HyperText Markup Language) An ASCII-based script-like language for creating hypertext documents like those on the World Wide Web.

HTTP (HyperText Transfer Protocol) Extremely fast protocol used for network file transfers in the WWW environment.

HTTP Over SSL (HTTPS) A secure form of HTTP, used commonly for Internet business transactions or any time where a secure connection is required. *See also* HTTP (HyperText Transfer Protocol) and SSL (Secure Sockets Layer).

Hub A hardware device that sits at the center of a star topology network, providing a common point for the connection of network devices. In a 10BaseT Ethernet network, the hub contains the electronic equivalent of a properly terminated bus cable; in a Token Ring network, the hub contains the electronic equivalent of a ring.

Hybrid A mix or blend of two different topologies. A star bus topology is a hybrid of the star and bus topologies.

HyperText A document that has been marked up to enable a user to select words or pictures within the document, click them, and connect to further information. The basis of the World Wide Web.

HyperText Transport Protocol with SSL (HTTPS) A protocol developed by Netscape for transmitting private documents over the Internet. HTTPS is a file or web page that uses SSL to encrypt sensitive data.

IANA (Internet Assigned Numbers Authority) The organization responsible for assigning public IP addresses.

IBM-Type Data Connector/Universal Data Connector (IDC/UDC) A unique hermaphroditic connector designed by IBM for Token Ring networks.

ICF (Internet Connection Firewall) A software firewall built into Windows XP that protects your system from unauthorized access from the Internet.

ICS (Internet Connection Sharing) Also known simply as *Internet sharing,* a term used to describe the technique of enabling more than one computer to access the Internet simultaneously using a single Internet connection. When you use Internet sharing, you connect an entire LAN to the Internet using a single public IP address.

IDE (Intelligent or Integrated Drive Electronics) A PC specification for small- to medium-sized hard drives in which the controlling electronics for the drive are part of the drive itself, speeding up transfer rates and leaving only a simple adapter (or *paddle*). IDE only supported two drives per system of no more than 504 megabytes each and has been completely supplanted by Enhanced IDE. EIDE supports four drives of over 8 gigabytes each and more than doubles the transfer rate. The more common name for PATA drives. *See* ATA (AT Attachment).

IEEE (Institute of Electronic and Electrical Engineers) IEEE is the leading standards-setting group in the United States.

IEEE 802.1 IEEE subcommittee that defined the standards for Higher Layer LAN Protocols.

IEEE 802.2 IEEE subcommittee that defined the standards for Logical Link Control.

IEEE 802.3 IEEE subcommittee that defined the standards for CSMA/CD (a.k.a. *Ethernet*).

IEEE 802.4 IEEE subcommittee that defined the standards for token bus.

IEEE 802.5 IEEE subcommittee that defined the standards for Token Ring.

IEEE 802.6 IEEE subcommittee that defined the standards for MAN (metropolitan area network).

IEEE 802.7 IEEE subcommittee that defined the standards for broadband.

IEEE 802.8 IEEE subcommittee that defined the standards for fiber optic.

IEEE 802.9   IEEE subcommittee that defined the standards for isochronous LAN.

IEEE 802.10   IEEE subcommittee that defined the standards for security.

IEEE 802.11   IEEE subcommittee that defined the standards for wireless.

IEEE 802.12   IEEE subcommittee that defined the standards for demand priority/ 100BaseVG.

IEEE 802.14   IEEE subcommittee that defined the standards for cable modems.

IETF (Internet Engineering Task Force)   The primary standards organization for the Internet.

IFCONFIG   A command-line utility for Linux servers and workstations that displays the current TCP/IP configuration of the machine, similar to IPCONFIG and WINIPCFG for Windows systems.

IMAP (Internet Message Access Protocol)   An alternative to POP3. IMAP retrieves e-mail from an e-mail server, like POP3; the main difference is that IMAP uses TCP/IP port 143.

Impedance   The amount of resistance to an electrical signal on a wire. It is used as a relative measure of the amount of data a cable can handle.

Incremental Backup   A type of backup that backs up all files that have their archive bits turned on, meaning they have been changed since the last backup. This type of backup turns the archive bits off after the files have been backed up.

Independent Basic Service Set (IBSS)   A basic unit of organization in wireless networks formed by two or more wireless nodes communicating in ad-hoc mode.

Infrastructure Mode   Wireless networks running in infrastructure mode use one or more wireless access points to connect the wireless network nodes centrally. This configuration is similar to the *star topology* of a wired network.

Inheritance   A method of assigning user permissions, in which folder permissions flow downward into subfolders.

Insulating Jacket   The insulating jacket is the outside part of a fiber-optic cable that holds it all together.

Interlaced   TV/video systems in which the electron beam writes every other line, then retraces itself to a second pass to complete the final framed image. Originally, this reduced magnetic line paring, but took twice as long to paint, which added some flicker in graphic images.

Internal Network   A LAN that resides behind a router, modem, or firewall.

Internal Network Address   A number added to MAC addresses on an IPX/SPX network that define the servers on that network.

Internal Threats   All the things that a network's own users do to create problems on the network. Examples include accidental deletion of files, accidental damage to hardware devices or cabling, and abuse of rights and permissions.

Internet Connection Firewall (ICF)   *See* ICF (Internet Connection Firewall).

Internet Connection Sharing (ICS)   *See* ICS (Internet Connection Sharing).

Internet Control Message Protocol (ICMP)   ICMP messages consist of a single packet and are connectionless. ICMP packets determine connectivity between two hosts.

Internet Protocol Version 4 (IPv4)   IPv4 addresses consist of four sets of numbers, each number being a value between 0 and 255, using a period to separate the numbers. This is often called *dotted decimal* format. No IPv4 address may be all 0s or all 1s (255). Examples include 192.168.0.1 and 64.176.19.164.

Internet Protocol Version 6 (IPv6)   IPv6 addresses consist of eight sets of four hexadecimal numbers, each number being a value between 0000 and FFFF, using a colon to separate the numbers. An example is FEDC:BA98:7654:3210:0800:200C:00CF:1234.

InterNIC   The organization that maintains the DNS services, registrations, and so forth run by Network Solutions, General Atomics, and AT&T.

Interrupt   A suspension of a process, such as the execution of a computer program, caused by an event initiated by a device on the computer and performed in such a way that the process can be resumed. Events of this kind include sensors monitoring laboratory equipment or a user pressing an interrupt key.

Intranet   A private network inside a company or organization that uses the same kinds of software and services you find on the public Internet, but that is only for internal use.

I/O (Input/Output)   A general term for reading and writing data to a computer. The term *input* includes data from a keyboard, pointing device (such as a mouse), and file from a disk. Output includes writing information to a disk, viewing it on a CRT, and printing it to a printer.

I/O Device   Pieces of hardware that enable a user to move data into or out of the computer, such as a mouse or a keyboard.

IP (Internet Protocol)   The Internet standard protocol that provides a common layer over dissimilar networks used to move packets among host computers and through gateways if necessary. Part of the TCP/IP protocol suite.

IP Address   The numeric address of a computer connected to a TCP/IP network, such as the Internet. The IP address is made up of 4 octets of 8-bit binary numbers that are translated by the computer into their shorthand numeric values; for example:

   11000000.10101000.00000100.00011010 = 192.168.4.26.

IP addresses must be matched with a valid subnet mask, which identifies the part of the IP address that is the network ID and the part that is the host ID.

IPCONFIG A command-line utility for Windows PCs that displays the current TCP/IP configuration of the machine; similar to UNIX/Linux's IFCONFIG and the graphical WINIPCFG available in Windows 9x and Windows XP.

IPSec (IP Security) A group of protocols used to encrypt IP packets. IPSec is most commonly seen on Virtual Private Networks. *See* VPN (Virtual Private Network).

IPX/SPX (Internetwork Packet Exchange/Sequence Packet Exchange) Protocol suite developed by Novell, primarily for supporting Novell NetWare–based networks.

IRC (Internet Relay Chat) A live online group discussion. IRC uses centralized IRC servers that manage all discussions for IRC clients. Usually shortened to simply *chat.*

IRQ (Interrupt Request) A signal from a hardware device, such as a modem or a mouse, indicating that it needs the CPU's attention. In PCs, IRQs are sent along specific IRQ channels associated with a particular device. For this reason, it's important to ensure that two devices do not share a common IRQ channel.

ISA (Industry Standard Architecture) A design found in the original IBM PC for the sockets on the motherboard that allowed additional hardware to be connected to the computer's motherboard. An 8-bit, 8.33-MHz expansion bus that was designed by IBM for its AT computer and released to the public domain. An improved 16-bit bus was also released to the public domain. Various other designs, such as IBM's MicroChannel and EISA bus, tried to improve on the design without much popularity. ISA only supports 8- and 16-bit data paths, so 32-bit alternatives such as PCI and AGP have become popular. Although ISA slots linger on a few motherboards, they are almost never seen in new systems.

ISDN (Integrated Services Digital Network) The CCITT (Comité Consutatif Internationale Téléphonique et Télégraphique) standard that defines a digital method for communications to replace the current analog telephone system. ISDN is superior to telephone lines because it supports up to 128 Kbps transfer rate for sending information from computer to computer. It also allows data and voice to share a common phone line.

ISP (Internet Service Provider) An institution that provides access to the Internet in some form, usually for a fee.

ISV (Independent Software Vendor) Firms that develop and market software.

IT (Information Technology) The business of computers, electronic communications, and electronic commerce.

Java A network-oriented programming language invented by Sun Microsystems and specifically designed for writing programs that can be safely downloaded to your computer through the Internet and immediately run without fear of viruses or other harm to your computer or files. Using small Java programs (called *applets*), web pages can include functions such as animations, calculators, and other fancy tricks.

JPEG (Joint Photographic Experts Group)   A method of formatting images for efficient storage and transfer across phone lines; JPEG files are often a factor of ten or more times smaller than non-compressed files. JPEG is a *lossy* format, meaning that some data is lost when an image is converted. Most JPEG conversion software allows the user to decide between more or less compression at the cost of image quality. JPEG supports 24-bit images (up to 16.8 million colors). Because computers running MS-DOS are limited in their filenames, this format is also referred to as *JPG*.

Jumper   A series of pairs of small pins that can be shorted with a *shunt* to configure many different aspects of PCs. Usually used in configurations that are rarely changed, such as master/slave settings on IDE drives.

Just a Bunch of Disks (JBOD)   An array of hard drives that are simply connected with no RAID implementations.

K-   Most commonly used as the suffix for the binary quantity 1024. 640 K means 640 × 1024 or 655360. Just to add some extra confusion to the IT industry, *K* is often mis-spoken as "kilo," the metric value for 1000. 10KB, for example, spoken as "10 kilobytes," means 10240 bytes rather than 10000 bytes.

Kbps (Kilobits Per Second)   Data transfer rate of 1000 bits per second. Note that this is not synonymous with KB, or 1024 bytes.

Kerberos   An authentication standard designed to allow different operating systems and applications to authenticate each other.

Kermit   A communications protocol that enables you to transfer files between your computer and online network systems. Kermit has built-in error correction and can handle binary (non-text) files.

Kern   The amount of distance between characters in a particular font.

Kernel   The core portion of a program that resides in memory and performs the most essential operating system tasks.

Kilohertz (KHz)   A unit of measure that equals a frequency of one thousand cycles per second.

Knowledge Base   A large collection of documents and FAQs that is maintained by Microsoft. Found on Microsoft's web site, the Knowledge Base is an excellent place to search for assistance on most operating system problems.

LAN (Local Area Network)   A group of PCs connected together via cabling, radio, or infrared, and using this connectivity to share resources such as printers and mass storage.

Laser Printer   An electrophotographic printer in which a laser is used as the light source.

Last Known Good Configuration   An option on the Advanced Startup Options menu in Windows NT/2000/XP/2003 that enables your system to revert to a previous configuration in order to troubleshoot and repair any major system problems.

Layer   A grouping of related tasks involving the transfer of information. Also, a particular level of the OSI reference model, for example, Physical layer, Data Link layer, and so forth.

Layer 2 Switch   Also known as a *bridge*. Filters and forwards data packets based on the MAC addresses of the sending and receiving machines.

Layer 3 Switch   Also known as a *router*. Filters and forwards data packets based on the network addresses of the sending and receiving machines.

LBA (Logical Block Addressing)   A translation (algorithm) of IDE drives promoted by Western Digital as a standardized method for breaking the 504-megabyte limit in IDE drives. Subsequently, LBA was universally adopted by the PC industry and is now standard on all PATA drives. Allows drives up to 8.4 gigabytes.

LCD (Liquid Crystal Display)   A display technology that relies on polarized light passing through a liquid medium, rather than on electron beams striking a phosphorescent surface.

LED (Light Emitting Diodes)   Solid state devices that light up when charged with electrical current.

Limited Account   A type of user account that has limited access to a system. Accounts of this type cannot alter system files, install new programs, and edit settings using the Control Panel.

Line Printer Daemon (LPD)   A TCP/IP function running on a UNIX/Linux system that works as a server and shares a local printer.

Line Printer Remote (LPR)   A TCP/IP function running on a UNIX/Linux system that wants to access a printer under the control of LPD.

Link Light   An LED on NICs, hubs, and switches that lights up to show good connection between the devices.

Link Segments   Segments that link other segments together but are unpopulated or have no computers directly attached to them. *See* 5-4-3 Rule.

Link State   The state describing whether a wireless device is connected.

Linux   Open-source, graphical UNIX-clone operating system invented by Linus Torvalds.

LMHOSTS File   A static text file that resides on a computer and is used to resolve NetBIOS names to IP addresses. The LMHOSTS file is checked before the machine sends a name resolution request to a WINS name server. The LMHOSTS file has no extension.

Local 1. Refers to systems connected to the same network segment, usually in the same physical site. Systems that are outside the local network segments are considered *remote*. 2. Refers to user accounts stored on a single computer system on a network.

Local Bus A high-speed data path that directly links the computer's CPU with one or more slots on the expansion bus. This direct link means signals from an adapter do not have to travel through the computer expansion bus, which is significantly slower.

Localhost An alias for the loopback address of 127.0.0.1, referring to the current machine.

LocalTalk A network protocol created by Apple computers to add networking to their computers. LocalTalk uses a bus topology, with each device daisy-chained to the next device on the segment, and a proprietary cabling with small round DIN-style connectors.

Local User Accounts The accounts for each local system on a Windows NT/2000/XP/2003 network. These accounts are stored in the local system's Registry.

Local Users and Groups The users and groups defined on each individual Windows NT/2000/XP/2003 system.

Logical Address An address that describes both a specific network and a specific machine on that network.

Logical Drives Sections of a hard drive that are formatted and assigned a drive letter, each of which is presented to the user as if it is a separate drive.

Logical Unit Numbers (LUNs) A specialized SCSI configuration that enables multiple devices to share a single SCSI ID. This type of arrangement is found most commonly in high-end servers that have large hard disk arrays.

Loopback Address Sometimes called the *localhost*, the loopback address is a reserved IP address used for internal testing: 127.0.0.1.

Loopback Test A special test often included in diagnostic software that sends data out of the NIC and checks to see if it comes back.

Low-Level Format Defining the physical location of magnetic tracks and sectors on a disk.

Luminescence The part of the video signal that controls the luminance/brightness of the picture. Also known as the *Y* portion of the component signal.

MAC (Media Access Control) 1. Unique 48-bit address assigned to each network card. IEEE assigns blocks of possible addresses to various NIC manufacturers to help ensure that each address is unique. 2. The sublayer of the Data Link layer of the OSI model uses MAC addresses for locating machines.

Machine Language A programming language or instruction code that is immediately interpretable by the hardware of the machine concerned.

Mac OS   The operating system used on Apple Macintosh computers.

Macro Virus   A specially written application macro (collection of commands) that performs the same functions as a virus. These macros normally autostart when the application is run and then make copies of themselves, often propagating across networks.

Mailbox   Special holding areas on an e-mail server that separates out e-mail for each user.

Mail Server   *See* E-mail Server.

Mainframe   Extremely powerful (and in most cases, physically large) computers that support thousands of user sessions simultaneously. Users access applications on the mainframe through dumb terminals. Mainframes typically have multiple CPUs, large amounts of RAM and disk storage space, and layers of hardware redundancy that enable hot-swapping of most hardware components. Mainframes are used extensively in industrial and scientific settings, banking, and in the military.

MAN (Metropolitan Area Network)   Defined as an IEEE 802.6 network, a MAN is a group of computers connected via cabling, radio, leased phone lines, or infrared, that use this connectivity to share resources such as printers and mass storage. Usually the distance is between that of a LAN and a WAN: different buildings, but within the same city. A typical example of a MAN is a college campus. No firm dividing lines dictate what is considered a WAN, MAN, or LAN.

Mapped Drive   A virtual drive set up on a computer that, in reality, links to a folder or drive on another computer.

Mapping   The process that links a shared folder or drive on another computer to the local one with a persistent link.

Mass Storage   Hard drives, CD-ROMs, removable media drives, and so forth.

Math Coprocessor   Also called *math unit, floating point unit,* or *FPU.* A secondary microprocessor whose function is the handling of floating point arithmetic. Although originally a physically separate chip, math coprocessors are now built into today's CPUs.

MAU (Multistation Access Unit)   A hub used in Token Ring networks. Also abbreviated as *MSAU.*

MB (Megabyte)   1,048,576 bytes.

MCA (MicroChannel Architecture)   Expansion bus architecture developed by IBM as the (unsuccessful) successor to ISA. MCA had a full 32-bit design and was self-configuring.

MCC (Memory Controller Chip)   The chip that handles memory requests from the CPU. Although once a special chip, it has been integrated into the chipset on all PCs today.

Media Certifier Tool   A device used by professional installers that can test the electrical characteristics of a cable and then generate a certification report to prove that your cable runs pass EIA/TIA standards.

Mega-   A prefix that usually stands for the binary quantity 1,048,576. One megabyte is 1,048,576 bytes. One megahertz, however, is a million hertz. Sometimes shortened to *meg*, as in "a 286 has an address space of 16 megs."

Memory   A device or medium that serves for temporary storage of programs and data during program execution. The term is synonymous with storage, although it is most frequently used for referring to the internal storage of a computer that can be directly addressed by operating instructions. A computer's temporary storage capacity is measured in kilobytes (KB) or megabytes (MB) of RAM (random access memory). Long-term data storage on disks is also measured in kilobytes, megabytes, gigabytes, and terabytes.

Mesh Topology   Each computer has a dedicated connection to every other computer in a network.

MHz (Megahertz)   A unit of measure that equals a frequency of 1 million cycles per second.

Microcomputer   A computer system in which the central processing unit is built as a single tiny semiconductor chip or as a small number of chips. The term is synonymous with personal computer (PC.)

Microprocessor   Main computer chip that provides speed and capabilities of the computer. Also called a *CPU*.

Microsoft Management Console (MMC)   The MMC provides a unified interface for a variety of configuration tools called *snap-ins*. Windows comes with a number of pre-defined consoles such as Computer Management, Users and Groups, and so on. Administrators can also create custom consoles that include snap-ins used to perform a specific task.

Microsoft Product Activation (MPA)   Introduced by Microsoft with the release of Windows XP, Microsoft Product Activation prevents unauthorized use of Microsoft's software by requiring a user to activate the software via the Internet or an automated phone system.

MIDI (Musical Instrument Digital Interface)   MIDI is a standard that describes the interface between a computer and a device for simulating musical instruments. Rather than sending large sound samples, a computer can simply send instructions to the instrument describing pitch, tone, and duration of a sound. MIDI files are, therefore, much more efficient. Because a MIDI file is made up of a set of instructions rather than a copy of the sound, it is easy to modify each component of the file. It also is possible to program many channels or *voices* of music to be played simultaneously, creating symphonic sound.

MIME (Multipurpose Internet Mail Extensions)   A standard for attaching binary files, such as executables and images, to the Internet's text-based mail (24-Kbps packet size).

Minicomputer   Minicomputers are similar to mainframe computers in that they are very powerful, multiprocessor systems with lots of hardware redundancy and hot-swapping capability. Instead of handling thousands of simultaneous user sessions, however, they handle hundreds and are smaller in size. Minicomputers are used extensively in the telecommunications industry.

MIPS (Millions of Instructions per Second)   A measurement of CPU performance used for processor benchmarks.

Mirroring   Also called *drive mirroring*. Reading and writing data at the same time to two drives for fault-tolerance purposes. Considered RAID level 1.

MMU (Memory-Management Unit)   A chip or circuit that translates virtual memory addresses to physical addresses and may implement memory protection.

Modem (MOdulator/DEModulator)   A device that converts both digital bit streams into analog signals (modulation) and incoming analog signals back into digital signals (demodulation). The analog communications channel is typically a telephone line and the analog signals are typically sounds.

Monitor   An electronic display device that shows text, graphics, and other functions performed by the computer.

Motherboard   The primary circuit board that holds all the core components of the computer.

Mounting Rack   Racks used in equipment rooms to mount servers, monitors, and other network hardware, thereby conserving space.

MP3 (MPEG-1 Audio Layer 3)   An audio compression scheme used extensively on the Internet.

MPEG (Motion Picture Experts Group)   A sophisticated video standard that enables digital video to be compressed using a form of JPEG image compression and a technique called *differencing*, in which only the differences between frames are recorded, rather than the frame itself.

MSAU (Multistation Access Unit)   A hub used in Token Ring networks. Also abbreviated as *MAU*.

MS-CHAP   Microsoft's variation of the CHAP protocol. It uses a slightly more advanced encryption protocol.

MSCONFIG   A utility found in Windows that enables a user to configure a system's boot files and critical system files.

Multimedia   A single work assembled using elements from more than one medium, such as high-resolution color images, sounds, video, and text that contains characters in multiple fonts and styles.

Multiplexer   A device that merges information from multiple input channels to a single output channel.

Multi-Speed Hub   Any hub that supports more than one network speed for otherwise similar cabling systems. Multispeed hubs come in two flavors: one has mostly dedicated slower ports, with a few dedicated faster ports, while the other has only special autosensing ports that automatically run at either the faster or the slower speed.

Multitasking   The process of running multiple programs or tasks on the same computer at the same time.

Name Resolution   A method that enables one computer on the network to locate another to establish a session. All network protocols perform name resolution in one of two ways: by *broadcasting* or by providing some form of *name server*.

Name Server   A computer whose job is to know the name of every other computer on the network.

NAT (Network Address Translation)   NAT works hand-in-hand with DHCP to mask the IP address of network clients behind a single public IP address. NAT devices (either dedicated hardware devices such as routers, or a PC with two NICs running the software NAT service) have two interfaces: one that connects to the Internet via an ISP-supplied IP address, and another that connects to the LAN. The NAT service converts (or *translates*) the IP addresses and TCP/UDP port numbers of data packets forwarded from the LAN interface from an address in the private IP address range to the public IP address. NAT enables multiple network clients to share a single Internet connection, and provides a level of firewall-like security.

NBTSTAT   A command-line utility used to check the current NetBIOS name cache on a particular machine. The utility compares NetBIOS names to their corresponding IP addresses.

NDS (Novell Directory Services)   Novell's directory service, supplied with NetWare versions 4.*x* and later. Administrators use NDS to organize users, servers, and groups into a hierarchical tree structure. Also called eDirectory.

NetBEUI (NetBIOS Extended User Interface)   NetBEUI is an extended version of the NetBIOS protocol that operates at the Transport layer of the OSI model. NetBEUI has been overshadowed by other protocols, such as IPX/SPX, mainly because NetBEUI is not routable and therefore unsuitable for connecting to the Internet. Microsoft is phasing support for NetBEUI out of their products, starting with Windows XP.

NetBIOS (Network Basic Input/Output System)   The NetBIOS protocol creates and manages connections based on the names of the computers involved. NetBIOS operates at the Session layer of the OSI seven-layer model.

NetBIOS Name   A computer name that identifies both the specific machine and the functions that machine performs. A NetBIOS name consists of 16 characters: the first 15 are an alphanumeric name, and the 16th is a special suffix that identifies the role the machine plays.

NetBIOS Over TCP/IP (NetBT)   A process used by Microsoft to transform NetBIOS into an application-layer function on a TCP/IP network, which added the flexibility of TCP/IP to NetBIOS support.

NETSTAT   A command-line utility used to examine the sockets-based connections open on a given host.

Network   A collection of two or more computers interconnected by telephone lines, coaxial cables, satellite links, radio, and/or some other communication technique. A computer *network* is a group of computers that are connected together and communicate with one another for a common purpose. Computer networks support "people and organization" networks, users who also share a common purpose for communicating.

Network ID   A number that identifies the network on which a device or machine exists. This number exists in both IP and IPX protocol suites.

Network Interface Card (NIC)   A hardware device that connects the PC to a network. NICs come as internal component cards that install onto the PC's motherboard, or as external devices the use the PC's USB or PC Card ports. NICs may have connections for coax, STP, UTP, or fiber-optic cabling, or 802.11- or Bluetooth-based wireless technology.

Network Layer   *See* OSI Seven-Layer Model.

Network Names   A 32-bit identification string that's inserted into the header of each data packet processed by a wireless access point. Usually known as the *Service Set Identification* (*SSID*). When properly configured, only wireless clients whose SSID matches that of the wireless access point are able to gain access to the wireless network.

Network Protocol   1. The rules and standards that define how computers communicate over a network. 2. The software applications and services that enable computers to access a network and establish sessions with remote computers. Examples of network protocols include TCP/IP, IPX/SPX, NetBEUI, DLC, and others.

Network Share   A logical representation of a resource on a network. A single resource, such as a printer, disk drive, or folder, may have numerous network shares configured under numerous names and with different access security settings.

Network Threats   Anything that endangers the integrity and security of data available on a network. Examples of network threats include unauthorized access, virus infection, deletion or manipulation of data, and loss of network services.

Network Topology   1. The physical structures that connect PCs to each other, including cabling, routers, hubs, patch panels, and other pieces of hardware. 2. The logical organization of a network, such as domains and workgroups.

Newsgroup   A discussion group on a public or private USENET network.

NFS (Network File System)   A file system that enables UNIX systems to treat files on a remote UNIX machine as though they were local files.

Node   1. A member of a network. 2. A point where one or more functional units interconnect transmission lines. 3. In the Windows MMC, a container object that enables access to snap-in consoles.

Noise   Undesirable signals bearing no desired information and frequently capable of introducing errors into the communication process.

Non-Discovery Mode   A setting for Bluetooth devices that prevents them from broadcasting their presence, effectively hiding them from other Bluetooth devices.

Normal Backup   A full backup of every selected file on a system. This type of backup turns off the archive bit after the backup.

Northbridge   The chip or chips that connect a CPU to memory, the PCI bus, Level 2 cache and AGP activities. The Northbridge chips communicate with the CPU through the FSB.

NOS (Network Operating System)   An operating system that provides basic file and supervisory services over a network. While each computer attached to the network does have its own OS, the NOS describes which actions are allowed by each user and coordinates distribution of networked files to the users who request them.

Novell NetWare   A popular and powerful network operating system that provides network services ranging from simple file storage and sharing to World Wide Web, e-mail, VPN, and other services. Novell NetWare is the only NOS that adheres to the strict definition of client/server.

Novell Storage Services (NSS)   A file format used in NetWare servers.

Ns (Nanosecond)   A billionth of a second. Light travels a little over 11 inches in one nanosecond.

NSLOOKUP   A handy tool that advanced techs use to query the functions of DNS servers.

NTFS (NT File System)   Microsoft's proprietary file system for hard drives that enables object-level security, long filename support, compression, and encryption. NTFS 4.0 debuted with Windows NT 4.0. Windows 2000/XP/2003 come with NTFS 5.0.

NTFS Permissions   Settings, or groups of settings, that enable administrators to control levels of access to files and folders on a per-user basis. There are two sets of NTFS permissions, special permissions and standard permissions. Special permissions include things such as Traverse Folders, Read Attributes, and Take Ownership (to name just a few) that enable or deny granular control over what a user or group can do to an NTFS resource. Standard permissions are pre-configured grouping of special permissions that are used to grant or deny more general access to resources, such as Modify, Read, and Write. Special permissions are rarely used, as standard permissions encompass the majority of actions that a user will ever need to take.

NTLDR A Windows NT/2000/XP/2003 boot file. Launched by the MBR or MFT, NTLDR looks at the BOOT.INI configuration file for any installed operating systems.

NWLink Also known as *IPX/SPX-compatible protocol*, this is Microsoft's implementation of IPX/SPX. *See also* IPX/SPX (Internetwork Packet Exchange/Sequence Packet Exchange).

Object A system component that is given a set of characteristics and can be managed by the operating system as a single entity.

OCR (Optical Character Recognition) The process of converting characters represented in a graphical format into ASCII. This is usually done in conjunction with a scanner to allow for editing of printed material.

OEM (Original Equipment Manufacturer) Contrary to the name, an OEM does not create original hardware, but rather purchases components from manufacturers and puts them together in systems under its own brand name. Dell Computers and Gateway 2000, for example, are for the most part OEMs. Apple Computers, which manufactures most of the components for its own Macintosh-branded machines, is not an OEM. Also known as *VARs (value-added resellers)*.

Ohm Electronic measurement of a cable's or an electronic component's impedance.

OLE (Object Linking and Embedding) The Microsoft Windows specification that enables objects created within one application to be placed, or embedded, in another application. The two applications are *linked*, meaning that when the original object is modified, the copy is updated automatically.

Open Shortest Path First (OSPF) An interior gateway routing protocol developed for IP networks based on the *shortest path first* or *link-state algorithm*.

Open Source Applications and operating systems that offer access to their source code; this enables developers to modify applications and operating systems easily to meet their specific needs.

Organizational Unit Also *OU*. A type of container used in Windows and NetWare network operating systems to enable grouping of user accounts for the purpose of administrative control.

OS (Operating System) The set of programming that enables a program to interact with the computer and provides an interface between the PC and the user. Examples are Microsoft Windows XP, Apple Macintosh OS X, and SUSE Linux.

Oscilloscope A device that gives a graphical/visual representation of signal levels over a period of time.

OSI (Open Systems Interconnection) An international standard suite of protocols defined by the International Organization for Standardization (ISO) that implements the OSI reference model for network communications between computers.

OSI Seven-Layer Model An architecture model based on the OSI protocol suite, which defines and standardizes the flow of data between computers. The seven layers are as follows:

- **Layer 1** The **Physical layer** defines hardware connections and turns binary into physical pulses (electrical or light). Repeaters and hubs operate at the Physical layer.

- **Layer 2** The **Data Link layer** identifies devices on the Physical layer. MAC addresses are part of the Data Link layer. Bridges operate at the Data Link layer.

- **Layer 3** The **Network layer** moves packets between computers on different networks. Routers operate at the Network layer. IP and IPX operate at the Network layer.

- **Layer 4** The **Transport layer** breaks data down into manageable chunks. TCP, UDP, SPX, and NetBEUI operate at the Transport layer.

- **Layer 5** The **Session layer** manages connections between machines. NetBIOS and Sockets operate at the Session layer.

- **Layer 6** The **Presentation layer**, which can also manage data encryption, hides the differences between various types of computer systems.

- **Layer 7** The **Application layer** provides tools for programs to use to access the network (and the lower layers). HTTP, FTP, SMTP, and POP3 are all examples of protocols that operate at the Application layer.

Overclocking To run a CPU or video processor faster than its rated speed.

Overdrive Generic name given to processors designed as aftermarket upgrades to computer systems.

Overscanning Displaying less than the complete area of an image to the viewer. Most monitors may slightly overscan. Also of value when using a Twain scanner to capture 2K × 2K images, and allowing playback in a smaller window, but moving beyond the normal borders to view close-up detail of portions of the image controlled by the mouse pointer.

Packet Basic component of communication over a network. A group of bits of fixed maximum size and well-defined format that is switched and transmitted as a complete whole through a network. It contains source and destination address, data, and control information. *See also* Frame.

Packet Filtering Packet filters, also known as *IP filters,* will block any incoming or outgoing packet from a particular IP address or range of IP addresses. Packet filters are far better at blocking outgoing IP addresses, because the network administrator knows and can specify the IP addresses of the internal systems.

Pad   Extra data added to an Ethernet frame to bring the data up to the minimum required size of 64 bytes.

PAP (Password Authentication Protocol)   The oldest and most basic form of authentication, it's also the least safe because it sends all passwords in clear text.

Parallel ATA (PATA)   A disk drive implementation that integrates the controller on the disk drive itself. *See also* ATA (AT Attachment).

Parallel Port   A connection for the synchronous, high-speed flow of data along parallel lines to a device, usually a printer.

Parameter   A value used to modify a routine or command. Synonymous with *argument*.

Parity   A method of error detection in which a small group of bits being transferred is compared to a single *parity* bit, which is set to make the total bits odd or even. The receiving device reads the parity bit and determines whether the data is valid based on the oddness or evenness of the parity bit.

Partition   A section of the storage area of a hard disk. A partition is created during initial preparation of the hard disk, before the disk is formatted.

Password   A series of characters that enable a user to gain access to a file, a folder, a PC, or a program.

Password Reset Disk   A special type of floppy disk that can allow a user to recover a lost password without losing access to any encrypted, or password-protected, data.

Patch Cables   Short UTP cables that connect patch panels to the hubs.

Patch Panel   A panel containing a row of female connectors (ports) that terminate the horizontal cabling in the equipment room. Patch panels facilitate cabling organization and provide protection to horizontal cabling.

Path   The route the operating system must follow to find an executable program stored in a subdirectory.

PBX (Private Branch Exchange)   A private phone system used within an organization.

PC (Personal Computer)   A more popular phrase than the more correct term *microcomputer*, PC means a small computer with its own processor and hard drive, as opposed to a dumb terminal connected to a central mainframe computer. Used in this fashion, the term *PC* indicates computers of many different manufacturers, using a variety of processors and operating systems. Although the term *PC* was around long before the original IBM PC was released, it has come to be almost synonymous with IBM-compatible computers, hence, the incorrect but common question, "Are you a Mac or a PC person?"

PCI (Peripheral Component Interconnect)   A design architecture for the sockets on the computer motherboard that enable system components to be added to the computer. PCI is a "local bus" standard, meaning that devices added to a computer through this port will use the processor at the motherboard's full speed (up to 33 MHz), rather than at the slower 8-MHz speed of the regular bus. In addition to moving data at a faster rate, PCI moves data 32 or 64 bits at a time, rather than the 8 or 16 bits that the older ISA buses supported.

PCMCIA (Personal Computer Memory Card International Association)   A consortium of computer manufacturers who devised the standard for credit card–sized adapter cards that add functionality in many notebook computers, PDAs, and other computer devices. The simpler term *PC Card* has become more common in referring to these cards.

PDA (Personal Digital Assistant)   Sometimes called *palmtop computers*, PDAs are computers small enough to fit into the palm of your hand. Early PDAs were used mainly as digital organizers, keeping track of contact lists, task lists, calendar events, and so on. Modern PDAs are much more powerful, and support chopped-down versions of productivity software such as Microsoft Office, multimedia, wireless networking, and telephone functions. PDAs run specialized operating systems, such as Palm OS or Microsoft Windows CE, Pocket PC, or Windows Mobile Edition. Popular PDAs include the various Palm models, HP's iPAQ, Sony Clie, and others. Most PDAs accept input via a *stylus* and special handwriting recognition software. Some come equipped with tiny keyboards.

Peer-to-Peer Networks   A decentralized network in which each machine acts as both a client and a server, and maintains its own security over its own shared resources.

Pentium   Name given to the fifth generation of Intel microprocessors, distinct with 32-bit address bus, 64-bit external data bus, and dual pipelining. Also used for subsequent generations of Intel processors: Pentium Pro, Pentium II, Pentium II Xeon, Pentium III, and Pentium 4.

Peripheral   Any device other than the motherboard components of the computer. The floppy drive is a peripheral; the CPU is not a peripheral.

Permissions   Sets of attributes that network administrators assign to resources to define what users and groups can do with them.

Persistent Connection   A connection to a shared folder or drive that the computer immediately reconnects to at logon.

Personal Area Networks (PAN)   The network created among Bluetooth devices such as PDAs, printers, keyboards, mice, and so on.

Phosphor   An electrofluorescent material used to coat the inside face of a Cathode Ray Tube (CRT). After being hit with an electron, phosphors glow for a fraction of a second.

Physical Address   A way of defining a specific machine without referencing its location or network. A MAC address is an example of a physical address.

Physical Layer   *See* OSI Seven-Layer Model.

PIM (Personal Information Manager)   A software application designed to hold and manage personal information such as phone numbers, contact notes, schedules, and to-do lists.

Ping (Packet Internet Groper)   Network utility that sends a small network message (ICMP ECHO) to a remote computer to check for presence and response time.

PIO (Programmable Input/Output)   Using the address bus to send communication to a peripheral. The most common way for the CPU to communicate with peripherals.

PIO Mode   A series of speed standards created by the Small Form Factor committee for the use of PIO by hard drives. The PIO modes range from PIO mode 0 to PIO mode 4.

Pixel (Picture Element)   In computer graphics, the smallest element of a display space that can be independently assigned color or intensity.

Platen   The cylinder that guides paper through an impact printer and provides a backing surface for the paper when images are impressed onto the page.

Platform   Hardware environment that supports the running of a computer system.

Plenum   1. The space between a building's false ceiling and the floor above it. Most of the wiring for networks is located in this space. 2. Plenum is also the fire rating of the grade of cable allowed to be installed in this location.

Plug and Play   Also known as *PnP*. A combination of smart PCs, smart devices, and smart operating systems that automatically configure all the necessary system resources and ports for peripheral devices.

Point Coordination Function (PCF)   A method of collision avoidance defined by the 802.11 standard, which has yet to be implemented.

Point-to-Multipoint   These devices can communicate with more than one other network segment.

POP (Post Office Protocol)   Also known as *Point Of Presence*, this refers to the way e-mail software such as Eudora gets mail from a mail server. When you obtain a SLIP, PPP, or shell account, you almost always get a POP account with it; and it is this POP account that you tell your e-mail software to use to get your mail. The current standard is called POP3.

Populated Segment   A segment that has one or more nodes directly attached to it.

Port   1. A logical endpoint through which computers send specific types of network or data traffic. For example, port 80 is reserved for HTTP communication. 2. A physical connector used to attach network or I/O device cabling to the PC, such as a parallel or USB port.

Port Filtering   Preventing the passage of any IP packets through any ports other than the ones prescribed by the system administrator.

Port Number   Number used to identify the requested service (such as SMTP or FTP) when connecting to a TCP/IP host. Some example port numbers include 80 (HTTP), 20 (FTP), 69 (TFTP), 25 (SMTP), and 110 (POP3).

PostScript   A language defined by Adobe Systems, Inc., for describing how to create an image on a page. The description is independent of the resolution of the device that will create the image. It includes a technology for defining the shape of a font and creating a raster image at many different resolutions and sizes.

Power Users   A user account that has the capability to do many, but not all, of the basic administrator functions.

PPP (Point-to-Point Protocol)   A protocol that enables a computer to connect to the Internet through a dial-in connection and to enjoy most of the benefits of a direct connection. PPP is considered to be superior to SLIP because of its error detection and data compression features, which SLIP lacks, and the capability to use dynamic IP addresses.

PPPoE (PPP over Ethernet)   A specialized implementation of PPP, specifically designed to allow Ethernet connections to enjoy some of the benefits of PPP, such as encryption. Used exclusively by ADSL.

PPTP (Point-to-Point Tunneling Protocol)   A protocol that works with PPP to provide a secure data link between computers using encryption.

Preamble   A 64-bit series of alternating ones and zeroes ending with 11 that begins every Ethernet frame. The preamble gives a receiving NIC time to realize a frame is coming and to know exactly where the frame starts.

Presentation Layer   *See* OSI Seven-Layer Model.

Program   A set of actions or instructions that a machine is capable of interpreting and executing. Used as a verb, it means to design, write, and test such instructions.

Promiscuous Mode   A mode of operation for a network interface card in which the NIC processes all packets that it sees on the cable.

Prompt   A character or message provided by an operating system or program to indicate that it is ready to accept input.

Proprietary   Term used to describe technology that is unique to, and owned by, a particular vendor.

Protected Mode   The operating mode of a CPU to allow more than one program to be run while ensuring that no program can corrupt another program currently running.

Protocol   An agreement that governs the procedures used to exchange information between cooperating entities; usually includes how much information is to be sent, how often it is sent, how to recover from transmission errors, and who is to receive the information.

Protocol Stack   The actual software that implements the protocol suite on a particular operating system.

Protocol Suite   A set of protocols that are commonly used together and operate at different levels of the OSI seven-layer model.

Proxy Server   A device that fetches Internet resources for a client without exposing that client directly to the Internet. Most proxy servers accept requests for HTTP, FTP, POP3, and SMTP resources. The proxy server will often cache a copy of the requested resource for later use.

PSTN (Public Switched Telephone Network)   Also known as *POTS (Plain Old Telephone Service)*. Most common type of phone connection that takes your sounds, translated into an analog waveform by the microphone, and transmits them to another phone.

Punchdown Tool   *See* 110-Punchdown Tool.

PVC (Polyvinyl Chloride)   A material used for the outside insulation and jacketing of most cables. Also a fire rating for a type of cable that has no significant fire protection.

QIC (Quarter-Inch Tape or Cartridge)/Travan Tape   Tape backup cartridges that use quarter-inch tape.

Queue   The waiting area for things to happen; or, as we say in America, the *line*. An example is the print queue, where print jobs wait until it is their turn to be printed.

RAID (Redundant Array of Independent [or Inexpensive] Devices [or Disks])   A way of creating a fault-tolerant storage system. There are six official levels. Level 0 uses byte-level striping and provides no fault tolerance. Level 1 uses mirroring or duplexing. Level 2 uses bit-level striping. Level 3 stores error correcting information (such as parity) on a separate disk, and uses data striping on the remaining drives. Level 4 is level 3 with block-level striping. Level 5 uses block-level and parity data striping. Other configurations are possible, such as RAID 10 (a mirrored set of two RAID 5 arrays), but these are uncommon. Many current motherboards sport something called RAID 0+1, a striped mirror that requires four hard drives.

RAM (Random Access Memory)   Expandable system memory in which any address can be written to or read from as easily as any other address. Typical system RAM is dynamic memory, meaning that RAM doesn't retail data after powering down the system.

Raster   The horizontal pattern of lines that forms an image on the monitor screen.

Real Mode   The original 64K segmented memory, single-tasking operating mode of the Intel 8086 and 8088 CPUs.

Real-Time   The processing of transactions as they occur, rather than batching them. Pertaining to an application in which response to input is fast enough to affect subsequent inputs and guide the process and in which records are updated immediately. Real-time systems are those with a response time of milliseconds; interactive systems respond in seconds, and batch systems may respond in hours or days.

Recovery Console   A DOS-like interface, accessed using Windows 2000/XP/2003 boot disks or CD-ROM, that can be used to repair a system that is suffering from massive operating system corruption or other problems.

Recycle Bin   When files are deleted from a modern Windows system, they are moved to the Recycle Bin. To permanently remove files from a system, they must be removed from the Recycle Bin.

Refresh   The process of repainting the CRT screen, causing the phosphors to remain lit (or change). Also refers to the process of recharging RAM.

REGEDIT.EXE   A 16-bit program used to edit the Windows 9*x* registry.

REGEDT32.EXE   32-bit version of the program used to edit the registry on Windows NT/2000/XP systems.

Remote   Any system that is non-local (i.e., another system on the same network segment, or a system that is on a different network segment.)

Remote Access   The capability to access a computer from outside a building in which it is housed. Remote access requires communications hardware, software, and actual physical links.

Remote Access Server (RAS)   Refers to both the hardware component (servers built to handle the unique stresses of a large number of clients calling in) and the software component (programs that work with the operating system to allow remote access to the network) of a remote access solution.

Remote Installation Services (RIS)   A service introduced with Windows 2000 used to initiate an image-based installation of the Windows operating system onto a PC via a network.

Repeater   A device that takes all of the data packets it receives on one Ethernet segment and re-creates them on another Ethernet segment. This allows for longer cables or more computers on a segment. Repeaters operate at Level 1 (Physical) of the OSI seven-layer model.

Replication   A fancy word meaning *copy*. During the replication process, data is copied from one PC to another. In the case of Windows 2000 Server/Server 2003 Active Directory domains, the AD database is replicated among all domain controllers (DCs), thus ensuring that each DC has a current and consistent copy of the database. Windows can also be configured to replicate user data files between file servers via the Distributed File Service (DFS) to ensure fault tolerance.

Resistance   The tendency for physical medium to impede electron flow. It is classically measured in a unit called *ohms*.

Resolution   A measurement expressed in horizontal and vertical dots or pixels for CRTs and/or printers. Higher resolutions provide sharper details, thus displaying better-looking images.

Resource   1. Any object, service, or device that can be shared with other PCs and users on a network. 2. Components of functions of a system used to perform tasks (i.e., memory addresses, channels to the CPU, and so on.)

Restore Point   A system snapshot created by the System Restore utility that is used to restore a malfunctioning system. *See also* System Restore.

Reverse Lookup Zones   A DNS setting that resolves IP addresses to FQDNs. In other words, it does exactly the reverse of what DNS normally accomplishes using Forward Lookup Zones.

RG-6   A type of coaxial cable that is virtually never installed in networks these days, but still has enough of an installed base that you should at least know about it. The cable used for cable TV is RG-6.

RG-8   Often referred to as *Thick Ethernet,* RG-8 is the oldest and least-used coaxial cabling type still in use. It gets the name Thick Ethernet because it is used exclusively for 802.5 Thick Ethernet networks. RG-8 is rated at 50 ohms and has a distinct yellow or orange/brown color.

RG-58   A type of coaxial cable that works with the still quite popular Thin Ethernet network technology. It is rated at 50 ohms.

RG-62   A type of coaxial cable used with ARCnet networks. Extremely rare today.

Rights   Novell NetWare's term for resource permissions.

Ring In   The Ring In port on a Token Ring MAU is used to connect to the Ring Out port on a second MAU, and vice versa, to form a single logical ring.

Ring Out   The Ring Out port on a Token Ring MAU is used to connect to the Ring In port on a second MAU, and vice versa, to form a single logical ring.

Ring Topology   A network topology in which all the computers on the network attach to a central ring of cable.

RJ (Registered Jack)   Connectors used for UTP cable for both telephone and network connections.

RJ-11   Type of connector with 4-wire UTP connections; usually found in telephone connections.

RJ-45 Type of connector with 8-wire UTP connections; usually found in network connections and used for 10BaseT networking.

ROM (Read-Only Memory) The generic term for non-volatile memory that can be read from but not written to. This means that code and data stored in ROM cannot be corrupted by accidental erasure. Additionally, ROM retains its data when power is removed, which makes it the perfect medium for storing BIOS data or information such as scientific constants.

Root Directory The top-level directory that contains all other subdirectories.

Router A device connecting separate networks, which forwards a packet from one network to another based only on the network address for the protocol being used. For example, an IP router looks only at the IP network number. Routers operate at Layer 3 (Network) of the OSI seven-layer model.

Routing Table A list of paths to various networks required by routers. This can be built either manually or dynamically via one of the routing protocols, such as RIP or OSPF.

RS-232C A standard port recommended by the Electronics Industry Association for serial devices.

Run The length of cable that connects nodes to the equipment room.

Samba A service that enables UNIX-based systems to communicate using SMB (Server Message Blocks). This, in turn, enables them to act as Microsoft clients and servers on the network.

Scalability The capability to support system or network growth.

Scanner A device that senses alterations of light and dark. It enables the user to import photographs, other physical images, and text into the computer in digital form.

SC Connector One of two special types of fiber-optic cable used in 10BaseFL networks.

SCSI (Small Computer System Interface) A powerful and flexible peripheral interface popularized on the Macintosh and used to connect hard drives, CD-ROM drives, tape drives, scanners, and other devices to PCs of all kinds. Because SCSI is less efficient at handling small drives than IDE, it did not become popular on IBM-compatible computers until price reductions made these large drives affordable. Normal SCSI enables up to seven devices to be connected through a single bus connection, whereas Wide SCSI can handle 15 devices attached to a single controller.

SCSI Chain A SCSI host adapter and all of the devices attached to it.

SDRAM (Synchronous DRAM) DRAM that is tied to the system clock and, thus, runs much faster than traditional FPM and EDO RAM.

Sector A segment of one of the concentric tracks encoded on the disk during a low-level format. A sector holds 512 bytes of data.

Secure Sockets Layer (SSL)   *See* SSL (Secure Sockets Layer).

Segment   The network bus that network clients connect to. *See* 5-4-3 rule.

Sequential   A method of storing and retrieving information that requires data to be written and read sequentially. Accessing any portion of the data requires reading all the preceding data.

Serial ATA (SATA)   A hard drive technology that offers many advantages over PATA (Parallel ATA) technology, including thinner cabling, keyed connectors, and lower power requirements. Current SATA drives transfer data at 150 megabytes per second. Future SATA drives will be much faster, while PATA drives are at the top speed the technology enables.

Server   A computer that shares its resources, such as printers and files, with other computers on the network. An example of this is a Network File System Server that shares its disk space with a workstation that has no disk drive of its own.

Server-Based Network   A network in which one or more systems function as dedicated file, print, or application servers, but do not function as clients.

Service Set Identification (SSID)   A 32-bit identification string, sometimes called a *network name*, that's inserted into the header of each data packet processed by a wireless access point.

Session   A networking term used to refer to the logical stream of data flowing between two programs and being communicated over a network. Many different sessions may be emanating from any one node on a network.

Session Layer   *See* OSI Seven-Layer Model.

Session Software   Session software handles the process of differentiating between various types of connections on a PC.

Share Level Security   A security system in which each resource has a password assigned to it at the network level, but not the local level. Access to the resource is typically password-based. *See* Share Permissions.

Share Permissions   Permissions that only control the access of other users on the network with whom you share your resource. They have no impact on you (or anyone else) sitting at the computer whose resource is being shared.

Shareware   Software that is distributed freely, enabling potential users to try before they buy. Shareware typically has a pre-configured trial period, after which it will cease to function unless the user opts to purchase a license. Most shareware is distributed with full functionality, but some vendors may disable advanced functions until a license is purchased.

Shell   A term that generally refers to the user interface of an operating system. A shell is the command processor that is the actual interface between the kernel and the user.

Short Circuit Allows electricity to pass between two conductive elements that weren't designed to interact together. Also called a *short*.

Shunt A tiny metal connector enclosed in plastic that creates an electrical connection between two posts of a jumper. Often incorrectly referred to as the jumper itself.

Signal Strength A measurement of how well your wireless device is connecting to other devices.

SIMM (Single In-Line Memory Module) A type of DRAM packaging distinct by having a number of small tabs that install into a special connector. Each side of each tab is the same signal. SIMMs come in two common sizes: 30-pin and 72-pin.

Simple Volume A type of volume created when setting up dynamic disks. A simple volume acts like a primary partition on a dynamic disk.

SL Enhanced A type of CPU that has the capability to turn off selected peripherals as well as run on low (3.3v or less) power. *See also* SMM (System Management Mode).

SLIP (Serial Line Interface Protocol) A protocol that enables a computer to connect to the Internet through a dial-in connection and enjoy most of the benefits of a direct connection. SLIP has been almost completely replaced by PPP, which is considered superior to SLIP because of its error detection and data compression—features that SLIP lacks—and the capability to use dynamic IP addresses.

SMB (Server Message Blocks) Protocol used by Microsoft clients and servers to share file and print resources.

SMM (System Management Mode) A special CPU mode that enables the CPU to reduce power consumption via the selective shutdown of peripherals.

SMTP (Simple Mail Transfer Protocol) The main protocol used to send electronic mail on the Internet.

Snap-Ins Small utilities that can be used with the Microsoft Management Console.

Sneakernet The term used for saving the file on a portable medium and physically walking it over to another computer.

SNMP (Simple Network Management Protocol) A protocol that enables communication and management of remote network hardware devices such as hubs, routers, and switches. The remote device in question must be SNMP-capable.

Social Engineering Methods of convincing network users to perform tasks on your behalf, such as revealing passwords or launching applications, that may compromise the network. Examples include impersonation of authority figures (law enforcement officers, network administrators, vendor support personnel), threats of punishment, promises of rewards, misdirection, and so on. Social engineering targets an unsuspecting user's natural inclination to help, or their fear of causing harm or losing their job.

Socket   A virtual endpoint for a network session. A combination of a port number and an IP address that uniquely identifies a connection.

Software   Programmatic instructions used to perform tasks on a PC. Examples of software include application programs, such as Microsoft Office, device drivers, protocol suites, client services, and the network operating system itself, among many others.

Solid Core   A cable that uses a single solid wire to transmit signals.

SONET (Synchronous Optical Network)   A standard for connecting fiber-optic transmission systems. SONET defines interface standards at the Physical layer of the OSI seven-layer model.

Source Code   The program in a language prepared by the programmer. This code cannot be directly executed by the computer and must first be translated into executable object code. Also, the building blocks of an operating system or application.

Southbridge   The Southbridge is part of a motherboard chipset. It handles all the inputs and outputs to the many devices in the PC.

Spool   A temporary storage area in memory that caches pending print jobs.

Spreadsheet   A software program that enables users to perform mathematical calculations in a tabular format, such as budgeting, keeping track of investments, or tracking grades.

SPS (Stand-by Power Supply or System)   A device that supplies continuous clean power to a computer system immediately following a power failure. *See also* UPS (Uninterruptible Power Supply).

SQL (Structured Query Language)   1. A language created by IBM that relies on simple English statements to perform database queries. SQL enables databases from different manufacturers to be queried using a standard syntax. 2. A Microsoft database application, *SQL Server*.

SRAM (Static RAM)   A type of RAM that uses a flip-flop type of circuit, rather than the typical transistor/capacitor of DRAM, to hold a bit of information. SRAM does not need to be refreshed and is faster than regular DRAM. Used primarily for cache.

SSL (Secure Sockets Layer)   A protocol developed by Netscape for transmitting private documents over the Internet. SSL works by using a public key to encrypt sensitive data. This encrypted data is sent over an SSL connection, and then decrypted at the receiving end using a private key.

ST506   A model of hard drive developed by Seagate. This drive, as well as the WD1003 controller developed by Western Digital, created the standard for the first generation of hard drives and controllers. As a result, drives that copied the connections and BIOS commands of the ST506 came to be known as ST506 drives.

Stackable Hub   Hubs with a special proprietary connection that enables them to function in groups, called *stacks*, as a single device.

Star Bus Topology   This is a hybrid of the Star and Bus topologies. This topology uses a physical star, where all nodes connect to a single wiring point such as a hub, and a logical bus that maintains the Ethernet standards. One benefit of a Star Bus topology is fault tolerance.

Star Ring Topology   A star ring is a hybrid of the Token Ring topology and the physical star.

Star Topology   A network topology in which all computers in the network connect to a central wiring point.

Static Routing   A process by which routers in an internetwork obtain information about paths to other routers. This information must be configured manually.

ST Connector   One of two special types of fiber-optic cable used in 10BaseFL networks.

Storage   A device or medium that can retain data for subsequent retrieval.

STP (Shielded Twisted Pair)   A popular cabling for networks composed of pairs of wires twisted around each other at specific intervals. The twists serve to reduce interference (also called *crosstalk*). The more twists, the less interference. The cable has metallic shielding to protect the wires from external interference. Token Ring networks are the only common network technology that uses STP, although Token Ring more often now uses UTP.

Stranded Core   A cable that uses a bundle of tiny wire strands to transmit signals. Stranded core is not quite as good a conductor as solid core, but it will stand up to substantial handling without breaking.

Stripe Set   A group of two or more disk drives that store data sequentially. Striped sets perform faster read and write operations than a single disk, but the threat of data loss is increased because no one disk in a striped set contains all pieces of file data.

Structured Cable   The practice of organizing the cables in a network for ease of repair and replacement.

Subnet   Sections of a TCP/IP network sharing a common IP addressing scheme. *See* Subnet Mask.

Subnet Mask   The value used in TCP/IP settings to divide the IP address of a host into its component parts: network ID and host ID.

Super User Account   A colloquial term that refers to the default administrator user account in Windows NT/2000/XP, and 2003. The administrator account, appropriately named *Administrator*, has complete authority to perform any tasks on the system, including accessing, moving, copying, and deleting files and folders, reconfiguring system settings, creating and disabling user accounts, installing programs, and so on.

SVGA   A graphics standard that specifies a monitor resolution of 800 × 600 at 256 colors.

Switch   1. A hardware device that filters and forwards data packets between network segments. 2. Synonymous with *parameter* or *argument*. 3. A hardware device that completes or terminates an electrical circuit.

Switched Ethernet   A network setup in which some devices are placed into their own collision domains. Logically, an Ethernet switch puts each device plugged into one of its switched ports into its own collision domain.

Synchronous   Describes a connection between two electronic devices where neither must acknowledge (ACK) when receiving data.

SYSCON   An ancient, but completely functional, program used to set up trustee rights, and create users and groups in NetWare 3.*x*.

Sysop (System Operator)   Anyone responsible for the physical operations of a computer system or network resource. A System Administrator decides how often backups and maintenance should be performed, and the System Operator performs those tasks.

System BIOS   The primary set of BIOS stored on an EPROM or Flash chip on the motherboard. Defines the BIOS for all the assumed hardware on the motherboard, such as keyboard controller, floppy drive, basic video, RAM, and so forth.

System Monitor   A utility that can be used to evaluate and monitor system resources, like CPU usage and memory usage.

System Resources   System resources are I/O addresses, IRQs, DMA channels, and memory addresses.

System Restore   A utility in Windows Me and XP that enables you to return your PC to a recent working configuration when something goes wrong. System Restore returns your computer's system settings to the way they were the last time you remember your system working correctly—all without affecting your personal files or e-mail.

T1   A leased-line connection capable of carrying data at 1,544,000 bits per second.

T3   A leased-line connection capable of carrying data at 44,736,000 bits per second.

T-Connector   A connector used in 10Base2 networks that is designed in a *T* shape. The stem of the T-connector plugs into the female connector on the Ethernet NIC, and the two pieces of coaxial cable are plugged into either end of the top bar.

TCP (Transmission Control Protocol)   Part of the TCP/IP protocol suite, TCP operates at Layer 4 (Transport) of the OSI seven-layer model. TCP is a connection-oriented protocol.

TCP/IP (Transmission Control Protocol/Internet Protocol)   A set of communication protocols, including TCP, IP, UDP, and others, developed by the U.S. Department of Defense that enables dissimilar computers to share information over a network.

TDR (Time Domain Reflectometer)   Advanced cable tester that tests the length of cables and their continuity or discontinuity, and identifies the location of any discontinuity due to a bend, break, unwanted crimp, and so on.

Telephony   The science of converting sound into electrical signals, moving those signals from one location to another, and then converting those signals back into sounds. This includes modems, telephone lines, the telephone system, and any products used to create a remote access link between a remote access client and server.

Telnet   A service that enables users on the Internet to log on to remote systems from their own host systems.

Tera-   A prefix that usually stands for the binary number 1,099,511,627,776, which is 2 to the 40th power. When used for mass storage, often shorthand usage for a trillion bytes.

Terabyte   1,099,511,627,776 bytes.

Terminal   A "dumb" device connected to a computer network that acts as a point for entry or retrieval of information.

Terminal Emulation   Software that enables a PC to communicate with another computer or network as if it were a specific type of hardware terminal.

Terminating Resistors   Any device that absorbs excess electrical signals off a wire. Examples include the device used at each end of a coaxial cable to absorb the excess electrical signals, which helps avoid signal bounce or reflection. The level of resistance in RG-58 coaxial cables requires them to have 50 ohm impedance. Another device with the same name is used to terminate the ends of a SCSI chain.

Terminator   1. *See* Terminating Resistors. 2. In a machine-dominated future, a type of cyborg designed to infiltrate groups of human resistance fighters. May be sent into the past to prevent the resistance leader from being born, thus ensuring the successful destruction of mankind.

Thick Ethernet (Thicknet)   Thick Ethernet, or Thicknet, also goes by the name *RG-8*. This is the oldest coax cabling type still in use.

Thin Ethernet (Thinnet)   Thin Ethernet, or Thinnet, is known also as *RG-58*. It stands alone as the only coax cable type still widely used in networks.

TIA/EIA   See EIA/TIA.

TIFF (Tagged Image File Format)   A graphical file format in which images are divided into discrete blocks or strips called *tags*. Each tag contains formatting information, such as width and number of colors, for the entire image. The TIFF format is useful because it can describe many different types of images, but it is also complex and writing software for it is difficult.

TLA (Three-Letter Acronym)   Any acronym of three letters, such as FAT (File Allocation Table) and GIF (Graphics Interchange Format).

Token   The token is a frame that enables the systems on a Token Ring network to effectively "take turns" sending data. The rule is that no device can transmit data unless it's currently holding the token.

Token Passing   The system used by Token Ring networks to control access to the ring. A node receives a token from its upstream neighbor and, when it is finished transmitting data, passes the token on to its downstream neighbor.

Token Ring   A LAN and protocol in which nodes are connected together in a ring, and a special packet called a token, passed from node to node around the ring, controls communication. A node can send data only when it receives the token and the token is not in use. This avoids the collision problems endemic to Ethernet networks.

Tone Generator   *See* Toners.

Tone Probe   *See* Toners.

Toners   Generic term for two devices used together—a tone generator and a tone locator (probe)—to trace cables by sending an electrical signal along a wire at a particular frequency. The tone locator then emits a sound when it distinguishes that frequency. An example of a tone generator/tone locator device is Triplett Corporation's *Fox and Hound*.

Topology   1. The pattern of interconnections in a communications system among devices, nodes, and associated input and output stations. 2. Also describes how computers connect to each other without regard to how they actually communicate. *See* Network Topology.

TRACERT (also TRACEROUTE)   A command-line utility used to follow the path a packet takes between two hosts.

Transceiver   The devices that transmit and receive signals on a cable.

Transport Layer   *See* OSI Seven-Layer Model.

Trivial File Transfer Protocol (TFTP)   A protocol that transfers files between servers and clients. Unlike FTP, TFTP requires no user login. Devices that need an operating system, but have no local hard disk (for example, diskless workstations and routers), often use TFTP to download their operating systems.

Trojan Virus   A virus that masquerades as a file with a legitimate purpose, so that a user will run it intentionally. The classic example is a file that runs a game, but also causes some type of damage to the player's system.

Trustee Rights   NetWare lingo for user and group permissions to a shared folder. Any user or group with rights to a certain shared folder is said to have trustee rights to that folder.

TSR (Terminate and Stay Resident)   A DOS program that mostly closes immediately after starting up, but leaves a tiny piece of itself in memory. TSRs are used to handle a broad cross-section of DOS-level system needs, such as running hardware (MOUSE.COM) or applying higher-level functionality to hardware already under the control of device drivers. MSCDEX.EXE, for example, assigns a drive letter to a CD-ROM drive after the CD-ROM driver has loaded in CONFIG.SYS.

TWAIN (Technology Without an Interesting Name)   A programming interface that enables a graphics application, such as a desktop publishing program, to activate a scanner, frame grabber, or other image-capturing device.

Twisted Pair   The most overwhelmingly common type of cabling used in networks consists of twisted pairs of cables. The two types of twisted pair cabling are UTP (Unshielded Twisted Pair) and STP (Shielded Twisted Pair). The twists serve to reduce interference, called *crosstalk*; the more twists, the less crosstalk.

Type I Connector   Another name for the IBM-designed hermaphroditic connector called either an *IBM-type Data Connector (IDC)* or a *Universal Data Connector (UDC)*.

UART (Universal Asynchronous Receiver/Transmitter)   A device that turns serial data into parallel data. The cornerstone of serial ports and modems.

UDP (User Datagram Protocol)   Part of the TCP/IP protocol suite, UDP is an alternative to TCP. UDP is a connectionless protocol.

UNC (Universal Naming Convention)   Describes any shared resource in a network using the convention \\\<server name>\<name of shared resource>.

Units (U)   The unique height measurement used with network equipment racks, expressed as *U*. One U equals 1.75 inches.

UNIX   A powerful, open source network operating system originally developed by Bell Laboratories in the 1970s. UNIX is widely used on many types of server systems.

Uplink Port   Special port in a hub used to connect to another hub by crossing the sending and receiving wires. *See* Crossover Port.

UPS (Uninterruptible Power Supply)   A device that supplies continuous clean power to a computer system the whole time the computer is on. Protects against power outages and sags. The term *UPS* is often used mistakenly when people mean SPS (Standby Power Supply or System).

Upstream Neighbor   The computer right before a node on a Token Ring network.

URL (Uniform Resource Locator)   A Uniform Resource Locator is an address that defines the location of a resource on the Internet and World Wide Web. URLs use the format *protocol://IP address or domain name/resource name*. Examples are http://www.totalsem.com/mikespc/mikesstuff/stuff.doc and ftp://63.31.12.159/srv/lovestruck.mp3

USB (Universal Serial Bus) A 12-Mbps serial interconnect for keyboards, printers, joysticks, and many other devices. Enables hot-swapping and daisy chaining of devices. USB 2.0 devices transfer data at up to 480 Mbps.

Usenet Started by Duke University and UNC-Chapel Hill. An information cooperative linking around 16,000 computer sites and millions of people. Usenet provides a series of "news groups" analogous to online conferences.

User Anyone who uses a computer. You. Me, too, for that matter.

User Account A container that identifies a user to the application, operating system, or network, including name, password, user name, groups to which the user belongs, and other information based on the user and the OS or NOS being used. Usually defines the rights and roles a user plays on a system.

User Datagram Protocol (UDP) A protocol used by some older applications, most prominently TFTP (Trivial FTP), to transfer files. UDP packets are both simpler and smaller than TCP packets, and they do most of the behind-the-scenes work in a TCP/IP network.

User Level Security A security system in which each user has an account, and access to resources is based on user identity.

User Profiles A collection of settings that corresponds to a specific user account and may follow the user, regardless of the computer at which he or she logs on. These settings enable the user to have customized environment and security settings.

UTP (Unshielded Twisted Pair) A popular cabling for telephone and networks composed of pairs of wires twisted around each other at specific intervals. The twists serve to reduce interference (also called *crosstalk*). The more twists, the less interference. The cable has *no* metallic shielding to protect the wires from external interference, unlike its cousin, *STP*. 10BaseT uses UTP, as do many other networking technologies. UTP is available in a variety of grades, called categories or CAT, as defined in the following:

- **Category 1 UTP** Regular analog phone lines, not used for data communications.
- **Category 2 UTP** Supports speeds up to 4 megabits per second.
- **Category 3 UTP** Supports speeds up to 16 megabits per second.
- **Category 4 UTP** Supports speeds up to 20 megabits per second.
- **Category 5 UTP** Supports speeds up to 100 megabits per second.
- **Category 5e UTP** Supports speeds up to 100 megabits per second with two pairs and up to 1000 megabits per second with four pairs.
- **Category 6 UTP** Improved support for speeds up to 1000 megabits per second.

V Standards Standards established by CCITT for modem manufacturers to follow (voluntarily) to ensure compatible speeds, compression, and error correction.

VESA (Video Electronics Standards Association)   A consortium of computer manufacturers that standardized improvements to common IBM PC components. VESA is responsible for the Super VGA video standard and the VLB bus architecture.

VGA (Video Graphics Array)   The standard for the video graphics adapter that was built into IBM's PS/2 computer. It supports 16 colors in a 640 × 480 pixel video display, and quickly replaced the older CGA (Color Graphics Adapter) and EGA (Extended Graphics Adapter).

Virtual   Pertaining to a device or facility that does not physically exist, yet behaves as if it does. Examples include *virtual memory*, *virtual device drivers*, *virtual private network*, and so on.

Virtual Device Driver (VxD)   A special type of driver file used to support older Windows programs. Windows protection errors take place when VxDs fail to load or unload. This usually occurs when a device somehow gets a device driver in both CONFIG.SYS and SYSTEM.INI or the Registry.

Virtual LAN (VLAN)   A LAN that, using smart, VLAN-capable switches, can place some (or any on the more expensive VLANs) systems on whatever collision domain you want.

Virus   A type of program containing malicious executable code. Viruses are designed to install themselves onto systems without the user's knowledge or permission, and cause varying degrees of damage to the system when executed. Some viruses cause no significant damage, while others may destroy data, corrupt the OS, render the system unbootable, or enable remote users to take control of the PC. Viruses are typically designed to propagate themselves by creating copies of themselves and transmitting the copies to other PCs via open network shares, e-mail, and unsecured ports.

Virus Definition or Data File   These files are also called *signature files*, depending on the virus protection software in use. These files enable the virus protection software to recognize the viruses on your system and clean them. These files should be updated often.

VLB (VESA Local Bus)   A design architecture for the sockets on the computer motherboard that enable system components to be added to the computer. VLB was the first *local bus* standard, meaning that devices added to a computer through this port would use the processor at its full speed, rather than at the slower 8-MHz speed of the regular bus. In addition to moving data at a faster rate, VLB moves data 32 bits at a time, rather than the 8 or 16 bits that the older ISA buses supported. Although VLB was common on machines using Intel's 486 CPU, modern computers now use PCI buses instead.

Volatile   1. Memory that must have constant electricity to retain data. 2. Any programmer six hours before deadline after a nonstop 48-hour coding session, running on nothing but caffeine and sugar.

Volts (V) The pressure of the electrons passing through a wire is called *voltage* and is measured in units called volts (V).

Volume 1. A physical unit of a storage medium, such as a tape reel or disk pack, that is capable of having data recorded on it and subsequently read. 2. A contiguous collection of cylinders or blocks on a disk that are treated as a separate unit.

VPN (Virtual Private Network) A network configuration that enables a remote user to access a private network via the Internet. VPNs employ an encryption methodology called *tunneling*, which protects the data from interception.

VRAM (Video RAM) A type of memory in a video display adapter that's used to create the image appearing on the CRT screen. VRAM uses dual-ported memory, which enables simultaneous reads and writes, making it much quicker than DRAM.

WAN (Wide Area Network) A geographically dispersed network created by linking various computers and LANs over long distances, generally using leased phone lines. There is no firm dividing line between a WAN and a LAN.

Warm Boot A system restart performed after the system has been powered and operating. This clears and resets the memory, but does not stop and start the hard drive.

Wattage (Watts or W) The amount of amps and volts needed by a particular device to function is expressed as how much wattage (watts or W) that device needs.

WAV (Windows Audio Format) The default sound format for Windows.

WB (Write Back) Defines a certain type of SRAM cache where instructions from the CPU to write changes are held in the cache until time is available to write the changes to main memory.

Web Server A server that enables access to HTML documents by remote users using the HTTP protocol.

Well-Known Ports Port numbers from 0 to 1204 that are used primarily by client applications to talk to server applications in TCP/IP networks.

Wi-Fi Protected Access (WPA) A wireless security protocol that addresses the weaknesses and acts as a sort of upgrade to WEP. WPA offers security enhancements such as dynamic encryption key generation (keys are issued on a per-user and per-session basis), an encryption key integrity-checking feature, user authentication through the industry-standard Extensible Authentication Protocol (EAP), and other advanced features that WEP lacks.

WIN32 A programming interface or API for an early PC 32-bit mode fully supported by Windows NT. Many functions are supported in Windows 3.*x*, and written to the Win32 subset to gain improved performance on a 386. Windows 3.*x* translates the 32-bit calls in an application into its native 16-bit calls.

Windows   A powerful and flexible network operating system developed by Microsoft in the 1980s. Windows comes in a variety of desktop and server versions, including Windows 9*x* (95, 98, 98 SE, Me), Windows NT Workstation and Server, Windows 2000 Professional and Server, Windows XP Home and Professional Editions, and Windows Server 2003. Many of these versions also have their own variations, such as Windows Server 2003 Small Business Edition, Terminal Server, Enterprise Edition, DataCenter, and so on.

WINIPCFG   A graphical program used on Windows 9*x*/Me/XP machines to display the current TCP/IP configuration of the machine; similar to Windows NT/2000/XP's IPCONFIG and UNIX/Linux's IFCONFIG.

WINS (Windows Internet Name Service)   A name resolution service that resolves NetBIOS names to IP addresses.

Winsock (WINdows SOCKets)   Microsoft Windows implementation of the TCP/IP Sockets interface.

WINS Relay Agent   A WINS relay agent forwards WINS broadcasts to a WINS server on the other side of a router to keep older systems from broadcasting in place of registering with the server.

Wireless Access Point   Connects wireless network nodes to wireless or wired networks. Many wireless access points are combination devices that act as high-speed hubs, switches, bridges, and routers, all rolled into one.

Wireless Equivalency Privacy (WEP)   A wireless security protocol that uses a 64-bit encryption algorithm to scramble data packets.

Wireless Fidelity (Wi-Fi)   The most widely adopted wireless networking type in use today. Technically, only wireless devices that conform to the extended versions of the 802.11 standard—802.11a, 802.11b, and 802.11g—are Wi-Fi certified.

Wireless Network   *See* Wireless Fidelity (Wi-Fi).

Word   A group of 16 binary digits or 2 bytes.

Word Processor   A program used to enter or edit text information in personal computers, often used to create a file before it is uploaded to a network. May also be used to process text after it has been downloaded.

Work Area   The work area in a basic structured cabling network is often simply an office or cubicle that potentially contains a PC attached to the network.

Workgroup   A convenient method of organizing computers under Network Neighborhood/My Network Places in Windows operating systems. Workgroups have flat namespaces and contain no method for applying security.

Workstation 1. A term used to differentiate a network client system from a server system. 2. A specialized type of high-end PC that has very powerful CPU(s), massive amounts of RAM, and other high-performance hardware making it suitable for advanced mathematical, scientific, or graphical applications. Sun and Silicon Graphics Inc. are two popular manufacturers of workstation-class PCs.

Worm A worm is a very special form of virus. Unlike other viruses, a worm does not infect other files on the computer. Instead, it replicates by making copies of itself on other systems on a network by taking advantage of security weaknesses in networking protocols.

WWW (World Wide Web) The system of servers supporting graphics and multimedia via HTTP. The WWW is a specialized use (some call it a layer) of the Internet, but is not synonymous with the Internet at large.

X.25 A type of packet switched network that enables remote devices to communicate with each other across high-speed digital links without the expense of individual leased lines.

XGA (Extended Graphics Array) IBM video display to bring 1,024 × 768 resolution to monitors. Can display 65,536 colors at low resolution, and 256 at high resolution.

Xmodem A file transfer protocol (FTP) that provides error-free asynchronous communications through telephone lines.

XMS (Extended Memory Services) The RAM above 1 megabyte that is installed directly on the motherboard, and directly accessible to the microprocessor. Usually shortened to simply "extended" memory.

Ymodem A file transfer protocol (FTP) that is more robust than Xmodem; it features a time and date stamp transfer, as well as batch file transfers.

ZIF Socket (Zero Insertion Force Socket) A type of socket for CPUs that enables insertion of a chip without much pressure. Intel promoted the ZIF socket with its overdrive upgrades. The chip is dropped into the socket's holes and a small lever is turned to lock it in. Somewhat replaced in modern motherboards by Slot 1 and Slot A architecture, ZIF is still in style in Super Socket 7 and Socket 370 motherboards.

Zmodem Streaming asynchronous file transfer protocol (FTP) used by communication software. Popular for downloading.

Zombie Attack A method of launching Denial of Service (DoS) attacks or spreading spam. Instigators of zombie attacks take over the function of numerous remote computers (via virus or worm), and use the remote systems to run malicious programs that flood the target system with requests or send mass e-mails. Zombie attacks make it difficult to trace the attack back to the original instigator.

INTERNATIONAL CONTACT INFORMATION

AUSTRALIA
McGraw-Hill Book Company
Australia Pty. Ltd.
TEL +61-2-9900-1800
FAX +61-2-9878-8881
http://www.mcgraw-hill.com.au
books-it_sydney@mcgraw-hill.com

CANADA
McGraw-Hill Ryerson Ltd.
TEL +905-430-5000
FAX +905-430-5020
http://www.mcgraw-hill.ca

**GREECE, MIDDLE EAST, & AFRICA
(Excluding South Africa)**
McGraw-Hill Hellas
TEL +30-210-6560-990
TEL +30-210-6560-993
TEL +30-210-6560-994
FAX +30-210-6545-525

MEXICO (Also serving Latin America)
McGraw-Hill Interamericana Editores
S.A. de C.V.
TEL +525-1500-5108
FAX +525-117-1589
http://www.mcgraw-hill.com.mx
carlos_ruiz@mcgraw-hill.com

SINGAPORE (Serving Asia)
McGraw-Hill Book Company
TEL +65-6863-1580
FAX +65-6862-3354
http://www.mcgraw-hill.com.sg
mghasia@mcgraw-hill.com

SOUTH AFRICA
McGraw-Hill South Africa
TEL +27-11-622-7512
FAX +27-11-622-9045
robyn_swanepoel@mcgraw-hill.com

SPAIN
McGraw-Hill/
Interamericana de España, S.A.U.
TEL +34-91-180-3000
FAX +34-91-372-8513
http://www.mcgraw-hill.es
professional@mcgraw-hill.es

**UNITED KINGDOM, NORTHERN,
EASTERN, & CENTRAL EUROPE**
McGraw-Hill Education Europe
TEL +44-1-628-502500
FAX +44-1-628-770224
http://www.mcgraw-hill.co.uk
emea_queries@mcgraw-hill.com

ALL OTHER INQUIRIES Contact:
McGraw-Hill/Osborne
TEL +1-510-420-7700
FAX +1-510-420-7703
http://www.osborne.com
omg_international@mcgraw-hill.com